MALCOLM X

ALSO BY MANNING MARABLE

Barack Obama and African-American Empowerment
(edited with Kristen Clarke)

Let Nobody Turn Us Around: An African-American Anthology
(edited with Leith Mullings)

Transnational Blackness: Navigating the Global Color Line
(edited with Vanessa Agard-Jones)

Living Black History: How Reimagining the African-American Past
Can Remake America's Racial Future

Race, Reform, and Rebellion: The Second Reconstruction and Beyond in
Black America, 1945–2006

W. E. B. Du Bois: Black Radical Democrat

Seeking Higher Ground: The Hurricane Katrina Crisis
(edited with Kristen Clarke)

The Great Wells of Democracy: The Meaning of Race in American Life

Freedom: A Photographic History of the African-American Freedom Struggle
(coauthored with Leith Mullings)

Black Leadership

Black Liberation in Conservative America

Speaking Truth to Power: Essays on Race, Radicalism, and Resistance

Racializing Justice, Disenfranchising Lives
(edited with Keesha Middlemass and Ian Steinberg)

Herbert Aptheker on Race and Democracy
(edited with Eric Foner)

The New Black Renaissance: The Souls Anthology
(editor)

Beyond Black and White: Transforming African-American Politics

The Crisis of Color and Democracy

African and Caribbean Politics

Black American Politics

*How Capitalism Underdeveloped Black America: Problems in Race,
Political Economy, and Society*

The Autobiography of Medgar Evers
(edited with Myrlie Evers-Williams)

*Freedom on My Mind: The Columbia Documentary Experience of the
African-American Experience*
(editor)

*Dispatches From the Ebony Tower: Intellectuals Confront the
African-American Experience*
(editor)

*Blackwater: Historical Studies in Race,
Class Consciousness, and Revolution*

MALCOLM X

A Life of Reinvention

Manning Marable

VIKING

VIKING

Published by the Penguin Group

Penguin Group (USA) Inc., 375 Hudson Street, New York, New York 10014, USA • Penguin Group (Canada),
90 Eglinton Avenue East, Suite 700, Toronto, Ontario M4P 2Y3, Canada (a division of Pearson Penguin Canada
Inc.) • Penguin Books Ltd, 80 Strand, London WC2R 0RL, England • Penguin Ireland, 25 St Stephen's Green,
Dublin 2, Ireland (a division of Penguin Books Ltd) • Penguin Group Australia Ltd, 250 Camberwell Road,
Camberwell, Victoria 3124, Australia (a division of Pearson Australia Group Pty Ltd) • Penguin Books India Pvt
Ltd, 11 Community Centre, Panchsheel Park, New Delhi - 110 017, India • Penguin Group (NZ), 67 Apollo Drive,
Rosedale, North Shore 0632, New Zealand (a division of Pearson New Zealand Ltd) • Penguin Books (South Africa)
(Pty) Ltd, 24 Sturdee Avenue, Rosebank, Johannesburg 2196, South Africa

Penguin Books Ltd, Registered Offices: 80 Strand, London WC2R 0RL, England

First published in 2011 by Viking Penguin, a member of Penguin Group (USA) Inc.

10   9   8   7   6   5   4   3   2   1

Grateful acknowledgment is made for permission to reprint excerpts from *The Autobiography of Malcolm X* by Malcolm X and Alex Haley. Copyright © 1964 by Alex Haley and Malcolm X. Copyright © 1965 by Alex Haley and Betty
Shabazz. Used by permission of Random House, Inc.

PHOTOGRAPH CREDITS
Insert p. 2 (top): Eve Arnold / Magnum Photos • p. 2 (bottom): Frank Scherschel / Getty Images • pp. 5 (bottom),
15: © Bob Adelman / Corbis • p. 6: © Hulton-Deutsch Collection / Corbis • p. 8: Keystone / Getty Images •
p. 10: Orlando Fernandez, New York World-Telegram and the Sun Newspaper Photograph Collection, Library of
Congress • p. 12: New York World-Telegram and the Sun Newspaper Photograph Collection, Library of Congress • All other photographs: © Bettman / Corbis

LIBRARY OF CONGRESS CATALOGING-IN-PUBLICATION DATA
Marable, Manning, 1950–
    Malcolm X : a life of reinvention / Manning Marable.
        p.   cm.
    Includes bibliographical references and index.
    ISBN 978-0-670-02220-5
    1. X, Malcolm, 1925–1965.   2. Black Muslims—Biography.   3. African Americans—Biography.   I. Title.
    BP223.Z8L57636   2011
    297.8'7092—dc22   2010025768
    [B]

Printed in the United States of America
Designed by Carla Bolte

No one has made more sacrifices to realize the completion of this work than Leith Mullings. For more than a decade, she has been my constant companion and intellectual compass as I have attempted to reconstruct the past.

This work is hers.

CONTENTS

Prologue Life Beyond the Legend | 1

Chapter 1 "Up, You Mighty Race!" | 15
1925–1941

Chapter 2 The Legend of Detroit Red | 39
1941–January 1946

Chapter 3 Becoming "X" | 70
January 1946–August 1952

Chapter 4 "They Don't Come Like the Minister" | 100
August 1952–May 1957

Chapter 5 "Brother, a Minister *Has* to Be Married" | 130
May 1957–March 1959

Chapter 6 "The Hate That Hate Produced" | 155
March 1959–January 1961

Chapter 7 "As Sure As God Made Green Apples" | 180
January 1961–May 1962

Chapter 8 From Prayer to Protest | 211
May 1962–March 1963

Chapter 9 "He Was Developing Too Fast" | 235
April–November 1963

Chapter 10 "The Chickens Coming Home to Roost" | 269
           December 1, 1963–March 12, 1964

Chapter 11 An Epiphany in the Hajj | 297
           March 12–May 21, 1964

Chapter 12 "Do Something About Malcolm X" | 321
           May 21–July 11, 1964

Chapter 13 "In the Struggle for Dignity" | 360
           July 11–November 24, 1964

Chapter 14 "Such a Man Is Worthy of Death" | 388
           November 24, 1964–February 14, 1965

Chapter 15 Death Comes on Time | 418
           February 14–February 21, 1965

Chapter 16 Life After Death | 450

Epilogue Reflections on a Revolutionary Vision | 479

        Acknowledgments and Research Notes | 489

        Notes | 495

        A Glossary of Terms | 559

        Bibliography | 563

        Index | 577

MALCOLM X

Life Beyond the Legend

In the early years of the last century, the neighborhood just north of Harlem, later to be named Washington Heights, was a sparsely settled suburb. Only the vision of a businessman, William Fox, led to the construction of an opulent entertainment center on Broadway between West 165th and 166th streets. Fox's instruction to the architect, Thomas W. Lamb, was to design a building more splendid than any theater on Broadway. By the time all was finished, in 1912, an expensive terra-cotta facade adorned the front walls, marble columns stood guard at the entrance, while carvings of exotic birds graced the foyer: it was these colorful motifs, inspired by the great nineteenth-century artist John James Audubon, that prompted Fox to name his pleasure palace the Audubon. On the building's first floor, Lamb designed a massive cinema, large enough to seat twenty-three hundred people. In subsequent years, the second floor was reserved for two spacious ballrooms: the Rose Ballroom, which could accommodate eight hundred patrons, and the larger Grand Ballroom, holding up to fifteen hundred.

Within a few decades, the neighborhood around the Audubon began to change, becoming increasingly black and working class. The Audubon's management catered to this new clientele by booking the most celebrated swing bands of the era, including Duke Ellington, Count Basie, and Chick Webb. The Audubon also became the home for many of the city's militant trade unionists, and from 1934 to 1937 the newly formed Transport Workers Union held its meetings there—accompanied by the occasional violent confrontation. One night in September 1929, for example, a four-hundred-strong party sponsored by the Lantern Athletic Club was disrupted by four gunshots. Two people were badly wounded.

During World War II, the Audubon was rented out for weddings, bar mitzvahs, political meetings, and graduation parties. After 1945, however, the neighborhood changed yet again, as many white middle-class residents sold their properties and fled to the suburbs. Columbia University's decision to expand its hospital at West 168th Street and Broadway into a major health sciences campus generated hundreds of new jobs for the black influx, while the Audubon adapted to economic realities by shutting down its cinema and subdividing the space it had occupied into rentals. However, both the Rose and Grand ballrooms remained.

By the mid-1960s, the building had surrendered most of its original grandeur. The main entrance for the ballrooms was small and drab. Customers had to climb a steep flight of stairs to the second-floor foyer, then maneuver past the manager's office and on into either the Rose, at the building's left (east) side, or the Grand, which faced Broadway. The larger room was about 180 feet by 60 feet, its north, east, and west walls housing about sixty-five separate booths, each of which could hold up to twelve people. Farthest from the building's main entrance, along the south wall, was a modest wooden stage, behind which was a cramped, poorly lit antechamber where musicians and speakers would muster before walking out to perform.

On the winter afternoon of Sunday, February 21, 1965, the Grand Ballroom had been reserved by the controversial Organization of Afro-American Unity (OAAU), a Harlem-based political group. For nearly a year, the Audubon's management had been renting the ballroom to the group, but it remained concerned about its leader, Malcolm X. About ten years before, he had arrived as the minister of Temple No. 7, the local headquarters for a militant Islamic sect, the Lost-Found Nation of Islam (NOI). Later commonly described in the press as Black Muslims, its members preached that whites were devils and that black Americans were the lost Asiatic tribe of Shabazz, forced into slavery in America's racial wilderness. The road to salvation required converts to reject their slave surnames, replacing them with the letter *X*, the symbol that represented the unknown. Members were told that, after years of personal dedication and spiritual growth, they would be given "original" surnames, in harmony with their true Asiatic identities. As the Nation's most public spokesman, Malcolm X gained notoriety for his provocative criticisms of both civil rights leaders and white politicians.

The previous March, Malcolm X had announced his independence from the Nation of Islam. He quickly established his own spiritual group, Muslim Mosque, Inc. (MMI), largely for those NOI members who had left the Nation in sympathy with him. Despite his break, he continued to make highly controversial statements. "There will be more violence than ever this year," he predicted to a *New York Times* reporter in March 1964, for instance. "The whites had better understand this while there is still time. The Negroes at the mass level are ready to act." The New York City police commissioner responded to this prediction by labeling Malcolm "another self-proclaimed 'leader' [who] openly advocates bloodshed and armed revolt and sneers at the sincere efforts of reasonable men to resolve the problem of equal rights by proper, peaceful and legitimate means." Malcolm was not intimidated by the attack. "The greatest compliment anyone can pay me," he responded, "is to say I'm irresponsible, because by responsible they mean Negroes who are responsible to white authorities—Negro Uncle Toms."

Several weeks later, Malcolm X appeared to experience a spiritual epiphany. In April, he visited the holy city of Mecca on a spiritual hajj, and on returning to the United States declared that he had converted to orthodox Sunni Islam. Repudiating his links to both the Nation of Islam and its leader, Elijah Muhammad, he announced his opposition to all forms of bigotry. He was now eager to cooperate with civil rights groups, he said, and to work with any white who genuinely supported black Americans. But despite these avowals, he continued to make controversial statements—for example, urging blacks to start gun clubs to protect their families against racists, and condemning the presidential candidates of the major parties, Lyndon Johnson and Barry Goldwater, as providing no real choice for blacks.

Most OAAU programs were choreographed as educational forums for the local community, encouraging audience participation. For the February 21 meeting, the featured speaker was Milton Galamison, a prominent Presbyterian minister who had organized protests against substandard schools in New York City's black and Latino neighborhoods. The OAAU had not directly participated, but Malcolm had publicly praised the minister's efforts, and his lieutenants may have desired an informal alliance.

Although the afternoon's program had been advertised to begin at two, by the starting time barely forty people had passed through the main entrance. The sparse early turnout may have been a reaction to fears of possible violence. For months, the Nation had been engaged in a well-publicized feud with its former national spokesman, and Malcolm's followers in Harlem and other cities had been physically assaulted. Only a week earlier, his own home, located in the quiet neighborhood of Elmhurst, Queens, had been firebombed in the middle of the night. To guard against a public confrontation, the NYPD had assigned a detachment of up to two dozen officers at OAAU rallies whenever held at the Audubon. One or more policemen, usually including the day's detail commander, would be stationed on the second floor in the business office, where they would have an uninterrupted view of everyone entering the main ballroom. Many of the others were prominently stationed at the main entrance, or located outside, directly across the street in a small playground area residents called Pigeon Park. On this particular afternoon, however, not a single officer was at the Audubon entrance, and only one, briefly, was stationed in the park. No one was seen inside the business office. In fact, just two uniformed patrolmen were placed inside the building, both having been ordered to remain in the smaller—and but for them unoccupied—Rose Ballroom, at a considerable distance from the featured event.

The absence of a substantial police presence would prove critical, because earlier that morning five men who had been planning for months to assassinate Malcolm X met together one final time. Although the venue of that meeting was in Paterson, New Jersey, all five were members of the Newark mosque of the Nation of Islam. Only one conspirator was an official of the mosque; the others were NOI laborers and assumed that their actions had been approved by the Nation's leadership. After meeting at the home of one of the conspirators, where they went over each man's assignment one final time, the five men then got into a Cadillac and headed for the George Washington Bridge. They exited in upper Manhattan and found a parking spot close to the Audubon that would also provide quick access back to the bridge, and an easy escape to New Jersey.

The sole security force inside the Grand Ballroom and at the main entrance was about twenty of Malcolm's followers. The head of Malcolm's security team was his personal bodyguard, Reuben X Francis, who earlier that afternoon had told William 64X George that the day's team would be undermanned, and that he would need his help. Usually, the dependable William would stand next to the speaker's podium (placed directly in the front center of the stage), where he could view the entire audience. On this particular day, however, Reuben instructed him to stand at the front entrance—about as far as he could have been from the stage.

Reuben also delegated some decisions to the event's security coordinator, John D. X, whose job was to supervise guards around the Grand Ballroom's perimeter. The normal protocol was for security teams to stand for up to thirty minutes—a demanding assignment, especially for those with no prior experience in policing crowds. Usually the most important positions went to former NOI members, all of whom had both security experience and martial arts training. If a known NOI sympathizer attempted to enter an event, he was to be questioned, quietly but firmly. Nation of Islam members who had personal histories of violence or were known for hostility toward Malcolm would be escorted from the building.

One such man was Linwood X Cathcart, a former member of Malcolm's Mosque No. 7 who had recently joined the Jersey City mosque. He had entered the Audubon at 1:45 and seated himself in the front row of wooden folding chairs that had been placed across the dance floor. Malcolm's team spotted him at once, reckoning that his presence could mean trouble. Cathcart now brazenly wore an NOI pin on his suit lapel. Reuben persuaded him to go with him to the rear of the ballroom, where, after exchanging words, he insisted that he remove the offending button if he wished to remain. Cathcart complied and returned to his seat. Malcolm's security people would later insist that he was the sole NOI loyalist they had spotted.

Handling the necessary custodial duties that afternoon was Anas M. Luqman (Langston Hughes Savage), another NOI member who had severed ties with the Nation out of loyalty to Malcolm. In his subsequent grand jury testimony, Luqman placed his arrival time at around 1:20. He briefly talked with a few people and, as he had done many times before, arranged the chairs onstage, positioned the speaker's podium, and removed some surplus equipment. He then "went out into the audience and just stood around until the meeting start[ed]." Sometime after two, he decided to recheck the doors, located at stage right, closest to the speaker's platform. For whatever reason, they were unlocked, which troubled him, but instead of notifying Malcolm's security people, he returned to his seat.

Despite the recent firebombing and the escalating threats of violence, Malcolm had insisted that none of his security team, with the sole exception of Reuben, should carry arms that Sunday. At an OAAU meeting some evenings before, his orders had been vigorously challenged. Malcolm's chief of staff, James 67X Warden, was convinced that the failure to tighten security that afternoon almost certainly would invite trouble. As he later explained his actions: "We wanted to check [for weapons]. But this was an OAAU [public] meeting. Malcolm said, 'These people are not accustomed to having anybody search them.' We're dealing with an entirely different group." As a result, as people entered the Audubon, many wearing bulky winter coats, no one was stopped. If Reuben was worried by this, he didn't appear so, and even left the ballroom to pay the manager that afternoon's $150 fee.

By this time, all the would-be assassins had entered the building. As they anticipated, no one searched them for weapons. The group then split up. The three designated shooters found chairs in the front row, either in front of or to the left of the speaker's podium. One shooter, a heavy-set, dark-complexioned man in his mid-twenties, was to deliver the initial hit. Two others were carrying handguns. Their task was to finish off Malcolm after the initial shots. The final two conspirators sat next to each other on the wooden chairs about seven rows back from the stage. Their assignment was to create a diversion. If possible, one of them was going to ignite a smoke bomb.

By two thirty p.m. the audience had grown to over two hundred, and they were becoming impatient. Benjamin 2X Goodman, Malcolm's assistant minister of Muslim Mosque, Inc., came onstage and began a thirty-minute warm-up. Because Benjamin was not among the featured speakers, most people continued talking or wandered about seeing friends. After about ten minutes, Benjamin's remarks began to attract attention, as he recalled recent themes in Malcolm's rally speeches, such as opposition to the Vietnam War. Everyone knew that Malcolm almost always came to the podium immediately following Benjamin's introductions.

Several minutes before three p.m., Benjamin was still exhorting the audience when, without warning, a tall, sandy-haired man walked briskly out and sat on a chair a few feet from the podium. Caught off guard by his leader's entrance, Benjamin hastily finished up his remarks, then turned to sit down on one of the folding chairs onstage. As a rule, for safety reasons, Malcolm was not permitted to be there alone. On this occasion, however, he stopped his colleague from sitting, whispering instructions into his ear. Looking puzzled, Benjamin stepped down and returned to the backstage room.

"*As-salaam alaikum,*" Malcolm proclaimed, extending the traditional Arabic greeting. "*Walaikum salaam,*" hundreds chanted back. But before he could say anything further, there was an unexpected disturbance about six or seven rows back from center stage. "Get your hands out of my pockets!" a man shouted to the person next to him. Both men stood up and began to tussle, diverting everyone's attention. From the stage, Malcolm yelled out, "Hold it! Hold it!"

The two principal rostrum guards, Charles X Blackwell and Robert 35X

Smith, scrambled to break up the men. Most of their colleagues also moved from their positions to quell the disruption, leaving Malcolm completely alone onstage. It was then that the conspirator in the first row stood up and walked briskly toward the rostrum. Beneath his winter coat, he cradled a sawed-off shotgun. About fifteen feet from the stage, he stopped, pulled back his coat, and lifted his weapon.

———

For many African Americans, February 21, 1965, is engraved in their memory as profoundly as the assassinations of John F. Kennedy and Martin Luther King, Jr., are for other Americans. In the turbulent aftermath of his death, Malcolm X's disciples embraced the slogan "Black Power" and elevated him to secular sainthood. By the late 1960s, he had come to embody the very ideal of blackness for an entire generation. Like W. E. B. Du Bois, Richard Wright, and James Baldwin, he had denounced the psychological and social costs that racism had imposed upon his people; he was also widely admired as a man of uncompromising action, the polar opposite of the nonviolent, middle-class-oriented Negro leadership that had dominated the civil rights movement before him.

The leader most closely linked to Malcolm in life and death was, of course, King. However, despite having spent much of his early life in urban Atlanta, King was rarely identified as a representative of ghetto blacks. In the decades following his assassination, he became associated with images of the largely rural and small-town South. Malcolm, conversely, was a product of the modern ghetto. The emotional rage he expressed was a reaction to racism in its urban context: segregated urban schools, substandard housing, high infant mortality rates, drugs, and crime. Since by the 1960s the overwhelming majority of African Americans lived in large cities, the conditions that defined their existence were more closely linked to what Malcolm spoke about than what King represented. Consequently, he was able to establish a strong audience among urban blacks, who perceived passive resistance as an insufficient tool for dismantling institutional racism.

Malcolm's later-day metamorphosis from angry black militant into a multicultural American icon was the product of the extraordinary success of *The Autobiography of Malcolm X*, coauthored by the writer Alex Haley and released nine months after the assassination. A best seller in its initial years of publication, the book soon established itself as a standard text in hundreds of college and university curricula. By the late 1960s, an entire generation of African-American poets and writers were producing a seemingly endless body of work paying homage to their fallen idol. In their imagination, Malcolm's image became permanently frozen: always displaying a broad, somewhat mischievous smile, spotlessly well attired, and devoted to advancing the interests and aspirations of his people.

From the moment of his murder, widely different groups, including Trotskyists, black cultural nationalists, and Sunni Muslims, claimed him. Hundreds of institutions and neighborhood clubs were renamed to honor the man whom actor Ossie Davis had eulogized as "our manhood, our living, black manhood." A Malcolm X Association was initiated by African Americans in the military. In Harlem, activists formed a Malcolm X Democrat Club. In 1968, the independent film producer Marvin Worth hired James Baldwin to write a screenplay based on the *Autobiography*, a project the novelist described as "my confession . . . it's the story of any black cat in this curious place and time." By the early 1970s, Betty Shabazz, Malcolm X's wife, was invited as an honored guest to a Washington, D.C., fundraising gala promoting the reelection of Richard Nixon.

The renaissance of Malcolm's popularity in the early 1990s was largely due to the rise of the "hip-hop nation." In the group Public Enemy's video "Shut 'Em Down," for example, the image of Malcolm is imposed over the face of George Washington on the U.S. dollar bill; another hip-hop group, Gang Starr, placed a portrait of Malcolm on the cover of one of its CDs. Political conservatives also continued their attempts to assimilate him into their pantheon. In the aftermath of the 1992 Los Angeles race riots, for instance, vice president Dan Quayle declared that he had acquired important insights into the reasons for such unrest by reading Malcolm's autobiography—an epiphany most African Americans viewed as absurd, with filmmaker Spike Lee quipping, "Every time Malcolm X talked about 'blue-eyed devils' Quayle should think he's talking about him."

With the release of Lee's three-hour biographical film *X* that same year, Malcolm reached a new generation. In a 1992 poll, 84 percent of African Americans between the ages of fifteen and twenty-four described him as "a hero for black Americans today." After years of relegating him to the periphery of modern black history, historians now began to see him as a central figure. He had become "an integral part of the scaffolding that supports a contemporary African-American identity," historian Gerald Horne wrote. "His fascination with music and dance and night clubs undergirded his bond with blacks." For many whites, however, his appeal was located in his conversion from militant black separatism to what might be described as multicultural universalism. His assimilation into the American mainstream occurred—ironically—at Harlem's Apollo Theater on January 20, 1999, when the United States Postal Service celebrated the release of a Malcolm X stamp there. In a press statement accompanying the stamp's issuance, the U.S. Postal Service claimed that, in the year prior to his assassination, Malcolm X had become an advocate of "a more integrationist solution to racial problems."

A closer reading of the *Autobiography* as well as the actual details of Malcolm's life reveals a more complicated history. Few of the book's reviewers appreciated that it was actually a joint endeavor—and particularly that Alex Haley, a retired twenty-year veteran of the U.S. Coast Guard, had an agenda of his own. A liberal Republican, Haley held the Nation of Islam's racial separatism and religious extremism in contempt, but he was fascinated by the tortured tale of Malcolm's personal life. In 1963, the beginning of the collaboration of these two very different men, Malcolm had labored to present a tale of moral uplift, to praise the power of the Nation's leader, Elijah Muhammad. After Malcolm's departure from the sect, he used his autobiography to explain his break from black separatism. Haley's purpose was quite different; for him, the autobiography was a cautionary tale about human waste and the tragedies produced by racial segregation. In many ways, the published book is more Haley's than its author's: because Malcolm died in February 1965, he had no opportunity to revise major elements of what would become known as his political testament.

My own curiosity about the *Autobiography* began more than two decades ago, when I was teaching it as part of a seminar on African-American political thought at Ohio State University. Among African-American leaders throughout history, Malcolm was unquestionably the most consummately "political" activist, a man who emphasized grassroots and participatory politics led by working-class and poor blacks. Yet the autobiography is virtually silent about his primary organization, the OAAU. Nowhere in the text does its agenda or its objectives appear. After years of research, I discovered that several chapters had been deleted prior to publication—chapters that envisioned the construction of a united front of Negroes, from a wide variety of political and social groups, led by the Black Muslims. According to Haley, the deletion had been at the author's request, after his return from Mecca. That probably is true; but Malcolm had absolutely no input on Haley's decision to preface the *Autobiography* with an introductory essay by *New York Times* journalist M. S. Handler, who had covered Malcolm extensively during previous years, nor on Haley's own rambling conclusion, which frames his subject firmly within mainstream civil rights respectability at the end of his life.

A deeper reading of the text also reveals numerous inconsistencies in names, dates, and facts. As both a historian and an African American, I was fascinated. How much isn't true, and how much hasn't been told?

The search for historical evidence and factual truth was made even more complicated by the complex and varied layers of the subject's life. A master of public rhetoric, he could artfully recount tales about his life that were partially fiction, yet the stories resonated as true to most blacks who had encountered racism. From an early age Malcolm Little (as he was born) had constructed multiple masks that distanced his inner self from the outside world. Years later, whether in a Massachusetts prison cell or traveling alone across the African continent during anticolonial revolutions, he maintained the dual ability to anticipate the actions of others and to package himself to maximum effect. He acquired the subtle tools of an ethnographer, crafting his language to fit the cultural contexts of his diverse audiences. As a result, different groups perceived his personality and his evolving message through their own particular lens. No matter the context, Malcolm exuded charm and a healthy sense of humor, placing ideological opponents off guard and allowing him to advance provocative and even outrageous arguments.

Malcolm always assumed an approachable and intimate outward style, yet also held something in reserve. These layers of personality were even expressed as a series of different names, some of which he created, while others were bestowed upon him: Malcolm Little, Homeboy, Jack Carlton, Detroit Red, Big Red, Satan, Malachi Shabazz, Malik Shabazz, El-Hajj Malik El-Shabazz. No single personality ever captured him fully. In this sense, his narrative is a brilliant series of reinventions, "Malcolm X" being just the best known.

Like a great method actor, Malcolm drew generously from his background, so that over time the distance between actual events and the public telling of them widened. After his death, other distortions—embellishments by devoted followers, friends, family members, and opponents—turned his life into a legend. Malcolm was fascinating to many whites in a sensual, animalistic way, and journalists who regularly covered his speeches picked up a subdued yet unmistakable sexual subtext. M. S. Handler, whose home Malcolm visited for an interview in early March of 1964, attributed his aura of physical prowess to his politics: "No man in our time aroused fear and hatred in the white man as did Malcolm, because in him the white man sensed an implacable foe who could not be had for any price—a man unreservedly committed to the cause of liberating the black man." Even Malcolm during his early years routinely employed evocative metaphors to describe his personality. For example, portraying his time in a Massachusetts prison in 1946, he likened his confinement to that of a trapped animal: "I would pace for hours like a caged leopard, viciously cursing aloud. . . . Eventually, the men in the cellblock had a name for me: 'Satan.'" Handler's wife, who had been present when Malcolm had visited her home, admitted to her husband, "You know, it was like having tea with a black panther."

To black Americans, however, Malcolm's appeal was rooted in entirely different cultural imagery. What made him truly original was that he presented himself as the embodiment of the two central figures of African-American folk culture, simultaneously the hustler/trickster and the preacher/minister. Janus-faced, the trickster is unpredictable, capable of outrageous transgressions; the minister saves souls, redeems shattered lives, and promises a new world. Malcolm was a committed student of black folk culture, and to make a political point he would constantly mix animal stories, rural metaphors, and trickster tales—for example, refashioning the fox vs. the wolf as Johnson vs. Goldwater. His speeches mesmerized audiences because he could orchestrate his themes into a narrative that promised ultimate salvation. He presented himself as an uncompromising man wholly dedicated to the empowerment of black people, without regard to his own personal safety. Even those who rejected his politics recognized his sincerity.

Obviously, the analogy between the actor as performer and the political leader as performer goes only so far, but the art of reinvention in politics does demand the selective rearrangement of a public figure's past lives (and the elimination of embarrassing episodes, as Bill Clinton has taught us). In Malcolm's case, the memoirs written by friends and relatives have illustrated that the notorious outlaw Detroit Red character Malcolm presented in his autobiography is highly exaggerated. The actual criminal record of Malcolm Little for the years 1941–46 supports the contention that he deliberately built up his criminal history, weaving elements of his past into an allegory documenting the destructive consequences of racism within the U.S. criminal justice and penal system. Self-invention was an effective way for him to reach the most marginalized sectors of the black community, giving justification to their hopes.

———

My primary purpose in this book is to go beyond the legend: to recount what actually occurred in Malcolm's life. I also present the facts that Malcolm himself could not know, such as the extent of illegal FBI and New York Police Department surveillance and acts of disruption against him, the truth about those among his supporters who betrayed him politically and personally, and the identification of those responsible for Malcolm's assassination.

One of the greatest challenges I encountered in reconstructing his life was the attempt to examine his activities inside the Nation of Islam. Most popular treatments focus heavily on his public career during his final two years. Part of the problem in unearthing his earlier speeches and letters from the 1950s was that the current NOI leadership, headed by the former Louis X Walcott, known today as Louis Farrakhan, had never permitted scholars to examine the sect's archives. After years of effort, I was able to initiate a dialogue with the Nation of Islam; in May 2005 I sat with Farrakhan for an extraordinary nine-hour meeting. The Nation subsequently made available to me fifty-year-old audiotapes of Malcolm's sermons and lectures delivered while he was still Mosque No. 7's leader, providing significant insights into his spiritual and political evolution. Veteran members also came forward to be interviewed, the most important of whom was Larry 4X Prescott, later known as Akbar Muhammad, a former assistant minister of Malcolm's who had sided with Elijah Muhammad during the sect's split in March 1964. These sources presented a perspective that had not been adequately represented before: the views of the Nation of Islam and its adherents.

Malcolm's journey of reinvention was in many ways centered on his lifelong quest to discern the meaning and substance of faith. As a prisoner, he embraced an antiwhite, quasi-Islamic sect that nevertheless validated his fragmented sense of humanity and ethnic identity. But as he traveled across the world, Malcolm learned that orthodox Islam was in many ways at odds with the racial stigmatization and intolerance at the center of the Nation of Islam's creed. Malcolm came to adopt true Islam's universalism, and its belief that all could find Allah's grace regardless of race. Islam was also the spiritual platform from which he constructed a politics of Third World revolution, with striking parallels to the Argentinean guerrilla and coleader of the 1959 Cuban revolution, Che Guevara. It was also the political bridge that brought Malcolm into contact with the Islamic Brotherhood in Lebanon, as well as in Egypt and Gaza, with the Palestine Liberation Organization. Soliciting the support of the government of Gamal Abdel

Nasser for his activities on behalf of orthodox Islam in the United States may have made it necessary to adopt Nasser's political positions, such as fierce opposition to Israel.

There also remain many unresolved questions about Malcolm's death, and what parties were responsible for the order to kill him. History is not a cold-case investigation; I have had to weigh forensic probabilities, not certainties. Although in 1966 three NOI members were convicted of the murder, extensive evidence suggests that two of those men were completely innocent of the crime, that both the FBI and the NYPD had advance knowledge of it, and that the New York County District Attorney's office may have cared more about protecting the identities of undercover police officers and informants than arresting the real killers. That the case has remained unsolved after more than forty years helps place it in a special category in the annals of African-American and U.S. history. Unlike the murders of Medgar Evers and Martin Luther King, Jr., gunned down by lone white supremacists, or the killing of George Jackson, carried out by California prison guards, Malcolm was killed before a large audience in the heart of urban black America. In the rush to judgment, his death was attributed solely to the Nation of Islam. The media-constructed image of Malcolm X as a dangerous demagogue made it impossible to conduct a thorough investigation of his death, and it was only within black American communities that he was seen as a political martyr. It would take most of white America almost three decades to alter its perceptions.

The great temptation for the biographer of an iconic figure is to portray him or her as a virtual saint, without the normal contradictions and blemishes that all human beings have. I have devoted so many years in the effort to understand the interior personality and mind of Malcolm that this temptation disappeared long ago. He was a truly historical figure in the sense that, more than any of his contemporaries, he embodied the spirit, vitality, and political mood of an entire population—black urban mid-twentieth-century America. He spoke with clarity, humor, and urgency, and black audiences both in the United States and throughout Africa responded enthusiastically. Even when he made controversial statements with which the majority of African Americans strongly disagreed, few questioned his sincerity and commitment. On the other hand, any comprehensive review of his public record reveals major mistakes of judgment, including negotiations with the Ku Klux Klan. But unlike many other leaders, Malcolm had the courage to admit his mistakes, and to seek out and apologize to those he had offended. Even when I have disagreed with him, I deeply admire the strength and integrity of his character, and the love he obviously felt toward the African-American people and their culture.

To appreciate how Malcolm's resurrection occurred, first among African Americans and later throughout America, we need to reconstruct the full contours of his remarkable life—a story that begins in a small black community on the north side of Omaha, Nebraska.

CHAPTER 1

"Up, You Mighty Race!"

1925–1941

Malcolm X's father, Earl Little, Sr., was born in Reynolds, Georgia, on July 29, 1890. A farmer's son who was frequently called Early, he had barely three years of formal schooling, although as a teenager he learned carpentry, which provided him with a livelihood. In 1909, he married a local African-American woman, Daisy Mason, and in quick succession had three children: Ella, Mary, and Earl, Jr.

Reynolds, a small town in Georgia's southwest corner, had a population of only twelve hundred people around 1910, but it was an impressive manufacturing hub with a large cotton milling factory, producing seven to eight thousand bales each year. Like most of the South in the decades after Reconstruction, it was also a dangerous and violent place for African Americans. Between 1882 and 1927, Georgia's white racists lynched more than five hundred blacks, putting the state second only to Mississippi in lynching deaths. The depression of the 1890s had hit Georgia particularly hard, unleashing a wave of business failures twice the rate of that in the rest of the United States. As jobs grew increasingly scarce, skilled white laborers faced increasing competition from blacks, especially in masonry, carpentry, and the mechanical trades. Earl's status as a skilled carpenter probably provoked tensions with local whites, and his parents and friends feared for his safety.

Well over six feet tall, muscular and dark skinned, Little frequently got into heated arguments with whites who resented his air of independence. Reynolds and surrounding towns had seen several lynchings and countless acts of violence against blacks. His home life was only slightly less tumultuous: Daisy's extended family liked neither his brawling nor the way he treated his wife. By 1917, tired both of fighting his in-laws and of white threats of violence, Earl abandoned his young wife and children as part of the great northern migration of Southern blacks that began with World War I. Following the path of the Seaboard Air Line railroad, a common route for blacks headed north from Georgia and the Carolinas, he stopped first in Philadelphia, then New York City, before finally settling in Montreal. He did not bother to get a legal divorce.

It was within Montreal's small, mostly Caribbean black community that Earl fell in love with a beautiful Grenadian, Louisa Langdon Norton. Born in St. Andrew, Grenada, in 1897, she had been raised by her maternal grandmother, Mary Jane Langdon. Louise, as she was known, had a fair complexion and dark, flowing hair; in everyday encounters she was often mistaken for white. Local blacks gossiped that she was the product of her mother's rape by a Scotsman. Unlike Earl, she had received an excellent Anglican elementary-level education, becoming a capable writer as well as fluent in French. Thoughtful and ambitious, she had emigrated to Canada at nineteen, seeking greater opportunities than her small island homeland could provide.

Perhaps it was the attraction of opposites that brought Louise and Earl together—although a more likely explanation is that they shared an interest in social justice, the well-being of their race, and, with it, politics. In 1917, black Montrealers started an informal chapter of the Universal Negro Improvement Association and African Communities League (UNIA), founded by a charismatic Jamaican activist, Marcus Garvey. Although not officially established as a branch organization until June 1919, the Montreal UNIA exerted tremendous influence on blacks throughout the city. It sponsored educational forums, recreational activities, and social events for blacks, even sending delegations to international conventions. The two militant Garveyites fell in love, and were married in Montreal on May 10, 1919. They decided to dedicate their lives and futures to the building of the Garvey movement in the United States. Garvey was to play a pivotal part in their lives and, a generation later, in that of their son Malcolm.

On the eve of America's entry into World War I, black American political culture was largely divided into two ideological camps: accommodationists and liberal reformers. Divisions in tactics, theory, and ultimate goals concerning race relations would persist through the century. Led by the conservative educator Booker T. Washington, the accommodationists accepted the reality of Jim Crow segregation and did not openly challenge black disenfranchisement, instead promoting the development of black-owned businesses, technical and agricultural schools, and land ownership. The reformers, chief among them the scholar W. E. B. Du Bois and the militant journalist William Monroe Trotter, called for full political and legal rights for black Americans, and ultimately the end of racial segregation itself. Like the nineteenth-century abolitionist Frederick Douglass, they believed in dismantling the barriers separating blacks and whites in society. The establishment of the liberal National Association for the Advancement of Colored People (NAACP) in 1910, led by Du Bois, and the death of Washington in 1915 advanced the national leadership of the reformers over their conservative rivals.

It was at this moment of intense political debates among blacks that the charismatic Marcus Garvey arrived in New York City, on March 24, 1916. Born in Jamaica in 1887, Garvey had been a printer and journalist in the Caribbean, Central America, and England. He had come to the United States at the urging of Booker T. Washington to garner support for a college in Jamaica, a project which came to naught but which launched the flamboyant young man on a different mission, a new and ambitious political and social movement for blacks. Inspired by Washington's conservative ideas, Garvey did not object to racial segregation laws or separate schools, but astutely he paired these ideas with a fiery polemical attack on white racism and white colonial rule. Unlike the NAACP, which appealed to a rising middle class, Garvey recruited the black poor, the working class, and rural workers. After establishing a small base of supporters in Harlem, he embarked on a yearlong national tour in which he appealed to blacks to see themselves as "a mighty race," linking their efforts not only with people of African descent from the Caribbean but with Africa itself. In uncompromising language, he preached self-respect, the necessity for blacks to establish their own educational organizations, and the cultivation of the religious and cultural institutions that nurtured black families. In January 1918, the New York UNIA branch was formally established, and later that year Garvey started his own newspaper, *Negro World*; the following year the UNIA set up its international headquarters in Harlem, naming their building Liberty Hall.

Central to Garvey's appeal were his enthusiastic embrace of capitalism and his gospel of success; self-mastery, willpower, and hard work would provide the steps to lift black Americans. "Be not deceived," he told his followers, "wealth is strength, wealth is power, wealth is influence, wealth is justice, is liberty, is real human rights." The purpose of the African Communities League was to set up, in his words, "commercial houses, distributing houses, and also to engage in business of all kinds, wholesale and retail." Starting in Harlem, the league opened grocery stores and restaurants, and even financed the purchase of a steam laundry. In 1920, Garvey incorporated the Negro Factories Corporation to supervise the movement's growing list of businesses. His best-known and most controversial start-up, however, was the Black Star Line, a steamship company backed by tens of thousands of blacks who bought five- and ten-dollar shares. Ironically, all this activity depended on the existence of *de facto* racial segregation, which limited competition from white businesses, all of which refused to invest in urban ghettos.

Racial separation, Garvey preached, was essential for his people's progress, not only in the States but worldwide. His program was an informal mélange of ideas extracted from such disparate sources as Frederick Douglass, Andrew Carnegie, Ralph Waldo Emerson, Horatio Alger, and Benjamin Franklin, set now in a framework of achievement occupying a separate sphere from whites. Blacks would never respect themselves as a people so long as they were dependent upon others for their employment, business, and financial affairs. Like Booker T. Washington, Garvey sensed that Jim Crow segregation would not disappear quickly. It was logical, therefore, to turn an inescapable evil into a cornerstone of group advancement. Blacks had to reject the divisive distinctions of class, religion, nationality, and ethnicity that had traditionally divided their communities. People of African descent were all part of a transnational "nation," a global race with a common destiny. The UNIA's initial manifesto of 1914 called for people of Negro or African parentage "to establish a Universal confraternity among the race; to promote the spirit of race, pride and love . . . [and] to assist in civilizing the backward tribes of Africa." Later, many middle-class blacks dismissed Garveyism as a hopelessly utopian back-to-Africa movement, which underplayed its radical global vision. What Garvey recognized was that the Old World and the New were inextricably linked: blacks throughout the Caribbean and the United States could never be fully free unless Africa itself was liberated. Pan-Africanism—the belief in Africa's ultimate political independence, and that of all colonial states in which blacks lived—was the essential goal.

Garvey also recognized that creating a mass movement required a cultural revolution. Generations of blacks had endured slavery, segregation, and colonialism, producing a widespread sense of submission to white authority. Black power depended on activities that could restore both self-respect and a sense of community—essentially the development of a united black culture. For these reasons, "cultural nationalism" occupied a central role in his project. Garveyites sponsored literary events and published the writings of their followers; they organized debates, held concerts, and paraded beneath gaudy banners of black, red, and green. They were encouraged to write nationalist anthems, most popular among these being the "Universal Ethiopian Anthem," which featured the powerful if ungainly chorus:

> *Advance, advance to victory,*
> *Let Africa be free;*
> *Advance to meet the foe*
> *With the might*
> *Of the red, the black and the green.*

Garvey used pageantry to great effect in building the culture of his movement. Exalted titles and colorful uniforms created a sense of historical import and seriousness, and gave poor African Americans a sense of pride and excitement. At a 1921 Harlem gathering, six thousand Garveyites launched the "inauguration of the Empire of Africa." Garvey himself was crowned president general of the UNIA and provisional president of Africa, who with one potentate and one supreme deputy potentate constituted the royalty of the empire. Garveyite leaders were bestowed titles as "Knights of the Nile, Knights of the Distinguished Service Order of Ethiopia and Dukes of Niger and of Uganda." The fact that Garvey's movement controlled no territory in colonial Africa or the Caribbean did not matter. Blacks were identifying themselves as a nobility in exile, working toward the day when Europeans would be expelled from the Motherland and they would claim inheritance.

The UNIA assimilated themes from various African-American religious rituals. Although a nominal Catholic, Garvey held that people of African descent had to embrace a black God and a black theology of liberation. This was not an open rejection of Christianity, although he did declare at one rally, "We have been worshipping a false god. . . . We just create a god of our own and give this new religion to the Negroes of the world." In 1929, Garvey went so far as to say that "the Universal Negro Improvement Association is fundamentally a religious institution."

Garveyism created a positive social environment for strengthening black households and families that confronted racial prejudice in their everyday lives. As in any all-encompassing social movement, enthusiastic members often find the best companionship within the group. Whatever initially brought Earl Little and Louise Norton together, they shared a commitment to Garvey's ideals that would sustain them in the future. They made their first home among Philadelphia's black community, where they would reside for nearly two years. By 1918, Philadelphia had become the hub of extensive UNIA activities, and soon the chapter's growth exploded; between 1919 and 1920, more than ten thousand people, mostly working class and poor, joined the local organization, putting Philadelphia behind only New York City in total membership. Here, the religious side of Garveyism drove its popularity, thanks largely to the commanding presence of the chapter's charismatic leader, Reverend James Walker Hood Eason. In 1918, Eason and his spiritual followers had formed the People's Metropolitan African Methodist Episcopal Zion Church. Disillusioned with the lack of militancy within the NAACP, Eason joined forces with Garvey, and his rise was immediate. In 1919, without consulting his congregation, the pastor sold the church building to Garvey's Black Star Line for twenty-five thousand dollars, and the next year Garvey appointed him "Leader of American Negroes" at UNIA's first International Convention of the Negro Peoples of the World. Known as "silver-tongued Eason," he was selected by the Harlem-based Liberty Party as its presidential candidate in the 1920 elections.

At the party's convention that year, before a crowd of twenty-one thousand in Madison Square Garden, Eason emphasized the international dimensions of the UNIA's mission. "We are talking from a world standpoint now," he proclaimed. "We do not represent the English Negro or the French Negro . . . we represent all Negroes." By 1920, there were at least a hundred thousand UNIA members worldwide in more than eight hundred branch organizations or chapters. Garveyites enthusiastically told the world their followers numbered in the millions. A more objective assessment would still place the total number of new members in the 1920s and 1930s at one million or more, making it one of the largest mass movements in black history.

The UNIA never acquired a formal affiliation with any religious denomination, but given Earl Little's lifelong background in the black Baptist Church, religious Garveyism had a special appeal, and no one in the country better personified it than Eason. With Louise at his side, Earl attended many of UNIA's conferences and lectures in Philadelphia and Harlem, where Eason was frequently the star attraction, and from whom Earl would learn practical lessons in public speaking. As he grew within the movement, so did his family; on February 12, 1920, Louise gave birth to the couple's first child, Wilfred, but they were not much longer for Philadelphia. The

UNIA routinely selected capable young activists as field organizers, and in mid-1921 the Littles agreed to move halfway across the continent to start a fledgling outpost in Omaha, Nebraska.

Their appointment coincided with the explosive rebirth of the Ku Klux Klan (KKK) in America's heartland. Created in the aftermath of the Civil War, the first Klan had been a white supremacist vigilante organization, employing violence and terror chiefly against newly freed African Americans. The second KKK, prompted by the waves of xenophobia among millions of white Americans following World War I, expanded its targets to include Jews, Catholics, Asians, and non-European "foreigners." Nebraska's local branch, called Klavern Number One, was set up in early 1921. Before that year's end, another twenty-four such groups had been born, initially recording an average of eight hundred new members statewide every week. Their forums were well advertised, and by 1923 membership totaled forty-five thousand. Within the year, Klan demonstrations, parades, and cross-burnings had become common throughout the state. According to Michael W. Schuyler, a leading local historian, the KKK's 1924 state convention in downtown Lincoln "featured 1,100 Klansmen in white robes. Klan dignitaries rode in open cars; hooded knights marched on foot, frequently carrying American flags; others rode horses." It was hardly the clandestine group it would be forced to become in later decades.

Omaha's small black community felt under siege. A few militants had already joined the NAACP, and they used their newspaper, the *Monitor*, to appeal to sympathetic local whites to join them against the KKK. In September 1921, the *Monitor* declared that with "the combined efforts of the Jews, the Catholics and the foreign-born, the Klan may expect the battle of its life. If actual bloodshed is desired, then the allies are prepared to do battle. If the war is a social and industrial one, then the allies are ready to meet that kind of warfare. The common enemy will drive the common allies together." Still, they found it difficult to match their rhetoric with action in the rigged political machinery of middle America. In January 1923, the anti-KKK coalition petitioned Nebraska's state legislature to outlaw citizens from holding public meetings while "in disguise to conceal their identities" and to require local police to protect individuals accused of crimes while in their custody. The bill easily passed the state house, sixty-five votes to thirty-four, but failed to garner the necessary two-thirds majority in the state senate, where Klan supporters ensured its failure.

By 1923, two to three million white Americans—including such rising politicians as Hugo Black of Alabama, and later Robert Byrd of West

Virginia—had joined the Klan, and it had become a force in national politics. The secret organization ran its members in both the Democratic and Republican parties, holding the balance of power in many state legislatures and hundreds of city councils. Their significant presence led Garvey to extrapolate that the KKK was both the face and soul of white America. "The Ku Klux Klan is the invisible government of the United States," he told his followers at Liberty Hall in 1922, and it "represents to a great extent the feelings of every real white American." Given this, he reasoned, it was only common sense to negotiate with them, and so he did, taking an infamous meeting with Klan leader Edward Young Clarke. From a practical standpoint, the groups shared considerable common ground, with both the KKK and the UNIA opposing interracial marriage and social intercourse between the races. However, many prominent Garveyites directly challenged Garvey's initiative, or simply broke from the UNIA in disgust. Even more members criticized their organization's chaotic business practices such as the Black Star Line, condemning the authoritarian way it was run. Many former UNIA members rallied around the leadership of Reverend Eason, who now created his own group, the Universal Negro Alliance, and whose popularity in some quarters exceeded Garvey's. Loyal Garveyites responded by isolating or, in some cases, eliminating their critics. In late 1922, Eason traveled to New Orleans to mobilize his supporters. After delivering an address at the city's St. John's Baptist Church, surrounded by hundreds of admirers, he was attacked by three gun-wielding assailants, shot in the back and through the forehead. He clung to life for several days, finally dying on January 4, 1923. There is no evidence directly linking Garvey to the murder; several key loyalists, including Amy Jacques Garvey, his articulate and ambitious second wife, were far more ruthless than their leader and may have been involved in Eason's assassination.

Neither dissension within the UNIA's national leadership nor their leader's erratic ideological shifts discouraged Louise and Earl. The young couple's life was hard; they had few resources, and Louise had given birth to two more children—Hilda in 1922 and Philbert in 1923. Earl supplemented the family's needs by hiring himself out for carpentry work; he shot game fowl with his rifle, and raised rabbits and chickens in their backyard. But his constant agitation on behalf of Garvey's cause led local blacks to fear KKK reprisals against their community. Earl's UNIA responsibilities occasionally required him to travel hundreds of miles; during one such trip, in the winter of 1925, hooded Klansmen rode out to the Little home in the middle of the night. Louise, pregnant again, bravely stepped onto her front porch to confront them. They demanded that Earl come out of the house immediately. Louise told them that she was alone with her three small children and that her husband was away, preaching, in Milwaukee. Frustrated in their objective, the Klan vigilantes warned Louise that she and her whole family should leave town, that Earl's "spreading trouble" within Omaha's black community would not be tolerated. To underline their message, the vigilantes proceeded to shatter every window. "Then they rode off," Malcolm wrote, recalling what he had been told about the event, "their torches flaring, as suddenly as they had come."

The apex of Klan activity in Nebraska came in the mid-1920s. By then the Klan numbered tens of thousands, drawn from nearly every social class. In 1925, a women's branch was established, and soon they were singing, listening to lectures by national spokeswomen, and joining their menfolk marching in parades. Thousands of white children were mobilized, boys joining the Junior Klan, girls the Tri-K clubs. Their influence in both Omaha and Nebraska was pervasive, some white churches even acquiescing when the Klan disrupted their services. That same year, 1925, the KKK's annual state convention was staged to coincide with the Nebraska State Fair, both held in Lincoln. Crosses were burned while a KKK parade with floats mustered fifteen hundred marchers and a public picnic drew twenty-five thousand followers.

It was during this terrible time that, on May 19, 1925, at Omaha's University Hospital, Louise gave birth to her fourth child. The boy, Earl's seventh child, was christened Malcolm.

———

Despite continuing threats, the Littles struggled to build a UNIA organization. On Sunday, May 8, 1926, the local branch held a meeting that featured "Mr. E. Little" as its principal speaker. In her role as secretary, Louise wrote, "This division is small but much alive to its part in carrying on the great work." By the fall of 1926, however, they concluded that their community, beleaguered by Klan depredations, could not sustain a militant organization. The UNIA's troubles nationally compounded their difficulties. The Justice Department had for years aggressively hounded UNIA leaders, and in 1923 Garvey had been convicted of mail fraud in connection with the financial dealings of his Black Star Line and given a five-year sentence. He spent the next two years exhausting his appeals before finally entering federal prison in Atlanta in February 1925. In many urban areas, especially in the Northeast, his imprisonment created major schisms and defections, but across the rural South and in the Midwest thousands continued to join the movement. Loyal Garveyites sent funds and letters of encouragement to local chapters and national offices, and made appeals to reverse Garvey's conviction.

Louise and Earl and their four children soon moved on to Milwaukee, Wisconsin, an urban center with an expanding African-American community. Between 1923 and 1928, industries in the city were hiring hundreds of new workers, and blacks migrated there in droves. In 1923, the black residential population was estimated at five thousand; by the end of the decade, it had grown by 50 percent. Common laborers' jobs paid up to seven dollars a day, higher than in many other cities. What also attracted the Littles was black Milwaukee's robust entrepreneurship and racial solidarity. There were a good number of black-owned restaurants, funeral parlors, boarding-houses, and hotels; many proprietors saw their entrepreneurial efforts as realizing "the dream of a black city within the city."

Though relations between Garvey and the national NAACP leadership were cold, if not frequently antagonistic, on the local level chapters of both groups often found themselves on the same side of issues and were open to collaboration. Despite their differing visions for the future of race relations, both could agree on the immediate need for less racial violence and more black jobs. In 1922, for instance, the local Milwaukee UNIA had drafted a resolution, endorsed by the NAACP, opposing the employment of blacks as strikebreakers on local railroads, aimed at preventing racial strife between striking workers. That year, the UNIA chapter claimed one hundred members; by the early 1930s more than four hundred had joined. This success was due largely to the efforts of a local clergyman, the Reverend Ernest Bland, under whose leadership the local UNIA pursued a strategy to appeal to low-income black workers, holding parades and cultural events and opening its own Liberty Hall. Many Milwaukee UNIA leaders also became Socialist Party activists; unlike at the national level, they frequently participated in civil rights protests and campaigns to elevate African Americans to elective office. Earl Little was involved as an officer in the International Industrial Club, a black working-class organization, and it was in that capacity, rather than as a UNIA leader, that he and two other club officers wrote to President Calvin Coolidge on June 8, 1927, asking for Garvey to be released. The Littles left town shortly after this petition was mailed, their departure delayed only by the birth of yet another son, Reginald. (Shortly after his birth Reginald was diagnosed with hernia problems; poor health would plague him into manhood.)

The family's next stop was East Chicago, Indiana, but their stay was even briefer, since the state proved to be another KKK hotbed. By 1929, they had moved on again, purchasing a one-and-a-half-story farmhouse on a small three-lot property on the outskirts of Lansing, Michigan. Curiously, it was a neighborhood where few blacks lived. The Littles failed to realize that the deed for the property contained a special provision—a racial exclusion clause that voided the sale to blacks. Within several months, their white neighbors, well aware of such clauses, filed to evict them, and a local judge granted the request. Earl retained the services of a lawyer, who filed an appeal.

Waiting on the due processes of law was not enough for local racists. Early in the morning of November 8, the Littles' house was shaken by an explosion that Earl would later attribute to several white men, none of whom he recognized, dousing the back of the house in gasoline and setting it afire. Within seconds, flames and thick smoke engulfed the farmhouse. Four-year-old Malcolm and his siblings would relive this event for the rest of their lives. "We heard a big boom," remembered Wilfred.

> When we woke up, fire was everywhere, and everybody was running into the walls and into each other, trying to get away. I could hear my mother yelling, my father yelling—they made sure they got us all rounded up and got us out. The fire was spreadin' so fast that they couldn't hardly bring anything else out. My mother began to run back and bring our bedclothing, whatever she could grab, and pulled it to the porch and then out into the yard. She made the mistake of laying my baby sister down on top of some quilts and things that were there and then went back for something else. When she came back, she didn't see the baby—what had happened, they'd put somethin' else on top of the baby. And my mother almost lost her mind. I mean they were hanging on to her to keep her from going back into the house. And then finally the baby cried, and they knew where the baby was.

The terrified family huddled together in the cold night air. Enraged, Earl "took a shot at somebody he said was running away from the house," Wilfred recalled. No fire wagon arrived to rescue them, and their home burned to the ground.

The police assigned Detective George W. Waterman to investigate the Little family's house-burning case. White residents in the neighborhood told the detective that a local gas station proprietor, Joseph Nicholson, had called the fire department but it had refused to come. Yet almost immediately, rumors circulated in the neighborhood that Earl had started the fire himself, and Waterman decided to pursue this line of inquiry vigorously. His suspicions were reinforced when he learned that Earl held a two-thousand-dollar home policy with the Westchester Fire Insurance Company, as well as a five-hundred-dollar policy on household contents with the Rouse Insurance Company. Waterman and another officer interviewed Nicholson, who claimed that Earl Little gave him a revolver the previous night. Nicholson produced the gun, which had five remaining bullets and one empty cylinder. Meanwhile, newly homeless, the Littles had decamped to Lansing, to stay temporarily with the family of a man named Herb Walker. That same evening, Waterman drove out to the Walkers' house while Earl was away and interviewed Louise, who explained to him that she had no knowledge of the fire until she was awakened by her husband. The police next interviewed Wilfred, then nine years old. It was dark by the time Earl finally returned to the Walker house, and Waterman and another officer took him outside to their car to interrogate him. Because some of Earl's responses did not exactly coincide with those of Louise and Wilfred, Waterman reported later, "We decided to lock Mr. Little up for further investigation." The police were now convinced that Little had set fire to his house to acquire the insurance money. Their problem was that the district attorney concluded there was insufficient evidence to prosecute Earl. Instead, he was charged only with being in possession of an unregistered handgun; he pled not guilty, and bond was set at five hundred dollars. The weak case was repeatedly delayed by the county prosecutor's office until February 26, 1930, when it was quickly dismissed.

Waterman's final report did not indicate that the investigation into Earl's possible arson had been closed. At the time of the fire, moreover, the Littles' attorney had been appealing their eviction to the Michigan State Supreme Court. Further, Earl had allowed one of the insurance policies on his home to lapse. On the morning after the fire, he visited a local insurance office and made a late payment on his old policy, saying nothing about the blaze that had just destroyed his home. His hasty actions indicate that he probably did not start the fire: had he intended to do so, he would surely have made the late payment first.

The destruction of a black family's home by racist whites was hardly unique in the Midwest at this time. In 1923, the Michigan State Supreme Court had upheld the legality of racially restrictive provisions in the sale of private homes. Most Michigan whites felt that blacks had no right to purchase homes in predominantly white communities. Four years before the Littles' fire, in June 1925, a black couple, Dr. Ossian Sweet and his wife, Gladys, purchased a single-family home in East Detroit, a white neighborhood, escaping Detroit's largest ghetto, known as the Black Bottom, and were forced to pay $18,500 even though the fair market value of the modest bungalow was under $13,000. On the night the Sweets moved in, despite the presence of a police inspector, hundreds of angry whites surrounded the house and began smashing its windows with rocks and bricks. Several of the Sweets' friends shot into the mob, killing one man and wounding another. Ossian and Gladys Sweet plus nine others were subsequently charged with murder. The NAACP vigorously took up the case, hiring celebrated defense attorney Clarence Darrow. Despite an all-white jury, eight of the eleven accused were acquitted; the jury divided on the remaining three. The judge subsequently declared a mistrial, and ultimately the Sweets were freed.

This latest setback did not destroy Earl Little's resolve. He was by now an experienced master carpenter, with the skills necessary to construct a new home. In only a few months, on the extreme south side of Lansing, close to the educational campus of what would later become a part of Michigan State University, the Littles found an inexpensive six-acre plot next to sprawling woodlands. Its owner, a white widow, agreed to sell it to them. Only a few months later, however, the Littles learned that a lien on one half of the property had been filed against her for nonpayment of back taxes. Once again frustrated by the law, they had no recourse but to forfeit the disputed land.

Earl's anger at his continued misfortunes was largely channeled into his work for the UNIA. Meanwhile, Malcolm, by then five years old, was fast becoming his favorite child, and the two would travel together to UNIA gatherings, usually held in a member's home. Such meetings rarely attracted more than two dozen people, but they were filled with energy and enthusiasm fueled by Earl's leadership. Malcolm remembered this vividly, writing, "The meetings always closed with my father saying several times and the people chanting after him, 'Up, you mighty race, you can accomplish what you will!'"

As he had in Omaha, however, Earl found recruitment in Lansing difficult. Although as early as 1850 several black families had lived in the area, even by 1910 blacks totaled only 354—about 1.1 percent of the town—of whom about one-fifth had migrated from Canada; the majority had been born in the upper South—states such as Kentucky, West Virginia, and Tennessee. The migration of millions of African Americans from the Deep South (beginning about 1915) drew a steady stream of poor blacks into Michigan's state capital, so that by 1930 1,409 lived there. It did not take long for class divisions to emerge. The earliest wave of migrants had possessed relatively high levels of education and vocational training. By the 1890s, the majority owned their own homes and some their own businesses, mostly in racially mixed neighborhoods. A small number were employed as stone and brick masons, teamsters, painters, carpenters, and plasterers. At the turn of the century, only 10 percent of the men had been classified as "unskilled and semiskilled." By contrast, most of those who arrived after 1915 often had no trade to speak of, and the sense of invasion brought about by their sheer numbers provoked new laws that drew sharper racial divisions. With the emergence of segregation laws in the late nineteenth and early twentieth centuries, restrictive racial covenants on the mortgages of private houses were widely adopted in many states, including Michigan. Such codes had the effect of forcing a second wave of black emigrants to occupy a poor neighborhood in west central Lansing. Although blacks were allowed to vote, their civil and legal rights were restricted in other ways. With only slight exaggeration, Wilfred Little later described blacks' lives in Michigan in the 1920s and 1930s as "the same as being in Mississippi. . . . When you went into the courts and when you had to deal with the police, it was the same as being down South."

When local Negroes resisted racial discrimination, whites would black-ball them. Because Earl Little persisted in trying to get blacks to organize themselves, he was considered just such a troublemaker. Yet Earl blamed his difficulties in securing regular employment on Lansing's black middle class, who looked askance at Garveyites. He frequently gave guest sermons in black churches, the paltry offerings he received meaning financial survival for the family. Yet Malcolm was taught to have little but scorn for the solid citizens who sat listening to his father. Lansing's black leaders were deluding themselves, he was convinced, about their real place within society. "I don't know a town with a higher percentage of complacent and misguided so-called 'middle class' Negroes—the typical status-symbol-oriented, integration-seeking type," than in Lansing. Yet this black bourgeoisie lacked the resources of a true upper class. "The real elite," Malcolm later wrote in his *Autobiography*, "'big shots,' the 'voices of the race,' were the waiters at the Lansing Country Club and the shoeshine boys at the state capitol." He was not being sarcastic: such men had indeed been his peers.

By the late 1920s, Garvey's once-massive movement had disintegrated in many of America's largest cities. In 1927, the UNIA's Liberty Hall headquarters in Harlem was sold at auction. That November, President Coolidge commuted Garvey's prison sentence, with the stipulation that he be deported and permanently barred from reentry. Garvey duly arrived in Jamaica on December 10, where he immediately went to work consolidating the remnants of his organization. The following year, he and Amy Garvey embarked on an international speaking tour, addressing thousands in England, Germany, France, Belgium, and Canada. In Jamaica, Garveyites launched the People's Political Party and started a daily newspaper, *Blackman*. Throughout the Caribbean, in Africa, and in rural and isolated black communities and small towns of the United States, Garveyism still flourished.

Perhaps because thousands of poor Southern migrants constituted the majority of Detroit's black working class, the city continued to be a Mecca for the cause. In 1924, Garveyites estimated membership in the city at seven thousand. Its African-American migrant population was predominantly between the ages of twenty and forty-four, and most were unmarried men, semiskilled or unskilled. Hundreds had found employment in Henry Ford's River Rouge plant, but others were routinely hired only in dangerous jobs in the foundries. These young migrant workers continued to be a prime constituency for the Garvey movement.

Even well into the early 1930s, Garveyite branches thrived in Michigan's smaller cities and towns, despite—or perhaps because of—the advent of the Great Depression. Between 1921 and 1933, fifteen UNIA divisions or branch organizations were established there. Earl organized fleets of cars of local Garveyites to travel to UNIA gatherings (usually held in Detroit) and imposed the movement's principles in his own household. African-American and even Caribbean newspapers were read at home, Wilfred Little recalled, and the children were regularly tutored about "what was going on in the Caribbean area and parts of Africa," as well as on news of the movement from around the country. From these educational efforts grew the Pan-African perspective that would become so crucial for Malcolm later in life.

The Little children were constantly drilled in the principles of Garveyism, to such an extent that they expressed their black nationalist values at school. For example, on one morning following the Pledge of Allegiance and the singing of the national anthem at school, Wilfred informed his teacher that blacks also had their own anthem. Instructed to sing it, Wilfred complied: "It began with the words . . . 'Ethiopia, the land of the free . . .' That creates some problems," Wilfred recalled, "because here is this little nigger that feels he is just equal to anybody else, he got his own little national anthem that he sings, and he's proud of it. . . . It wasn't the way they wanted things to go."

As the family continued to grow, Louise did her best to care for them all with a meager income. To learn the Garveyite principles of self-sufficiency and personal responsibility, each older child was allotted a personal patch of garden. They continued to raise chickens and rabbits, but the daily pressures of poverty and their reputation as Garveyite oddballs took its toll. Earl was prone to physical violence with his wife and most of his children. Yet Malcolm, who idolized his father, would routinely escape punishment. Somehow the small boy sensed that his light color served as a kind of shield from Earl's beatings. As an adult, Malcolm recalled the violent incidents, admitting that his parents quarreled frequently; however, nearly all of his whippings as a boy came from his mother.

As the Great Depression deepened, impoverished whites in the Midwest became attracted to a new vigilante formation, the Black Legion. Starting as the Klan Guard in late 1924 or early 1925 in Bellaire, Ohio, the formation employed a blend of anti-black and anti-Catholic rhetoric. Black robes instead of white were used; "burning crosses on midnight hillsides were in; noontime parades down Main Street were out." The Black Legion successfully attracted many law enforcement personnel and some union members in public transport. By the early 1930s, its members routinely engaged in night riding and policing of town and village morals, with their victims subjected to any number of humiliations, including whippings, being tarred and feathered, or just being run out of town.

Early in the evening of September 8, 1931, shortly after supper, Earl went into his bedroom to clean up before setting off for Lansing's north side to collect "chicken money" from families that had purchased his poultry. Louise had a bad feeling about the trip and implored him not to go. Earl dismissed her fears and left. A few hours later, Louise and the children went to bed. Late in the night, she was awakened by a loud knock on the front door and sprang from her bed in terror. When she cautiously opened the door, she found a young Michigan state police officer, Lawrence G. Baril, who brought dreadful and long-feared news: her husband had been critically injured in an accident and was in the local hospital.

Several hours earlier Baril had been summoned to the scene of a streetcar accident. This was the first serious accident that the young officer had investigated; his vivid impression, his widow, Florentina, later recalled, was that "the man had been cut in two . . . the accident was quite violent." Police had immediately hypothesized that Earl had somehow slipped and fallen while boarding a moving streetcar at night. Perhaps he'd lost his footing and was pulled under the streetcar's rear wheels, they speculated. The possibility that Earl could have been the victim of racist violence was never considered.

Earl suffered terrible pain for several hours after being taken to hospital. His left arm had been crushed, his left leg nearly severed from his torso. By the time Louise reached him, he was dead. The Lansing coroner ruled Earl's death accidental, and the Lansing newspaper account presented the story that way as well. Yet the memories of Lansing blacks as set down in oral histories tell a different story, one that suggested foul play and the involvement of the Black Legion.

Wilfred recalled attending the funeral and viewing his father's corpse. "While my mother was talking, I slipped into the back where they had the body on the table," he remembered. "The streetcar had cut him just below the torso and it had cut his left leg completely off and had crushed the right leg, because the streetcar . . . had just run right over him. He ended up bleeding to death." Malcolm's most vivid memory of his father's funeral was his mother's hysteria, and later her difficulty in coping with what had happened. He believed that he and his siblings "adjusted" to the challenging reality of Early Little's death better than Louise did. Nevertheless, the children were deeply disturbed by swirling rumors about their father's violent death. Philbert, then eight years old, was told that "somebody had hit my father from behind with a car and knocked him under the streetcar. Then I learned later that somebody had shoved him under that car."

A forensic reconstruction of Earl Little's death suggests that the story Philbert had heard may have been true. Before leaving home on the night of his death, Earl had told his wife that he was traveling to North Lansing. However, according to a local newspaper, his body was discovered at the intersection of Detroit Street and East Michigan Avenue, one block east of the town's boundary line. Few blacks lived in the area. The odd location of the body suggests the possibility that Earl was struck by a car or perhaps bludgeoned in one location, and then moved under a streetcar at another site, making it appear to have been a terrible accident. Earl Little's possible murder may have served the same purpose that lynchings did in the South—to terrorize local blacks and to suppress their acts of resistance.

Louise harbored no doubts that her husband had been murdered, possibly by the Black Legion. Although she identified Earl's body, she does not appear to have challenged the police report or otherwise tried to search out the truth. Malcolm remained throughout his life both haunted by his father's tragic end and ambivalent about how it occurred. In 1963, while visiting Michigan State University, he described Earl's death as accidental, yet the following year cast his father as a martyr for black liberation.

With their patriarch's sudden death, the Little family was plunged into an abyss of poverty. Earl held a one-thousand-dollar life insurance policy, which was now paid to Louise, but she was not allowed to keep the money for long. The news of her husband's death brought a host of irate petitioners to the probate court, demanding payment for past services. Local physician U. S. Bagley, for one, came asking for ninety-nine dollars, claiming he had assisted at the births of Louise and Earl's youngest children, Yvonne and Wesley, in addition to his household visits to treat Philbert for pneumonia. Dentist bills, rental fees, roof repairs—all of these added up; even the funeral company was still owed close to four hundred dollars, including burial expenses in Georgia. Almost none of the petitioners received anything, because the estate was worth only a thousand dollars— the equivalent of about $15,000 in 2010. Louise had petitioned the court for a "widow's allowance," requesting eighteen dollars per month "for the maintenance of myself and the family." Nearly $750 from the insurance payment went to cover the widow's allowance. After paying the court fees and the probate administrator, the policy payout was almost exhausted.

At first, Louise fought desperately to maintain stability. "My mother had a lot of pride," Yvonne Little Woodward, Malcolm's younger sister, would recall. "She crocheted gloves for people. . . . She rented out garden space, she sharecropped with the man that would come and rent garden space. We had a dump behind our house—she rented that out." Hilda, almost ten years old, became the surrogate mother, taking care of her younger siblings while finding occasional employment as a babysitter. Wilfred used his father's rifle to hunt game for the family's suppers. The only children who apparently failed to rally were Philbert and Malcolm, who took no part in the household obligations. After school, at Lansing's Pleasant Grove Elementary, the two boys would hang out with local whites "to create mischief," as Philbert later admitted. On one such occasion, they deliberately moved the outhouse of a neighbor who routinely "used to give them a bad time," one of Malcolm's childhood friends, Cyril McGuine, recalled. "When he came out to chase them, all of a sudden he just dropped out of sight with a scream and fell into the hole that they had prepared."

Even at seven, Malcolm had a knack for avoiding hard work. Yvonne recalled her mother sending a group of the children out to work in the garden. Almost immediately, "Malcolm would start talking, and we would start working. . . . I can remember Malcolm lying under a tree with a straw in his mouth. [He] was telling these stories, but we were so happy to be around him that we worked." Wilfred noticed that his younger brother already possessed an unusual self-confidence. "When a group [of children] would start playing, [Malcolm] would end up being the one that was leading." When the local white children played in the woods behind the Littles' property, "Malcolm would say, 'Let's go play Robin Hood.' Well, we'd go back there, and Robin Hood was Malcolm. And these white kids would go along with it—a Black Robin Hood!"

Already difficult, things grew more frustrating when Louise was forced to contend with Michigan's bedeviling welfare bureaucracy. The state had passed its first comprehensive pension law in 1913, providing financial support for poor children whose mothers were judged suitable guardians. This established a statewide standard of three dollars per week per child, but in reality—the result of a 1931 state law that separated "poor relief" from the administration of "mothers' pensions"—the average weekly payment was no more than $1.75. In some cases, women who headed households with six or more children received payments covering only three. Recipients had few rights. Unlike those on poor relief, who were required to live in a particular county for a full year before they could become eligible, mothers could move throughout the state without surrendering benefits. However, because the pensions were administered by counties, local administrators and probate judges exercised considerable discretion. Although state law required equal access for African-American mothers, discrimination based on marital status, race, and other factors was widespread. Louise's pension payments never covered even basic needs. "The checks helped," Malcolm admitted, "but they weren't enough, as many as there were."

The year 1934 was especially trying. Michigan's welfare department was constantly investigating the Little household, and Louise just as constantly faced down its officers, protesting at the "meddling in our lives." Hunger was the family's constant companion, and occasionally Malcolm and his siblings became dizzy from malnourishment. By the fall, a subtle psychological shift had taken place; the Garveyite sense of pride and self-sufficiency began to fade. The Littles started to see themselves as victims of the state's bureaucracy.

Louise desperately continued to seek ways to keep her family afloat. She was careful to maintain a household routine that would nurture order and a sense of family. At the end of the day, they "would all gather around the stove," said Wilfred, "and my mother would tell us stories. Or we would sing our alphabets, or we would sing our math, and then she taught us French. . . . And then she would tell us stories about our ancestry." For Louise, the family increasingly became her only enduring source of support. The small network of Garveyites with whom she and her husband had worked had unraveled during the Great Depression. She solicited help from members of a nearby Seventh-Day Adventist Church, but their assistance came with the price of assimilation. With Wilfred, she read through the Adventists' many pamphlets, modifying the family's food intake to conform to what the church taught. This included a ban on pork and rabbit, two staples of their diet.

At school, Malcolm's stigmatization as a child on relief affected him deeply; Michigan's schools were integrated, and it was difficult enough to be black, much less black and on welfare. Before long he began stealing food from local stores, both as a way of acting out and to satisfy his hunger. It was still far from enough. For days at a time, when the Littles had no food, Malcolm started showing up around suppertime at the home of their neighbors Thornton and Mabel Gohanna. The Gohannas "were nice, older people, and great churchgoers. I had watched them lead the jumping and shouting when my father preached," Malcolm recalled. Their household always included a number of interesting drifters and the indigent who needed care. The Gohannas were soon lavishing attention on the growing boy. After Malcolm had been caught stealing several times, his petty thievery became a contentious issue for county welfare workers, who approached the Gohanna family to see if they were willing to take him in as a foster child. The Gohannas consented. "My mother threw a fit, though," Malcolm related.

The fabric of life seemed to be worn increasingly threadbare by daily events, large and small. Yvonne recalled an incident when her mother had managed to scrape enough together to buy some new bedroom furniture. One day soon afterward, a truck pulled up in front of her home, and the driver explained that he had been ordered to return the purchases to the store. "My mother kept saying, 'I have paid this. I have the receipt,'" but the driver refused to listen. The next day, Louise went downtown to rectify the problem, and the furniture was returned to her. Still, the incident rattled her, as it compounded the stress of poverty by challenging her efforts to keep up appearances in front of her white neighbors. "How many of them saw [the furniture] come back?" Yvonne questioned. "They didn't know that [it] was paid for. The store apologized, but look what they put my mother through." In another incident, someone killed the family's dog. Wilfred explained, "They shot [it] just for the purpose of seeing to it that you don't have a dog. I guess, just to give you a hard time." Local whites, with few exceptions, treated Louise and her children with contempt. "When they would come to the house," Wilfred recalled, "they would speak to my mother in a way where they were trying to get her to kneel . . . because she was independent."

Louise was not yet forty and, despite these hardships, remained an extremely attractive woman. Sometime in 1935 or 1936, she began dating a local African American. Malcolm described the man's physical appearance as similar to his father's, noting that Louise would brighten whenever her suitor came by. The man—never identified in Malcolm's account—was self-employed and possessed modest resources. His presence in their lives offered a glimpse of promise: only the security of marriage could guarantee that welfare officers would keep out of the Little family's lives. For a time a proposal seemed likely; then, in late 1937, Louise became pregnant with the man's child. Once he discovered she was pregnant, Malcolm recalled, he "jilted my mother suddenly."

It was either just before or during the pregnancy, when Malcolm was eleven or twelve, that welfare workers placed him in the Gohannas' home. He resisted the move, but Louise could no longer look after the whole household. "We children," Malcolm reflected, "watched our anchor giving way." He was unhappy at first, but put on a good face when his transfer to his foster neighbors was made official: the new arrangement eased the financial burden on his mother, and he was close enough to visit frequently. The Gohanna family, out of its religious convictions, was also known for welcoming ex-convicts into their home. Perhaps it was here that the genesis of Malcolm's later strategy of "fishing" for religious converts among the homeless and former prisoners was born.

As the winter of 1938 turned into spring, the Littles' slender hopes disintegrated. Physically and psychologically, Louise grew weaker. That summer, she gave birth to her eighth child, Robert. Several weeks later, in the fall, Malcolm was enrolled in West Grove Junior High School in Lansing. By all indications, he performed well academically and easily established friendships with other children, black and white. At home, though, the new baby had pushed Louise beyond her breaking point. Days before Christmas, police officers found her trudging barefoot along a snow-covered road, her new child clutched to her chest. She appeared traumatized and did not know who or where she was. In early January 1939, a physician certified that she was "an insane person and her condition is such as to require care and treatment in an institution." On January 31, 1939, Louise was received at Kalamazoo State Hospital, accompanied by Sheriff Frank Clone, Deputy

Sheriff Ray Pinchet, and Wilfred Little. She would be confined to the state hospital's grounds for the next twenty-four years.

Michigan's mental health facilities were primitive by the era's standards, in some cases no better than old-fashioned asylums where the mentally ill were warehoused. Their wards were frequently overcrowded, and recovery rates remained low. Kalamazoo State Hospital had been established in 1859 as the Michigan Asylum for the Insane, and by the time Louise arrived, it wore its age plainly; throughout the 1930s, its administrators complained of chronic understaffing, which contributed to neglect and improper diagnoses. A 1903 Michigan law on insanity had mandated that asylums "use every proper means to furnish employment to such patients as may be benefited by regular labor suited to their capacity and strength." Beginning in the 1920s, female patients were routinely assigned to weave rugs and construct mattresses in the asylum's industrial building. Elsewhere, women patients cooked, ironed and mended clothing, and kept house. Louise was expected to carry out such tasks. Given her diagnosis of severe depression, her treatment at the time seems likely to have included electroconvulsive therapy. Whatever the treatment, it offered her little relief, and she drifted in and out of a dazed state for years.

Malcolm would rarely visit his mother, and seldom spoke of her: he was deeply ashamed of her illness. The experience etched into him the conviction that all women were, by nature, weak and unreliable. He may also have believed that his mother's love affair and subsequent out-of-wedlock pregnancy were, in some way, a betrayal of his father.

Welfare officials determined that Wilfred, twenty, and Hilda, eighteen, were old enough to be responsible for the household. That summer, however, a state worker decided that the Gohannas could no longer provide for the now fourteen-year-old Malcolm and recommended that he be reassigned to the Ingham County Juvenile Home in Mason, ten miles south of Lansing. The town was virtually all white, as was the school to which Malcolm would be forced to transfer. During his time with the Gohannas, Malcolm had often spent weekends at home with his family, but the reassignment severely limited such access.

At first, he adjusted easily to Mason's junior high school—he was elected class president during his second semester, and finished academically near the top of his class. The handsome black boy began to develop crushes on several white female classmates. Tall and painfully thin, he was noticeably unathletic; his two attempts at boxing were comic disasters, and he was a poor performer in basketball. Yet his charm and verbal and intellectual skills won him admirers. He was a natural leader, and others enjoyed being around him. White teens nicknamed him "Harpy," because he kept "harping" on pet themes or talking loudly and rapidly over others. Within Lansing's black community, however, he received a different nickname—"Red," due to the color of his hair.

With Malcolm separated from the family, and Wilfred and Hilda struggling to support the rest of their siblings after their mother's institutionalization, help arrived from Boston in late 1939 or early 1940 in the form of Ella Little, their oldest half sister. One of Earl's children from his first marriage, Ella had moved north from Georgia with other family members in the 1930s. Though she had never met—or at least had never been much involved with—Earl's second family, when news reached her of their troubles in Lansing, she set out to take an active role in the children's supervision. To the fifteen-year-old Malcolm, she was an assertive, no-nonsense woman. During Ella's visit, the Little children accompanied her to Kalamazoo to call on their mother. Malcolm was particularly affected by the physical differences between the two women; Ella's jet-black skin and robust physique provided a striking contrast to Louise's much lighter complexion. Several days later, just prior to her return home, Ella urged Malcolm to write to her regularly. Perhaps, she ventured, he might even spend part of the summer with her in Boston. "I jumped at the chance," Malcolm recalled.

When Malcolm made the trip in the summer of 1940, he was overwhelmed by the city's sights. Ella was only twenty-six, but seemed worldly and independent. She lived with her second husband in a comfortable single-family home on Waumbeck Street in the racially mixed Hill district of Boston. Her younger brother, Earl, Jr., and her shy younger sister, Mary, resided there as well. On the weekends, thousands of blacks congregated in Boston's busy streets—shopping, going to restaurants or movies. For the first time in his life, Malcolm saw black–white couples walking together easily, without obvious fear. He was fascinated by the sounds and rhythms of jazz, which poured forth from clubs like Wally's Paradise and the Savoy Café, along Massachusetts Avenue between Columbus and Huntington avenues. It was a thrilling world, a lively, urban environment, and its magic took hold of his imagination in a lasting way.

When he returned home that fall, he made some efforts to readjust to small-town life. Despite his physical awkwardness, he tried out for, and made, Mason's football team. Over two decades later a local newspaper published a photograph of Mason's 1940 squad, which included Malcolm;

the paper claimed that he "showed a preference for tackling ball-carriers . . . instead of tackling the white race as he is doing today." "When Malcolm went to Mason, you could see a change in him," Wilfred recalled. "Some for the better, some for the worse. . . . He would complain about some of the things the teachers would try to do—they would try to discourage him from taking courses that black people weren't supposed to take; in other words, keep him in his place." It hadn't bothered him particularly during the previous year when white students who had befriended him continued to call him nigger. But now Malcolm was keenly aware of the social distance between himself and others. An English teacher, Richard Kaminska, sharply discouraged him from becoming a lawyer. "You've got to be realistic about being a nigger," Kaminska advised him. "A lawyer—that's no realistic goal for a nigger. . . . Why don't you plan on carpentry?" Malcolm's grades plummeted and his truculence increased. Within several months, he found himself expelled.

Already burdened by the demands of a large family, Wilfred and Hilda soon found they could not handle their wayward younger brother. Once again, Ella felt compelled to intervene. Several months earlier, in a letter to Malcolm, she had written:

> We miss you so much. Don't swell up and bust but honest everything seems dead here. Lots of boys called for you. . . . I would like for you to come back but under one condition. Your mind is made up. If I would send your fare could you pay all your bills? Let me know real soon.

Ella believed that Malcolm would be better off under her care, and his older siblings agreed. In early February 1941, three months shy of sixteen, nearly six feet tall and still growing, Malcolm boarded the Greyhound bus at Lansing's depot. He took pains to wear his best suit, a dark green; the sleeves stopped some way short of his wrists. He wore a narrow-collared light green topcoat. Twenty hours later, his first major reinvention would begin.

CHAPTER 2

The Legend of Detroit Red

1941–January 1946

Even before the bus carrying Malcolm Little pulled into Boston's main bus terminal, Ella had decided that her half brother would no longer make his own decisions about school. Without checking with him, she enrolled him in a private all-boys' academy in downtown Boston. Malcolm made at least a halfhearted effort. He arrived at the school the first morning, learned that there were no girls there, and promptly walked out, never to return to a classroom.

It was the first test of wills between the two siblings. As headstrong as her young charge, Ella did not normally allow herself to be overruled. Born on December 13, 1913, in Georgia, she had moved north as a teenager at the beginning of the Great Depression. For a short time she lived in New York City, employed as a floorwalker at a major department store. Standing five feet nine and at 145 pounds, with jet-black skin, Ella cut an imposing figure; store executives "decided she looked evil enough to possibly frighten off potential shoplifters." After about six months, suspecting her job was going nowhere, she quit. Relocating to Everett, a suburb of Boston, she met and married Lloyd Oxley, a physician at Boston City Hospital. Oxley, a Jamaican, was a strong supporter of Garvey, which she found admirable, but tensions over money, and Ella's refusal to be dominated, led to divorce in 1934.

Sometime after her marriage ended, Ella began seeing a married man named Johnson, but her money troubles continued. According to her son, Rodnell P. Collins, Ella had used her time catching shoplifters to learn their tricks, and soon she had joined their ranks. Boosting clothing and food items became almost routine as Ella scrambled to assist her relatives. Her transgressions quickly escalated to more serious crimes, and in August 1936 she was charged with assault and battery with a dangerous weapon and "lewd and lascivious cohabitation." She was given a year's probation on the latter charge, while she pled guilty and received additional probation on the assault and battery. Over the next three years Ella was arrested on three separate occasions, including another charge of assault and battery in 1939. By the time Malcolm moved to Boston, Ella was already planning to end her second marriage, and on July 31, 1941, filed a suit charging "cruel and abusive treatment."

It probably did not take Malcolm long, once he reached Boston that February of 1941, to realize that his half sister's idyllic middle-class existence hid an erratic lifestyle supported by petty crime. In temperament, Ella turned out to be neither a stable parental figure nor a particularly pleasant housemate. Her repeated run-ins with the law testify to her belligerent and paranoid behavior, a recklessness that only worsened through the years. Two decades after these events, she was admitted to the Massachusetts Mental Health Center, after charges of being armed with a dangerous weapon. There, she was interviewed by the center's director of psychiatry, Dr. Elvin Semrad. Even though he reported that she had been "a model patient, entirely reasonable, showing wit, intelligence, and charm," he was far from won over. Ella was also "a paranoid character," he observed, who "because of the militant nature of her character . . . could be considered a dangerous individual."

During Ella's trip to Lansing to check in on her siblings, she had met Kenneth Collins, a twenty-four-year-old blessed with good looks and a suave dancing style, and the two became involved. Early in 1941, Collins had moved to Boston, whereupon he almost immediately enraged Ella by hanging out with her brother, Earl, Jr., at dance halls and nightclubs. Still, on June 20, 1942, she married him anyway.

In the 1940s, Ella Collins and her family lived among a growing cluster of black homeowners and renters in the Waumbeck and Humboldt Avenue section of Boston, known colloquially as the Hill. This neighborhood was one of several distinctly different black communities that developed in the city during the first half of the twentieth century. The most important, and largest, was Boston's South End, home to working-class and low-income blacks, with its heart located along Columbus and Massachusetts avenues. Another was the Intown section, located in Lower Roxbury and the blocks just beyond the South End. Yet these inner-city areas had not become all-black ghettos—yet. Thousands of white ethnic immigrants—Lithuanians, Greeks, Armenians, Syrians, and others—who had arrived earlier in the century, still lived together in close proximity with their new black neighbors. Like other cities in the Northeast at that time, Boston was multiethnic and expanding.

The Hill was a neighborhood in transition. A pleasant community of middle- and working-class families, largely single-family houses, and smaller apartment buildings, it had been predominantly Jewish at the turn of the century, but saw its racial composition change with the rising fortunes of blacks in the years leading up to World War II. Even before Pearl Harbor, Boston's employment began picking up. Local industries and companies that had previously hired few or no blacks began lifting the color bar, including the Navy Yard, the Quincy Shipyard, and passenger railroad companies. Plus a new era of black migration had opened. In the years just before and during World War II, nearly two million Southern blacks relocated to other sections of the United States, with extended families first sending one or two of their members to a city to find work and locate housing before the rest followed. Relatives on Ella's mother's side of her family, the Masons, moved in large numbers to Boston. Rodnell Collins estimated that by the mid-1940s Ella had as many as fifty members of her extended family living in greater Boston.

The population influx, combined with new opportunities and income for African Americans, created a major shift in the demographics of Boston neighborhoods. By the late 1930s hundreds of Boston blacks had risen to become police officers, clerical workers, schoolteachers, and white-collar professionals, and their success led them to seek out better housing in places like the Hill. It was this kind of life, a good bourgeois middle-class life, to which Ella aspired. But to scale the class hierarchy of black Boston, Ella needed money, and crime was, unfortunately, the only way she saw to get it. At the same time, she was still her Garveyite father's daughter. She was sympathetic especially to Garvey's notions of black enterprise and upward mobility, and a strong proponent of both capitalism and a kind of proto–black nationalism. She was no integrationist, passionately opposed to interracial dating and marriage.

Malcolm must have pondered what his parents would have thought about his new neighborhood. He would later recall that initially he believed Ella's neighbors were high class and educated, and echoing his father's distaste for the black bourgeoisie, would observe that "what I was really seeing was only a big-city version of those 'successful' Negro bootblacks and janitors back in Lansing." Looking back, he said he could quickly see the chasms of nationality, ethnicity, and class that subdivided black Bostonians. The older black bourgeois families, whose kinfolk extended back multiple generations in New England, perceived themselves as socially superior to immigrants from the South and the Caribbean; but the newcomers embraced an aggressive entrepreneurial spirit. Malcolm observed with approval that it was the Southerners and the West Indians, more frequently than blacks from the North, who appeared to open up businesses and restaurants. Malcolm was also acutely aware that he was something of a country bumpkin who knew little about the big city: "I had never tasted a sip of liquor, never even smoked a cigarette, and here I saw little black children, ten and twelve years old, shooting craps, playing cards."

At fifteen, Malcolm was entering an early adulthood with little sense of how to carry himself in the world. He continued to feel connected to the memory of his father, and remembered the evenings they had spent together for Garvey's great cause, but unlike Earl he had not been given a trade and seemed to lack the constitution for hard work. Living with Ella may have reinforced the importance of politics and racial identity, prized by his parents, but her example also gave him a different set of ideas on how to get on in the world. Over a twenty-year period, Ella was arrested an astonishing twenty-one times, and yet convicted only once. Her criminal behavior and knack for evading responsibility presented him with a vivid message. Unchecked by any moral counterforce, he was set on an unsteady path that would define the next phase of his youth. Years later he would describe this time as a "destructive detour" in an otherwise purpose-driven life.

Without a guide or mentor, Malcolm fashioned his own version of adult behavior whole cloth, learning to present himself as being older, more sober, and more worldly than he really was. He studied carefully the different types of adult males he met. His eye was drawn first to his half brother, Earl Little, Jr. Dark skinned, handsome, and flashy (like his comrade-in-arms, Kenneth Collins), Earl at that time was trying to break into show business, performing as a singer in dance halls and nightclubs under the stage name Jimmy Carlton. Within months of his nephew's move to the city, however, he contracted tuberculosis and before year's end was dead. Around this time a much longer-lasting male influence also came into Malcolm's life. One night at a local Boston pool hall, as he remembered it, a "dark, stubby conked-headed fellow" approached him and introduced himself as "Shorty." The two teenagers were pleased to discover that they were both from Lansing, and Shorty immediately dubbed his new friend "Homeboy."

This was Malcolm "Shorty" Jarvis, who would soon become, as Rodnell Collins described it, "Malcolm's guide and companion in the Boston street life and nightclub scene." Two years older than his redheaded friend (though Malcolm would put it at ten in the *Autobiography*), Shorty was already a minor figure in Boston's black nightlife. An accomplished trumpet player despite his youth, he regularly sat in at one-nighters for big bands, including Count Basie's and Duke Ellington's. At home in the flashy world of bars and clubs, Shorty took great pleasure in sexual adventures, and gave his young friend a tour of the city's nightlife, equally well informed whether pointing out gamblers or pimps.

Malcolm proved a quick study. He soon learned all about smoking "reefer"—marijuana cigarettes—hustling, petty thievery, and seducing fast women. Soon he had even mastered the economic fundamentals of the numbers racket. Every day, thousands of habitual bettors would place wagers on numbers, usually between 001 and 999. Numbers "runners," in turn, would collect "policies"—bets on slips of paper—and take them to a central collection "bank." The racketeers who ran the scam generally took at least 40 percent of the gross revenue, redistributing the remainder as daily winnings.

Malcolm's obvious attraction to the ghetto's underworld caused tensions back at his new home, and partially to placate Ella he found part-time employment as a shoeshine boy at the Roseland Ballroom. It was at the Roseland that he began to develop his lifelong fascination with black celebrities—men and women of talent and ability who had overcome the barrier of race to achieve public recognition. As at its more famous counterpart, Harlem's Savoy Ballroom, at the Roseland black and white mingled, danced, and drank, showing the teenager that there was also a celebratory side to success. At the humble shoeshine stand, he solicited praise and tips from African Americans playing gigs at the ballroom. Decades later he recalled the jazz legends whose shoes he had once proudly buffed: "Duke Ellington, Count Basie, Lionel Hampton, Cootie Williams, Jimmie Lunceford were just a few." To make a favorable impression, the spunky teenager soon learned to make "my shine rag sound like someone had set off Chinese firecrackers." During his breaks, he would gawk, openmouthed, listen to the rocking rhythms of the music, and, most especially, admire the brilliance and athleticism of the ballroom dancers doing the Lindy Hop, the standard dance performed to syncopated big band jazz. Occasionally Malcolm would sneak away from his job just to watch the dancers go through their paces.

An impressionable young black man in search of roles and images in the movies and media, however, would have found a sorry set of models. In the forties, the dominant representation of the African American was the comic minstrel, typified by the national radio show *Amos 'n' Andy*. (Ironically, of course, the original actors in the series were white, mimicking black dialect.) In films, blacks were generally presented as clowns or mental incompetents. *Gone With the Wind*, Hollywood's 1939 extravaganza celebrating the prewar slave South, offered up the servant Mammy, docile yet loyal, obese and hardworking. One of the few Hollywood movies of the period that departed slightly from crude stereotypes was Warner Brothers' *Bullets or Ballots*, featuring black actress Louise Beavers as the notorious Nellie LaFleur, the numbers queen. It is likely that Malcolm saw this film as well as dozens of others that addressed racial themes; decades later he would recall Hollywood's distortions of black people as part of his general indictment of white racism. Even the title of the Warner Brothers' film may have been recycled in Malcolm's 1964 address "The Ballot or the Bullet."

Off-screen, however, there were ample models of militancy and resistance. Some of the figures who would lead the postwar civil rights movement were rising to prominence by focusing on the war and the opportunities and obstacles it presented to African Americans. One of Garvey's former critics on the socialist left, labor union leader A. Philip Randolph, was pushing the Roosevelt administration to adopt reforms that would increase black employment and undermine Jim Crow segregation. Randolph boldly urged thousands of blacks to launch a civil disobedience campaign in what was called the Negro March on Washington Movement. One of his demands included the desegregation of the U.S. military. To stop the march, Roosevelt agreed to sign Executive Order 8802 on June 25, 1941; his directive outlawed racially discriminatory hiring policies in defense industries and also created the Fair Employment Practices Committee. Three decades later, Order 8802 would become the legal foundation for equal opportunity and affirmative action laws, but both Randolph's campaigning and Roosevelt's response would have profound consequences even for the life of young Malcolm Little.

Though he posed to the outside world as an urban sophisticate, the anxious teen mailed a constant stream of letters to his family, as well as occasional ones to school friends. A lively correspondence continued throughout 1941 and early 1942. One old classmate brought Malcolm up to speed on the latest gossip at Mason High School. Another sketched in Mason's basketball season, and some former sweethearts also kept in touch. For his part, he had dutifully written home within days of arriving in Boston, but his sloppy handwriting provoked Philbert to urge him to write more clearly in the future. Reginald, the brother to whom he was closest, asked whether he had yet enrolled at a high school—and also detailed his budding relationships with several Lansing girls. Malcolm kept quiet about his decision to give up his formal education.

He was determined to transform his outward appearance to fit into his cool new world. Although not naturally athletic, he patiently learned to dance by watching others at neighborhood house parties and then trying out his techniques on the Roseland's fabled dance floor. At Shorty's insistence, he purchased his first colorful "zoot suit" on credit. Shorty administered a cultural rite of passage by "conking" his hair, using a "jelly-like, starchy-looking glop" produced from lye, several potatoes, and two eggs. The mixture burned intensely, but the final product, viewed from a mirror, more than satisfied. "I'd seen some pretty conks, but when it's the first time, on your own head," Malcolm wrote, "the transformation, after a lifetime of kinks, is staggering."

Hair styles in the African-American community then, as now, carried a certain weight or meaning, and whether or not to straighten one's hair—conking it with various chemicals—was a contentious issue. Until he went to prison five years later, Malcolm would continue to conk his hair, though he eventually came to disdain the practice. As an NOI leader, he would routinely recite this episode from his early life as the ultimate act of self-debasement. Yet the 1940s aesthetic of the conk was far more complicated than the mature Malcolm could admit. Most middle-class black males, as well as many popular jazz artists, rarely tortured their hair in this way, preferring a short, natural style. The conk was the emblem of the hippest, street-savvy black, the choice of hustlers, pimps, professional gamblers, and criminals. It was directly influenced by wavy-haired Latinos, whom blacks sought to emulate.

Similarly, the zoot suit uniform was an act of defiance against white standards of behavior. In the wave of national patriotism following Pearl Harbor and the United States' going to war, zoot-suiters were widely identified with draft-dodging. For this reason, in 1942 the War Production Board banned their production and sale. In 1943, hundreds of Mexican Americans and blacks wearing the suits were beaten up by uniformed sailors in Los Angeles's streets, prompting the city council to declare the wearing of a zoot suit a misdemeanor. Similar smaller riots took place in Baltimore, Detroit, San Diego, and New York City. Malcolm's obsession with jazz, Lindy Hopping, zoot suits, and illegal hustling encompassed the various symbols of the cultural war waged between oppressed urban black youth and the black bourgeoisie.

By the fall of 1941 Malcolm, who was now generally known as "Red," had gained confidence and skill as a dancer. He had also begun romancing a black Roxbury girl, Gloria Strother. Since she was from a middle-class family, the aspiring Ella approved of the relationship, perhaps hoping it might curb her charge's fascination with the underworld. But he had many other girls on his mind, and despite beseeching letters from a more than willing Gloria, refused to commit himself. The girl's grandmother and guardian soon grew frustrated enough to write him, inquiring about his intentions, but to no avail. Gloria, too, continued writing, even after Malcolm had moved to Harlem in early 1942, but he does not appear to have responded.

Of the many women who diverted Malcolm's attention from Gloria, none enchanted him quite so much as a blonde Armenian named Bea Caragulian. Surprisingly little is known about this ethnic white woman who, with the exception of Betty Shabazz, maintained the longest intimate relationship with Malcolm. Several years his senior, Bea had been a professional dancer at small-time clubs. She was pleasant looking, but not stunning. It is difficult to know her motives for having an open sexual relationship with a black teenager, and Malcolm himself did little to illuminate them; in his *Autobiography*, he devoted far more attention to the plight of Gloria than to any discussion of Bea, who is referred to as "Sophia." He placed their initial meeting at the Roseland, culminating in sex mere hours later, but this story, like Bea's pseudonym, was a fabrication—the two actually met at the far less glamorous Tick Tock Club. Within several weeks, Bea was showering Malcolm with gifts and small amounts of money, while he proudly paraded his blonde conquest at nightclubs throughout black Boston, to the envy of his friends. Their sexual relationship was yet another violated taboo in a society still defined by race and class, but Bea's obvious desire created, for Malcolm, a sense of masculine authority and power. To the world of hustlers, he had arrived as a serious player.

The liaison infuriated Ella, who was incensed at the thought of her brother dating a white woman. According to Rodnell Collins, she saw Bea as "a thrill[-seeker] for whom young black men like Malcolm are just another wild adventure." Late one night, Malcolm attempted to sneak Bea up into his second-floor bedroom. Ella heard the couple and, in comic-opera style, pushed a bookcase down the stairs right on top of them. Malcolm was not yet legally an adult, however, and lacked the resources to maintain his own living quarters elsewhere. For the time being he had to stay put.

He next found work as a soda fountain clerk at Roxbury's Townsend

Drugstore, but with the new job came fresh frustrations. Forced to serve his middle-class betters, he was yet again irritated by "those penny-ante squares who came in there putting on their millionaires' airs, the young ones and the old ones both." He did not last long; with his ghetto persona enhanced by his very public liaison with Caragulian, the job of lowly soda clerk quickly lost its appeal. With Bea's financial help, he finally left Ella's home for Shorty's apartment. Over four months he drifted through a series of menial jobs: at a South Boston wallpaper company warehouse; washing dishes at a restaurant; then briefly in Boston's elite hotel, the Parker House, working in the dining room as a waiter.

Although Bea was now his regular girlfriend, Malcolm continued to see other women. In late 1941 through mid-1942, he maintained a lively correspondence with several who lived in either Boston or Michigan, and nurtured intimate relationships with a number of them. In a November 1941 letter to Zolma Holman of Jackson, Michigan, for instance, Malcolm bragged that he had already traveled through twenty-three different states. Apparently writing from a train, he noted that he was heading toward Florida, and that he hoped to travel to California soon. Then there were Roberta Jo of Kalamazoo, Edyth Robertson of Boston, a Charlotte from Jackson, and Catherine Haines, dashing off a one-page letter from her summer resort at Martha's Vineyard, describing her boredom. These diverse contacts may have reinforced Malcolm's growing belief that most women were dishonest and could not be trusted. He later bluntly warned: "Never ask a woman about other men. Either she'll tell you a lie, and you still won't know, or if she tells you the truth, you might not have wanted to hear it in the first place."

———

The formal entry of the United States into World War II on December 9, 1941, prompted several million American boys and men to volunteer for service. Harlem had a long history of sending its sons to war. The Harlem Hellfighters, the all-black 369th U.S. Infantry, had fought with distinction alongside the French army during World War I. In June 1945, the 369th fought again at Okinawa, and by the end of hostilities about sixty thousand blacks from New York City had served their country.

The immediate impact of the war mobilization was that almost overnight hundreds of thousands of white men's jobs became vacant. Many employers were forced to hire blacks and women. In critical industries such as the railroads—in the 1940s, the principal means of national transportation—the demand for workers became acute. It wasn't difficult for sixteen-year-old Malcolm, despite his abysmal employment record, to secure a job on a railroad line as a fourth-class cook.

His first assignment was on the *Colonial*, which ran from Boston to Washington, D.C., and provided him with the chance to visit big cities he had longed to see for years. During the *Colonial*'s routine layover in Washington, Malcolm, dressed in a zoot suit, would tour the city's sprawling black neighborhoods. He was not impressed. "I was astounded to find in the nation's capital, just a few blocks from Capitol Hill, thousands of Negroes living worse than any I'd ever seen in the poorest sections of Roxbury." One source of the terrible poverty, he suspected, was the backwardness of the city's Negro middle class, which he felt possessed the intelligence and education to have reached a better station in life than what it had settled for. Malcolm later claimed that veteran black employees on the *Colonial* talked disparagingly about Washington's "'middle-class' Negroes with Howard University degrees, who were working as laborers, janitors, guards, taxi-drivers and the like."

For the first time in his young life, Malcolm made an effort to retain a job beyond a few months. He loved traveling, and railroad work made this possible and affordable, though it often meant playing demeaning service roles. Reassigned to the *Yankee Clipper*, the train traveling the New York–Boston route, he was expected to lug a box of sandwiches, candy, and ice cream along with a heavy, five-gallon aluminum coffeepot up and down the aisles of the train, soliciting sales. As they had done when he was a shoeshine boy, customers frequently gave larger tips to workers who displayed enthusiasm and a happy face, and Malcolm was soon mimicking the jovial dining car waiters to obtain tips. He became so proficient that his coworkers began to call him "Sandwich Red."

His frequent stops in New York meant that he could finally visit that fabled black Mecca, Harlem. Louise and Earl had regaled their children with stories about the shining city's legendary institutions, its broad boulevards, its vibrant political and cultural life. Yet nothing, not even Boston's glamour and excitement, prepared the teenager for his first encounter with the neighborhood with which he would one day become identified. "New York was heaven to me," he remembered. "And Harlem was Seventh Heaven!"

Like a frantic tourist on a tight schedule, he rushed from site to celebrated site. His first stop was the popular bar and nightclub Small's Paradise. Opened in October 1925 at the height of Prohibition, Small's was racially integrated from the outset. With seating accommodations for up to fifteen hundred, it quickly became a hot spot for the jazz era's greatest entertainers, one of Harlem's "big three" venues along with the Cotton Club and Connie's Inn. "No Negro place of business had ever impressed me so much," Malcolm recalled of his first time there. "Around the big, luxurious-looking, circular bar were thirty or forty Negroes, mostly men, drinking and talking."

Next on his itinerary was the grand Apollo Theater on West 125th Street. Built some thirty years before as a whites-only burlesque house, it had become nationally known as an entertainment center featuring black performers. A few blocks east was the celebrated Hotel Theresa. Designed in a neo-Renaissance style, the hotel first opened in 1913. Until the late 1930s it had accepted only white guests, but with new management African Americans began staying there. A host of black celebrities, including Duke Ellington, Sugar Ray Robinson, Josephine Baker, and Lena Horne, made the Hotel Theresa their headquarters in the city. Since New York's major hotels in midtown refused Negro guests throughout the 1940s and the early 1950s, the Theresa became the center for all black elites—in entertainment, business, civic associations, and politics. When Malcolm first saw the hotel in early 1942, it may have already been known to him for hosting boxer Joe Louis's celebration with thousands of Negroes after he won the heavyweight championship. By that evening, Malcolm made what would be a fateful decision: "I had left Boston and Roxbury forever."

In most respects, he had already left. Most nights he spent in transit, either working or sleeping on the train, and when he was in New York he sometimes stayed at the Harlem YMCA on West 135th Street. He took to visiting Small's on a regular basis, as he did the nearby bar at the Braddock Hotel on West 126th Street, a hangout for the Apollo's entertainers. Before long, he was living a double life. At work, on the *Yankee Clipper*, he excelled as Sandwich Red, entertaining white patrons with his harmless clowning. In Harlem, he was simply "Red," a wild, cocky kid, learning the language of the streets. He began supplementing his income by peddling marijuana, casually at first, then more aggressively. Bea frequently came down from Boston to visit, and Malcolm showed her off at his favorite nightspots. For a boy who on May 19, 1942, had reached only his seventeenth birthday, barely more than a year after settling in the Northeast, his reinvention was remarkable.

For an irresponsible, headstrong young man, trying to compartmentalize these two wildly different personas would prove impossible. Malcolm's behavior on the *Yankee Clipper* soon grew erratic and confrontational, aggravated all the more by his frequent pot smoking. He provoked arguments with customers, and especially with servicemen. In October 1942, he was fired, but the shortage of experienced workers on the railroads was so severe that he was hired again on two further occasions, and he used these short-term jobs to transport and sell marijuana across the country. Malcolm would return from long hauls "with two of the biggest suitcases you ever saw, full of that stuff . . . marijuana pressed into bricks, you know . . . but they would pay him a thousand dollars a trip," his brother Wilfred claimed. It is highly unlikely that the trafficking was that substantial or lucrative, but the barrier between legal and illegal activity no longer mattered, and Malcolm was more than willing to jeopardize his job to profit from an illegal hustle. His career in drugs was relatively penny ante—literally selling reefers stuffed in his socks or shirt—but it still took him over a line.

Life on the railroads influenced Malcolm in other ways. The sounds of the trains have been woven into the fabric of jazz, blues, and even rhythm and blues. As the writer Albert Murray has observed, railroads have long been a central metaphor in African-American folklore because of the nineteenth-century abolitionists' Underground Railroad that spirited thousands of enslaved blacks to freedom. Malcolm's Harlem style helped him meet and learn from the jazz musicians who were his marijuana customers. More important, the experiences on the railroad began Malcolm's love affair with travel itself, the excitement and adventure of encountering new cities and different people. These trips provided an essential education about the physical vastness and tremendous diversity of the country; they also provided lessons in the conditions in which blacks lived and worked. He saw some cut off from any hope, and others squandering their privileges, opportunities, and gifts. As he looked around Washington, Boston, and New York, the seeds of his later antibourgeois attitudes were sown.

His siblings continued writing to him, but his replies became sporadic. Reginald and Hilda both sent letters asking for money, although they knew that Malcolm was hardly making enough money to support himself. Bea's occasional gifts of cash augmented his meager wages, but went only so far. Several tailoring establishments sent him bills for clothing he had obtained on credit, but he had no intention of paying. One or more creditors turned over their claims to the Boyle Brothers collection agency, which threatened legal action. Before he was fired, Malcolm was even behind in his dues to the Dining Car Employees Union.

In late 1942, he returned to Lansing to show off his new appearance, and had the satisfactory effect of shocking his family. "My conk and whole costume were so wild that I might have been taken as a man from Mars," he recalled. Attending a neighborhood hop at Lincoln High School, he showed off his dance steps before admiring crowds, a true celebrity. Without a hint of embarrassment, he even signed autographs for admiring teenagers with the bold signature "Harlem Red."

Malcolm's autobiography implies that his trip home was brief—Harlem, after all, had become the center of his new life—but he actually stayed in Lansing for at least two months. His evenings were spent pursuing a number of different women. During the day he was scrambling to find money—for himself and his family, which had continued to struggle financially in his absence. For a few weeks he worked at Shaw's jewelry store, then at nearby Flint's A/C spark plug company. But his return home was also about receiving family validation and support. Still a teenager, Malcolm depended on the love of his siblings. He didn't expect them to understand Harlem's jazz culture or his zoot suit costumes, but he needed them to recognize that he had become successful. He finally returned to Harlem in late February 1943. Once again he was hired by the New Haven Railroad, only to be fired seventeen days later for insubordination.

Malcolm wrote in his autobiography that he'd stopped seriously looking for work after 1942 and had instead devoted himself to increasingly violent crime. He dated his employment at Small's Paradise from sometime in mid-1942, just after he had turned seventeen, till early 1943. Yet either his memory was faulty or he was at work on his legend, because he was still in Lansing at that time. His job at Small's actually began in late March 1943 and was terminated less than two months later, when he asked an undercover military detective posing as a Small's patron "if he wanted a woman"—prompting arrest for solicitation, and another firing.

From 1942 to 1944, he worked sporadically at a much less glamorous site, Jimmy's Chicken Shack, a late-night Harlem hot spot for black artists and entertainers. Even washing dishes, he was in esteemed company: Charlie Parker had done the same in the thirties when Art Tatum held court at the piano. Clarence Atkins, Malcolm's close friend at that time, recalled that Malcolm was "flunking for Jimmy . . . doing anything, like washing dishes, mopping floors, or whatever . . . because he could eat, and Jimmy had a place upstairs, over the place where he could sleep." One of his fellow employees was a black dishwasher, John Elroy Sanford, who had aspirations to be a professional comedian. Both Malcolm and Sanford had red hair, and to distinguish the two Sanford was called "Chicago Red," referring to his original hometown. Since no one had even heard of Lansing, Malcolm was eager to be known as "Detroit Red." Years later, Sanford would become famous as the comedian Redd Foxx.

The Detroit Red of the *Autobiography* is a young black man almost completely uninterested in, even alienated from, politics. Yet the childhood lessons of black pride and self-sufficiency had not been entirely abandoned. Malcolm spoke frequently about black nationalist ideas at Jimmy's Chicken Shack. "He would talk often," Atkins explained, "about how his father used to get brutalized and beat up on the corner selling Marcus Garvey's paper, and he would talk a lot about Garvey's concepts in terms of how they could benefit us as a people."

During his time in Harlem, Malcolm was not directly involved in activities that could be described as political—rent strikes, picketing stores that refused to hire Negroes, registering black voters, and so forth. Yet to his credit, even at this stage in his life he was an extraordinary observer of people. In his description of one of his early forays into Harlem, he mentions the presence of communist organizers: "Negro and white canvassers sidled up alongside you, talking fast as they tried to get you to buy a copy of the *Daily Worker*: 'This paper's trying to keep your rent controlled. . . . Make that greedy landlord kill them rats in your apartment. . . . Who do you think fought the hardest to help free those Scottsboro boys?'" Longtime Harlem residents had schooled Detroit Red about the neighborhood's racial demography, an urban transformation that he later characterized as the "immigrant musical chairs game." His own telling of that shift captured both the directness and the broad strokes of his style. New York's earliest black neighborhoods, he explained, had been confined in lower Manhattan. "Then, in 1910, a Negro real estate man somehow got two or three Negro families into one Jewish Harlem apartment house. The Jews fled from that house, then from that block, and more Negroes came in to fill their apartments. Then whole blocks of Jews ran . . . until in a short time, Harlem was like it still is today—virtually all black."

———

Malcolm's impressions about the origins and evolution of black Harlem were only partially accurate. He correctly noted blacks' northward movement within the island of Manhattan, but missed the larger forces that prompted it. At the heart of every community are its social institutions; black Harlem was formed largely from the migration of venerable black churches and organizations from lower Manhattan to above 110th Street.

St. Philip's Episcopal Church, founded in 1809 and a central institution for the African-American middle class, left Manhattan's Tenderloin district on West 34th Street and constructed a beautiful new church—in early Gothic style—on West 134th Street in 1909. Abyssinian Baptist Church, also founded in the early nineteenth century, moved to West 138th Street in 1923, where it became for several decades the largest Protestant congregation in America. Bethel African Methodist Episcopal Church had existed for a century prior to its relocation to 60 West 132nd Street. Many of these churches made large profits when they sold their downtown locations, and the relative cheapness of land in Harlem allowed them to buy up not only sites for new churches but also large blocks of real estate that were then rented out to Negroes who followed them north.

Public and privately owned apartment complexes also were centers of social interaction and cultural activity in the neighborhood. One prime example was the Dunbar Apartments, built in 1926–27 by John D. Rockefeller, Jr. Opened in 1928 and located between Seventh and Eighth avenues at West 149th and 150th streets, the Dunbar Apartments were designed as the first housing cooperative for blacks. The residences claimed many famous tenants, including Bill "Bojangles" Robinson, Paul and Eslanda Robeson, and W. E. B. and Nina Du Bois. Harlem's famous YMCA, a center for public lectures and cultural events, was located on West 135th Street and opened in 1933. These and hundreds of other institutions were part of the cultural bedrock of black Harlem.

Equally important to Harlem was the racial transformation of New York City. In 1910, only 91,700 blacks lived in metropolitan New York; 60,500 African Americans resided in Manhattan, of whom only 14,300 had been born in New York State. The great majority of blacks had been Southern born. With the onset in 1915 of the Great Migration from the rural South, hundreds of thousands of blacks began to make their way to Gotham. The city's total black population steadily increased: 152,500 in 1920; 327,700 in 1930. The Census Bureau estimated that 54,724 black New Yorkers in 1930 were foreign born. Much of this increase was confined to the Harlem ghetto. In 1910, Harlem's total population regardless of race was 49,600. In 1920, Harlem's population was 73,000, of which about two-thirds were black. By the 1920s, Harlem became the urban capital of the black diaspora, a lively center for the extraordinary flowering of literature, plays, dance, and the arts, a period that would come to be known as the Harlem Renaissance. Harlem's music, jazz, traversed the Atlantic, found a loving home in Paris, and became a global expression for youth culture.

Malcolm could not have lived in Harlem during World War II without being deeply affected by its turbulent history and cultural activities. By any standard, it had by 1940 become the cosmopolitan center for black political activity, not only in America but worldwide. Roughly one-quarter of its black population consisted of Caribbean immigrants, nearly all of whom had established political associations, parties, and clubs of all kinds. One of the most influential West Indian politicians, Hulan Jack, originally from St. Lucia, had been elected to represent the neighborhood in the New York State Assembly in 1940. Harlem was also the national center of black labor activism, headed by A. Philip Randolph, who began his legendary career as a public orator even before Garvey's arrival in the United States. Thousands of Harlem residents were active members and supporters of the Communist Party; figures like Claudia Jones and Benjamin Davis, Jr., were widely respected and popular leaders.

Despite the demise of the Garvey movement, Harlem's militancy had grown more intense, chiefly through the Depression-era 1930s and largely in response to social inequalities the black community was no longer willing to tolerate. For example, black workers in public laundries routinely earned three dollars per week less than whites performing identical work. Employment discrimination was rampant. One 1920–28 survey of 258 Harlem businesses employing more than 2,000 workers found that only 163 employees were black, and all held low-wage jobs. As the depression deepened, joblessness soared. Black youth unemployment for the period was estimated at well above 50 percent. In 1935, the federal Works Progress Administration (WPA), which had determined that the cost of living for a New York City household at "maintenance level" was $1,375 annually, estimated the average black family's income at $1,025.

The economic pressure exerted by these conditions found a release as black citizens began to organize in protest. In 1931, the Harlem Housewives League initiated a campaign at local chain stores, insisting that they employ African Americans. Many former Garveyites joined the movement, urging blacks to support a "buy black" effort. In 1932, the Harlem Labor Union was created, which picketed white-owned stores that refused to hire blacks. A year later, the newly formed Citizens' League for Fair Play, a popular coalition including women's groups and religious and fraternal organizations, demanded greater black employment in business. In March 1935, such protests sparked a riot along 125th Street, involving several thousand people. Dozens of white-owned stores were looted; fifty-seven civilians and seven police officers were injured, and seventy-five people, mostly African

Americans, were arrested on charges ranging from inciting to riot and malicious mischief to felonious assault and burglary. The NYPD's brutal treatment of the rioters was subsequently documented by Mayor Fiorello LaGuardia's Commission on Conditions in Harlem. Its report found that police had made "derogatory and threatening remarks"; one officer shot and killed a young black man, without warning, while another "called to arrest an unarmed drunk, hit the drunk so hard that he died."

The commission's report included recommendations for improving conditions, and the liberal LaGuardia administration sought to defuse the escalating racial tension by implementing many of them. From 1936 to 1941, the mayor's administration backed the construction of two new schools, the Harlem River Houses public housing complex, and the Women's Pavilion at Harlem Hospital. But LaGuardia's concessions did little to alter the widespread residential segregation, poverty, and discontent among Harlem's working class. When in 1938 the Supreme Court declared that public picketing of private business establishments over "racially based complaints" was constitutional, a new round of protests ensued. A "Don't Buy Where You Can't Work" coalition quickly won major concessions; within several years about one-third of all clerks and white-collar employees in Harlem were African Americans. In parallel efforts, blacks won concessions to work as telephone repairmen and operators, to drive buses for the Fifth Avenue and New York Omnibus companies, and to hold white-collar positions at Consolidated Edison.

Through these struggles Harlem established a dynamic model of social reform and urban protest that would be repeated across America. Mass agitation, mostly by grassroots associations, culminated in a series of well-publicized demonstrations, followed by urban insurrection. A liberal government, supported by white and black elites, subsequently granted major concessions in the form of hospitals, public housing, and expanded opportunities in both the public and private sectors. This in turn spawned new African-American victories within electoral politics, the courts, and government. These key tactics, which would become the protest strategy during the civil rights movement, were developed in Harlem a generation before.

The primary political beneficiary of these struggles and reforms was the Reverend Adam Clayton Powell, Jr., a man who would later become Malcolm's ally and occasional rival. Born in 1908, he was the handsome son of the powerful pastor of Harlem's Abyssinian Baptist Church, Adam Clayton Powell, Sr. The junior Powell followed his father into the ministry, but his interests were not chiefly spiritual. In 1931, he led a protest at New York

City's Board of Estimate that successfully halted the exclusion of five African-American physicians from Harlem Hospital. Seven years later, he helped launch the Greater New York Coordinating Committee for Employment, which used pickets and nonviolent protests to secure jobs. Succeeding his father as Abyssinian's pastor in 1937, Powell possessed a strong religious constituency as well as a growing army of political supporters. Ideologically and politically, he was a pragmatic liberal, at the national level endorsing Roosevelt's New Deal, while in Harlem working with the Communist Party and supporting LaGuardia's reelection campaign in 1941. That same year, Powell started the People's Committee, a Harlem-based organization of eighteen hundred campaign workers and eight offices dedicated to electing him to the city council. Powell's challengers on his left and right, American Labor Party candidate Dr. Max Yergan and Republican candidate Channing Tobias, pulled out of the contest in his favor. LaGuardia endorsed him, and the two liberals campaigned together—and both won.

On the city council, Powell consistently fought for Harlem's interests. When Yergan, a history instructor at the nearly all-white City College located in West Harlem, was not reappointed, Powell introduced a resolution that outlawed racial discrimination in academic appointments. In May 1942, his organization sponsored a mass rally at the Golden Gate Ballroom to protest against the NYPD's beating and killing of a black man, Wallace Armstrong. The next year, when the LaGuardia administration granted the navy permission to establish training facilities for the racially segregated Women's Reserve (WAVES) at Manhattan's Hunter College and Walton High School, Powell denounced the action.

Powell's bold position was embraced by civil rights organizations, black labor, and the Communist Party. His fierce opposition to Jim Crow, moreover, was in harmony with the black press's "Double V" campaign of 1942–43, which called for victory over fascism abroad and racial discrimination at home. In response to blacks' modest gains in employment, thousands of white workers participated in "hate strikes" during the war years, demanding exclusion of Negroes, especially in skilled positions. In July 1943, for example, white racists briefly paralyzed part of Baltimore's Bethlehem Shipyards. In August the following year, white streetcar drivers in Philadelphia, outraged at the assignment of eight black motormen, staged a six-day strike. In response, Roosevelt dispatched five thousand troops and issued an executive order placing the streetcar company under army control.

None of the meaning of these events was lost upon African Americans, many of whom began to question their support for America's war effort.

Years later, James Baldwin recalled, "The treatment accorded the Negro during the Second World War marks, for me, a turning point in the Negro's relation to America. . . . A certain hope died, a certain respect for white Americans faded." Although the vast majority of blacks still supported the war, a militant minority of young African-American males refused to register for the draft; others sought to disqualify themselves due to health reasons or other disabilities.

After a relatively calm period in black–white relations—or perhaps better put, one with a less aggressive push by blacks for equality—a new era was opening, characterized by black resistance and militancy. The Negro March on Washington and the civil rights rallies and demonstrations led by Powell in Harlem provoked fear and reaction among whites. Government authorities tried to derail the burgeoning movement by restricting the freedoms or activities of African Americans and to impose Jim Crow even in cities and states without legal racial segregation laws. Some targets were auspiciously outside politics—most notably, in Harlem, the world famous Savoy Ballroom.

Since its grand opening in 1926, the Savoy, located on Lenox Avenue between 140th and 141st streets, had quickly become the most significant cultural institution of Harlem. The great ballroom contained two large bandstands, richly carpeted lounges, and mirrored walls. During its heyday, about seven hundred thousand customers visited each year. Frequent white patrons included Orson Welles, Greta Garbo, Lana Turner, and even the rising Republican star Thomas E. Dewey. In a period when downtown hotels and dance halls still remained racially segregated, the Savoy was the center for interracial dancing and entertainment.

On April 22, 1943, the Savoy was padlocked by the NYPD, on the grounds that servicemen had been solicited by prostitutes there. New York City's Bureau of Social Hygiene cited evidence that, over a nine-month period, 164 individuals had "met the source of their [venereal] disease at the Savoy Ballroom." These alleged cases all came from armed services or coast guard personnel. Bureau officials offered absolutely no explanation as to how they had determined that the servicemen contracted diseases specifically from Savoy hookers. The appellate division of the New York State Supreme Court ruled unanimously to uphold the police action, with Mayor LaGuardia declaring that he was powerless to stop the ballroom from being closed down.

The Savoy remained closed throughout the summer of 1943. On October 15, the police announced that the establishment's license had been renewed, and a "grand reopening" took place the following week. For Malcolm, the whole episode was clear evidence of the limitations of white liberalism's racial tolerance: "City Hall kept the Savoy closed for a long time. It was just another one of the 'liberal North' actions that didn't help Harlem to love the white man any."

Meanwhile, plans were afoot downtown for a major urban development project that was designed to exclude black New Yorkers entirely. Only weeks after the Savoy's closing, the LaGuardia administration made public its agreement with Metropolitan Life Insurance Company to construct Stuyvesant Town, a semipublic housing complex located on the east side of Manhattan by Gramercy. Metropolitan Life had received generous tax exemptions, eminent domain authority, and control of tenant selection. When the company admitted that it would bar black tenants, blacks and many white liberals were outraged. Powell accused LaGuardia of once again capitulating to racism. His newspaper boldly editorialized, "Hitler won a victory in New York City." At one rally attracting twenty thousand protesters, Powell demanded LaGuardia be impeached. Not until 1944 did LaGuardia broker a compromise. Stuyvesant Town was constructed under the original terms; however, the mayor signed Local Law No. 20, barring all racial discrimination in tenant selection in future housing projects constructed under the city's authority.

In Detroit, the hub for Malcolm's family, escalating racial tensions erupted in a massive riot on June 20, 1943. In only its first six hours, the toll from Detroit's unrest was thirty-four deaths, seven hundred injured, and two million dollars worth of property damage. Five thousand federal troops had been sent in to patrol the streets; military vehicles were assigned to escort trolley cars and buses. New York City's authorities should have recognized that the conditions for a similar insurrection were ripe in Harlem. The neighborhood's turn duly came on August 1, when a policeman shot a black serviceman in uniform. Within minutes, rioting erupted; white-owned businesses were attacked throughout the neighborhood—along 125th Street and on Harlem's major north–south boulevards, Lenox, Seventh, and Eighth avenues, north from Central Park up to 145th Street. Before midnight, 1,450 stores had been vandalized, 6 people killed, 189 injured, and more than 600 blacks arrested. Significantly, unlike the 1935 riot, eyewitness accounts described the rioters as both middle class and low income. Even one police report recognized that: "Those actually committing malicious acts of violence were irresponsible, ignorant individuals. [But] the probability is that many decent citizens were in various groups, who in the

most instances are intelligent and law abiding, and while not actually taking part in the physical disturbances, aided and abetted indirectly."

The afternoon of the riot, Malcolm was walking south on St. Nicholas
Avenue when he encountered blacks running uptown "loaded down with
armfuls of stuff." Along West 125th Street, he discovered, "Negroes were
smashing store windows, and taking everything they could grab and carry—
furniture, food, jewelry, clothes, whisky." Within an hour, the NYPD had
dispatched what appeared to be "every New York City cop" into Harlem.
Malcolm went on to describe the semicomic scene of NAACP leader Walter
White accompanying Mayor LaGuardia, driving along 125th Street in a
bright red fire car appealing to blacks to "please go home and stay inside."

———

The real world finally intruded into Malcolm's life in the spring of 1943: he
was called up for duty in the U.S. Army.

While the majority of African Americans had patriotically pledged their
services since the first days of war, there had always been a vocal minority
who saw little reason to enter a segregated service to fight in a white man's
war. By 1943–44, dissent among blacks within the armed forces had escalated. Hundreds of black soldiers were simply going AWOL. When the
military induction notice addressed to Malcolm arrived at Ella's house in
Boston, she informed the authorities that her half brother no longer resided
there. Malcolm did eventually receive the notice, deciding that he would
avoid service by any means necessary.

In his autobiography, he recalled with approval Shorty Jarvis's attitude:
"Whitey owns everything. He wants us to go and bleed for him? Let him
fight." Malcolm may have heard about the well-publicized case of Winfred
W. Lynn, an African American who had refused to be inducted because he
opposed racially segregated military units. Lynn had lost the case, but his
protest provoked widespread sympathy.

Writing about the day of his scheduled induction at Local Draft Board
#59 on June 1, 1943, Malcolm recalled, "I costumed like an actor . . . I frizzled
my hair up into a reddish bush of conk." He addressed one white soldier,
sitting at the receptionist desk, as "Crazy-o." Eventually pulled from the
induction line, the zoot-suited hustler was interrogated by a military psychiatrist to determine his fitness to serve. Malcolm rambled incessantly
before whispering in the psychiatrist's ear, "I want to get sent down South.
Organize them nigger soldiers, you dig? Steal us some guns, and kill us
crackers!" The medic, stunned, uttered, "That will be all," later marking

him as 4-F, unfit for duty. "A 4-F card came to me in the mail," Malcolm concluded triumphantly, "and I never heard from the Army anymore."

A subsequent FBI report released in January 1955 gave the official version of Malcolm's rejection: "The subject was found mentally disqualified for military service for the following reasons: psychopathic personality inadequate, sexual perversion, psychiatric rejection."

Harlem's racial grievances—employment discrimination, widespread lack of jobs, the closing of the Savoy, the Stuyvesant Town agreement, and the August 1943 race riot—color all of Malcolm's actions concerning his military induction. He was pushed in new directions largely by external events. Malcolm's zoot-suited performance at the induction center was a different version of his Sandwich Red routine on the railroad. Both were examples of buffoonery, designed to achieve, respectively, financial reward and a permanent deferment from military service; both directly repudiated the forward, militant, and assertive model of his father. Though he had objected in principle to going to war, his choice of method for avoiding service was pointedly the opposite of actually embodying that principle.

Malcolm had learned well how to play the role of the clown or buffoon, but this pose was beginning to come up against his slowly forming new political attitude. Adam Clayton Powell, Jr.'s leadership during these years had deeply impressed him, reminding him of the more positive heritage of active engagement once practiced by his parents. What made Earl Little and Powell different from Detroit Red, or other tricksters, was their sense of responsibility to others within their community, and to African Americans generally. The trickster or hustler "getting over" was the ultimate opportunist who would use others to achieve his own ends. Malcolm would soon have to choose which model of black masculinity he would claim.

———

The *Autobiography*'s narrative suggests that, in 1944–45, Malcolm had ceased seeking legitimate work and had graduated from small-time street hustling into burglary, armed robbery, and prostitution, in order to pay for what was becoming a regular drug habit. The narrative's key character during this destructive phase is appropriately called "Sammy the Pimp," later identified as Sammy McKnight. As Malcolm would have it, over a six-to-eight-month period he pulled a series of robberies and burglaries outside New York City. During one heist, the robbery encountered "some bad luck. A bullet grazed Sammy. We just barely escaped." Malcolm subsequently described his involvement in the numbers racket: "My job now was to ride a bus across the George Washington Bridge where a fellow was waiting for me to hand him a bag of betting slips. We never spoke. . . . You didn't ask questions in the rackets." He also claimed to work as a "steerer" in Times Square, making connections with potential johns and placing them with white and Negro prostitutes working out of Harlem apartments. Through these criminal activities, Detroit Red was witnessing what he viewed as the filth and hypocrisy of the white man.

Without question, some elements of Detroit Red's gangster tale are accurate. But if by 1944 Malcolm had graduated from marijuana to cocaine, as seems possible, he probably was in no condition to engineer a series of well-executed burglaries without at some point being discovered. An investigation of the NYPD's arrest record for Malcolm Little years later failed to turn up any criminal charges or arrests.

Clarence Atkins, Malcolm's friend, asserted, "He was never no big-time racketeer or thug." A more realistic appraisal of his criminal activity speculates that Malcolm and Sammy may have occasionally burglarized "Harlem's popular nightspots, such as LaFamille," and subsequently "divide[d] the spoils." Crimes of this nature, during the racially segregated 1940s, were frequently not taken seriously by the nearly all-white NYPD, and Malcolm's possible burglaries could well have escaped police attention. But the politics of race that underscore the entire *Autobiography*'s narrative are careful to place the most nihilistic, destructive aspects of Malcolm's criminal history well *outside* Harlem. Perhaps this explains Malcolm's description of his string of successful burglaries in 1944 as taking place in New York City's nearly all-white suburbs. His role as a steerer for prostitutes also usually occurred in Times Square, not on 125th Street.

What seems plain is that between 1944 and 1946 Malcolm Little was struggling to survive. His sporadic work at Jimmy's Chicken Shack had dried up, leaving him to find other ways to scrape by. Reginald Little, who had visited his brother on several occasions in 1942–43, had left the merchant marine and by that time settled in Harlem, where Malcolm set him up in a "legal" con operation. "For a small fee, Reginald obtained a 'regular city peddler's license,'" Malcolm wrote. "Then I took him to a manufacturers' outlet where we bought a supply of cheap imperfect 'seconds'—shirts, underwear, cheap rings, watches, all kinds of quick-sale items." Reginald then sold this merchandise, giving buyers the impression that the goods had been stolen. If approached by the police, Reginald could simply produce his peddler's license and sales receipts from the purchase of the goods. This gambit was a classic grifter's short-con, manipulating the expectations of the victim to profit from a perfectly legitimate transaction. Malcolm's efforts to shield his younger brother from serious criminality revealed the continued responsibility he felt toward his siblings. But it also suggests that he was never himself a hardened criminal.

As the war continued to drag on overseas, it had a powerful if unanticipated impact upon black culture in cities back home—and particularly in music. Big band jazz and swing music's enormous popularity among white middle-class Americans during the war years had brought it from the margins of entertainment to wide prominence in mainstream popular culture. Around 1943, however, there was a precipitous drop in popularity for swing bands and their showmanship. It was a consequence of both practical concerns and aesthetic ones. Many big bands lost their best musicians to the armed forces. Gasoline was rationed, making it difficult for thirty-piece orchestras to travel. Then, in 1942, the Musicians Union initiated a strike because its members did not receive royalty payments when their records were played on the radio. In solidarity, union members boycotted record production until September 1943, and the lack of new big band singles sapped the genre's popularity. But the production strike gave artists the space for experimentation and innovation. It was the younger black musicians, the hepcats, who broke most sharply from swing, developing a black-oriented sound at the margins of musical taste and commercialism.

A new sound developed in dark Manhattan, in smoky late-night sessions. Musicians no longer attempted to present themselves as entertainers. They limited the time of songs by stripping down the melodic form, emphasizing improvisation as well as complex chord changes and complicated beats. When this music, which came to be called bebop, was reproduced on records after the strike, the sound seemed bizarre, almost alien to some jazz enthusiasts. But the new movement's key artists, such as Charlie Parker, Dizzy Gillespie, and Thelonious Monk, were constructing an experimental form in a radically different environment from the Depression-era thirties that had fostered swing. Bebop reflected the anger of the zoot-suiters and the enterprise of black artists who opposed mainstream white culture. These musicians sought to create a protest sound that could not be so easily exploited and commodified.

Many who favored the radical new jazz coming from Harlem nightclubs described the 1943 insurrection as another "zoot suit riot." The term had become a common metaphor for black activities that seemed subversive to white order. One zoot-suiter who had taken part in the Harlem riot linked black resistance to the U.S. war effort with urban unrest: "I'm not a spy or a saboteur, but I don't like goin' over there fightin' for the white man—so be it." Even African-American social psychologist Kenneth Clarke character- ized the new militancy he had observed in Harlem as "the Zoot Effect." As the critic Frank Kofsky observed of the bebop movement, "Jazz inevitably functioned not solely as music, but also as a vehicle for the expression of outraged protest."

Malcolm was thoroughly immersed in this world, and well aware of the new sound and its implications—the frisson of outsiders shaking up main- stream culture. Like the zoot-suiters, beboppers implicitly rejected assimi- lation into standards established by whites and were contemptuous of the police and the power of the U.S. government over black people's lives. Both sought to carve out identities that blacks could claim for themselves. Jazz artists recognized the parallels and, not surprisingly, later became Mal- colm's avid supporters in the 1960s. His version of militant black national- ism appealed to their spirit of rebellion and artistic nonconformity.

One major lesson Malcolm absorbed from the jazz artists' performances in the forties was the power of black art to convey celebrity status. Young Malcolm wistfully dreamt about the adoration of the crowd. In Harlem, he would escort Reginald backstage to join the artists and the musicians at the Roxy or the Paramount, intimating that they knew who he was. "After sell- ing reefers with the bands as they traveled, I was known to almost every popular Negro musician around New York in 1944–45," he would boast. In July 1944, he even found work at the Lobster Pond nightclub on Forty- second Street. The proprietor, Abe Goldstein, is identified as "Hymie" in the *Autobiography*:

> "Red, I'm a Jew and you're black," he would say. "These Gentiles don't like either one of us."
>
> Hymie paid me good money while I was with him, sometimes two hundred and three hundred a week. I would have done anything for Hymie. I did do all kinds of things. But my main job was transporting bootleg that Hymie supplied, usually to those spruced-up bars which he had sold to someone.

What the *Autobiography* fails to reveal is that Detroit Red, under the stage name Jack Carlton, was allowed to perform as a bar entertainer. At last, on a lighted nightclub stage, Malcolm could display his dancing ability; he even sometimes played the drums. The stage name was his way of honor- ing his late half brother, Earl, Jr., who had performed as Jimmy Carlton. It isn't clear whether Goldstein paid Malcolm primarily to entertain or to transport illegal alcohol (if his account is true). But in October 1944, Malcolm was fired. A few years later, on the occasion of another arrest, Goldstein described his former employee as "a bit unstable and neurotic but under proper guidance, a good boy."

Unemployed and desperate, and probably nursing a drug habit, Malcolm soon drifted back to Boston, and to Ella. He may have reasoned that, given her own continuing illegal activities, she could hardly turn her back on him, and he tried to convince her that he would turn over a new leaf and return to the upright upwardly mobile life she still thought to be her own destiny. To demonstrate his sobriety, in late October he obtained a menial job at a Sears Roebuck warehouse. The wages were a paltry twenty dollars a week, and the work strenuous. Malcolm had never been physically strong; years of alcohol addiction and cocaine use could not have helped. Over a six-week period, he failed to get to work six times. By Thanksgiving, he had had enough, and quit. In desperation, he stole a fur coat from Ella's home, pawning it for five dollars. The coat belonged to Ella's sister, Grace; Ella was so outraged that she summoned the police. Malcolm was duly arrested and taken to jail. The Roxbury court gave him a three-month suspended sentence, with probation to last one full year. This was Detroit Red's first offense to result in arrest and conviction. He was nineteen years old.

The Christmas season was only weeks away, and Goldstein consented to let Red work for him in New York City for a few weeks. In January 1945, with several hundred dollars in his pocket, Malcolm set off for Lansing. He had sent home small sums of money since 1941 and figured that his family owed him. Through Ella or Reginald, the Little siblings undoubtedly knew about their brother's downward slide, and his drug dependency. He anticipated resistance, especially from Wilfred, Hilda, and Philbert, so he arrived wearing a conservative-looking suit. His days of crime, he claimed, were long gone. For several weeks, seemingly true to his word, he worked at East Lansing's Coral Gables bar, then as a busboy at the city's Mayfair Ballroom. But he used these jobs as opportunities for petty theft. Traveling into Detroit, he brazenly robbed an acquaintance, a black man named Douglas Haynes, at gunpoint. Haynes filed a complaint with the Detroit police, who contacted the Lansing police. On March 17, 1945, Malcolm was arrested and turned over to the Detroit Police Department, charged with grand larceny. Wilfred posted a bond of a thousand dollars, and for a short time Malcolm found menial jobs at a Lansing mattress maker and then a truck factory. When his trial was postponed, he decided that his best move was to get out of town. Sometime in August 1945, he fled the jurisdiction; a warrant was issued for his arrest.

The *Autobiography* is completely silent about these events. Undoubtedly, Malcolm was profoundly ashamed about this phase of his past. He likely felt that the deepest violation he had committed was the humiliation he inflicted on his family through his career as a petty criminal. But he may have also dropped these incidents from his history as part of the attempt to shape his legend. His amateurish efforts at gangsterism in Boston and Lansing—the clumsy theft of his aunt's coat, the ridiculous armed robbery of an acquaintance—undermined the credibility of his supposed criminal exploits in New York, and even he must have realized that the Michigan arrest warrant, combined with his parole violation from Massachusetts, would follow him across the country. If he was ever arrested again for even a minor crime, these other violations would be brought against him.

He first returned to New York City and subsequently to Boston, desperately trying to survive through a variety of hustles. It was during this time that Malcolm encountered a man named William Paul Lennon, and the uncertain particulars of their intimate relationship would generate much controversy and speculation in the years following Malcolm's death.

Lennon was born on March 25, 1888, in Pawtucket, Rhode Island, to Bernard and Nellie F. Lennon. His father was a successful merchant and newspaper publisher and active in local Democratic Party politics. The eldest son of eight children, Lennon enrolled in Brown University in 1906 as a "special student," described in the school's catalog as a category for "mature persons of good character who desire to pursue some special subject and who have had the requisite preliminary training." After attending Brown for several years, Lennon drifted, seeking to establish himself in some suitable profession. During World War I, he served as chief petty officer in the navy, stationed out of Newport, Rhode Island, and upon his discharge he lived briefly with his parents before getting hired as a hotel manager in Pawtucket. Within five years he had become manager of Manhattan's Dorset Hotel, just off Fifth Avenue in midtown. Apparently he embarked on a successful career in hotel management, but—contrary to Malcolm's later assertions that his patron was a multimillionaire—there is no record indicating that Lennon ever became truly wealthy. Sometime during the 1930s or early 1940s, Lennon had relocated to Boston, where he began to employ male secretaries in his home.

Malcolm's initial contact with Lennon may have come through classified advertisements placed in New York newspapers. What is certain is that sometime in 1944 Malcolm had begun working for Lennon as a "butler and occasional house worker" at Lennon's Boston home, on an affluent stretch of Arlington Street overlooking the Public Garden. Soon something deeper than an employer–employee relationship developed. (After Malcolm's later arrest, in 1946, he would give the police Lennon's name and address as a previous employer, convinced that Lennon would use his financial resources and other contacts to help him during his time in prison.) The *Autobiography* describes sexual contacts with Lennon, except that Malcolm falsely attributed them to a character named Rudy:

> [Rudy] had a side deal going, a hustle that took me right back to the old steering days in Harlem. Once a week, Rudy went to the home of this old, rich Boston blueblood, pillar-of-society aristocrat. He paid Rudy to undress them both, then pick up the old man like a baby, lay him on his bed, then stand over him and sprinkle him all over with *talcum powder*. Rudy said the old man would actually reach his climax from that.

Based on circumstantial but strong evidence, Malcolm was probably describing his own homosexual encounters with Paul Lennon. The revelation of his involvement with Lennon produced much speculation about Malcolm's sexual orientation, but the experience appears to have been limited. There is no evidence from his prison record in Massachusetts or from his personal life after 1952 that he was actively homosexual. More credible, perhaps, is Rodnell Collins's insight about his uncle: "Malcolm basically lived two lives." When he was around Ella, "he enthusiastically participated in family picnics and family dinners. . . . He saved some of his money to send to his brothers and sisters in Lansing." But in his Detroit Red life, he participated in prostitution, marijuana sales, cocaine sessions, numbers running, the occasional robbery, and, apparently, paid homosexual encounters. Keeping the two lives separate from each other was never easy, due to his unstable material circumstances. But Malcolm had the intelligence and ingenuity to mask his most illegal and potentially upsetting activities from his family and friends.

Well-to-do white men were one thing, white women another. During the war, his old paramour Bea Caragulian had married a white man, Mehan Bazarian, but he was serving in the military and was largely away. Malcolm's sexual relationship with Bea had continued after her marriage, although it eventually grew chaotic and frequently abusive. By early December 1945, he was back in Boston, with no place to go except Ella's. Once again, his disgusted half sister had no choice but to allow him to stay; after all, blood was blood. Malcolm quickly ran down Shorty Jarvis, who complained to him about his wife and their money problems. Within several days, Malcolm organized a gang, with the intention of robbing homes in Boston's affluent neighborhoods. His motley crew consisted of another African American, Francis E. "Sonny" Brown; Bea; her younger sister, Joyce Caragulian; a third Armenian woman, Kora Marderosian; and Shorty. Early in the evening of December 14, 1945, Malcolm and Brown robbed a Brookline home, absconding with $2,400 worth of fur coats, silverware, jewelry, and other items. The next night, they struck a second Brookline house, stealing several rugs and silverware valued at nearly $400, in addition to liquor, jewelry, and linen. For these break-ins, the gang followed a general pattern. Sonny would jimmy the home's rear door, then open the front door for Malcolm and Shorty. The premises was quickly looted, with a focus on items that could easily be sold on the black market. The women stayed in the automobile, acting as lookouts. On December 16 they drove to New York City to sell part of their merchandise. Some items that failed to find a buyer were dumped, but most of the loot was distributed among gang members, a mistake no veteran burglar would ever have made.

One of the gang's most lucrative hauls took place the day after their trip to New York. Entering a home in Newton, Massachusetts, the young criminals managed to grab jewelry, a watch, a vacuum cleaner, bed linen, silver candlesticks, earrings, a gold pendant and chain, and additional merchandise, with a total value estimated by police at $6,275. Over a period of one month, they robbed about eight homes. When they were finally caught, Malcolm was primarily responsible for tipping their hand. He gave a watch to a relative as a Christmas gift; the relative sold it on to a Boston jeweler, who, suspecting it had been stolen, contacted the police. The authorities bided their time. In early January 1946, Malcolm took another stolen watch to a repair shop. When he returned for it, local police were on hand to arrest him. Malcolm was carrying a loaded .32 caliber pistol at the time. During his interrogation, detectives disingenuously promised not to prosecute him on the gun charge if he agreed to give up his accomplices. He readily complied, naming his whole crew. With the exception of Sonny Brown, who managed to elude authorities, everyone in the gang was promptly arrested.

Malcolm was charged with the illegal possession of a firearm in Roxbury court on January 15. The next day, at the Quincy court, charges of larceny and breaking and entering were added. The court set a bail of ten thousand dollars. Because the burglaries had taken place in two Massachusetts counties, Norfolk and Middlesex, two trials were held. Shorty Jarvis's account provides a vivid description of his and Malcolm's ordeal: "We were urged by the district attorney and our white lawyers to plead guilty as charged; we were also told that if we did, things would go real easy and well in our favor (meaning the sentence)." Both men had been "damn fools" not to have anticipated a legal double cross. Bea was subpoenaed and turned the state's evidence against Malcolm, largely reading the script the prosecutors wrote for her. Jarvis claimed that the district attorney had even attempted unsuccessfully "to get the girls to testify that we had raped them; this was so he could ask the judge for a fifteen-to-twenty-year sentence or life in prison." To Malcolm and Shorty, as well as to Ella, it seemed that the prime motivation for their prosecution was racial. "As long as I live," Shorty reflected, "I will never forget how the judge told me I had had no business associating with white women." Ella's son, Rodnell, observed: "In court [Ella] said, the men were described by one lawyer as 'schvartze bastards' and by another as 'minor Al Capones.' The arresting officer meanwhile referred to [the women] as 'poor, unfortunate, friendless, scared lost girls.'"

Both Malcolm Little and Shorty Jarvis pled guilty and were sentenced in a Middlesex County court to four concurrent eight-to-ten-year sentences, to be served in prison. While this was read out, they were confined behind bars in a steel cage in the courtroom. Shorty snapped, shaking the bars and screaming at the presiding judge, "Why don't you kill me? Why don't you kill me? I would rather be dead than do ten years." In Norfolk County Superior Court eight weeks later, Malcolm received three concurrent six-to-eight-year sentences. The court could hardly have imposed more. When Malcolm remarked to a defense attorney that "we seem to be getting sentenced because of those girls," the lawyer replied angrily, "You had no business with white girls!" Bea pleaded to the courts that she and the other white women were innocent victims of Malcolm's vicious criminal enterprise. He had coerced them. "We lived in constant fear," she told the court with emotion. She ultimately served only seven months of a five-year sentence.

Bea's self-serving actions left a profound impression on Malcolm. "All women, by their nature, are fragile and weak," he observed. "They are attracted to the male in whom they see strength." His misogyny had been reinforced during his time as a steerer for Harlem prostitutes. Reflecting on his experiences, Malcolm wrote, "I got my first schooling about the cesspool morals of the white man from the best possible source, from his own women." Bea's actions underlined what he perceived as women's deceptive, opportunistic tendencies. Malcolm rarely examined his own behavior—his broken relationship with Gloria Strother, his physical abuse of Bea Caragulian—let alone his betrayal of his partners.

CHAPTER 3

Becoming "X"

January 1946–August 1952

O n March 8, 1946, a Massachusetts state psychiatrist interviewed prisoner number 22843. "He got called every filthy name I could think of," Malcolm remembered. He described himself as being "physically miserable and as evil-tempered as a snake." The "Psychometric Report," written nearly two months later, however, described him as attentive and apparently cooperative. Malcolm blithely informed his interviewer that his parents had been missionaries and his mother a "white Scot" whose marriage to a black man had led to Malcolm's being taunted by racial abuse throughout his childhood. Other misinformation followed. The psychiatrist, apparently troubled by all he had heard, observed that the prisoner "has fatalistic views, is moody, cynical, and has a sardonic smile which seems to be affected because of his sensitiveness to color."

His defense lawyer had prevented his speaking on his own behalf during the trials, and Malcolm was convinced that his lengthy sentence was due solely to his involvement with Bea and the other white women. He also dreaded, being not yet twenty-one years old, the challenges of prison life, a dangerous world about which he knew only horror stories. During the weeks he was held in county jails prior to his transfer to the state penitentiary, Malcolm decided he had to exaggerate his criminal experiences, making himself appear tougher and more violent than he really was. He would also present a made-up history of his own family, making it almost impossible for the authorities to know his true background. He already felt outraged by how corrections officers recognized only a convict's number, rather than his name. In prison, "you never heard your name, only your number," he would recall years later. "On all of your clothing, every item was your number, stenciled. It grew stenciled on your brain."

Two months later, another caseworker filed a report on Malcolm. "Subject is a tall light-complexioned negro," it ran in part, "unmarried, a child of a broken home, who has grown up indifferently into a pattern of life he liked, colorful, cynical, a-moral, fatalistic." The report indicated that the prison authorities viewed him as the ringleader of the burglary ring. Perhaps Malcolm once again launched into a string of profanities, for the caseworker judged his prognosis as "poor. His present 'hard' attitude will no doubt increase in bitterness. . . . Subject may prove an intermediate security risk as he will find it hard to adjust from the accelerated tempo of night spots to the slow pace of institution life at Charlestown [prison]."

Both Malcolm and Shorty Jarvis had been assigned to Charlestown State Prison, at that time the oldest penal facility in continuous use in the world. It had been constructed in 1804–5 on the west banks of the Charlestown peninsula along the Boston Harbor, and its physical conditions were wretched: its mice-infested cells were tiny—seven feet by eight—and devoid of plumbing and running water. Prisoners relieved themselves in buckets that were emptied only once in twenty-four hours. There was no common dining room, so prisoners were forced to eat in their cells. The atmosphere was hardly improved by the prison's grotesque history of executions, the most notorious being the 1927 electrocution of anarchists Nicola Sacco and Bartolomeo Vanzetti, who had previously been unfairly convicted for a 1920 robbery and double homicide. The place was so beastly that in May 1952, shortly before Malcolm's release, state governor Paul A. Dever described it as "a Bastille that eclipses in infamy any current prison in the United States."

At first Malcolm had great difficulty accepting his sentence, and especially what he perceived as Bea's betrayal in the trial. His fits of outrage and alienation were plain. Shorty, still upset with Malcolm for turning him in, began calling him the "Green-Eyed Monster." During his first months, Malcolm routinely insulted guards and prisoners alike. He had never been particularly religious, but he now concentrated his profanities against God and religion in general. Other prisoners, listening to Malcolm's tirades, came up with a further nickname for him: "Satan." In the Middlesex jail during his trial, Malcolm had been forced to get clean, but once in Charlestown he soon resumed his old drug habit, first getting high on ground nutmeg. In small amounts—roughly four to eight teaspoons—nutmeg is a mild hallucinogen, creating euphoria and visual distortions; when taken in large amounts, as Malcolm may have done, it has similar effects to those of ecstasy. Nutmeg users can achieve highs lasting as long as seventy-two hours, but can also suffer mental breakdown. Some of the symptoms Malcolm described during his early months at Charlestown sound like the effects of nutmeg poisoning, especially the episodes of depression and paranoia. When Ella started sending small amounts of money, he used it to purchase drugs from corrupt guards who were happy to conduct business. Prisoners could obtain almost any drugs they wanted, from hash to heroin.

Malcolm had lived for years in a close web of family and stayed in relatively constant touch through mail and visits wherever he moved, but now, in his anger and shame about what had happened to him, he was reluctant to contact his siblings, especially Ella. During his first year in prison, he wrote only a few letters, including one or more to William Paul Lennon. The first one he received was from Philbert, to say that he had become a member of an evangelical church in Detroit. Philbert's assurance that the entire congregation was praying for the soul of his younger brother enraged Malcolm. "I scrawled him a reply I'm ashamed to think of today," he later admitted. Things went no better when Ella visited. On one occasion, about fifty prisoners and visitors were crowded into the small visitation center, all of them surrounded by armed guards. Ella attempted to exchange pleasantries, but was so upset that it was almost impossible for her to talk. Malcolm became so defensive that he "wished she hadn't come at all."

His attitude soon left him isolated, but he was not without visitors entirely. Malcolm's most regular, and perhaps most sympathetic, visitor was a teenager, Evelyn Lorene Williams. Evelyn's foster mother, Dorothy Young, was a close friend of Ella's. Indeed, the two women were such good friends that Ella's son, Rodnell, referred to Young as Aunt Dot. Malcolm had occasionally dated Evelyn during his years in Boston, and Ella had strongly encouraged the relationship. Malcolm had little sexual interest in Evelyn—compared, say, with the chemistry he had with Bea. Evelyn, however, seems to have fallen deeply in love with Malcolm.

Another frequent visitor was Jackie Mason, a Boston woman who had been sexually involved with Malcolm before his incarceration. Ella sharply disapproved of Mason, describing her as a "common street woman" unfit for her brother. Her attitude, according to Rodnell Collins, was that she "was well aware of how much havoc [an] older, experienced predatory woman could wreak on a teenaged, adventurous, highly impressionable" boy.

When Ella did go to see him, she was not happy with what she found—

that he was not reflecting in any serious way on why he had wound up in prison or what its consequences might be for him. She was upset about his continuing contact with Paul Lennon, and was scandalized by his resumption of drug use. After several disappointing visits, Ella decided not to see her brother again. When Malcolm learned about this, he appeared contrite. In a plaintive letter dated September 10, he thanked Ella for mailing photos of family members, and for small amounts of cash. But then he incensed her again by trying to get her to contact Paul Lennon on his behalf. "The person that you said called me is a very good friend of mine," Malcolm explained. "He's only worth some fourteen million dollars. If you read the society pages you'd know who he is. He knows where I am now because I've written and told him, but I didn't say what for." Without mentioning Lennon's name, he appealed to Ella to be cordial. "He may call and ask you. Whatever answer you give him will have to do with my entire future but I still depend on you." Apparently Malcolm was convinced that Lennon could use his wealth and political contacts to reduce his prison term. According to Collins, Lennon never contacted Ella. In her words, though, she was "outraged" that her half brother had given her phone number to Lennon and that he had asked her to act as a go-between. Lennon, she thought, was obviously "one of those decadent whites whom he had been hustling."

In the end Malcolm was forced to confront the challenges of prison life by himself. And it didn't help matters that his attitude toward prison work detail was noncooperative. During his first seven months at Charlestown, he was assigned to the prison auto shop; then, that October, to work as a laborer in the yard. The month following, he was moved again, this time to sew in the underwear shop. Here he immediately ran into problems, being charged with shirking his duties; for this he was given three days' detention. His work performance improved somewhat when he was reassigned to the foundry, where he was considered "cooperative, poor in skill, and average to poor in effort." It was also here that he met a tall, light-complexioned former burglar named John Elton Bembry: the man who would change his life.

Bembry, who was about twenty years older than Malcolm, dazzled the young man with his mind. He was the first black man Malcolm would meet in prison (and possibly outside of prison as well) who seemed knowledgeable about virtually every subject and had the verbal skills to command nearly every conversation. Intellectually, Bembry had an astonishing range of interests, able to address the works of Thoreau at one moment, and then the institutional history of Massachusetts's Concord prison at another.

Malcolm was especially attracted to Bembry's ability to "put the atheist philosophy in a framework."

Malcolm's brain came alive under Bembry's tutelage. Here, finally, was an older man with both intellectual curiosity and a sense of discipline to impart to his young follower. Both men were assigned to the license plate shop, where after work inmates and even a few guards would cluster around to listen to Bembry's wide-ranging discourses on any number of topics. For weeks, Bembry carefully noted the wild behavior of his young workmate. Finally, taking Malcolm aside, he challenged him to employ his intellect to improve his situation. Bembry urged him to enroll in correspondence courses and to use the library, Malcolm recalled. Hilda had already offered similar advice, imploring her brother to "study English and penmanship." Malcolm consented: "So, feeling I had time on my hands, I did."

It is possible that the details Bembry ("Bimbi" in the *Autobiography*) related to other convicts about his successful history of thefts found their way into Malcolm's tales about his own burglary exploits, but above all Malcolm envied Bembry's reputation as an intellectual. There was also a strong motive of self-interest: his own newfound enthusiasm for study and self-improvement might get him recommended for a transfer to the system's most lenient facility, Massachusetts's Norfolk Prison Colony. The bait of increased freedom was enough to instill discipline within Malcolm, such that he finally chose to pursue a self-directed course of formal study. During 1946–47, he devoted himself to a rigorous program, fulfilling the requirements for university extension courses that included English and elementary Latin and German. He devoured books from Charlestown's small library, particularly those on linguistics and etymology. Following Bembry's advice, he began studying a dictionary, memorizing the definitions of both commonly used and obscure words. Education now had a clear, practical goal: it offered a way out, to a prison with better conditions, and maybe even a reduction in prison time. Ironically, it also had the side benefit of making him a more persuasive con man. Refining his oratorical skills, he found new success in hustles of various kinds, including betting on baseball.

Malcolm was duly transferred in January 1947—but to the Massachusetts Reformatory at Concord, only a slight improvement over Charlestown. Concord maintained a so-called mark system of discipline, which set a confusing schedule of penalties and the loss of prisoners' freedoms for acts of misconduct. No inmate council existed to negotiate the conditions of work and supervision. The new regulations and the lack of prisoners' rights probably contributed to Malcolm's continued acts of noncompliance.

During his incarceration at Concord he received a total of thirty-four visits. Among them were five from Ella, three from Reginald, and nineteen from "friends" (according to the redacted files)—undoubtedly Jackie Mason and Evelyn Williams, and possibly William Paul Lennon.

His hard work and professions about wanting to become a better man seem to have convinced Ella that he was finally committed to transforming his life, and she launched a letter-writing campaign to officials urging that he be relocated to the Norfolk Prison Colony. She encouraged Malcolm to write directly to the administrator in charge of transfers there. On July 28, in just such a letter, Malcolm employed his enhanced language skills to good effect: "Since my confinement I've already received a diploma in Elementary English through the State Correspondence Courses. I'm very much dissatisfied, though. There are many things that I would like to learn that would be of use to me when I regain my freedom." Still, he undermined his efforts by continuing to cause trouble. Throughout 1947, he was assigned to the prison's furniture shop, where he was evaluated as a "poor and uncooperative worker." In April, he had been suspected of possessing "contraband"—in this case, a knife. In September he would be charged with disruptive behavior, and on two more occasions penalized for poor work. But Malcolm was as adept as Ella in skirting penalties. After each infraction he improved his job performance sufficiently so as to avoid severe discipline.

In early 1948, a curious letter arrived from his brother Philbert, one that would have enormous consequences. Philbert explained that he and other family members had all converted to Islam. Malcolm was not surprised by the sudden enthusiasm, and did not take this particular turn very seriously. Philbert "was forever joining something," he recalled. Philbert now asked his brother to "pray to Allah for deliverance." Malcolm was not impressed. His reply, written in proper English, was completely dismissive.

Philbert's letter was in fact the opening salvo in a family campaign to convert Malcolm to a nascent movement called the Nation of Islam. As Wilfred later explained, "It was a program designed to help black people. And they had the best program going." They were determined to get Malcolm on board. After Philbert's letter had no effect, the family decided that an overture from Reginald might be more effective. Reginald wrote a "newsy" missive that contained no overt references to the Nation of Islam, but concluded with a cryptic promise: "Don't eat any more pork, and don't smoke any more cigarettes. I'll show you how to get out of prison." For days, Malcolm was puzzled. Was this some new way to hustle? He still had many doubts, but decided to follow the advice and stopped smoking. His new refusal to eat pork provoked surprise among inmates at the dining hall.

Meanwhile, Ella's appeals and letter writing finally won out: in late March 1948, Malcolm was transferred to the Norfolk Prison Colony. Established in 1927 as a model of correctional reform, the facility was located twenty-three miles from Boston, near Walpole, on a thirty-five-acre, oval-shaped property that looked more like a college campus than a traditional prison. However, it did possess strong escape deterrents, most prominently a five-thousand-foot-long, nineteen-foot-high wall surrounding the entire grounds, topped by three inches of electrified barbed wire. The philosophy behind the prison was rehabilitation and reentry into society. Prisoners lived in compounds of twenty-four houses, with individual and group rooms, all with windows and doors.

———

Compared to Charlestown, Malcolm had a life as eased of restrictions as one might find in a state penitentiary. First and foremost, he was treated like a human being. He was not locked into a room at night. He had two lockers, one in his room for personal clothes and toiletries, the other in his housing unit's basement, for his work uniform. Two inmates in each house were responsible for serving meals, cleaning the dining and common rooms, and minor repairs. There were meetings every Saturday night, at which inmates' concerns were addressed. Prisoners could elect their own representatives to house committees, and an inmate chairman was responsible for running them. Norfolk encouraged the prisoners to participate in all sorts of educational activities, such as the debating club and the prison newspaper, the *Colony*. Entertainment, which consisted of both outside groups and inmate-initiated shows, was organized on Sunday evenings. Religious services were held weekly for Roman Catholics, Protestants, Christian Scientists, and Theosophists, while monthly group meetings and religious holiday observances were permitted for "Hebrews."

This new life suited the newly disciplined Malcolm well, and he continued his plan to educate himself broadly. He eagerly participated in the facility's activities, and extended his reading agenda to include works on Buddhism. Unfortunately, his new commitment to self-improvement did not extend to improved work habits. In the prison laundry and on kitchen duty, his work performance was once again rated as substandard, his supervisors describing him as "lazy, detested work in any form, and accepted and performed given work seemingly in silent disgust." He was careful, however, to work just enough to avoid any major infraction, which would have jeopardized his place at Norfolk. He also stopped cursing the guards and fellow prisoners.

Reginald was the first relative to visit Malcolm in the new place. First he filled him in on family gossip and told him about a recent visit to Harlem he'd made, but eventually he turned the conversation to a new subject: Islam, or the "no pork and cigarettes riddle," as described in the *Autobiography*.

"If a man knew every imaginable thing that there is to know, who would he be?" Reginald asked.

"Some kind of a god," replied Malcolm.

Reginald explained that such a man did exist—"his real name is Allah"— and had made himself known years before to an African American named Elijah—"a black man, just like us." Allah had identified all whites, without exception, as devils. At first, Malcolm found this extremely difficult to accept. Not even Garveyism had prepared him for such an extreme antiwhite message. But afterward, when he had carefully cataloged each significant relationship he had ever developed with a white person, he concluded that every white he had ever known had held a deep animus toward blacks.

The seed was sown. Not long after this conversation, Hilda paid a visit and filled in the backdrop to the family's conversion. It had begun quietly and casually. Sometime in 1947, while waiting at a bus stop, Wilfred had struck up a conversation with a young, well-dressed black man, who began discussing religion and black nationalism and invited him to visit the Nation of Islam's Temple No. 1 in Detroit. When Wilfred went, he found a modest storefront church. It was a rental property with a hall that could probably accommodate about two hundred people, though there seemed to be fewer than a hundred actual members. What Wilfred heard there sounded comfortingly familiar: a message of black separatism, self-reliance, and a black deity that reminded him instantly of Earl Little's Garveyite sermons.

It took only a few months for Hilda, Philbert, Wesley, and Reginald to also become members. Wilfred would later explain, "We already had been indoctrinated with Marcus Garvey's philosophy, so that was just a good place for us. They didn't have to convince us we were black and should be proud or anything like that." There were personal connections to the NOI's first family, Clara and Elijah Poole, that made the family's attraction to the

Nation of Islam natural. When Earl had been living in Georgia, he had occasionally preached in the town of Perry, the home of Clara Poole's parents. Ella had grown to adulthood in Georgia before moving to the North, and she had met both Clara and Elijah Poole years before they were linked to the Nation.

During her visit, Hilda also explained to Malcolm the central tenet of Nation of Islam theology, Yacub's History, which told how an evil black scientist named Yacub had genetically engineered the creation of the entire white race. Allah, in the person of an Asiatic black man, had come into the world to reveal this extraordinary story, and to explain the legacies of the white race's monstrous crimes against blacks. Only through complete racial separation, Hilda explained, could blacks survive. She urged Malcolm to write directly to the Nation of Islam's supreme leader, Elijah Muhammad—as Elijah Poole had renamed himself—who was based in Chicago. He would satisfy any doubts Malcolm might have. Malcolm was amazed by his sister's obvious devotion, and afterward wrote, "I don't know if I was able to open my mouth and say goodbye."

Over the next few weeks, he grappled with what he had been told. The black nationalist message of racial pride, a rejection of integration, and self-sufficiency rekindled strong connections with the driving faith of his parents. The NOI's condemnation of all-white institutions, especially Christianity, also fitted with his experiences. Yet the bitter young nonbeliever had never shown the least interest in organized religion or the spiritual life. For Malcolm, the lure was more secular: Nation of Islam held out the possibility of finding self-respect and even dignity as a black man. This was a faith that said blacks had nothing for which to be ashamed or apologetic.

But above any spiritual or political goals was one important personal one: conversion was a way to keep the Little family together. As all the Little children had reached adulthood, the possibility of the family's disintegration had again become a problem. By 1948, both Wilfred and Philbert had been married for several years. In 1949, Yvonne Little married Robert Jones, and the couple relocated to Grand Rapids. As the family grew and spread across new communities, the Nation of Islam would provide a common ground. Malcolm was the last to join, but his commitment was complete, and he embraced this opportunity to enact a wholesale change in his future life. Malcolm—Detroit Red, Satan, hustler, onetime pimp, drug addict and drug dealer, homosexual lover, ladies' man, numbers racketeer, burglar Jack Carlton, and convicted thief—had convinced himself that a total revolution in his identity and beliefs was called for. After redrafting a one-page letter to Elijah Muhammad "at least twenty-five times," he mailed it off. It wasn't long before he received Muhammad's reply, together with a five-dollar bill. He had taken his first decisive step toward Allah.

———

Although Malcolm did not realize it, by becoming members of the Nation of Islam, his brothers and sisters had entered into the richly heterodox community of global Islam. Extremely sectarian by the standards of orthodox Islam, the Nation of Islam nevertheless became the starting point for a spiritual journey that would consume Malcolm's life.

Islam was established in what is today Saudi Arabia in the early seventh century CE by a man known as the Prophet Muhammad. Over the course of more than two decades, from roughly 610 CE to 632 CE, hundreds of beautiful verses were revealed to Muhammad and passed on by poetic recitations, just like Homer's stories or the love songs of the troubadours. These verses became known as the *Qur'an*, and Islam's enduring power as a religion rests, in part, on its elegance and simplicity. At its core is the metaphor of the five pillars. The first pillar is the profession of faith, or *sha-hada*: "There is no god but God, and Muhammad is God's Messenger." The other four are acts a devout Muslim must perform: daily prayers (*salat*); tithing, or alms to those less fortunate (*zakat*); fasting during the month of Ramadan; and making a pilgrimage to Mecca (*hajj*). Many Muslims characterize *jihad*, meaning "striving" or "struggle," as a sixth pillar, separating it into two types: the "greater jihad" that refers to a believer's internal struggle to adhere to Islam's creed, and the "lesser jihad," the struggle against those who oppose Muhammad's message.

In the Prophet's day, Islam was an embracing, not excluding, religion that drew on the practices of other contemporaries. Muhammad had taught that both Jews and Christians were *ahl al-Kitab* (People of the Book), and that the Torah, the Gospels, and the Holy Qur'an were all a single divine scripture. Early Islamic rituals drew directly upon Jewish traditions. At first, Muslims prayed in the direction of Jerusalem, not Mecca. The Prophet's mandatory fast was initiated each year on the tenth day (*Ashura*) of the first month of the Jewish calendar, the day more commonly known as Yom Kippur. Muhammad also adopted many Jewish dietary laws and purity requirements, and encouraged his followers to marry Jews, as he himself did. Second only to the Qur'an, and also central to Islam, is the *Sunna*, the collective traditions associated with Muhammad, which include thousands of stories, or *hadith*, all roughly based on the actions or words of the Prophet or those of his closest disciples.

What was truly revolutionary about the Islamic concept was its transethnic, nonracial character. Islam is primarily defined by a series of actions and obligations that all believers follow. In theory, differences in native language, race, ethnicity, geography, and social class become irrelevant. Indeed, from the beginning, individuals of African descent have become Muslims (literally, "those who submit" to God). Muhammad had encouraged the emancipation of African slaves held by Arabs; his first *muezzin* (the individual who calls believers to prayer) was an Ethiopian former slave named Bilal.

Over time, the religious pluralism of the *ummah*—the transnational Islamic community—gave way to an exclusive monotheism. After the Prophet's death, Jews and Christians were perceived to be excluded from the community; centuries later, Islamic legal scholars would divide the entire world into two, the *dar al-Islam* (House of Islam) and the *dar al-Harb* (House of War), or those who oppose the believers.

By the eighth century, Islam dominated northern Africa, soon penetrating the Sudan and, in West Africa, the sub-Saharan regions. The Arab elite within this growing Muslim world had a long tradition of slavery, and over the centuries millions of black Africans were subjugated and transported to what today is the Middle East, northern Africa, and the Iberian peninsula. There were, however, many prominent examples of black converts to Islam who came into power in the Muslim world—such as Yaqub al-Mansur, the twelfth-century black ruler of Morocco and parts of what are today Portugal and Spain. Several great Islamic empires dominated West Africa from the fourteenth through the sixteenth centuries. As European states colonized the Americas and the Caribbean in the sixteenth century, they ultimately transported about fifteen million chattel slaves into their respective colonies. A significant minority were Muslims: of the approximately 650,000 involuntarily taken to what would become the United States, Muslims made up about 7 or 8 percent.

During the nineteenth century, a series of black intellectuals from the Caribbean and the United States were attracted to Islam. This was an era of evangelical Christianity, and social Darwinism, which promoted religious and scientific justifications for white supremacy. People of African descent increasingly became attracted to Islam as an alternative to Christianity. By far the most influential black intellectual of the period was Edward Wilmot Blyden (1832–1912), who came to the United States from the Danish West Indies as a candidate for the Presbyterian ministry. After the passage of the Fugitive Slave Act, which permitted blacks to be arrested and deported to the slave South, Blyden left for Liberia in 1851. During the next sixty years he had an extraordinary career as a scholar, traveler, and diplomat.

Blyden's contributions to Malcolm Little's spiritual and political journey were threefold. First, long before W. E. B. Du Bois's *The Souls of Black Folk* (1903), Blyden argued that the black race possessed certain spiritual and cultural strengths, a collective personality, uniting black humanity through-out the world. During the 1960s, this insight would form the basis for what would be called "black cultural nationalism"—a deep pride in African antiquity, history, and culture, together with the celebration of rituals and aesthetics drawing upon Africa and the black diaspora.

Second, long before Garvey, Blyden had envisioned a program of "Pan-Africanism"—the political and social unity of black people worldwide—leading to a strategy of group migration back to Africa. Blyden was convinced that conditions for American blacks would eventually become so oppressive that millions would return to the land of their ancestors. His writings on Pan-Africanism paved the way for the back-to-Africa move-ment among Southern blacks in the 1890s, and provided the intellectual arguments for Garveyites a generation later.

His most original contribution, however, was to link Pan-Africanism with West African Islam. In his classic 1888 treatise, *Christianity, Islam and the Negro Race*, he argued that Christianity, despite its Middle Eastern origins, had evolved into a distinctly European religion that was discrimi-natory and oppressive. He insisted that among the world's great religions, only Islam permitted Africans to retain their traditions with integrity.

By the early twentieth century, the first significant religious organization in the United States that identified itself as Islamic was the Moorish Science Temple of America. The group's founder, a North Carolina–born African American named Timothy Drew, established the cult in Newark, New Jersey, in 1913, as the Canaanite Temple. Proclaiming himself Noble Drew Ali, he told followers that he was the second prophet of Islam, Mahdi, or redeemer. In orthodox Islam, Muhammad is widely described as the Seal of the Prophets, the last of a line of Qur'anic prophets beginning with Adam. Any such claim to the status of prophet is inherently blasphemous, but Ali's deviation from Islam's five pillars didn't stop there. The sacred text of his cult was the *Holy Koran*, also known as the *Circle Seven Koran*, a sixty-four-page synthesis that drew on four sources: the Qur'an, the Bible, the *Aquarian Gospels of Jesus Christ* (an occult version of the New Testament), and *Unto Thee I Grant* (a publication of the Rosicrucian Brotherhood, a Masonic order influenced by the Egyptian mystery schools).

Noble Drew Ali's major appeal to black Americans paralleled Blyden's arguments. He claimed that Islam was the spiritual home for all Asiatics, a term that embraced Arabs, Egyptians, Chinese, Japanese, black Americans, as well as several other ethnicities and nationalities. African Americans were not Negroes at all, Ali insisted, but "an olive-skinned Asiatic people who were the descendants of Moroccans." Members consequently acquired "Islamic" names, as well as new identities as "Asiatic" blacks, or Moroccans. The Moorish Science Temple preached that blacks' authentic religion was Islam; their national identity was not American, but Moorish; and their genealogy extended back to Christ. Ali's strange quasi-Masonic creed attracted hundreds of followers in Newark, chiefly drawn from illiterate sharecroppers and landless workers who had trekked from the rural South during the initial wave of the Great Migration. By the late 1920s, the Moorish Science Temple claimed thirty thousand members, with temples in Philadelphia, Baltimore, Richmond, Petersburg (Virginia), Cleveland, Youngstown (Ohio), Lansing, Chicago, and Milwaukee, among others.

Ali's awareness of orthodox Islam's core tenets was sketchy at best. He demanded that followers adhere to many of Islam's dietary laws; the eating of pork was forbidden. There was some overlap between the Temple people and Garveyism, but the two movements differed in fundamental ways. The Moorish Science Temple was essentially a cult, while the Universal Negro Improvement Association was a popular movement with many different local leaders. However, as the UNIA fragmented, some of its former members joined the Temple, or began to influence it. In March 1929, Ali was arrested on suspicion of murdering an opposition leader, Sheikh Claude Greene. Released on bail, he died mysteriously several months later. His movement almost immediately split into feuding factions. The two major groups were led, respectively, by Ali's former chauffeur, John Givens-El, who announced he was the reincarnation of Ali, and by Kirkman Bey, "Grand Sheikh" and president of the Moorish Science Temple Corporation. By the 1940s, Kirkman's followers came under intense scrutiny by the FBI, and a significant number of their temples were investigated for sedition. The Moorish Science Temple largely disintegrated after World

War II, with fewer than ten thousand members remaining nationwide, but it had prepared the path for more orthodox expressions of Islam within black America.

From a theological standpoint, the most successful sect in America was the Ahmadiyya movement, which had been founded by Hazrat Mirza Ghulam Ahmad (c. 1835–1908) in the Punjab. At first, it adhered to the core tenets of Islam, but in 1891 Ahmad declared himself Islam's Mahdi, as well as an avatar of Krishna to the Hindus and Messiah to the Christians. Several years later, he further asserted that Christ did not die on the cross, but survived and made his way to India, where he did finally die and physically ascended into heaven. Such claims outraged Muslims, who declared the sect blasphemous and heretical. Following Ahmad's own death in 1908, the Ahmadiyya cause fractured into the Qadianis, the more conservative faction connected with landowners and the merchant classes, who supported strict adherence to Ghulam Ahmad's version of Islam, and a more liberal group, the Lahoris, who supported rapprochement with orthodox Islam.

Between 1921 and 1925, Ahmadiyya made its first great inroads in America when the first Qadiani Ahmadi missionary, Mufti Muhammad Sadiq, persuaded more than one thousand Americans to convert, both white and black. Many African-American Ahmadi Muslims joined the faith in Chicago and Detroit, cities where the UNIA was also strong. In July 1921, Sadiq initiated the first Muslim publication in the United States, the *Moslem Sunrise*, through which he reached out to Garveyites, encouraging them to link Islam with their advocacy of black nationalism and Pan-Africanism. In a January 1923 issue, he declared:

> My Dear American Negro . . . the Christian profiteers brought you out of your native lands of Africa and in Christianizing you made you forsake the religion and language of your forefathers—which were Islam and Arabic. You have experienced Christianity for so many years and it has proved to be no good. It is a failure. Christianity cannot bring real brotherhood to the nations. Now leave it alone. And join Islam, the real faith of Universal Brotherhood, which at once does away with all distinctions of race, color and creed.

For all his proselytizing, however, Sadiq was not a natural leader. By the late 1920s, the movement languished; but it did not die away completely. Under the guidance of a new leader, Sufi Bengalee, the Ahmadi movement surged again. In 1929–30 Bengalee delivered over seventy public lectures throughout the United States, reaching thousands. Many of these events were designed to attract black and interracial groups. For example, in November 1931 the Ahmadi-sponsored program "How Can We Overcome Color and Race Prejudice?" attracted more than two thousand attendees at one Chicago venue. By 1940, through its extensive missionary work, the Ahmadis claimed between five and ten thousand American converts, half of them African Americans. The Ahmadis' primary missionary centers were based in Washington, D.C., Pittsburgh, Cleveland, Chicago, and Kansas City (Missouri). The movement was largely responsible for introducing the Qur'an and Islamic literature to a large African-American audience. Because many of the proselytizers Sadiq selected were African Americans, some Garveyites were attracted to the movement, although the multiracial character of the Ahmadiyya made it difficult for most black Garveyites to convert. By the Great Depression their numbers were still significantly smaller than those of the Moorish Science Temple.

It was within this rapidly changing social context that an olive-skinned peddler calling himself Wallace D. Fard made his appearance in Detroit's black ghetto. He regaled his poor audiences with exotic tales of the Orient, which he mixed with the militant, antiwhite views of the staunch Garveyite. Little is known of his origins. Years later, when he commanded a large number of followers, a story circulated that he had been born in Mecca, the son of wealthy parents of the tribe of the Koreish, which connected in ancestry to Muhammad. Others believed that Fard had been a Moorish Science Temple local leader on the West Coast.

Fard (pronounced *FA-rod*) preached in the emotional style of a Pentecostal minister, exhorting audiences to avoid alcohol and tobacco, and praising the virtues of marital fidelity and family life. Blacks should work hard, save their meager resources, and if possible own their homes and businesses. Within months, after he had attracted a sympathetic following, his message took an apocalyptic turn when he "revealed" that he was actually a prophet, sent by God to preach a message of salvation. African Americans were not Negroes at all, he announced, "but members of the lost tribe of Shabazz, stolen by traders from the Holy City of Mecca 379 years ago. . . . The original people must regain their religion, which is Islam, their language, which is Arabic, and their culture, which is astronomy and higher mathematics, especially calculus."

Fard employed elementary physics to challenge his audience's unquestioned belief in the Bible. As one follower later explained:

The very first time I went to a meeting I heard him say: "The Bible tells you that the Sun rises and sets. That is not so. The Sun stands still. All your lives you have been thinking that the Earth never moved. Stand and look toward the Sun and know that it is the Earth that you are standing on which is moving." Up to that day I always went to the Baptist church. After I heard that sermon from the prophet, I was turned around completely.

Fard did not claim to be divine: he presented himself as a prophet, like Muhammad, and added Muhammad to his name. By 1931, news of his controversial addresses attracted hundreds of blacks, many desperately seeking a message of hope as the country sank into depression. Fard wrote two basic texts: "The Secret Ritual of the Nation of Islam," a pamphlet which was generally presented orally and which adherents were to memorize, and the manual "Teaching for the Lost-Found Nation of Islam in a Mathematical Way." Formal membership in the "Lost-Found Nation" required converts "to return to the holy original Nation." Members were required to surrender their surnames, which Fard ridiculed as being identified with slavery. In turn, he promised to bestow upon each new member "an Original name," printed on a national identification card that showed its bearer to be a righteous Muslim. Members were given sets of questions and answers to be memorized perfectly:

Q: "Why does [Fard] Muhammad and any Moslem murder the devil? What is the duty of each Moslem in regard to four devils? What reward does a Moslem receive by presenting the four devils at one time?"

A: "Because he is one percent wicked and will not keep and obey the laws of Islam. His ways and actions are like a snake of the grafted type. So Mohammed learned that he could not reform the devils, so they had to be murdered. All Moslem will murder the devil because they know he is a snake and also if he be allowed to live, he would sting someone else. Each Moslem is required to bring four devils, and by bringing and presenting four at one time, his reward is a button to wear on the lapel of his coat, also a free transportation to the Holy City of Mecca."

The most controversial dimension of Fard's preaching concerned Euro-Americans. Since black Americans were both Asiatics and Earth's Original People, what were whites? The reason that both Marcus Garvey and Noble Drew Ali had failed, Fard taught, was that neither had fully grasped the true nature of whites: as Malcolm Little was to learn, they were "devils." To explain this, Fard presented his parable, Yacub's History, centered on the genetic plot of an evil "Big Head" scientist named Yacub, who lived thousands of years ago. A member of the exalted tribe of Shabazz, Yacub nevertheless used his scientific skills to produce genetic mutations that culminated in the creation of the white race. Although the naturally crafty and violent whites were banished to the caves of Caucasus, they ultimately achieved control over the entire earth. The Original People, Fard taught, subsequently "went to sleep" mentally and spiritually. The task of the Nation of Islam was to bring into consciousness the "lost-found" Asiatic black man from his centuries-long slumber.

The demonizing of the white race, the glorification of blacks, and the bombastic blend of orthodox Islam, Moorish science, and numerology were a seductive message to unemployed and disillusioned African Americans casting about for a new rallying cause after the disintegration of Garveyism and the inadequacies of the Moorish Science Temple. One evening in August 1931, Fard gave a lecture to an audience of hundreds at the former UNIA hall on West Lake Street in Detroit. One young man in particular, a thirty-three-year-old migrant from Georgia named Elijah Poole, found the address mesmerizing. Recalling it later, he approached Fard and said softly, "I know who you are, you're God himself."

"That's right," Fard quietly replied, "but don't tell it now. It is not yet time for me to be known."

Born in Sandersville, Georgia, in 1897, Poole had been a skilled laborer for years, working in his home state as a foreman at a brick-making company. Thin, wirily built, and of below average height, at the age of twenty-two he moved to Detroit along with his wife, Clara, where he quickly became an active member of the UNIA. After Garvey's imprisonment and exile in 1927, Poole had been searching for a new movement dedicated to black racial pride. In Fard, he felt the presence of a messianic leader who could realize the shattered dreams of Garveyites.

The large number of converts to the Lost-Found Nation of Islam required Fard to institute rudimentary administrative units, a level of lieutenants and captains, and a small number of assistant ministers. He set about promoting his most dedicated followers. In 1932, the sect established a small parochial school in Detroit, followed by another in Chicago two years later. For the male members, he established the Fruit of Islam (FOI), a paramilitary police corps which quickly became the organization's security force. Women and girls were coordinated through Muslim Girls Training (MGT) classes, which instructed them in their roles as Muslim wives.

In the desperate months of 1932, as black unemployment rates in Detroit reached 50 percent, the sect surrounding Fard expanded exponentially, and with its rising fortunes grew those of Elijah Poole. Although Poole was a poor public speaker, without charisma or even basic language skills, Fard saw something in him, bestowing on him an original name, Elijah Karriem, and a new title, "top laborer." He was soon representing Fard in a number of capacities, but what neither man anticipated was the surveillance and harassment by Detroit police. On the night of November 20, 1932, Robert Harris, a Nation of Islam member, was arrested for a gruesome ritualistic murder; he had hung up his victim to die on a wooden cross. Under questioning, Harris ranted that his actions were necessary to permit his "voluntary" victim to become a "savior." The story made headlines, and the Nation of Islam was quickly dubbed the "Voodoo Cult." Police broke into the group's headquarters, arresting Fard and one of his lieutenants. Harris was subsequently committed to a mental institution, but the Nation of Islam remained under intense police scrutiny; Fard was arrested on two further occasions. Finally, on May 26, 1933, he fled Detroit for Chicago, where his recent missionary efforts had been particularly well received.

Fard named Karriem to be the "supreme minister." A bitter feud sprang up among those who had been passed over, most of whom were better educated than Karriem, and more articulate. But the dissent only reinforced Fard's conviction that Elijah was the most suitable candidate. He renamed his chief lieutenant once more, this time as Elijah Muhammad.

Then, in 1934, Fard simply vanished. The last public notice of any kind to mention him is a Chicago police record, dated September 26, 1933, citing his arrest for disorderly conduct.

Even before this mysterious disappearance, his followers had split sharply over who should succeed him. A vocal majority in Detroit strongly opposed Elijah's elevation; Muhammad had little choice but to take his wife and children and a handful of supporters into exile to Chicago. Even here, his leadership was soon challenged by his youngest brother, Kallat Muhammad, who had been appointed "supreme captain" by Fard. One of Elijah's assistant ministers in Chicago, Augustus Muhammad, defected to Detroit, and later helped initiate the pro-Japanese black American organization, Development of Our Own. Over the next decade, the majority of Nation members quit the cult, either drifting into Christian sects or becoming

Ahmadi Muslims. Elijah Muhammad stubbornly refused to give up, traveling the road for years like an itinerant evangelist, eking out his existence
by soliciting donations for his sermons. In later years, NOI loyalists would
see parallels in the Prophet Muhammad's flight from Mecca in 622 CE and
Elijah Muhammad's wanderings. Elijah was never a charismatic speaker,
but his sheer persistence earned him followers.

Still under FBI surveillance, on May 8, 1942, Elijah was arrested in
Washington, D.C., and charged with failure to register for the draft and for
counseling his followers to resist military service. Convicted, he did not
emerge from federal prison until August 1946. Somehow the Lost-Found
Nation of Islam managed to survive, largely due to the administrative talents of his wife, Clara, who became especially active in the running of the
Chicago temple, corresponding regularly with her husband and visiting
him in prison. But the hard years living underground and the demands of
prison life took their toll. Muhammad's asthma and other chronic health
problems became worse, his body frail and thin, but the experience of
enforced isolation provided him ample time to redesign his tiny sect in his
own image. He would use his "martyrdom" to convince former members
to return to the Nation.

Even years before his incarceration, Elijah Muhammad had revealed to
his closest followers that Fard had informed him privately that he, Fard,
was God in person. Fard's elevation from prophet to savior also thrust Elijah into the exalted role of being the sole "Messenger of Allah." Elijah later
explained that an angel had descended from heaven with a message of truth
for the black race. "This angel can be no other than Master W. D. Muhammad who came from the Holy City of Mecca, Arabia, in 1930." Thus the
recipient of one message became himself the messenger to his people.

Malcolm learned of all this—Fard's teachings, his persecution, his disappearance, and the ultimate triumph of Elijah Karriem—at Norfolk. Reading
the letters from his siblings and the occasional letters from Elijah himself,
with whom Malcolm had struck up a correspondence, he drew further into
the world and worldview of the Nation of Islam. He soon convinced himself about Fard's divinity. "The greatest and mightiest God who appeared
on the earth was Master W. D. Fard," Malcolm would eventually profess.
"He came from the East to the West, appearing at a time when the history
and prophecy that is written was coming to realization, as the non-white
people all over the world began to rise, and as the devil white civilization,
condemned by Allah, was, through its devilish nature, destroying itself."

Under Fard, the Nation's preachers had always mentioned the cosmic inevitability of the white race's decline, associating this with an apocalyptic vision of the final days. Fard and Elijah Muhammad both used the Torah's tale of Ezekiel's Wheel to explain the existence of a mechanical device from heaven that could save the faithful. In his most widely read work, *Message to the Blackman in America*, Elijah gave even greater emphasis to this than Fard, as well as the specific details for the pending apocalypse:

> There is a similar wheel in the sky today which very well answers the description of Ezekiel's vision. . . . The Great Wheel which many of us see in the sky today is . . . a plane made like a wheel. The like of this wheel-like plane was never seen before. . . . The present wheel-shaped plane known as the Mother Plane, is one-half of a half-mile and is the largest mechanical manmade object in the sky. It is a small human planet made for the purpose of destroying the present world of the enemies of Allah. . . . It is capable of staying in outer space six to twelve months at a time without coming into the earth's gravity. It carried fifteen hundred bombing planes with the most deadliest explosives—the type used in bringing up mountains on the earth. The very same method is to be used in the destruction of this world.

To Elijah Muhammad, the world was divided into two: the community of devout believers, which included "Asiatics" and "Asiatic blacks" such as American Negroes who might be converted; and, in orthodox Islamic terms, the "House of War," all Europeans or white people, the devils. No reconciliation or integration was possible or even conceivable. If the millions of black Americans could not physically return to Africa, then a partition of the United States along racial lines had to be instituted. Middle-aged and older African Americans who had belonged to the UNIA immediately recognized Muhammad's program as similar to Garvey's, but with a kind of divinely based apocalyptic fury, and it ignited a revolutionary spark that touched Malcolm in a way Garveyism never would have.

Since neither wholesale emigration nor the secession of several Southern U.S. states under blacks' authority was immediately likely, Muhammad counseled his followers to withdraw from active civic life. America's political institutions would never grant equality to the Original People. Muhammad preached that registering to vote or mobilizing blacks to petition the courts, as the NAACP did, was a waste of time. In the years prior to *Brown v. Board of Education*, the May 1954 Supreme Court decision that outlawed racial segregation in the country's public schools, Muhammad's arguments could be reasonably defended, but his "audience" among blacks still remained small. By 1947, he had consolidated control over Fard's followers in only four cities—in Washington, D.C., Detroit, Milwaukee, and at his headquarters in Chicago. The Nation's combined membership was four hundred, an insignificant number compared to the thousands of African-American members of the growing Ahmadiyya movement, or even the fading remnants of the Moorish Science Temple.

Yet there was also a growing group of black prisoners converting to the Nation of Islam while still in prison, where the depression caused by long confinement made inmates particularly vulnerable. Muhammad's own prison experience had taught him to channel his recruitment efforts at convicted felons, alcoholics, drug addicts, and prostitutes. Malcolm numbered among these, and as he sat in isolation, anxiously writing letters to Elijah on an almost daily basis, the intensity of his commitment grew until he reached total acceptance.

———

Prison life can shatter the soul and will of anyone who experiences it. "It destroys thought utterly," Antonio Gramsci observed in his prison notebooks. "It operates like the master craftsman who was given a fine trunk of seasoned olive wood with which to carve a statue of Saint Peter; he carved away, a piece here, a piece there, shaped the wood roughly, modified it, corrected it—and ended up with a handle for the cobbler's awl." Confined to Mussolini's prisons for over a decade, Gramsci struggled fiercely to maintain his sense of purpose, and eventually realized that only through a dedicated program of intellectual engagement could he endure the physical hardships. He wrote, "I want, following a fixed plan, to devote myself intensely and systematically to some subject that will absorb me and give a focus to my inner life." Faced with a similar dilemma, Malcolm committed himself to a rigorous course of study. In doing so, he consciously remade himself into Gramsci's now famous "organic intellectual," creating the habits that, years later, would become legendary. His powers of dedication and self-discipline were extraordinary, and directly opposite to the wayward drifting of his earlier years. The trickster disappeared, the clowning side of disobedience, leaving the willful challenger to authority.

At Norfolk, the prisoners in the debate club engaged in weekly exchanges on a variety of issues. Malcolm and Shorty, who had also been transferred to Norfolk, found a forum for Malcolm's new beliefs and arguments. "Right there, in the prison, debating, speaking to a crowd, was as exhilarating to me as the discovery of knowledge through reading," Malcolm wrote. "Standing up there, the faces looking up at me, things in my head coming out of my mouth, while my brain searched for the next best thing to follow what I was saying, and if I could sway them to my side by handling it right, then I had won the debate—once my feet got wet, I was gone on debating." It soon did not matter what the formal topic was. Malcolm had by now become an expert debater, thoroughly researching his subjects in the prison library and planning his arguments accordingly. The common theme of his public discourses, however, was his indictment of white supremacy.

Malcolm now began perfecting what would become his distinctive speaking style. He possessed an excellent tenor voice, which helped him attract listeners. But even more unusual was how he employed his voice to convey his thoughts. Coming into maturity during the big band era, he quickly picked up on the cadence and percussive sounds of jazz music, and inevitably his evolving speaking style borrowed its cadences.

Once he had started reeducating himself, there was no limit to his search for fact and inspiration. Through Norfolk's library, Malcolm devoured the writings of influential scholars such as W. E. B. Du Bois, Carter G. Woodson, and J. A. Rogers. He studied the history of the transatlantic slave trade, the impact of the "peculiar institution" of chattel slavery in the United States, and African-American revolts. He learned with satisfaction about Nat Turner's 1831 uprising in Virginia, which to him provided a clear example of black resistance: "Turner wasn't going around preaching pie-in-the-sky and 'non-violent' freedom for the black man." Nor did Malcolm restrict his studies to black history. He plowed through Herodotus, Kant, Nietzsche, and other historians and philosophers of Western civilization. He was impressed by Mahatma Gandhi's accounts of the struggle to drive the British out of India; he was appalled by the history of China's opium wars, and the European and American suppression of the 1901 Boxer Rebellion. "I could spend the rest of my life reading," he reflected. "I don't think anybody ever got more out of going to prison than I did." Malcolm had undertaken his studies with the idea of becoming, like Bembry, the well-respected figure of wisdom behind the prison's walls. But as 1948 drew to a close, his breadth of understanding had transformed him into a trenchant critic of white Western values and institutions. There was something passive about teaching, and Malcolm was not passive.

His routine at Norfolk provided him with the leisure time to correspond extensively with family members and friends, and he now became a devoted letter writer. In an undated note to Philbert, probably written mid-1948, he was preoccupied with family gossip. "Phil, I love all my brothers and sisters. In fact, they are the only ones in the world I love or have. However," he emphasized, "never say 'we are happy to own you as a brother.'" Such language smacked of tolerance rather than love. "Under no circumstances don't ever preach to me," he warned. Malcolm also continued to correspond with Elijah Muhammad, and by late November the tone of his letters to Philbert had been transformed. He now opened each letter with the declaration: "In the Name of 'Allah,' the Beneficent, the Merciful, the Great God of the Universe . . . and in the Name of His Holy Servant and Apostle, the Honorable Elijah Muhammad . . ." He praised family members for bringing him into the grace of Elijah Muhammad's guidance. Now a devoted NOI follower, he shared his belief that "things are jumping out there . . . I'm unaware of what is actually occurring, but I know it is being Directed by the Hand of Allah and will rid the planet of these wretched devils." Malcolm's new commitment undoubtedly provided another reason to figure out some way out of prison.

His letters were also filled with lines of verse. He explained, "I'm a real bug for poetry. When you think back over all of our past lives, only poetry could best fit into the vast emptiness created by men." Later that same month, he wrote, "I will have three years in [prison] on the 27th of this month. I want to get *out this year* if I can." But he recognized how improbable his parole would be. "It's my own fault I'm here," he admitted. "The whole ordeal, though, has benefited me immensely because I have fully awakened to what I'm surrounded by. I certainly woke up the hard way, hmm?"

In another letter to Philbert, his thoughts turned to racial politics. "Yes, I'm aware many Brothers were put into the federal institutions for not taking active part in the war. Surely you must remember, I would have taken imprisonment first also." Although he had not been aware of Elijah's teachings during World War II, Malcolm claims that "I was even at that time aware of the devil and knew it to be foolish for yours truly to risk his neck fighting for something that didn't exist." He also expressed a new appreciation for their mother.

Reginald visited in late 1949, but all was not well. Malcolm was dumbfounded when his brother began to speak ill of Elijah Muhammad. He learned subsequently that Reginald had been expelled from the Nation of Islam for having sexual relations with the female secretary of the New York

City temple. Reginald was his closest Little sibling, and his disaffection provoked a crisis of faith within Malcolm, which he only partially revealed later in the *Autobiography*. How could a religion devoted to the redemption of all black men expel Reginald? Frustrated and confused, he promptly wrote to Elijah in his brother's defense. The next night, in the solitude of his prison cell, he thought he had been awakened by a vision of someone next to him:

> He had on a dark suit. I remember. I could see him as plainly as I see anyone I look at. He wasn't black, and he wasn't white. He was light-brown-skinned, an Asiatic cast of countenance, and he had oily black hair. I looked right into his face. I didn't get frightened. I knew I wasn't dreaming. I couldn't move, I didn't speak, and he didn't. . . . He just sat there. Then, suddenly as he had come, he was gone.

He would come to believe that his vision had been that of "Master W. D. Fard, the Messiah." Days later, Elijah Muhammad sent a stern reply, chastising his new disciple for his pleas. "If you once believed in the truth, and now you are beginning to doubt the truth, you didn't believe the truth in the first place," he charged.

Such a letter of rebuke, combined with the twilight vision of "Master Fard," convinced Malcolm that Reginald's censure was not only justified but absolutely necessary. His actions could not be tolerated within the Nation's small community. Months later, when Reginald visited again, Malcolm noted his physical and mental deterioration, and reasoned that this was evidence of "Allah's chastisement." Several years later, Reginald's complete mental collapse led to his being institutionalized. To Malcolm, struggling to make sense of his brother's fate, there was only one explanation: Reginald had been used by Allah "as a bait, as a minnow, to reach into the ocean of blackness where I was to save me."

By early 1950, Malcolm had converted several black inmates, including Shorty. The small group began to demand concessions from the prison administrators, on the grounds that they were exercising their rights of religious freedom. They requested that Norfolk's menu be changed, to accommodate the dietary restrictions of Muslims, and also refused to submit to standard medical inoculations. Norfolk's officials viewed these requests as disruptive, and in March 1950 Malcolm and Shorty were told that they would be transferred back to Charlestown along with several other

Black Muslims. Norfolk's officials also recorded that Malcolm's letters provided indisputable evidence of "his dislike for the white race."

Malcolm rationalized the transfer as best he could. "Norfolk was getting on my nerves in many ways, and I didn't have as much Solitude as I wished for," he complained to Philbert. "Here we are in our cells for seventeen of the twenty-four hours in each day . . ." He also recounted a brief visit by their sister. "Ella wants to try to get me out. What should I do? Previously when she had asked me if I wanted out I have said 'not particularly.' But Saturday I told her to do whatever she can."

He began agitating for even greater concessions, impelled by the requirements of his faith. He and other Muslims not only insisted on changes in their food and on the rules governing typhoid inoculations; they asked to be moved into cells that faced east, so that they could pray more easily toward Mecca. When the warden rejected their requests, Malcolm threatened to take their grievances to the Egyptian consul's U.S. office, at which point the warden backed down. The local media learned about the controversy, and several articles soon appeared, the first to present Malcolm to a public audience. On April 20, 1950, the *Boston Herald* reported the incident under the headline "Four Convicts Turn Moslems, Get Cells Looking to Mecca." More colorful and descriptive was the *Springfield Union*: "Local Criminals, in Prison, Claim Moslem Faith Now: Grow Beards, Won't Eat Pork, Demand East-Facing Cells to Facilitate 'Prayers to Allah.'"

In the middle of the controversy, Malcolm sent a sober, detailed letter to the commissioner of the Massachusetts Department of Correction. His purpose was to provide examples of discrimination against Muslims, appealing for greater religious freedom. He highlighted the case of one Muslim who had been placed in solitary confinement at Norfolk for four months. "He wholeheartedly embraced Islam," Malcolm argued, "and by doing this he incurred the wrath [of prison authorities]. Because the Brother wishes to be *Black* (instead of negro or collared [*sic*]), because of his desire to be a good Muslim . . . he is being maliciously prosecuted."

In a second letter to the commissioner, and in subsequent correspondence, he shifted his argument, accusing Charlestown's authorities of severely restricting the books by black authors that were available in the prison library. The tone was intellectual but increasingly intense and argumentative. "Is it actually against the 'law' for a Black man to read about himself? (let me laugh!)," he complained. He deplored the harassment experienced by Muslims who he claimed had done nothing wrong, and contrasted the example of one Black Muslim who had been rejected from enrolling in a prison literacy workshop with "the homosexual perverts" behind bars who "can get job-changes whenever they wish to change or acquire new 'husbands.'" In more explicit language than ever before, he warned the commissioner that the Muslims would prefer to be kept separate from other prisoners, but if denied fair treatment they would be forced to become disruptive. "If it becomes the Will of Allah for peace to cease," Malcolm predicted, "peace will cease!" This was a step beyond self-invention: Malcolm was in effect developing his powers of protest. He was teaching himself to be a great orator.

In June 1950, the United States initiated military actions in Korea, under the auspices of the United Nations, to suppress communist insurgency. On June 29, Malcolm brazenly wrote a letter to President Truman, declaring his opposition to the conflict. "I have always been a Communist," he wrote. "I have tried to enlist in the Japanese Army, last war, now they will never draft or accept me in the U.S. Army. Everyone has always said MALCOLM is crazy so it isn't hard to convince people that I am."

It was this letter that brought Malcolm to the attention of the FBI, which opened a file on him that would never be closed. It also marked the beginning of their surveillance of him, which would continue until his death.

Malcolm kept up his letter-writing campaign throughout 1950 and into 1951, even reaching back to people who had known him as a juvenile delinquent. One such letter, dated November 14, 1950, was addressed to the Reverend Samuel L. Laviscount of Roxbury. Apparently, Malcolm had occasionally attended meetings at Laviscount's St. Mark's Congregational Church in 1941. "Dear Brother Samuel," he began. "When I was a child I behaved like a child, but since becoming a man I have endeavored to put away childish things. . . . When I was a wild youth, you often gave me some timely advice; now that I have matured I desire to return the favor." He recounted his involvement in crime, his arrest, and subsequent incarceration. But "this sojourn in prison has proved to be a blessing in disguise, for it provided me with the Solitude that produced many nights of Meditation." The experiences of imprisonment had confirmed the validity of Elijah Muhammad's indictments. Malcolm proclaimed that he had subsequently "reversed my attitude toward my black brothers," and "in my guilt and shame I began to catch every chance I could to recruit for Mr. Muhammad." The task of emancipating black people from the effects of racial oppression, he explained, required a fundamental rejection of white values: "The devil['s] strongest weapon is his ability to conventionalize our Thought . . . we willfully remain the humble servants of every one else's ideas except our own . . . we have made ourselves the helpless slaves of the wicked accidental world."

After months back in Charlestown, however, the terrible conditions there took their toll. In a letter to Philbert sent in December 1950, Malcolm complained, "I have ulcers or something but I've had my fill of hospitals since being here. Ole man, I think I'm actually falling apart physically. Nothing more physically wrecks a man, than a steady prison diet." He explained that he was "reading the Bible diligently," but worried whether his interpretations of scriptures were "sound, or even on the correct track," and looked forward to when he could listen to Elijah Muhammad's latest teachings. For the first time, he signed his name, "Malcolm X (surprised?)." He also revealed that "a very wealthy man for whom I once worked, visited me today and is going to try and get me a recommendation from the parole board (Insha Allah) The Will of Allah will be done." The "wealthy man" almost certainly was Paul Lennon. The most striking aspect of Malcolm's continuing contacts with Lennon was that his affluent benefactor was white; given Malcolm's professed hatred of all "white devils" (and his comments on homosexual inmates), his continuing contacts with Lennon may have indicated that his determination to get out of prison exceeded his commitment to Yacub's History. Or perhaps the physical intimacies between the two men created a bond. Malcolm uncharacteristically stumbled somewhat as he explained, "By the way, he's not an original"—meaning that he was not a Negro. "However he can give me a home and a job . . . ."

Malcolm's choice of words—"a home"—implies more than a business association. The fact that Lennon went to see Malcolm behind bars suggests a degree of friendship. But Malcolm's commitment to the Nation eventually made any kind of continued contact with Lennon impossible. No correspondence between Malcolm and Lennon has been found following Malcolm's prison sentence ending in 1952. Malcolm firmly put behind him the episodes with Lennon, along with some other events from Detroit Red's life of drugs and criminality. Malcolm Little, petty criminal and trickster, had transformed himself into Malcolm X, a serious political intellectual and Black Muslim. That metamorphosis left no space for a rich gay white man.

Malcolm's subsequent FBI files cite a revealing letter, written in January 1951, to someone whose name has been redacted in its records, but from the tone of the correspondence may have been Elijah Muhammad. "You once told me that I had a persecution complex," it runs. "Quite naturally I refused to agree with you. . . . I was blinded by my own ignorance." The letter recounts a visit to Charlestown by several family members, who raised with him the wrongs that he had committed:

With great remorse I now think of the hate and revenge that I have been preaching in the past. But from here on in my words shall all be of Love and Justice. . . . Now that the Way has been made clear to me my sole desire is to replace the seeds of hate and revenge, that I have sown into the hearts of others, with the seed of Love and Justice . . . and to be Just in all that I think, speak and do.

Malcolm's further "apology for the unrest and misrepresentation of the Truth" was probably prompted by Elijah's disapproval over the publicity surrounding the campaign for Muslim prisoners' rights. For months, Malcolm had attempted to "embarrass" penal authorities by sending a stream of letters to local and state officials. Given Muhammad's own prison hardships, the NOI leader recognized that any adverse publicity could threaten the sect's survival. He also feared that prisoners who had converted to the Nation of Islam in other institutions might become targets of harassment by prison guards.

Malcolm had himself already experienced such harassment at Charlestown. When prison cooks learned about the Muslims' refusal to eat pork, they frequently served Malcolm's food from utensils that had been used to process the meat, and made sure Malcolm and his fellow Muslims knew. In response, over his final two years in prison Malcolm existed on a diet composed primarily of bread and cheese. Such deprivations, combined with the lack of competent medical care while in prison, caused him health problems that would plague him the rest of his life. After arriving back at Charlestown, he was diagnosed with astigmatism and received his first pair of glasses. He came to believe that his impaired vision had been caused at Norfolk because he had "read so much by the lights-out glow in my room."

In late 1950, Malcolm had submitted a petition to the commissioner of corrections requesting an official pardon from Massachusetts governor Paul A. Dever. On December 13 the district attorney for the Northern District of the Commonwealth of Massachusetts recommended the petition be denied. Not surprisingly, Dever agreed.

That same month, Charlestown's officials had refused to allow Muslim prisoners to leave their beds after lights-out curfew, to face east in solemn prayer. Writing in protest, Malcolm condemned the ban as an attack upon religious rights and warned that such an abridgment might require him to issue an appeal for redress to "the *Whole Body* of Islam"—that is, Islamic countries throughout the world. There might have been differences between the rituals of the Nation of Islam and orthodox Islam, but Malcolm saw himself in a global community.

His next request to be paroled would be considered on June 4, 1952. After a review of his prison records, he was granted parole on condition that he go to Detroit to live with Wilfred. On August 4 the Massachusetts supervisor of parole, Philip J. Flynn, informed the parole board that Malcolm had obtained full-time employment at the Cut Rate department stores in Detroit. The date for his release was set for August 7. Wilfred's willingness to sponsor Malcolm in his home and to secure a job for him was a collective decision by Little family members, including Ella. Given their brother's chaotic histories in both Roxbury and Harlem, they must have decided that it was preferable for him to be in Detroit. At the time, Wilfred was working at Cut Rate and persuaded his boss to take his younger brother on as a salesman.

Just weeks before Malcolm's release, however, the state experienced several prison uprisings. On July 1, 1952, 41 out of approximately 680 men at Concord prison rioted. This may have inspired some inmates at Charlestown to plan their own revolt. On July 22 about forty prisoners there staged an even more destructive outburst. Two prison guards were seized as hostages. When state police at last retook the facility, everybody who had taken part was placed in solitary confinement; some were also prosecuted. The two officers who had been hostages were retired, and fourteen guards were added to the prison staff for greater security. Eventually an inmates' council was established, elected by prisoners, which regularly met with the warden to resolve grievances. Malcolm was not involved in the uprising and it did not affect his release. Indeed, he would have felt little sense of solidarity with rioting white inmates.

Malcolm was finally released on August 7. He later described the occasion as just one more humiliation: "They gave me a lecture, a cheap L'il Abner suit, and a small amount of money, and I walked out of the gate. I never looked back . . ." Hilda was waiting outside. After the two embraced, they went to Boston to spend the night at Ella's house. That evening, Malcolm visited a Turkish bath, to get "some of that physical feeling of prison-taint off me." To start his new life, he purchased a new pair of glasses, a suitcase, and a wristwatch. Reflecting on his purchases, he wrote, "I was preparing for what my life was about to become." He would see more, he would travel, and he would seize the time.

CHAPTER 4

"They Don't Come Like the Minister"

August 1952–May 1957

M alcolm's elder brother Wilfred and his wife, Ruth, lived in the quiet, suburban black neighborhood of Inkster, just outside Detroit, at 4336 Williams Street. This was to be Malcolm's base for the seven months after his release from prison. In his autobiography, Malcolm recounted the morning routine that Wilfred supervised. "'In the name of Allah, I perform the ablution,' he would say before washing first his right hand, then his left." After the family had showered, completing "the whole body's purification," it was ready for morning prayers. Part of this ritual was similar to practices of orthodox Islam; however, like many of the NOI's methods, it also had special elements. First, Nation of Islam members, like Moorish Science Temple followers, faced east and raised their hands when praying, but did not prostrate themselves. They also did not recite the *shahada* or practice any other of the five pillars. At one point, when Elijah Muhammad felt slighted by Arab Muslims, he briefly commanded NOI members to face the direction of Chicago rather than Mecca for their prayers.

Shortly after moving back to Michigan, Malcolm started working at the Cut Rate department store to fulfill the conditions of his parole. He was grateful to have a job, but soon described his experiences with some bitterness:

"Nothing Down" advertisements drew poor Negroes into that store like [flies to] flypaper. It was a shame, the way they paid three and four times what the furniture had cost, because they could get credit from those Jews. It was the same kind of cheap, gaudy-looking junk that you can see in any of the black furniture stores today. . . . I would see clumsy, work-hardened, calloused hands scrawling and scratching signatures on the contract, agreeing to highway-robbery interest rates in the fine print that never was read.

It was his first work experience of the outside world since his conversion, and the episode had a profound impact on Malcolm. It was the first time he had offered a strongly negative generalization about Jews, categorizing them as a group.

Established in 1932, downtown Detroit's Temple No. 1 was the Nation of Islam's oldest, but after twenty years it still had barely one hundred formal members. Its minister, Lemuel (Anderson) Hassan, like all NOI clergy, had been selected personally by Elijah Muhammad, to whom he was required to report each week. Despite its modest size, the temple possessed an active religious and social life. "The men were quietly, tastefully dressed," Malcolm recalled. Seating arrangements were by gender, men to the right, women to the left. Unlike in an orthodox Muslim *masjid* (mosque), which had no furniture, members sat upright in chairs throughout all services, which largely consisted of lectures about Elijah's teachings. It did not take long for Malcolm to wonder why, after two decades of existence, Temple No. 1's membership was so tiny, and he was surprised to learn that Hassan and other senior members were not eager to proselytize. Malcolm voiced his frustration to his family, but Wilfred advised patience.

That August Malcolm asked his parole officer if he might travel to Chicago to visit Elijah Muhammad, explaining that he would be accompanied by three of his brothers. Approval granted, Malcolm participated in Temple No. 1's automobile caravan, consisting of ten cars, to make the trip. Arriving in Chicago's sprawling South Side, Malcolm waited impatiently at the temple for the formal program to start. Finally Allah's Messenger entered, surrounded by Fruit of Islam guards in dark suits, white shirts, and bow ties. In a soft voice, Muhammad—wearing a gold-embroidered fez—reminded his audience about the personal sacrifices he had made for over two decades. African Americans were truly the Original People, he said, unjustly stolen to North America. Only the Nation of Islam's teachings could restore black people to their rightful place. Malcolm "sat riveted"—then, unbelievably, Elijah called out his name. Stunned, he stood up before several hundred congregants as Muhammad explained that Malcolm had been so devoted while in prison that he had written to him daily; such peerless example recalled Job.

After the service, Malcolm and his whole group were invited to dinner. The Messenger's family had only recently moved into an eighteen-room mansion at 4847 South Woodlawn Avenue, in the exclusive Hyde Park section of Chicago's South Side, purchased with funds tithed by the Nation's increasing membership. During the meal, Malcolm mustered the courage to ask how Detroit's Nation of Islam should reach out to recruits. Muhammad counseled him to concentrate on young people—"The older ones will follow through shame," he explained. The point went home.

In orthodox Islam, evangelical work is known as *da'wa*. In Western countries, it has two purposes: to promote Muslim practices and values among nonbelievers, and to reinforce what the scholar Ismail al-Faruqi termed "Islamicity." In the Nation of Islam, *da'wa* was called "fishing for converts." Almost immediately after his return home Malcolm plunged into Detroit's bars, pool halls, nightclubs, and back alleys, aggressively "fishing." Night after night, he attempted to interest his "poor, ignorant, brain-washed black brothers" in Muhammad's message. At first, only a trickle of the curious came to temple meetings, but persistence soon paid off. Within a few months temple membership had almost tripled.

Malcolm's most remarkable convert during this time was a young man named Joseph Gravitt, who would become for a time one of his closest confidants and an important figure in the Nation of Islam over the next decade. Born in Detroit in 1927, Gravitt served in the army in 1946–47, winning, according to his own account, the "World War II Victory Medal"; his official army record shows evaluations that ranged from "unknown" to "excellent." Returning to civilian life, he found it difficult to get work, soon becoming addicted to drugs and alcohol and developing a reputation for violence against women. In November 1949, police charged him with "indecent and obscene conduct in a public place."

By the time Malcolm encountered him, Gravitt was sleeping in Detroit's alleys, but Malcolm sensed his potential, and personally supervised his rehabilitation. Having experienced military discipline, Gravitt responded well under Malcolm's stern authority. Within days, his entire life was taken up by the Nation of Islam: during the daytime he worked as the short-order cook and waiter at the temple restaurant; in the evenings he directed Fruit of Islam members in the martial arts, and he sacked out to sleep in the restaurant at night. Within months he had become a devoted—even fanatical—Fruit of Islam leader, his metamorphosis adding to Malcolm's reputation.

As he was devoting an increasing amount of time to the Nation of Islam, Malcolm struggled to find regular work that he could tolerate. In January 1953, he was taken on at the new Ford assembly plant in Wayne as a "final assembler" on the production line. Although he was employed for only one week, it was long enough for him to become a member of United Auto Workers Local 900. A short time later, he was hired at Gar Wood Industries, a company famous for its innovations in truck equipment, cranes, and road machinery. By the 1950s, Gar Wood was one of Detroit's major employers, but many of the jobs made available to blacks were dirty and dangerous. Malcolm's technical classification was as a grinder, defined as a "worker who pulverizes material or grinds surface objects." It paid a little better than his previous employment, but it was a miserable, monotonous job, and Malcolm felt caged.

Wilfred, in whom he confided, may have conveyed his brother's discontent to Minister Hassan; or perhaps, with his eye for identifying talent, Elijah suggested a new assignment for his young disciple. When in early 1953 Malcolm was approached about becoming an NOI minister, he must have felt profound relief, as well as justifiable pride, yet he also recognized that the inner council surrounding Elijah demanded humility. He duly responded that he was "happy and willing to serve Mr. Muhammad in the lowliest capacity," reluctantly agreeing to deliver a brief talk to Temple No. 1 about "what Mr. Muhammad's teachings had done for me." The lecture went off well, and as a follow-up he gave another, devoted to "my favorite subject . . . Christianity and the horrors of slavery." He came to look back nostalgically on these early efforts as the beginnings of his life as a minister.

The Massachusetts Parole Board certified Malcolm's discharge from parole on May 4, 1953; Michigan's discharge followed shortly thereafter. Malcolm X—as he was now known within the Nation of Islam—was free to travel throughout the United States. One day that same month, during his work shift, he was pulled off the production line by his supervisor. Waiting to see him was an FBI field agent, who ordered Malcolm to accompany him to his supervisor's office. Once there, he was asked why he had not registered for the Korean War draft. Malcolm was aware that Elijah Muhammad had encouraged the evasion of the draft during World War II, but instead of citing the Messenger's example, he informed the agent that he had just been released from prison and thought that former prisoners were not allowed to register. He was allowed to leave, and a few days later registered at the local Selective Service office, claiming conscientious objector status. According to FBI records, he wrote that his country of citizenship was Asia. He also asserted that his "mental attitude and outlook in general regarding war and religion" merited "disqualification from military service." On May 25 he was given a physical exam for the draft and failed: the subject "had [an] asocial personality with paranoid trends."

That summer, Malcolm became Detroit Temple No. 1's assistant minister. He was already commuting regularly between Detroit and Chicago, where he was preparing for the ministry, much of his tutelage being directly under the supervision of Elijah Muhammad. "I was treated as if I had been one of the sons of Mr. Muhammad and his dark, good wife Sister Clara," Malcolm recalled fondly. "In the Muslim-owned combination grocery-drug store on Wentworth and 31st Street, Mr. Muhammad would sweep the floor or something like that . . . as an example to his followers." Malcolm relished the opportunity to ask questions of the man he believed to embody perfection. "The way we were with each other," he recalled, "it would make me think of Socrates on the steps of the Athens marketplace, spreading his wisdom to his students."

In June, Malcolm quit his job at Gar Wood and began working full-time for the Nation of Islam. Technically, NOI clergy were not employees; the income they received from temple offerings was deemed an informal contribution for voluntary services. Throughout the remainder of that year, Malcolm continued to steer scores of fresh converts into Detroit's temple. He also gained confidence in his ability to speak in public, lecturing on a range of topics. By late 1953, Elijah Muhammad decided that his protégé should be promoted to minister and be assigned to establishing a temple where the Nation of Islam had few followers. Boston was the logical choice: Malcolm had lived there for several years and had numerous relatives and old friends in the city. One NOI member who lived in the city, Lloyd X, agreed to house him and invite small groups to his home to hear the young minister. Years later, Malcolm could recall the appeal he delivered to one such gathering in early January 1954. What he could not have known was that within his audience was an FBI informant. The fact that the Boston field office of the FBI thought it prudent to conduct surveillance even of tiny NOI gatherings, in their homes, reveals just how potentially dangerous the sect was believed to be.

Within the Nation of Islam, each successful temple had four decision-making officers who exercised authority over routine activities, though always under Muhammad's autocratic guidance: the minister, the temple's secretary-treasurer, the women's captain of Muslim Girls Training (MGT), and the men's captain, the head of the Fruit of Islam (FOI). These personnel were frequently selected directly by the national secretariat in Chicago, which in effect included Muhammad, national captain of the Fruit of Islam Raymond Sharrieff, Sharrieff's wife and Muhammad's daughter, national

MGT captain Ethel Sharrieff, and the national secretary-treasurer; indirectly, Elijah Muhammad, Jr., Herbert Muhammad, and other relatives were involved in the process. At local levels, the minister was the public face of the temple, the Nation of Islam's chief representative to the outside world. Internally, his role was pastoral. But in terms of how the temple functioned as a social organization, as a kind of secret society whose borders had to be policed constantly, no one was more important than the Fruit of Islam captain. Forever on the lookout for acts of disobedience or disloyalty, his disciplinary rod was essential in maintaining a well-run temple.

Although Malcolm's initial activities focused on Boston, he traveled up and down the East Coast and as far west as Chicago. Sometime that first January back east, he went to several meetings at New York City's tiny Temple No. 7 in Harlem. In February he served as a guide for pilgrims coming to Chicago to attend the Nation of Islam's major annual event, the Saviour's Day convention, celebrating the birth and divinity of its founder, Wallace D. Fard. This marked the first time that the young apprentice took the stage as a featured speaker before a national audience. FBI surveillance indicated that he "spoke against the 'white devils'" and encouraged "greater hatred on the part of the cult towards the white race."

By late February, Malcolm's recruitment efforts had been so successful that there were sufficient converts to create a new temple in Boston, No. 11. At one of his larger public gatherings, he was delighted to see Ella, but she remained a stubborn holdout against the Nation's call. With its focus on recruiting prisoners and the poor, the Nation didn't fit with her notions of black middle-class respectability, and she was skeptical of Muhammad's claim to be Allah's Messenger. Knowing Ella's stubborn temperament, Malcolm doubted that his words would ever change her negative view of the Nation. "I wouldn't have expected anyone short of Allah Himself to have been able to convert Ella." During this time, it's possible that Malcolm also reconnected with his former girlfriend Evelyn Williams, who continued to harbor deep feelings for him. She subsequently joined the NOI, and when Malcolm moved to New York later that year, she followed him there.

His next assignment, as minister of Philadelphia's temple, required both diplomacy and a firm administrative hand. The temple was run by Willie Sharrieff (no relation to Raymond). Malcolm spoke at one of its meetings, informing his stunned audience that he had been authorized to "shake things up." Along with Isaiah X Edwards, the minister of Baltimore's temple, he had conducted a preliminary investigation of the temple's affairs. The day before the meeting, March 5, Sharrieff had been removed from his position. Eugene X Bee, who had been appointed Fruit of Islam temple captain as well as assistant minister by Sharrieff, was also dismissed. Malcolm assumed the titles "teacher" and "acting minister." To consolidate his position, he led or participated in a series of eight temple meetings throughout the last three weeks of March.

Malcolm's progress was carefully monitored by the FOI's supreme captain, Raymond Sharrieff. In 1949, Sharrieff had married Muhammad's second oldest child, Ethel, and before long exercised administrative authority that went well beyond the Fruit of Islam, overseeing the Nation's growing real estate and commercial ventures in Chicago. For years, the Nation of Islam had lacked a substantial institutional presence in many key cities, but its failure to grow was now shown not to have been due to a lack of interest in its message but to poor local leadership. In Detroit, Malcolm had exposed Lemuel Hassan as, at best, a mediocre minister. By 1957 Hassan would be reassigned to the less prestigious temple in Cincinnati, Ohio, and Malcolm's brother Wilfred elevated to become minister of Detroit's Temple No. 1, second in status only to Chicago. Malcolm's rise and Hassan's demotion infuriated Hassan's brother, James X, who was the assistant minister of Chicago Temple No. 2, as well as assistant principal of the University of Islam. James's hostility toward Malcolm would, within several years, be shared by most of the Nation of Islam's ruling elite in Chicago.

Both Muhammad and Sharrieff may also have worried that Malcolm, still only twenty-nine, might be moving too quickly. One of them initiated the order in early 1954 to Joseph X Gravitt to travel first to Boston, then to the Philadelphia temple, to aid in the reconsolidation of both temples' Fruit of Islam as their new captain. Joseph's immediate supervisor, however, was not to be Malcolm, but Sharrieff.

Joseph's presence in Philadelphia afforded Malcolm the rare luxury of having occasional mornings and afternoons off, and whenever he could he explored sites such as the city's art museum and libraries. Most of his time, however, was taken up by his administrative duties throughout the Northeast, which kept him constantly in transit. His absence required Joseph to speak frequently at Philadelphia's Temple No. 12. The subject of one May 1954 speech was "the duty of Muslims to take the heads of four devils for which they will win a free trip to Mecca." He explained that this meant "the bringing of a lost Muslim into the Nation of Islam and thereby cutting off a devil's head." Such hell-and-damnation rhetoric lacked even the sophistication of the young Malcolm, but in an organization that lived by disclipline such a no-nonsense manner had its advantages.

Side by side, both living in Philadelphia (Malcolm in a rented flat at 1522 North Twenty-sixth Street), the two men seemed an unlikely duo, but over these months they formed bonds of trust and codependence. Malcolm was six feet, three inches tall and weighed no more than 170 pounds; he was youthful, passionate, constantly in motion, intent on honing his language. Joseph, at five feet, six inches, possessed a muscular build, and was small but very tough at 145 pounds; he was quiet and cautious, yet volatile. As in Boston, much of the credit for getting the Philadelphia temple in order went to Malcolm, and indeed in June, in recognition of his outstanding efforts, Muhammad named him the new minister of Harlem's Temple No. 7. Yet during the two and a half months after Joseph's arrival in Philadelphia, Malcolm had participated in only four local meetings: Joseph had absolutely been in charge, both as head of the Fruit of Islam and as substitute minister. In the *Autobiography*, Malcolm is silent about Joseph's contributions.

In less than a year, Malcolm had gone from line worker at Gar Wood to full minister of the Nation of Islam in one of the most important black centers in the United States. He was keenly aware of the challenge ahead of him. He would later recall, "Nowhere in America was such a single temple potential available as in New York's five boroughs. They contained over a million black people."

―――

Sometime in June 1954, Malcolm relocated to New York City. For another three months he continued to serve as the principal minister in both Harlem and Philadelphia, but he devoted most of his time trying to make sense of the situation in New York. His first step was to appoint a man named James 7X as his assistant minister, but not until August was Joseph X transferred to New York, to join him at Temple No. 7 as its FOI captain.

Malcolm found himself with a membership that numbered only a few dozen people. Even that figure is an informed guess: neither he nor any other NOI minister ever revealed publicly the actual numbers, in part because they were so low. From 1952 to early 1953, there were probably fewer than one thousand members throughout the country.

Malcolm found to his dismay that Harlem's Temple No. 7 was even more disorganized than Philadelphia. For six months he labored to reproduce the growth he had created in Boston and Philadelphia, but without success. The *Autobiography* offers several explanations. First, Harlem was still filled with ex-Garveyites and a variety of aggressive nationalist groups all pushing their agendas. "We were only one among the many voices of black discontent," Malcolm noted. "I had nothing against anyone trying to promote independence and unity among black men, but they still were making it tough for Mr. Muhammad's voice to be heard." He also mentioned the social apathy and lack of political awareness to which Harlem blacks seemed to have succumbed. "Every time I lectured my heart out and then asked those who wanted to follow Mr. Muhammad to stand, only two or three would . . . sometimes not that many."

The challenges were more complicated than he was willing to admit. The postwar economic boom had left much of African America behind. The conditions of Harlem's tenements had deteriorated significantly from the neighborhood's more glorious times in the 1920s. Many buildings were vermin- and rat-infested; it was not unusual even along major thoroughfares for disgruntled tenants to throw their garbage into the streets. Asthma, drug addiction, venereal disease, and tuberculosis were rampant. In 1952, for example, central Harlem's tuberculosis mortality rate was nearly fifteen times that for nearly all-white Flushing, Queens.

Despite these problems, in the decade after World War II Harlem had also developed a small, status-conscious black middle class that was wealthier and politically more influential than during the depression. New York City's farther suburbs were still largely segregated, but slowly middle-class blacks began to move to the outer boroughs of the Bronx, Queens, and Brooklyn. The number of black professionals grew, but many were still only beginning to escape from the ghettos of Harlem and Brooklyn.

The heavy concentration of black voters in Manhattan also led to expanding political power. The 1953 election of Harlem resident Hulan Jack as the first black president of the borough of Manhattan symbolized that growing clout. Constantly pushing Harlem's political agenda was of course Adam Clayton Powell, Jr., who by the time of Malcolm's return had been in Congress for a decade. In March 1955, Powell called for a boycott of Harlem savings banks that "practice 'Jim Crow-ism' and 'economic lynching.'" He urged Abyssinian Baptist Church's fifteen thousand members to withdraw their funds from white-owned banks and transfer them to either the black-owned Carver Federal Savings in Harlem or the black-owned Tri-State Bank in Memphis, Tennessee. At the national level, he disrupted the Democratic Party's presidential campaign for Adlai Stevenson by his surprise endorsement of Dwight Eisenhower, who in the election that November received nearly 40 percent of the African-American vote nationally. Powell's justification was the domination of Southern "Dixiecrats" who controlled the Democratic Party in Congress. He explained, "This does not necessarily mean a shift to the Republican party. It does mean that the Negro people are standing up as American men and women, thinking for themselves and voting as independents." Malcolm probably admired the black congressman's feisty independence from the Tammany Hall Democratic Party machine. Powell's model of political independence, as a black man who could not be dominated by whites, would influence how Malcolm defined independent politics after his departure from the Nation of Islam.

Harlem was also a common site for many civil rights protests. One of the largest, soon after Malcolm's arrival, occurred on September 25, 1955. More than ten thousand people gathered at the Williams Institutional Church on Seventh Avenue at West 132nd Street to denounce the acquittal by an all-white jury of two white men accused of murdering Emmett Till, a fourteen-year-old black boy in Mississippi. The rally demanded that President Eisenhower "convene a special session of Congress and . . . recommend the immediate passage of a Federal anti-lynching bill." Abyssinian's associate pastor, the Reverend David N. Licorish, who represented Powell, called upon blacks to protest in Washington, D.C. The NAACP leader, Roy Wilkins, urged black New Yorkers to address racial discrimination in the city.

Far from being a community overwhelmed and silenced by the weight of racial oppression, Harlem continued to be a lively political environment. The level of participation was high and in full evidence: public rallies, boycotts, and fund-raisers were common. Street philosophers and orators would climb up ladders placed along major thoroughfares, primarily 125th Street, and declaim their ideas to passersby. The Nation found it difficult to make headway, largely because its appeal was *apolitical*; Elijah Muhammad's resistance to involvement in political issues affecting blacks, and his opposition to NOI members registering to vote and becoming civically engaged, would have struck most Harlemites as self-defeating.

Many in the neighborhood had already been introduced to a more orthodox Islam through the extensive missionary activities of the Ahmadiyya Muslims. The sect had won the respect of many blacks through its vigorous opposition to legal segregation and its criticism of Christian denominations for accepting Jim Crow. In 1943, for example, the Ahmadis' *Moslem Sunrise* had characterized Detroit's race riot as a "dark blot on this country's good name." The colored world would recognize "that black-skinned people are killing and being killed by white-skinned people in free America." Five years later, the magazine published a survey of nearly 13,600 Presbyterian,

Unitarian, Lutheran, and Congregational churches documenting that only 1,331 of them had any nonwhite members. Racism within Christian churches led many African-American artists, writers, and intellectuals in the 1940s and 1950s to consider converting to some version of Islam. Recruiting was particularly effective in the bebop world. A key figure was Antigua-born Alfonso Nelson Rainey (Talib Dawud), onetime member of Dizzy Gillespie's band. Dawud's own conversion persuaded tenor saxophonist Bill Evans to become a Muslim, acquiring the name Yusef Lateef; his conversion was followed by Lynn Hope's (Hajj Rashid) and drummer Kenny Clarke's (Liaqat Ali Salaam). Based in Philadelphia, Dawud developed a working relationship with Harlem's International Muslim Brotherhood, throughout which a supportive network was established linking largely black *masjids* in Providence, Washington, D.C., and Boston. Dozens of other popular jazz artists became associated with Ahmadi Islam, including Art Blakey, Ahmad Jamal, McCoy Tyner, Sahib Shihab, and Talib Dawud's wife, the vocalist Dakota Staton (who changed her name to Aliyah Rabia after conversion). Even those who did not formally convert, like John Coltrane, were heavily influenced by the Ahmadiyya.

In Cleveland, an Ahmadiyya mosque had been established during the Great Depression; by the 1950s it had more than one hundred African-American congregants. Indeed, the Cleveland mosque's Ahmadi leader, Wali Akram, became perhaps the first black American awarded a visa for a pilgrimage to Mecca, in 1957. All of these activities created among many African Americans a general awareness of different types of Islam, beyond that represented by the Nation of Islam. This was particularly true in Harlem, which made winning converts difficult.

Not until September 1954 did Malcolm secure permanent living quarters in the New York area: at 25-35 Humphrey Street, in the quiet neighborhood of East Elmhurst, Queens. The property was owned and shared by a black couple, Curtis and Susie Kenner. Although Malcolm's principal responsibility was now Temple No. 7, he was informally promoted to be Elijah Muhammad's chief troubleshooter along the East Coast, and even in the Midwest. He continued to lecture regularly at the Philadelphia temple throughout the fall and winter months of 1954–55, and also made trips by automobile to Springfield, Massachusetts, and Cincinnati, Ohio, to support local initiatives.

Even more than in the Philadelphia temple, he came to rely on Captain Joseph, routinely dictating instructions to his lieutenant, who in turn barked out orders to subordinates. One Sunday when Malcolm was away, a guest sermon was delivered by the minister from the Baltimore temple. The meeting, however, actually belonged to Joseph, who opened the proceedings by upbraiding all the male members who had missed meetings or turned up late, demanding "explanations of their delinquencies in attendance." Joseph praised Baltimore's minister as "a man of peace," but sharply reminded the faithful that he (Joseph) "was not."

Despite Joseph's hard work, nearly all the praise for the successes in New York centered increasingly on Malcolm. At this time, Joseph was living in a small basement apartment far uptown in West Harlem. He received no salary for his labors as FOI head and worked as a cook at a restaurant owned by an NOI member, the Shabazz restaurant on Fifth Avenue. Sometime during his assignment in Philadelphia, he started dating a woman in the Philadelphia temple, and by early 1956 she had moved in with him. If Joseph planned to start a family, Malcolm must have realized, the Nation owed him a more dependable income. Perhaps for these reasons, Malcolm started praising Joseph during his temple sermons or remarks to the Fruit of Islam. The Nation of Islam's administrators in Chicago also recognized Joseph's contributions and considered reassigning him to a more prestigious position. Two weeks prior to the Saviour's Day convention in February 1955, Joseph was summoned to Chicago, probably by Raymond Sharrieff, and told of a new national program in which he would supervise the recruitment and training of a thousand recruits. For several weeks it appeared that he would be transferred, and at Temple No. 7's Fruit of Islam meeting on February 21 members received word that he would no longer be with them. But, for reasons still unclear, in early March it was announced that he would be remaining in New York.

Malcolm and Joseph's efforts in Boston, Philadelphia, and New York, combined with other evangelical efforts by Malcolm in various cities, had increased NOI membership by perhaps a thousand new followers. This unprecedented growth signaled to the FBI, which had been tracking the Nation of Islam for decades, that something was stirring, something that they should take seriously. For years, the Bureau had monitored what it still described derisively in internal documents as the "Moslem Cult of Islam" (MCI). Its surveillance now indicated that an ex-convict, one Malcolm K. Little, was largely responsible for the cult's new evangelical fervor. Malcolm had been on their radar, and under watch, since his letter-writing days at Norfolk and Charlestown, and on January 10, 1955, two FBI agents arranged to see him in New York. They subsequently reported that the subject had been "very uncooperative." He "refused to furnish any information concerning the officers, names of members, to furnish doctrines or beliefs of the MCI or family background data on himself." The ex-convict did, however, express several theological and political opinions, describing Elijah Muhammad as "the greatest prophet of all, being the last and greatest Apostle." When the agents challenged him about the NOI's "alleged teachings [of] racial hatred," he replied, "They do not teach hatred but the truth, that the 'black man' has been enslaved in the United States by the 'white man.'" When asked whether he would serve in the armed forces, Malcolm refused to answer. "The subject did, however, admit that during World War II he had admired the Japanese people and soldiers and that he would have liked to join the Japanese Army." Malcolm also denied ever having been a member of the Communist Party. His responses were far more confrontational than his interview with the FBI field agent several years earlier. He was unafraid to identify himself completely with Elijah Muhammad's creed and his organization, regardless of the political consequences. Malcolm subsequently warned members of Temple No. 7 not to cooperate with FBI agents who might contact them.

The February Saviour's Day convention of 1955 was symbolically Malcolm's coming out party as the Nation of Islam's uncrowned prince. In less than two years, he had tripled the size of Detroit's temple, established thriving temples in Boston and Philadelphia, and with Joseph's assistance was finally beginning to recruit members into Harlem's Temple No. 7. He had become a favorite guest minister in Cincinnati, Cleveland, Detroit, Springfield, and other cities. The FBI surveillance of the NOI convention observed that throughout the proceedings "the subject appeared to be enjoying Elijah Mohammed's confidence, and seemed to have a free hand." Malcolm even set aside time to escort NOI members on a tour of Chicago's Museum of Natural History and "placed his various interpretations on the exhibits at the Museum as portraying the creation of the white man by the 'black man.'"

Attending the convention was an ambitious twenty-one-year-old singer and nightclub performer named Louis Eugene Walcott. Born in New York City on May 11, 1933, Walcott was raised as an Episcopalian in Roxbury. He would recall that both his parents, like Malcolm's, had been militant black nationalists: "My father was a Garveyite," he explained, "so I couldn't grow up in this society without the touch of Mr. Garvey in my soul, in my mind, and in my spirit." Both Walcott's parents had emigrated from the Caribbean, and as in the Little household from an early age he had been encouraged by his mother to read books and magazines documenting the issues affecting blacks. A track star in high school, he also excelled as a debater, violinist, and singer. After graduating from Winston-Salem State University in North Carolina, he began his career in show business as a calypso artist, calling himself "the Charmer." Like Malcolm, he eventually came to remake himself, first as Louis X, and then as Louis Farrakhan.

It was in Boston in 1954 that "the Charmer" first encountered Malcolm. Walcott and his wife were living in a small apartment on Massachusetts Avenue—only a few doors away from the apartment of Martin Luther King, Jr., who was in graduate school completing his Ph.D. Not far away was the nightclub where Walcott performed, and between his musical sets he would occasionally grab a quick dinner at a nearby restaurant, the Chicken Lane. It was here that he was introduced to Malcolm, who "had on a brown tam, brown coat, brown suit, and brown gloves." The minister made an immediate impression. "He was an imposing man," Farrakhan remembered, "talking so bad about white folks, I was scared of him."

Walcott's first real experience of the Nation of Islam occurred at the 1955 Saviour's Day convention. He was headlining a show, "Calypso Follies," at the Blue Angel nightclub on Chicago's North Side, when a friend invited him to the Nation's festival. The supreme minister had been told that Walcott, who was a minor celebrity in the music and nightclub business, would be present in the audience. Aides later informed Muhammad exactly where the young man was sitting. Well into his talk, Muhammad turned and began speaking directly to him. Farrakhan later described the moment as "instant love." His wife enthusiastically joined the Nation that night, and although he still harbored reservations, he agreed to join as well. The young couple duly completed the obligatory letter of request for membership and mailed it off to the Chicago office. They heard nothing for five months. That July, Walcott was in New York City, performing in Greenwich Village. He decided to attend a service at Harlem's Temple No. 7, primarily to hear Malcolm, whose oratory captivated him and who convinced him to dedicate his life to the Nation. "I had never heard a black man in my life talk the way this brother talked," Farrakhan recalled.

By the mid-1950s, the number of established jazz artists and popular musicians who had joined the Nation of Islam caused some consternation within the Chicago headquarters, which worried that their prominence might make them more independent than other members. The Nation demanded a conservative, sober lifestyle, something quite at odds with the way most musicians lived. In late 1955, the temples were informed that no

NOI member would henceforth be permitted to work as a professional entertainer. Walcott first heard about the edict while in New York when visiting the Nation's restaurant on West 116th Street at Lenox Avenue. For him, with a wife and young child, it was a serious blow. Walcott walked several blocks, confused over what course to take. Somehow he came to a halt, turned around, and headed back to the restaurant with the intention of remaining faithful to the Nation. He was met by Captain Joseph, who was furious that someone had leaked the information prematurely. Malcolm had the job of subsequently informing Louis that he had been granted four additional weeks, but thereafter would have to quit the music business.

Louis had enrolled in the Monday FOI class, and Joseph asked him to deliver a talk. His brief oration, which explained the reasons leading to his conversion, proved mesmerizing. Decades later, NOI veterans who were there could still recite Louis's words: "I will take the message of the Honorable Elijah Muhammad to every nook and cranny in the United States of America." Louis's talent as an orator convinced Malcolm to put the young apprentice into his small assistant minister class. It was here, during the first six months of 1956, that Louis flourished, carefully modeling his presentations on Malcolm's, even studying his mentor's mannerisms and dietary habits. It was clear that he brought to the ministry certain skills from his nightclub act. Not only did Malcolm not mind; he took genuine pride in Louis's accomplishments, and a bond developed. Eventually, Louis described Malcolm as "the father I never had."

In June or July, Louis was named FOI captain for Boston's Temple No. 11. In the years since Malcolm's initial proselytizing efforts, the temple had suffered a membership decline and was in need of an energy boost. Within a year Louis was elevated to minister. Chicago officials were thrilled with their convert. They even allowed him to revive his singing career, but in the service of the Honorable Elijah Muhammad; he wrote and performed several "Islamic-inspired" gospel songs that became wildly popular among temple members.

Louis became Malcolm's first true protégé. Many other young men would follow, fashioning their sermons and temple activities on Malcolm's dynamic model. It was not long before they were widely, and sometimes disparagingly, known within the Nation as "Malcolm's Ministers."

Malcolm believed that Muslim clergy could be divided into two categories— evangelists and pastors. Few outstanding evangelists excelled as pastors, which called for skill in providing comfort and support to congregants, while relatively few pastors could call their congregations to embrace a spiritual vision in the manner of a great evangelist. "My desire has always been to be good at both," he said. Several years later, he would equate himself with the greatest Christian evangelist of his time, Billy Graham.

He considered every sermon he delivered an evangelical opportunity, because usually the congregation included a small number of first-time guests. A typical NOI service was very different from most Christian services. The temple's secretary or captains might open the meeting with announcements; then the minister would lecture, frequently using a blackboard or posters to reinforce points being made. Malcolm would encourage his audience to ask questions, and even welcomed banter and debate with visitors. At one typical Philadelphia meeting, Malcolm declared that the Nation was "the only place in the 'wilderness of North America' that the 'black man and black woman' [hear] the truth about themselves." The lecture hammered at two themes. First, Malcolm repeatedly emphasized that blacks were spiritually dead as a group, and that their reawakening depended solely on their acknowledgment of the truth, represented by Elijah Muhammad. Second, Malcolm discussed the Nation's expectations of how women and men should relate to each other. Urging men to "respect their women," he also warned women to dress modestly. Women who attracted the amorous attentions of men by "the display of their bodies," Malcolm declared, "were as common as the dog we see chasing the other dog in the streets."

At another 1955 Philadelphia temple sermon he used experiences of racial oppression to explain why whites had no right to describe the Nation of Islam as subversive:

Here is a man who has raped your mother and hung your father on his tree, is he subversive? Here is a man who robbed you of all knowledge of your nation and your religion and is he subversive? Here is a man who lied to you and trick[ed] you about all things, is he subversive? . . . This is a man who the Almighty God Allah is subversive against. Black men all over the planet are subversive to this devil and you come in here and get mad at us. You's better listen or you will be taken off the planet along with the devil. This wicked government must be destroyed and those of you who want to follow after the serpent and commit evil also. This is a warning to you that you are living in the last day and you must decide tonight, whether you want to survive the war of Armageddon. . . .

Throughout the Philadelphia sermon, Malcolm presented a vivid picture of damnation for those who continued their allegiance to white values, though as an orator he had learned how to modulate his tone. Frequently he employed humor, and occasionally even references to bebop slang. "North America is already smothering with fire," he warned. "You think you are so hep and, Jack, you can't even smell the smoke." He even "ran the dozens," in the colloquial language of black folk culture, by making negative references to black mothers: "Your mother is a prostitute when you are not respecting women—you might as well say this because this is what is proven by your actions." He declared that he had no fear of government surveillance: "The FBI follows me all over the country and they cannot do anything about this teaching unless it is the will of Allah. The devils have lost their power now and the only thing they can do is try to frighten the black men who are still dead."

As the sermon ended, he observed that, while there had been a large number of male converts recently, "there is something very wrong that sisters are not coming in." Instead of questioning the Nation's sexist practices that discouraged the recruitment of new female members, Malcolm blamed the excessive gossiping of the temple's females. "I'd rather put all of the sisters out for bickering and go out and get a lot of prostitutes. That sounds harsh, but I cannot stand this disunity." Tirades like these earned Malcolm a reputation for being aggressively hostile to black women and suspicious of the institution of marriage. Taking his cue, many Fruit members applauded and imitated the minister's sexist attitudes and rhetoric.

Malcolm frequently cited episodes in American history, emphasizing the legacy of the slave trade to condemn both Christianity and the U.S. government. In another sermon, he remarked that all Negroes were "American citizens, but you cannot prove this because you have been fighting for civil rights ever since the enemy brought you to Jamestown, Virginia, in the year of 1555. You do not own any state in North America but today you say you are American." Black people could not look to whites to redeem their lives. "Today the white man does not have any power left and it is only the black man who has any chance to save himself." On another occasion, he reminded members that people of European descent were hopelessly outnumbered globally by Africans, Asians, and other nonwhites. "There are only two kinds of people, the white and the black, so if you are not white you must be black." He urged NOI members to patronize businesses managed or owned by Muslims. Without mentioning Wilfred by name, he noted that, in Detroit, "one of the brothers is the manager of a large department store and hires as many members . . . as he possibly can."

By 1955, Malcolm's popularity had become so intense that NOI head-quarters called on him to relocate to Chicago for three weeks, to promote a membership drive in Temple No. 2. Recruitment efforts were ongoing, and during the mid-1950s the Nation of Islam seems to have looked closely at the model of Islamic proselytizing practiced by the controversial Ahmadi Muslims. Despite the Ahmadis' refusal to consider the Prophet Muhammad the Seal of the Prophets, which deeply disturbed nearly all orthodox Mus-lims, and at a time when the Pakistani government was moving to designate the sect a non-Muslim religious group, emigrant Ahmadis had successfully formed political coalitions and working relationships with Sunni Muslims in the United States and frequently worshipped side by side with them. By the late 1950s a significant number of African-American Ahmadis had joined the Nation, partially due to its explicitly black identification. In doing so, they introduced a more orthodox interpretation of classical Islam, as well as a long-standing commitment to the international Islamic community. No matter how sectarian and heretical the NOI's theological tenets, Elijah Muhammad always insisted that his ministers present his creed as part of a global community of Muslims. These factors helped shape Malcolm's version of *da'wa*, and his pastoral duties. This was the main reason why, in the early 1960s, Malcolm would so vigorously criticize the phrase "Black Muslims" to describe the Nation of Islam.

As the Nation grew, it began to interact with traditional or orthodox Muslims in different ways. And despite the Nation's adherence to the theo-logically bizarre tenets of Yacub's History, the fundamental spiritual terrain that defined Islam's contours had a direct and inescapable pull on the NOI's evolution. Within orthodox Islam, there are two great divisions: the Sunni, who represent the overwhelming majority of Muslims, and the Shi'a, a group who believe that Ali, the Prophet's nephew and son-in-law, and his descendants were the sole successors to Muhammad. For Sunnis, ordained clergy do not exist. The leader of the observance of *salat*, or prayer service, may be anyone knowledgeable. This leader, the *imam*, strives to be "a pat-tern for the rest to follow, so as to preserve the required precision and order of the service." In Islam, the imam may also be a prominent theologian or legal scholar. The Shi'a, by contrast, perceive their imams as divinely inspired. Two main branches of the Shi'a, the Isma'ilis and Imanis, define their imams by hereditary descent and believe that their leaders possess a

god-given understanding of Islam, first represented by Ali. The imams possess the powers of the "cycle of prophecy" (*nubuwwa*) and, as one Islamic
scholar puts it, "they serve as intercessors between humans and God."

Over centuries, Islamic political thought evolved in two strikingly different directions. For most Sunnis, the foundation of all religious teachings
is the *sharia*, the law, which in turn is grounded in *haqiqat*, a literal interpretation of the Qur'an. For the Shi'as, spiritual knowledge is esoteric, hidden,
secret. The Shi'a Muslim approaches the Qur'an not for the construction of
laws but for knowledge that reveals truth. Because Shi'as frequently functioned as persecuted minorities in predominantly Sunni societies, they withdrew from politics and civil society. The Shi'as view most political leaders
as illegitimate, and except in states like Iran in which they control the government, they generally have not participated in politics.

Although the Lost-Found Nation of Islam can hardly be considered orthodox, it shares striking parallels with Shi'ism. Both view their faiths from
the vantage point of persecuted minorities; both are convinced that all civil
authorities and politics are corrupt; both espouse what in Arabic is called
hikmat' At-tadrij, the gradual communication of religious knowledge and
truth over time. When Elijah Muhammad elevated Wallace D. Fard to the
status of Allah, Muhammad immediately became the sect's sole conduit
with God. Muhammad also acquired the authoritative power of prophecy
and, as in the case of Shi'a Muslims, an infallibility that could not be challenged. Also like most Shi'a, Elijah Muhammad firmly believed that key
positions within the temple's leadership should be linked, either through
genetic connections (for example, Ethel Muhammad Sharrieff, Herbert
Muhammad, Elijah Muhammad, Jr., Wallace Muhammad) or through marriage (for example, Raymond Sharrieff). For this reason, despite Malcolm's
filial relationship with Muhammad, most members of the patriarch's family strongly rejected him as a potential heir apparent because he was not
related by blood. On a lower level, it was not unusual for local leaders to
be relatives. By the late 1950s, for instance, three Little brothers were ministers of important temples—Wilfred in Detroit, Philbert in Lansing, and
Malcolm in Harlem.

Despite the NOI's heterodoxy, Elijah Muhammad perceived his sect as
part of a global brotherhood, the *ummah*, which transcended the distinctions
of ethnicity, nationality, class, and even race. NOI ministers were trained to
see themselves as dedicated warriors in a spiritual struggle against God's
enemies. Such an imam can be described as a *mujahid*, one who devotes his
life to the service of Allah, but who also practices spiritual self-discipline.

Members of the Nation of Islam with a more sophisticated knowledge of orthodox Islam found allegorical reasons for believing that the sect would ultimately grow away from its heretical roots and rejoin more conventional Islam. They compared Elijah's flight from Detroit to Chicago and the *hegira* of the Prophet Muhammad from Mecca to Medina. The persecution of the first Muslims was subsequently experienced by Elijah and his early followers who resisted the U.S. draft. Perhaps most persuasively, all Muslims knew that the Holy Qur'an was a book of Muhammad's recitations compiled over a period of twenty-two years. Muslims believe that the work contains a unitary message; nevertheless, the focus and content of the *surahs*, or chapters, changed over time. In a similar fashion, Elijah distributed "lessons" to his followers to be studied and committed to memory. Each lesson reflected a "divine truth," yet together they were incomplete, to be superseded by subsequent revelations. As Elijah's connections with the larger Islamic world grew, the likelihood for some sort of theological evolution, or "Islamization," also increased. In fact, this is exactly what happened upon Elijah's death in 1975, when his rebellious son Wallace took over the leadership of the Nation; he instituted a total rejection of the Nation's dissident religious dogma and accepted orthodox Islam.

One decisive step occurred, curiously enough, through global politics. The Nation of Islam had always viewed African Americans as "black Asiatics," and in its realm of the saved there was no distinction between Asians and Africans. Consequently, the NOI took special note when in April 1955 representatives from twenty-nine African and Asian nations met in Bandung, Indonesia, to plan how they might cooperate politically. Participating states included Burma, Cambodia, the People's Republic of China, India, Thailand, North Vietnam, South Vietnam, Ethiopia, and the Gold Coast, but by far the largest contingent was made up by nations with majority Muslim populations: Afghanistan, Indonesia, Iran, Iraq, Egypt, Libya, Jordan, Lebanon, Pakistan, Saudi Arabia, Syria, Sudan, Turkey, and Yemen. In the opening address, the Indonesian president Achmed Sukarno declared the gathering the first transnational conference of colored peoples in history.

Revolution against the old colonial rule had been in the air. The conference came only six years after the triumph of the Communist Party over the Kuomintang in China. In Vietnam in 1952, the popular forces of Ho Chi Minh had routed the French colonial army at Dien Bien Phu, leading to a French withdrawal two years later. In Sudan, a revolt broke out in August 1955, forcing the British to airlift eighteen thousand troops into rebel areas. But it was in the Muslim *ummah* that the struggles for independence were most inspirational. In Morocco, the French decision to depose Sultan Mohammed V in 1953 had led to massive protests. Fresh from their defeat in Vietnam, the French permitted the sultan to return, and independence was granted in March 1956. In Tunisia, internal autonomy from the French had been achieved in 1955, and full independence was won the following March. In November 1954, the struggle in Algeria had erupted into war. What was significant was that the Algerian nationalists, while Muslims, did not perceive the conflict as a jihad, or holy war, but rather a nationalist one. The guerrilla fighters, numbering about twenty thousand, confronted over one million French colonists and the French army. By the end of the war a quarter of a million Algerians had been killed and two million displaced from their homes, many into camps. Perhaps the most dramatic confrontation between the Arab world and the West occurred in Egypt with the Suez crisis. In July 1956, President Gamal Abdel Nasser nationalized the Suez Canal. In response, on October 30 the Israelis invaded Egypt, and the British followed. The United States, under Eisenhower, opposed the invasion, forcing the Israelis and the British to withdraw. Throughout the Muslim world Nasser was celebrated as the leader of anti-Western sentiment and Arab nationalism. Malcolm closely monitored these events, which to him fulfilled the divine prophecy foretelling the decline and fall of European and U.S. power. As Malcolm explained to a Temple No. 7 audience, "The 'black man' are united all over the world to fight the 'devils.'"

The Bandung gathering represented the opening of a new epoch, and firmly fixed in Malcolm's mind the possibilities of unifying internationally and nationally with other African Americans and followers of Islam. Black American leaders, Malcolm now urged, must "hold a Bandung Conference in Harlem." The principles of nonaggression and cooperation that had characterized the Bandung Conference should inform the strategy of black "Asiatics" inside the United States. "We must come together and hear each other before we can agree . . . ," he argued. "And the enemy must be recognized by all of us [as] a common enemy . . . before we can put forth a united effort against him." Delivered at a meeting of the African Freedom Day Rally, Malcolm's remarks echoed those of Blyden nearly a century before, illustrating the connections that were forming within his politics between Pan-Africanism, Pan-Islam, and Third World liberation. More than any other NOI leader, he recognized the religious and political significance of Bandung. His sermons made increased references to events in Asia, Africa, and other Third World regions, and he emphasized the kinship black Americans had with non-Western dark humanity, but he was also careful to integrate this new emphasis into his presentations gradually, without seeming to break from the traditional script demanded by Elijah Muhammad.

———

By as early as 1956, Captain Joseph began using such expressions as "Hey, ain't none like Malcolm" and "They don't come like the Minister." He was careful to speak playfully, almost mocking Malcolm, but he was acknowledging an undeniable truth: Malcolm was standing apart. He had earned a reputation as the Nation's most extreme taskmaster, a zealot whose life was consumed by his service of Allah and unquestioned dedication to Elijah Muhammad. Malcolm held each member of his temple to the strictest standards; he would never hesitate to levy sanctions against even his closest lieutenants or to oust loyal members from the temple for weeks at a time for minor infractions, such as smoking cigarettes. He could be so demanding, his chief lieutenant James 67X Warden explained, because he was hardest on himself. Louis Farrakhan confirmed this:

> Nobody could handle Malcolm. He had a brilliant mind. He was disciplined . . . I never saw Malcolm smoke. I never heard Malcolm curse. I never saw Malcolm wink at a woman. I never saw Malcolm eat in between meals. He ate one meal a day. He got up at 5 o'clock in the morning to say his prayers. I never saw Malcolm late for an appointment. Malcolm was like a clock.

Elijah Muhammad preached that the Bible was a book not of history but of prophecy. "So Malcolm saw himself biblically," James 67X related, "not as someone who had been, but as [one who] was becoming, had been described prophetically. He saw himself as poor, and he saw himself as a fisher of men." Malcolm sought no monetary reward; the pride he felt in bringing in thousands of "lost-founds" was sufficient compensation. But James also understood that much of Malcolm's success, especially in New York, was "based upon what was happening outside the mosque"—that is, the conditions that confronted most blacks in daily life.

Essential to the Nation's functioning was discipline—and swift punishment for infractions. Members were constantly urged to report to officers anything that constituted suspicious behavior. Under Elijah Muhammad's postwar regime, the Nation developed a strict disciplinary procedure in which, for example, members were expected to eat only one meal a day, usually in late afternoon or early evening. Muslims who were judged overweight were technically in violation of the NOI's dietary rules. Penalties imposed were usually "time out," a period when the offender was barred from attending temple functions. More severe was "silencing," when the offender was barred not only from the temple but also from communicating with other members. In a 1955 lecture at the Philadelphia temple, Malcolm ordered the local leaders to purchase scales and to "weigh the members" every Monday and Thursday. "Those who are overweight," he warned, "will be given two weeks to lose ten pounds or will be given time out." He anticipated that his draconian edict would not be popular: "I'd better not hear anyone mentioning my name in criticism or I will give them indefinite time out of the temple and might keep you out of here for good. Is there anyone who wants to question me or doesn't think I am being fair? Raise your hand. Good thing you didn't, because you would have gotten out of the temple."

Malcolm's reputation for severity, especially toward those who questioned the infallibility of Elijah Muhammad, was demonstrated in an incident that occurred probably in May 1955. He and a trusted lieutenant, Jeremiah X (later Shabazz), were driving a car through Detroit's streets when they recognized Malcolm's younger brother Reginald, who had been expelled from the Nation years before. Malcolm stopped the car and beckoned him over; his brother appeared deranged and disheveled. According to Jeremiah, Malcolm then drove away, leaving Reginald adrift on the city's sidewalks. Malcolm explained to Jeremiah X that his brother had fallen under "divine chastisement" for his self-destructive opposition to Elijah Muhammad.

Malcolm cut back on his travels throughout the remainder of 1955 and all of 1956, but still maintained a demanding schedule. His recruitment trip to Lansing and Detroit in May 1955 consumed at least two weeks. Over that summer, administrative problems at the temple in Philadelphia again forced him to divide his work largely between that city and New York. His energy for recruiting new members and expanding the Nation's base was undiminished, however. In 1955 alone, he was instrumental in establishing three successful temples: No. 13 in Springfield, Massachusetts; No. 14 in Hartford, Connecticut; and No. 15 in Atlanta. To build the organization in Springfield, he relied on the leadership of an old acquaintance, Osborne Thaxton, whom he had converted to the Nation of Islam while both were serving time in prison. Temple No. 14 came about practically from nothing when a woman from Hartford attended a service at Springfield and asked Malcolm to come to her hometown the following Thursday, traditionally domestic servants' day off. Malcolm made the journey, and into her housing project apartment trooped about fifteen maids, cooks, chauffeurs, and household workers employed in the Hartford area. Within a few months more than forty new converts had been won.

These evangelical efforts had a profound impact on the internal culture of the Nation of Islam. Hundreds of converts were joining every month. Hundreds of letters requesting membership had to be reviewed and processed every week. The administrative burdens multiplied accordingly. Local temple secretaries had to be instructed about new applications and members. New administrative teams—ministers, secretaries, FOI and MGT captains—had to be selected, or in many cases moved from one city to another. Between 1953 and 1955, the Nation of Islam more than quadrupled, from about twelve hundred to nearly six thousand members. From 1956 until 1961, it would expand more than tenfold, to between fifty thousand and seventy-five thousand members. Although many continued to be recruited from prisons, unemployment lines, and ghettos, the Nation began to capture a broader audience. Thousands now came from the middle class, or were highly paid skilled workers and trade unionists.

Part of the Nation's newfound appeal had to do with the black reaction to Southern whites' "massive resistance" to desegregation beginning in 1955. The growth of White Citizens' Councils across the South and the slayings of local NAACP and civil rights workers in the late fifties convinced a minority of African Americans that the NOI was right: whites would never grant full equality to blacks. If Jim Crow was inescapable, then the Nation's strategy of building all-black economic and social institutions in the face of implacable white hostility made sense to many.

Civil rights activity was intensifying across the country, on multiple fronts. The struggle during the bus boycott in 1955–56 unfolding in Montgomery, Alabama, put the movement, and its radiant (and then virtually unknown) young leader, in the headlines. Blacks couldn't understand why, years after the Supreme Court had outlawed racial segregation on interstate buses, the laws weren't being enforced. In Montgomery, thousands of working- and middle-class Negroes risked their jobs and personal safety to support a nonviolent protest, led by twenty-six-year-old minister Martin Luther King, Jr.

The goal of King and the majority of civil rights activists was integration— they had had enough of separation, which was so dramatically trapping African Americans in poverty and inequality. Malcolm was wise enough not to criticize the boycott for its integrationist goals when asked to comment on King's efforts. Instead, he focused his criticisms on the U.S. government, "the seat of every kind of evil. . . . America is the modern Babylon where there is greater crime, persecution and injustice than in every place in the world." Alluding to the Bandung model of Asian–African solidarity, he stated in another address that the "'black men' all over the planet Earth are uniting, and all have one object in mind—the destruction of the 'devil.'"

The thousands of recruits Malcolm and others were bringing into the Nation represented hundreds of thousands of dollars in additional revenue, thanks to the group's strict tithing requirements. All members were expected to donate at minimum one-tenth of their household income to the temple, but many gave significantly more. Under Sharrieff's supervision, the NOI began purchasing commercial real estate on Chicago's South Side. Muhammad's adult children, at Malcolm's urging, were added to the NOI's payroll. Elijah Muhammad could not have failed to notice the growing power of his brilliant protégé. New temples required the training and supervision of new ministers, and since Malcolm was personally responsible for establishing the four new temples and for successfully reviving those in Philadelphia and New York, he directly managed or influenced the selection of personnel. No previous minister had ever been granted such authority. It is probably for this reason that, sometime in 1956, temple ministers were ordered by Chicago to audiotape their weekly sermons and mail the tapes to NOI headquarters. Either Elijah or his associates would then monitor the lectures, to ensure no deviation from official dogma. The edict coincided with a new attitude Muhammad displayed toward Malcolm, perhaps meant to temper his young minister's growth. Now when Malcolm visited Muhammad at his Hyde Park estate, he would be criticized on some point or other.

These criticisms had their effect. Malcolm's frenetic travel schedule was somewhat reduced. However, even a relatively scaled-down schedule meant that he was on the road for at least four months of the twelve between mid-1956 and mid-1957. His basic message made few major deviations from Elijah's script, but transcripts from FBI informants also reveal a degree of political emphasis in Malcolm's polemics against white racism that were largely missing from Elijah Muhammad's jeremiads.

By the end of 1955 the Harlem temple had grown from several dozen followers to 227 "registered members"—either official converts or individuals who had submitted letters to join. Registered members generally attended Sunday services but participated irregularly in other temple activities. Within this group, only seventy-five individuals were considered "active members": participating in all FOI or MGT meetings, attending all lectures and services, volunteering for special duties, and regularly tithing. The administrative routine had become well established. Although Malcolm continued to be out of town for weeks at a time, he tried to keep involved in all important business decisions, relying on Joseph to maintain discipline and for the development and expansion of the temple. Occasionally, however, the two men traveled together to nearby cities where new temples had been started, to supervise training and the selection of captains.

Given Malcolm's legendary strictness, the NOI's highly punitive culture, and tension that may have rippled beneath the surface of his relationship with Joseph over issues of credit and control, it seems surprising that the two men took so long to find themselves at odds. But in 1956 their productive partnership was finally ruptured. The specific reasons for the break remain contested. Some believe that Malcolm had blocked Joseph's advancement as the Nation's supreme captain. Others blame Joseph for the break, accusing him of failing to report to Malcolm a damaging rumor about Elijah Muhammad that had been circulating. But within months their fraternal association soured and Joseph grew to hate Malcolm for what transpired next.

In September 1956, Joseph stood accused of beating his wife, and Malcolm, as judge and jury, conducted the trial before the entire membership of the temple. Prior to bringing up the case, Malcolm had addressed several others. Brother Adam and Sister Naomi, who'd admitted to the sin of fornication, were banished for five years. Sister Eunice, who had joined the Nation of Islam as a child, was charged with adultery. Malcolm observed that Eunice's husband was a "registered" Muslim, a man "who was in prison. How do you think he feels?" After listening to her responses, Malcolm coldly meted out his version of justice: "Sister, I have no alternative other than to give you five years out of the Nation of Islam, during which I would advise you to fast and pray to Allah, ask him for forgiveness, ask your husband for forgiveness. . . . In no way can I show you any sympathy, pity, or anything, because you should know better."

When Joseph stepped up, Malcolm sternly announced, "This is the day of manifestation of defects." He then addressed Joseph: "You are charged with putting your hands on your wife. Guilty or not guilty?" Joseph curtly replied, "Guilty." Malcolm ruled that Joseph had been convicted of a "class F" judgment, meaning that he was no longer considered in good standing. For the next ninety days, he was stripped of his FOI rank and banned from temple functions and even from speaking with other members except officials. Malcolm used Joseph's shame as an opportunity to instruct his congregation about the standards that were expected:

> You know the laws of Islam, brother. You teach them. You taught them. You were Captain of the Fruit in Boston, and you've been Captain of the Fruit in

Philadelphia, and you've been Captain of the Fruit right here. . . . You know, as well as I, and better perhaps than most brothers here, that any brother that puts his hand on his wife . . . if it comes to my knowledge, automatically has ninety days out of the Temple of Islam. . . . I hope and pray Allah will bless you to remain strong and come back into the Temple of Islam and do the good work for Allah and his Messenger in the Nation.

Joseph was asked if he had anything to say in his own defense; he declined to speak, and was told to leave the room. Malcolm informed temple members that the original charge of spousal abuse had been filed eight months before—implying that the case had been considered by the Messenger himself, so delaying the final decision. Then he launched into a vigorous defense of Joseph's character. "Many of you may not like him. Many of you may have grievances against him . . . But also, many of you won't make the sacrifice that he would make." Without question, Joseph was a "good brother," but for the next three months he was to be treated as an outcast. "And all of those Muslims that follow him are outcasts."

The FBI watched these internal conflicts with interest. On October 23 its New York office reported to the director that Gravitt had been removed as Temple No. 7's FOI captain, but that he had been allowed to hold a job as a night cook at the temple's restaurant. A second report, dated December 12, indicated that Gravitt still remained under suspension; if accurate, this was beyond the ninety-day period that Malcolm had mandated. By the celebration of Saviour's Day in Chicago in late February 1957, Joseph had been fully restored to his rank. Yet the experience of becoming a temple "outcast" likely left him feeling a profound sense of humiliation and a loss of status. He was no longer, at least within the confines of the temple, Malcolm's partner and equal; he was his subordinate, a hardworking but flawed lieutenant who had proven incapable of adhering to Malcolm's high moral standards.

While Joseph grew angrier, Malcolm continued to be unhappy with the slow growth of Harlem's Temple No. 7. He had begun making overtures to the Abyssinian Baptist Church, and also recruited several members from Powell's powerful Baptist church. The most productive fishing grounds by far had been the tiny Pentecostal churches, whose members were working-class blacks. But Malcolm must have seen that the most well-attended institutions in Harlem were those involved in civil rights advocacy, electoral politics, and social reform. The NOI's culture was designed to look inward, to reject the "devil" and all his works. However, if neither heaven nor hell existed, as Elijah Muhammad taught, and the Negro's "hell" was here, in the United States, did not Muslims have an obligation to wage jihad?

Despite the absence of legal Jim Crow, New York City in the mid-1950s remained highly segregated. As the *New York Times* observed, "There is gross discrimination against Negroes here, and in many respects they are the oppressed class of the city." Blacks as a rule were barred from most private housing, and were shepherded into ghettos like Harlem. The zoning of public schools confined most of their children to a substandard education, and there were frequent examples of police brutality toward blacks. For the NOI to break through to a mass audience, Malcolm would have to speak directly to these issues. Like Powell and other political ministers, he would have to leave his sanctuary and shift his focus beyond simply recruiting congregants for the Nation. He would have to address the real-world conditions of African Americans.

Though he did not realize it at the time, Malcolm's career as a national civil rights leader began late on the afternoon of April 26, 1957, near the corner of Lenox Avenue and 125th Street, in the heart of Harlem. Two police officers were attempting to arrest a black man, Reese V. Poe, of 120 West 126th Street, following a street altercation. They were working over Poe with their nightsticks when three black men attempted to intervene: Frankie Lee Potts, twenty-three, as well as two members of Temple No. 7, Lypsie Tall, twenty-eight, and Johnson Hinton, thirty-two. The men yelled, "You're not in Alabama. This is New York." One of the patrolmen, interpreting this as a provocation, attempted to arrest Hinton, on the grounds of failure to move and resisting arrest. He delivered several powerful blows to Hinton's face and skull, which surgeons later diagnosed as causing lacerations of the scalp, a brain contusion, and subdural hemorrhaging. The three Muslims were then arrested along with Poe and hauled to the 28th Precinct station house.

A woman who had observed the assault rushed to the NOI's restaurant several blocks away with the news. Captain Joseph promptly mobilized members by telephone. At sundown, Malcolm and a small group of Muslims went to the station house and demanded to see brother Johnson. At first, the duty officer denied that any Muslims were there, but as a crowd of angry Harlemites swelled to about five hundred, the police changed their minds and Malcolm was allowed to speak briefly with him. Despite his pain and disorientation, Hinton explained that when they had arrived at the station house and he attempted to fall down on his knees to pray, an officer struck him across the mouth and shins with his nightstick. Malcolm quickly took in Hinton's physical condition and demanded that he be properly treated. The police relented; Hinton was transported in an ambulance to Harlem Hospital—followed by about a hundred Muslims who walked in formation north up Lenox Avenue. Malcolm knew exactly what effect this march would have down the busiest thoroughfare in Harlem. While Hinton received treatment, the crowd outside swelled to two thousand. Alarmed, the NYPD called "all available cops" to provide backup. Then, amazingly, they released Johnson X Hinton from the hospital—back to the 28th Precinct jail. The protesters marched back to the station house angrier than before, returning this time down West 125th Street, Harlem's central business corridor. Within an hour, at least four thousand people were jammed in front of the station house. A confrontation appeared inevitable.

When Malcolm finally walked into the station house, it was well past midnight. Escorting him was Harlem attorney Charles J. Beavers, who made bail arrangements for Potts and Tall and asked to see Hinton. The police allowed this but adamantly refused to return Hinton to the hospital, insisting that he had to be incarcerated overnight to appear in court the next day. At about two thirty a.m., with thousands of angry Harlemites still gathered outside, Malcolm sensed a stalemate. As if to underscore his authority in front of the police, he walked outside and gave a hand signal to his FOI phalanx. Silently and immediately, the FOI marched away, with orders to regroup at the NOI restaurant at four a.m. Following their lead, the protesting Harlemites also dispersed in minutes.

The police had never seen anything like it. One stunned officer, groping for an explanation, admitted to the New York *Amsterdam News* editor James Hicks, "No one man should have that much power."

The next morning, bail of $2,500 was paid by the NOI, but the police still refused to deliver Hinton to his attorney or to Malcolm. Still bleeding and disoriented, he was dumped out into the street outside the city's felony courthouse. Malcolm's men subsequently drove him to Harlem's Sydenham Hospital, where doctors estimated that he had a fifty-fifty chance of surviving. The next day, a crowd of more than four hundred Muslims and Harlemites gathered for a vigil at a small park facing the hospital; NOI members from Boston, Washington, D.C., Baltimore, Hartford, and other cities had driven in to take part. In a private meeting with a delegation of police administrators, Malcolm made the Nation's position clear: "We do not look for trouble . . . we do not carry knives or guns. But we are also taught that when one finds something that is worthwhile getting into trouble about, he should be ready to die, then and there, for that particular thing." As James Hicks observed, "Though they were stern in their protest they were as orderly as a battalion of Marines."

All three men who had been arrested were subsequently acquitted. Johnson X Hinton and the Muslims filed a successful lawsuit against the NYPD, receiving more than seventy thousand dollars, the largest police brutality judgment that a New York jury had ever awarded. But the incident had also set in motion the forces culminating in Malcolm's inevitable rupture with the Nation of Islam. Elijah Muhammad could maintain his personal authority only by forcing his followers away from the outside world; Malcolm knew that the Nation's future growth depended on its being immersed in the black community's struggles of daily existence. His evangelism had expanded the NOI's membership, giving it greater impact, but it was also forcing him to address the problems of non-Muslim black Americans in new ways. Eventually, he would have to choose: whether to remain loyal to Elijah Muhammad, or to be "on the side of my people."

CHAPTER 5

"Brother, a Minister *Has* to Be Married"

May 1957–March 1959

The Johnson Hinton controversy introduced the Nation of Islam to hundreds of thousands of blacks, and Malcolm was quick to take advantage. He had already begun publishing a regular column outlining the NOI's views, "God's Angry Men," in the *Amsterdam News*, and now he worked to broaden the group's appeal. Elijah Muhammad, Malcolm argued in one column, was "a modern-day Moses who . . . would ask God . . . to destroy this wicked race and their slave empire with plagues of cancer, polio, [and] heart disease."

Hundreds of new blacks, both those who had been inspired by the Hinton incident and those who were simply curious, started attending temple lectures. Instead of preaching to the converted, Malcolm now gave more attention to crafting a popular message, and he rarely failed to deliver a command performance. Slowly, he began to incorporate into his talks his growing awareness of global events, merging the situations and goals of repressed peoples around the world with those of blacks in America. At his June 21 sermon at Temple No. 7, for example, he linked Bandung's theme of Third World solidarity with Elijah Muhammad's apocalyptic vision:

Who is the Original Man? . . . It is the Asiatic Black Man. . . . The brown, red and yellow man along with the black outnumber the white man eleven to one. And he knows it. If ever they all got together to reclaim what the white man has taken from them the whites would not have a chance. How blind we are that we cannot see how badly our people, all our people, need to unite. But the Honorable Elijah Muhammad is here to unite us. The day is near. In the UN there is a pact of nations called the African-Asia block. It is a block comprised of some of the black nations on this earth. They are becoming stronger and it is just a bit more proof that the Black Men are beginning to realize that there is strength in numbers.

The summer of 1957 was one of tremendous growth for Malcolm, as he continued to make inroads to building greater legitimacy for the Nation while keeping up a demanding speaking schedule. In July, Temple No. 7 hosted an extravagant event, the Feast of the Followers of Messenger Muhammad, at Harlem's Park Palace dance club. More than two thousand attended, including Rafik Asha, leader of the Syrian mission to the UN, and Ahmad Zaki el-Barail, the Egyptian attaché. The presence of the Muslim diplomats was an indication that Elijah Muhammad's long-standing efforts to acquire greater legitimacy in the Islamic world were producing results. The featured speaker was not Malcolm but twenty-four-year-old Wallace Muhammad, born on October 30, 1933, and seventh among the children of Clara and Elijah. Wallace was an assistant minister in the Chicago temple, and his participation in New York City was significant. He had been tutored in Arabic as a teenager, and by the mid-1950s, troubled by the inconsistencies between his father's teachings and the classical tenets of Islam, he relished the opportunity to make overtures to officials of Muslim nations. He may have expressed his doubts to Malcolm; what is certain is that this event initiated a closer relationship between the two young men.

In August, Malcolm took great strides toward bringing an older generation of Harlemites into the NOI fold. That month, a festival in honor of Marcus Garvey was organized in Harlem by a committee of local activists, including James Lawson's African Nationalist Movement and the United African Nationalist Movement. A huge outdoor stand was erected to accommodate the performers, and an impressive lineup of speakers was present. Without question, however, Malcolm stole the show. "Moslem Speaker Electrifies Garvey Crowd," reported the local Harlem paper, noting that "the fiery Mr. X . . . attacked the white race for being 'responsible for the plight of the so-called Negroes in America' and condemned the Negroes' political and religious leaders as being nothing but 'puppets for the white man.'" His bravura performance in front of the police station had captured respect, but it was his speech at this festival that converted hundreds of old-line Garveyites to his cause.

Malcolm and the Nation's rising profile helped boost membership significantly, but it also put them more prominently in the sights of local and federal authorities. In the aftermath of the Hinton beating, the NYPD's secret operations unit, the Bureau of Special Services and Investigation (BOSS or BOSSI) began to take a special interest. BOSS was an elite unit staffed with detectives and charged with providing security to dignitaries and public leaders visiting the city. It also engaged in covert activities, such as the wiretapping of telephones and the infiltration of organizations deemed politically subversive. On May 15, 1957, NYPD chief inspector Thomas A. Nielson sent a series of urgent telegrams and letters to various law enforcement agencies around the country requesting information about Malcolm. He wrote the Detroit Police Department; the Michigan parole commission; the police chiefs of Dedham and Milton, Massachusetts, and of Lansing, Michigan; and the superintendent of the Massachusetts Reformatory at Concord. From each, Nielson asked for "complete background [of] criminal information with photo showing full description." The NYPD also began (or stepped up) tracking Malcolm at NOI public gatherings.

Late that summer, Elijah Muhammad gave Malcolm permission to deliver a four-week series of lectures at Temple No. 1 in Detroit, by now relocated to significantly larger quarters at 5401 John C. Lodge Street. Interest in the series was so extensive that the *Pittsburgh Courier*, one of the country's most prominent black newspapers, ran an interview with Malcolm in which he denounced the Eisenhower administration, particularly its failure to support the desegregation of public schools across the South. "The root of the trouble and center of the arena is in Washington, D.C.," he declared, "where the modern-day 'Pharaoh's Magicians' are putting on a great show, fooling most of the so-called Negroes by pretending to be divided against each other." The worst offender was Eisenhower himself, "the 'Master Magician'" who was "too busy playing golf to speak out—and with the expert timing of a master general, when he does speak out, he is always too late." Unlike Elijah Muhammad, who after his spell in prison rarely criticized the government and almost never cited individual officials, Malcolm was both outspoken and named names.

The Detroit public lectures were both a long-awaited homecoming and an announcement of what the future had in store for black militancy. Through family and friends, Malcolm's remarkable story from criminality to public leadership was well known in black Detroit. The reporter for the *Los Angeles Dispatch* covering Malcolm's talk on August 10, 1957, noted, "More than 4,000 Moslems and non-Moslems filled Muhammad's Detroit Temple of Islam to capacity to hear young Malcolm X." The paper quoted Malcolm describing the position of black Americans within the U.S. political system as both strategic and unique. For, although the Negroes are deprived of most of their voting powers yet their diluted vote will swing the balance of power in the Presidential or any other election in this country. What would the role and the position of the Negro be if he had a full voting voice? . . . No wonder, then, the freedom or equal rights struggle of the Negro people is so greatly feared. . . . If the present leaders of the so-called American Negro don't unite soon, and take a firm stand with positive steps designed to eliminate immediately the brutal atrocities that are being committed daily against our people, and, if the so-called Negro intelligentsia, intellectuals and educators won't unite to help alter this nasty and most degrading situation; then the little man in the street will henceforth begin to take matters into his own hands.

This is an extraordinary passage on several levels. First, it anticipates the presidential election of 1960, which Kennedy narrowly won with 72 percent of the black vote. Years before the successful passage of the 1965 Voting Rights Act, Malcolm appears to be linking the general empowerment of African Americans to the struggle for voter registration and education. Years before King, Malcolm understands the potential power of black bloc voting. Second, it proposes a broad-based coalition of civil rights organizations and other groups—presumably including the NOI—to address the collective problems of blacks. Third, the final sentence of the passage implies a stark warning to the Negro intelligentsia and middle class that the truly disadvantaged among the black masses might, out of impatience or despair, rise up violently. This theme would become the basis for Malcolm's most famous address, his "Message to the Grassroots," delivered in Detroit on November 10, 1963. The speech also anticipates his April 3, 1964, "Ballot or the Bullet" speech that envisioned a bloodless revolution led by blacks exercising their democratic voting rights.

What was truly paradoxical about the August 10, 1957, address was that the NOI was at this time strictly opposed to its members becoming involved in electoral politics, or even registering to vote. What remained paradoxical about the Nation was that, despite being organized to achieve power, its core philosophy was apolitical. Temple members were never encouraged to register in civil rights demonstrations or disrupt public places by engaging in civil disobedience. They were hardly "revolutionaries." Perhaps one explanation is Congressman Powell's growing influence on Malcolm. Abyssinian's fifteen-thousand-strong voting bloc illustrated just how powerful a single black institution could be in the context of New York City's fractious politics. Malcolm may have floated these ideas as part of an attempt to change Elijah Muhammad's rigid antipolitics position.

Finally, the speech's flowing construction displayed Malcolm's growing rhetorical confidence. Although the talk was formally hosted by the Nation of Islam, its focus and style were profoundly secular: Malcolm no longer saw himself exclusively as an NOI minister, but someone who could speak to black politics.

The FBI of course monitored this and later lectures. One of its spies advised the Bureau that in September Malcolm had been named acting minister of Detroit's temple. The informant added that "Little is well liked in Detroit and the meetings at which he spoke were well attended." Two months on, Wilfred X Little would become head minister of Temple No. 1. The *Amsterdam News* also followed Malcolm's Midwest road tour, reporting back that he had "been a great hit with the general Detroit Public." His speaking venues in that city were "packed to capacity," and his evangelical drive, the paper noted, had produced major gains for the Nation.

Malcolm's high-impact speaking schedule kept members flowing in and media interest high, but it also battered his already weakened body. For a month after the Detroit lectures, he got by on only two to four hours of sleep each night, eating once daily, and keeping himself awake on coffee. Several days after a lecture on October 23, he began to feel severe pains in his chest and stomach. Fearing that he might have a coronary condition, he checked himself in to Harlem's Sydenham Hospital. The physicians diagnosed heart palpitations and inflammation around the ribs, but attributed the problems to exhaustion and stress. They strongly advised that he take time off, but he adamantly refused.

Checking out of Sydenham after a two-day stay, he rushed up to Boston to preside over the dedication of a new temple and to offer support for his protégé Louis X, the Boston temple minister. Introduced as "the founder of the Boston temple," Malcolm reminded his audience about the inequality that existed throughout America. Blacks "have died for this country and yet we are not [full] citizens." Even other discriminated-against groups, such as the Jews, received better treatment. "A Jew is in the White House, Jews in the State House, the Jews run the country. You and I can't go into a white hotel down south," he argued, "but a Jew can."

Malcolm continued his public criticisms of New York's police department, writing a telegram to the police commissioner in which he demanded that the officers directly involved in the Hinton incident be suspended. In October, when a New York County grand jury opted not to indict those responsible, Malcolm condemned the decision. "Harlem is already a potential powder keg," he warned. "If these ignorant white officers are allowed to remain in the Harlem area, their presence is not only a menace to society, but to world peace." BOSS considered Malcolm's words as a threat against the police and increased its surveillance by placing black undercover officers inside the Nation. On November 7, BOSS detective Walter A. Upshur visited William Traynham, the administrator of Sydenham Hospital in Harlem, to investigate Malcolm's recent hospitalization. The detective learned that Malcolm's "admitting diagnosis was coronary" and obtained the name and address of his private physician.

By November 10, Malcolm was back in Detroit, and soon after departed on a nearly three-week-long tour of the West Coast with the goal of establishing a strong temple in Los Angeles. Following this, he made an unscheduled return stop in Detroit to tell a standing-room-only audience that Islam was "spreading like a flaming fire awakening and uniting Negroes where it is heard." Although Malcolm usually spoke at Muslim temples, his audiences increasingly consisted of both Muslim and non-Muslim blacks. In his language and style, Malcolm reached out to recruit black Christians to his cause.

His breakthrough as a national speaker generated a financial windfall for the Nation. Between five hundred and one thousand African Americans were joining almost every month. The demand for new temples must have seemed endless. Much of the new revenue went into commercial ventures overseen by Raymond Sharrieff, mostly in Chicago: a restaurant, a dry cleaning and laundry establishment, a bakery, a barbershop, a well-stocked grocery store. The Nation also purchased an apartment building on Chicago's South Side, as well as a farm and a house in White Cloud, Michigan, valued at sixteen thousand dollars. The economic success of these ventures may have been responsible for Elijah Muhammad's decision to stop mentioning some of the original tenets of Wallace D. Fard's Islam—in particular the bizarre Yacub's History—and to give greater emphasis to the Garveyite thesis that a self-sustainable, all-black capitalist economy was a viable strategy.

Malcolm's popularity gave him unprecedented leverage with Muhammad, allowing him to achieve major concessions, such as NOI ministers being permitted the surname Shabazz rather than the standard X. Since, according to NOI theology, Shabazz was the original tribal identity of the lost-founds, it could be claimed as a legitimate surname. Contrary to the perception that "Malcolm Shabazz" emerged only after Malcolm's break with the Nation in 1964, he was using this name widely by 1957.

Muhammad's pride in Malcolm's strategic judgments allowed the young minister to develop regional recruitment campaigns in areas where the NOI had never previously canvassed. The best, and in many ways the most problematic, example was in the South. Despite Malcolm's establishment of the Atlanta temple in 1955, the NOI had virtually no presence below the Mason-Dixon line. Yet in the recent years of the Nation's greatest growth, the region had become a racial powder keg. In Montgomery, Alabama, the successful bus boycott of 1955–56, initiated by Rosa Parks's refusal to surrender her seat on a segregated bus, had brought to national attention the struggle to abolish legal Jim Crow. Since the Nation of Islam's position favored racial separation, Malcolm thought it important that integrationist reformers like Dr. Martin Luther King, Jr., not be allowed to exercise too great an influence—Elijah Muhammad's message of black solidarity, black capitalism, and racial separatism had to be carried into Dixie. These arguments made sense to Muhammad, who gave him permission to launch a Southern campaign. Though eager, Malcolm moved with some caution: when the press asked his opinions on the Montgomery boycott, he praised Rosa Parks's courage, describing her as a "good, hard-working, Christian-believing black woman." Rarely would he directly criticize the protests espoused by King.

Malcolm already had some experience stumping for the Nation of Islam in the South. In August 1956, one year after establishing the Atlanta temple, he had been the featured speaker for the first Southern Goodwill Tour of the Brotherhood of Islam. The convention attracted hundreds of people across the region, but to ensure an impressive turnout NOI temples from as far away as Atlantic City and Lansing sent their members. By the conclusion of the tour, the Atlanta temple had doubled its membership. The next February, Malcolm was again called to the South, this time to Alabama. While en route to attend the Saviour's Day convention in Chicago that year, a group of NOI members tangled with police at a train station in the small town of Flomaton. Two Muslim women had violated an ordinance by sitting on a whites-only bench, and police moved to confront them. When two young Muslim men, Joe Allen and George R. White, sought to protect the women, the local police chief, "Red" Hemby, pulled his revolver. In the struggle, Allen and White disarmed and severely beat the officer. Minutes later they were arrested and charged with attempted murder. Arriving in Flomaton, Malcolm used his influence to secure their release with only minor fines.

His second major Southern tour, the centerpiece of the campaign that Muhammad had approved, took place in September and October of 1958, beginning in Atlanta, which, with its flourishing temple, remained one of the few urban centers in the region to have a significant NOI presence. By September 29 he was in Florida, and over the next two weeks the state's NOI members coordinated public lectures for him in Miami, Tampa, and Jacksonville. Apparently Malcolm did not modify his talks to address regional issues that were particularly relevant in the South. Nevertheless, his speeches did attract modest media coverage, and the tour enhanced the Nation's profile, especially in Miami.

The NOI never captured the following in the South that it achieved in the mostly urban industrial Midwest, on the East Coast, and in California. Its organizational weakness in the region was compounded by several critical errors it made in its response to newly emerging desegregation campaigns. Following Muhammad's lead, NOI leaders believed that white Southerners were at least honest in their hatred of blacks. The NOI could not imagine a political future where Jim Crow segregation would ever become outlawed. Consequently, Malcolm concluded, "the advantage of this is the Southern black man never has been under any illusions about the opposition he is dealing with." Since white supremacy would always be a reality, blacks were better off reaching a working relationship with racist whites rather than allying themselves with Northern liberals. This was a tragic replay of Garvey's disastrous thesis that culminated in his overtures to white supremacist organizations. "You can say for many Southern white people that, individually, they have been paternalistically helpful to many individual Negroes," Malcolm was to argue in *Autobiography*. "I know nothing about the South. I am a creation of the Northern white man."

Even though Malcolm's Southern campaign ultimately scored limited gains, that effort paled in comparison to his remarkable success in growing the Nation of Islam across the country. Of the thousands of new converts he made in 1956–57, two would figure in his own life in ways he could not have imagined. One was James Warden, a New York City native and son of a labor organizer who may once have been a member of the Communist Party. After graduating from the Bronx High School of Science, Warden attended Lincoln University in Pennsylvania and then served a two-year stint in the military, returning home to enroll in an M.A. program at Columbia University's East Asian Institute. Sometime in 1957, when he was twenty-five, a black friend persuaded him to go to the NOI temple to hear Malcolm. He took some convincing: Warden disliked everything he had heard about this strange, racist cult. "I was convinced that these people were saying, 'The white man is the devil,'" he recalled. "I figured, hey, it's some crazy group, [but] America is full of them." Upon entering the temple at West 116th Street and Lenox Avenue, he was offended to find he had to submit to a physical search. When the program began, he met with further frustration; the evening's speaker was not Malcolm but Louis X Walcott. As Louis launched wildly into his sermon, a bewildered Warden asked himself, "Has this man lost his mind?" The concept of whites literally as devils seemed ridiculous. Warden vowed to himself, "If I get out of this place without being arrested, I will never come back."

But curiosity got the better of him. Five nights later he returned, but once again was disappointed when yet another minister addressed the congregation. Still, he persisted, and two nights later finally heard Malcolm. The experience was a revelation. On display was Malcolm's great strength not merely as an orator, but as a teacher. For this sermon, as for many, he used a chalkboard as part of his presentation and employed evidence from academic sources to buttress his arguments. He also didn't mind being challenged. When Warden left that night, he realized he wanted to return. For the next nine months, he continued to attend meetings regularly, though he stopped short of joining formally. What finally put him over was finding himself the target of racial insults from schoolmates at Columbia. When they ridiculed him as a "nigger," he became infuriated. "I felt that I was in classrooms with people who because of our mutual interests had some kind of appreciation or respect for me as a person," he said. "This was not the case." Giving himself over to the Nation, Warden flourished, and by 1960 was named an FOI lieutenant. It was in this capacity that his friendship with Malcolm grew to dedication. Short, pugnacious, fluent in three foreign languages including Japanese, the workaholic Warden—renamed James 67X—would eventually become one of Malcolm's most steadfast advisers.

Another significant recruit was Betty Sanders. Born on May 28, 1934, like Malcolm she had been raised in a household where race issues played a prominent role. Her foster parents, Lorenzo and Helen Malloy, had taken her in from a broken home as a young girl and provided her with a stable middle-class existence. Lorenzo Malloy was a graduate of Tuskegee Institute and a businessman who owned a shoe repair shop in Detroit. Helen Malloy was active in civil rights, serving as an officer in the National Housewives League, a group that initiated boycotts of white-owned businesses that refused to hire blacks or sell black products . She also belonged to the NAACP and to Mary McLeod Bethune's National Council of Negro Women, two pillars of the black bourgeoisie. Betty attended Detroit's Northern High

School, and upon receiving her diploma in 1952 enrolled in the Tuskegee Institute, intent on studying education. After two years, she switched her major to nursing; against her parents' advice she transferred to Brooklyn State College School of Nursing, where she earned her undergraduate degree in 1956, and soon began her clinical studies at the Bronx's Montefiore Hospital.

Betty's discovery of the NOI was, like Warden's, entirely fortuitous. One Friday night in mid-1956, an older nurse at Montefiore invited her to an NOI-sponsored dinner, followed by a temple sermon. Betty found the main lecturer "bewildering." With serious reservations, she consented to go one more time, and on this occasion Malcolm spoke. As she noted his thin frame, her first impression was one of concern. "This man is totally malnourished!" she thought. Following the lecture, she was introduced to him, and as they conversed Betty was struck by Malcolm's relaxed manner. Onstage, he had seemed soldierly and stern; in private, he was personable, even charming. Intrigued, she began attending Temple No. 7 sermons, at first hiding her fascination with the Muslims from her parents. By that fall, Betty Sanders officially joined, becoming Betty X, and serving as a health instructor in the MGT's General Civilization Class. Her friends outside the temple believed that her newfound dedication to the Nation had a lot to do with her feelings for Minister Malcolm.

———

In late 1958, an African-American FBI informant candidly evaluated both Malcolm's character and his standing within the NOI:

> Brother MALCOLM ranks about third in influence. He has unlimited freedom of movement in all states, and outside of the Messenger's immediate family he is the most trusted follower. He is an excellent speaker, forceful and convincing. He is an expert organizer and an untiring worker. . . . MALCOLM has a strong hatred for the "blue eyed devils," but this hatred is not likely to erupt in violence as he is much too clever and intelligent for that. . . . He is fearless and cannot be intimidated by words or threats of personal harm. He has most of the answers at his fingertips and should be carefully dealt with. He is not likely to violate any ordinances or laws. He neither smokes nor drinks and is of high moral character.

This assessment underscored the FBI's problem. Though the Bureau saw Malcolm as a potential threat to national security, his rigid behavioral code and strong leadership skills would make him hard to discredit. He did not have obvious vulnerabilities, nor was he likely to be baited into making a mistake. Yet what the evaluation also gathered, quite astutely, was that Malcolm's authority within the sect emanated directly from his closeness to Elijah Muhammad. It would not take the Bureau long to deduce that any conflict provoked between Muhammad and Malcolm could weaken the Nation as a whole.

By late 1957, Malcolm was becoming the NOI's version of Adam Clayton Powell, Jr.—a celebrity minister based in New York City, but whose larger role took him on the road for weeks at a time. His responsibilities still growing, he led a pressurized existence, his life often a blur of planes and trains, speeches and sermons. At some level, he must have felt a great weight of loneliness and frustration, especially as the freshness of new initiatives gave way to the inevitability of routine. The acclaim he found so intoxicating at the beginning came with equally significant burdens: the difficulties and humiliations that all blacks encountered when traveling across the country during these years; the administrative and budgetary puzzles of managing thousands of people; the challenges involved in pastoral work—going to see members in hospitals, overseeing funerals, preparing sermons and prayers. When he was in New York, he was expected to be a nightly presence in his temple, while the week's schedule was strictly regimented. Every Monday was FOI night, where men were drilled in martial arts, as well as "the responsibilities of a husband and father," as Malcolm put it. Tuesday evenings were "Unity Night, where the brothers and sisters enjoy each other's conversational company." Wednesday was Student Enrollment, with lectures explaining NOI theology. Thursdays were reserved for the MGT and General Civilization Class, at which Malcolm frequently lectured. Fridays were Civilization Night, with classes "for brothers and sisters in the area of the domestic relations, emphasizing how both husbands and wives must understand and respect each other's true natures." On Saturdays, members were free to visit each other's homes, with Sundays reserved for the week's main religious service.

Whether prompted by a gnawing sense of emptiness in his life or something less emotional, Malcolm's thoughts turned to marriage. Such a move would have practical benefits; Malcolm calculated that he could be a more effective representative of Elijah Muhammad if he married. He had heard the many rumors about his romantic attachments, and had tried to suppress them. Everyone in Temple No. 7 undoubtedly knew about their minister's long-term relationship with Evelyn Williams. It is impossible to know whether the minister rekindled sexual intimacies with his longtime lover, or if Islamic sanctions against premarital sex affected their behavior. In 1956, Malcolm proposed marriage and Evelyn accepted, but a few days later he retracted his offer. Of all the women with whom he was involved, Malcolm would later write to Elijah Muhammad, "Sister Evelyn is the only one who had a legitiment [*sic*] beef against me . . . and I do bear witness that if she complains she is justified."

But Evelyn was not the only recipient of a marriage proposal from Malcolm in 1956. That same year, he asked another NOI woman, Betty Sue Williams. Little is known of her, though she was likely the sister of Robert X Williams, minister of the Buffalo temple. Both women, in different ways, were unsuitable choices. Malcolm sensed that he had built bonds of trust and spiritual kinship between himself, his religious followers, and to a growing extent the Harlem community. The woman he chose as his wife would impact all these relationships. Romantic love and sexual attractiveness, he reasoned, had little to do with fulfilling his primary roles as a minister and role model. Evelyn had known and loved him when he was Detroit Red, and though he had changed drastically, her claim on him by virtue of their shared past would always compete with his commitment to the Nation. For this reason, Malcolm believed it necessary for his spouse to have no knowledge of or connection to his prior life. And Betty Sue, who probably lived in Buffalo, four hundred miles from Harlem, was not a member of Temple No. 7's intimate community. Malcolm was proud of the bonds he had established with both the members of Temple No. 7 and the Harlem community generally. The minister's wife, he felt, was an extension of himself; she would sometimes be his representative at public occasions, and would have to possess the same commitment to Muhammad and the NOI that he had. Malcolm's failed proposals in 1956 surely increased his sense of personal isolation and private loneliness.

If practical reasons came to dominate the way Malcolm thought about choosing a wife, it may have had much to do with the sense of betrayal he long harbored about his mistreatment at the hands of partners past, especially Bea. He had come to fear that it was impossible for him to love or trust any woman. "I'd had too much experience that women were only tricky, deceitful, untrustworthy flesh," he complained. "To tell a woman not to talk too much was like telling Jesse James not to carry a gun, or telling a hen not to cackle." And knowing when not to talk was a crucial skill for anyone who was to be Mrs. Malcolm Shabazz.

Malcolm also possessed firm ideas about the role a wife should play.

"Islam has very strict laws and teachings about women," he observed. "The true nature of a man is to be strong, and a woman's true nature is to be weak . . . [a man] must control her if he expects to get her respect." Because he viewed all women as inherently inferior and subordinate to males, he was not looking for a spouse with whom he would share his innermost feelings. He expected his wife to be obedient and chaste, to bear his children and to maintain a Muslim household.

These sentiments were much in keeping with those of the Nation at large, which were in turn similar to those of orthodox Islam. In the Qur'anic tradition, the primary objectives of marriage (*nikah*) are sexual reproduction and the transfer and inheritance of private property from one generation to the next. *Nikah* also controls the temptation toward promiscuity. Carnal knowledge can easily lead to social chaos, or *fitna*, if not tightly controlled. To most Muslims, premarital sex, homosexuality, prostitution, and extramarital sexual intercourse are all absolutely forbidden.

Throughout the Islamic world, marriage is perceived as the uniting of two families or kinship lines rather than an act dictated by two individuals. In the negotiations with the relatives of the husband-to-be, a first-time bride is often represented by a *wali*, or guardian, who is normally a father or elder male relative. Premarital meetings between women and men are strictly supervised. Marriage is perceived as based on mutual respect, friendship, and a joint commitment toward an Islamic lifestyle. These processes, unfortunately, have tended to reinforce Islamic structures of patriarchy and domestic violence against women down through the centuries.

The Holy Qur'an is quite specific regarding Islamic expectations for the duties of women. *Surah XXIV*, verse 33, instructs "believing women":

> to lower their gaze and be modest, and to display of their adornment only that which is apparent, and to draw their veils over their bosoms, and not to reveal their adornment save to their own husband or fathers or husband's fathers, or their sons or their husband's sons, or their brothers or their brothers' sons or sisters' sons, or their women, or their slaves, or male attendants who lack vigour, or children who know naught of women's nakedness. And let them not stamp their feet so as to reveal what they hide of their adornment.

The Nation attempted to incorporate some of these values within its own catechism. Elijah Muhammad's views about gender relations would be set out in his 1965 manifesto *Message to the Blackman in America*. To Muhammad, males and females occupied separate spheres. Black women had been the mothers of civilization, and they would play a central role in the construction of the world to come. Metaphorically, they were the field in which a mighty Nation would grow; thus it was essential for black men to keep the devil, the white man, away from his "field," because the black woman was far more valuable than any cash crop. There was no question that all women had to be controlled; the question was, who should exercise that control, the white man or the black? He also warned against birth control, a devilish plot to carry out genocide against black babies. It was precisely a woman's ability to produce children that gave the weaker sex its value. "Who wants a sterile wom[a]n?" he asked rhetorically.

What attracted so many intelligent, independent African-American women to such a patriarchal sect? The sexist and racist world of the 1940s and 1950s provides part of the answer. Many African-American women in the paid labor force were private household workers and routinely experienced sexual harassment by their white employers. The NOI, by contrast, offered them the protections of private patriarchy. Like their middle-class white counterparts, African-American women in the Nation were not expected to hold full-time jobs, and even if Malcolm's frequent misogynistic statements, especially in his sermons, were extreme even by the sexist standards of the NOI, it offered protection, stability, and a kind of leadership. Malcolm's emphasis on the sanctity of the black home made an explicit promise "that families won't be abandoned, that women will be cherished and protected, [and] that there will be economic stability."

Temple women during those years rarely perceived themselves as being subjugated. The MGT was its own center of activity, in which members participated in neighborhood activities and were encouraged to monitor their children's progress in school. At the Newark NOI temple, not far from Temple No. 7, women were involved in establishing small businesses. They also took an active role in working with their local board of education as well as other community concerns. It is likely that Harlem's women made similar efforts. As with those who were working in civil rights, women in the NOI had in mind the future of the black community. What attracted them to the Nation was the possibility of strong, healthy families, supportive relationships, and personal engagement in building crime-free black neighborhoods and ultimately an independent black nation.

In the *Autobiography*, Malcolm tells how his relationship with Betty Sanders evolved within the parameters defined by both Islam and the NOI. By early 1957 he was aware that Betty had joined Temple No. 7. He soon learned that she was from Detroit, had attended Tuskegee, and was currently at nursing school in the city. She was physically attractive—medium brown in color, dark hair, brown eyes, and a lively smile. Her education had given her the confidence and experience to stand before groups and lecture, and to direct the work of others. Malcolm began dropping in on Betty's classes at the temple on Thursday evenings. His attitude toward her was formal but friendly. He eventually overcame his reservations to invite her out—to New York's Museum of Natural History. As he recounted their first date, his sole purpose was to view several museum displays that would help her in her lectures. Betty agreed to go and an afternoon outing was set. Hours before their meeting, however, Malcolm got cold feet, calling her to say that he had to cancel; another matter had come up. Betty's rejoinder was surprisingly blunt: "Well, you sure waited long enough to tell me, Brother Minister, I was just ready to walk out of the door." Embarrassed, he recanted, and hastily agreed to keep the date after all. The afternoon went off well, and he was pleasantly surprised to be "halfway impressed by her intelligence and also her education." The two continued to meet and work together, but Malcolm was paralyzed by the thought that if he showed he was romantically attracted to her she might reject him.

The NOI by now possessed the financial resources to fly Malcolm to Chicago each month to consult with Elijah Muhammad. At one of these meetings, Malcolm admitted that he might ask Betty to marry him. Since her foster parents were opposed to her membership in the Nation, Muhammad decided to investigate her suitability for his prized disciple. On the pretext of several days' training at national headquarters, he invited Betty to Chicago. During her time there, she was the houseguest of Elijah and Clara Muhammad. Afterward, Muhammad told Malcolm approvingly that he thought Betty X was "a fine sister."

In Malcolm's telling (and in Spike Lee's film), sexual attraction was the primary force drawing the two together, yet some of those who worked closely with Malcolm saw things differently. James 67X recalled that the minister saw his marriage as the fulfillment of an obligation to the Nation. Any personal feelings were secondary. "Brother, a minister *has* to be married," Malcolm told him, alluding to the Islamic precepts. To avoid *fitna*, the threats of scandal and sin, even a loveless marriage could become a haven. Another confidant, Charles 37X Morris, became convinced that Malcolm "didn't have no feelings for a woman," an ambiguous statement that nonetheless suggests that his minister was not enthusiastic about marriage. Charles believed that it was Elijah, not Malcolm, who was the chief instigator of his lieutenant's marriage. Years after Malcolm's death, Louis Farrakhan insisted that Malcolm continued to be deeply in love with Evelyn Williams. Yet Betty herself—or Dr. Betty Shabazz, as she became known—would always insist that Malcolm had pursued her "persistently and correctly."

Still, the unusual way Malcolm proposed to Betty suggests that his former lieutenants may have had a point. Early in the morning on Sunday, January 12, 1958, he stood in a pay telephone booth at a gas station in Detroit, having driven all night from New York City. He reached her at her hospital dormitory and immediately blurted out, "Look, do you want to get married?" Betty, overcome, dropped the receiver, but as soon as she had it in hand again said, "Yes." She promptly packed her suitcase and immediately flew to Detroit.

As soon as Betty was in Detroit, the young couple went together to the Malloys, who were stunned. Betty recalled leaving Malcolm in the living room as she retreated with her parents to the back of the house to tell them the news. They did not respond well. Helen Malloy sobbed uncontrollably, complaining that Malcolm was too old and "not even a Christian." Her father was even more direct: "What have we done to make you hate us so?" Betty began to weep as well, but she was determined to have her way. What Malcolm surmised from the raised voices and gales of sobbing is hard to know. He simply recalled that the Malloys "were very friendly, and happily surprised."

The news received a better reception from the Littles. Malcolm's siblings in the Detroit area were overjoyed, and probably extremely relieved, that their thirty-two-year-old brother was finally settling down. On January 14, Malcolm and Betty drove to nearby northern Indiana, where liberal marriage laws would make it easy to wed quickly. However, the state had recently established a mandatory waiting period, so the two went on to Philbert's home in Lansing, where they learned it was possible to marry within two days. They obtained the necessary blood tests, bought a pair of rings, and filled out a marriage certificate. Then came the ceremony itself, on January 4. Malcolm's rendering is both semicomical and bittersweet, because it reveals little sense of joy. "An old hunchback white man," a justice of the peace, performed the ceremony. Wilfred and Philbert were there, although in Malcolm's version of events all the witnesses were white. Malcolm was most offended when the justice of the peace instructed him to "kiss your bride." Malcolm protested, "I got her out of there. All that Hollywood stuff!" He ridiculed "these movie and television-addicted women expecting some bouquets and kissing and hugging . . . like Cinderella." The newlyweds spent the night at a hotel, Betty flying back to New York the next day to attend her classes.

When the news of Minister Malcolm's nuptials reached Temple No. 7, there was pandemonium, and not all of it celebratory. The NOI was predominantly an organization in which males fraternized easily with each other, hugging and embracing in public. While physical contact between genders was prohibited, male-to-male contact, especially within the martial arts context, was routine. It was not a surprise to Malcolm, therefore, when some brothers at Temple No. 7 "looked at me as though I had betrayed them." Malcolm was seen as a modern-day Abelard, the priest who had surrendered to earthly passions, abandoning his true calling. But he was far more intrigued with the temple sisters' response to Betty. "I never will forget hearing one exclaim, 'You got him!' That's like I was telling you, the *nature* of women. That's part of why I never have been able to shake it out of my mind that she knew something—all the time. Maybe she did get me!"

Evelyn, who was at the temple when the news of Malcolm's marriage was announced, ran from the building screaming. Undoubtedly Malcolm felt guilty; if, as Farrakhan suggested, he continued to harbor feelings for her, the formal ending of their relationship may have been almost as difficult for Malcolm. But just as practical considerations had motivated his desire to be married, it now drove his resolve to restore order within the temple. He consulted with Muhammad, and it was decided that Evelyn would relocate to Chicago, where the national office would employ her as one of Muhammad's secretaries. This must have seemed like the best solution to Malcolm, because, even if he had heard the rumors that occasionally surfaced in the temple about the Messenger, he could not have guessed how the move would come to complicate his life.

The unease Malcolm had shown toward marrying Betty almost immediately manifested itself in their lives together as man and wife. The challenges they faced were linked, in part, to the general problems that many black Americans encounter when adopting Qur'anic standards for marriage. Many basic beliefs Muslims have about its purposes and duties are at odds with Western Christian values. Another serious issue is the concept of machismo that some African-American males carry into Islam. The Nation had long drawn its converts from the lowest rungs of black society, and many of its flock came from difficult or self-destructive backgrounds. Those who, like Malcolm, had converted while in prison often continued to bear painful scars, both physical and psychological, from that experience. Trauma can last an entire lifetime, and the Nation had no self-help program to assist men in overcoming such emotional problems. Malcolm's prior sexual history had been largely defined by encounters with prostitutes and women like Bea Caragulian. Now he would have an obligation not only to provide financially for Betty, but to address her emotional and sexual needs.

He did at least try. At the beginning of 1958, the newlyweds moved into a duplex house at 25-26 Ninety-ninth Street in East Elmhurst, Queens. Betty and Malcolm shared the upstairs living quarters with temple secretary John X Simmons, his wife, Minnie, and their four-month-old baby; also living there were an Edward 3X Robinson and his wife. Occupants in the basement and ground-level residence included John X and Yvonne X Molette, Mildred Crosby, Alice Rice, and her baby daughter, Zinina. All either were NOI members or were connected to the NOI through family ties. Betty quickly became pregnant and gave up her nursing career. For several months, Malcolm stopped extensive touring and tried to appear happy about the pregnancy. From the beginning, however, Betty's behavior displeased him. Just as she had defied her parents' wishes by transferring to nursing school and by marrying Malcolm, she retained an independent streak that her demanding husband found unacceptable. Even her continued attendance at MGT classes bothered him. For her part, Betty confided to one girlfriend that while Malcolm's word was final inside the temple, in the privacy of their home "that attitude just didn't go." James 67X later characterized Betty's combative opposition to the patriarchal behavior of both her husband and the NOI hierarchy as "continuous," explaining with a smile that "no woman who has been brought up under the devil can accept this." Although Betty's foster parents were black, their entrenched Christian values and middle-class norms, as far as James 67X was concerned, were like those of whites.

Years after Malcolm's assassination, Betty would describe her marriage as "hectic, beautiful, and unforgettable—the greatest thing in my life." In reality, the twenty-three-year-old was poorly prepared for married life. She had never learned to cook. Even after she joined the Nation, she knew how to make little more than bean dishes and a few beef and chicken recipes. Malcolm never cooked, so it was up to her to plan nutritious and varied meals on a limited budget. Any romantic fantasies she may have had about her future life were largely extinguished by the end of their first year together. Malcolm rarely, if ever, displayed affection toward her. They almost never spent the night out in each other's company—throughout their seven years of marriage, he took her to a movie only once, in 1963. The most caring moments occurred around the births of their children. For example, Malcolm personally drove Betty for her regular appointments with her obstetrician, Dr. Josephine English (he'd made it clear that no male physician would touch his spouse). To allow for Malcolm's hectic schedule, Dr. English set Betty's appointments at seven a.m. at her hospital. Malcolm had convinced himself that his firstborn child would be male; indeed, he had told associates that the only name he had come up with was a boy's. Then, on November 16, 1958, a girl was born and given the name Attallah. Whether Malcolm was disappointed or simply believed he had little postpartum role to play, he virtually disappeared following the birth. The next day he drove north to Albany to speak at an NOI gathering. Two days later, he was in Hartford, Connecticut, before moving along to Newark, New Jersey. He was back on the road, carrying on as though little had changed.

His reaction dismayed Betty. Shortly after Attallah's birth, she collected some clothing and her daughter and took the subway to the home of Ruth Summerford, a distant cousin. When Malcolm arrived back to discover his wife and child missing, he guessed where they had gone. He sensed that Betty was upset with his behavior, but he had no intention of offering an apology. Instead, he waited nearly two days before he drove over to Summerford's house and ordered his wife to pick up their daughter and get into the car. Betty did as she was told.

Marriage continued to be filled with surprises. During her years as a single woman, Betty had collected a small number of debts. Malcolm had no knowledge about these before their marriage, but now thought it best not to let his young wife think that "she had married a good thing," so he allowed her to continue working to clear these debts. Still, he did not make it easy for her. When Betty asked him to drive her to work, which began at six a.m., he curtly refused. By keeping firm control of the family finances and denying Betty the opportunity to earn income beyond what was needed for the repayments, he kept his wife "in jail financially," as he put it.

If long days on the road had once turned Malcolm's thoughts to marriage and stability, the difficulties of his marriage now renewed the road's appeal, offering him a way to find solace and distance from his troubles. His first significant trip after his marriage was a monthlong visit to Los Angeles in the spring of 1958, which was in many ways as significant as his extended series of speeches in Detroit in the summer of 1957. Malcolm was determined to establish a strong NOI base on the West Coast. He also wanted to establish the NOI's Islamic credentials by engaging in public activities with Middle Eastern and Asian Muslim representatives in the region. In late

March and early April, Malcolm addressed NOI members at meetings held at the Normandie Hall in Los Angeles. While in the city, he also attended a gala reception honoring the Republic of Pakistan, and spoke at a press conference at the Roosevelt Hotel in Hollywood, coordinated by Mohammad T. Mendi of Karbala, Iraq, using the platform to say it was "absurd" for the Arabs to expect fair treatment from the white media "since it is controlled by the Zionists." On April 20 he was again the featured speaker at a public event designed to be an interfaith dialogue between Muslims and Christians. Three preachers walked out in protest when Malcolm criticized the wealth of some African-American churches and the poverty of their worshippers. He also arranged with Louis X to deliver a sermon at Boston's temple in May. At its conclusion, Malcolm asked the audience if anyone wished to convert to the NOI. He was astonished to find among those standing his sister Ella; somehow their lives had come full circle.

Malcolm grew increasingly troubled by Betty's behavior. In a letter sent to Elijah in March 1959, he confessed that "the main source of our trouble was based upon *SEX*":

> [S]he placed a great deal more stress upon it than I was *physically* capable of doing. Please forgive me for this topic, but I feel compelled to tell you of it, and would tell it to no one else but you. At a time when I was going all out to keep her satisfied (sexually), one day she told me that we were incompatible sexually because I had never given her any real satisfaction. From then on, try as I may, I began to become very cool toward her. I didn't ever again feel right (free) with her in that sense, for no matter how happy she would act I'd see it only as a pretense. . . . She stayed miserable during her expectancy, and those were the nine most miserable months of my life . . . she often cursed the day she married and of being pregnant, and *she cursed me too.*

From Betty's perspective, marriage to Temple No. 7's minister meant constantly sharing her husband with others, leaving little time for her. She also sensed that she had become the object of vicious gossip. Malcolm had grown too powerful to criticize openly, but Betty was an easy target. Some of the rumors circulating about her were cruel. For example, when she gave birth to a series of daughters, temple gossipmongers suggested that Allah was punishing her for her constant challenges to the male-dominated hierarchy. She would not be able to bear sons, they whispered, until she first learned to control her behavior. The more criticism that came Betty's way, the more assertive she became. She also began to develop a circle of women friends inside the temple, providing some measure of support. But to critics, her group displayed arrogance and the willingness to divide MGT into feuding factions. "She made sure that you appreciated the distance between you and her," James 67X tartly observed. "Because of her relationship with Malcolm, you and her were no longer equals."

In February 1959, Betty was again sent to an NOI training program at Chicago headquarters. It lasted several weeks. Upon her return, Malcolm informed Muhammad, "She said to me that if I didn't watch out she was going to embarrass me and herself (which under questioning she later said she was going to seek satisfaction elsewhere)." For a Muslim male, cuckoldry was intolerable. For Malcolm, it would not only end his marriage but jeopardize his position as a minister. Perhaps he reasoned that the only way to keep Betty under control, or less sexually desirable to other males, was to keep her perpetually pregnant, so after six months of abstinence, he began having sex with his wife again. Betty's response was to heap ridicule on her husband. She "told me that I was *impotent* . . . and even tho [sic] I could father a child I was like an old man (not able to engage in the act long enough to satisfy her)." Complicating matters, the entire temple knew about their disharmony; the other Muslims living in the same duplex as the battling couple kept Captain Joseph well apprised.

Since their bitter break, Joseph's feelings toward Malcolm had grown increasingly hostile, and he may have seized on Malcolm's marital distractions to tip the balance of power in the Nation back in his direction. He undoubtedly reported Malcolm's marital problems to his superior, Supreme Captain Raymond Sharrieff. Through Sharrieff, other members of Muhammad's family would have learned about their difficulties. In the late fifties, the Chicago headquarters expanded Joseph's authority to all temples in the northeastern United States, which gave him authority over the deployment of thousands of FOI members. Joseph could now influence the selection of captains across the country. Malcolm's only means to contest this, and to minimize the stigma over his marital woes, was to throw himself even more single-mindedly into NOI affairs.

———

On May 14, 1958, as Malcolm was lecturing in Boston, two detectives from the Astoria precinct, Joseph Kiernan and Michael Bonura, came to the front door of his East Elmhurst home. They had been ordered to serve a federal bench warrant issued for a woman named Margaret Dorsey, whose official residence was on East 165th Street in the Bronx but who supposedly lived on the ground floor of the Littles' duplex. (Malcolm would later claim to BOSS detectives that the police officers had not asked for Dorsey, but for Alvin Crosby, age twenty-four, who resided with other families either in the ground-floor living quarters or in the basement.) The detectives were met at the front door by twenty-seven-year-old Yvonne X Molette, who politely explained that she would not admit them without a search warrant. The police tried to overpower her and enter the house. Several other women who were inside heard the commotion and ran to Yvonne's aid. Together, they managed to slam the door shut. The detectives vowed that they would call again, this time with a warrant.

They returned at about eight thirty p.m., with U.S. Postal Inspector Herbert Halls. Halls knocked on the front door, while Kiernan and Bonura went around to the duplex's side entrance. There they were met by John X Molette, who had returned home after his wife called him about the detectives' first attempt to enter. The police told Molette that they were looking for Margaret Dorsey, at which point Molette stepped outside, closing the door behind him. Impatient, Kiernan complained they "didn't have time for all that foolishness." He pushed Molette aside and tried to open the door and barge his way inside. As the three men wrestled in the doorway, Molette was pushed backward into the house, and with the assistance of his mother-in-law he managed to force the two policemen out and close the door. Undaunted, Kiernan shattered one of the door's glass panels and reached inside to let himself in. As the fight continued, Detective Bonura was struck by a bottle that had been hurled from an upper window. At this, Kiernan pulled his revolver and fired two shots through the door.

The gunfire had a dramatic effect. The residents scattered and the police entered the house, following the occupants up the stairs. When they reached the top, they found the door to the Littles' apartment locked. The officers threatened to shoot through the door unless the occupants opened it, and the women—Betty Shabazz and Minnie Simmons—did so. After searching the house, the police took both women as well as Yvonne and John Molette outside and lined them up against a wall next to the driveway. When a police patrol wagon arrived, they were taken to the 114th Precinct station house. Two others were also arrested, and all were eventually released on bail.

When word of the incident reached Malcolm in Boston, it galvanized him, just as the showdown over Johnson X Hinton had done the year before. He flew immediately to New York City and launched into a media tirade against the NYPD, drawing parallels between "the [G]estapo tactics of white police who control the black belts" of American ghettos and occupation forces in controlling hostile territory. "Where else and under what circumstances," he asked, "could you find situations where police can freely invade private homes, break down doors, threaten to beat pregnant women, and even try to shoot a 13-year-old girl . . . but right here in American Negro neighborhoods, where the 'occupying army' is in disguise as police officers?" The NOI immediately placed a picket line of silent protesters in front of the 114th Precinct, a bold move that, according to one press account, utterly amazed the police. The Hinton affair had taught Malcolm to put the authorities on the defensive with such demonstrations, a maneuver that also sent a signal to black non-Muslims that the conflict was a civil rights issue.

Although neither Malcolm nor Betty probably realized it, her marriage to the NOI minister had triggered her surveillance by the FBI. As early as June 1958, FBI informants were reporting to the Bureau's New York office that Betty had attended the Afro-Asian Educational and Crafts Display sponsored by Temple No. 7 and held at the Park Palace on February 8, 1958; they also noted her participation in the 1958 Saviour's Day festivities in Chicago. Betty's indictment for assaulting a police officer and for "conspiracy" led to more extensive FBI digging. Her credit history was thoroughly checked, and the FBI learned that Betty had a series of money problems that predated her marriage to Malcolm. For example, in late 1957, two separate judgments were filed against Betty in Westchester County, New York, one for $546.57 owed to Budget Charge Account, Inc., and another for $742.42 to Sacks Quality Stores, Inc. What emerges from the FBI surveillance of her is a confident, independent-minded black nationalist who expressed herself well. An FBI informant observing a talk Betty gave in Chicago in early 1959 noted that she praised Elijah Muhammad "for providing jobs and opportunity to all of us." In her address, Betty outlined her own vision for the Nation's economic growth:

> We are going to have a bank of our own here in Chicago and we are going to loan money. This bank is being organized on paper now. Everytime there are enough members to get a number for a temple we are going to have a restaurant, dress shop, and bakery just like we have in Chicago. We are also going to open a health center here. We want educated members with college degrees to help us so they can help their own people.

Betty's lecture illustrates that she possessed a clear and expansive view of the NOI's future, based on an educated black middle class—people like herself. The point here is that she was not being manipulated by events; she was a committed, determined follower of Elijah Muhammad in her own right.

The case took nearly a year to go to trial, and in the intervening months Malcolm frequently made reference to what had happened. He also gave several speeches primarily based on the event. When in March 1959 the case was tried, only four of the six individuals originally arrested were prosecuted, including Betty Shabazz. The hearing lasted three weeks and at the time was the longest assault trial ever recorded in Queens County. Sixteen witnesses testified, as the defendants decried the police's actions as a blatant violation of their property and constitutional rights. The Nation was determined to dominate the environment of the trial. It brought its own stenographers and deployed FOI guards at the court's doors; anyone who entered the hallway leading to the trial room had their picture taken by one of three roaming NOI photographers.

After the defense rested, the jury, which included three African Americans, deliberated for thirteen hours. At three p.m. on March 18, the jury informed Judge Peter T. Farrell that it had reached a verdict, but the judge was so intimidated by the presence of hundreds of angry Muslims in the courthouse that he took the unusual step of clearing all spectators before the jury revealed its decision. Two of those charged, Betty Shabazz and Minnie Simmons, were exonerated. The jury deadlocked over Yvonne and John Molette without reaching a unanimous decision, freeing them, but subject to a second prosecution. After the verdict was read, the jury was escorted to the subway under a tense police guard, surrounded by hundreds of shouting Muslims. Standing before his members on the courthouse steps, Malcolm instructed, "Any policeman who abuses you belongs in the cemetery. Be peaceful, firm and aggressive but if one of them so much as touch your finger, die." The jury's inability to acquit all the accused, according to Malcolm, was the fault of Judge Farrell, who had employed "kangaroo tactics" to protect the police. He harshly criticized Farrell's "ambiguous interpretations of the law, and failure to charge the jury properly on key points that forced the jury into a deadlock."

Although Malcolm seldom referred to the case after 1960 or so, it was just as significant as the Johnson Hinton incident. The resolution to fight the case, and to identify it in civil rights terminology, created sympathy and solidarity among most blacks, even those who did not share the NOI's separatist views. Malcolm absorbed this lesson from this chaotic event: when the NOI came out in solidarity with civil rights and civil liberties groups addressing problems like police brutality that affected nearly all blacks, the NOI was rewarded with favorable media attention and swelling membership. Meanwhile, the FBI's New York office informed its director that it would "continue to follow LITTLE's activities" and issue a surveillance update every six months.

The FBI had the resources to hire scores of black informants to infiltrate the Nation, but it failed to comprehend the nature of the sect it had deemed so dangerous. It was convinced that the NOI was subversive because it promoted "black hate."

The FBI never understood that the NOI did not seek the destruction of America's legal and socioeconomic institutions; the Black Muslims were not radicals, but profound conservatives under Muhammad. They praised capitalism, so long as it served what they deemed blacks' interests. Their fundamental mistake was their unshakable belief that whites as a group would never transcend their hatred of blacks. The FBI also viewed the Islamic elements of the Nation as fraudulent. As a result, the Bureau never grasped the underlying concerns that motivated Malcolm and Elijah Muhammad, and how both men had constructed a dynamic organization that attracted the membership of tens of thousands of African Americans and the admiration of millions more. The NOI's theology certainly "demonized" whites, yet its program in many ways merely channeled the profound sense of alienation that already existed among working-class blacks, born of the reality of Southern Jim Crow segregation and Northern discrimination.

Malcolm and Muhammad did not look to the American political system to redeem itself or to solve the problems of "black Asiatics" in America. It would only be through the grace of Allah, and the building of strong black institutions, that blacks would rediscover their strengths. Malcolm at this time did not consider his pubic addresses "political," but rather spiritually inspired, based on the prophetic teachings of both the Qur'an and the Bible, in anticipation of the final days. A time would soon come, however, when the separation between spirituality and politics was no longer a tenable position.

CHAPTER 6

"The Hate That Hate Produced"

March 1959–January 1961

The questions Malcolm faced at the end of 1959 about the necessity of bold political action were not his alone to ponder. During the 1950s, as the civil rights movement grew, it contended with powerful internal struggles over how to move forward. There was not general agreement on the direction that black activism should take or even on the goals that needed to be achieved. While the NOI stood virtually alone in its rejection of direct action, many black leaders, including Malcolm, grew increasingly enamored with the ideals and successes of Third World revolutionaries. Some saw in the Marxist struggle a better way of defining and addressing racial conflict. In the era of McCarthyism, this ideological identification put additional pressure on civil rights groups as black leaders came under intense scrutiny from government agencies. Malcolm was by no means the only one deemed a threat to national security by the FBI.

Despite this pressure, and the general political swing toward conservatism in the postwar years, black activists continued to make significant advances. In December 1952, when *Brown v. Board of Education* came before the Supreme Court, the political world was still rigidly coded by black and white. "Separate but equal," as defined by the precedent of the Supreme Court's 1896 *Plessy v. Ferguson* decision, remained the law of the land. Yet the years leading up to the 1954 *Brown* decision saw changing circumstances that presaged its outcome. With the outlawing of the whites-only primary elections by the Supreme Court in 1944, many blacks throughout much of the South began voting for the first time. Between 1944 and 1952, the number of black registered voters there soared, from about 250,000 to nearly 1.25 million. In 1946, in its *Morgan v. Virginia* decision, the Supreme Court declared unconstitutional any state law requiring Jim Crow sections on interstate buses, a decision that prompted a new civil rights organization, the Congress of Racial Equality (CORE), to launch a series of nonviolent protests challenging local segregation laws on interstate public transport. In late 1955, King was catapulted to international prominence by his role in the Montgomery bus boycott, while in nearby Tuskegee, Alabama, blacks staged a three-year-long economic boycott of local white merchants in response to that state legislature's gerrymandering of nearly all black voters outside the town's boundaries. In 1960, the Supreme Court sided with Tuskegee's black protesters by declaring racial gerrymandering illegal.

These successes were the fruits of concerted efforts by a new generation of African-American leaders that supported confrontational challenge. In New York City, Ella Baker was elected branch president of New York City's NAACP in 1952, and went on to build interracial coalitions around two issues that affected nearly all blacks—police brutality and public school desegregation. Meanwhile, in Mississippi, NAACP field secretary Medgar Evers eschewed King's nonviolent approach for one of armed self-defense, committing himself to investigating and publicizing racist crimes. In 1957, Baker, Bayard Rustin, and liberal attorney/activist Stanley Levison drafted a series of papers to develop what would become the agenda of the new Southern Christian Leadership Conference (SCLC). What these individuals shared was a willingness to place their own lives at risk. They were all critical of the slow pace of reforms by older civil rights leaders; economic boycotts, civil disobedience, and youth organizing, they believed, should spearhead their protests.

The frightening specter of McCarthyism and virulent anticommunism had taken its toll among black liberals. America's most prominent African-American sociologist, E. Franklin Frazier, for example, had been investigated by the FBI for belonging to the Negro People's Committee to Aid Spanish Democracy in the 1930s. Educator and Eleanor Roosevelt confidante Mary McLeod Bethune was grilled by authorities for membership in the American Committee for the Protection of the Foreign Born. But the political virus had run its course, and as the anticommunist demagogues retreated, there was a rebirth of a black left, whose resurgent fortunes were symbolized by the status of controversial singer and actor Paul Robeson. Banished from stage and screen during the years of McCarthy repression, Robeson had had his passport confiscated by the State Department, yet in 1958 his comeback tour across the United States received strong support from the black community. These concerts coincided with the publication of his manifesto *Here I Stand*, part memoir and part political commentary, which emphasized the struggles for independence in Africa as well as the fight for civil rights within the United States. The book was widely praised in the African-American press, yet did little to endear Robeson to white authorities. When the prime minister of India, Jawaharlal Nehru, called for a national celebration of the singer's sixtieth birthday, the United States tried unsuccessfully to pressure his government to cancel the event.

Perhaps no single person better symbolized the trends toward militancy than Robert F. Williams. After serving in the military and working as a laborer, Williams returned home to North Carolina in 1955, where he soon joined campaigns for civil rights. His charisma and militancy attracted followers, and he was soon elected head of the Monroe, North Carolina, branch of the NAACP. Controversy first beset him in 1959 when, following the acquittal of a white man who had assaulted an African-American woman, Williams told the press that maybe blacks should "meet violence with violence in order to protect themselves." The NAACP national leader, Roy Wilkins, publicly distanced the association from these remarks and had Williams suspended. In turn, Williams's supporters condemned Wilkins's actions, which sparked a long-suppressed debate within the civil rights community.

Williams subsequently became involved in a well-publicized "kissing case," in which he defended two black boys—ages eight and ten—who had been jailed in Monroe for the crime of kissing a white girl. By mid-1961, tensions in Monroe surrounding the case had reached a boiling point. When the civil rights organizer James Forman visited the town, he was assaulted and thrown in jail simply for being associated with Williams. White gangs cruised the streets after dark searching for blacks to terrorize, to which the black community responded by arming itself. When a white couple mistakenly drove into a cordoned-off black district, Williams ordered that they be detained, to ensure their safety. Local authorities, however, promptly charged him with kidnapping.

The collective impact of Baker, Williams, and other militants pushed organizations like the NAACP toward greater activism, pressuring both major political parties to adopt new legislation. In 1957, Congress passed a weak civil rights act that established an advisory group, the Commission on Civil Rights. The SCLC responded by initiating the Crusade for Citizenship Campaign, which broadened its strategic agenda to include voter registration and civic education. Organized by Ella Baker, the campaign held press conferences and rallies in more than two dozen cities.

The fire of this new activism burned brightest in the South, but it also had a profound effect on Northern black communities, where legal segregation may not have existed but patterns of exclusion were deep and long-standing. In September 1957, inspired by the struggle earlier that year to desegregate Little Rock, Arkansas's Central High School, New York activists picketed city hall in protest against racial discrimination in public schools.

Some activists concluded that they should run for office, perhaps figuring that creating legislation would be more effective than merely agitating for it. Their model was attorney Benjamin Davis, Jr., a communist who represented Harlem in the New York City Council from 1943 to 1949. Even after his political views got him convicted for violating the 1940 Alien Registration Act, known generally as the Smith Act, in a losing bid for Manhattan reelection in 1949, Davis won more Harlem votes than in his previous elections. On a similarly progressive agenda, Ella Baker ran unsuccessfully for the New York City Council in both 1951 and 1953. The attorney Pauli Murray, who would later defend Robert Williams before a national hearing of the NAACP, also ran for the council. But although Hulan Jack was elected Manhattan's first African-American borough president in 1953, New York blacks continued to be underrepresented. In 1954, for instance, more than one million of the state's fourteen million residents were African Americans, yet they had only one of New York's forty-three members of Congress; one of its fifty-eight state senators; just five of the 150 state assembly members; and ten of its 189 judges.

In Harlem, activism took a cultural turn. From 1951 to 1955, radicals there published a newspaper called *Freedom*. Some anticommunist black nationalists, such as the writer Harold Cruse, criticized the paper's orientation as "nothing more than integration, couched in left-wing phraseology." The paper soon closed, but in early 1961 many of its old staff established a new quarterly, *Freedomways*, as a link between black communists, independent radicals, and the left wing of the civil rights movement. For nationalists like Cruse, however, even the new magazine was compromised, due to its associations with the Marxist left.

Despite such ideological misgivings, the majority of the new generation of radicals increasingly came under the influence of the black left, best illustrated by the growing African-American fascination with Cuba. In January 1959, an unlikely band of guerrilla fighters led by Fidel Castro had wrested control of the country from dictator Fulgencio Batista. Though Castro traveled to Washington in April to reassure the Eisenhower administration of his good intentions, the U.S. government quickly concluded that the new regime was anti-American and set to work trying to destabilize it. American radicals who sympathized with the young revolution responded by establishing the Fair Play for Cuba Committee, which attracted such notable intellectuals as Allen Ginsberg, C. Wright Mills, and I. F. Stone. A significant number of African-American artists and political activists joined the committee, or at least publicly endorsed Castro's revolution. These included journalists William Worthy and Richard Gibson, writers James Baldwin, John Oliver Killens, and Julian Mayfield—and, unsurprisingly, Robert Williams.

In June 1960, the committee sponsored Williams's first trip to Cuba, and the following month organized an African-American delegation, which he led. Its members included Mayfield, playwright/poet LeRoi Jones (later Amiri Baraka), historian John Henrik Clarke, and Harold Cruse. Even for bitter anticommunists like Cruse, the experience was inspirational. "The ideology of a new revolutionary wave in the world at large," he observed, "had lifted us out of anonymity of lonely struggle in the United States to the glorified rank of visiting dignitaries." But Cruse struggled to maintain his objectivity—much as Malcolm did under similar circumstances several years later when he visited Africa. To Cruse the fundamental questions to be answered were, "What did it all mean and how did it relate to the Negro in America?" A significant lesson, he wrote, reflecting the increasingly militant feelings among black activists, was "the relevance of force and violence to successful revolutions."

As the civil rights movement adopted an increasingly confrontational approach involving a mix of protest and politics, Malcolm and the NOI watched from a distance. Holding fast to its doctrine of strict separatism, the Nation had little to contribute to the dialogue over how best to change the existing order. Many of the Nation's leaders did not truly understand the growing civil rights struggle; they were still convinced that they should distance themselves from anything controversial or subversive. Yet when it came to competing for the minds of black Americans, the issue-based platforms and forceful personalities within the Black Freedom Movement presented a direct challenge to the NOI. The positive press coverage received by King and other civil rights leaders gave them a relevance to political realities that the NOI lacked.

In a letter written in April 1959 to James 3X Shabazz, the newly appointed minister of Temple No. 25 in Newark, Muhammad expressed concern about "the all too frequent clashes with Law Enforcement Agents that we, the

Believers of Islam, are being involved in." He was troubled by the confrontation in Malcolm's home between the NYPD and the NOI members, as well as by the publicity surrounding the subsequent trial. "Whenever an officer comes to serve a notice or to arrest you, you should not resist whether you are innocent or guilty," he instructed. "We must *remember* that we are not in power in Washington, nor where we live, to dictate to the authorities. . . . Lawyers, bonds and fines are expensive, and being beat up and bruised is too painful to bear for nothing." Allah would ultimately punish those who had mistreated his followers. "But, *remember* that you should not be the *cause* for them to take the opportunity to mistreat you, since you now know that the devil has no Justice for you."

Privately, Malcolm disagreed. The extensive press coverage around the trial of the Molettes, Minnie Simmons, and Betty, he thought, generally presented the Nation of Islam in a favorable light. "If it had not been for the on-the-spot reporting of the *Amsterdam News* from the very beginning of the case," he wrote in a public letter, "these innocent people would now be behind bars." He astutely linked the NOI's confrontation with the police to the larger struggle for civil rights and the need for a crusading African-American press. Some of "Malcolm's Ministers" inside the NOI surely felt the same way.

He was looking beyond the NOI, to non-Islamic black Americans, and making overtures to blacks outside the Nation—as indeed he had done for several years. It was during this time that he was contacted by a young African-American representative of the local television station WNTA Channel 13, Louis Lomax, who was preparing a series of television programs about the NOI. Lomax was working on the project with another journalist, Mike Wallace, who by the late 1950s had become a familiar presence on New York–area television.

The two men had different reasons for approaching the NOI. Wallace was in his late thirties and had extensive media experience, but was still looking for his big break. Given Malcolm's and the Nation's rising profile, he sensed the possibility of controversy in exposing the NOI's divisive racial ideas before a large audience. Lomax's interests were more complicated. Born in 1922 in Valdosta, Georgia, he had earned a bachelor's degree from Paine College, as well as master's degrees from American University and Yale (in 1944 and 1947 respectively). While studying at Yale, he had flourished, hosting a weekly radio program that "marked the first time a Negro had written and presented his own dramatic skits over the air in the District of Columbia." But by 1949 he had fallen on harder times. After moving to

Chicago's South Side, he became involved in a scam leasing rental cars in Indiana and driving them to Chicago to be sold. The police easily tracked down the stolen cars and busted him; he was convicted of a series of larcenies and remained behind bars until paroled in November 1954, during which time his wife had divorced him.

In 1956, he had an unexpected reversal of fortune. That February, his parole officer gave him permission to work for the Associated Negro Press in Washington. The opportunity revitalized Lomax; during the next three years, he placed articles in such newspapers as the *New York Daily News* and the *New York Daily Mirror* and analytical pieces in magazines such as *Pageant, Coronet,* and *The Nation.* Through these his name reached Wallace, who offered him the job of conducting preinterviews with guests prior to their appearance on his show. It was Lomax who came up with the idea of a series devoted to the NOI, having secured Elijah Muhammad's approval through Malcolm. Lomax may also have shared with Malcolm his history in prison, which would have strengthened their relationship.

Ideologically Lomax was an integrationist, yet he found much to admire in the self-sufficiency and racial pride exuded by Nation members. The NOI gave him permission to film Muhammad at a rally in Washington on May 31. After weeks compiling footage, Lomax delivered the reels to Wallace, who edited and narrated the series for maximum shock value. The confrontational title, *The Hate That Hate Produced,* was a covert appeal to white liberals, which reflected Wallace's politics. After all, white America had tolerated slavery and racial segregation for centuries. Was it really so surprising that a minority of Negroes had become as racist as many whites?

The Wallace/Lomax series appeared on New York City's WNTA-TV in five half-hour installments, from July 13 to July 17. One week later, the channel aired a one-hour documentary hosted by Wallace on the black supremacy movement, comprising segments from the earlier broadcasts. It was probably fortunate that Malcolm was out of the country when the programs appeared, because they sparked a firestorm. Civil rights leaders, sensing a publicity disaster, could not move quickly enough to distance themselves. Arnold Forster, head of the Anti-Defamation League's civil rights division, charged that Wallace had exaggerated the size of the NOI and given it an "importance that was not warranted." Other critics took issue with the series itself. In the *New York Times,* Jack Gould declared: "The periodic tendency of Mike Wallace to pursue sensationalism as an end in itself backfired. . . . To transmit the wild statements of rabble-rousers without at least some pertinent facts in refutation is not conscientious or constructive reporting." Malcolm himself thought the show had demonized the Nation, and likened its impact to "what happened back in the 1930s when Orson Welles frightened America with a radio program describing, as though it was actually happening, an invasion by 'men from Mars.'" But part of Malcolm always believed that even negative publicity was better than none at all.

Outcry notwithstanding, the show had effectively brought the NOI to a much wider audience. There was an "instant avalanche of public reaction," recalled Malcolm. "Hundreds of thousands of New Yorkers, black and white, were exclaiming 'Did you hear it? Did you see it? Preaching *hate* of white people!'" The controversy spread quickly. After the negative response from the New York press, the national weeklies followed, characterizing the NOI as "black racists," "black fascists," and even "possibly Communist-inspired." Faced with heated criticism from the African-American community, Malcolm dismissed his black middle-class opponents as Uncle Toms.

The intense publicity changed the lives of nearly everyone connected with the series. It gave Wallace the break he needed; the national exposure led to an offer from a group of Westinghouse-owned stations to cover the 1960 presidential campaign, and in three years he was hosting the national morning news for CBS. Later, he would turn down Republican presidential candidate Richard Nixon's offer to become his press secretary, instead accepting a new assignment as a reporter on CBS's *60 Minutes*, which became the longest-running news feature program in television history. Lomax also achieved success, in 1960 publishing his first book, *The Reluctant African*, which won the Anisfield-Wolf award. His reports on civil rights issues were regularly featured on network television. Both Wallace and Lomax continued to exploit their connections with the NOI. On July 26, 1959, however, the NOI barred Wallace from a massive rally at New York's St. Nicholas Arena, which featured Elijah Muhammad as keynote speaker. At this event Muhammad accused Wallace and other white journalists of attempting to divide the NOI into factions. "Does he classify the truth as Hate?" he asked. "No enemy wants to see the so-called American Negro free and united."

Inside the Nation, Malcolm's critics blamed him for the negative publicity surrounding *Hate*. NOI ministers who were against media interviews now felt justified in banning members from talking to the press. The view from Chicago headquarters, however, was much less severe. When a young doctoral student, C. Eric Lincoln, asked for help with his dissertation about the NOI, Muhammad, Malcolm, and other Muslims consented. Lincoln's study, published in 1961 under the title *The Black Muslims in America*, became the standard work for decades. As the dust settled, even Lomax found his way back into the Nation's good graces. When he subsequently approached the NOI to write his own book about the sect, its leaders were generous with their time. Lomax's 1963 study *When the Word Is Given* is perhaps the single best resource about the NOI's inner workings prior to Malcolm's split from the sect. Despite his own commitment to racial integration, Lomax tried to present a balanced, objective critique of the NOI's strengths and weaknesses. He correctly identified the malaise among working-class blacks that several years later would feed the anger beneath Black Power. Lomax quoted the ever-eloquent James Baldwin: "Deep down in their hearts the black masses don't believe in white people anymore. They don't believe in Malcolm, either, except when he articulates their disbelief in white people. . . . The Negro masses neither join nor denounce the Black Muslims. They just sit at home in the ghetto amid the heat, the roaches, the rats, the vice, the disgrace, and rue the fact that come daylight they must meet the man—the white man—and work at a job that leads only to a dead end."

Within the Nation itself, the most lasting impact of the series was the recognition that the sect had to exert greater control over its image. This required, at a minimum, a regularly published magazine or newspaper. In the fall of 1959, Malcolm produced his first attempt, *Messenger Magazine*; he may have been drawing upon an older Harlem tradition, as a previous paper named the *Messenger*, edited by A. Philip Randolph and Chandler Owen, had been published from 1917 to 1928. The *Amsterdam News* advertisement promoting the journal promised it would present "Mr. Muhammad's aims and accomplishments" and "the truth about the amazing success of the Moslems' economic, educational, and spiritual growth among the Negroes of America." The magazine failed to gain an audience, however, as did several other publishing ventures, until in 1960 Malcolm started printing a monthly newspaper, *Muhammad Speaks*. Temples began receiving hundreds of copies, and the publication quickly attracted tens of thousands of regular readers, the vast majority of them non-Muslims. The keys to its success were twofold. First, the publication hired legitimate, well-qualified journalists, who were given some leeway to cover their interests. Over time, the newspaper developed a schizophrenic character, with some articles praising Muhammad and promoting the NOI and the rest of the paper providing detailed coverage of black American issues, Africa, and the Third

World. But the second reason was that all temples were ordered to sell a certain number of copies per week; the papers were doled out to individual FOI laborers, who were expected to place *Muhammad Speaks* everywhere.

Malcolm used the shake-up from *Hate* to recommend Temple No. 7's secretary, John X Simmons, for the position of national secretary. Within a year Simmons would move to Chicago and be given an original name, John Ali, by Elijah Muhammad. The promotion pleased Malcolm, who believed he would have another strong ally in Chicago. He did not imagine that Ali would become one of his sharpest critics in the national headquarters.

———

After the ordeal of Betty's trial, Malcolm decided that she and Attallah needed to be sent temporarily to her parents' home in Detroit. Betty was opposed to the move, but she bent to Malcolm's will. Her feelings did not change upon settling in, however, and in late March 1959 she complained to her husband about the arrangement, though he had little sympathy. He encouraged her to think about her absence from New York as a vacation. Though Betty worried for him in her absence, he assured her that he would survive. He missed her cooking, writing her that he had been eating regularly at the Temple's restaurant. He found it difficult to express romantic love, or even to give Betty a compliment without qualifying it with a statement related to the NOI. For instance, he praised Betty's cooking, but then added, "What would we Brothers do without our wonderful MGT Sisters? (smile)."

Betty's involuntary "vacation" may have given Malcolm space, but it further taxed his already strained finances. On April 1 he sent her a second letter, enclosing twenty dollars. Malcolm urged her to spend as little as possible, reminding her that he was experiencing a "great financial burden." He then reminded her that the airfare to Detroit had been expensive and that staying in Detroit would also be costly. Malcolm went on to offer a statement that seems almost comically paradoxical. He urged her again to "enjoy yourself but don't buy anything" except items that were absolutely essential. To save money he instructed her not to phone him, but instead write a letter. He even enclosed some stamps in the envelope he mailed to her. Feeling spurned and stranded, Betty once again fell into a depression and entertained thoughts about fleeing her marriage. By this time Malcolm viewed his wife largely as a nuisance—someone he was obliged to put up with—rather than as a loving life partner. The wounds from Betty's sexual taunting were still too fresh. He focused his energies instead on the Nation and the major events it had planned for 1959.

The largest public occasion involving Malcolm that year was a major rally and speech by Elijah Muhammad in July, at New York City's St. Nicholas Arena. Muhammad declared that he and the Nation were "backed by 500 million people, who are lifting their voices to Allah five times a day." In effect, he was laying claim to full membership within Islam's global community, a notion that would have been vigorously rejected by the vast majority of orthodox Muslims in the United States. Within the small, mostly Sunni emigrant communities that traced their lineage to the Middle East, southern Asia, and northern Africa, Muslims understood the NOI to have little in common with their faith. "Let us fervently pray that the readers of *The Courier* will not confuse the sect of Mr. Muhammad with that of true Islam," wrote Yasuf Ibrahim, an Algerian, in a letter to the Pittsburgh paper. "Believers in Allah recognize no such thing as race."

Perhaps to quell outside critics, the Nation took several measures to affirm its connections with the global Islamic community. Muhammad began his 1960 publication *Message to the Blackman in America* with a Qur'anic verse: "He it is who sent His Messenger with the guidance and the true religion, that He may make it overcome the religions, all of them, though the polytheists may be adverse." One regular feature in *Muhammad Speaks*, Muslim Cookbook, provided recipes that adhered to *halal* criteria. Arabic-language instructors were hired in NOI schools, and ministers were encouraged to make references to the Qur'an during their sermons. The most prominent woman of Temple No. 7, Tynetta Deanar, started a column in *Muhammad Speaks* on the global achievements of Islamic women.

It was in this spirit of confraternity that the NOI had cabled its congratulations to the Afro-Asian Solidarity Conference, held from December 26, 1957, to January 1, 1958, in Cairo, under the auspices of Egypt's president, Gamal Abdel Nasser. The sect had much to gain from recognition or even acknowledgment by major Muslim states, and Egypt. Nasser reciprocated the gesture the following year by sending greetings to Elijah Muhammad at the Saviour's Day convention. This was followed by an invitation from Nasser's government to Muhammad to visit Egypt and to make the hajj to Mecca. Muhammad planned to visit the Middle East, but he encountered some difficulties from the U.S. government regarding overseas travel. The decision was made to send Malcolm first, as Muhammad's emissary. Malcolm would establish the necessary contacts for Muhammad and members of his family to follow.

Malcolm was undoubtedly thrilled to receive the assignment, but in proper NOI tradition he could not display excessive enthusiasm. He duly applied for a passport. His stated itinerary was to visit the United Kingdom, Germany, Italy, Greece, Egypt, Lebanon, Turkey, Saudi Arabia, and Sudan, intending to depart on June 5 in order to attend "the annual sacred Moslem Pilgrimage Rites at the Holy City of Mecca," scheduled from June 9 to June 16. For various reasons, however, his journey was delayed, so he continued carrying out his duties throughout June.

When he finally arrived in Cairo on July 4, it marked the beginning of a transformative experience. Malcolm was now an international traveler, the welcome guest of heads of state, and a pilgrim in the lands of the faith that had pulled him up from despair. In Egypt, deputy premier Anwar el-Sadat met with him several times, and he was well received by religious leaders at Al-Azhar University. Nasser offered to meet him personally, but Malcolm politely demurred, explaining that "he was just the forerunner and humble servant of Elijah Muhammad." He planned to stay briefly in Egypt before visiting Mecca and touring Saudi Arabia at length, but shortly after his arrival he fell ill with dysentery and ended up spending eleven days there. During his stay, a series of prominent Egyptians extended overnight accommodations in their homes to him. Having long practiced the NOI's peculiar version of Islam, Malcolm found himself embarrassed at times by his lack of formal knowledge of the Muslim religion. While in Egypt he was expected to participate in prayers with others five times daily, but confessed to an acquaintance that he didn't understand the Arabic language, and had "only a sketchy notion of the [prayer] ritual."

When his dysentery finally abated, he traveled to Saudi Arabia, where enslavement of people of African descent had existed for more than fifteen hundred years. From the perspective of most black Americans, Saudi Arabia would have appeared to be a nonwhite society, with blacks relegated to the bottom. Writing from the Kandara Palace hotel in Jeddah, he described the physical appearance of the Saudi population as ranging "from regal black to rich brown, but none are white." Most Arabs, he noted, "would be right at home in Harlem. And all of them refer warmly to our people in America as their 'brothers of color.'" His own race, so long the prism of his self-definition, receded in importance. "Many Egyptians didn't identify him as negroid because of his color until they saw him closer," noted one of his fellow travelers. The episode taught Malcolm that racial identities were not fixed: what was "black" in one country could be white or mulatto in another. The absence of a rigid color line apparently suggested to Malcolm that "there is no color prejudice among Moslems, for Islam teaches that all mortals are equal and brothers."

Three weeks of mixing with commoners and statesmen in the Middle East also reinforced Malcolm's commitment to Pan-Africanism. "Africa is the land of the future," he wrote in a letter home that was eventually published by the *Pittsburgh Courier*.

Only yesterday, America was the New World, a world with a future—but now, we suddenly realize Africa is the New World—the world with the brightest future—a future in which the so-called American Negroes are destined to play a key role.

Throughout his trip, he kept listeners rapt with talk of the importance of the NOI, and of the cruel suppression American blacks faced at the hands of whites. Writing of their outraged reaction, he explained that "the increasing hordes of intelligent Africans find it difficult to understand" why black Americans continued to be oppressed, "without real freedom, without public school rights, and above all, relegated to slums. . . . The chief instrument by which East and West are being divided, day and night, is resentment in Africa and Asia for administrative jim-crow in the United States." This insight underlined the need to broaden the international perspective within the Black Freedom Movement. By cultivating alliances with Third World nations, black Americans could gain leverage to achieve racial empowerment.

There were several reasons to believe that such a strategy could produce results. First, a significant number of African leaders, like Ghana's Kwame Nkrumah, either had attended U.S. universities or had visited the United States and were familiar with its system of racial oppression. Black churches, colleges, and civic associations since the mid-nineteenth century had contacts or exchanges with African institutions. This was especially the case in South Africa, where the parallels between apartheid and legal Jim Crow were obvious. Finally, a good number of revolutionary anticolonial movements, such as Algeria's National Liberation Front, were noncommunist. Black Americans could work with representatives of such movements without being red-baited at home.

Malcolm's letter, filled with new ideas about Islam and Afro-Asian solidarity, found him at a philosophical crossroads. The attitudes toward race expressed by Muslims he encountered on his trip had revealed to him fundamental contradictions within NOI theology. Islam was in theory color-blind; members of the *ummah* could be any nationality or race, so long as they practiced the five pillars and other essential traditions. Whites could not be categorically demonized. Malcolm came to realize during this trip that if the NOI were to continue growing, its sectarian concepts and practices, such as Yacub's History, might have to be abandoned, and the assimilation of orthodox Islam would need to be accelerated. Pan-Africanism presented a different problem. Using Third World solidarity to leverage change in America came to seem increasingly viable, yet this premise contradicted the NOI's dogma that reforms were impossible to achieve under white rule and that peace required a separate black state. Most troublingly, there was the question of leadership. The *shahada* confirms that only Muhammad is the final prophet of God; to move closer to true Islam meant that Elijah's claim to be "Allah's Messenger" would inevitably have to be questioned.

Perhaps because the trip marked the beginning of Malcolm's private concerns with the NOI's organization, he was virtually silent about it in the *Autobiography*. He could obviously see the discrepancies between what he had been taught by Elijah Muhammad compared to the richly diverse cultures that he had observed. All Muslims clearly were not "black." Malcolm's letter to the *Pittsburgh Courier*, however, as well as stories he recalled of his experiences, conveyed how vividly the trip impressed itself on his mind. Its lessons continued to be heard in the developing philosophy that he expressed through his public speeches.

Malcolm's 1959 tour was widely publicized both within the NOI and by African-American newspapers. Yet after he returned on July 22, he spoke only briefly about his trip, focusing instead on the controversy created by *The Hate That Hate Produced*. He tried to convey what he had learned about the Islamic world to Temple No. 7 members, and even then he spoke carefully, perhaps trying to avoid presenting ideas that might seem at odds with the NOI's basic tenets. "Muslims in the Far East," he said, "were intensely curious to learn how it was that he professed to be Muslim, yet spoke no Arabic." He had explained to them that he had been "kidnapped 400 years ago, robbed of his language, of religion and robbed of his name and wisdom."

Plans moved forward for Elijah Muhammad to make his own trip. Sometime during the first half of November 1959, Muhammad set out with two of his sons, Herbert and Akbar. He later claimed to have accomplished a hajj, but because his journey to Mecca took place outside of the officially sanctioned hajj season, technically he had made *umrah*, a spiritually motivated visit, even though the *umrah* is widely accepted throughout the Muslim world as a legitimate pilgrimage. More important was the official acceptance of Muhammad and his small delegation by Saudi authorities, who controlled access to the city for worshippers.

Muhammad arrived back home on January 6, 1960. Like Malcolm, he had been profoundly affected, and set about implementing changes to give the NOI a stronger Islamic character. At the next month's Saviour's Day convention, he ordered that the NOI's temples would henceforth be called mosques, in keeping with orthodox Islam. More significantly, the pace of Islamization was accelerated. Arabic-language instruction increased, and he sent his son Akbar to study at Al-Azhar University in Cairo; yet he must have seen, as Malcolm had, that his own position presented special challenges when it came to reconciling the NOI with orthodox Islam. His authority, and indeed much of the wealth and property he had accrued, derived from his special (if fictive) status as Allah's Messenger—a status he had no intention of relinquishing. To maintain his supremacy while remaking the face of the NOI would prove a difficult balancing act.

"1960 may well prove to be a year of decision for the American Negro." Thus spoke radical attorney William Kunstler, opening a debate between Malcolm and the Reverend William M. James on New York City's WMCA radio early that year. Across the South sit-ins and protests had been multiplying, with Negro students refusing to vacate their seats at lunch counters that would not serve them and standing firm in stores that asked them to leave. The mixed experience Malcolm had had with *The Hate That Hate Produced* reinforced the value of presenting the NOI's views in a favorable light, so when early in 1960 New York local radio station WMCA proposed a debate between him and James, the liberal pastor of Metropolitan Community United Methodist Church in Harlem, he accepted the invitation.

Kunstler pressed Malcolm right away. "Roy Wilkins, the executive director of the NAACP, has described your Temple of Islam as being no better than the Ku Klux Klan. You think this is an adequate comment?" Malcolm at once characterized Wilkins's comment as ignorant: "I very much doubt, if Mr. Wilkins was familiar with Mr. Muhammad and his program, that he would make such charges." When Kunstler grew agitated and cited press accounts of NOI members calling whites "inhuman devils," Malcolm defended the cause of "racial extremism" by framing it as a form of exceptionalism common to religious groups. Catholics and Baptists, he pointed out, both claimed the only way to get to heaven was through membership in their respective churches. "And Jews themselves for thousands of years have been taught that they alone are God's chosen people . . . I find it difficult for Catholics and Christians to accuse us of teaching or advancing any kind of racial supremacy or racial hatred, because their history and their own teachings are filled with it."

Whether or not 1960 proved to be the year of the American Negro, it saw Malcolm finding an audience beyond the black community, and his fame growing. He tried hard to maintain a regular presence at Mosque No. 7, but his speaking engagements continued at a rapid clip. In March, he lectured to students from Harvard, Boston, and MIT at a seminar hosted at Boston University. His formal remarks lasted barely ten minutes; the question and answer exchange went on for more than two hours. He also delivered a lecture at an NAACP-sponsored event at Queens College in May, significant because it marked the first time that the civil rights organization had provided a platform to a black leader who so sharply opposed its policies.

However, the most important address he gave that year was on May 28 at the Harlem Freedom Rally, which the NOI organized with more than a dozen other local black groups. The rally was held at the intersection of Harlem's West 125th Street and Seventh Avenue, where an estimated four thousand people attending the five-hour-long program were packed in shoulder to shoulder in the streets and along the sidewalks. Before the rally started, loudspeakers blared out Louis X's calypso song "A White Man's Heaven Is a Black Man's Hell." When Malcolm took to the stage, he delivered a speech that departed from his typical remarks of the time. He made a consciously broad appeal, focusing not on the NOI but on "the black people of Harlem, the black people of America, and the black people all over this earth." At times, he even sounded King-like: "We are not here at this rally because we have already gained freedom. No! We are gathered here rallying for the freedom which we have long been promised, but have as yet not received." Throughout his remarks, he used the racially inclusive language of the civil rights cause—"freedom," "equality," and "justice"—as the framework for building an all-black militant coalition based in the Harlem ghetto. Negroes aligned with the NAACP and National Urban League would find it difficult to argue against such rhetoric, which had neatly appropriated their own.

A central purpose of the rally, Malcolm told his audience, was to listen to a variety of African-American leaders, including some "who have been acting as our spokesmen, and representing us to the white man downtown." He offered no criticism of moderates, instead emphasizing the necessity for Harlem's blacks to overcome the divisions in their community. His emphasis on the need for a united front projected an image of pragmatism and moderation, a remarkable turn for a man who only months earlier had attacked integrationist leaders as Uncle Toms. The speech met with tremendous success and was largely responsible for transforming Malcolm into a respected political leader in Harlem's civic life. Whether the NYPD's BOSS division knew ahead of time about his intentions, it assigned six detectives to attend the rally. One, a black officer named Ernest B. Latty, was apparently so disturbed by the song "A White Man's Heaven" that he purchased the record and attached it to his report. Reactions among the detectives in general raised enough concern to result in a significant increase in BOSS's surveillance.

As Malcolm's schedule of media appearances, college lectures, and speeches grew throughout 1960, so did criticism of him within the NOI. To demonstrate his loyalty, he attended many of Muhammad's public talks, while keeping track of local mosques and devoting himself to Mosque No. 7 at all hours. He also promoted a cult around Muhammad, suggesting that the "apostle" could commit no sins or errors of judgment. "If you look at the development of the Nation of Islam," Louis Farrakhan explained, "it was Brother Malcolm who started referring to Elijah as 'the Honorable' Elijah, and who started making us say—over and over again—'Messenger Elijah Muhammad taught me' or 'Messenger Elijah Muhammad teaches us.' He was driving the point home that Elijah Muhammad was a messenger of God."

Malcolm's high profile continued to generate speaking invitations at major universities, which introduced him to a significantly larger—and whiter—audience than any of his coworkers inside the Nation. FBI informants even reported that Malcolm might run for public office. On October 20, at Yale Law School auditorium, he was matched with Herbert Wright, the NAACP's national youth secretary. Before a standing-room-only crowd, Wright predictably promoted the cause of racial integration, calling for the use of "litigation, education, and legislation" to achieve reforms. Malcolm rejected this in favor of the total separation of the races. At the end of the debate, NOI members circulated among the throng of white students, selling records featuring "A White Man's Heaven Is a Black Man's Hell." The debate with Wright represented, on balance, a retreat from the positions favoring civil rights that Malcolm had expressed at the Harlem rally only months before. The emphasis on strict racial separation probably was prompted by Malcolm's desire to make a clear distinction with the NAACP in front of a mostly white audience.

The brutal pace of travel continued throughout the second half of 1960. Although NOI-related business consumed most of his energies, Malcolm continued to look for ways to reach a wider public. The radio interviews and debates reached a largely intellectual and middle-class audience. What he was looking for was a way to establish himself on a par with other national and international leaders.

As fate would have it, an opportunity to crash international headlines came gift wrapped from the Cuban Revolution. In September 1960, Cuban prime minister Fidel Castro traveled to New York City to attend the United Nations General Assembly. Across Harlem, news of his impending trip set off great excitement among leaders of the local black left. They quickly arranged a welcoming committee, which Malcolm joined. When the Cuban delegation arrived, it checked in to the well-appointed Shelburne Hotel on Lexington Avenue at 37th Street. Tensions soon ran high: the Cubans already felt insulted by the State Department, which had confined the eighty-five-member delegation's freedom of travel to Manhattan Island. Then a dispute arose over the bill at the Shelburne, with an outraged Castro accusing the hotel of making "unacceptable cash demands." At first, he threatened to move his entourage to Central Park. "We are mountain people," he explained proudly. "We are used to sleeping in the open air." United Nations secretary-general Dag Hammarskjöld scrambled to secure lodgings for them at the midtown Commodore Hotel, but he was too late: Malcolm and the Harlem welcoming committee had swooped in and invited the Cubans to stay at the Hotel Theresa, at Seventh Avenue and 125th Street. The eleven-story hotel had three hundred guest rooms; the new guests reserved forty of them, in addition to two suites, one of which was for Fidel.

A *Washington Post* writer speculated that "Castro, who has made overtures to U.S. Negro leaders to support his left-leaning revolution, apparently was trying to get as much propaganda as possible out of his move." The Soviet premier, Nikita Khrushchev, who was attending the same UN session, immediately sensed an opportunity, and within hours drove uptown and met with Castro for the first time. Meanwhile, thousands of Harlemites thronged the hotel to witness the comings and goings of the delegation and the various visits by international dignitaries. It wasn't long before a mix of political groups entered the crowd, pushing their own agendas: black nationalists who promoted the cause of deposed Congolese premier Patrice Lumumba, civil rights activists favoring desegregation, pro-Castro demonstrators, and even some beatniks from Greenwich Village. One placard read: "Man, like us cats dig Fidel the most. He knows what's hip and bugs the squares."

Malcolm's membership on the welcoming committee put him in a prime position to turn the visit into an opportunity. Late in the evening of September 19, he and a few NOI lieutenants were granted an hour with Castro. Details of their conversation are at best sketchy; Benjamin 2X Goodman later claimed that Malcolm attempted to "fish" Castro, inviting him to join the NOI. Yet Malcolm surely sensed that any official relationship, while useful, would create great difficulties for him with the authorities. One report suggests that, after the meeting, Malcolm was repeatedly invited to visit Cuba, but made no commitments. Whatever transpired, he was clearly impressed by Castro personally and viewed this new connection as a diplomatic resource that the NOI could exploit. On September 21, speaking at Mosque No. 7, Malcolm instructed all FOI members to stand on "twenty-four-hour alert" so long as Castro remained in Harlem. He added that Castro was "friendly" to the Muslims. An FBI informant reported that "the FOI was being alerted to assist Castro in the event of any anti-Castro demonstrations."

Though *Muhammad Speaks* eventually became a staunch defender of the Cuban Revolution, at the time Elijah Muhammad was extremely unhappy about the meeting between Malcolm and Castro. Since his return from the Middle East, his chronic pulmonary illness had worsened, and for all Malcolm's efforts to venerate Muhammad, speculation remained rife throughout the Nation over whether Malcolm or Wallace Muhammad might soon assume the role of national leader. Since speaking together at the Feast of the Followers in 1957, Malcolm and Wallace had grown closer, despite Wallace's increasing rejection of his father's theology and his disgust with what he saw as graft on the part of advisers like Raymond and Ethel Sharrieff. Malcolm's militant attitude rubbed off on Wallace to the point that some NOI leaders worried about the potency of a potential alliance. Mosque No. 4 minister Lucius X Brown complained that the duo might "talk Elijah Muhammad into marching on the White House." Even if Muhammad did not want to, Lucius suggested, "Malcolm and Wallace were after Muhammad's job and Muhammad might do it to save face."

The possibility of this power pairing appeared to be dashed on March 23, 1960, when Wallace Muhammad was convicted in federal court for refusing to be drafted into the military. In June of that same year, he was sentenced to three years' incarceration. Wallace's attorney appealed the decision, claiming him as a conscientious objector. While the appeal crawled through the system, Wallace continued his activities building the Philadelphia mosque, and he was a frequent visitor to Harlem Mosque No. 7. For example, on January 29, 1961, when Malcolm was away on an extended lecture tour, Wallace was advertised as the featured speaker at Mosque No. 7 in the *Amsterdam News*. At an October 1961 hearing, Wallace's appeal was finally denied, and he was ordered to turn himself in for incarceration in a federal prison. On October 30, Wallace began serving a three-year term at the Federal Correctional Institution in Sandstone, Minnesota. Wallace Muhammad was paroled on January 10, 1963, and he immediately returned to resume his minister's appointment at Mosque No. 12 in Philadelphia.

Wallace's absence from NOI organizational life tended to increase paranoid rumors and fears about Malcolm, especially among Elijah Muhammad's other children. Some of the hostility directed at Malcolm grew from his organizational function. As a national overseer, his responsibilities included resolving local feuds between members of various mosques. The role of troubleshooter was an unenviable one, because Malcolm was frequently forced to impose the authority of Chicago headquarters over local leaders who sought the semiautonomy and flexibility that he himself enjoyed.

Facing growing strife, Malcolm was concerned about protecting his allies within the NOI. No one was more important to him than Louis X Walcott. Louis had worked directly under Malcolm in New York City from October 1955 to July 1956, enough time for him to incorporate Malcolm's oratorical style into his own. But when he had become Boston's minister in 1957, he had considerable difficulty handling the job. He feared that he was unqualified, with the mosque having attracted a number of professionals far more experienced in business and civic affairs than he was. Farrakhan recalled: "[Malcolm] would come and look after his little brother and give me pointers. And Malcolm would go out in the street, man, and listen to the people, go in barbershops—'What do you think about the mosque?' And he would get the outside view of me and us. And he would come back and tell me what the people were saying and correct me."

Malcolm was determined that his protégé become a national figure in his own right, and encouraged him to write two plays, *Orgena* and *The Trial*, both of which became wildly popular when performed before Muslim audiences. But before long Louis needed a different kind of help. Ella Collins, newly converted to the NOI, had quickly become leader of those who wanted Louis deposed. Years later he would describe her as a "genius woman," then adding, "But in my weakness in administrative skill, she saw that weakness and raised a group in opposition to me." With the same boundless energy with which she had established educational programs within the temple, she threw herself into battle. As tensions mounted, a fire broke out in Louis's home; no one was injured, but most NOI members believed that Collins was responsible.

Both sides appealed to Elijah Muhammad. Louis argued that Ella continued to undermine his authority and should be disciplined, if not expelled. Ella urged Muhammad to name her captain of Mosque No. 11 and to fire Louis. Muhammad first offered a compromise: Louis would remain the minister, but none of the programs Ella had initiated at the mosque would be canceled. Ella tried to adhere to this plan, but her dislike for Louis was too strong, and she soon stopped attending the mosque. But the matter did not end there. Malcolm was invited to Boston as a mediator, where he explained to Louis that Ella was an extremely dangerous person. "Ella is the type of woman that—brother, she'll kill you." Malcolm had little choice but to back Louis's decision to expel her, making her the second of his siblings, after Reginald, that Malcolm would sacrifice to his loyalty to the Nation.

———

By 1960, the black activist Bayard Rustin was almost fifty years old. Though his tireless civil rights work brought him into association with younger men like King, his agitation on behalf of African Americans had begun decades earlier. Rustin had briefly joined the Communist Party in the late 1930s, then in 1941 worked with A. Philip Randolph's Negro March on Washington Movement, which forced President Roosevelt to outlaw racial discrimination in the defense industry. Like Malcolm, he had opposed black involvement in World War II, and his refusal to join the military landed him a three-year prison sentence. After his release, he participated in nonviolent demonstrations, challenging Jim Crow laws on public buses in the upper South; by the mid-1950s he had become an invaluable adviser and fund-raiser to King.

However, as the decade turned and the bitter taste of McCarthyism lingered in the mouths of the left, Rustin found himself suddenly marginalized. It was not only on account of his brief communist membership, but also his sexuality: Rustin was gay, and in 1953 had been jailed in California for public sexual activity. In April 1960, he had become involved with a new organization initiated by Ella Baker, the Student Nonviolent Coordinating Committee (SNCC), which would become the radical wing of the desegregationist struggle. Throughout that summer, he had assisted SNCC's new president, Marion Barry, in planning what was to be a major conference on nonviolence in October. Rustin's name was even listed on the conference program. But when the AFL-CIO's executive council, which was funding the conference, expressed opposition to his participation based on his sexual orientation and brief communist past, Barry and other student coordinators caved in and "disinvited" him. Rustin's public banning was not unusual for African-American leftists, however. In academic year 1961–62, communist Benjamin Davis, Jr., was banned from speaking on many college campuses, sparking student protests at City University of New York.

Rustin's isolation from the Black Freedom Movement and his desire to use the publicity surrounding Malcolm to reestablish his own credentials may help to explain his growing interest in the Nation of Islam. On November 7, 1960, the two men debated each other on New York City's WBAI radio, the beginning of a friendship that would endure despite their divergent agendas. Malcolm, speaking first, began by distinguishing the NOI's approach from that of black nationalism. A nationalist, Malcolm explained, shared the same aim of a Muslim. "But the difference is in method. We say the only solution is the religious approach; this is why we stress the importance of a moral reformation." He denied any commitment to practical politics, asserting Elijah Muhammad was "not a politician."

Malcolm had by this time garnered much experience as a debater, but Rustin had more, and he worked over his younger opponent; it didn't help that the holes in Malcolm's argument were easy to spot. Rustin attacked Malcolm's separatist position as conservative, even passive. The vast majority of blacks, he said, were "seeking to become full-fledged citizens," and the purpose of civil rights protests was to further this cause. Malcolm denied the possibility that "full-fledged" citizenship was attainable. "We feel that if a hundred years after the so-called Emancipation Proclamation the black man is still not free, then we don't feel that what Lincoln did set them free in the first place." Rustin quickly pointed out that Malcolm was avoiding the question.

The older man's superior debating skills kept his opponent on the defensive. At one point, Malcolm denied that integration was ever going to happen, but admitted that "if the white man were to accept us, without laws being passed, then we would go for it." This alone was a significant concession, except Rustin wanted to force Malcolm to the logical end point of this argument: that if change was impossible to achieve in America, blacks would have to set up a separate state elsewhere. When Malcolm finally admitted as much, Rustin closed the trap. It was relatively easy for him to recount the major reforms that had taken place, and the practical impossibility of a black state. "The great majority of Negroes [are] feeling that things can improve here. Until you have some place to go, they're going to want to stay."

In a matter of minutes, the essential weakness of the Nation of Islam had been exposed. It presented itself as a religious movement, with no direct interest in politics. Yet, as King had shown, when it came to driving change, religion and politics did not need to be mutually exclusive. Hundreds of black Christian ministers were already using their churches as centers for mobilizing civil disobedience and voter registration efforts. The Nation saw the white government as the enemy; Elijah Muhammad often claimed in speeches that the government had failed black Americans. But with John F. Kennedy's election in November 1960, largely on the wings of significant support by blacks, reforms seemed to be on the horizon. And even if those reforms were limited, the Garveyite notion of one or more separate black states was never a realizable alternative.

Most devastating for Malcolm was that he knew Rustin was right. For all the strides the Nation had made in promoting self-improvement in the lives of its members, its political isolation had left it powerless to change the external conditions that bounded their freedoms. Malcolm himself had already embraced the necessity of direct political action when he marched down Harlem's busiest thoroughfares and blockaded a police station to secure the safety of Johnson X Hinton. And the Third World movements he embraced—from the postcolonial struggles inspired by Pan-Africanism to his identification with Castro—were driven fundamentally by a commitment to politics. Rustin showed that Malcolm was defending a conservative, apolitical program that, by his own actions, he did not endorse.

Had Malcolm been quicker to grasp the practical implications of Rustin's logic, he might have avoided one of the great disasters of his career. Soon after the debate, he was charged with leading the NOI's mobilization in Dixie. By the late 1950s, most civil rights organizations were devoting their resources to support campaigns across the South, and the NOI did not want to be caught out. In 1960 in Jackson, Mississippi, thousands of blacks had participated in an economic boycott of segregationist white merchants that proved to be 90 to 95 percent effective. That August NAACP field secretary Medgar Evers investigated and publicized police brutality cases in the state. CORE was also poised for growth, when in December 1960 the Supreme Court ruled in *Boynton v. Virginia* that racial segregation was outlawed in all interstate transportation terminals, much as the earlier *Morgan v. Virginia* had done for interstate bus travel itself. In early 1961, under new director James Farmer, CORE would initiate "Freedom Rides" of desegregationist protesters into the Deep South.

Unlike these civil rights groups, however, the Nation's Southern strategy would be anchored to its program of black separatism. Elijah Muhammad and Malcolm had together constructed an anti-integrationist strategy that they hoped would find a receptive audience among Southern blacks. A key element of their approach was to brand African-American Christian clergy, especially those involved in nonviolent protests, as "Toms"—even though such an ugly attack directly contradicted Malcolm's public commitment to the building of a black united front. The plan also called for the construction of new NOI mosques across the region.

In December, Malcolm traveled to Atlanta, announcing his presence there in an interview on that city's WERD radio. He attended meetings and gave lectures at Atlanta's Mosque No. 15 on at least five occasions, before moving on to an interdenominational ministers' conference in Alabama and other meetings in Tampa, Miami, and Jacksonville.

Malcolm returned home for the Christmas Day birth of his second daughter, Qubilah, named in honor of Mongol emperor Kublai Khan, but by late January he was back in Atlanta, ostensibly to participate in local NOI meetings. The main purpose of this trip, however, was to establish an understanding with the Ku Klux Klan.

No single incident in Malcolm's entire career has generated more controversy than his private caucus with the Klan in January 1961. Most of the details about the planning and logistics of this meeting are still sketchy. What is established is that, despite a previous exchange of hostile letters between KKK leader J. B. Stoner and Elijah Muhammad, both the Klan and the NOI saw advantages to crafting a secret alliance. On January 28, Malcolm and Atlanta NOI leader Jeremiah X met in Atlanta with KKK representatives. Apparently, the Nation was interested in purchasing tracts of farmland and other properties in the South and, as Malcolm explained, wanted to solicit "the aid of the Klan to obtain the land." According to FBI surveillance, Malcolm assured the white racists that "his people wanted complete segregation from the white race." If sufficient territory were obtainable, blacks could establish their own racially separate businesses and even government. Explaining that the Nation exercised strict discipline over its members, he urged white racists in Georgia to do likewise: to eliminate those white "traitors who assisted integration leaders."

Malcolm himself seems to have viewed the entire affair with distaste, as he complained about it afterward to Elijah Muhammad and did not publicly admit his role until years later. Even then, he worked to distance himself, claiming that he had no knowledge about NOI–Klan contacts after January 1961, though this seems highly unlikely. Jeremiah X, who was actively involved in the Klan negotiations, participated in a daylight Klan rally in Atlanta in 1964, receiving the public praise of Ku Klux Klan Imperial Wizard Robert M. Shelton.

To sit down with white supremacists to negotiate common interests, at a moment in black history when the KKK was harassing, victimizing, and even killing civil rights workers and ordinary black citizens, was despicable. Malcolm's apologetics about negotiating with white racists were insufficient. He had also told the Klansmen that "the Jew is behind the integration movement, using the Negro as a tool." He had to know that this overture would be used to undermine the struggle for blacks' equal rights, that Klansmen and white supremacists were committed to murdering civil rights leaders in the region. Malcolm's uncritical adoption of Elijah Muhammad's conservative, black separatist policies had led him to an ugly dead end.

CHAPTER 7

"As Sure As God Made Green Apples"

January 1961–May 1962

Betty was suffering. For the three weeks prior to the birth of Qubilah, Malcolm had been traveling. On the day of her birth itself, he had devoted most of his time to the mass trial of members from Mosque No. 7. Now her husband was once again away. Within weeks, she would pack up Attallah and Qubilah and journey south to North Philadelphia, this time seeking temporary refuge at the home of her birth father, Shelman Sandlin.

As Malcolm waited in Atlanta to negotiate with the Ku Klux Klan, he worried that relations with Betty might have reached a point of no return. On January 25, 1961, they spoke by phone, but their conversation only troubled him further. Later that day he decided to write to her. Malcolm observed that his wife had undergone a meaningful change of character during recent weeks. Perhaps expressing his appreciation for the strength and sacrifices Betty had made, especially during her pregnancy and Qubilah's birth, Malcolm conveyed his love for her. In an act of uncharacteristic generosity—for him—he even stuffed forty dollars into the envelope with the love letter.

These expressions of affection probably were insufficient to reassure Betty about his love. She had come to resent the fact that for Malcolm, the work of the Nation always came first—the letter had even included a request for Betty to iron out details about the possibility of an NOI show at Carnegie Hall. With little in the way of an emotional connection to build from, inviting his spouse to share in his duties for the NOI may have been his way of trying to bridge the distance between them.

If the great difficulties Malcolm encountered with Betty ever led him to wonder whether he'd made the right choice of partners, he must have been surprised to learn, sometime in late 1959, that Evelyn Williams, the woman he had turned away, was pregnant. Unmarried, she had been working for only a short time in the secretarial pool at the Nation's Chicago headquarters, and her scandalous condition brought upon her the full weight of the NOI's draconian policy of punishment and scorn. Yet what no one including Malcolm knew, and would not know until 1963, was that the unborn child's father was none other than the Messenger himself, Elijah Muhammad.

With his network of informants throughout the NOI, Muhammad was well aware of the troubles between Malcolm and Betty, and he certainly knew of the romantic feelings Evelyn still harbored toward Malcolm. And yet he selfishly chose to have her anyway. His decision, however, set off a chain reaction that quickly tested the limits of his control. Evelyn became pregnant in the middle of 1959, and by October she began phoning Muhammad at his home, demanding money. She strongly implied that she would cause trouble for him if it was revealed that she was carrying his child. Muhammad was outraged, convinced that he was being blackmailed. "You must think I'm a fool or Santa Claus," he told her. After another telephone conversation with Evelyn, Muhammad turned to a minister who had heard the exchange and said coldly, "It looks like she will have to be put down." In an organization where members were routinely beaten for transgressions as innocuous as smoking a cigarette, this statement could not be simply dismissed as tough talk. But Muhammad did nothing to harm Evelyn, and she gave birth to their daughter, Eva Marie, at St. Francis Hospital, in Lynwood, California, on March 30, 1960.

It would be easy to ascribe Muhammad's trysts with Evelyn to some secret jealousy he felt over Malcolm's growing media profile, but Evelyn's case was not unique. Three months before her child was born, another unmarried NOI secretary, Lucille X Rosary, also gave birth to a child; two more children were born to NOI secretaries that year, in April and December. All were the progeny of Elijah Muhammad, who had taken advantage of the weeklong Chicago MGT tutorials—such as the one Betty had attended—to select attractive and talented young women for service in the national headquarters' secretarial staff. Once they arrived, it took little for him to get what he wanted from them.

On the surface, Muhammad was not an impressive-looking man. He was short, mostly bald, homely, and his thin body had been crippled by severe bronchitis. But these external features obscured the attractive power that he exercised over his followers. They were convinced that he had actually spoken to God, and that his mission on earth was to redeem the black race.

Muhammad radiated power and authority. When he demanded sex from a woman in his organization, it was inconceivable to him that his overtures would be rejected, or even questioned. The fact that his actions directly violated his own sect's rules regarding sexual transgressions and morality were irrelevant to him.

For a time Muhammad's long-suffering wife, Clara, pretended that she was unaware of her husband's lascivious behavior, talking only to her daughter, Ethel Sharrieff, and other female confidantes. She complained bitterly to Ethel, for instance, when she discovered a love letter from one of his mistresses. When she refused to turn it over to him, he angrily stopped speaking to her. Clara Muhammad told her daughter, "I don't know what he thinks my heart is, flesh and bone or a piece of wood or what." Leading up to the February 1960 Saviour's Day, Clara became overwhelmed by news of additional relations concerning her husband. On February 13, 1960, after a shrill argument, Elijah abruptly abandoned his home. Tearfully, Clara complained to Ethel, "I'm sick of being treated like a dog."

Thanks to its wiretaps and informants, the FBI was fully apprised of Muhammad's infidelities. Having been frustrated in their attempts to find Malcolm's weaknesses, Bureau officials now considered ways to turn Muhammad's actions to their advantage. On May 22, 1960, FBI assistant director Cartha De Loach approved the text of a fictive anonymous letter to be sent to Clara Muhammad and several NOI ministers. The letter provocatively charged that "there appears to be a tremendous occupational hazard in being a young unmarried secretary employed in the household of Elijah Muhammad." He had "preached against extramarital relationships but he doesn't seem to be able to keep things under control in his own household." To ensure greater privacy with his mistresses when in Chicago, Muhammad rented a love-nest apartment on South Vernon Avenue, but the Bureau kept one step ahead of him: its Chicago field office contacted the director, who gave approval for telephone taps and electronic bugging devices in the apartment. The Chicago field agent explained, "Muhammad, feeling he is secure in his 'hideaway,' may converse more freely with high officials of the NOI and his personal contacts. Through this it is hoped to obtain policy and future plans of Muhammad."

By 1961, Muhammad had purchased a second, luxurious home at 2118 East Violet Drive in sunny Phoenix; NOI members were informed that due to the deterioration of Muhammad's health from severe bronchitis, it was beneficial for him to spend most of the year in the arid southwest. The family home in Chicago, however, was retained. The new property also afforded

Muhammad yet another layer of privacy for his sexual adventures. By early October the FBI counted at least five different NOI women who were regularly having sexual intercourse with Muhammad, two of whom were sisters. Like a young gigolo, Elijah tried to play one woman against the others as they competed for his affections.

Soon there were so many illegitimate children to take care of that new household arrangements were necessary. In October 1961, Muhammad telephoned Evelyn Williams in Chicago and asked her if she would be willing to raise and supervise his illegitimate children in a large home located on the West Coast. He approached with flattery, telling her that he needed to have his "Sweet and Honey come and stay with me for two or three months . . . or years." Faced with financial burdens and a child, Evelyn agreed, but it didn't take long for the new arrangement to sour. In July 1962, she phoned Muhammad demanding more money, and accused him of treating his illegitimate children like "stray dogs." "You don't allow your other children to live on $300 a month," she argued. "All I want is money to pay the rent and to get some food and clothing."

Muhammad once again complained of blackmail. "I won't speak to you," he told her, "or give you one red cent!" Stymied, Evelyn and Lucille Rosary took their children to Muhammad's Phoenix home, and when no one answered the front door, they left the children at the entrance. Raymond Sharrieff eventually came to the front door and called out to the women to take their children back. Evelyn and Lucille refused, and left. Sharrieff went back inside and called the police, reporting that several small children had been abandoned on their doorstep. The children were subsequently turned over to social workers for investigation. The next day, Muhammad called Evelyn in a fury, but she refused to back down. "From now on, I'm not going to protect you in any way, shape or form," she warned him. "If you want trouble, you'll get it." She told Muhammad that calling the police on his own children was "the dirtiest thing you could do." Yet whether out of fear, love, or a lingering sense of loyalty, when police interrogated Evelyn about the father of her child, she would not divulge his name. Both Lucille and Evelyn were placed on notice for "child neglect," but neither was formally charged. These emotional and legal conflicts could not be entirely suppressed or contained by national secretary John Ali, Raymond Sharrieff, or other Chicago officials. By mid-1962 rumors of Muhammad's messy sex life were circulating widely in Chicago. Malcolm undoubtedly heard these rumors but continued to refuse to examine whether they were true and never imagined that Evelyn was involved.

Before leaving Atlanta during his travel to the South in January and February 1961, Malcolm attended an hourlong lecture delivered by the Pulitzer Prize–winning historian Arthur Schlesinger, Jr., at Atlanta University on January 17. At the time, Schlesinger was also a prominent adviser to president-elect John F. Kennedy. Schlesinger's talk, "America's Domestic Future, Its Perils and Prospects," was given before a standing-room-only audience and included a passing reference to the Nation of Islam: "Nothing can obstruct . . . recognition of the brotherhood of the human community more than the racist doctrines preached by the White Citizens Councils, the Ku Klux Klan, and the Black Muslims." Schlesinger praised Thurgood Marshall and Roy Wilkins for advancing "effective ways to [achieve] equality through the courts," and applauded Dr. Martin Luther King, Jr., for promoting nonviolence as "the best way to attack prejudice." After the talk, Schlesinger moved to the much smaller Dean Sage Auditorium on the Clark College campus to field questions; Malcolm was waiting.

Identifying himself only as "a Muslim," he demanded to know on "what do you base your charge that the Black Muslims are racists and black supremacists?" Schlesinger cited a recent article by the black journalist William Worthy. "But, sir, how can a man of your intelligence, a professor of history, who knows the value of thorough research, come here from Harvard and attack the Black Muslims, basing your conclusions on one small article?" Schlesinger asked if Malcolm had read Worthy's article. Malcolm acknowledged that he had read it but noted that the article, which had quoted Schlesinger, did not attack the NOI as racist, but instead had focused on the negative conditions all blacks endured that had produced the Nation. The mostly black audience favored Malcolm's arguments, but Schlesinger still insisted that the white racists and the "Black Muslims are two sides of the same coin." He had no way of knowing how right he was, given Malcolm's upcoming détente with the Klan. The black press, however, judged the confrontation between the Kennedy adviser and the NOI minister as a clear-cut victory for Malcolm. The *Pittsburgh Courier* declared that "the fiery Mr. X victoriously crossed swords" with Schlesinger, forcing the Harvard historian "into a 'diplomatic withdrawal' of his earlier statement." The February 4, 1961, issue of the *New Jersey Herald* also covered the debate with the headline "Muslims Give the JFK Man a Fit." The informal debate with Schlesinger reinforced Malcolm's belief that the Nation had to confront its critics. And there was no better venue for such confrontations than American universities.

During the next five months, he planned appearances at a series of colleges. Within the Nation, he explained that his purpose was to present the views of Elijah Muhammad and to challenge distortions about their religion. In fact, his objectives were to turn upside down the standard racial dialectic of black subordination and white supremacy, and to show off his rhetorical skill at the expense of white authorities and Negro integrationists. He had become convinced that the Nation's elders were making a big mistake in shying away from public confrontations. The NOI's survival depended on its ability to answer its critics, to divide white opinion about the group, and to win over converts.

Nowhere in the academic world was Malcolm's and the NOI's divisiveness within the black community more prominently on display than at Howard University, the historically black college in Washington, D.C. The Howard campus chapter of the NAACP invited Malcolm to speak on February 14, 1961, as part of Negro History Week, a tradition established by the historian Carter G. Woodson and which would later be expanded into Black History Month. Though the national organization still found Malcolm too hot to touch, his growing reputation as a militant appealed to the NAACP's younger members, who increasingly sought him out for debates and speeches despite the reticence of the old guard. The invitation by Howard students rattled the school's administrators, almost all of whom were staunch integrationists and who could little afford to have the university's federal funding threatened by appearing to embrace the Nation of Islam's most prominent spokesman. When the student group failed to clear approval with the student activities office, the lecture had to be canceled. Undaunted, the NAACP chapter then secured the use of New Bethel Baptist Church, but—probably under pressure from the university—it too decided to cancel, using the excuse that the sanctuary was too small to accommodate the anticipated audience. Writing to Elijah Muhammad, Malcolm explained that the whole affair was fortunate: "We really threw a 'stone of stumbling' onto the Howard University campus because they are all divided and arguing now, and it places us in an even better position to pour 'boiling water' on them when we get there."

It was not until October 30, 1961, that Malcolm finally appeared at Howard, thanks largely to the efforts of E. Franklin Frazier. The author of *Black Bourgeoisie*, Frazier had been associated with Howard since 1934. A leftist during his early years, he had long been critical of the black middle class's lack of social responsibility toward the black poor. He convinced the school administration to sanction Malcolm's appearance, but as a concession the format would now be a debate, to ensure the presentation of a counterpoint to Malcolm's opinions. To provide the opposing view, the school secured an appearance by the man who had frustrated and outmaneuvered Malcolm in the radio debate just a year earlier, Bayard Rustin.

The Howard debate would enter history as an important moment for both Bayard Rustin and Malcolm X. That evening, fifteen hundred people packed Howard's brand-new Cramton Auditorium, and five hundred more crowded the building's entrance in hopes of getting in. Malcolm had not forgotten the drubbing he had taken from Rustin during their first encounter, and he carefully worked on what he would say. Unlike the first debate, which had taken place in the isolation of a radio station studio, this appearance would give Malcolm the advantage of addressing a large black crowd and allow him to draw on his tremendous strength as a public speaker. He went for the rafters from his opening statement, telling the audience members that he stood before them not as a partisan of any major political party, or by religion or nationality: Malcolm announced that his only credential for speaking the truth was his identity as *"A BLACK MAN!"*

Throughout the speech he hammered home the thesis of Frazier's *Black Bourgeoisie*—that the privileged African-American middle class had not played the leadership role it should assume to advance the black masses. At the center of Malcolm's attack was his relentless criticism of "so-called Negro leaders. . . . The black man in America will never be equal to the white man as long as he attempts to force himself into his house." Malcolm suggested that the entire philosophy of racial integration was doomed to failure, because the great majority of whites would never acquiesce to racial assimilation. As a result, a fraudulent black leadership had developed that did not effectively advocate the interests and concerns of African Americans. "The anemic Negro leader," Malcolm sneered, "who survives and thrives off of gifts from white people, is dependent upon the white man whom he gives false information about the masses of black people." Frequently employing humor in his presentation, Malcolm praised Elijah Muhammad's method of isolating "ourselves from the white man long enough to analyze this great hypocrisy and begin to think black, and now we speak black." He urged students not to seek the white man's "love," but rather to "demand his respect."

It was not in Rustin's character to abandon a fight, and he vigorously challenged Malcolm. At one point, a *Chicago Defender* reporter noted that Rustin "received loud cheers," when he said to Malcolm, "you say America constituted is a sinking ship, and Negroes should abandon this ship, for another called 'Separation' or another state. If this ship sinks," Rustin asked, "what possible chance do you think your 'separate' state would have?" But in front of a youthful black audience, Rustin's warnings seemed tired and stale. As the reporter observed, it was Malcolm who effectively drew upon "reference(s) to history and his many sharp criticisms of current practices won over the majority of students."

One other aspect of Malcolm's address that was especially effective in appealing to civil rights organizers and leftists was proletarian appeal. He claimed that Muhammad and the Nation represented blacks who were unemployed, impoverished, and angry. The majority of urban blacks were confined to the ghetto, where they were subjected to police brutality; indeed, law enforcement authorities functioned like an occupying army under colonial conditions. In effect, Malcolm was using the analogy of postcolonial Africa to define the political conflict between black leaders in the United States. Although Frantz Fanon's writings would not be known or translated in the United States until the late 1960s, Malcolm's analysis anticipated Fanon's famous "Wretched of the Earth" thesis. By the end of the great debate, despite the older man's point-scoring, however, it was Malcolm who was largely setting the agenda now, capturing the militancy of most college students, black and white. As one bewildered faculty member at the debate admitted, "Howard will never be the same. I feel a reluctance to face my class tomorrow."

Malcolm's oratory brought him not just to the heights of esteemed black institutions, but to landmark locales in the upper-crust white world as well. On March 24 of the following year, he was invited to debate the black attorney Walter C. Carrington at the Harvard Law School Forum. The excitement generated by Malcolm's appearance was so intense that at the last minute the venue was changed from Lowell Hall to Sanders Theatre, Harvard's largest auditorium. There, on the stage that had hosted American presidents and foreign heads of state, Malcolm presented the NOI program to a record-breaking crowd. "Allah is now giving America every chance to repent and change before He destroys this wicked Caucasian world," he declared. He went on to argue that desegregated public facilities and integrated schools were not enough. America's twenty million blacks "number a nation in their own right." For that nation to be successful, blacks "must have some land of our own." Louis X, who had come out for the debate from the Boston mosque, recalled Malcolm's powerful presence onstage. The white audience at Harvard, he remembered, was enamored with this black man who could handle their questions with ease. If Malcolm's abrupt shift from political and international themes to jeremiads about the coming destruction of white civilization seemed jarring, this hodgepodge construction was not of

his design; Elijah Muhammad, ever vigilant about Malcolm's growing platform, would often dictate parts of his speeches; the Harvard debate was
probably no exception. Chicago headquarters also insisted that Malcolm's
lectures be audio-recorded, with copies forwarded to them, so that both
Muhammad and John Ali could monitor the addresses.

Through the spring of 1961, Malcolm's campus speaking engagements
took him far and wide, rarely failing to generate controversy or to prompt
blistering debates about free speech. In California, for instance, students
at UC Berkeley were scheduled to hear Malcolm, but the university
administration banned the lecture, which had to be relocated to the local
YMCA. On April 19, Malcolm was back in the Ivy League, at Yale, to debate
Louis Lomax, and four days later he appeared on the NBC television program
Open Mind as part of a panel that included the conservative George Schuyler
and the writer James Baldwin. When host Eric Goldman introduced Malcolm
as the NOI's "number two man," at the first opportunity Malcolm denied
that such a position existed. More important, the show's taping marked the
beginning of a lifelong friendship between Malcolm and Baldwin.

Although most of Malcolm's public lectures were now aimed at university audiences, he also tried to establish an interfaith dialogue between the
Nation and African-American Christians. As the Nation continued to deny
the necessity of politics, it became even more important to establish its
legitimacy within the black community as a real religious organization;
acknowledgment by important Christian groups brought it closer to that
goal. To this end, Malcolm organized events that brought groups of Muslims
to a black church, where he would deliver a sermon focused on the connections between Christianity and Islam. Probably the first of these occurred
on June 16, 1961, at Elder Solomon Lightfoot Michaux's New York Church
of God. In his sermon, Malcolm exuded praise "to Allah for putting into
Elder Michaux's heart to invite those of us who are Muslims here this evening to explain what the Honorable Elijah Muhammad is teaching." He
explained that the NOI did not believe in politics, because no "president
that has ever sat in the White House" has ever kept his promises to black
people. Instead, he advised, we must "turn toward the God of our forefa-
thers," by emulating what "Moses taught his people to do in the house of
bondage four thousand years ago." If these interfaith gestures brought new
respect to the Nation from outsiders, Malcolm's internal speeches often
undermined their sincerity. Speaking on July 14, only four weeks after his
eloquent appeal at Elder Michaux's Church of God, he bluntly told followers at the mosque that "Christianity is evil and also America is evil." And

he continued to characterize as "Uncle Toms" the mainstream civil rights leaders and integrationists, many of whom professed a deep Christian faith.

Increasingly, Malcolm had to address a growing variety of competing issues and demands: problems within the NOI, street demonstrations, debates with civil rights leaders and organizations. But he continued to balance these new obligations with his commitment to building Mosque No. 7. He still set aside a significant share of time for the Nation, even if his extensive travels in the early sixties left relatively little room for his mosque. His first sermon there after his January 1961 meeting with the Ku Klux Klan had been on February 6, when he melodramatically asserted that if a white man should hit a Muslim in the South, it could very well be "the start of a holy war." But the next controversy involving the NOI did not begin in Dixie, but rather on Manhattan's east side.

In the early dawn of independence in postcolonial Africa, Congolese prime minister Patrice Lumumba came to be recognized as a symbol for postcolonial African aspirations. He would not be beholden to colonial Western powers or the United States. On January 17, 1961, he was murdered by Belgian mercenaries in Congo's Katanga province. The delayed news of Lumumba's death was finally announced on February 13, leading to militant demonstrations throughout the world. The Soviets blamed UN troops stationed in the Congo for failing to protect Lumumba, and demanded secretary Dag Hammarskjöld's firing. On February 15 a coalition of widely divergent groups put up several long picket lines blocking the entrance to the UN building in New York. One organization taking part, the Cultural Association for Women of African Heritage, included an individual who would later influence Malcolm's life: the writer Maya Angelou, the association's director. As the crowd grew, scuffles broke out between demonstrators and security guards. In the ensuing mêlée, forty-one people were injured, including eighteen UN personnel. Reporters and press photographers claimed they had been attacked by rioters with brass knuckles and knives. United States diplomats accused the demonstrators of being "Communist-inspired, linked [to] mob violence against Belgian embassies in Moscow, Cairo and Warsaw over the death" of Lumumba. New York police commissioner Stephen P. Kennedy blamed the rioting on the "Muslim Brotherhood, a fanatic Negro national cult, which is one of the most dangerous gangs in the city." Somehow the police along with the U.S. ambassador to the UN, Adlai Stevenson, believed that the Muslim Brotherhood "gang" was affiliated with the NOI and Malcolm X. "It wasn't us," Malcolm responded bluntly. "We don't involve ourselves in any politics, whether local, national, or international." But Malcolm could not resist expressing Pan-Africanist solidarity with the protesters: "I refuse to condemn the demonstrations . . . because I am not Moise Tshombe, and will permit no one to use me against the nationalists."

Several days after the UN riot, Maya Angelou and an associate contacted the NOI to arrange a meeting with Malcolm. The two went uptown to the NOI restaurant and met the minister in a rear room. "His aura was too bright and his masculine force affected me physically," Angelou recalled years later. "A hot desert storm eddied around him and rushed to me, making my skin contract, and my pores slam shut. . . . His hair was the color of burning embers and his eyes pierced." As representatives of the Cultural Association of Women of African Heritage, the women explained, they had been involved in the UN demonstration, but had not anticipated thousands of protesters turning out. Malcolm responded that the Muslims had not been involved in the protest. "You were wrong in your direction," Malcolm said, chastising his guests. United Nations demonstrations "and carrying placards will not win freedom for anyone, nor will it keep the white devils from killing another African leader." Angelou had anticipated receiving Malcolm's endorsement of the protest and tried hard not to display her disappointment. But then, surprisingly, Malcolm's voice softened, she remembered, "and for a time the Islamic preacher disappeared." Malcolm warned the women that conservative African-American leaders would be used by the white power structure to denounce them as "dangerous and probably communists." He promised that he would make a statement to the press describing the demonstration as "symbolic of the anger in this country." Although Angelou left feeling the "fog of defeat," her encounter with Malcolm struck her to the core. She would eagerly renew her acquaintance with him several years later, after she had moved to Ghana.

Throughout mid-1961, Malcolm would devote more time to his pastoral duties in Mosque No. 7. Lecturing there on July 9, for instance, he explained the Nation's official interpretation of what would unfold during the final days. "In the next war, the War of Armageddon," he predicted, "it will be a race war and will not be a 'spooky war.'" Using a blackboard, he explained why the ideals of freedom, justice, and equality were impossible to achieve under the "American flag."

He was also actively involved with many of the business-related aspects of the NOI. For instance, Elijah Muhammad wrote Malcolm in March asking whether C. Eric Lincoln's book *The Black Muslims in America* should be carried by the Nation despite its criticism of the sect. The book's publisher had agreed to sell five thousand copies at "a very good commission to the Muslims." But Elijah also stressed in his letter, "THIS IS NOT TO BE MEN-TIONED IN PUBLIC." Astutely, he realized that the deal was good business if not good publicity. Apparently the sale agreement went ahead and the NOI duly sold discounted copies of the book.

On August 11, Malcolm unexpectedly received a telegram from labor leader A. Philip Randolph: "I am appointing you to the Ad Hoc Working Committee of Unity for Action. First meeting scheduled for 3 p.m., Monday, August fourteenth, 217 West 125th Street." Nothing in Randolph's communication indicated what the committee's agenda might be, or who else had been invited.

At the time, Randolph was a lion of the civil rights effort and, even at age seventy-two, had lost little of his enthusiasm for leading the charge; he remained the most powerful black labor leader in the United States. Still based in Harlem, he had seen the fight shift in recent years from demanding more black jobs at businesses on 125th Street to seeking full representation for blacks within the political system. Such an effort required a united front from Harlem's black community, and Randolph knew that Malcolm represented an increasingly significant constituency. But his admiration for Malcolm likely had an ideological component. Almost fifty years before, Randolph had introduced newcomer Marcus Garvey to a Harlem audience, and though he never endorsed black nationalism, he maintained throughout his career a sense of admiration for its fundamental embrace of black pride and self-respect. Randolph was old enough to take the historical long view, and he saw Malcolm as a legitimate voice in the militant tradition of Garvey and Martin R. Delaney.

The respect was mutual; Malcolm put aside his reservations and attended the meeting. The goal of the committee, he learned, was to establish a broad coalition—from black nationalists to moderate integrationists—to address social and political problems in Harlem. To join officially, Malcolm realized, meant to go beyond the limited venture he had made into politics up to that time. Though he was interested, he knew he would have to justify his participation to the Nation.

Fortunately, Elijah Muhammad gave him an unintentional loophole. Throughout much of August, Malcolm and Mosque No. 7 were busily preparing to host a major address by Muhammad, to be held on August 23 at Harlem's 369th Infantry Armory. Before an audience estimated at between five and eight thousand, the Messenger of Allah offered a bleak and dire vision:

It is not the nature of the white man to call the Negro a brother. The Negro ministers are taught to preach by white people. They are given licenses by white people and if they do not teach like white people want them to they are cut down. . . . Harlem should elect its own leaders and should not accept the leaders set up for them by the white man. We must elect our leaders and if they do not do right we should cut their heads off. We cannot integrate with the white man, we must separate.

In the call for Harlem to elect its own leaders, Malcolm saw an opportunity. Although Muhammad's outlook was anchored to a separatist partition, he encouraged NOI members to support black-owned businesses and to back black leaders, and it was on this slender basis that Malcolm consented to work with Randolph's committee. Its members, he found, were drawn largely from the Negro American Labor Council; many were representatives from business, civic, and faith institutions. One such member was Percy Sutton, a prominent Harlem lawyer who also served as branch president of the New York NAACP. Malcolm and Sutton came to respect each other, and within several years Malcolm would seek Sutton's legal counsel on a range of sensitive matters. Bayard Rustin, who by that time had worked with Randolph for over twenty years, was also on the committee, and his presence may have further intrigued Malcolm about the group's potential.

The first public event staged by what was then called the Emergency Committee was a rally in front of the Hotel Theresa in early September. Randolph carefully crafted the speakers' list to reflect the range of Harlem politics. For the nationalists, there were black bookstore proprietor Lewis Michaux and James Lawson, head of the United African Nationalist Movement; for black labor, the militant Cleveland Robinson, secretary-treasurer for the Retail, Wholesale and Department Store Union's District 65, as well as Richard Parrish, national treasurer of the Negro American Labor Council. About one thousand people attended. The *Pittsburgh Courier*, which covered the event, observed that the "most exciting speaker was Malcolm X, whom many in the audience had never heard before." Malcolm won praise for his sharp condemnation of the NYPD, whom he blamed for the escalation of illegal narcotics, prostitution, and violence in New York's black neighborhoods. What was curious, however, was his deferential approach to the police. He assured the crowd that he would encourage "his people" to obey the law, denied that NOI members had participated in any recent "uprisings in Harlem," and denounced the call for a "march on the 28th

Precinct Police Station," which had been outlined in a leaflet distributed through the crowd. "We do not think this will accomplish anything," he declared. The speech toed the line. It was forceful, yet conservative on action. Activists like Rustin would have noted that Malcolm had virtually replicated the paradox of the NOI: he had identified and condemned the problem yet refused to go further in embracing a working solution. Black Harlemites could no more escape interaction with the local police than set up a separate state.

Still, the importance of Malcolm's role on the Emergency Committee is central to interpreting what happened to him after he broke with the NOI in 1964. The committee was the only black united front–type organization in which he participated during his years inside the Nation, and although it featured a range of ideological opinions, it was Randolph who controlled who was invited to join the committee, who spoke at the rallies, and what the program of action would be. His model of top-down leadership would later be uncritically adopted by Malcolm in the development of the Organization of Afro-American Unity.

In early October, the Emergency Committee produced a blueprint to combat the "social and economic deterioration" of New York City's black communities. It called for a series of reforms, including the establishment of a citywide minimum wage set at $1.50; the creation of a Fair Employment Practices Committee, with powers that would include jail terms for violators; an investigation of all contracts, with the goal of eliminating discriminatory practices; and forcing one of the city's major employers, Consolidated Edison, to improve its record in the hiring and advancement of black employees. The blueprint identified Malcolm as a member of the committee, but next to his name, in parentheses, was written "Malik el-Shabazz." Since the late 1950s, Elijah Muhammad had permitted his ministers who had not yet received original names to use Shabazz as a surname. For Malcolm, Malik el-Shabazz was an identity that rooted him to the NOI's imaginary history while at the same time granting him the freedom to operate as an individual in the secular world of politics.

Due to his speaking commitments, Malcolm's presence at his home mosque became ever more limited throughout the rest of 1961. He began relying on his assistant ministers, especially Benjamin 2X Goodman. His absences also gave Joseph Gravitt unfettered authority over decisions, including disciplinary actions. This may have been part of the reason that, when Malcolm did speak at Mosque No. 7, he tended to adhere to Elijah Muhammad's conservative, antiwhite positions. On December 1, for instance, he lectured on the nature of the devil. For those attending an NOI meeting for the first time, he said, he was "not speaking of something under the ground. . . . The devil is not a spirit, rather he has blue eyes, blond hair, and he has a white skin."

Early in December, FOI captain Raymond Sharrieff, accompanied by his wife, Ethel, visited the mosque for several days. A visit from Sharrieff was second in import only to a visit from the Messenger himself, and when the couple arrived, they were treated like royalty. Malcolm went to considerable effort to ensure that their stay was memorable, summoning FOI members from Philadelphia and New Jersey and arranging for a karate performance to be held in their honor. At a mosque meeting on December 4, Sharrieff informed his troops: "All organizations follow their leaders. The ability to take an order is a Muslim's number one duty. There should never be any dissension." Though Sharrieff talked hard and, by virtue of his title, was head of the Nation's paramilitary wing, he was not a thug like some local FOI captains. These men, often violent and unstable characters, carried out much of the Nation's dirty work, organizing groups to mete out punishments that ran to beatings or worse, and Sharrieff understood keenly how important it was to reinforce his position at the top of the command structure.

Before the couple departed Harlem, the mosque put on a grand dinner. Sharrieff had already called upon members to donate money to Muhammad's family in honor of the upcoming Saviour's Day, but on top of this he now asked them to give money toward a new luxury automobile for Sharrieff himself. James 67X was outraged: "That was the straw that broke the camel's back. I said, 'I'm riding the number seven bus, and I'm supposed to contribute to his Lincoln Continental?'" The Nation had changed; for some members, it seemed as though the national leadership increasingly viewed the rank and file as a cash register, and resentment began to grow. At the dinner, however, anger over extortion soon gave way to confusion as the Sharrieffs launched into a pair of bizarre and inappropriate monologues. Ethel addressed the audience first and, according to James, "publicly started talking about some of the men not being able to fulfill the sexual requirements of their wives." Even more surprising was her husband's speech. The stern FOI leader came to the speaker's podium and began riffing on his wife's talk, "making jokes about sexual nonperformance."

The ribald, sex-oriented burlesque was designed to humiliate one person alone—Malcolm. The Sharrieffs had evidently read Malcolm's heartfelt March 1959 letter to Elijah Muhammad about problems in his marriage.

They wanted Malcolm to understand that there was no privileged communication with the Messenger. They also apparently wanted to convey
their total contempt, and to ridicule him as a man. For Malcolm, the whole
performance must have contributed to his doubts about his role within
the NOI.

At some point in 1961, Elijah Muhammad may have briefly reduced
Sharrieff's authority over the FOI by making local captains directly responsible to Malcolm. If this is true, it might explain Sharrieff's behavior. However, Malcolm had no ambitions to run the FOI; his interests were pastoral
and political. At Mosque No. 7's regular FOI meeting on December 18, he
seemed to confirm Joseph's role as boss of all NOI captains nationally; it
is unclear what that would have meant for Sharrieff's continued authority. Possibly, the endorsement was based merely on Joseph's effective
management.

What is certain is that, by 1962, the internal life of the Nation had moved
to a new and unsettled place. Elijah Muhammad now spent most of his time
in Arizona; when in Chicago, he was preoccupied with one or more of his
mistresses in his hideaway apartment on the South Side, largely divorced
from the Nation's growing business affairs. Freed from his oversight, Sharrieff and John Ali became the de facto administrative heads of the NOI, and
they reinvested the incoming cash from the members' tithing into Nation-
owned businesses and real estate of all kinds. Muhammad's sons also took
on a greater role in the NOI's affairs. Elijah, Jr., despite possessing a mediocre mind and poor language skills, traveled across the country as an
enforcer, pressing mosques to produce more revenue for the Chicago headquarters. Malcolm was asked to cede editorship of *Muhammad Speaks* to
Herbert Muhammad, who quickly made it clear to all mosques that they
were expected to increase their quotas of newspapers, with all revenue
remitted to Chicago. The success and growth of the NOI ironically created
new problems with old business partners, who increasingly viewed the
group as a competitor. Papers that for years had provided generous coverage to the Nation, such as the *Chicago Defender* and the *Amsterdam News*,
sharply restricted their coverage with the emergence of *Muhammad Speaks*.
By 1963, the *Cleveland Call and Post*, a black Republican paper, declared that
the NOI was encountering "growing disenchantment among the masses
they would lead to a black Utopia."

Mosque No. 7 did not experience the intense upheaval that characterized
many mosques during these years. Despite their personal feelings of hostility, Malcolm and Captain Joseph appeared to work closely together in pub-

lic and generally agreed on all mosque matters. By 1962, only a minority of congregants could remember Joseph's 1956 trial and humiliation. And as hundreds of new members continued to pour into the mosque, memories of the old conflicts faded. By 1959, Temple No. 7 had 1,125 members, 569 of them active. By 1961, the renamed Mosque No. 7 had 2,369 registered members, of whom 737 were defined as active. What types of individuals joined during these years? At a time when the vast majority of Negro leaders were promoting racial integration, the NOI stood almost alone. The vision of building a self-confident nation that blacks themselves controlled began to attract African Americans from different income groups and educational backgrounds. Each new convert seemed to have a unique explanation for joining. James 67X suspected that it was the Black Muslims' reputation for being outside society's mainstream, beyond the boundaries of "normalcy," that drew in blacks who also felt frustrated and bitter. "Normalcy is something that is not highly regarded in the ghetto," James advised. "Everybody got a story."

One bearer of many different stories, who would within several years become extremely close to Malcolm, was Charles Morris. Born in Boston in 1921, as a teenager he had received training as a dental technician, but like Detroit Red he was drawn to show business, joining the Brown Skin Models show at a Seventh Avenue nightclub. In September 1942, he was inducted into the army and was eventually posted to Camp Shelby, Mississippi. For a proud black man raised in the North, being assigned to the segregated South was a disaster waiting to happen. On November 25, 1944, Morris was convicted by general court martial of organizing a mutiny, fighting with another private, and disrespecting a superior officer. He was sentenced to hard labor for six years, and after serving part of his sentence was discharged on September 13, 1946.

In later years, Morris would tell the FBI that he first met Malcolm in Detroit, where the latter was assistant minister. He was impressed by the young preacher, but not by the NOI's message. After Malcolm departed for Boston, he decided not to join the sect. By 1960, Morris had relocated to the Bronx and began to attend NOI meetings again. Finally, he converted, receiving the name Charles 37X, but although he became a familiar figure around the mosque, some of his fellow members thought there was something not quite right about him. The new recruit dressed extravagantly, laughed loudly, and used his charm and personality to curry favors. In retrospect, James 67X coolly observed, "he thought he was a whole lot more than he was, and he was very dangerous." From August 1961 on, Charles was confined for several months at the Rockland State Hospital in Orange-burg, New York, evaluated as having "psychoneurosis—mixed type, mildly depressed but cooperative." Despite this, from 1962 until his resignation from the mosque in 1964, he cultivated a network of friends, most promi-nently Malcolm. Charles was eager to provide security for Malcolm and appeared to be devoted to him. And despite James 67X's deep misgivings, Malcolm developed bonds of trust and respect for his fellow ex-con—the man whom he would later refer to as "my best friend."

Others entered the Nation searching for stability or for restored health—by ending their dependency on narcotics, for example. The complex journey of Thomas Arthur Johnson, Jr., was typical. Born in Pennsylvania in the mid-1930s and raised by his grandparents near Atlantic City, Johnson had what he described as a "really beautiful childhood." He inherited a lifelong love of music from his grandfather, who had played the tuba and slide trombone in the Barnum & Bailey circus's sideshow. As a teenager he spent much of his time loitering around jazz clubs. By the age of fifteen he had been ordered out of the house because of heroin use. In 1958, after several arrests, he was sentenced to twelve months in prison.

In the Islamic faith, the Arabic word *ingadh* means "to save, rescue, bring relief or salvation." The faithful have a duty to save those in distress. In Thomas's case, the call to *ingadh* had first come to his cell mate, a Times Square pickpocket who explained to him the fundamentals of the NOI, including Yacub's History and Elijah's role as Allah's Messenger. All of it made complete sense to Johnson. Once free, he immediately went to Tem-ple No. 7. Before long, his grandparents were stunned by the positive changes in his behavior: permanently off drugs, he dressed neatly in suits and adhered rigidly to Muslim dietary laws.

For Johnson, the NOI was like a combat organization. "I didn't see any-body making a stand, representing us in any way that would alleviate a lot of oppression and the abuse and the things that was going on in the South . . . the waves of killing African-American people," he would later explain. After receiving his X—becoming Thomas 15X—he came to the attention of Captain Joseph for what were considered outstanding displays of devotion. "It was a very hostile atmosphere at that time, and we didn't take no crap from nobody, see, so . . . they called me [the] 'Reactor,' because I was always jumping at everything," he recalled. "[If] somebody threatened a Muslim or they beat up a Muslim or something, I would be the first one on the scene."

Joseph decided that Thomas should be assigned to provide security for

Malcolm, which included doing routine errands and odd jobs for his family. At that time, Thomas thought Malcolm was "the greatest thing walking ... I don't know any commentator, news people, that could handle him." Thomas's daily duties usually began when Malcolm traveled from his home in Queens to the Harlem mosque. Regardless of the weather, Thomas was expected to stand outside, reserving a parking spot for the minister's car. He also drove Malcolm to appointments. Once a month, Betty gave him a list of household items to purchase at the Shabazz supermarket in Brooklyn, driving back afterward to unpack. He noticed that Malcolm avoided going home "if he could." Malcolm confided, "'Man, if I go [home], all them women . . . no telling what I might say, how I'm going to respond.' And he'd say, 'Let's go down to Foley Square.' So we would." Sometimes Malcolm would be deeply engrossed in reading some book very obscure to Thomas. One author he vividly recalled was philosopher G. W. F. Hegel. "Hegel was his man," Thomas recalled, possibly referring to the same passages on "lordship and bondage" that had also fascinated Frantz Fanon.

And yet something about Thomas made Malcolm uneasy. On one occasion he voiced his concerns to Joseph, saying that he was uncomfortable simply because Thomas rarely talked. Thomas, for his part, told Joseph, "I didn't think I was qualified to interject and have a lot of conversation with him. I was just interested in doing my job." Things remained as they were.

Within a growing number of mosques—most notably the Newark, New Jersey, mosque—a storm of criticism against Malcolm began to gather. The standard charges were that he coveted the Messenger's position, that he craved material possessions, and that he was using the Nation to advance himself politically and in the media. Malcolm routinely responded to such barbs by building up the cult around Elijah, which he felt was the most effective way to dispel doubts. Muhammad appreciated such labors on his behalf, and around this time told Malcolm that he wanted him to "become well known," because it was through his fame that Elijah's message would be heard. But Malcolm needed to realize, he added, "You will grow to be hated when you become well known."

———

George Lincoln Rockwell may have thought himself white America's answer to Malcolm X. Square jawed and solidly built, he cut a striking figure when commanding the stage at rallies held by the group he had founded and led, the American Nazi Party. Rockwell's extreme conservatism had grown at first along conventional lines; a longtime naval reservist, he opposed racial integration and despised communism, and for a brief time was employed by William F. Buckley, Jr., the editor of *National Review*. Only after reading *Mein Kampf* and the *Protocols of the Elders of Zion* did his supremacist beliefs merge with a deep hatred for Jews. In March 1959, he established the World Union of Free Enterprise National Socialists, which soon became the American Nazi Party. Despite his loathsome politics, Rockwell possessed a gift for manipulating the media that brought the party outsized attention. On April 3, 1960, he delivered a two-hour speech on the National Mall in Washington that attracted more journalists than supporters; yet, even within the fringes of the far right, he managed to maintain substantial press coverage, creating a greatly inflated image of his party's actual number.

In its early years, the American Nazi Party's literature routinely described African Americans as "niggers," morally and mentally inferior to whites. However, once Rockwell learned of the Nation of Islam's anti-integrationist positions, he became fascinated by the concept of a white supremacist–black nationalist united front. He even praised the NOI to his followers, arguing that Elijah Muhammad had "gathered millions of the dirty, immoral, drunken, filthy-mouthed, lazy and repulsive people sneeringly called 'niggers' and inspired them to the point where they are clean, sober, honest, hard-working, dignified, dedicated and admirable human beings in spite of their color."

At some time in early 1961, Rockwell's group had talks with Muhammad and several top aides in Chicago; Rockwell and Muhammad may even have met privately to work out an "agreement of mutual assistance." The main concession that Rockwell wrung from Muhammad was permission to bring his Nazi storm troopers into NOI rallies, which he knew would provoke press coverage. For Muhammad, the attention carried greater risk, but he believed that it was outweighed by the opportunity to put on display the true nature of the white man. Rockwell's group may have been at the fringe, but Muhammad saw its racial hatred and anti-Semitism as an honest representation of white America's core beliefs. But there was another reason for the pairing: the authoritarianism of the NOI was in harmony with the racist authoritarianism of the white supremacists. Both groups, after all, dreamed of a segregated world in which interracial marriages were outlawed and the races dwelled in separate states.

On June 25, 1961, the Nation of Islam held a major rally in Washington, D.C. Before an audience of eight thousand, Rockwell and ten storm troopers—all crisply dressed in tan fatigues and bright swastika armbands—were escorted to seats near the stage in the center of the arena. Representatives of the African-American press, stunned to see Nazis there, shouted questions to Rockwell, who announced, "I am fully in concert with [the NOI's] program and I have the highest respect for Mr. Elijah Muhammad." Although Muhammad had been advertised as the keynote speaker, once again he was too ill, and it was left to Malcolm to make the main address. After his speech, the audience was asked for contributions, and when Rockwell put in twenty dollars, Malcolm asked who had donated the money. A storm trooper shouted, "George Lincoln Rockwell!" which generated polite applause from the Muslims. Rockwell was invited to stand up; the Nazi leader again received mild applause. Malcolm could not resist commenting, "You got the biggest hand you ever got."

Malcolm's joke belied his deeper feelings about this alliance with the lunatic right, which had been engineered entirely by Elijah Muhammad and the Chicago headquarters. The stain of the Nazis could not quite match that of the Klan, but those meetings had been conducted in secret. Now Malcolm was receiving a cash donation from the leader of a notorious white hate group in front of an audience of thousands. However he felt about Rockwell's usefulness to the NOI, he knew that the appearance would only hurt him with the black leaders who had recently begun courting his opinion.

For his part, Rockwell came away from his contacts with the NOI impressed by their organization and discipline. "Muhammad understands the vicious fraud of the Jewish exploitation of the Negro people," he later observed. "[T]he Muslims are the key to solving the Negro problem, both in the North and the South. And this guy Malcolm X is no mealy-mouth pansy like so many of the disgusting 'integrationist' leaders, both black and white. He is a MAN, whom it is impossible not to admire, even when blasting the White Race for its mishandling of the Black Man." The following February, Rockwell attended NOI's Saviour's Day, held in Chicago before an audience of twelve thousand Muslims. After Elijah Muhammad finished his sermon, Rockwell was invited to speak and strolled to the stage, flanked by two bodyguards. "You know that we call you niggers," he began. "But wouldn't you rather be confronted by honest white men who tell you to your face what the others say behind your back?" He pledged to "do everything in my power to help the Honorable Elijah Muhammad carry out his inspired plan for land of your own in Africa. Elijah Muhammad is right—separation or death!"

Most studies devoted to Malcolm X ignore or do not examine the connections between the NOI and the American Nazi Party. Even the scholar Claude Andrew Clegg, who is highly critical of Muhammad's decision to allow Rockwell to speak in 1962, argues that the Nazi leader "was a sort of bugbear that Muhammad used to scare blacks into the NOI." This underestimates the common ground involved. In the April 1962 issue of *Muhammad Speaks,* Muhammad praised Rockwell as a man who had "endorsed the stand for self that you and I are taking. Why should not you applaud?" The Nazis "have taken a stand to see that you be separated to get justice and freedom." For several years, Rockwell continued to endorse the NOI's program. At an address in October 1962, for example, he stated: "[Elijah Muhammad] is a black supremacist and I'm a white supremacist: that doesn't necessarily mean we gotta kill each other."

Dining with the devil requires more than a long spoon. Like the tête-à-tête with the Klan, the NOI's public identification with the Nazis undermined Malcolm's efforts to reach out to moderate audiences, people who might have agreed with his critique of American racism but rejected his solutions. This was the challenge he faced when he again confronted Bayard Rustin, on January 23, 1962. The debate was held at Manhattan's Community Church, a liberal east side congregation. The topic—"Separation or Integration?"—should have favored Rustin. The audience consisted largely of white liberals who strongly supported civil rights. However, Malcolm astutely did not condemn all whites as "devils," emphasizing instead the negative effects of institutional racism on the black community. His arguments were persuasive to many whites in the audience. Rustin was forced to complain that too many whites in the gallery, including some of his own friends, were applauding Malcolm's statements more vigorously than the Negroes in the audience: "May I explain the process. . . . It is, my friends, that many white people love to hear their kind damned to high water while they sit saying, 'Isn't it wonderful that that nice black man gives *those* white people hell? But he couldn't be talking about *me*—I'm the liberal.'"

Malcolm's lectures and sermons in early 1962 rarely mentioned the core values of the Nation's theology, and increasingly he was pulled into larger debates over the political future of black America. Probably to silence

his critics within the NOI, he tried to give more attention to organiza-
tional matters. In January, both he and Joseph visited Mosque No. 23 in
Buffalo, New York. And at the end of the same month he supervised the
NOI's sponsorship of an African-Asian Bazaar at Harlem's Rockland Palace.
He also continued to use his speeches to build up the cult around Elijah
Muhammad. The Messenger appreciated such labors on his behalf; yet
before long, Muhammad's opinion began to shift. He read the transcripts
and recordings from Malcolm's speeches and could see the political direction of his increasingly famous minister's mind. He decided to tighten the
reins.

On February 14, Muhammad wrote Malcolm formally about his schedule. "[W]hen you go to these Colleges and Universities to represent the
Teachings that Allah has revealed to me for our people, do not go too much
into the details of the political side; nor into the subject of a separate state
here for us." Muhammad instructed him to "speak only what you know
they have heard me say or that which you yourself have heard me say."
Malcolm was forbidden to express his independent opinions, even on
questions that had no relationship with the NOI. The aging patriarch sought
to reclaim his right to be the sole interpreter of Muslim teachings. "Make
the public seek me for the answers," he wrote. "Do not you see how I reject
the devils on such subjects, by telling them I will say WHERE when the
Government shows interest?" The NOI was a religious movement, not a
political cause; Malcolm no longer had the authority to address issues like
a separate black state or to speak about current events of a political nature,
unless Muhammad gave his permission. Yet, of course, any discussion of
black Americans' affairs inevitably centered on the struggle for civil rights;
Muhammad was making Malcolm's position untenable.

An opportunity soon arose to test Muhammad's boundaries. On March 7,
Cornell University invited Malcolm and CORE executive director James
Farmer to debate the theme "Segregation or Integration?" During the previous year, Farmer's Freedom Riders had grabbed national headlines with
their challenges to segregated bus systems in the South, and the promise of
real gains to be made through concerted activism gave him a strong chip
to play against Malcolm. In his opening remarks, Malcolm emphasized that
black Americans were part of the "non-white world." And just as "our
African and Asian brothers wanted to have their own land, wanted to have
their own country, wanted to exercise control over themselves," it was reasonable for black Americans to desire the same. "It is not integration that

Negroes in America want, it is human dignity." Once more, he attacked integration as a scheme benefiting only the black bourgeoisie:

> We who are black in the black belt, or black community, or black neighbor-hood can easily see that our people who settle for integration are usually the middle-class so-called Negroes, who are in the minority. Why? Because they have confidence in the white man . . . they believe that there is still hope in the American dream. But what to them is an American dream to us is an American nightmare, and we don't think that it is possible for the American white man in sincerity to take the action necessary to correct the unjust conditions that 20 million black people are made to suffer, morning, noon and night.

But Farmer, like Rustin, was not intimidated, aggressively going after the conservatism and weaknesses in the NOI's program. "We are seeking an open society . . . where people will be accepted for what they are worth, will be able to contribute fully to the total culture and the total life of the nation," he declared. Racism was America's greatest problem. Turning to Malcolm, he asked, "We know the disease, physician, what is your cure? What is your program and how do you hope to bring it into effect?" Malcolm had been long on rhetoric but short on details. "We need to have it spelled out," Farmer pressed him. "Is it a separate Negro society in each city? As a Harlem [or] a South Side Chicago?" He also effectively countered Malcolm's claim that only the black middle class favored integration by pointing out that the majority of student Freedom Riders were from working-class and low-income families. In fact, Farmer argued, the opposite was true: black entrepreneurial capitalists favored Jim Crow, because it created a self-segregated black consumer market without white competition; it was usually the black middle class that opposed desegregation. Malcolm sensed that he was losing the debate and, to score points, resorted to mentioning that Farmer was married to a white woman.

Unlike the NAACP representatives that Malcolm had previously debated, Farmer was able to explain the tactics of the Black Freedom Movement in clear, everyday terms. To Malcolm's claim that desegregated lunch counters were unimportant, for instance, he had a sensible response: "Are we not to travel? Picket lines and boycotts brought Woolworth's to its knees." CORE's Freedom Riders had "helped to create desegregation in cities throughout the South." What Malcolm undoubtedly grasped that night was that CORE's approach to desegregation was fundamentally different from that of the older civil rights establishment, which relied on litigation and legislation. CORE was actively committed to building mass protests in the streets—in Farmer's words, "The picketing and the nationwide demonstrations are the reason that the walls came down in the South, because people were in motion with their own bodies marching with picket signs, sitting in, boycotting, withholding their patronage." Ironically, the net result of the Farmer–Malcolm debate, which was widely discussed among movement activists, was to give greater legitimacy to the Black Muslim leader. Even integrationists who sharply rejected black nationalism found Malcolm's argument persuasive. Within two years, entire branch organizations of CORE, especially in Cleveland, Detroit, Brooklyn, and Harlem, would become oriented toward Malcolm X.

Perhaps Malcolm's most important public address during the first half of 1962 was at Harlem's Abyssinian Baptist Church, where Congressman Powell had invited him as part of a lecture series on the theme "Which Way the Negro?" Abyssinian church administrators informed the press that the overwhelming response they had received was larger "than all the previous Harlem 'leaders' combined." To an audience of two thousand, Malcolm repeated his thesis. "We don't think it is within the nature of the white man to change in his attitude toward the black man," he argued, while also responding to charges that, although the NOI talked a militant line, it didn't involve itself in the black community's politics. "Just because a man doesn't throw a punch doesn't mean he can't do so whenever he gets ready, so don't play the Muslims and the [black] nationalists cheap." Wisely, he praised Powell as a model of independent leadership. "Adam Clayton Powell is the only black politician who has been able to come off the white man's political plantation, buck against the white political machine downtown, and still hold his seat in Congress." Malcolm's comments set the stage for what would become a much closer partnership between the two men in the year to come.

Still, the divergence between his own views and those at the core of the NOI continued to trouble him, and he increasingly solicited the advice of those he trusted, though at times he found this circumstantially difficult. In Boston, a natural confidant would have been Louis X. However, throughout most of 1962, Louis was preoccupied with his fierce power struggle with Clarence 2X Gill over demands for selling bulk copies of *Muhammad Speaks*. Although Ella was no longer a member of the Boston mosque, Malcolm continued to be in touch, and may have reached out to her. She had also become interested in orthodox Islam during these years, which helped to draw them closer after their falling out over the power struggle in Boston.

Despite the continuing tensions in their marriage, Malcolm also occasionally consulted Betty, who worried about their stability. Over the years she had become comfortable with many of the perks that were bestowed on her as the wife of the mosque's minister. Her grocery shopping, done by others, was dutifully boxed and dropped off at her kitchen; Thomas 15X Johnson or other FOI members chauffeured her to NOI events. At official occasions Betty enjoyed front-row seats, and the applause of the adoring crowd. And occasionally, when the Messenger visited New York City, it was at Betty and Malcolm's house that the honor of hosting him was extended. As James 67X later observed, "Every woman would have liked to [have been] in her position."

Unlike Malcolm, however, Betty was growing increasingly suspicious of the NOI leadership. Because of her husband's high position in the hierarchy, she had ample opportunity to observe for herself the greedy behavior of Muhammad's family and entourage. By comparison, she and Malcolm lived almost in poverty, owning virtually nothing beyond a small amount of household furniture, their clothing, and personal items. His Oldsmobile belonged to the NOI; likewise, the title to his home was not in his name, but the mosque's. Through the early 1960s Malcolm received around three thousand dollars every month to cover his transportation, overnight accommodations, and meals when traveling. He kept meticulous records, collecting receipts for every expenditure to justify his account. The NOI forbade ministers from purchasing life insurance, Betty claimed, perhaps to make their representatives totally dependent on the sect. Quietly at first, then more forcefully, she pleaded with her husband to take appropriate measures to protect his family financially. She tried him with the Garveyite argument that black families should at least own their own homes. Malcolm's stern response was that if anything should happen to him, the Nation would certainly provide for Betty and their children.

———

Malcolm may have publicly commanded his followers to obey the law, but this did little to lessen suspicion of the Muslims by law enforcement in major cities. Nowhere did tensions run hotter than in Los Angeles, where Malcolm had established Temple No. 27 in 1957. For most whites who migrated to the city, Los Angeles was the quintessential city of dreams. For black migrants, the city of endless possibilities offered some of the same Jim Crow restrictions they had sought to escape by moving west. As early as 1915, black Los Angeles residents were protesting against racially restrictive housing covenants; such racial covenants as well as blatant discrimination by real estate firms continued to be a problem well into the 1960s. The real growth of the black community in Southern California only began to take place during the two decades after 1945. During this twenty-year period, when the black population of New York City increased by nearly 250 percent, the black population of Los Angeles jumped 800 percent. Blacks were also increasingly important in local trade unions, and in the economy generally. For example, between 1940 and 1960, the percentage of black males in LA working as factory operatives increased from 15 percent to 24 percent; the proportion of African-American men employed in crafts during the same period rose from 7 percent to 14 percent. By 1960, 468,000 blacks resided in Los Angeles County, approximately 20 percent of the county's population.

These were some of the reasons that Malcolm had invested so much energy and effort to build the NOI's presence in Southern California, and especially the development of Mosque No. 27. Having recruited the mosque's leaders, he flew out to settle a local factional dispute in October 1961. Such activities were noticed and monitored by the California Senate Fact-Finding Committee on Un-American Activities, which feared that the NOI had "Communist affiliations." The state committee concluded that there was an "interesting parallel between the Negro Muslim movement and the Communist Party, and that is the advocacy of the overthrow of a hated regime by force, violence or any other means." On September 2, 1961, several Muslims selling *Muhammad Speaks* in a South Central Los Angeles grocery store parking lot were harassed by two white store detectives. The detectives later claimed that when they had attempted to stop the Muslims from selling the paper, they were "stomped and beaten." The version of this incident described in *Muhammad Speaks* was strikingly different, with the paper claiming that "the two 'detectives' produced guns, and attempted to make a 'citizen's arrest.' Grocery packers rushed out to help the detectives . . . and black residents of the area who had gathered also became involved. For 45 minutes bedlam reigned." About forty Los Angeles Police Department officers were dispatched to the scene to restore order. Five Muslims were arrested. At their subsequent trial, the store's owner and manager confirmed that the NOI had been given permission to peddle their newspapers in the parking lot. An all-white jury acquitted the Muslims on all charges.

Following the parking lot mêlée, the LAPD was primed for retaliation against the local NOI. The city's police commissioner, William H. Parker, had even read Lincoln's *The Black Muslims in America*, and viewed the sect as subversive and dangerous, capable of producing widespread unrest. He instructed his officers to closely monitor the mosque's activities, which is why, just after midnight on April 27, 1962, when two officers observed what looked to them like men taking clothes out of the back of a car outside the mosque, they approached with suspicion. What happened next is a matter of dispute, yet whether the police were jumped, as they claimed, or the Muslim men were shoved and beaten without provocation, as seems likely, the commotion brought a stream of angry Muslims out of the mosque. The police threatened to respond with deadly force, but when one officer attempted to intimidate the growing crowd of bystanders, he was disarmed by the crowd. Somehow one officer's revolver went off, shooting and wounding his partner in the elbow. Backup squad cars soon arrived ferrying more than seventy officers, and a full-scale battle ensued. Within minutes dozens of cops raided the mosque itself, randomly beating NOI members. It took fifteen minutes for the fighting to die down. In the end, seven Muslims were shot, including NOI member William X Rogers, who was shot in the back and paralyzed for life. NOI officer Ronald Stokes, a Korean War veteran, had attempted to surrender to the police by raising his hands over his head. Police responded by shooting him from the rear; a bullet pierced his heart, killing him. A coroner's inquest determined that Stokes's death was "justifiable." A number of Muslims were indicted.

News of the raid shattered Malcolm; he wept for the reliable and trustworthy Stokes, whom he had known well from his many trips to the West Coast. The desecration of the mosque and the violence brought upon its members pushed Malcolm to a dark place. He was finally ready for the Nation to throw a punch. Malcolm told Mosque No. 7's Fruit of Islam that the time had come for retribution, an eye for an eye, and he began to recruit members for an assassination team to target LAPD officers. Charles 37X, who attended one of these meetings, recalled him in a rage, shouting to the assembled Fruit, "What are you here for? What the *hell* are you here for?" As Louis Farrakhan related, "Brother Malcolm had a gangsterlike past. And coming into the Nation, and especially in New York, he had a tremendous sway over men that came out of the street with gangster leanings." It was especially from these hardened men that Malcolm demanded action, and they rose to his cry. Mosque No. 7 intended to "send somebody to Los

Angeles to kill [the police] as sure as God made green apples," said James 67X. "Brothers volunteered for it."

As he made plans to bring his killers to Los Angeles, Malcolm sought the approval of Elijah Muhammad, in what he assumed would be a formality. The time had come for action, and surely Muhammad would see the necessity in summoning the Nation's strength for the battle. But the Messenger denied him. "Brother, you don't go to war over a provocation," he told Malcolm. "They could kill a few of my followers, but I'm not going to go out and do something silly." He ordered the entire FOI to stand down. Malcolm was stunned; he acquiesced, but with bitter disappointment. Farrakhan believes Malcolm concluded that Muhammad was trying "to protect the wealth that he had acquired, rather than go out with the struggle of our people."

A few days later Malcolm flew to Los Angeles, and on May 4 he held a press conference about the shootings at the Statler Hilton. The next day he presided over Stokes's funeral. More than two thousand people attended the service, and an estimated one thousand joined in the automobile procession to the cemetery. Yet the matter was far from resolved. If Malcolm could not kill the officers involved, he was determined that both the police and the political establishment in Los Angeles should be forced to acknowledge their responsibility. The only way to accomplish this, he believed, was for the NOI to work with civil rights organizations, local black politicians, and religious groups. On May 20, Malcolm participated in a major rally against police brutality that attracted the support of many white liberals, as well as communists. "You're brutalized because you're black," he declared at the demonstration. "And when they lay a club on the side of your head, they do not ask your religion. You're black—that's enough."

He threw himself into organizing a black united front against the police in Southern California, but once more Elijah Muhammad stepped in, ordering his stubborn lieutenant to halt all efforts. "Brother, stay where I put you," ran his edict, "because they [civil rights organizations] have no place to go. Hold your position." Muhammad was convinced that integration could not be achieved; the civil rights groups would ultimately gravitate toward the Nation of Islam. When desegregation failed, he explained to Malcolm (and later to Farrakhan), "they will have no place to go but what you and I represent." Consequently, he vetoed any cooperation with civil rights groups even on a matter as contentious as Stokes's murder. Louis X saw this as an important turning point in the deteriorating relationship between Malcolm and Muhammad. By 1962, Malcolm was "speaking less and less about the teachings [of Muhammad]," recalled Farrakhan. "And he was fascinated by the civil rights movement, the action of the civil rights participants, and the lack of action of the followers of the Honorable Elijah."

At heart, the disagreement between Malcolm X and Elijah Muhammad went deeper than the practical question of how to respond to the Los Angeles police assault. Almost from the moment Muhammad had been informed about the raid and Stokes's death, he viewed the tragedy as stemming from a lack of courage by Mosque No. 27's members. "Every one of the Muslims should have died," he was reported to have said, "before they allowed an aggressor to come into their mosque." Muhammad believed Stokes had died from weakness, because he had attempted to surrender to the police. Malcolm could hardly stomach such an idea, but having submitted to the Messenger's authority, he repeated the arguments as his own inside Mosque No. 7. James 67X listened as Malcolm told the congregation, "We are not Christian(s). We are not to turn the other cheek, but the laborers [NOI members] have gotten so comfortable that in dealing with the devil they will submit to him. . . . If a blow is struck against you, fight back." The brothers in the Los Angeles mosque who resisted had lived. Roland Stokes submitted and was killed.

Some of Malcolm's closest associates were persuaded that Elijah Muhammad had made the correct decision, at least on the issue of retaliation. Benjamin 2X Goodman, for one, would later declare, "Mr. Muhammad said, 'All in good time' . . . and he was right. The police were ready. It would have been a trap." But Malcolm himself was humiliated by the NOI's failure to defend its own members. Everything that he had experienced over the previous years—from mobilizing thousands in the streets around Hinton's beating in 1957 to working with Philip Randolph to build a local black united front in 1961–62—told him that the Nation could protect its members only through joint action with civil rights organizations and other religious groups. One could not simply leave everything to Allah.

The Stokes murder brought to a close the first phase of Malcolm's career within the NOI. He had become convinced that Elijah Muhammad's passive position could not be justified. Malcolm had spent almost a decade in the Nation, and for all his speeches, he could point to no progress on the creation of a separate black state. Meanwhile, in the state that existed, the black men and women who looked to him for leadership were suffering and dying. Political agitation and public protests, along the lines of CORE and SNCC, were essential to challenging institutional racism. Malcolm hoped that, at least within the confines of Mosque No. 7, he would be allowed to pursue a more aggressive strategy, in concert with independent black leaders like Powell and Randolph. In doing so, he speculated, perhaps the entire Nation of Islam could be reborn.

CHAPTER 8

From Prayer to Protest

May 1962–March 1963

Within days of his return from Los Angeles, Malcolm began to quietly pursue a strategy of limited political engagement. His muzzling by Elijah Muhammad continued to rankle, as did Muhammad's belittling theory about Ronald X Stokes's death resulting from his submission to the authorities. Before leaving Los Angeles on May 22, Malcolm had told an electrified crowd that Stokes "displayed the highest form of morals of any black person anywhere on this earth," and he arrived in New York a few days later feeling charged with purpose. Though Muhammad had restrained him from coalition building with non-Muslim moderates in Los Angeles, on Malcolm's home turf he held much greater latitude. On May 26, Mosque No. 7 organized a rally in front of the Hotel Theresa. The press release advertising this event linked the "cold-blooded murder of Ronald T. Stokes and the shooting of seven other innocent, unarmed Negroes" in Los Angeles with the Freedom Riders in Alabama and the then current mass desegregation campaign led by King in Georgia. Malcolm invited the two candidates competing for Harlem's congressional seat to attend, Powell and attorney Paul Zuber, and he called for all Harlem leaders to support a coalition against police brutality. He was challenging Elijah Muhammad and his Chicago superiors by carrying out in New York the civil rights approach he had planned for Southern California.

Malcolm's critics in the Nation of Islam took this as proof that he had become mesmerized by the media, diverting his attention from religious matters into the dangerous realm of politics. Even Los Angeles minister John Shabazz, whose mosque stood at the center of the political maelstrom and who was presently a defendant in the LAPD's criminal suit against the

Muslims, kept to the party line. In a June 1962 letter addressed to "Brother Minister" and copied to Malcolm, Shabazz argued that excessive force by the police could not be ended primarily through politics: The letter declared that "a *religious* solution will fit the problem of Police Brutality."

Undaunted, Malcolm's frustration pushed him forward, yet it soon led him to make a misstep that put him sharply on the defensive. On June 3 an airplane crashed in Paris, killing 121 well-to-do white citizens of Atlanta; given its timing, Malcolm found the tragedy too tempting a target. Before an audience of fifteen hundred in Los Angeles, he described the disaster as "a very beautiful thing," proof that God answers prayers. "We call on our God—He gets rid of 120 of them." The following month, the press picked up the statement, and many prominent Negroes wasted little time in denouncing both Malcolm and the NOI. Dr. Rufus Clement, president of Atlanta's University Center, described Malcolm's remarks as "unchristian and inhuman," while NAACP leader Roy Wilkins referred to the crash as "a mass tragedy," adding in bewilderment, "Even when Negroes had their most violent [white] enemies against them, they did not descend to any glad feelings over death." But the most eloquent—and damning—statement came from Martin Luther King, Jr., who sought to reassure white Americans "that the hatred expressed toward whites by Malcolm X [was not] shared by the vast majority of Negroes in the United States. While there is a great deal of legitimate discontent and righteous indignation in the Negro community, it has never developed into a large-scale hatred of whites." Above all, Malcolm's statement was a public relations disaster. It made it much easier for Negro moderates in groups like the NAACP and National Urban League to refuse to cooperate with the NOI, and it almost certainly increased the level of FBI infiltration. It was probably even what prompted the Bureau to discredit him in France; shortly thereafter, J. Edgar Hoover contacted the French government's legal attaché in Paris, warning that a French film director, Pierre-Dominique Gaisseau, had recently been in contact with Malcolm, leader of a "fanatical" and "anti-white organization."

Even more than the 1959 television series *The Hate That Hate Produced*, Malcolm's comments on the crash reinforced his reputation as a demagogue. He may have considered his remark as part of a polemical jihad of words, designed to place Christian whites on the defensive, but it reinforced the Lomax-Wallace thesis that the NOI was the product of black hate. For Malcolm's critics in the civil rights movement, the statement, and others like it, marked him as representative of white society's failure to integrate.

Yet in retrospect, many of Malcolm's most outrageous statements about the necessity of extremism in the achievement of political freedom and liberty were not unlike the views expressed by the 1964 Republican presidential candidate Barry Goldwater, who declared that "extremism in the defense of liberty is no vice, and moderation in the pursuit of justice is no virtue." Nearly two years before, in 1962, Malcolm argued, "Death is the price of liberty. If you're not ready to die for it, put the word 'freedom' out of your vocabulary."

For a few weeks Malcolm avoided speaking to the press while attempting to smooth things over within the NOI. On June 9 he attended a two-day rally featuring Elijah Muhammad at Detroit's Olympia Stadium. After the end of the second public event, all NOI members were ordered to stay. Malcolm had the unpleasant responsibility of reading to the crowd a letter from Raymond Sharrieff that had already been sent to all FOI captains, ordering "every Muslim to begin obtaining no less than two new subscriptions to *Muhammad Speaks* per day." The subscription drive would continue for three months. The letter ended noting that "those who failed to comply would be eliminated from the mosque." This new edict showed Chicago's determination to turn the budding success of its newspaper into a cash cow. Members were already tithing from their wages to their mosques as well as voluntarily donating funds to Muhammad and his family; now they were expected to generate even more money.

The Nation's craven financial squeeze began to cause unrest at mosques throughout the country, and tensions in Boston rattled the organization. By 1962, Louis X was earning about $110 weekly serving as minister, yet as former Boston NOI official Aubrey Barnette would later note, "Each member was supposed to donate $2.95 a week toward Louis's upkeep, which means that if 100 members were contributing regularly he was receiving another $15,000 a year in expense money." Technically, none of the other mosque officials drew salaries, but in practice the FOI captain received eighty-five dollars weekly and the mosque secretary another thirty-five dollars each week, plus "frequent contributions from the membership." During the three-year period that Barnette and his wife, Ruth, belonged to the mosque, they donated one thousand dollars, about one-fifth of Barnette's income, which was itself slightly above average for NOI members at the time. Moreover, a cult of violence and intimidation began to grow around FOI captain Clarence 2X Gill. Barnette recalled Captain Clarence as "a stocky man of medium height" who looked "like an ex–middleweight boxer . . . and is arrogant, suspicious, dictatorial." Members could not speak to Clarence directly, but were forced instead to communicate through intermediaries. At his Monday night FOI sessions, he put Fruit members through a two-hour-long "mishmash of drill, hygiene lectures, current events briefings, pep talks, physical exercise and miscellaneous instruction." His legendary paranoia infected the ranks, as members were constantly instructed to look out for possible FBI informants. When Barnette urged him to dial down the rants, Clarence immediately accused him of being an "FBI spy."

The push to increase sales of *Muhammad Speaks* sparked an already disgruntled Boston membership to open revolt. About fifty black businessmen—small merchants and entrepreneurs mostly—had joined the mosque in part for their enthusiasm for Louis X. They didn't mind the weekly payments to sustain officials' salaries and to cover administrative costs. But they balked when told they were each to sell two hundred copies of *Muhammad Speaks* at fifteen cents per issue, and that they'd be responsible for a full financial account whether or not the papers were sold. Elijah Muhammad, Jr., by then the FOI's assistant supreme captain, flew to Boston to quell potential dissent, warning Boston's Fruit that "if you don't want to sell the paper, then don't even bother to come in here. I'm the judge tonight, and you are guilty." He even reminded members "that in the old days recalcitrant brothers were killed."

The threats and physical intimidation backfired. Within days, forty-two men, all businessmen, resigned from the mosque. Faced with shrinking membership and commensurately shrinking income, Louis X announced a "general amnesty" and invited all those who had left the mosque to attend a meeting. He promised them that the newspaper quotas would no longer be enforced, and that Clarence was out. But when the Chicago headquarters learned about Louis's leniency, he was overruled. Two days later, Louis spoke to the entire mosque: "Some of you seem to have misunderstood me." Upon learning that nothing had changed, Barnette immediately walked out, never to return to the mosque. But matters weren't finished as far as Captain Clarence was concerned. Months later, as Barnette and another ex-Muslim drove past the mosque on a busy Roxbury street, a pink Cadillac pulled from the curb and cut in front of Barnette's car. Six or more Muslims rushed both sides of Barnette's blocked automobile, pulling the two men out. In plain daylight and in public, Barnette and the second man, John Thomas, were punched, kicked, and stomped repeatedly. Barnette suffered a broken ankle, a fractured vertebra, fractured ribs, damaged kidneys, and internal bleeding, placing him in the hospital for a week. "I believe we were beaten as punishment for quitting and also as a warning to keep our mouths shut," he said.

In New York, where Malcolm and Joseph exerted a firmer grasp on the membership, such troubles were largely avoided. Instead, increased sales-manship of *Muhammad Speaks* drew hassles from local cops. On July 2, Malcolm addressed Mosque No. 7, warning that if police bothered the NOI for selling the paper, then members should do what the officers instructed. But he also suggested that Muslims had a legal right to sell their publica-tion, as guaranteed by the Constitution. He went on to predict, "The time will come when the Muslims will not be able to leave their homes." NOI members should never carry weapons, he explained, but "if attacked, self-defense is granted throughout the world."

A week later, he flew to Chicago to participate in a rally featuring Elijah Muhammad, at which the Nation would unveil the two pieces of literature that would later come to define it. Although the NOI had grown rapidly, it had not participated in the desegregation struggles across the South that had won the respect and admiration of people throughout the world. To blacks, it was abundantly clear what groups like the NAACP and CORE wanted; the NOI, by contrast and largely by design, had no clear social program that realistically could be implemented. Since it was unlikely that blacks could seize a separate territory for themselves inside the United States, what did the NOI propose to do? For as much as Muhammad dis-liked and discouraged Malcolm's inclinations toward activism, he was not a fool when it came to surveying the landscape of black politics and cali-brating the NOI's place within it.

By the middle of 1962, CORE had come to national prominence for its Freedom Rides, and King was back in Albany, Georgia, where he was lead-ing a desegregation campaign that found him briefly jailed until the chief of police released him to avoid further negative media coverage. The suc-cesses of the civil rights movement had emboldened America's black com-munities and made the NOI's strict noninterventionist, antiactivist platform seem out of step or, worse, backward. To bolster his case in the court of public opinion, Muhammad and his Chicago lieutenants developed a ten-point policy statement that he unveiled in his address at the rally. Before a large crowd at the Arie Crown Theater on Lake Shore Drive, he presented a list of demands that preserved the Nation's anti-integrationist stance—later codified as "What the Muslims Want"—and included religious free-dom, an end to police brutality, and the release "of all Believers of Islam now held in federal prisons." But the statement also astutely contained major concessions to the civil rights movement. "As long as we are not allowed to establish a state or territory of our own, we demand not only equal justice under the laws of the United States, but equal employment opportunities, *now!*" Muhammad followed this statement with a twelve-point "What the Muslims Believe," a summary of the Nation of Islam's basic creed. Over the next thirteen years, until Muhammad's death in 1975, these two statements would become the most widely disseminated of NOI manifestos. For Malcolm, who had pushed for greater involvement with the movement, the revelation was bittersweet; he had moved toward these ideas long before Chicago.

His own push for action renewed shortly in New York, where Mosque No. 7 now organized rallies almost every other week, focused mainly on bringing broad change to Harlem's impoverished and embattled blacks. Malcolm's involvement with A. Philip Randolph's Emergency Committee continued to shape his efforts, and on July 21 he addressed a crowd of two thousand packed in front of the Hotel Theresa. The five-hour program featured a saxophone, drum, and bass trio, which helped attract onlookers. Fruit of Islam members circulated through the crowd, selling *Muhammad Speaks* and NOI-produced records featuring Louis X. Malcolm focused largely on Harlem's social and economic conditions. "Unemployment, juvenile delinquency, prostitution, gambling, the dope traffic and other forms of organized crimes are on the rise," he explained:

> Even our women, young girls and boys, are falling victim to the organized evils that are destroying the moral fiber of the Negro community. The fuse has already been lit . . . if something is not done immediately, there will be an explosive situation in the Negro community more dangerous and destructive than a hundred megaton bombs.

The intensity of the speech reflected the growing depths of his own commitment to embracing a united black community. Covering the event, the *Chicago Defender* noted that Malcolm's words contained such "sentiment and emotional drive" that the cries from the audience "became at times almost a chant, coming at the cadenced pauses in his oratory." But the most significant feature of this largely NOI-sponsored rally was the list of guest speakers, which ran to far more moderate figures and included none other than Malcolm's old sparring partner, Bayard Rustin.

The very next day, Betty gave birth to the couple's third daughter. She was named Ilyasah, the feminized Arabic version of Elijah. By now, Malcolm's quick departures after the births of his children had become almost routine; that same day, he ducked out and joined several FOI members to watch a labor rally of mostly blacks and Latinos held on Manhattan's Upper East Side and organized by the Committee for Justice to Hospital Workers. Although forbidden to participate in civil rights–style demonstrations, the Muslims expressed their support from the sidelines. Malcolm even briefly addressed the strikers—technically a violation of Muhammad's orders, but once again he presumably reasoned that in his own territory, so long as he sang Muhammad's praises, neither Raymond Sharrieff nor anyone else had the power to stop him.

Ongoing legal issues stemming from events in Los Angeles continued to consume him throughout the summer. The day after Ilyasah's birth, he was in Connecticut, raising funds on behalf of the late Ronald Stokes's family. On July 28 he returned to New York, having heard that Los Angeles mayor Sam Yorty would be speaking at a symposium at the Waldorf-Astoria on the subject of the urban crisis. Shortly after the assault, Yorty had given LAPD commissioner William Parker his full backing on the mosque shootings and went so far as to meet with attorney general Robert Kennedy in hopes of prompting a federal investigation of the NOI. When Malcolm, having gained admittance to the audience, spoke up from the floor, Yorty was apoplectic: "I didn't fly here to be questioned by Malcolm X," he retorted. "I regard the Black Muslim movement as a Nazi-type of movement preaching hate." Malcolm responded by telling the *New York Times*, "I'd rather be a Nazi than whatever Mr. Yorty is."

The next month, together with a large group of Muslims, Malcolm packed a hearing room in the Los Angeles County Superior Court to express support for the NOI members who had been indicted for assault on April 27. Through repeated entreaties, he had convinced Earl Broady, a criminal attorney and former Los Angeles police officer, to represent the thirteen Muslims facing charges. Race promised to play a prominent role in determining the course of the case. The FBI agent monitoring the proceedings noted, "It is understood that these defendants would argue that there was an improper[ly] impaneled jury because of the lack of sufficient numbers of Negroes."

For several days in mid-August, Malcolm visited St. Louis for a local NOI rally. Although he spoke, most attention was focused on Muhammad, who was promoted as the featured speaker. Sometime during this visit, Muhammad expressed concern to Malcolm about recent damage to the

NOI's image. He was especially agitated about Malcolm's university lectures, which he felt "gained no converts and only provided an opportunity for the NOI to be blasted in public." Malcolm had little choice except to cancel all his remaining college appearances. Internal FBI documents establish that the Bureau almost immediately knew about these cancellations; someone with direct access to the highest level inside the NOI was providing information to the agency. The most likely such person was national secretary John Ali; all business-related correspondence and ministers' weekly reports went across Ali's desk. Ali personally knew, and could demand the firing of, every local mosque's secretary. The FBI would have easily recognized the value of his strategic place inside the Nation's hierarchy.

While Malcolm was in St. Louis, he kept an interview appointment with a white journalist who had recently caught his attention with a series of thoughtful pieces on the city's somewhat sleepy mosque. Peter Goldman was a news writer for the *St. Louis Globe-Democrat*, a conservative newspaper that also had on its editorial staff a young Patrick Buchanan. Goldman's interest in the NOI went back two years to his postgraduate fellowship at Harvard in 1960, where he had started reading Lincoln's *The Black Muslims in America* and then had seen Malcolm's remarkable debate with Walter Carrington at Sanders Theatre. Though Goldman had become a liberal integrationist in college, going so far as to join CORE and attend local sit-ins in the fifties, Malcolm's performance in the debate profoundly affected him. Goldman was stunned by both the man and his message, and he was especially impressed by Malcolm's bearing, recalling it as "both soldierly and priestly. His carriage was amazing." He also was struck by the NOI members who accompanied Malcolm: "There were members of the Brothers of Islam in the hall, a protective presence, and as I left, I could see them spotted around the nearby campus. There'd be a guy standing under a tree with the narrow tie and the sort of Ivy League suit (and bald head)."

When Goldman returned to St. Louis and landed at the *Globe-Democrat*, he quickly began writing about the local mosque, and though his series' chief effect was probably to bring the local NOI under greater scrutiny from the authorities, it also earned him Malcolm's attention. Several weeks after the articles appeared, he called Goldman to explain that he was about to visit the city. "Would you like to get together," he asked, the better to "understand the Nation of Islam?"

An interview was arranged through the local mosque, to take place at the Shabazz Frosti Kreem, an NOI-affiliated luncheonette in the North Side ghetto. Goldman was extremely nervous: "I was then prisoner to all the white liberal views of the world, of race in America, including the view that the locus of tragedy was the American South, that Jim Crow was the central struggle." Helen Dudar, Goldman's wife and also a journalist, accompanied him to the meeting, and together they waited outside the luncheonette for their subject to arrive. After a few minutes a car pulled up, with Malcolm sitting "sort of jackknifed in the backseat." As soon as he got out, Goldman recalled, "Just from the moment you saw him, [you felt] this incredible presence." The three of them, accompanied by the local minister, Clyde X, went inside and sat at a table. Malcolm quickly gravitated to the jukebox. Dropping in a coin, he chose Louis X's "A White Man's Heaven Is a Black Man's Hell."

To Goldman's surprise, the interview lasted nearly three hours. Malcolm "told us perfectly pleasantly that whites were inherently the enemies of Negroes; that integration was impossible without a great bloodletting and was undesirable anyway; [and] that nonviolence—'this mealy-mouth beg-in, wait-in, lead-in kind of action'—was only a device for disarming the blacks and, worse still, unmanning them." Although Malcolm was impressive, Goldman remained a committed liberal who struggled to overcome his ideological prejudices to write about the Nation fairly.

Over the next three years, Goldman conducted at least five lengthy interviews with Malcolm. They spoke over the telephone on individual stories frequently. Sometimes Goldman was simply seeking a publishable quote; but he sensed that for some reason he had become part of "a relatively small target group of media people whom [Malcolm wanted to] *seduce*." These were the journalists Malcolm trusted "to get the serious message out." For most people, however, his normal approach was "the cocked fist . . . It was very easy to scare the pants off most white reporters . . . Their attention span was the quote—the most inflammatory quote you can put on the air, and Malcolm liked to serve those up." But Goldman also sensed that Malcolm knew, deep down, "if you create an atmosphere of threat, a sense of threat . . . , never throw the punch, because if you throw the punch, people will be out on the street dying." So he was never an "advocate of suicidal activity," still believing "the threat was useful."

———

Another journalist who would have a profound impact on Malcolm's life and legacy was Alex Haley. Born in 1921, Haley had just retired after twenty years' service in the U.S. Coast Guard. A liberal Republican, Haley completely rejected the racial separatism and intolerance of the NOI. He believed the Nation was the consequence of mainstream America's failure to assimilate Negroes into the existing system. Yet in the wake of the publicity surrounding *The Hate That Hate Produced* in 1959, Haley drafted a short article about the group, "Mr. Muhammad Speaks," that was published in the March 1960 issue of *Reader's Digest*. Although Haley had characterized the Nation as a "potent, racist cult," NOI leaders generally praised the article's objectivity. The essay focused primarily on Elijah Muhammad's history and leadership of the sect; Malcolm was mentioned but only as a secondary figure. In 1962, Haley contacted the NOI again, requesting its cooperation for a longer story to be published in the widely read *Saturday Evening Post*. It would be coauthored with a white journalist, Alfred Balk, who had apparently been recruited to convince white readers that the piece reflected an integrationist viewpoint, despite the fact that Haley himself was an avowed integrationist. On the strength of Haley's previous article, he and Balk were given substantial access to NOI activities throughout the country. Malcolm even agreed to give Haley a detailed interview about his life prior to becoming a follower of Muhammad. What the Muslims could not have known was that simultaneously Balk was talking to the FBI, meeting on October 9 with an agent in their Crime Research Section in Chicago. Balk explained that his and Haley's story had "to give an accurate and realistic appraisal of the Nation of Islam" while illustrating "that many of the statements about the successes of the organization among the Negro people are also exaggerated." The Bureau agreed to funnel them selective information about the NOI, based on its years of covert surveillance, but none of it could be attributed.

The Nation was facing unanticipated challenges resulting from its rapid expansion. The real estate investments and the forced "taxation" on NOI members to obtain thousands of *Muhammad Speaks* subscriptions—despite the resistance it raised in many members—generated impressive sums for the Chicago headquarters, and for Muhammad's family. Raymond Sharrieff and John Ali had consolidated their control over the organization's day-to-day operations, and they did not share the Messenger's paternal fondness for Malcolm, nor did Muhammad's children appreciate the close bond their father had developed with his greatest protégé. It made for an awkward and strained relationship between the Nation's largest branch, in New York, and Chicago. Malcolm's tireless barnstorming over the previous few years and his magnetic personality had driven much of the Nation's growth—and in turn the growth in its coffers—yet continued press speculation that he was Muhammad's heir apparent challenged everyone's sense of security, despite Malcolm's constant efforts to keep the spotlight on Elijah.

By 1962, the secretary of every mosque was directly reporting to John Ali, who had become firmly allied with Malcolm's critics. Farrakhan recalled that "the captains were under Raymond Sharrieff and Elijah, Junior . . . and the sister captains were under Ethel Sharrieff or Lottie, [the] Messenger's daughter. . . . They had these positions that they wanted to keep, [so] they began to persecute brother Malcolm from headquarters." *Muhammad Speaks* began reducing its coverage of his speeches. "He would speak in places, and really he'd do a lot of great work," said Farrakhan, "but our paper would hardly say anything." Occasionally Malcolm expressed his disappointments to his Boston friend. "He would say things to me—he said, 'You know, I work hard for the Nation, and, man, for me to be doing this and I get no recognition.' So it began eating away at [my] brother." Malcolm kept quiet about his unhappiness to his subordinates, but rather, following Muhammad's instructions, began turning down college engagements—for instance, canceling a speaking event at the University of Bridgeport because of "throat trouble."

To counter the animosity building against him in Chicago, he also drew closer to the allies that surrounded him in New York, chief among them Mosque No. 7's assistant minister Benjamin 2X Goodman. Like many in the NOI, Goodman had come to the organization following an unhappy tenure in the armed forces during the years after World War II. Having enlisted in the air force in 1949, he was cited for "company punishment" four times before being court-martialed in August 1951 and discharged in late 1952. The experience hardly endeared him to white authority, and in 1957, shortly after his arrival in New York, he became a member of the Harlem temple. He showed immediate promise, and two years later, nearing his thirtieth birthday, he was named the instructor for the Great Black Man's History course in Temple No. 7's adult education program. To support himself, he started a bookselling business, and also found employment as a building supervisor. In 1961, NOI literature described Benjamin as manager of Crescent Book Sales, a "specialist in Islamic literature and history."

Though Benjamin 2X had begun serving as a ministry assistant in 1958, it was not until the early 1960s that Malcolm came to rely on him for a wide variety of duties. Although Henry X remained Mosque No. 7's official chief assistant minister, everyone knew that Benjamin was the closest to Malcolm. The spiritual bond between the two was second only to that between Malcolm and Louis X. In 1961–62, Benjamin's role within the mosque significantly changed, and consequently so did his relationship with Malcolm. The FBI noted that Benjamin was increasingly given additional assignments. For example, from September 1961 until August 1962, he attended meetings to establish an NOI mosque in Bridgeport, Connecticut. During May and June 1962, he was one of several featured speakers at Philadelphia's Mosque No. 12, and in mid-July of that year was named the mosque's "main speaker." He also increasingly accompanied Malcolm on out-of-town engagements.

His greatest value, so far as Malcolm was concerned, lay in the humble attitude he brought to his position. By all accounts, his disposition was pastoral and spiritual; he sought the meaning of his faith through the good works he did. Over the years, he enjoyed meals and other forms of fellowship in Malcolm's home hundreds of times. He knew, and lovingly admired, his senior minister, making him the pastoral counterbalance to James 67X, the men representing two distinctive aspects of Malcolm's personality. Yet unlike James, who was the only man who would vigorously argue with Malcolm to his face, there was always a distance, an absence of intimacy, between Benjamin and Malcolm. "He used to send me out of town, and I'd come back and go to his house maybe at one in the morning and we'd talk," Benjamin recalled. "But we didn't get close. Not in the buddy sense. He was always in *command*."

After his Sunday sermons at Mosque No. 7, Malcolm usually invited his assistants back home for dinner. The young ministers thought of such occasions as tutorials. Increasingly, however, they witnessed tense confrontations between Betty and Malcolm. Betty's anger and anxiety became so overwhelming that by early 1963 she had fled again, to Detroit. When Malcolm arrived back home one evening after being away, he discovered his spouse and children were gone. This time he didn't go looking. After a few days, Betty grew terribly worried; perhaps she finally had pushed her husband too far. Eventually Malcolm learned where she was, and he contacted her: "I don't have a job where I can leave at a certain time. . . . You knew that when you married me. If you leave again, I'm not coming after you." Sometimes, when the couple was experiencing difficulties, he dispatched Betty and the children to stay at the Boston home of Louis Farrakhan and his wife. "Because he knew I loved him," Farrakhan explained, "and he knew that I would defend him. . . . It was a good place for Betty to be."

By the early fall of 1962, Malcolm had decided that he would not seek an open confrontation with his critics inside the Nation. He greatly reduced the number of interviews and television appearances he accepted, to dispel the impression that he saw himself as Muhammad's successor. Nevertheless, he still did some radio and television. On the night of September 30, when thousands of federal troops were occupying the University of Mississippi to ensure the enrollment of James Meredith, he was on the Barry Gray radio show, denouncing racial intermarriage. As for Meredith, Malcolm curtly commented, "One little black man going to a school in Mississippi in no way compensates for the fact that a million black people don't even get to the grade school level in Mississippi." At every opportunity he made plain his boundless belief in Elijah Muhammad's perfection. At a Mosque No. 7 meeting on October 19, he drew attention to a negative newspaper article about the Messenger. No one, he preached, must be permitted "to defame the name of Elijah Muhammad," adding that if he saw the reporter of the article on the street he would punch him "right in the mouth."

One part of Malcolm's strategy to promote the cult around Muhammad involved taking a more aggressive role in defending the Islamic legitimacy of the NOI's religious views, especially when criticized by orthodox Muslims, who often took great offense at Muhammad's claim of connection with the divine. Near the end of the summer a Sudanese Muslim college student, Yahya Hayari, publicly criticized the NOI, prompting Malcolm to write him a letter of protest, not so much addressing the meat of Hayari's critique, but taking him to task for airing his complaint publicly. It is "difficult for me to believe that you're a Muslim from the Sudan," Malcolm began. "No real Muslim will ever attack another Muslim just to gain the friendship of Christians." Differences, he suggested, should be settled "in private . . . but never to the public delight of Jews and Christians." Malcolm drew upon international conflicts to explain the dangers of Muslim disunity: "The Europeans are still in the Congo because the Congolese have been kept busy fighting each other. . . . It would be quite foolish for Muslim students to come here from the Sudan or any other part of Africa and allow themselves to be used to attack us in a Christian country, a white country, a country in which 20 million of their own 'Darker Brothers' are yet being held as Second-Class Citizens, which is only a modified form of 20th Century Colonialism." Hayari's criticisms against the Nation continued, prompting Malcolm to send a letter of protest to the *Pittsburgh Courier*. Hayari "has been in Christian America too long," Malcolm advised, because he "sounds like . . . [a] brainwashed, American Negro." Malcolm minimized the theological differences between his sect and global Islam, arguing that the tactics of "the police of the enemies of Islam have always been 'divide and conquer.'"

Hayari was clearly among those who "suffer" from a "colonial mentality." Hayari's response appeared in the October 27, 1962, issue of the *Pittsburgh Courier*. "Mr. Elijah does not believe in or teach Islam," Hayari insisted. "What he teaches in the name of Islam is his own social theory." Because of Muhammad's heresies, "all those that follow him should know that they are being led straight to Hell."

On November 24, Malcolm's letter criticizing an Afghani Muslim's critique of the NOI appeared in the *Amsterdam News*. To demonstrate his fidelity to Islamic orthodoxy, Malcolm responded by citing verses from the Qur'an. "Messenger Elijah Muhammad's followers here in America live by a higher moral code and practice a more strict form of religious discipline than Muslims do anywhere else on this earth," Malcolm insisted. "Oh, you who believe, take not the Jews and the Christians for friends . . . And whoever takes them for friends he is indeed one of them," Malcolm praised Elijah Muhammad as "Allah's last messenger today, and by accepting his divine message we receive such strong spiritual strength from him that we are able to reform ourselves from the evils of this Christian world overnight."

Also in 1962, another Sudanese Muslim, Ahmed Osman, studying at Dartmouth College, attended Mosque No. 7 services and directly challenged Malcolm X during a question and answer period. Osman was particularly agitated by the NOI's claims that Elijah Muhammad was the "Messenger of God," and that whites were literally "devils." Osman came away "greatly impressed with Malcolm," but "unsatisfied" with his answers. He began sending literature from the Islamic Center in Geneva, Switzerland, and writing to him about the "true Islam." Malcolm appreciated the literature and asked Osman for more. Yet despite his exposure to orthodox Islam, Malcolm was still unprepared to break from the Nation.

Yet the more challengers he engaged on the question of Islam, the more emerged to confront him. In March 1963, he debated Louis Lomax and others as part of a program on Los Angeles Channel 11, during which he appeared to distance himself from Muhammad. He explained, "One becomes a Muslim only by accepting the religion of Islam, which means belief in one God, Allah. Christians call him Christ, Jews call him Jehovah." This statement was a tacit rejection of Yacub's History, and of the NOI demonology of whites. Despite such modification, Malcolm adhered to other aspects of NOI orthodoxy, stating at one point in the debate, "The Honorable Elijah Muhammad teaches us that God taught him that the white race is a race of devils and what a white person should do if he is not a devil is prove it. As far as I'm concerned, the history of the white race as it has been taught to us by the Honorable Elijah Muhammad is pretty strong evidence against that particular race." The debate ran late, and he and Lomax did not leave the television studio until after one thirty in the morning. When they reached the parking lot, they were confronted by a group of angry Arab students from UCLA who had viewed with dismay Malcolm's "white devil" statements, which directly contradicted the color-blind, abstract orthodoxy of Islam. Malcolm explained that the phrase "white devils" was essential "in waking up the deaf, dumb and blind American Negro," but the students were unconvinced. Malcolm, upset, left in a waiting automobile. What he was beginning to comprehend was that he could no longer claim to be part of Islam's *ummah* while reviling all whites as a race beyond redemption. He would have to choose.

———

On November 15, 1962, aging boxing legend Archie Moore climbed into the ring in Los Angeles for a late-career fight against an opponent almost half his age. By round four he was finished, giving another victory to his brash challenger, who was as yet unbeaten in sixteen professional fights. In New York, Malcolm, due in the city the next week, kept an eye out for news of the fight. Though the Nation looked unfavorably upon boxing, and though Malcolm himself had never shown much interest in the sport, this particular young fighter presented a special case. Earlier that year, in Detroit, Malcolm had been relaxing at the Students' Luncheonette next door to Mosque No. 1 when he was approached by a handsome, well-built black man who excitedly thrust out his hand to introduce himself: "I'm Cassius Clay." Just nineteen years old, he and his brother, Rudy, had driven all the way from Louisville to hear Elijah Muhammad speak.

Few men would play such an outsized role in Malcolm's life as this enigmatic, irrepressible figure, who would become legendary as Muhammad Ali. The two men shared important childhood connections: though Clay's father, Cassius, Sr., remained very much alive well into his son's life, like Earl Little he had been deeply influenced by Marcus Garvey and had imparted the lessons of black pride and self-sufficiency to his son. Born on January 17, 1942, Cassius, Jr., had taken up boxing at the age of twelve under the guidance of a local police officer, at once excelling. However, at first he won more plaudits for his charm than for his pugilistic skills, making a name for himself by spouting comedic rhymes celebrating his prowess. He broke through in 1960 by winning a gold medal in the 175-pound light heavyweight division at the Rome Olympics. Promptly turning professional, Clay was backed by a syndicate of wealthy white men calling themselves the Louisville Sponsoring Group.

Clay's fierce individualism and Garvey-inspired sense of pride made him a natural fit for the Nation of Islam, and when he first encountered the group in 1959, it caught his attention. He had traveled to Chicago to fight in a Golden Gloves tournament and returned to Louisville clutching a long-playing record of Elijah Muhammad's speeches. Still in high school, he pestered one of his teachers, unsuccessfully, to be allowed to write a paper about the sect. In March 1961, by this time a professional training in Miami, Clay encountered Captain Sam X Saxon (later Abdul Rahman) selling copies of *Muhammad Speaks* on the street. He struck up a conversation and Saxon invited him to attend the city's small mosque. From his very first visit, the young boxer was fascinated. "This minister started teaching, and the things he said really shook me up," he told Alex Haley.

> Things like that we twenty million black people in America didn't know our true identities, or even our true family names. And we were the direct descendants of black men and women stolen from the rich black continent and brought here and stripped of all knowledge of themselves and taught to hate themselves and their kind. And that's how us so-called "Negroes" had come to be the only race among mankind that loves its enemies. Now, I'm the kind that catches on quick. I said to myself, listen, this man's *saying* something!

He later claimed that it was "the first time I ever felt spiritual in my life." Soon he started reading *Muhammad Speaks* regularly and developed friendships with NOI members, eventually coming to the attention of Jeremiah X, Atlanta's minister and the NOI's regional boss, who traveled to Miami on several occasions to see him. Through Saxon, Clay obtained the services of a Muslim cook, who helped him observe Muslim dietary requirements.

To Malcolm, Clay was a jovial, "clean-cut, down-to-earth youngster." He saw through Clay's clown routine, which perhaps reminded him of his own comedic antics as Sandwich Red while serving whites on trains during the war. After their introduction at the luncheonette in early 1962, the two men stayed in contact throughout the year, and soon Malcolm asked his friend Archie Richardson (later Osman Karriem) to watch over Clay in Miami. Malcolm sensed that Clay had potential as a fighter; his conversion to the

NOI could allow the sect to reach an entirely different audience. Ferdie Pacheco, Clay's trainer, later observed, "Malcolm X and Ali were like very close brothers. It was almost like they were in love with each other." To Clay, Malcolm was "the smartest black man on the face of the earth." Even Pacheco was impressed. "Malcolm X was bright as hell, convincing, charismatic in the way that great leaders and martyrs are. It certainly rubbed off on Ali."

Four days after Clay's fight with Moore, Malcolm touched down in Los Angeles, where, according to the *Los Angeles Herald-Dispatch,* he would be helping out with a fund-raising drive and teaching classes for two weeks. But this was only part of Malcolm's new plan. He had decided to quietly countermand Elijah's ban on cooperation with civil rights and non-Muslim groups. To that end, between November 19 and 24, he participated in forums on "Integration or Separation" and "Militants in Negro Leadership," the latter largely organized by the Afro-American Association. Founded earlier in 1962 by activist Donald Warden, the association was a progressive network of largely militant black students. Some of the activists who emerged from this group would soon have a major impact on the Black Freedom Movement. The association chapter in the Bay Area claimed future Black Panther Party founder Huey P. Newton as a member, and in Los Angeles the local leader was Ron Everett, who subsequently became the high priest of black cultural nationalism, known as Maulana Karenga.

Although the conference and rally managed to bring out only four hundred people—much smaller than the thousands of Harlemites that Mosque No. 7 regularly massed—it attracted the attention of the *New York Times* as well as the national black press. The daylong program featured a series of workshops under the theme "The Mind of the Ghetto." In the plenary session, Wilfred Ussery of the Afro-American Association vigorously propounded CORE's nonviolent approach, but the crowd was overwhelmingly for Malcolm. The *Times* observed, "There appeared to be a considerable number of Black Muslim supporters, judging from shouts of approval that punctuated the statements made by Malcolm X."

The cheers reflected the increasing complexity of Malcolm's relationship with the leftmost wing of the civil rights movement. Unlike the NAACP, whose discrete units largely moved in lockstep thanks to its rigid, multi-tiered hierarchy, CORE had a freer organizing structure with less oversight from national headquarters. Local branches often took on a different, more militant character that found greater common ground with the NOI's black nationalism. Whereas Malcolm and James Farmer had long disagreed on philosophy and tactics, in the CORE outposts more and more activists were aligning themselves with Malcolm.

At the conference, Malcolm did not obscure his political differences with CORE, criticizing the Freedom Rides as a waste of resources and repeatedly underscoring the fundamental difference that separated integrationist liberals from black nationalists: the former believed that the predominantly white political system possessed the capacity to reform itself on matters of race, whereas the latter viewed that as impossible. "Our problem will never be solved by the white man," said Malcolm. "We must solve it for ourselves." When eventually he returned from the Los Angeles visit, he had reached certain conclusions about his future. Despite Muhammad's warnings, he would return to the lecture circuit. He also favored direct involvement in civil rights, engaging in frequently critical dialogues with militants in SNCC, CORE, and local groups such as the Afro-American Association. CORE may have moved toward Malcolm, but he was not himself unmoved.

This strategy would soon be tested. On Christmas Day 1962, two Muslims were arrested while selling *Muhammad Speaks* in Times Square. Three days later, at a Mosque No. 7 meeting, Malcolm told his followers that it grieved him every time that the NOI had to go to court, but he could not condone cowardice. On January 2 he sent a telegram to New York City mayor Robert Wagner, with copies to the district attorney, Frank Hogan, and police commissioner Michael Murphy, challenging the arrests. Malcolm denounced the arrests as a suppression of press freedom, and "the freedom of religious expression."

But the Nation's legal troubles continued to mount. In Rochester, on January 6, police invaded the city's mosque during a service, after receiving a call claiming that a man with a gun was inside the building where the mosque was located. Two policemen said they were beaten during the raid, and more than a dozen Muslims were arrested. Malcolm at once flew to Rochester. "We allow no intrusions at ou[r] religious services and will give our lives if necessary to protect their sanctity," he told the press, before filing formal complaints. Returning to New York City, he led a nonviolent demonstration in front of Manhattan's Criminal Court. The flyers circulated at the protest could have been written by SNCC radicals. "America has become a Police-state for 20 Million Negroes," one declared. "We must let [Rochester's NOI members] know they are not alone. We must let them know that the *whole Dark World is with them*." Later that evening, Malcolm told a crowd at a Mosque No. 7 meeting that he was "tired of hearing about

Muslims being pistol-whipped." On January 25 the two Muslim newspaper salesmen were sentenced to sixty days in jail.

That same week Malcolm's new militancy was on full display at Michigan State University. Before an audience of more than a thousand, he sounded out many familiar themes, but with a new twist:

> So you have two types of Negro. . . . Most of you know the old type . . . during slavery he was called "Uncle Tom." He was the house Negro. And during slavery you had two Negroes. You had the house Negro and the field Negro. The house Negro usually lived close to his master. He dressed like his master. He wore his master's second-hand clothes. He ate food that his master left on the table. And he lived in his master's house . . . he always identified himself in the same sense that his master identified himself. When his master said, "We have good food," the house Negro would say, "Yes we have plenty of good food." . . . When the master would be sick, the house Negro identified himself so much with his master he'd say, "What's the matter boss, we sick?" . . . But then you had another Negro out in the field. The house Negro was in the minority. The masses—the field Negroes were the masses. They were in the majority. When the master got sick, they prayed that he'd die. If his house caught on fire, they'd pray for a wind to come along and fan the breeze.

The address also showcased his evolving ideas about race. For decades, the NOI had preached that the ethnic identity of black Americans was Asiatic, descendants of the lost tribe of Shabazz that had its origins in the Middle East. But now Malcolm affirmed the common cultural heritage that united Africans with African Americans. "The man that you call Negro is nothing but an African himself," he explained. "The unity of Africans abroad and the unity of Africans here in this country can bring about practically any kind of achievement or accomplishment that black people want." During the question and answer period, Malcolm also denounced South African apartheid, making a sharp distinction between that system and the separatism advocated by Muhammad. Once more, he criticized CORE's James Farmer for his marriage to a white woman, quipping that it "almost makes him a white man." He turned finally to the Jewish people as an appropriate role model for black empowerment. "Whenever the Jews have been segregated and Jim Crowed, they haven't sat-in," he insisted. "They usually go and use the economic weapon."

The mosque assault in Rochester animated Malcolm, as it provided a counterpoint and companion piece to the legal proceedings unfolding against the Muslims in Los Angeles. Preliminary hearings had begun there at the end of 1962, and the trial itself was scheduled for the upcoming spring. But the high profile of the Los Angeles case meant that Malcolm had little room to maneuver or make way on his protest plans; Muhammad and his Chicago lieutenants would be watching. In Rochester, however, deep in upstate New York, he could be more vocal. On January 28 he addressed an audience of four hundred at the city's university, where his speech moved him even closer to openly promoting equality over racial separation. "Americans have come to realize that the black man is capable of doing things equal to him," he told his largely student audience. "But they are not fully prepared to accept that the black man can take a role in political and economic society." Without acknowledging his shift, Malcolm had drawn closer to both Rustin and Farmer. If African Americans received the full measure of their constitutional rights and equal opportunities across the board, could racism be abolished? In the Rochester talk, Malcolm answered: no race problem would exist in the United States "if the Negro could 'speak as an American.'"

He seemed more than ever of two minds, pulled both by his loyalty to Muhammad and by a need to engage in the struggle. Having just ventured to discuss the role of the black man in society, he quickly shifted gears. On February 3, during an interview broadcast on radio and television, he again pressed Elijah Muhammad's plan for a separate black state inside the United States. Then, turning back to protest ten days later, he led a Manhattan street demonstration of about 230 Fruit of Islam members to denounce police harassment. The police had cautioned him that protest rallies were illegal in Times Square and that he and his men would be subject to arrest. Malcolm replied that he was going to walk through Times Square as an individual, which was his constitutional right. If others voluntarily walked in file behind him, that was not his responsibility. No one was arrested.

Word soon reached him that twelve of the Muslims jailed after the police raid on Rochester's mosque were planning a hunger strike, and he quickly came to their support. He informed the press that the protesting Muslims were prepared to fast "until they die." Alluding to the Black Freedom Movement, he boasted that soon "Rochester will be better known than Oxford, Mississippi," the Southern town where thousands of angry whites erupted in street violence attempting to halt the desegregation of Ole Miss. The very next day, February 16, the *Rochester Times* reported that twelve of the thirteen prisoners had been released, pending charges. The funds for their bail had been forwarded by Elijah Muhammad. The same day, Malcolm addressed another Harlem rally, organized around the theme that "America has become a police state for 20 million Negroes." Following the demonstration, he once again led hundreds of protesters down affluent midtown Manhattan streets.

———

The *Saturday Evening Post* published Alex Haley and Alfred Balk's collaboration "Black Merchants of Hate" on January 26, 1963, giving the story six full pages and including numerous illustrations. The article brought into stark relief the tensions simmering between Malcolm and the Chicago headquarters, and for anyone paying close attention it marked the shift in public perception of both the Nation and Malcolm in the previous two years. The article differed from "Mr. Muhammad Speaks" in several significant ways, opening with the dramatic story of Johnson X Hinton's beating and the provocative response led by Malcolm. It briefly covered Elijah Muhammad's personal history and role within the sect, whose national membership it estimated at the absurdly low figure of five to six thousand, with another fifty thousand sympathizers. Haley and Balk emphasized that the Nation of Islam was never part of the larger Muslim world: "Muhammad himself has no known tie with orthodox Islam." But the greatest discontinuity from the initial article was the coverage given to Malcolm, whom the authors moved to center stage, succinctly charting his father's terrifying death, the vices and crimes of Harlem's Detroit Red—incorrectly placing his incarceration "at the age of 19"—and his ultimate salvation as an NOI zealot:

> Articulate, single-minded, the fire of bitterness still burning in his soul, Malcolm X travels the country, organizing, encouraging, trouble-shooting . . . While Muhammad appears to be training his son Wallace to succeed him when he retires or dies, many Muslims feel that Malcolm is too powerful to be denied the leadership if he wants it.

By building up Malcolm's role at Muhammad's expense, and suggesting a possible internal conflict, "Black Merchants of Hate" fostered even greater jealousy and dissent within the NOI's ranks: exactly what the FBI had hoped for when it agreed to feed information to Balk. Still, the piece was so successful that Haley, who had begun conducting interviews for *Playboy* magazine, proposed Malcolm as his next subject, and the two men met over several days in the winter of 1963 at the NOI's restaurant in Harlem to generate material.

As Saviour's Day 1963 approached, Malcolm found himself increasingly at odds with Muhammad's children and John Ali. Paranoid that the gravy train afforded them by the flow of tithe money to Chicago might be disrupted if Muhammad died, they had not been reassured by the tone of "Black Merchants of Hate." By late 1962, the tales of their father's sexual adventures had reached New York City and the West Coast, further complicating matters and heightening their suspicions of Malcolm. For his part, Malcolm pretended that he knew nothing about the rumors, desperately hoping that somehow they would go away. In past years, he had traveled to Chicago a week or more in advance of Saviour's Day to prepare for the celebration, but now the antiharassment campaign in New York kept him mercifully busy. Meanwhile, NOI officials announced that the chronic illnesses of Elijah Muhammad had forced the patriarch to cancel his own appearances; Chicago headquarters reduced the program to one day, February 26, and placed Malcolm in charge. The absence of Muhammad and the shortened program reduced the turnout to three thousand NOI faithful, but the crowd still buzzed with whispers of impropriety. Muhammad's illness surely made it ill-advised for him to fly up from Phoenix, but his decision to skip Saviour's Day was also partially motivated by a desire to discourage mosques from sending large delegations and to limit the discussions of swirling rumors. He also may have been reacting to the uninvited presence in Chicago of several unwed mothers of his illegitimate children. Writing later in his diary, Malcolm observed that Ola Hughes, the mother of Muhammad's illegitimate two-year-old son, Kamal, was "telling everybody" and had a "very nasty attitude."

At the convention, Muhammad's family turned its embarrassment into angry tirades against Malcolm. Family members had sent notes demanding that Wallace Muhammad, recently released from prison, be permitted to address the assembly during Malcolm's major Saviour's Day address. Yet Wallace, who had grown even more skeptical of his father's dogma while incarcerated, wanted no part of it, and he and Malcolm had agreed that Malcolm would find a way around the family's demands. From the podium, Malcolm announced that, due to the program's delayed start, there was no time left for Wallace to speak; but in a gesture of appreciation, he recognized Muhammad's family members in the hall and solicited applause from the audience. It did little good: as FBI informants observed, "The family was especially resentful of [Malcolm's] attempts to advise and tell the family what to do."

Although there was pressing business at home, Malcolm remained in Chicago for several weeks, hoping to investigate for himself the rumors about Muhammad. The family thought that shortening the Saviour's Day program had solved the problem, but after Malcolm consulted with Wallace, who confirmed that the rumors were true, he knew that more needed to be done. In the next weeks, he met with three of Muhammad's former secretaries, including Evelyn, and found they all had similar stories. Once their pregnancies had been discovered, they had been summoned before secret NOI courts and received sentences of isolation. Muhammad provided little or no financial support for his out-of-wedlock children.

The revelations should not have been a complete surprise to Malcolm, who first heard hints about Muhammad's sexual misconduct in the mid-1950s. Yet for years, it had been impossible for Malcolm to imagine that the sect's little lamb was using his exalted position to sexually molest his secretarial staff. Only when Malcolm confronted the women themselves did he see the truth—not just of the affairs, but of the way the Messenger had frequently talked him down to others. "From their own mouths I heard that Elijah Muhammad had told them I was the best, the greatest minister he ever had," Malcolm recalled, "but that someday I would leave him, turn against him—so I was 'dangerous.' . . . While he was praising me to my face, he was tearing me apart behind my back."

Hearing this broke Malcolm's heart, but his greatest anguish was reserved for the violation of Evelyn, though she told him that she believed her pregnancy "to be prophetic" and reserved her hostility for the entourage surrounding the Messenger. Malcolm had known for years about Evelyn's pregnancy and the birth of her daughter, but had simply assumed the father was a member of Mosque No. 2. Yet Evelyn was never far from his mind. At times, his unhappiness with Betty was so profound that he considered reestablishing his love affair with Evelyn. He even unburdened himself to Louis X, who sharply rebuked him, saying, "You are a married man!" Louis worried that Malcolm "would really hurt Betty." Malcolm had agreed to back away from any involvement with Evelyn, at least for the time being. But now, with the realization that the father of Evelyn's child was Muhammad, Malcolm must have felt a deep sense of betrayal. Two decades before, Malcolm had posed as a pimp, hustling prostitutes in Harlem. Now, unwittingly, he had been maneuvered into becoming Elijah Muhammad's pimp, even bringing the woman he had loved to be violated.

Many NOI observers who did not know of Malcolm's detective work interpreted his lingering presence in Chicago as a personal affront; to some it seemed he was merely indulging in media appearances. Spurred on by his angry children, Muhammad may have instructed Malcolm to return to New York City, which he did on March 10, canceling several scheduled appearances with the excuse that Betty had fallen and broken her leg. Arriving home, he mulled a course of action. He now sensed the outlines of the spiritual and moral journey that he knew lay ahead, but decided that he would try to find a way to remain inside the NOI if he could. He wrote to Muhammad requesting a meeting, and in early April flew to Phoenix to learn his future.

CHAPTER 9

"He Was Developing Too Fast"

April–November 1963

Malcolm arrived at Muhammad's residence on or around April 1. The two men embraced, and Elijah led the way to the rear of his home, where they strolled around the compound's swimming pool. Malcolm recounted what was being said about Muhammad's extramarital affairs and, without waiting for a reply, suggested a way forward. "Loyal Muslims could be taught that a man's accomplishments in his life outweigh his personal, human weaknesses . . . Wallace Muhammad helped me to review the Quran and the Bible for documentation. David's adultery with Bathsheba weighed less on history's scales, for instance, than the positive fact of David's killing Goliath."

Muhammad immediately focused on Malcolm's solution. "Son, I'm not surprised. You always have had such a good understanding of prophecy, and of spiritual things." He did not focus on his sexual relationships with specific women, but chose instead to look to the biblical past to justify his behavior. "When you read about how David took another man's wife, I'm that David," he told Malcolm. Although the two men parted in friendship, in retrospect it is clear they already held two strikingly different agendas. Muhammad wanted to have the rumors suppressed. If Malcolm, in his sermons, employed Qur'anic and biblical teachings to justify his conduct, that was acceptable. Malcolm, however, left the meeting feeling more troubled than when he had arrived. As he tried to cope with the Messenger having confirmed his worst suspicions, he also knew that it would require careful work on his own part to protect the Nation going forward. He saw the rumors as a virus that could lead to an epidemic, and his goal was to "inoculate" the Nation's rank and file.

Almost immediately he set to work, speaking first in Philadelphia and then several times over the course of four days at Mosque No. 7, at each event unfolding the new language that he hoped would ease the news of Muhammad's transgressions. James 67X quickly noticed the shift in the minister's argument. "Malcolm had always taught that every two thousand years or so, the scriptures change. A new messenger is needed, because that which has preceded has become corrupt." He assumed that this was Malcolm's way of establishing the superiority of Islam over Christianity, and also of affirming Fard's divine status. "Then, one day, Malcolm . . . said something that shocked me. He said, 'A prophet is in a scale. If he does more good than he did bad, then he's considered good . . . A prophet, like everybody else, is weighed in the balance.' I said to myself, 'Well, what happened to this business about them always doing the right thing?'" James realized that Malcolm must be discussing Elijah Muhammad, but was reluctant to bring it up with him.

Malcolm's increasing interest in discussing practical concerns now offered him an attractive alternative to speaking at length about the Messenger and his theology. Throughout 1963, he wrote in his *Autobiography,* "I spoke less and less of religion. I taught social doctrine to Muslims, and current events, and politics." He significantly reduced his references to Muhammad while continuing to affirm his public loyalty. Muhammad acknowledged this at the end of April by greatly expanding Malcolm's responsibilities. On April 25 he sent a letter addressed to "Malcolm Shabazz," confirming his appointment as interim minister of Washington, D.C.'s Mosque No. 4. The former minister, Lucius X Brown, had been "dismissed from the ministry." What was needed, he wrote Malcolm, was a minister "who has not only the love of Allah and Islam in his heart, but has enough intelligence and educational training to demand the respect of the Believers there in No. 4, and also the devils in that city." This was not a maneuver to take Malcolm away from New York: he was expected to maintain his ministerial role at Mosque No. 7 while providing supervision in D.C. The appointment actually confirmed Muhammad's continued trust in him, despite their recent confrontation. Malcolm told Mosque No. 7's FOI that he would shuttle between Washington and New York each week. He also admitted that former minister Brown had been fired due to his "negative attitude" toward *Muhammad Speaks.* It is unclear whether Lucius's complaints were about the paper's contents or the aggressive sales policies forced upon members.

But if Muhammad still believed Malcolm to be trustworthy and dependable, the Chicago headquarters saw an opportunity in Malcolm's frequent absences from New York, and John Ali began contacting Joseph directly on mosque matters. On April 25, Chicago had also widely circulated a letter bearing Elijah Muhammad's signature and calling upon "all Ministers, Secretaries, and Captains . . . to get our paper, *Muhammad Speaks*, into the hands of our poor, blind, deaf, and dumb brothers and sisters. . . ." The paper, the letter stated, "will get to people who will not speak to us in the public; it will convert behind the door a hundred of our people to our one from the Speaker's Stand!" It was an unmistakable attack on Malcolm. Meanwhile, the information blackout of Malcolm in the paper itself became virtually complete.

The *Washington Post* reported Malcolm's new appointment to the D.C. mosque, describing him as "the No. 2 man of the Black Muslim sect." For Malcolm, the expanded responsibilities opened new doors; here was a chance to transplant much of the community building he had been pushing in New York to another city. Already the Nation had found great success in Harlem with several of their black improvement projects, most notably in combating juvenile delinquency. Washington's desolate ghettos, in no better shape than Malcolm had found them during his Detroit Red years, offered an attractive new proving ground. He would also now be operating in the nation's capital, close to the power center. At a press conference in Washington's National airport, Malcolm insisted that he was not second in command, that the Nation did not "preach hatred of white people," and that he intended to hold a series of blacks-only meetings over a four-week period to examine the causes and cures for black street crime in the nation's capital.

On the same day that Malcolm had returned from Phoenix to begin dealing with the rumors surrounding Elijah Muhammad, the landscape of the Black Freedom Movement entered a tumultuous phase, sending tremors throughout the country. On April 3, Martin Luther King, Jr., and the SCLC began the long and devastating sit-in campaign to break segregation in Birmingham, Alabama. More than any previous protest, Birmingham focused the eyes of the nation on the civil rights struggle, as over the course of five weeks more than seven hundred nonviolent protesters, many of them children, faced arrest and jail time. Black newspapers like the *Pittsburgh Courier* and the *Los Angeles Herald-Dispatch* reacted with cautious optimism; the public outcry over the protesters' brutal treatment at the hands of Birmingham police chief Bull Connor and his men had set the gears of Washington turning, and talk of new civil rights legislation percolated beyond the capital. More than ever, the time seemed ripe for action, yet Malcolm knew that with tensions between himself and Chicago still unresolved, his options remained limited. Several reporters had heard rumors that Malcolm was planning to go to Birmingham, although he himself announced that he would travel there only on the direct orders of Muhammad, or at the invitation of NOI regional leader, minister Jeremiah X. Asked about the protests, Malcolm chose to address King's tactics rather than his goals: "I'll say this, if anybody sets a dog on a black man, the black man should kill that dog—whether he is a four-legged dog or a two-legged dog."

Despite his extensive travels, Malcolm kept a close eye on the legal struggles of the Los Angeles mosque. The trial of fourteen Muslims stemming from the mosque raid began on April 8, 1963. Thirteen were tried on felony assault and resisting arrest with force. The *Los Angeles Times* reported that "members of the cult, the men dressed in neat dark suits, and the women in ankle-length, flowing dresses and white or pastel-colored scarves, quickly filled . . . 200 seats. Four additional bailiffs were assigned to the courtroom to maintain order and numerous policemen and deputy sheriffs, in plain clothes and uniforms, circulated in a dense crowd outside." The prospective jurors sitting in the courtroom audience were given flyers by NOI members, detailing examples of police brutality. Judge David Coleman instructed prospective jurors that they should disregard the content of the flyers, explaining, "I am not too critical of the distribution of the leaflets . . . because I realize there is a great deal of interest in this trial and there is a great deal of emotion involved." On April 25, 1963, an all-white jury of eleven women and one man was sworn in.

As the trial began, the Muslim women asked the bailiffs to arrange a separate seating area for them, segregated from white spectators. The bailiffs consented, and a separate section was created for the women. The judge, however, put a halt to the racially designated seating, ordering that all seating would be allotted on a first-come, first-served basis. Malcolm arrived back in Los Angeles and attended the trial on May 3, insisting that "the defendants are not getting a fair trial." The district attorney had "scientifically eliminated" blacks from the jury, Malcolm declared. During a recess, Malcolm sought out Donald L. Weese, the police officer who had killed Stokes, and provocatively took several photos of him. The unstated implication was that they might be used by Fruit members to identify him on the street, to launch their retaliation. One day, among the hundreds attending the proceedings was George Lincoln Rockwell, who informed the press that most blacks "are in complete agreement with the Muslims and their ideals, just as most of the white people of the country are in agreement with the Nazis."

As the trial progressed, the prosecution made a vigorous case against the Muslims. Defense attorney Earl Broady was so frustrated by Judge Coleman's constant overruling of his motions of objection that at one point he simply sat with his head in his hands for five minutes. When queried by reporters, Broady replied, "No, I'm not ill. I just thought I might lose my temper." Malcolm made the local news again by claiming that he and another Muslim had been held at gunpoint upon his arrival: "They [the police] tried in every way to provoke us into an offensive act . . . so they would have a reason to shoot us." On May 4, Malcolm addressed an audience of about two hundred at the Elks Lodge in South Central Los Angeles. Outside, two black men, one of whom was the actor Caleb Peterson, the head of the Hollywood Race Relations Bureau, began picketing against the Muslims. A tense confrontation took place in which the other integrationist picketer, Phil Waddell, was punched in the face by a Muslim. The police were called, but on their appearance Malcolm warned them, "If you don't get these pickets away from here, I will not be responsible for anything that happens to them." The pickets decided they had made their point, and beat a hasty retreat.

Final arguments were made on Friday, May 25, with the jury beginning its deliberations the next Monday. After setting a new Los Angeles court record for longest deliberations, on Friday, June 14, the jury found that nine of the defendants were guilty of assault charges; two men were acquitted, and the jury failed to reach unanimous verdicts on two others. On July 31 four of the convicted Muslims received prison terms of one to five years. The other convicted Muslims received probation, with one being sentenced to serve time in the county jail. The day after the sentences were handed down, three female jurors and three alternates told the media they did not believe "justice was done." The women had met secretly with the judge on July 6 to lobby for leniency for the convicted Muslims. One juror announced that she planned to testify at the prisoners' probation hearing on their behalf. Despite their convictions, the Muslims had made an effective and convincing case that the LAPD had employed excessive force in the mosque incident, generating sympathy even among whites.

Long before the resolution of the Los Angeles trial, Malcolm was back on the East Coast. He returned to Washington, D.C., to make what was to have been his maiden appearance before a congressional committee. Several newspaper reports on the success of the Nation's juvenile delinquency programs had found their way to the desk of Congresswoman Edith Green of Oregon, and she had subsequently invited Malcolm to explain these initiatives to the House of Representatives Subcommittee on Education and Labor, which she chaired, on the morning of May 16. For reasons that remain unclear, his appearance was canceled. Instead, he met privately with Green for two hours. When the Capitol Hill media learned about his presence, a press conference was hastily arranged outside Green's office shortly after midday. Malcolm attributed the hearing's cancellation to "some segment of the power structure," but he also used the opportunity to criticize Kennedy's handling of the Birmingham crisis. "President Kennedy did not send troops to Alabama when dogs were biting black babies," he observed. "He waited three weeks until the situation exploded. He then sent troops after the Negroes had demonstrated their ability to defend themselves."

During the previous few years, Malcolm's criticism of Kennedy had grown sharper and more frequent, despite Elijah Muhammad's requests that he avoid targeting the president. Malcolm frequently attacked Kennedy by mentioning his religion, much as his opponents had during the election. For the Nation, Kennedy's Catholicism served as easy shorthand for the antagonist, racist Christianity of whites that was soon to be supplanted by Islam. Malcolm also saw Kennedy as a liberal, and attributed to him all the disingenuousness he perceived in that ilk. During the fifties, Malcolm had not shied from denouncing the conservative Eisenhower, but never with quite the same intensity or general tone of ill regard. Kennedy was also popular among blacks, though the Nation saw this sentiment as misguided, and Malcolm believed he could bolster the Nation's separatist position by working to increase doubts about Kennedy's sincerity. On May 12 he attended an NOI meeting of four hundred people held at WUST Radio Music Hall, using the occasion to pillory both Kennedy and Alabama's segregationist governor, George Wallace, as "the fox versus the wolf." "Neither one loves you," he warned. "The only difference is that the fox will eat you with a smile instead of a scowl."

From his new position in Washington, Malcolm pushed for expanding the NOI's access to America's prisons. The issue was not altogether new for him. After all, his very first political actions had come during his own prison tenure; this experience, and the understanding that poor blacks in prison were prime conversion targets for the NOI, led him to focus more on his efforts in this area. A year before, he had become involved with the case of five African Americans at the Attica state prison in upstate New York. Converting to the NOI while behind bars, the men demanded the right to hold religious services. The state commissioner of corrections rejected their request, calling the NOI a hate group. The prisoners filed a civil suit in federal court, and throughout their hearing were chained inside the courtroom—an example of excessive coercion that caused Congressman Adam Clayton Powell, Jr., to question the practice against felons. Malcolm testified as an expert witness for the Nation. "Muhammad never taught us to hate anybody," he informed the court. When the judge inquired whether he could attend an NOI religious service, Malcolm responded, "Whites never come to our religious services. Many whites have a guilt complex about the race issue and think that when Negroes come together hate is discussed. The Muslim who has proper religious training and guidance gets along better with whites than Negroes who are Christians." His testimony rarely mentioned Elijah Muhammad by name, placing emphasis instead on the obligations of his faith: "The only way that we can be recognized as a righteous people, we must abstain from alcohol, nicotine, tobacco, narcotics, profanity, gambling, lying, cheating, stealing . . . all forms of vice."

That same year, a federal judge had ruled that NOI member William T. X Fulwood had the constitutional right to attend religious services at the Lorton Reformatory, located in Virginia. Black prisoners all over the country were eagerly joining the NOI and demanding their right to religious services. Malcolm and Quinton X Roosevelt Edwards of Mosque No. 4 had conducted a service at Lorton back in May. In June, however, corrections officials turned down Malcolm's request to continue services there, saying that he was a convicted felon and an "incendiary" who disrupted prison life. The D.C. branch of the American Civil Liberties Union at once took up the issue.

The oppressive reality of prison had a clear effect on Malcolm's rhetoric, to the point where he began using it as a metaphor for the condition of being black in America. During an interview with psychologist Kenneth Clark on June 4, he asserted that the NOI was not a Black Muslim religion, saying, "We are black people who are Muslims because we have accepted the religion of Islam." Malcolm then asserted that all black Americans, regardless of their religious views, were in effect prisoners under a racist system. Increasingly, a growing majority of blacks saw themselves as "inmates"; the American president, Malcolm added, was "just another [prison] warden."

As the summer began, black Americans experienced twin polarities of joy and devastation. First, President Kennedy, ignoring his advisers, went on television and announced to the country the broad outlines of his new civil rights legislation. Then, a few hours later, a sniper assassinated NAACP field secretary Medgar Evers outside his home in Jackson, Mississippi. With each new piece of news, the stakes grew higher, fueling black hopes and, in many places, white animosity.

Malcolm's extensive engagement with the civil rights movement, and the well-publicized public protests by Mosque No. 7, had inspired Muslims in other cities to become involved in protests, but Chicago headquarters was anxious to quell the new mood. On June 21, Raymond Sharrieff warned a crowd in Chicago: "The whites are watching the Muslims to see what kind of stand they will take on demonstrations. . . . The NOI stands on total separation." Therefore, "peaceful demonstrations" could accomplish nothing. Sharrieff informed Mosque No. 2 that he had been "shocked and surprised that some of the FOI want to take part in the so-called peaceful demonstrations by the so-called Negroes," predicting that after his fellow blacks suffered mistreatment by the police and were "lied to" by King, "the so-called Negroes will be easy to get for Islam." He then threatened, "If this is not plain enough for you, let me put it more clearly to you. Do not participate in any way in these demonstrations. If you are caught, you will wish you were dead."

———

By the early sixties, some brothers inside the Nation were almost impossible to control. To a man, they were enthusiastic, loyal, and devoted, yet their propensity for violence and lockstep obedience to the Nation's rigid chain of command made them useful tools only so long as they could be tethered. Gladly willing to sacrifice their lives for the NOI's cause, these men had become familiar faces to passersby in Harlem, Detroit, Miami, and Chicago, aggressively hawking *Muhammad Speaks* on street corners, in driving rain and freezing snow. Veteran captains like Joseph closely studied them and channeled their energies into the martial arts. The most aggressive were selected for the task of disciplining NOI members who had committed an infraction that required penitence. Louis X's brother, based in New York, was soon recruited into the secret "pipe squad" inside Mosque No. 7, although to Louis its disciplinary actions seemed excessive. "If a brother committed adultery, he would get time out, but the brothers would go by and visit him and beat him down. And this was sanctioned," he recalled. Over the years, a "thuggish kind of behavior" was institutionalized under the leadership of NOI's most influential captains, such as Joseph in New York, Clarence in Boston, and Jeremiah in Philadelphia. Matters frequently got out of hand. "Carelessness in what you say to somebody," explained Farrakhan, "could lead to harm and hurt to people who disliked Elijah Muhammad, whatever their reason." As a lieutenant, Thomas 15X Johnson was expected to perform disciplinary duties. "Say a brother got caught smoking a cigarette. [The lieutenants] would throw him down a flight of stairs," he explained. If someone "disrespected the captain [Joseph] on their way out [of the mosque], he would have an 'accident' and he would just fall down the stairs." Joseph almost always gave his disciplinary orders to a first lieutenant, who communicated what was to be done to the group of fellow lieutenants, or other FOI "enforcers." NOI members who became victims of assaults "didn't deserve to be beat up," Farrakhan confessed. "They didn't deserve to be blinded. They didn't deserve even to be killed."

The ministers occupied a difficult position when it came to discipline. As the de facto head of a mosque, a minister needed to know what was happening with his members, yet the unpleasant, often criminal nature of the punitive violence made it sensible to maintain a degree of deniability. In the vast majority of cases, ministers like Malcolm were deliberately kept ignorant of the actions of enforcers. "Whatever took place, we had a policy: don't let the minister know," said Thomas 15X. "Don't involve him in this . . . because that puts him in a bad position." Years later, Farrakhan implied that Malcolm had carefully insulated himself from direct involvement but was fully aware of the crimes being committed. He recalled saying to Malcolm, "Look, do you realize that when a man who is taught that this black man is his brother, and we're giving a law to put him out the society, and then he's visited, with every blow that you hit that man in the head, you're killing the love that was in you for your brother?" Malcolm listened, then chided him, saying, "Brother, you're just spiritual." Louis took this to mean that the Nation needed men who were religiously oriented, but also men who would resort to violence without remorse to maintain discipline. If murder became necessary to set an example, so be it.

Most members of the Fruit would never question authority. "Nobody would even think about making a move if there wasn't a direct order from a lieutenant which comes down from the top," explained Thomas 15X Johnson. By the early 1960s, Joseph was well aware that his mosque had been infiltrated by FBI informants, so when he gave an order to discipline an individual, he carefully limited his contact with the men carrying it out. "Captain Joseph never talked to us directly," Johnson said. "He would talk to the first lieutenant," who in turn would communicate that order to one or more second lieutenants, who could select his own group of Fruit for that particular assignment.

Punishment ran from simple beatings for routine transgressions to far, far worse. Elijah Muhammad, Jr.'s stern reminder to the Fruit that "in the old days" brothers who stepped out of line had been killed was inaccurate only its suggestion that such punishment remained in the past. Johnson was involved in a number of extreme disciplinary actions, at least one of which exacted the ultimate price. "A brother got killed in the Bronx, okay?" he recounted in a calm, matter-of-fact voice. "He was a man worthy of death. I mean, there was no question about that, but he got killed." In another incident, an NOI minister was discovered both with marijuana in his apartment and engaging in "fornication." "They went up there and they damned near kicked his spleen out," Johnson recalled. Still, like many who embraced the strictness of the Nation's rules, he thought the beating was justified: "They kicked him out because, like I say, that's unheard of, man, violating like that."

One incident involved a member who reportedly made threats against Muhammad's life. "Because Elijah was coming [to speak at] the 369th Armory . . . [this man] put out the word that he was going to kill Elijah. So me and my crew were posted in the lobby there, because we knew who this guy was." Finally, the man was spotted in the crowd, at the top of a staircase. According to Johnson, he and his men

> picked him up and we handed him down the ranks, because there was all soldiers on the staircase. . . . We got him down to the bottom, and we put [him in] a circle. We stomped him pretty bad. Making a threat like that on Elijah Muhammad—hey, as far as we were concerned, man, he should have gotten murdered right there. Police just stood around and waited. . . . They said, "Okay, well, y'all proved your point here." I said, "Well, we'll decide whether we've proved our point or not." And after we were satisfied, we dispersed, and they called the ambulance and they took him away. But they wouldn't intervene. . . . They [knew] that if they touched one of us they would have to touch all of us. Everybody knew it. This was a law. It was untouchable.

The disciplining of an NOI minister was especially serious. Johnson explained, "A lieutenant cannot discipline a minister. The only one can do that is the captain, and that had to be done through the supreme captain [Raymond Sharrieff] in Chicago."

The mosque also continued to attract young people both who were dedicated to Elijah Muhammad and who did not challenge the chain of command. One outstanding example was Lawrence (Larry) Prescott, Jr. Born in the early 1940s in Hampton, Virginia, he moved to New York City when a child. As a teenager still in high school, Larry first went to hear Malcolm speak on February 13, 1960, but found that he had been replaced that evening by Wallace Muhammad. Sitting eagerly in the front row, Larry vividly remembered Wallace's provocative statement that "Negroes are afraid of everything" at the same time that he dramatically threw a Bible to the floor. "Everybody, especially those first few rows where we were . . . jumped back," Larry recalled. Wallace then shamed his audience, saying, "Look at you. You think a lightning bolt is going to come through and strike me?"

Larry began attending Mosque No. 7 meetings, and by age eighteen was on the verge of dedicating himself to the NOI. Two enthusiasms stood in the way: his passion for jazz and a fondness for marijuana. But one Friday night, after listening to a fiery speech by Malcolm on the radio, he collected his entire marijuana stash—about one pound—went to a friend's home, and after announcing his determination to become a Muslim, handed it over. Larry laughed, explaining, "So he put the word out in South Jamaica [Queens]. He said, 'Larry has lost his mind. He's messing with them Muslims!'"

By 1962, Larry 4X was an assistant minister at Mosque No. 7, a proud junior member of Malcolm's entourage. Unlike many at the mosque, he sensed the tensions developing between his mentor and Chicago. "Malcolm had more visibility than any minister in the Nation," he recalled in 2006. "And his charisma added to that—people just hung on to Malcolm's word." After the police invasion of the Los Angeles mosque in 1962, "Malcolm handled it in his very strident way . . . saying that these devils that killed one of our brothers and Elijah will make them pay. And when that plane went down with all of them white folks from Georgia on it, he said, 'Elijah answered our prayers.'"

Larry developed a close friendship with Maceo X after learning that the mosque's secretary had been a jazz piano player, and he also nurtured a deep respect for the strict disciplinarian Captain Joseph, but as far as he was concerned, Malcolm was the "boss of the bosses." What he appreciated most was Malcolm's approach in tutorials with the junior ministers. "It was a one-way street. He did the talking; we did the listening." Malcolm always insisted that his students be thoroughly prepared before giving a lecture. Never shoot from the hip, he cautioned; always state the subject of a talk clearly at the beginning. "He would always talk about how you have to remember and do the loop in your subject and bring the people back." By 1963 Larry was sometimes given the responsibility of introducing his mentor at events. "There [was] a joke in the ministry class that when Malcolm walked onto the rostrum—say, if I was opening up for him—he would say, 'Make it plain.' He would sit down, you know, and he would sit there for a minute and let you make your point; he'd smile and maybe applaud. Then he'd say, 'Make it plain.' That was the signal: close out and bring him on."

In May, Alex Haley's *Playboy* interview with Malcolm hit the newsstands, further bolstering his national profile. On the one hand, the interview benefited from having been mostly conducted before Malcolm's confrontation with Muhammad, yet the timing of its appearance hardly endeared him further to the Chicago headquarters. In the introduction, Haley presented Malcolm as standing "on the right hand of God's Messenger" in the NOI, wielding "all but absolute authority over the movement and its membership as Muhammad's business manager, trouble-shooter, prime minister and heir apparent." Throughout the interview, however, Malcolm tried to express total devotion to Muhammad, explaining, "[T]o faithfully serve and follow the Honorable Elijah Muhammad is the guiding goal of every Muslim. Mr. Muhammad teaches us the knowledge of our own selves and of our own people." One innovative argument Malcolm did advance was that the NOI had "the sympathy of ninety percent of the black people" in the United States. "A Muslim to us is somebody who is for the black man; I don't care if he goes to the Baptist Church seven days a week." This merger of religious, political, and ethnic identities empowered Malcolm to speak on behalf of millions of non-Islamic African Americans.

Malcolm used the interview to make a number of arguments guaranteed to offend white middle America. When asked about his plane crash comments, he replied, "Sir, as I see the law of justice, it says as you sow, so shall you reap . . . We Muslims believe that the white race, which is guilty of having oppressed and exploited and enslaved our people here in America, should and will be the victims of God's divine wrath." The interview also contained several anti-Semitic slurs. "The Jew cries louder than anybody else if anybody criticizes him," Malcolm complained. "The Jew is always anxious to *advise* the black man. But they never advise him how to solve his problem the way the Jews solved their problem." Through their economic clout, he observed, Jews owned Atlantic City and Miami Beach, and not only these. "Who owns Hollywood? Who runs the garment industry, the largest industry in New York City? . . . When there's something worth owning, the Jew's got it." He went on to argue that Jewish money controlled civil rights groups like the NAACP, pushing Negroes into adopting a strategy of integration that was doomed to failure. His comments would be deemed so controversial, he said, that *Playboy* would never print them in their entirety. Haley felt vindicated, however, when the magazine indeed printed the interview exactly as transcribed: "[Malcolm] was very much taken aback when *Playboy* kept its word."

That same month, following the publication of the interview, Haley contacted Malcolm with a new proposition—to tell his life story in a book. "It was one of the few times I have ever seen him uncertain," Haley recalled. Malcolm asked for some time to consider the idea, but just two days later telephoned to say he would do the autobiography, on two conditions. All royalties to which he was entitled would go to the NOI. And second, Haley must personally request permission from Elijah Muhammad. Haley flew to see Muhammad at his home in Phoenix, but without knowing that only weeks before Malcolm and Elijah had discussed the charges of adultery. Muhammad felt that the scandal placed him at a disadvantage in considering Haley's request. He interpreted the book project as evidence of Malcolm's vanity, but believed it was probably in his own best interest, at least temporarily, to cater to this. "Allah approves," Muhammad managed to say to Haley between bouts of coughing. "Malcolm is one of my most outstanding ministers." Whether he meant it or not, he had almost completely misread Malcolm's intentions for the project, which were nearly the opposite of what Muhammad thought. Concerned about his increasingly strained relations with his mentor, Malcolm hoped to use the book as a reconciliation tactic, presenting his life as a tribute to the genius and good works of the Messenger.

Shortly after Haley had returned to New York City and secured a book contract with Doubleday for twenty thousand dollars, Malcolm presented him with a piece of paper containing a statement written in longhand. He told Haley, "This is the book's dedication." It read: "This book I dedicate to The Honorable Elijah Muhammad, who found me here in the muck and mire of the filthiest civilization and society on this earth, and pulled me out, cleaned me up, and stood me on my feet, and made me the man that I am today." None of this language, of course, appeared in the final text of the *Autobiography*, a casualty to Malcolm's spiritual and political transformation in the remaining years of his life.

On May 27, 1963, a "Memorandum of Agreement" was signed between Malcolm X—also described as "sometimes called Malik Shabazz"—Alex Haley, and a representative of Doubleday. The work was described as "an untitled non-fiction book," with a length of eighty thousand to one hundred thousand words. The royalty advance of twenty thousand dollars was to be split equally between Haley and Malcolm. Upon signing the contract, the two men each received twenty-five hundred dollars. In a second document sent to Malcolm from Haley, the key terms of the contract were restated, calling for a book manuscript of 224 pages. Haley acknowledged Malcolm's request that his royalty share be granted directly to NOI Mosque No. 2 in Chicago. A deadline of October 1963 was set for the completion of the book. With the contracts secure, the Doubleday staff began calculating how much it stood to gain financially from publishing Malcolm's autobiography. On June 6, 1963, Doubleday estimated that the *Autobiography*, priced at $3.95 in paperback and $4.95 in cloth cover, should sell fifteen thousand copies in its initial year of publication, with projected total sales of twenty thousand.

Haley drafted clear ground rules for their collaboration. "It is understood," he declared, "that nothing can be in the manuscript, whether a sentence, a paragraph, or a chapter, or more that you do not completely approve of. It is further understood that anything must be in the manuscript that you want in the manuscript." Despite this reassurance, it took Malcolm at least a month to relax sufficiently to talk frankly about his personal life. The two men made an uneasy pair: the integrationist former coast guard man and the separatist preacher; each was skeptical of the other's ideas, yet both could see what they stood to gain from their collaboration. From June until early October, they would usually meet at Haley's Greenwich Village studio apartment, Malcolm arriving around nine p.m. and staying until midnight. Haley took detailed notes, but Malcolm would also scribble his own notes on scrap paper as he talked. After he had left, Haley would attempt to decipher the scrawls. By midsummer, the project was making progress, despite the reservations both men retained. "I had heard him bitterly attack other Negro writers as 'Uncle Toms,'" Haley complained in the *Autobiography*'s epilogue. And Malcolm continually made it plain that Haley personified the do-nothing Negro petty bourgeoisie that he enjoyed ridiculing.

As work on the *Autobiography* progressed, Haley peppered his agent, Paul Reynolds, and his editors at Doubleday with requests of all sorts. On August 5, Haley informed Reynolds's assistant that he should replace the designation "Co-authored by Alex Haley" with "As told to Alex Haley." He explained in a letter that he was "sometimes awed by [Malcolm's] skill as a demagogue," but wanted to assert a clear separation between Malcolm's political perspectives and his own. "'Co-authoring with Malcolm X' would, to me, imply sharing his views—when mine are almost a complete antithesis of his." One month later, after an "18-hour" session with Malcolm, Haley asked Reynolds for a five-hundred-dollar advance to fly to Chicago for an interview with Elijah Muhammad. Despite his many requests, work progressed slowly, and on September 22 Haley forwarded to Reynolds the book's first two chapters. He was optimistic that he could complete the entire work by the end of October 1963. Still, he was having trouble working through the early phases of Malcolm's life, and near the end of September he pressed Malcolm, trying to break through the minister's reserve and lingering mistrust. Haley urged him "to make more gripping your catharsis of decision involving Reginald. I must build up your regard and respect for [him] when the two of you were earlier in Harlem." He pleaded with Malcolm to give him three consecutive days that week to collaborate on the book, arguing that "night sessions here, such as we had, will be the most productive."

Malcolm also sought to present Elijah Muhammad's views about black women in a positive light. This may explain the *New York Herald Tribune*'s feature story about Betty Shabazz, published on June 30, 1963. For her first press interview, Betty presented an impressive figure:

> She acknowledged us impressively, as a queen might greet a subject. She was wearing white gloves and a white veil over her hair, brushed smooth across her forehead. Her grey tweed two-piece cotton dress, buttoned to the neck, reached to the floor. Her manner was as formal as her dress, as neat and attractive as that of her husband.

The reporter was informed that Muslim women avoided publicity. The primary tasks of NOI women were caring for their families and "obeying the moral tenets dictated to them by Elijah Muhammad." Betty stated that MGT leader Ethel Sharrieff represented the standard by which Muslim women judged themselves. "All of us try in some ways to copy her," Betty explained to the reporter. Betty was reticent to reveal basic facts about her own life, such as at which New York hospital she had been employed as a nurse. She admitted that she did not "know the Koran very well," but said that she read "the history of black people" to her children. Both Betty and Malcolm presented themselves as loyal followers of Muhammad. But Malcolm added, "Elijah teaches us that no two people should stay together who can't get along."

The idea of organizing a march on Washington, D.C., was born in the Harlem office of A. Philip Randolph sometime in December 1962, when Bayard

Rustin visited Randolph there. The two old friends began talking about the Negro March on Washington Movement of 1941 that had pressured the Roosevelt administration into an executive order that outlawed hiring discrimination by defense plants. That mass mobilization never culminated in an actual event, but now Rustin conceived of a new march on a more ambitious scale, climaxing with two days of public activities. His draft proposal emphasized the acceleration of "integration in the fields of education, housing, transportation and public accommodations" and "broad national government action . . . to meet the problem of unemployment, especially as it related to minority groups." At the outset, CORE's Norman Hill was appointed director of field staff, traveling the country to build support at local levels, while SNCC would send John Lewis, its national chair, to represent the organization.

In the wake of his desegregation victory in Birmingham, Martin Luther King, Jr., also favored placing greater pressure on the Kennedy administration. For more than a year, he and the SCLC had pushed for a presidential order outlawing segregation. At first, King supported the tactics of simultaneous demonstrations to take place all over the country, but in the end was persuaded to support the Washington march. The more conservative wing of the black freedom struggle, the NAACP and National Urban League, was at best cool. Roy Wilkins demanded that Rustin be fired as coordinator because of his homosexuality and record of arrests. A compromise was reached, with Randolph accepting the public role of march chairman and Rustin, as vice chair, functioning essentially as executive director. The Kennedy administration was also deeply unhappy, fearing that the presence of several hundred thousand demonstrators on the National Mall might invite widespread violence. But Rustin recruited hundreds of out-of-uniform African-American police, who would be deployed as a barrier between the marchers and the mostly white D.C. police and National Park Service officers. As the project gathered momentum, some of the mobilization's more radical demands were jettisoned to accommodate the support of organized labor and white liberal religious groups. The expanded presence of whites was just enough to convince a reluctant Kennedy administration to offer its endorsement.

Although the Nation of Islam was firmly opposed to the march's integrationist goals, it would have been impossible for Malcolm not to have been affected by such an unprecedented mobilization. For one thing, Rustin's headquarters was in Harlem—on West 130th Street. Throughout the summer, the black press speculated on whether the march would be successful, both in terms of turnout and in its ability to change Washington priorities. Despite the NOI's ban on participation in such demonstrations, Mosque No. 7 continued to be involved in similar activities. On June 29 it sponsored another major street rally, at the corner of Lenox Avenue and West 115th Street. The NOI's press release targeted "the Uncle-Tom Negro leaders" for doing little to halt "the dope traffic, alcoholism, gambling, prostitution, and other forms of organized crime . . . destroying the very moral fiber of the Black Community." Despite such strident attacks, Malcolm extended speaking invitations to NAACP head Roy Wilkins, National Urban League director Whitney Young, CORE's James Farmer, Martin Luther King, Jr., and Adam Clayton Powell, Jr. Only Powell seems to have responded, indicating that business commitments made it impossible for him to address the rally. The program brought out about two thousand people. The attitude of the NYPD was that of mild harassment, and FOI members were dispatched to the rooftops to observe both crowd and cops.

On July 13, Mosque No. 7 threw a large banquet to celebrate a formal visit from the youngest son of Elijah Muhammad, Akbar Muhammad, and his wife, Harriet. The couple was in the process of returning home after a two-year stay in Cairo, where the twenty-five-year-old Akbar had been a student of Islamic jurisprudence. His arrival pleased Malcolm. After Wallace, Akbar had come to be counted first among Malcolm's allies in Muhammad's family. The youngest of the Messenger's children, he found that his time in the Middle East had accomplished for him what prison had done for Wallace: basically, completely disabuse him of any belief in his father's peculiar brand of Islam. Two days after his arrival in New York, the NOI held another public rally, drawing a crowd of four thousand, and Akbar was invited to speak. His talk had been advertised as a "Special Report on Africa for the People of Harlem, but once on his feet he called for a comprehensive united front of African Americans." "We must have unity among Negroes," he told the crowd. "It is time for all of us—CORE, the NAACP, Dr. Martin Luther King, Jr., the Student Nonviolent Coordinating Committee, and the Black Muslims—to sit down together. . . . We must stop calling Dr. King names, and he must stop talking about us before the enemy." For Akbar, the distinction between black separatism, symbolized by his father, and racial integration was secondary to the need to force coalitions. If such unity could be achieved, leaders of independent African states were "ready to help us win our freedom."

Akbar then made an extraordinary comment, sending murmurs through the crowd and certainly drawing Malcolm's complete attention. "I don't hate any man because of the color of his skin," he declared. "I look at a man's heart, I watch his actions, and I make my conclusions on the basis of what he does, rather than how he looks." Listening to the speech, Louis Lomax recalled that Malcolm had preached a similar approach several years earlier, but he had also continued to denigrate King and other civil rights leaders. Akbar Muhammad's address marked a potential schism. Here was a son of the Messenger, the one who had most thoroughly immersed himself in the world of orthodox Islam, offering a clear refutation of the very foundation of the Nation's theology. Akbar's position, said Lomax, "reflects the Arabs' involvement with black unity throughout the world. . . . Malcolm X is closer to Elijah Muhammad, in terms of just what the American Negro should do, than is Elijah's own son." Akbar's emergence meant that "the Black Muslims will become more 'Islamic' and more 'political' in the days just ahead."

Though Akbar's speech challenged Nation of Islam orthodoxy far more directly than Malcolm had ever dared, Malcolm was well aware that the NOI's pace of Islamization had to be accelerated. He had been forced to continue his public defense of the Nation's religious legitimacy, as more and more orthodox Muslims came forward to challenge the sect's racial exclusivity. On July 15, the *Chicago Defender* published a story on Egypt's powerful Muslim League, which "flatly disagrees with the anti-white, anti-Christian, anti-Jew, and anti-integration preachments of America's Black Muslims." The story also cited complaints from the Jami'at al-Islam Humanitarian Foundation of the United States, whose director, Ahmad Kamal, characterized Elijah Muhammad's views as "anti-Muslim." To this, Elijah Muhammad responded personally and forcefully: "Neither Jeddah nor Mecca have sent me! I am sent from Allah and not from the Secretary General of the Muslim League. There is no Muslim in Arabia that has authority to stop me from delivering this message that I have been assigned to."

As the summer progressed, Malcolm stepped up his involvement with on-the-ground demonstrations in support of civil rights. On July 22 he attended the picketing of a Brooklyn hospital construction site by more than a thousand workers who charged racial discrimination in the building industry. Hundreds of picketers began blocking huge construction trucks beginning at seven a.m. and the demonstration continued for nine hours; although the protesters observed nonviolent tactics, three hundred of them were dragged away by police. Malcolm carefully stood across the street, but he shook hands and expressed his support with participants. When asked by journalists why he wasn't directly involved, he evaded the issue:

"It would not be fair. You would see a different situation here. We would never let these policemen put us into those paddy wagons." Joining him at a second demonstration was playwright/actor Ossie Davis, who briefly blocked the access of one construction truck. Malcolm brought along a 35-millimeter camera and busied himself taking photographs. "If there were no captions for these pictures, you'd think this was Mississippi or Nazi Germany," he informed one *New York Times* reporter. "Only difference between the Gestapo and the New York police is that this is 1963." Five days later, he turned up at a civil rights rally in Brooklyn that brought out more than three hundred people. Addressing the crowd, Malcolm emphasized the need for "unity" and said that there were "no real differences" between the various civil rights groups.

The March on Washington was scheduled for August 28, and as it approached, Malcolm's increased involvement in the business of pickets and protests began to expose yet another weakness in the Nation's ideology. For years, mainstream civil rights leaders like Rustin and Farmer had criticized the NOI for having no real political plan. Now, as black activists increasingly found themselves facing the business end of billy clubs and fire hoses, the Nation risked further revealing itself as unable to live up to its militant rhetoric. For years, Malcolm had warned listeners not to underestimate the Muslims; he consistently told anyone who would listen that while his people were to be cooperative with police, if a Muslim was physically assaulted or attacked, it would bring down a rain of retributive violence. At an FOI meeting at the end of July that summer, he talked about the problem of police brutality. "When the NOI demonstrates, it demonstrates all the way." He told the Fruit that while he did not publicly say so, he believed in violence to defend his rights, even claiming that he was prepared to "use his teeth" if he had to protect himself. Yet for all his talk of willingness to use violence, the only real damage the Nation had inflicted in the past half decade had targeted its own misbehaving members. It was a contradiction that increasingly troubled Malcolm.

Still, he could point to some progress, certainly in terms of his increased recognition. His many media appearances and his public activities in the D.C. area even caught the attention of President Kennedy, who, referring to a controversy over the TFX fighter plane in early June, quipped, "We have had an interesting six months . . . with TFX and now we are going to have his brother Malcolm for the next six." Muhammad continued to monitor these public addresses by his star lieutenant. It was now difficult for him to restrain Malcolm from tackling political issues, given Akbar's speech, which had been widely covered. But he continued to be troubled by Malcolm's frequent criticisms of Kennedy, who despite his administration's sluggish record on civil rights remained popular among blacks. In a letter to Malcolm dated August 1, Muhammad advised, "Be careful about mentioning Kennedy in your talks and printed matters by name; use U.S.A. or the American Government."

As excitement about the March on Washington grew, Malcolm decided to increase the Harlem mosque's outreach efforts. On August 10, Malcolm told a crowd of about eight hundred that the Nation would not participate in the march, but Elijah Muhammad was planning to be in Washington during that week to ensure that "there would be no skullduggery, no flim-flam, no sell-out." Malcolm also tried out, for the first time, his counterargument against the march, implying that it had been taken over by the Kennedy administration. This strategy characterized the main thrust of Malcolm's attacks against both Kennedy and King. By taking aim at the top of the power structure and assuming a populist tone, he hoped to drive a wedge between average blacks and their leadership, to better bring them to the Nation's position. Now he set about portraying the march as another example of the grassroots being co-opted by the establishment, which of course had its own selfish agenda. "When the white man found out he couldn't stop [the march], he joined it," Malcolm told the crowd. Four days later, Raymond Sharrieff gave a talk at Mosque No. 7, and he too discouraged participation by NOI members. "Some so-called Negroes believe in Martin King, and this is well and good," he declared diplomatically. Elijah Muhammad and King "should be tried as leaders," but ultimately Muhammad would be "on top because his works are greater." He then warned, "In Islam today a test of the Muslim belief is being waged. You should be wise in your decision when choosing."

On August 18, Malcolm was in Washington, speaking at a local NOI meeting. In the speech, he described the current situation as the "gravest crisis since the civil war." The vast majority of blacks had "lost all confidence in the false promises of hypocritical white politicians." His chief animus, however, was aimed at the "white liberals, who have been making a great fuss over the South, only to blind us to what is happening here in the North." The root causes of American racism were to be found in the nation's history. "The Revolutionary War and the Civil War were two wars fought on American soil, supposedly for freedom and democracy—but if these two wars were really for freedom and human dignity of *all* men, why are 20 million of our people still confined and enslaved?" A majority of the "founding fathers," men who signed the Declaration of Independence, owned slaves.

In the typed manuscript of this address, Malcolm made a handwritten correction that directly attacked the Kennedy administration, despite Muhammad's advice. Crossing out the words "the American government," he inscribed, "this present Catholic administration." He correctly anticipated the white backlash against the affirmative action and equal opportunity policies that within a few years would drive millions of Southern Democrats and white workers into the Republican Party, but he still could not imagine the passage of landmark civil rights legislation, least of all led by a Southern Democrat and taking place within one year

On August 23, Malcolm answered listeners' questions on WNOR radio, in Norfolk, Virginia, saying that Wallace D. Fard's coming in the 1930s represented the realization of Jewish prophecies, as well as the fulfillment of Islamic expectations. He described Fard as "the son of Man," making him divine—a status that Fard never claimed, at least not publicly. The day before, he had explained to a crowd the basics of the Nation's strange cosmology, complete with the story of Yacub and the white devils. It seemed incongruous with the rest of his rhetoric, but either he still firmly accepted the key tenets of Elijah Muhammad's world or he found it expedient to make it seem as though he did publicly. Politically, he was clearer: "The Muslims who follow the Honorable Elijah Muhammad won't have anything to do whatsoever with the March," he insisted. It would not benefit blacks to "go down to a dead man's statue—a dead President's monument—who was supposed to have issued an Emancipation Proclamation a hundred years ago."

It took only a few days before his negative comments about the forthcoming march began circulating in the national press. Meanwhile, thousands began to descend on Washington: the supposedly "Uncle Tom" leaders like Rustin, Randolph, and King had mobilized a quarter of a million people, well beyond the NOI's outreach. Across the country, tens of thousands of working-class blacks were also engaged in smaller protests. As Malcolm took in the march's tremendous drawing power, he must have been of two minds. The turnout let him take the temperature of the nation's black community; the massive mobilization showed that the gains made by King and other civil rights leaders in Birmingham and Montgomery had had a galvanizing effect. He could hardly deny their effectiveness in mobilizing blacks on a large scale. Yet he also believed that the NOI needed to delegitimize the march, to push back on the idea that this dramatic display of numbers could have any real effect on black Americans' lives. According to Larry 4X Prescott, several days before the march Malcolm met with Mosque No. 7 members, instructing them again that Elijah Muhammad had forbidden them to participate, though he also informed Larry and others that he himself would be attending, having received permission from the Messenger. On the night before the march, hundreds of buses were stationed at departure points throughout New York City. NOI laborers went to virtually every bus to distribute copies of *Muhammad Speaks*. Malcolm was letting it be known, Larry explained, that this was "a part of history that we should be a part of."

And yet publicly he was communicating the opposite. At an NOI rally just before the march, Malcolm pilloried the gathering as "the Farce on Washington," decrying its effectiveness and challenging the idea that the march as planned represented the will of the majority of blacks. He argued that the mobilization "actually began as a spontaneous and angry action of protest from the dissatisfied black masses." This had occurred, he admitted, because black people were overwhelmingly opposed to racial segregation. Malcolm claimed that the original intention was for black groups to tie up the Capitol through sit-ins and other civic disruptions. Inevitably, though, powerful whites began to influence events. Wilkins, Randolph, King, and other civil rights leaders supposedly had been ordered to call off the march. They informed the Kennedy administration that they were not in charge of the mobilization—that the black masses had taken control. Malcolm argued that the Kennedy administration decided to "co-opt" the demonstration. The president not only publicly endorsed the march's goals, but encouraged Negroes to participate in it. Malcolm's thesis was that the civil rights leaders were so craven and bankrupt that they were duped by whites in power.

This version of events was a gross distortion of the facts—yet it contained enough truth to capture an audience of unhappy black militants who had wanted the march to spearhead strikes and widespread civil disobedience. For all of Malcolm's calls for unity, and for whatever the march represented in its mass outpouring of support, the Black Freedom Movement continued to be pulled in different directions. Many on the left, including much of SNCC, were inclined to agree with Malcolm's position on the march's ineffectiveness. They saw the event as representative of the overly cautious strategies of middle-class Negro leaders, and believed more forceful action would be necessary to make real gains. These disagreements played themselves out in backroom deals leading up to the march, most notably when

SNCC's John Lewis found himself embroiled in controversy over his planned speech, which said essentially that the march was too little, too late; at the last minute, more conservative leaders pressured him to cut its most inflammatory passages. Malcolm's rhetoric, unburdened by factors of diplomacy, did not shy away from making such points.

On the night before the march, Peter Goldman ran into Louis Lomax in a Washington hotel lobby. Goldman recalled that Lomax led him to a large suite crowded with about fifty middle-class African Americans:

> And there [in the center] was Malcolm. And until I saw him, I had no clue that was what Lomax was leading me to. His attitude, his public attitude toward the march, was that this is a picnic, it's a circus, it's meaningless. . . . He was doing a very much muted version of that. He wasn't addressing them. It was more kind of a cocktail party setting. Indeed, there were a lot of bourbons splashing, including into my glass. . . . There's always one power center at a cocktail party, and he was it. . . . He knew that that was the capital . . . the epicenter of black America on that day.

Malcolm was indeed the center of attention wherever he went, usually followed by a gaggle of newsmen. Attorney Floyd McKissick, who in 1965 would become head of CORE, ran into him at the Washington Hilton. The two men hugged each other and began conversing before panicked CORE staffers hustled McKissick away, worried that any association with Malcolm would damage their image. Rustin encountered Malcolm on at least three occasions that night and the following day. The first time, he was leaving a strategy session with the march's major speakers when he saw Malcolm holding court with some reporters. Instead of getting angry, he knew his old debating partner well enough by now to use humor to deflate him. "Now, Malcolm, be careful," he warned. "There are going to be a half-million people here tomorrow, and you don't want to tell *them* this is nothing but a picnic." Malcolm replied, "What I tell them is one thing. What I tell the press is something else." Sometime later, Malcolm was with a group of marchers. Walking by, Rustin shouted out, "Why don't you tell them this is just a picnic?" This time Malcolm just smiled. The next day, with the demonstration concluded, Rustin saw him one more time. Malcolm said seriously, "You know, this dream of King's is going to be a nightmare before it's over." "You're probably right," Rustin replied.

The March on Washington is today largely remembered for King's "I Have a Dream" address, which drew heavily upon public speeches he had given in Birmingham that April and in Detroit two months earlier. The democratic vision he evoked—"that one day on the red hills of Georgia, the sons of former slaves and the sons of former slaveholders will be able to sit down together at the table of brotherhood"—spoke to the possibility of transforming the nation's political culture and making it fully inclusive for the first time in history. King's speech was much more than a rhetorical achievement: it was a challenge to white America to break with its racist past, and to embrace a multiracial future. Not widely known is that King's most memorable remarks that day were completely extemporaneous. However, as central as King's role was, what Rustin did following the "I Have a Dream" address was nearly as important. Going to the podium, he reviewed the march's objectives, which included passage of Kennedy's civil rights bill, a federal initiative to address unemployment, the desegregation of schools, and an increase in the federal minimum hourly wage to two dollars. The vast audience gave its consent for every demand.

From a distance, Malcolm witnessed it all. Roy Wilkins's nephew Roger Wilkins, then a young attorney working in the Justice Department, spotted Malcolm's unmistakable profile under a shady tree, looking out over the crowd. It is probable that several hundred NOI members participated in the march, defying Muhammad and the national leadership. Among their numbers was included Herbert Muhammad, who used his connections with *Muhammad Speaks* to be admitted as an "official photographer" to the grandstand at the speaker's platform. As Malcolm returned to New York, he must have realized that he had to present an action-oriented program of demands that would place the Nation of Islam on the side of black protest.

The NOI's national leaders finally felt confident enough that the rumors of Muhammad's sexual infidelities were sufficiently under control to schedule a major address by the Messenger in Philadelphia on September 29. At this rally, Muhammad voiced his direct opposition to the spirit of the March, which continued to dominate discussions a month later. In his judgment, it was "a waste of time for Negro leaders to go to Washington for justice." American whites were "snakelike in nature" and "were created for the purpose of murdering black people." Negroes had to choose complete racial separation, and if not, "they will die." The 1963 Philadelphia rally was also significant because it was the final time that both Muhammad and Malcolm appeared on a public stage together. Throughout 1961–63, Malcolm had presented himself to the media as Muhammad's national representative. But at the Philadelphia rally, Muhammad announced that Malcolm had been named national minister. The new appointment, which surely generated opposition from Muhammad's inner circle and family members, elevated Malcolm above all other NOI ministers. "This is my most faithful, hard-working minister," Muhammad told his audience. "He will follow me until he dies."

During these autumn weeks, Malcolm continued his sessions with Alex Haley, which he may have come to consider as a kind of therapy. In the writer's studio, telling his story, Malcolm discovered that he could relax a bit, and a looser, more casual side of his personality emerged. On one occasion, Haley recalled Malcolm's playfulness as he discussed his Harlem exploits: "Incredibly, the fearsome black demagogue was scat-singing and popping his fingers, 're-bop-de-bop-blap-blam—' and then grabbing a vertical pipe with one hand (as the girl partner) he went jubilantly lindy-hopping around . . ." In late September, Haley contacted Malcolm by letter, with words of praise: "I've never heard, when its full sweep is reflected upon, a more dramatic life account." He promised Malcolm that "whatever professional techniques" he possessed, they would "be brought into the effort to do the material that you have given me full justice." He asked assistance in "filling holes," and once again gave as an example Malcolm's complex relationship with Reginald. To make the break with his brother "gripping," Haley explained, "I must build up your regard and respect for Reginald when the two of you were earlier in Harlem—and, as of now, I have nothing about him there." Finally, Haley urged for as many hours as Malcolm could spare. "I badly need it. Justice to what the book can do for the Muslims needs it."

As the calendar turned to October, Reynolds and Doubleday became worried about the slow pace of Haley's productivity on the autobiography. On the first of the month, Wolcott (Tony) Gibbs, Jr., an assistant editor at Doubleday, suggested that Haley come up with a more "realistic manuscript delivery date," reminding him that it was crucial for the *Autobiography* to "have a publication date before the 1964 election is in full swing." Inspired by his editors and assisted by Malcolm's availability, Haley rapidly produced a series of draft chapters. On October 11, Haley forwarded Chapter 9, "The Negro," and promised additional chapters to come. This new material, he told Gibbs, "will present the style of Malcolm, the demagogue, sometimes ragged at the edges, sometimes quasi-dulcet, sometimes pounding . . . without obvious intrusion by the 'as told to' writer."

When compared to the final published version of *The Autobiography of Malcolm X*, which appeared in late 1965, the October 1963 version of the book had similarities, but also striking differences. Both the 1963 manuscript and the 1965 published book included these chapters: "Nightmare," "Mascot," "Homeboy," "Detroit Red," "Caught," "Satan," "Saved," "Savior," and "Minister Malcolm X." The 1965 version additionally contains "Laura," "Harlemite," "Hustler," "Trapped," and "Black Muslims." These chapters formed the core of the autobiographical narrative, and the majority of the book as a whole. Malcolm's objective was to present to the general reader the transformative power of the apostle Elijah Muhammad, who had taken him from a life of criminality and drugs to one of sobriety and commitment. In his lengthy conversations with Haley, Malcolm deliberately exaggerated his gangster exploits—the number of his burglaries, the amount of marijuana he sold to musicians, and the like—to illustrate how depraved he had become. Malcolm told Haley stories about himself that were largely true, but frequently presented himself as being more illiterate and backward than he really was. Malcolm's overriding mission was to show himself in the worst possible light, which would illustrate the power of Muhammad's message in changing people's lives. He also hoped that the narrative would stand as a testament to his continued devotion to and adoration of the Messenger. It might even quiet his growing chorus of critics in Muhammad's family.

In the 1963 version, Haley had planned a chapter, "The Messenger's Advocate," which he described as "the man today . . . speaking at Harvard Law School." This was to be followed by three essays outlining Malcolm's religious views and social philosophy. To an extent these three essays contained Malcolm's response to the striking success of the March on Washington. With a civil rights bill then being debated in the U.S. Senate, Malcolm not only had to make a case for black separation; he also had to outline an affirmative strategy for African-American resistance that was as dynamic as the Freedom Rides and sit-in protests. Drawing upon his experiences working with Randolph in Harlem, Malcolm called for a black united front embracing virtually all Negroes around a program of self-respect, economic development, and group empowerment. He believed that the NOI could play a vanguard role in building such a coalition, working with black elected officials, businesspeople, labor leaders, intellectuals, and others. Malcolm was taking the experiences he'd had in Harlem with Mosque No. 7 organizing mass rallies in the streets, and advocating an alternative to the peaceful, nonviolent demonstrations of King.

By the end of October, the *Autobiography* appeared to be taking shape. On October 27, Haley informed Gibbs that the book would be somewhat larger than originally planned, at roughly 120,000 words. The text would include ten chapters, three essays, and an afterword. The initial ten chapters were designed to tell "the unfolding, snowballing drama of this man's life." The final essays—"The Negro," "The End of Christianity," and "Twenty Million Black Muslims"—were designed to be a summation of Malcolm's religious and political point of view. In his afterword, Haley intended to write "as a Christian Negro," describing "the demagogue as I see him." Haley wanted to explain "what I critically feel about his life, and what he signifies, and represents, to Negroes, to white people, to America." He also mentioned to Gibbs that Malcolm had given him thirty to forty photographs to use for the book, including one of a young Malcolm alongside singer Billie Holiday. Nearly three weeks later, Haley wrote to his agent, editors, and Malcolm. Contacting executive editor Kenneth McCormick, Gibbs, and Reynolds, Haley revealed he was at the point at which the process of writing the *Autobiography* was changing him: "when the material begins to direct you and command you into what must be done with it." Writing separately to Malcolm the same day, Haley explained: "[I] am being careful, careful in developing the nuances as it unfolds, each stage, because viewed overall, your whole life is so incredible that no stage, especially in the early developing stages, may the reader be left with gaps, for if so it would strain the plausibility, believability of the truly fantastic 'Detroit Red'—and, then, the galvanic, absolute conversion."

As Haley worked to finish the manuscript, Malcolm made what would be his last tour of the West Coast as an NOI leader. He opened by holding a press conference in San Francisco on October 10, followed the next day by a panel discussion at the University of California at Berkeley. His speech took less than thirty minutes, but contained nearly twenty specific references to "the Honorable Elijah Muhammad." Yet in other respects its tone was profoundly secular and political. "It's not my intention to discuss the Muslim religious group today nor the Muslim religion," he explained. The nature of the crisis confronting America was "the increase of racial hostility, and the increase of outright racial hatred. We see masses of Black people who have lost all confidence in the false promises of the hypocritical white politicians." The discrimination that blacks confronted in the liberal North "is even more cruel and more vicious" than Southern racism.

Even more sharply than before, Malcolm pitted the Negro elite against the interests of the struggling black masses. "The wealthy, educated black bourgeoisie, those uppity Negroes who do escape, never reach back and pull the rest of our people out with them. The blacks remain trapped in the slum." The solution was not "token integration." When blacks tried to desegregate housing, whites fled these residential areas. "After the 1954 Supreme Court decision," Malcolm explained, "the same thing happened when our people tried to integrate the schools. All the white students disappeared into the suburbs." Now black leaders "are demanding a certain quota, a percentage, of white people's jobs." Such a demand would cause "violence and bloodshed." This was another instance in which Malcolm's imagined future led him to the wrong conclusion: only six years later a Republican president, Richard M. Nixon, with millions of whites sharply opposed, would implement affirmative action and programs such as minority economic set-asides. Such reforms were enacted without the "violence and bloodshed" Malcolm had predicted.

During the question and answer period following his short lecture, Malcolm was asked about discrimination in Cuba. He observed that "Castro has made a great accomplishment and contribution" toward the achievement of greater equality for blacks. But the Cubans generally "don't refer to themselves either as white people or Black," just as people. The same thing held true for Muslims: "When you become a Muslim, you don't look at a man as being black, brown, red, or white. You look upon him as being a man." This interpretation directly contradicted NOI theology. On another issue, Malcolm was asked, "Why can't a Negro infiltrate the political machine and use power politics to his own end?" His reply was again at odds with the NOI's position: "If he studies the science of politics, he probably would." There were some African-American elected officials who effectively represented "the Black masses. . . . Adam Powell is one of the best examples."

For a week, he traveled throughout California. In Los Angeles, at the Embassy Auditorium, an audience of two thousand heard him deliver his blistering "Farce on Washington" speech. Malcolm accused the demonstration of being "instigated by the white liberals to stem the real revolution, the black revolution." On October 18, Malcolm returned to New York, where he delivered a talk at Mosque No. 7 on "the condition of Negroes on the West Coast." In mid-October, Lonnie X Cross, who had been an undergraduate classmate of James 67X while at Lincoln University, was appointed the new minister of Mosque No. 4 in Washington, D.C., allowing Malcolm to relinquish his responsibilities there. Lonnie had joined the Nation only eighteen months earlier, and in September had resigned his faculty position as chairman of the mathematics department at Atlanta University to give "full time to the truth of Mr. Elijah Muhammad."

On October 29, Malcolm traveled to Hartford, Connecticut, where student groups at the University of Hartford had invited him to speak. Interest expressed in the visit was so strong that his talk, which had originally been set for the two-hundred-seat Auerbach Auditorium, was moved to an open-air arena accommodating seven hundred people. Buffeted by cold winds, Malcolm addressed his audience, saying, "Maybe some of what I have to say will make you hot." Much of what he said repeated his lecture at Berkeley. On November 5 he traveled to Philadelphia to address the local NOI mosque. Four days later, Malcolm engaged in a public dialogue with James Baldwin. Hardly a week went by without Malcolm making at least three public appearances, often more.

———

Perhaps unsurprisingly, the success of the March on Washington generated great dissension inside the Black Freedom Movement. The suppression of John Lewis's controversial speech highlighted the deeper issues that divided black activists, and as 1963 wore on, the split between the conservative old guard and the militants bubbled to the surface. Those increasingly influenced by Malcolm's black nationalism included sections of CORE, progressives in several Christian denominations, and secular activists from colleges, labor unions, and in Northern inner-city communities. When Detroit's Council for Human Rights began planning a Northern Negro Leadership Conference, many representatives of these independent, radical, and black nationalist groups were excluded from the program. In response, the charismatic minister the Reverend Albert B. Cleage, Jr., withdrew from the Northern Negro Leadership Conference and announced the holding of a second, more militant meeting that same weekend in Detroit. This insurgent gathering was largely put together by a Detroit network, the Group on Advanced Leadership (GOAL), which included two independent Marxists, James and Grace Lee Boggs. A former Trotskyist, Grace Lee Boggs had for years been an associate of the celebrated Trinidadian Marxist C. L. R. James, and was an astute Marxist theorist in her own right. Her husband, James Boggs, had extensive experience in labor organizing, and soon would become one of Black Power's most influential writers and social theorists.

Another radical constituency in Detroit intensely interested in Malcolm was the Socialist Workers Party (SWP). Its key figure, who would subsequently help shape Malcolm's intellectual legacy through the publication of several books by and about him, was George Breitman. The editor of the SWP's newspaper, *The Militant*, Breitman also initiated the successful Friday Night Socialist Forum hosted at Wayne State University in the 1960s. The SWP also supported efforts to establish the Freedom Now Party, an independent black third party formed in Michigan. Consequently, when Malcolm accepted an invitation to address the Reverend Cleage's Grassroots Conference, he may not have realized that thousands of his local supporters considered themselves more militant than he was. They, too, rejected the gradualism of the NAACP and SCLC and the nonviolent activism of Rustin and Farmer, and were sharply critical of the Negro bourgeoisie. With the collapse of McCarthyism and the most extreme forms of government harassment, American leftists and socialists were eager to participate in the national struggle for blacks' rights. They looked to Malcolm X as a possible leader of that new movement.

When, on the evening of November 10, Malcolm walked up to the King Solomon Baptist Church's pulpit, he saw a sea of two thousand mostly black faces. He probably had not intended to break new political ground. Certainly he had not planned to repudiate his allegiance to the NOI. Yet as he delivered his "Message to the Grassroots" address, his life was fundamentally changed—not unlike King's, in the aftermath of "I Have a Dream." In his address, Malcolm incorporated sections from recent speeches, especially "The Farce on Washington," but he also drew parallels between the black freedom struggle in the United States, the Bandung Conference, and anti-colonial movements across Asia and Africa. He drew a sharp distinction between what he called a "Negro revolution" versus a black one. A true revolution, he declared, was represented by the Chinese communists— "There are no Uncle Toms" in China, he said—and by the Algerian revolution against French colonial rule. The "Negro revolution," based on nonviolent direct action, was no revolution at all:

> Revolution is bloody, revolution is hostile, revolution knows no compromise, revolution overturns and destroys everything that gets in its way. And you, sitting around here like a knot on a wall, saying, "I'm going to love these folks no matter how much they hate me." No, you need a revolution. Whoever heard of a revolution where they lock arms, as Rev. Cleage was pointing out beautifully, singing "We Shall Overcome"? You don't do that in a revolution. You don't do any singing; you're too busy swinging. It's based on land. A revolutionary wants land so he can set up his own nation, an independent nation. . . . If you're afraid of black nationalism you're afraid of revolution. And if you love revolution, you love black nationalism.

In the second half of his address came the dichotomy of the house Negro and the field Negro. Malcolm ridiculed the "modern house Negroes" such as King and Wilkins, casting himself as a modern-day slave rebel. He denounced the March on Washington as a "sellout." "And every one of those Toms was put out of town by sundown," he added, to gales of laughter. The major Negro endorsers of the march should even receive Academy Awards "for the best supporting cast." As he finished, the response was electrifying: people cheered and waved their hands. The talk had some obligatory references to Muhammad, but these were deleted from the tape recording several months later, when "Message to the Grassroots" was released as a record. The enthusiasm was provoked by the crowd's recognition that Malcolm appeared to have broken free politically. Grace Lee Boggs, who was sitting next to the Reverend Cleage on the speakers' platform, thought that Malcolm's "speech was so analytical, so much less [black] nationalist and more internationalist" than all his previous talks. Excited, Boggs whispered to Cleage, "Malcolm's going to split with Elijah Muhammad."

In mid-November, he revealed to Haley that when he visited Michigan in late October, he had driven with Philbert to Kalamazoo and secured the release of his mother from the state mental hospital. "It may shock you to learn that two weeks ago," he wrote, "I had dinner with my mother for the first time in 25 years, and she is now home and residing with my brother Philbert in Lansing." Haley meanwhile pushed on. He had just relocated from lower Manhattan to a small house in rural Rome, New York. He explained to Malcolm, "I don't want [a telephone] even here," until most of the *Autobiography* was completed. When he heard about Louise's release, he responded: "Shocked? No, friend, I was most sincerely—moved very much . . . professionally, I was happy as I can be that there is added to the book for the millions of readers that it will have, this graphic human interest story, this caliber of a 'happy ending.'"

———

Wallace Muhammad had invited Louis X to his Chicago home after Saviour's Day 1963. Over hot chocolate, he asked, "I want you to tell brother Malcolm that I would like to see him and you together. There's something that I want to tell you both." As fate would have it, for several months he was unable to schedule a meeting with Louis and Malcolm at the same time. He sat down with Malcolm alone in October, telling him that his father's extramarital sexual activity was "as bad as it ever was."

Malcolm now had a choice. He could have stayed silent, continuing to give biblical and Qur'anic analogies to explain away Muhammad's errors in judgment. However, he felt that a more aggressive approach was needed, both to protect Muhammad and to stop the hemorrhaging of disillusioned members. He consulted with six or seven ministers whom he trusted. Among their number was, of course, Louis X—who knew significantly more than Malcolm suspected.

Malcolm's initial conversation with Louis about the Messenger's transgressions had occurred in New York; as was his custom after their meeting, Malcolm drove Louis to the airport. According to Farrakhan, as Malcolm was driving to LaGuardia airport, Louis casually told him that he would have to inform Muhammad that Malcolm had been discussing the infidelities with other ministers. There was a brief silence. Then Malcolm, looking straight ahead, said, "Give me two weeks." Malcolm wanted to explain his contacts with NOI ministers about the scandal first. Louis consented to Malcolm's request. And although neither man knew this at the time, their roles and futures within the Nation would fundamentally change at that moment. When Louis gave his version of these events to Elijah Muhammad, the apostle would never fully trust Malcolm again, and he began to look at Louis as Malcolm's possible successor.

It would be too easy to argue that the root cause of Malcolm's disaffection from Elijah Muhammad was the knowledge that Evelyn, the woman with whom he had been romantically involved for years, had been impregnated by the Messenger. Farrakhan is the only one of his intimate friends to claim Malcolm was considering leaving Betty for Evelyn; no one else—not even James 67X—has made such a claim. Farrakhan may have a vested interest in exaggerating Malcolm's anger about Evelyn in order to promote a nontheological reason for his break with the NOI, which set the stage for Farrakhan's own rise to prominence. There is no doubt that Malcolm was extremely upset by this information, but in itself it seems unlikely he would have quit the NOI solely based on the incident with Evelyn.

Malcolm continued his hectic pace throughout the remainder of November. On November 20 he addressed a class at the journalism school of Columbia University. The short talk, followed by a lengthy discussion period, was an artful dance, incorporating politics, traditional NOI dogma, and classical tenets of Sunni Islam.

This class discussion represents one of the most revealing sessions ever conducted with Malcolm, because of the broad spectrum of issues covered. For example, in one of his rare comments about the nonblack Islamic community, Malcolm accused this group of largely Asian and Middle Eastern immigrants of not living up to the true tenets of the Islamic faith. These

Muslims should give Elijah Muhammad credit for recruiting thousands to Islam and "not question his religious authenticity," he said. When one student raised the American Nazi Party's interest in the NOI, Malcolm responded, "More white people in the county are in sympathy with Nazism than they are with practicing democracy. . . . I don't think any white is in a moral position to ask me what I think about Nazis in light of the fact you're living in a country which in 1963 permits the bombing of Negro churches and the murder of little innocent and defenseless black children." Without explaining why the NOI permitted Nazis to attend their gatherings, he insisted that "Rockwell couldn't do what he's doing . . . if there weren't a large segment of whites in this country who think exactly like Rockwell does." When asked about the administration's civil rights policy, he stammered, "What about it?" Once again, he expressed his contempt for Kennedy: "Any time a man can become president, and after three years in office do as little for Negroes as he has done despite the fact that Negroes went for him 80 percent . . . I'll have to say he's the foxiest of the foxy."

Even here, Malcolm continued to portray the NOI as a coiled snake ready to strike, despite all the missed chances to do so; he bragged that Muhammad taught Muslims to respect the law, "but any time anybody puts their hands on us, we should send them straight to the cemetery." Someone asked about his attitude toward the newly created Freedom Now Party, for which he offered a convoluted quasi-endorsement. Because the NOI's position was to discourage its members from voting, he could not officially endorse any party, but he noted with interest the eight million unregistered black voters nationally. Imagine what "presidential candidates and others" would have to do if this group became active. "Why, they would upset the entire political picture."

Although Malcolm's responsibilities were now truly national, he tried hard not to neglect racial issues in New York City. Notably, he attended and supported a series of civil rights demonstrations occurring across the city. Herman Ferguson, a thirty-nine-year-old public school assistant principal who was actively involved in leading civil rights demonstrations in Queens, was pleasantly surprised when assistant minister Larry 4X and other Muslims offered their support. "Lots of them [Muslims] I had taught in school," Ferguson explained. "They couldn't become [directly] involved because they were not allowed to." An agreement was reached where the Muslims would show up at the civil rights demonstrations to sell *Muhammad Speaks* but would also distribute the civil rights coalition's flyers. Malcolm sent word through Larry that he supported the demonstrations, and he extended an invitation to Ferguson and other Queens activists to visit Mosque No. 7. Ferguson and the Queens activists began attending lectures there, and were deeply impressed. It was Ferguson who suggested organizing a major speaking event featuring Malcolm in Queens, an invitation Malcolm accepted. The Nation paid a New Jersey printer to produce attractive posters that were distributed throughout the largely black Queens neighborhood of South Jamaica.

Malcolm's lecture was scheduled for the evening of Thanksgiving Day. Hundreds came out to attend, and the NYPD was also there in force. "It was like half the police force in Queens was assigned to that place that day," Ferguson later recalled. "We didn't realize the drawing power of Malcolm," even on the Thanksgiving holiday.

There was an incident that day involving Malcolm that Ferguson would never forget. Shortly before going to the podium to speak, Malcolm was busily scrawling on a yellow legal pad, and Ferguson simply assumed the minister was making final notes on his speech. So he was truly surprised when Malcolm, looking out at the audience, said, "'That fellow there is going with that white girl there,'" Ferguson recalled. "Now, there was quite a distance, a lot of space between them. . . . There was no indication, nobody would have known or suspected that there was anything going on." Yet Malcolm was absolutely correct. Nearly every great speaker, like Malcolm, must also be a student of people and cultures. "He observed people and things that were going on around him, and from time to time he would make little comments, to let you know that he had picked up on something that was happening around him."

Yet the central irony of Malcolm's career was that his critical powers of observation, so important in fashioning his dynamic public addresses, virtually disappeared in his mundane evaluations of those in his day-to-day personal circle. Especially in the final years of his life, nearly every individual he trusted would betray that trust. As late as November 1963, Malcolm did not recognize that the political path he had deliberately chosen would quickly lead to his expulsion from the Nation. This was apparent, even to Ferguson, in 1963: "I felt that . . . eventually [he] would have to leave the Nation of Islam. He was just too political. . . . He was developing too fast."

CHAPTER 10

"The Chickens Coming Home to Roost"

December 1, 1963–March 12, 1964

John F. Kennedy was assassinated in the early afternoon of Friday, November 22, 1963. When Elijah Muhammad was told, he was taken aback. He had frequently warned Malcolm of criticizing Kennedy, knowing of the president's considerable popularity with black Americans, and now he took steps to ensure that the NOI would not be caught in the storm of anger and disbelief that was already roiling the nation. He released a short statement expressing shock "over the loss of our president," and then arranged for his next column in *Muhammad Speaks* to be moved to the front page alongside a photo of Kennedy. He informed all NOI ministers to say nothing in public, going so far as to have one of his sons call Malcolm so he could dictate over the phone what he wanted his national minister to say if questioned about the assassination. With the stakes high and Malcolm already bridling at Chicago's attempts to control him, Muhammad would leave nothing to chance.

Yet fate interceded when the Messenger was forced to cancel a long-planned speaking engagement at the Manhattan Center in midtown New York City on December 1. The Nation could not get out of its rental agreement, so Malcolm was selected as a substitute speaker for what would be the first major speech delivered by an NOI leader since the assassination. To make certain that the public program was handled properly, John Ali flew from Chicago to help out, and the decision was made to allow all reporters, including whites, to cover the speech. Malcolm's advertised title, "God's Judgment of White America," was deliberately provocative, but he, Ali, and all the other NOI officials involved knew of Muhammad's instruction to avoid any references to Kennedy.

The talk was an important one for Malcolm, and he prepared carefully, first drafting a detailed outline of the key issues he wanted to cover, then typing out the actual lecture he planned to deliver. The lecture reflected the two divergent realms of black consciousness that Malcolm occupied: the spiritual domain of the Nation of Islam and the political worlds of black nationalism, Pan-Africanism, and Third World revolution. He was sufficiently astute to express the obligatory remarks of homage to Elijah Muhammad, but also clearly visible was the militant political language of "Message to the Grassroots," along with calls for a black global revolution and the destruction of white power. He knew that John Ali would be in the audience and would immediately report back to Muhammad with a negative review of the speech. By choosing to be provocative, Malcolm would push the NOI toward a more militant posture.

An audience of about seven hundred attended, a majority of them congregants of Mosque No. 7, but a significant minority were non-Muslim blacks. Captain Joseph had ordered Larry 4X to serve on Malcolm's security detail; as instructed, he drove out to the minister's home in Queens and tailed Malcolm's Oldsmobile on its way to the Manhattan Center. Once Malcolm was secure in the building, Larry directed other Fruit of Islam to bar any whites, except reporters, from entering.

"God's Judgment of White America" began with a sophisticated argument about political economies. "The Honorable Elijah Muhammad teaches us . . . it was the evil of slavery that caused the downfall and destruction of ancient Egypt and Babylon, and of ancient Greece, as well as ancient Rome," Malcolm told his audience. In similar fashion, colonialism contributed to "the collapse of the white nations in present-day Europe as world powers." The exploitation of African Americans will, in turn, "bring white America to her hour of judgment, to her downfall as a respected nation." Malcolm's core argument was that America, like the ancient civilizations of Greece and Rome, was in moral decline. The greatest example of its moral bankruptcy, Malcolm argued, was its hypocrisy. "White America pretends to ask herself, 'What do these Negroes want?' White America knows that four hundred years of cruel bondage has made these twenty-two million ex-slaves too (mentally) [Malcolm's parentheses] blind to see what they really want."

"God's Judgment" made an effort to put the NOI's religious practices and beliefs within the larger Muslim world. Malcolm explained that Elijah Muhammad's "divine mission" was essentially that of a modern prophet, not unlike "Noah, Moses, and Daniel. He is a warrior to our white oppressor, but a savior to the oppressed." This claim that Elijah merited the status of prophet directly contradicted orthodox Islam's interpretation of Muhammad of the Qur'an as being the Seal of the Prophets. Despite this deviation, Malcolm insisted that "the Honorable Elijah Muhammad teaches us not only the principles of Muslim belief but the principles of Muslim practice." Nation of Islam members, he insisted, adhered to the five pillars of Islam, including prayer five times daily, tithing, fasting, and making "the pilgrimage to the Holy City, Mecca, at least [once] during our lifetime." He observed that Elijah and two of his sons had visited Mecca in 1959, adding that "others of his followers have been making [the Mecca pilgrimage] since then." He deliberately avoided presenting Islam as a black religion, portraying it as a faith with an emancipatory message for African Americans.

There was an urgent emphasis on the coming apocalypse, which, while part of the Nation of Islam's theology, was merged into a political jeremiad of destruction. A Muslim world could not come into existence unless God himself destroyed "this evil Western world, the white world, a wicked world, ruled by a race of devils, that preaches falsehood, practices slavery, and thrives on indecency and immorality." America had now reached "that great Doomsday, the final hour," where all the wicked would perish and only those who believed in Allah as God and who affirmed Islam as their faith would be saved.

Midway through this apocalyptic vision, however, Malcolm did an about-face, turning from eschatology to racial politics. He accused the government of "trying to trick her twenty-two million ex-slaves with promises she never intends to keep." To retain power, liberals and conservatives alike cynically manipulate civil rights issues and Negro leaders who align themselves with white liberals "sell out our people for just a few crumbs of token recognition and token gains." He equated the approximately three million blacks who were registered to vote as of 1960 with the "black bourgeoisie," "who have been educated to think as patriotic 'individualists' with no racial pride, and who therefore look forward hopefully to the future integrated-*intermarried* [Malcolm's emphasis] society promised them by white liberals and the Negro 'leaders.'" But no racial progress was possible so long as those in power listened to this "white-minded minority" of Negro leaders and registered voters. "The white man should try to learn what the black masses want . . . by listening to the man who speaks for the black masses of America"—that is, Elijah Muhammad. Malcolm's attempt to make the Messenger a black working-class hero and to equate bourgeois status with the act of voter registration were clever, if fraudulent. He certainly was aware that in 1963 millions of African Americans who wanted to vote were being denied franchisement, through harassment, intimidation, and murder, as in the case of Medgar Evers. The overwhelming majority were demanding access to public accommodations and full voting rights, issues that had nothing to do with upward class mobility or a lack of "racial pride." This was Malcolm's easy way to attack middle-class blacks.

Finally, he argued that it was the U.S. government and white liberals that controlled the Negro revolution. But far greater was the "black revolution . . . the struggle of the nonwhites of this earth against their white oppressors." Black revolutionaries had already "swept white supremacy" out of Asia and Africa, and were about to do so in Latin America. "Revolutions," Malcolm explained, "are based on *land* [Malcolm's emphasis]. Revolutionaries are the landless against the landlord." In an obvious reference to King, he echoed his language from "Grassroots": "Revolutions are never peaceful, never loving, never nonviolent. Nor are they compromising. Revolutions are destructive and bloody." The apocalypse would come about through the black masses and the wretched of the earth seizing the citadels of power. It was a powerful vision, but not one that Elijah Muhammad had in mind.

Throughout his speech, Malcolm had been careful to avoid references to the late president, but in the question and answer session following the talk, his sense of humor and his tendency to banter with representatives of the press got the better of him. When asked about the assassination, he initially charged that the media had tried to trap the Nation of Islam into making a "fanatic, inflexibly dogmatic statement." What the press wanted from the Muslims, he declared, was a remark like "Hooray, hooray! I'm glad he got it!" Members of the audience laughed and applauded, and the crowd's encouragement led Malcolm down the path from which Elijah Muhammad had tried to steer him. Now he was fired up, finally unmuzzled, and the criticism began to flow freely. Kennedy had been "twiddling his thumbs" when South Vietnamese president Ngo Dinh Diem and his brother Ngo Dinh Nhu were murdered recently. The Dallas assassination, Malcolm said, was an instance of "the chickens coming home to roost." America had fomented violence, so it was not a surprise that the president had become a victim.

Had Malcolm stopped there, he might have escaped unscathed, or at least invited less trouble than would soon unfold for him. These comments, while certainly offensive, could at least be understood in the context of previous speeches and the generally understood opinions of the Nation of

Islam. But then he added, with a rhetorical flourish, "Being an old farm boy myself, chickens coming home to roost never did make me sad; they've always made me glad." There was further laughter and applause by audience members, but this extra sentence condemned him as gleeful and celebratory over the president's death. When the FBI later noted the speech in a report, it characterized the "chickens" remarks as suggesting that the assassination brought Malcolm pleasure, which, if not quite the thrust of his much quoted phrase, was certainly the sentiment driven home by the "old farm boy" quip that followed.

Though the comments would almost instantly cause a furor outside the Manhattan Center, inside the reaction was almost entirely the opposite. "The crowd just started applauding," remembered Larry 4X. "When he made the statement, I didn't think anything about it." Herman Ferguson, the assistant school principal who had arranged Malcolm's Thanksgiving speech in Queens the previous month, was also in attendance, and saw little to get agitated about: "It was an innocuous comment, and nobody paid any particular attention to it."

Nobody, perhaps, except for John Ali and Captain Joseph, who had been standing only a few feet away from Malcolm as he delivered his remarks. Ali was livid, and within moments he was searching for a phone to call Elijah Muhammad. Malcolm had challenged a direct order, jeopardizing the interests of the Nation. The comments would certainly intensify the scrutiny of the FBI and local law enforcement, making it harder for the Nation to operate without being hassled, and the blowback threatened to bring a halt to the recruitment gains made over the last five years. Chicago headquarters had other worries as well. By now there were hundreds of Muslims inside federal and state prisons, all of them vulnerable to harassment and physical abuse. If correction officials believed that the Black Muslims celebrated Kennedy's murder, these Muslim prisoners could become targets for retribution. Finally, Ali probably raised with Elijah Muhammad what would have been, for him, the disturbing second half of Malcolm's address. The news of Malcolm's speech wounded the Messenger. His most trusted minister had directly disobeyed him; challenged, he would have no choice but to push back hard. Yet it undoubtedly also gave comfort to Malcolm's enemies within the Nation: here was a chance for Sharrieff, Ali, Elijah, Jr., Herbert Muhammad, and others to freeze Malcolm out. His inflammatory statement had given them a wedge by which he might be forced from the Nation of Islam. They counseled Muhammad immediately to establish a public distance between Malcolm and the Nation. By disciplining the Nation's national spokesman, Elijah Muhammad would reassert his personal authority throughout the sect. And if Malcolm chose to challenge him, he would give Ali and others sufficient reason to push for his expulsion.

The next day, Monday, December 2, Malcolm flew to Chicago for his regular monthly meeting with Muhammad. That morning, the *New York Times* headlined its story "Malcolm X Scores U.S. and Kennedy: Likens Slaying to 'Chickens Coming Home to Roost.'" When he arrived, as customary the two men embraced, but Malcolm immediately sensed that something was wrong. "That was a very bad statement," Muhammad told him. "The president of the country is our president, too." This was an odd formulation, given that NOI members had been discouraged from voting in elections. Muhammad then told Malcolm that he was suspended for the next ninety days, during which time he would be removed from his post as minister of Mosque No. 7. Though he would not be allowed to preach or even enter the mosque, he was expected to continue performing the administrative tasks of the minister—approving invoices, answering correspondence, and maintaining records. Marilyn E.X., his secretary, would continue working for him.

The gears turned quickly to spread news of the punishment. Late that afternoon, as Malcolm was returning to the Chicago airport to fly back to New York City, Ali and his aides contacted press organizations throughout the country about Malcolm's "silencing." In a widely circulated telegram to media outlets, the NOI stated, "Minister Malcolm did not speak for Muhammad or the Nation of Islam or any of Mr. Muhammad's followers. . . . The correct statement on the death of the President is: 'We with the world are very shocked at the assassination of President Kennedy.'" An *Amsterdam News* reporter reached Malcolm at his home and asked for a comment. Technically his "silence" should have meant that he had no direct contact with the media, but instead, in a small act of defiance, he responded, saying, "Yes, I'm wrong. I disobeyed Muhammad's order. He was justified 100 percent. I agree I need to withdraw from public appearance." The news about Malcolm's suspension from the Nation of Islam was widely covered in the white press. The *Los Angeles Times* story, for example, was titled "Malcolm X Hit for Glee Over Kennedy Death." *Newsweek* speculated that the suspension had left Malcolm "only with his intramural duties as New York's Muslim minister—and even that job reportedly was in doubt."

When Mosque No. 7 learned about Malcolm's ninety-day suspension, there was uncertainty but not panic. Putting individuals "out of the mosque" for disciplinary reasons was routine. Veteran members could recall Captain Joseph being ousted from his privileged post as head of the Fruit of Islam back in 1956. Nearly everyone assumed that the minister would simply acquiesce to the decision and three months later resume his customary role. Much continued as it had before. Larry 4X continued to make sure that Malcolm received his office mail. "He would go to the restaurant, he would talk to the staff," recalled Larry, "but he would make no public speeches."

Yet during the initial days of the suspension, many mosque members were unsure about the boundaries that should be set for the minister. James 67X was at the speaker's rostrum, opening a meeting at the mosque, when Malcolm walked through the double-door entrance at the back of the hall only to have Captain Joseph quickly step forward and block him. "Malcolm had to turn around and go back out," recalled James, "and I said, 'Oh-oh, something funny is going on.'"

By this time James was the mosque's circulation manager for *Muhammad Speaks*, responsible for managing thousands of dollars in revenue each week. His close working relationship with Malcolm had let him see just how great a toll the internal tumult had taken. In the fall of 1963, he had sensed that Malcolm was physically and mentally exhausted, and took it upon himself to write a letter to Muhammad, requesting leave for the minister. He wrote a second letter to Captain Joseph, who treated it with ridicule. Now he found it difficult to get further details on what was happening with Malcolm. He and other office staff were simply told that the minister had been expelled for only ninety days; no mosque member in good standing was permitted to speak to him. "At first," said James, "I figured, well, Mr. Muhammad is making an astute political move." But within several weeks, James began hearing complaints about Malcolm. Some said, "Big Red, yeah, he never was with the Messenger." Others blamed him for the public fiascos with the American Nazi Party.

The situation was extremely difficult for Betty, too. As of January 1964, she was three months pregnant with their fourth child. Her husband was increasingly the object of ridicule and open condemnation, but as a Muslim in good standing she was expected to attend mosque functions, making it hard to avoid awkward situations. All the warnings she had given Malcolm about reckoning his future beyond the Nation seemed prophetic, and any hesitation he may have shown now about distancing himself financially or otherwise surely heightened the tension between them. But there was no way for Malcolm to shield his wife from the gathering storm, or the consequences when his salary stopped.

On December 6, the *New York Times* ran a story, "Malcolm Expected to Be Replaced." The news, surely generated by a leak from those closest to Muhammad, surprised not just Malcolm and his family, but his supporters as well. The *Times* indicated that sources close to the Black Muslims had confirmed that Elijah Muhammad had already selected a successor for Mosque No. 7. The most likely candidates were Muhammad's youngest son, Akbar Muhammad; Jeremiah X, minister of the Atlanta and Birmingham mosques; and Washington, D.C., minister Lonnie X. Sources to the *Times* also indicated that "Malcolm had become 'so powerful' that he had emerged as a 'personality,' rather than as a spokesman for the movement." The story was most striking in its detail, which confirmed that it had come from close to up high: the naming of specific ministers in key positions could have been authorized only by either the Nation's secretariat in Chicago or Captain Joseph. Asked for a comment, Malcolm denied the rumors. "I am the minister of the mosque," he insisted, "and I shall be carrying out my responsibilities for the mosque whatever they may entail. I will just exclude public speaking engagements." Technically, his statement represented a violation of Elijah Muhammad's silencing order. But no further action was taken against him for the time being.

To his critics inside the Nation, Malcolm was simply going through the motions, only appearing to be contrite. He had informed Mosque No. 7 officials that he had begun working on a manuscript based on the wisdom expressed by Elijah Muhammad during their many dinner conversations over the years, yet beyond making rough outlines, Malcolm never really worked on the project. Instead, he continued to express himself in the national press, against Muhammad's order. In the *Chicago Defender*, for instance, he blasted black Republican Jackie Robinson for negative comments he had made against Adam Clayton Powell, Jr., and the Nation of Islam. Dripping with satire, his polemic ridiculed the former baseball great as someone who never knows "what is going on in the Negro community until the white man tells you." He accused Robinson of attempting to influence blacks into supporting New York governor Nelson Rockefeller, asking, "Just who are you playing ball for today, good friend?" He also warned Robinson that if he ever dared to exhibit the militant courage of a Medgar Evers, "the same whites whom you now take to be your friends will be the first to put the bullet or the dagger in your back, just as they put it in the back of Medgar Evers." Further, Elijah Muhammad probably was not pleased when the *Amsterdam News* reported that Doubleday was planning to publish Malcolm's autobiography. Muhammad reaffirmed to the press that his troublesome deputy still retained the title of minister, "but he will not be permitted to speak in public."

Malcolm felt almost completely adrift. After years of traveling cross-country to make speeches and organize the Nation's affairs, he now found himself saddled with a new and oddly unpleasant burden: free time. To keep occupied, he answered letters. To an African-American student at Colgate University who had expressed interest in starting an Islamic society on campus, he explained that while the acquisition of knowledge was commendable, to be useful, education had to be culturally relevant. "Our cultural roots must be restored before life (incentive) can flow into us; because just as a tree without roots is dead, a people without cultural roots are automatically dead."

The best evidence of Malcolm's state of mind is in an interview he gave to Louis Lomax, in which he vigorously denied implying "that Kennedy's death was a reason for rejoicing." His central point was that the president's assassination "was the result of a long line of violent acts, the culmination of hate and suspicion and doubt in this country." Muhammad "had warned me not to say anything about the death of the president, and I omitted any references to that tragedy in my main speech." While he accepted his suspension, he assured the journalist that "I don't think it will be permanent." Most significantly, when Lomax inquired about "differences" that were rumored to exist between himself and Muhammad, Malcolm snapped, "It's a lie. . . . How could there be any difference between the Messenger and me? I am his slave, his servant, his son. He is the leader, the only spokesman for the Black Muslims."

Elijah Muhammad was at first satisfied with the general reaction to Malcolm's suspension. In telephone conversations recorded by the FBI, he described his punishment of Malcolm as an act of parental authority: "Papa" had to discipline the child, who would receive even more censure "if he sticks out his lip and starts popping off." But as the Kennedy controversy faded from the headlines, Elijah was confronted with other concerns. The continued shunning of the Nation's golden child led many to believe that the Kennedy statement was only a pretense for punishment, and that this was simply the long-awaited showdown between Malcolm and the NOI secretariat in Chicago over the future direction of the Nation of Islam. The major issue, however, was the continuing rumors of Muhammad's sexual infidelities, which had only grown more widespread. Muhammad now knew that Malcolm had told Louis X and other ministers, with Malcolm explaining his course of action as an attempt to control sentiments among the rank and file. But John Ali, Sharrieff, and others told Muhammad that Malcolm had deliberately spread this information to undermine him and argued that Malcolm's actions were destroying confidence in Muhammad and in the Nation. They were helped along by the FBI, which had tracked the dissension with interest and now moved with a new series of planted letters meant to corroborate Malcolm's supposed rumormongering.

This constant drumbeat of derision had its desired effect. Sometime in mid-December 1963, Muhammad decided not to return Malcolm to his position in Mosque No. 7. He had permitted Malcolm to become too powerful. By publicly humiliating him, he could reclaim his supremacy over the sect in such a manner that no other minister would dare challenge him. Although the Chicago officials wanted to expel Malcolm and his supporters outright, it is unlikely that Elijah shared their views, at least at that time. Keeping Malcolm within the sect but muzzled and stripped of his offices seemed a more effective demonstration of the Messenger's power. He would eliminate Malcolm's institutional base but leave him in place as the national minister to work in a lower-profile administrative capacity. Malcolm, for his part, still clung to the hope that Muhammad would eventually reinstate him. By the end of 1963, both men stood at the precipice, but neither believed that a total split was inevitable.

The new year, however, saw the situation continue to worsen. On January 2, 1964, Muhammad phoned Malcolm to discuss the suspension; Sharrieff and Ali were probably listening in. Malcolm, he said, had discussed his conduct with NOI ministers in a manner that was highly irresponsible. Charges of extramarital affairs and out-of-wedlock children were akin to a "fire" that could devastate the Nation. A second concern for Muhammad was the continuing rivalry between his family and Malcolm. Malcolm offered no opposition or rebuttal. Even when Muhammad hinted that his suspension could continue indefinitely, Malcolm replied calmly that he had profited from his mentor's advice and actions, adding that he was praying to atone for his errors.

Perhaps Malcolm failed to express his remorse sufficiently, for it was after this phone call that Muhammad concluded the time had come to strip him of all authority. The next day, Joseph was informed that a new minister would replace Malcolm at Mosque No. 7; however, the decision-making authority in running the mosque would now be Joseph's. On January 5, Muhammad promoted James 3X (McGregor) Shabazz, the head of Newark's mosque, as the new minister. Malcolm was ordered to fly to Phoenix for a judicial hearing, at which Elijah Muhammad, Ali, and Sharrieff were all present. It was probably only at this formal session that Malcolm finally grasped what was happening to him. He confessed to the "court" that he had revealed details about Muhammad's private life to Captain Joseph and to a handful of NOI ministers, and went on to plead for the opportunity to continue to serve Muhammad. But he also insisted upon the right to a judicial hearing before members of his own mosque, a right that had been long established for those accused of violations in the Nation. Muhammad's response was "Go back and put out the fire you started." Henceforth, Malcolm was to be quarantined: no member in good standing was permitted to speak to him or to interact with him in any manner. As Peter Goldman astutely observed, "For a faithful Muslim, this order was tantamount to being forced to the edge of that grave the rest of us call the world. The evidence soon accumulated that somebody in the Nation had another, less metaphorical grave in mind."

As the weeks lurched forward, the Nation boiled over with enmity toward Malcolm, spurred on by John Ali and Raymond Sharrieff, who used their positions at the top of the NOI hierarchy to trigger a cascade of invective down through the ranks. Gross rumors of Malcolm's disloyalty to Muhammad swept through the Nation, at first whispered at MGT meetings or discussed among the Fruit, yet eventually declaimed openly by ministers, even by James 3X Shabazz from Malcolm's own former pulpit. Not long after returning from Phoenix, Malcolm and NOI member Charles 37X Morris were walking along Amsterdam Avenue in Harlem when they encountered a young Muslim brother on the sidewalk staring at them. His fists were clenched and he appeared ready to hurl himself at them. Mosque No. 7 officials had told the angry young Fruit, "If you knew what Malcolm had said about the Dear Holy Apostle, you'd kill him yourself." Charles defiantly told the young man to go back to the mosque official and ask why he didn't do his own killing. The moment passed without further incident, but it illustrated all too plainly that hundreds of Nation of Islam members were being made to view Malcolm as the enemy of their sect. The degree of anger and hatred generated by the anti-Malcolm campaign would make it almost impossible for the minister to return, even with Muhammad's permission. Malcolm desperately tried to maintain a routine, a pattern of work and responsibility, to keep his bearings. On January 14, he met with Alex Haley to work on the *Autobiography*. Their session lasted over seven hours, deep into the night. As he worked with Haley to shape the story of his past, he found the shape of his present was changing too quickly to pin down.

Since Cassius Clay had walked into the Students' Luncheonette in Detroit and into Malcolm's life, his reputation had continued to grow; after knocking out Archie Moore in July 1962, he proceeded to put down three more fighters, remaining undefeated and earning himself a title shot against the much favored heavyweight champion Sonny Liston. While training for the fight in Miami in the winter of 1963, Clay invited Malcolm and his family down to his camp in Miami Beach for a vacation. Grateful for the chance to escape New York, Malcolm accepted, and on January 15 he, Betty, and their three daughters flew south. His trip, and the fight, mustered little attention from Muhammad. Although the Chicago headquarters appreciated the young boxer's interest in the Nation of Islam, the Messenger made it known that he disapproved of the sport as a profession. Beyond this, NOI leaders were convinced that the loudmouthed Clay had no chance to defeat Liston, who had just annihilated the former heavyweight champion Floyd Patterson. Publicly embracing him, they believed, would bring only embarrassment after his all but certain loss. But Malcolm, who had developed a solid friendship with Clay, possessed a surer sense of the boxer's skills. He also saw that Cassius was intelligent and possessed the charisma that could attract young blacks to Islam. And it probably occurred to him that, in the event of a showdown with the Chicago leaders, having Clay on his side was a plus.

The Miami Beach excursion was the one and only vacation that Betty and Malcolm would ever share. Malcolm's family was probably surprised when the young boxer himself met them at the Miami airport. This unexpected encounter was relayed to the local FBI office by an informant. Apparently, the Bureau had not yet established any connections between Clay and black separatists, and the FBI office in Miami found itself sufficiently nonplussed that it failed to forward the information to Washington, D.C., until January 21. For several days, the family did mostly tourist things: lounging at the beach, taking photos, buying postcards. Malcolm was able to set aside informal time with Clay, building up the young fighter's confidence. He also tried to use the trip as an opportunity to recraft his image, perhaps realizing finally the need to start presenting himself independent of the Nation. In a notebook he kept of the trip, he drafted several paragraphs about his family's visit to Clay's training camp that were designed to be the basis for a feature news story, "Malcolm X, the Family Man." Most of his notes were captions designed to accompany photographs he had taken. One note indicated that he and Betty were celebrating their sixth wedding anniversary on the trip, that they were the parents of three daughters and were expecting their fourth child that June. This attempt to moderate his public image proved successful. The *Chicago Defender* published a beautiful portrait of the family, with Clay at the right, holding the couple's youngest daughter, Ilyasah. A similar photograph was published in the *Amsterdam News*, and together they would mark the first time Malcolm presented his family to the public. They represented the beginning of what would prove to be Malcolm's final reinvention, one that would culminate a few months later during his trip to Mecca for the hajj.

Betty and the children returned home on January 19, but Malcolm lingered to spend more time alone with Cassius Clay. A few days later, when Malcolm flew back to New York, Clay went with him. He did not bother to ask his trainer, Angelo Dundee, for permission to leave, and though it is unheard of for a boxer to break camp one month before a championship fight, Dundee did not try to stop him. Arriving in New York on January 21, Clay finally discovered a city big enough to hold his outsized personality. He and Malcolm set about touring Harlem and other sights of the city, and Clay attended an NOI rally held at the Rockland Palace, though Malcolm stayed away, observing his suspension. Afterward Clay returned to Miami and resumed training.

It was not long before news of Clay's and Malcolm's relationship made its way into the press. On January 25, the *Amsterdam News* noted Malcolm's vacation in Florida with his family "as the guests of heavyweight boxer Cassius Clay." The publicity caused great difficulties in Clay's fight camp in Miami. As his fame had grown in the boxing world, the question of his involvement with the Nation had dogged him. With the sect identified primarily with antagonistic feelings toward whites, his affiliation threatened to damage him professionally, and so he had come to dance around the issue when questioned about it by the press. But now, in the days leading up to the Liston fight, Malcolm's influence pushed him closer to open support. The *Amsterdam News* reported Clay's twenty-minute-long remarks at the Rockland Palace: "I'm a race man, and every time I go to a Muslim meeting I get inspired." On February 3, the Louisville *Courier-Journal* published an interview with Clay in which he all but admitted membership in the Nation. "Sure I talked to the Muslims and I'm going back again," he declared. "Integration is wrong. The white people don't want integration, I don't want integration. I don't believe in forcing it, and the Muslims don't believe in it. So what's wrong with the Muslims?"

Throughout most of February Malcolm continued to appeal to Muhammad for reinstatement, but to no avail. He was now forced to consider emergency household issues. The Nation paid out a household stipend to its ministers to provide food, clothing, and household items. For Malcolm this amounted to about $150 per month. He was still considered a minister and technically could claim the stipend, but if fully stripped of his title he would have no monthly income and no claim on his family's East Elmhurst home. According to an estimate by James 67X, from 1960 to 1963 Malcolm also received an expense account from the Nation of about $3,000 per month, covering his travel, hotel accommodations, meals, and incidental expenses. For Malcolm to exert the impact on the national media that he had in the early 1960s, a considerable investment by the Nation was required. For example, whenever he traveled to a city with a Nation of Islam mosque, local leaders were expected to take off from work and make automobiles, drivers, and security personnel available. If his itinerary involved a locale with no NOI presence, he frequently traveled with one or more FOI security members. His secretary at the mosque handled his routine correspondence. It was this elaborate infrastructure that helped turn a prominent local leader into a national figure. The question Malcolm now confronted was, what would happen if all this was taken away? What financial resources could he provide for Betty and the children? He had virtually no savings, and no insurance. He had even arranged for his future book royalties to go to the Nation. His faith in the Nation of Islam had been complete and unquestioning, leaving him no fallback, no path of escape if it turned out to be misplaced.

It was this position of vulnerability that forced Malcolm to plead to Muhammad to allow him to be reinstated, in any capacity. In a notebook he kept during the last two weeks of January, he tried to work out his thoughts on the best way to present his case to Muhammad. "Had no bad motive. Had good intention," he wrote.

> Feeling innocent, have felt extremely persecuted. Have felt lied about. Unjustly and unnecessarily . . . forced to find some way to defend myself, to retaliate against those enemies without hurting you. . . . If I'm wrong in these feelings and conclusions, I'm at least being truthful and not hypocritical, chance to serve Allah and you . . .
>
> As my last letter stated: 1. I believe in Our Savior, you and your program. 2. I know only what you taught me. 3. And am only what you have made me. 4. I have never exalted myself above you. 5. I have never acted independently. I made a serious mistake by not coming straight to you—and that mistake, led to my making others. I am sincerely sorry and pray to Allah for

forgiveness, and I ask you to pray to Allah for my forgiveness. I cannot be an enemy to you without being an enemy to myself. I cannot speak against you without speaking against myself.

Between January and late February, he wrote Muhammad a series of letters requesting reinstatement, appealing to their close personal relationship and casting the Chicago leadership as jealous and bent on driving them apart. The "others," he wrote, leaving no question as to whom he meant, desired the end of their partnership "because they know Allah has blessed me to be your best representative as well as your best defender. . . . The only ones there who may think against you are the ones that are not really with you themselves. This is a dangerous position to be in, because it only adds division upon division." Few of these letters have survived; there is also a good chance that Muhammad never read them, because his access to correspondence with Nation officials was controlled by Ali and his aides.

Yet as his suspension persisted and Muhammad seemed unsympathetic, Malcolm eventually came to believe he had misjudged the situation. For all his difficulties with Chicago, he finally began to see that the real problem was not with John Ali or Raymond Sharrieff, but with Muhammad himself. In his diary, Malcolm drafted a four-item critique of Elijah Muhammad that had been suggested by Wallace: "1. John not to blame[,] you behind all John's moves," he wrote in his notebook. "2. You use John. 3. You not interested in Muslims, but self. 4. You use money to control all those around you." Malcolm observed that he and Wallace shared extensive common ground in their complaints about the Nation's leadership. Under the heading "Wallace's analysis of [Mosque] No. 2," Malcolm noted: "1. Chi[cago] officials scared and had changed (agreed). 2. Cold, impersonal, inconsiderate & hard on members (agreed). 3. Force & authority instead of *instructions* (agreed). 4. Protecting self, not you or the nation (agreed)." He complained to Wallace that under Joseph's influence the FOI had been turned into an internal surveillance system. "Joseph had become a cop, and ceased being a bro (two-thirds a cop) same situation everywhere. Captains have become anti-Minister."

These notebook fragments are significant in explaining the differences that led to Malcolm's split from the sect, and subsequently to his assassination. Most of Muhammad's family and the Chicago secretariat opposed Malcolm for two basic reasons. First, they were convinced that he coveted the Messenger's position: that once Elijah was incapacitated, or dead, Malcolm would easily take command. Their material benefits derived from being the "royal family" would abruptly end. But equally important was the second reason: Malcolm's militant politics of 1962–63 represented a radical break with the Nation of Islam's apolitical black nationalism. Herbert Muhammad had already barred any publicity in *Muhammad Speaks* related to Malcolm one full year prior to the official silencing. To ensure that Chicago maintained tight control, officials increasingly deployed the Fruit of Islam as a surveillance and intimidation unit. As Malcolm noted, Joseph had "become a cop," not a brother, a not so subtle reference to the beatings he inflicted. But Muhammad's family totally misread Malcolm's motives. He never saw himself as the heir apparent; if anyone should be groomed for the Messenger's role, Malcolm believed, it was Wallace. He preferred the itinerant life of an evangelist. He respected and loved Wallace and would have supported him as the successor had the Messenger died. Malcolm's tragic mistake was believing that his militant political aims—the creation of an all-inclusive black united front against U.S. racism—could be constructed with the full participation of the Nation of Islam. The Nation was prepared to undergo Islamization, but it wasn't ready for civil rights demonstrations, Third World revolution, or Pan-Africanism. It was politics, not personalities, that severed Malcolm's relationship with the Nation of Islam.

Only in February 1964 was Malcolm emotionally prepared to contemplate the possibility of life after the Nation of Islam. Politically, he would have to relate to a range of activist organizations, from the NAACP to the socialist left, in an entirely new way. Like many Harlemites, he respected the antiracist political work the Communist Party had done over four decades. But dialogue with them was difficult: they were atheists and, even worse, staunch integrationists. Their key theoreticians on race, notably James E. Jackson and Claude Lightfoot, had examined the Black Muslim phenomenon, characterizing black nationalism as a "conditioned reflex to white chauvinism": a response to Jim Crow, job discrimination, and the social isolation of the ghetto. However, the Black Muslim emphasis on the teaching of Negro history and culture, and its opposition to drugs, alcoholism, and black-on-black crime, were all positive contributions to the black community. So, on balance, while the communists vigorously disagreed with the sect's tenets, they favored what Lightfoot called "united front" coalitions on a case-by-case basis. There is evidence that Malcolm may have met with the leaders of the Communist Party's Harlem branch in mid-February. However, there were no subsequent sessions, even after Malcolm had established the Organization of Afro-American Unity.

Part of Malcolm's inner turmoil over these months was caused by doubts about his faith. Leaving the Nation of Islam meant much more than departing a religious cult; he would be abandoning an entire spiritual geography. At many NOI lectures, a display about the future of black identity was depicted on a blackboard. On one side of the board was drawn the American flag, accompanied by a Christian cross and the words "Slavery," "Suffering," and "Death." On the other was depicted the Muslim Crescent, with the words "Islam," "Freedom," "Justice," and "Equality." Beneath both sets of symbols and words was a question: "Which will survive the War of Armageddon?" The Nation of Islam's purpose here was twofold. First, Muhammad preached that not only was Islam the "natural religion" of all blacks, but it was *only* through the knowledge of Islam that African Americans could achieve their goals. Second, the Nation of Islam argued that Americanism and Christianity had brought blacks only slavery and social death. Thus the Nation presented to its converts a comprehensive global system of race, "pitting black Islam against white Christianity in a worldwide and historic struggle." The essential tenets for the Nation's religious remapping of the world rested on Yacub's History—that whites were the devil, that Wallace D. Fard Muhammad was God in person, and that Elijah Muhammad had indeed been chosen by that God to represent his interests on earth. Despite Malcolm's support for the Nation's moves toward Islamization, as late as December 1963 he agreed with Yacub's History and embraced the notion that Muhammad's contacts with Fard were with Allah in human form. In his interview with Lomax in late December 1963, he insisted vigorously that Elijah had talked with God personally. When Wallace Muhammad in early 1964 expressed his belief that Fard was neither Allah nor God, Malcolm dissented.

Yet if Elijah Muhammad's greatest sin was not in impregnating his subordinates but in fraudulently representing himself as Allah's Messenger, then the Fard narrative was a myth. Were Yacub's History also false, then people of European descent were not devils to be fought against, but individuals who could oppose racism. Even at the level of NOI class instruction, a new religious remapping of the world based on orthodox Islam would not necessarily stigmatize or isolate the United States because of its history of slavery and racial discrimination. Instead of a bloody jihad, a holy Armageddon, perhaps America could experience a nonviolent, bloodless revolution. At some point, Malcolm must have pondered the unthinkable: it was possible to be black, a Muslim, *and* an American.

There were also the practical implications of leaving the Nation. Without its backing, Malcolm would lack the financial means to travel across the country, to hold press conferences or give public speeches. He recognized that if he was to continue as a public figure, he would need to establish a secular organization, dedicated to his own political ideals and staffed by devoted assistants. With such a group, he could negotiate new relationships with civil rights organizations and their leaders.

———

By the time Malcolm returned to Miami Beach only a few days before the Clay-Liston fight, wild rumors were swirling. Publicity about Clay's NOI affiliations had swept through Miami, pleasing no one except perhaps Malcolm. The fight's promoter, Bill MacDonald, had to gross $800,000 to break even, and the stories were turning off white fans and depressing the box office. Days before the fight, scheduled for February 25, less than one half of the Miami Convention Hall's 15,744 seats had been sold. When Malcolm returned to Miami to rejoin Clay's entourage, MacDonald threatened to cancel. A compromise was reached when Malcolm agreed to maintain a lower profile, at least until the night of the fight. In return, the Muslim minister would receive celebrity treatment and a ringside view—seat 7, his favorite number.

Malcolm primarily saw his role as Clay's spiritual mentor. No one gave the brash pretender any chance of winning. Yet Malcolm reassured Clay that his impending victory had been prophesied centuries earlier. Clay's win, he predicted, would not only be a triumph for the Nation of Islam, but for seven hundred million Muslims across the globe. But Malcolm's continuing fascination with Clay, and the outcome of this particular bout, was at least in part influenced by his problematic status inside the Nation. The fight would be held only one day prior to the annual Saviour's Day convention, and here Malcolm saw an opportunity. He contacted Chicago headquarters and offered a deal: he would accompany Clay, once victorious over Liston, directly to Chicago to appear at the convention, in return for his full reinstatement. Chicago rejected the offer, in part because officials still doubted Clay's boxing abilities, but primarily because by late February they had no intention of allowing Malcolm back in.

On fight night, Malcolm wandered through the crowd at ease, secure in his knowledge that both he and Clay would soon be vindicated by victory. Shortly before the bout he retired to the dressing room to join Clay, whose Muslim entourage—stocked mostly by minor flunkies sent from Chicago—was fueling the fighter's paranoia over the rumors and threats of violence against him that had been circulating in the last twenty-four hours. Cutting through this, Malcolm took Clay and his brother, Rudy, aside and led them in prayer. Then he returned to the arena and settled into his ringside seat, not too far from football legend Jim Brown and singer Sam Cooke. Soon the fighters emerged, and ring announcer Frank Wyman's booming voice filled the room as he introduced them, starting with Clay. Then, finally, the bell loosed them from their corners.

Clay's match strategy was to take the fight to Liston in the initial rounds, coast during the third, fourth, and fifth, then fight "full steam" from the sixth through the ninth, with any luck scoring a knockout. Liston, big but slow, would tire early, making him vulnerable after about the fifth round. All of Clay's and Angelo Dundee's plans ended up being correct tactically, except for one near mishap. In a moment of desperation, one of Liston's handlers rubbed some ointment on the boxer's gloves, blinding Clay for an entire round. With his eyes blazing, Clay kept dancing across the ring, just outside Liston's lumbering reach. In the sixth round, as his eyes began to clear, Clay destroyed Liston with multiple jabs and combinations. By the end of its three minutes, Liston was exhausted, unable even to raise his arms to defend himself. At the start of the seventh round he squatted sadly on his corner stool, refusing to come out. Stunned, Clay ran around the ring, yelling hysterically: "I am the greatest thing that ever lived! I don't have a mark on my face, and I upset Sonny Liston, and I just turned twenty-two years old. I must be the greatest! I showed the world! I talk to God every day! I'm the king of the world!"

Cheering from his ringside seat, Malcolm experienced a sweetness unlike any he had felt in some time. He had prepared a victory party in his room back at the Hampton House motel in one of Miami's black neighbor-hoods, and just after midnight Clay arrived for the festivities. In keeping with the Muslims' sober image, celebrants were given bowls of ice cream. The next day, Clay confirmed his membership in the Nation of Islam, and despite the speaking ban Malcolm explained to the press why the new convert's triumph held political as well as religious significance, giving a sage assessment of Clay's still forming legacy: "Clay is the finest Negro athlete I have ever known, the man who will mean more to his people than any athlete before him. He is more than Jackie Robinson was, because Robinson is the white man's hero. The white press wanted him to lose. They wanted him to lose because he is a Muslim. You notice nobody cares about the religion of other athletes. But their prejudice against Clay blinded them to his ability."

Clay's victory caught the Nation's leadership off guard. They had never given a thought that he might win, and with Malcolm now standing proudly at his side before the entire country, he had instantly become another point of leverage from which Malcolm must be separated. The day after the fight, Clay duly flew to Chicago to attend the Saviour's Day convention, where he finally threw off the ambiguity of previous statements and officially announced his membership in the Nation of Islam. Without missing a beat, Elijah Muhammad embraced his new convert, claiming that Clay's triumph was the work of both Allah and his Messenger. Despite this public declaration, Clay continued to view Malcolm as his prime mentor. On March 1 he drove to New York City, rented two three-room suites in the Hotel Theresa, and immediately contacted Malcolm. Accompanying him was his brother, Rudy, and an entourage of six. Malcolm relished Clay's time in the spotlight and astutely played the press for maximum advantage. On March 4 the two men went on a two-hour tour of the United Nations. At an impromptu press gathering, Clay surprised reporters by claiming that he intended to "live forever" in New York. "I'm so popular I need a big town so all the people who want to watch me can do it," Clay explained. When asked whether he had played any role in the heavyweight champ's decision to relocate to New York City, Malcolm replied, "He's got a mind of his own." For several days, in fact, he and Clay had been talking about the advantages of moving to New York. Malcolm even drove Clay out to Queens, looking at houses near his East Elmhurst home.

The prospect that Clay might move to New York City, in part under the influence of Malcolm, infuriated the Nation's Chicago headquarters. But far more threatening were two press reports. On March 2, the *Chicago Tribune* noted that "Clay, recently crowned heavyweight champion of the world, arrived in Harlem unexpectedly yesterday for a secret conference with Malcolm X." That same day, the *Chicago Defender* broke the news that the two men were planning to launch a new, rival organization to the Nation of Islam. This series of events and reports finally ended any faint possibility of Malcolm's readmission into the Nation. By this time, the Chicago headquarters recognized how seriously mistaken it had been in its handling of Clay. Permitting him to travel to New York and to continue his public affiliation with Malcolm undermined the Nation of Islam's authority. What truly frightened Muhammad and his lieutenants was that Clay and Malcolm were popular and had national audiences in their own right; the duo might easily split the Nation into warring factions. Was this Malcolm's intention, to use his close relationship with Clay either to reform the Nation from within or to establish a new Muslim movement outside of the Nation? During these chaotic days, Malcolm was largely unsure himself. But from the vantage point of Chicago headquarters, there could be no doubt: Clay was the Nation of Islam's prized property and had to be retained. Malcolm X was the enemy.

It took Malcolm longer than might be expected to see just how serious Chicago was, and to what lengths it would go in attacking him. As late as February 22 an article appeared in the *Amsterdam News* quoting sources close to Malcolm as saying that he expected to "return in full swing" on March 1. Yet all around him, the anger toward him driven by Chicago spread throughout the mosque's membership, poisoning any idea that his future efforts might be tied to the Nation, or that post-Nation life would be easy. James 67X and Reuben X Francis, another FOI lieutenant loyal to Malcolm, were employed as waiters at the Mosque No. 7 luncheonette, and by early February the diner's boss, Charles 24X, had begun slandering Malcolm in public. "This business came about," remembered James, "talking about 'Oh, don't call him Malcolm, call him Red; oh, let's kill Malcolm.' . . . I was sitting in the restaurant at the time, so I figured that Joseph was doing this to try to find out which way I would bend." James still considered himself a loyal follower of Elijah Muhammad. "I was with Mr. Muhammad 100 percent," he explained. "But when they started talking about killing Malcolm, I said, 'Well, if they'd kill Malcolm, they'll kill me.'"

A turning point came when John Ali visited the mosque and announced that Chicago was "getting letters from the East Coast threatening to take the Little Lamb's life." James phoned Malcolm's home again, warning Betty to "tell my big brother [to] be very careful." Subsequently, he and Malcolm talked on the phone, and James told him, "They're talking about killing you." Malcolm laughed. "Listen, brother," he said. "I'm no Sunday Muslim. I put in twelve years of my life into the Nation. . . . If somebody tried to do me some harm the Nation would raise up against them." Malcolm simply didn't grasp that John Ali and other NOI officials were laying the groundwork for his permanent expulsion or assassination. But he asked James to see him later that evening. "Well, I thought, because I said I ain't supposed to be talking to this guy," James grumbled, but nevertheless agreed. To avoid any possibility of detection, they arranged to meet at the corner of East 116th Street and Second Avenue "in the middle of the night."

Malcolm picked up James and drove west to Morningside Park, pulling his blue Oldsmobile Ninety-Eight to the curb between West 113th and West 114th streets. In the dark car, Malcolm finally began to talk, unburdening himself. "I didn't argue with him," James recalled. "I just listened. . . . He talked about corruption in the Nation and a whole bunch of other stuff." James had already heard about Muhammad's extramarital relationships, and wasn't dismayed. When Malcolm brought up Muhammad's out-of-wedlock children, James explained, "Not to be coarse, I said, 'So Mr. Muhammad's been getting some nookie.' I mean, that's part of power, you know? . . . So that kind of puzzled me. So I said, 'Islamic leader, there is a philosophical concept of polygamy.'" But Malcolm just talked on, justifying his actions and explaining how he might be readmitted to the Nation. James was stunned. It was obvious to him that Malcolm didn't comprehend his dire situation. "My position was very simple. I said, 'They're talking about killing you.'" This time he ensured he would not be misunderstood, repeating, "'Look, brother, you were seen in favor by Mr. Muhammad. And I hope you will return to his favor. [But] no, you're not going back in the Nation. People are talking about killing you.'"

Malcolm finally fell silent. James realized that he had to decide, then and there, whether he would leave the Nation of Islam with Malcolm. Against his better judgment, he said, "Listen, I don't know what your plans are. But I will help you for a year." He had only one condition: "Don't chump me off. Don't tell me something that's not true, or tell me something that is true that's not. . . . I'm not asking what you're going to do, how you're going to do it, just don't lie to me." Malcolm took James back to his apartment building, and drove off into the darkness.

Sometime in late February, Captain Joseph contacted a Fruit member named Anas Luqman, James 67X's roommate, to arrange a private meeting. Luqman had joined the Nation only a few years earlier, but his navy training and considerable skill as a martial artist had landed him an important role in the Fruit of Islam. Partnered with Thomas 15X Johnson and several others, he served as part of a top security squad whose purpose, he later explained, was finding an "inconspicuous way of dissolving a bad situation." The squad members avoided using guns and strove for discretion. "You had to know how to do it another way," he recalled, "because we didn't want to upset the general public any more than necessary." Luqman found Malcolm extremely impressive, and disliked and distrusted Joseph in equal measure. A private meeting with the FOI captain sounded unappealing, but Luqman agreed to meet him outside the NOI restaurant. At the rendezvous Joseph immediately made plain his purpose. He knew about Luqman's naval training and had somehow gathered the impression that he had experience with ballistics, which was not the case. He gave Luqman a direct order: "Plant a bomb in [Malcolm's] '63 Oldsmobile that will take care of him." The command was highly unusual in that it violated routine protocol for carrying out disciplinary matters. Luqman knew that Joseph never gave direct orders to FOI members; he only dictated instructions to individual lieutenants, who served as buffers between Joseph and those who carried out the mission. "There were no witnesses. Joseph wasn't stupid. He had me by myself, outside, and that's the way it was."

After the two men parted, Luqman felt uneasy. He had joined the Nation not for its spiritual agenda but for its principled positions on race—the emphasis on land ownership, business development, and black solidarity. He had cheered Malcolm's decision to protest the harassment and jailing of *Muhammad Speaks* salesmen, even participating in the Times Square demonstration of January 1963. By late that year he was growing impatient with the Nation of Islam's gradualism, and now he was being asked to execute the one man in the organization who might push black politics forward. It was too much, he thought, "I got to break with all of them." Out of loyalty to Malcolm, Luqman went and told him about Joseph's order. In retrospect, it seems likely that the FOI captain did not intend to kill Malcolm at this time, but to lay a trap for him and Luqman. "Joseph was as slick as goose grease, man," recalled James 67X. "He was no fool. Joseph told me once, 'Generals come and generals go, but J. Edgar Hoover—he been there all the time. He ain't been removed.'" Joseph already sensed where Luqman's loyalties lay, that he would surely tell Malcolm about the car bomb. If Malcolm still intended to remain in the Nation, security protocol required him to report the alleged plot to Chicago. If he did not report it, he must be planning to leave.

Around this same period, Malcolm met with his old friend and protégé Louis X for the final time. By now, after Louis had reported back to Muhammad Malcolm's discussion of his affairs, it had become clear that Louis's loyalty to Elijah Muhammad was paramount. Still, though their friendship had been severely strained, the feelings between them persisted. Louis was asked to speak in Malcolm's place on several Sundays during his suspension, and when Louis came down from Boston, he met with Malcolm despite the prohibition against contacting a member under sanctions. Malcolm even drove him to the mosque to deliver the Sunday speeches.

Farrakhan later came to interpret Malcolm's split with the Nation of Islam in somewhat unusual terms: he believed that Elijah Muhammad had been testing Malcolm for leadership, and that he had failed that test. But by the time of their final meeting, Louis had already been chosen by Muhammad as Malcolm's replacement speaker for the 1964 Saviour's Day, and the Boston minister was clearly being groomed to assume a significant leadership role, probably Malcolm's. If his mentor had failed a test, it would be one that he himself would soon pass. He also believed that Muhammad's impregnation of Evelyn Williams was a major source of Malcolm's anger. After learning about the pregnancy, Farrakhan recalled, "Malcolm began speaking less and less about the teachings [of Elijah Muhammad and] became more and more political."

On their last outing together, Farrakhan remembered, they cruised the city late into the night in Malcolm's automobile.

> He told me of his love for Evelyn and he was going to bring her to New York. I said, "Brother, please don't do that, you would really hurt Betty if you did that." I said, "It's best that you leave Evelyn where she is." We had that type of conversation. And he sat with me and he said, "Brother, my enemies will one day be your enemies." He named people that I would have to look out for in the Nation. And then he said these words to me: "I wish it was you being an example for me, rather than me being an example for you." That's the last conversation that I held with my brother.

Malcolm not only foresaw Louis taking his place as the major national spokesman of the Nation, he predicted the hatred and hostility of Captain Joseph, Raymond Sharrieff, and other NOI leaders toward him. But what Farrakhan could not have anticipated was that, in little more than a decade, he too would be cast out.

———

Late in the evening of March 6, an audiotaped broadcast of an Elijah Muhammad address was aired on WWRL radio in New York City as well as on a Chicago radio station. Muhammad's immediate purpose was to secure Cassius Clay's continued allegiance. In doing so, he would take away Malcolm's last chip. "This Clay name has no divine meaning," Muhammad announced. "I hope he will accept being called by a better name. Muhammad Ali is what I will give to him as long as he believes in Allah and follows me." Malcolm heard Muhammad's address over his car radio and was stunned. Malcolm's response was "That's a political move! He did it to prevent him from coming with me." NOI representatives were already meeting with Ali at the Hotel Theresa. Among the prized items they promised to deliver him was a wife, and if he desired, it could be one of the Messenger's own granddaughters. Malcolm had actually discouraged Ali from leaving the Nation, perhaps thinking the young boxer might be more inclined to join him if he wasn't pressured. Within a few days, Ali chose to side with Muhammad. In an interview with Alex Haley, he admitted that one factor in his calculation was fear. "You don't just buck Mr. Muhammad and get away with it," he told Haley, and of Malcolm he said, "I don't want to talk about him no more." On March 10, the *New York Times* reported that "the twenty-two-year-old heavyweight champion indicated that he would remain with the Black Muslim sect headed by Elijah Muhammad and would not join with Malcolm X." By March 21, the *Pittsburgh Courier* announced that "the all-out efforts of Malcolm X . . . to 'sell' himself, and a brand new program, the 'Black Mosque' to heavyweight boxing champion Cassius X Clay, has completely failed."

Malcolm's entire life seemed to be spinning out of control. On March 6 he was pulled over by the police while speeding over New York's Triborough Bridge and given a ticket. The day before, he had received a letter from Muhammad, indicating that he was suspended indefinitely. This, combined with Muhammad Ali's siding with Muhammad, left Malcolm stranded. His monthly household stipend would be cut off. Speaker's fees from colleges and public lectures could provide a modest stream of revenue, and he could draw a bit more of his book advance from Doubleday if necessary, but he could not afford to delay his decision to break from the organization any longer.

On March 8 he drove to the home of *New York Times* reporter M. S. Handler, and in the presence of Handler's wife, announced his decision to leave the Nation. Handler's story, "Malcolm X Splits with Muhammad," appeared the following day. Initially, he went out of his way to avoid confrontation with the Nation of Islam. "I want it clearly understood that my advice to all Muslims is that they stay in the Nation of Islam under the spiritual guidance of the Honorable Elijah Muhammad," he declared. "It is not my desire to encourage any of them to follow me." Malcolm suggested that his departure from the sect was inspired by a desire to help promote the Nation's agenda. "I have reached the conclusion that I can best spread Mr. Muhammad's message by staying out of the Nation of Islam and continuing to work on my own among America's 22 million non-Muslim Negroes." He offered an olive branch to his critics in the civil rights movement, affirming his commitment "to cooperate in local civil rights actions in the South and elsewhere." To secular black nationalists and independent activists, he declared his support for building "a politically oriented black nationalist party" that would "seek to convert the Negro population from nonviolence to active self-defense against white supremacists in all parts of the country." Mindful of his need for funds, he also announced, "I shall also accept all important speaking engagements at colleges and universities."

If Malcolm had left matters there, Muhammad and the NOI officials might not have retaliated with the degree of viciousness they did. But much like his "chickens" comment, he was incapable of pulling himself back from the brink. When Handler inquired about the reasons for his departure, the minister replied, "Envy blinds men and makes it impossible for them to think clearly. This is what happened." Malcolm accused the Nation of Islam of restricting his political independence and involvement inside the civil rights movement. "It is going to be different now," he vowed. "I'm going to join in the fight wherever Negroes ask for my help." These comments almost certainly guaranteed an escalation of polemical, and possibly physical, attacks against him.

Malcolm may have discouraged members from leaving the Nation, in part, to reduce the level of criticism against him. But from a practical standpoint, it was clear that he had not thought things through, because many members were already in the process of leaving. First, there was a cadre of lieutenants and confidants—James 67X Warden, Charles 37X Morris (also called Charles Kenyatta), Anas Luqman, Reuben X Francis, and many others—who were leaving the Nation primarily out of personal loyalty to Malcolm. Because of their past extensive involvement in the sect—for example, their knowledge of the pipe squads' brutal activities—their lives were also in jeopardy. Another group included NOI members who were disgusted by the diatribes against Malcolm that they had heard at Mosque No. 7 and the restaurant for several months, and who believed that the minister should have been afforded his right to defend himself before the entire congregation. After Malcolm's ouster, there was a handful of Original People, perhaps a dozen, who bravely defended their former minister inside the mosque. It is impossible to know exactly how many Muslims left Mosque No. 7 in March and April during the controversy over Malcolm, but it is likely that no more than two hundred members in good standing quit the sect: less than 5 percent of all mosque congregants.

Some of those who left to join Malcolm were longtime members. But a surprising number were new converts who knew little about the sources of tension between the NOI's rival factions. One of these was William 64X George. William had been an inmate at Rikers Island when another prisoner recruited him to the Nation. In June 1963, he formally joined Mosque No. 7.

He quit the Nation for two major reasons. In early 1964 the NOI began making increased demands on FOI members to sell thousands of *Muhammad Speaks*. William was instructed to sell a minimum of 150 copies each week, representing hundreds of dollars. Second, he was concerned about the threatening talk led by Captain Joseph and Mosque No. 7's acting minister, James 3X Shabazz, describing Malcolm as a "hypocrite, and that he should be killed." In April, William left the sect and would soon join Malcolm's group, becoming one of his key security men.

On March 9, Malcolm and a small cadre of supporters held a meeting at 23-11 Ninety-seventh Street in Queens. It was decided to incorporate under the name Muslim Mosque, Incorporated (MMI), with Malcolm, journalist Earl Grant, and James 67X elected as its trustees to serve until the first Sunday of March 1965, at which time a second election would be held. Muslim Mosque, Inc., was designed to offer African-American Muslims a spiritual alternative to the Nation of Islam. James, who had been designated as MMI's vice president, had advised Malcolm to encourage "those who are in the mosque to stay in the mosque" at MMI's initial press conference, which would be held on March 12. James later estimated that the core of MMI's dedicated activists had never been larger than fifty, all of whom had been former NOI members. But the act of incorporating MMI, viewed from the NOI, was seen as a deliberate provocation. Later that day, Malcolm did several interviews, including one with reporter Joe Durso of New York's WNDT, Channel 13. On March 10, Malcolm received a certified letter from the Nation, requesting that he and his family vacate their East Elmhurst, Queens, home. One month later, Maceo X, Mosque No. 7's secretary, would file a lawsuit in Queens Civil Court to have Malcolm evicted.

On March 11, Malcolm sent a telegram to Elijah Muhammad, outlining some of the reasons for his public departure. The contents were published in the *Amsterdam News* along with an interview with Malcolm. He also held a press conference at the Park Sheraton hotel in Manhattan the next morning. There, before a group of reporters and supporters, he read his March 11 telegram, again explaining his reasons for leaving the Nation. Malcolm stated that his new headquarters would be at the Hotel Theresa and he revealed his intention to open a new mosque. Sympathetic whites could donate funds to assist his new movement, but they would never be permitted to join because "when whites join an organization they usually take control of it." Although he had pledged to cooperate with civil rights groups, much of his language at the conference seemed to revel in apocalyptic violence. "Negroes on the mass level," he predicted, were now ready to start "self-defense" efforts, rejecting nonviolence as a strategy. "There will be more violence than ever this year. . . . White people will be shocked when they discover that the passive little Negro they had known turns out to be a roaring lion. The whites had better understand this while there is still time."

The press conference was a disaster at nearly every level. Somehow Malcolm had raised the money to rent the posh Tapestry Suite at the Sheraton, but it left MMI without financial resources. Handler's follow-up article in the *Times* mentioned that despite Malcolm's earlier statement "that he would not seek to take members away from Elijah Muhammad's movement," there was every indication that he intended to launch a rival organization. And to civil rights leaders still committed to racial integration and nonviolence, Malcolm's predictions of blood in the streets reconfirmed his reputation for nihilism and violence. Instead of broadening his potential base, his immediate actions following his break from Muhammad only isolated him further.

It is highly unlikely that Malcolm consulted Betty about his decision to leave the Nation; he still saw her largely as a passive observer. "I never had a moment's question that Betty, after initial amazement, would change her thinking to join mine," Malcolm would later explain. As he made grand pronouncements of his intentions, his wife worried about practical problems. A fourth child was well on the way. How would their household survive financially? Betty feared, correctly, that they would soon be evicted from their home. She also detected her husband's ambivalence about Elijah Muhammad and the Nation—throughout most of March he continued to praise the Nation of Islam's program. "The final cord," Betty would later observe, "had yet to be broken."

CHAPTER 11

An Epiphany in the Hajj

March 12–May 21, 1964

Malcolm's departure from the Nation of Islam coincided with one of the most intense periods of the civil rights struggle, a time at which the fragile unity that had made possible the great efforts in Montgomery and Birmingham was showing signs of strain. The arguments between radicals like John Lewis and more mainstream black leaders like King and Ralph Abernathy had not abated, and as long-desired goals finally came within sight, they had the peculiar effect of further splintering the movement. The success of the March on Washington in 1963 should have consolidated King's power, yet almost immediately afterward many black leaders sought to move away from marches and public protests toward working to directly influence Democratic Party politics. The legislation for the long-awaited Civil Rights Act had reached the Senate by the end of 1963, yet two months later the deadlock forced by recalcitrant Southern senators gave no hint of breaking. As the weeks, and then months, wore on, frustration mounted, exacerbated by the backlash to the increasing American military action in Vietnam.

Out of the Nation yet hardly liberated, Malcolm found himself forced to grapple with the past and the future at once. His decision to cut ties made him a kind of free agent, and some groups and leaders realized the potential advantage in bringing him into the civil rights fold. Yet Malcolm was still working to consolidate his own ideas, on both Islam and politics, and the wounds left by his break with the Nation of Islam were still too fresh to give him a truly clean start. In these early weeks, he alternated between reaffirming his loyalty to Elijah Muhammad's ideas and decrying his flawed morality, sometimes in speeches only days apart. At the same time, he struggled to stake out ground for Muslim Mosque, Inc., apart from the Nation, and here the most promising path was that which Elijah Muhammad had circumscribed: civil rights. In some way it must have been freeing; without John Ali and Raymond Sharrieff constantly looking over his shoulder, he could cast off the last vestiges of restraint. One of the MMI's initial press statements declared: "Concerning nonviolence: it is criminal to teach a man not to defend himself when he is the constant victim of brutal attacks. It is legal and lawful to own a shotgun or a rifle. . . . When our people are being bitten by dogs, they are within their rights to kill those dogs." When New York police commissioner Michael Murphy condemned such comments as "irresponsible," Malcolm responded that such a condemnation was a "compliment."

In his efforts to establish himself as a solo force, he cast a wide intellectual net, swinging from powerful arguments on the importance of black nationalism to occasional expressions of support for desegregation. On March 14 he attended a meeting in Chester, Pennsylvania, of East Coast civil rights leaders, including the most prominent public school desegregation leader in metropolitan New York, the Reverend Milton Galamison; the comedian and social activist Dick Gregory; and the Cambridge, Maryland, activist Gloria Richardson. Only weeks earlier, he had still been in the Nation of Islam routinely denouncing integration, yet here he was embracing efforts to promote school desegregation and improvements in the quality of blacks' public education. It marked an early, tentative concession to the idea that perhaps blacks could someday become empowered within the existing system. That same day he had given an interview to the *Amsterdam News*, during which he accused the Nation of attempting to murder him, a reference to the plot cooked up by Captain Joseph that Anas Luqman had divulged. While these comments were certain to provoke an angry response from the Nation, they also afforded Malcolm some breathing room. With the threat made public, it would be harder for the NOI to move against him. Still, Malcolm's assertions were probably not widely believed by most observers of the Nation. Up to 1964 the Nation's routine violence and beatings of its members had largely escaped public scrutiny. It was also well known that the Fruit never carried weapons, and Malcolm's reputation for hyperbole and extremism probably led police and most blacks to dismiss his claims.

On March 16, Muslim Mosque, Inc., became a legal entity, filing a certificate of incorporation with the County of New York, listing its address as Hotel Theresa, Suite 128, 2090 Seventh Avenue—in reality, a large room located on the hotel's mezzanine. Two days later at Harvard University,

Malcolm set to work defining the goals of the organization. The black man, he said, had to "control the politics in his own residential areas by voting . . . and investing in the businesses within the Negro areas." African Americans had become "disillusioned with nonviolence" and were now "ready for any action which will get immediate results." In these remarks stirred the beginnings of what would evolve a few years later into the Black Power movement. According to FBI surveillance, during the question and answer session at Harvard he was asked whether he was advocating bloody revolution. Malcolm said no, although he did note that the African American "has bled all the time, but the white man does not recognize this as bloodshed and will not until the white man himself bleeds a little." It was not an endorsement of violence, but this statement and others like it made it difficult for critics to gauge whether his militancy was receding. The following day, he gave a lengthy interview to the African-American writer A. B. Spellman, which appeared in the independent Marxist journal *Monthly Review* that May, and once again he denied his advocacy of violence. Yet if he sought to avoid controversy in that respect, his comments in the interview concerning Jews did nothing to endear him to progressives. "We are not racists at all," he stated, but then continued, "The Jews have been the tradesmen and the business people of the 'black community' for such a long time that it is normal that they feel guilty when one says that the exploiters of the blacks are the Jews. This does not say that we are anti-Semitic. We are simply against exploitation."

Along with crafting the MMI's agenda, Malcolm also hoped to establish the organization's legitimacy. In the Nation, he had represented a group that numbered between seventy-five thousand and one hundred thousand, but with the MMI he started virtually from scratch. It was probably for this reason that he exaggerated the group's size when a few days later he appeared on the show *Listening Post*, hosted by Joe Rainey on WDAS in Philadelphia. When Rainey asked whether MMI was a nationwide organization, Malcolm grandly proclaimed that "student groups from coast to coast" had requested information on how to join up. Yet though the group struggled early to put members on its rolls, Malcolm himself continued to attract sizable crowds. On March 22 he was the featured speaker at an MMI-sponsored rally held at the Rockland Palace that drew one thousand people, a surprisingly large audience given Malcolm's recent death threat charges. Reporters covering the event speculated that Malcolm was planning to form "a black nationalist army."

The work of building any kind of army would promise to be slow and labored. By name and nature the MMI was a religious organization, which limited its growth to Muslims; Malcolm had yet to establish a secular branch that could gather non-Muslims around his cause, so he now looked to members of the Nation that he might peel away, despite urgent warnings by James 67X and others that he should avoid conflict with the Nation. Scheduled to appear on the Bob Kennedy show on Boston radio on March 24, Malcolm decided to drive up early. Accompanied by James 67X and probably also by Charles 37X Kenyatta, he held meetings with several NOI members, almost certainly to discuss potential recruitment. Though he risked trouble by poaching on Louis X's grounds, the trip made strategic sense. Malcolm had established the Boston mosque himself, and Ella's presence in the city gave him an especially strong foothold in a certain part of the black community.

The subject of discussion on Bob Kennedy's radio program had originally been billed as "Negro—Separation and Supremacy," but Kennedy wanted Malcolm to explain how he had changed his views since leaving the Nation of Islam. Here Malcolm was forced to negotiate difficult terrain. Despite all that had transpired, he felt a lingering loyalty to the man who, more than any other in his life, had fulfilled a paternal role, and he responded by reaffirming his spiritual and ideological fidelity to the Messenger. "Everything" he knew, he asserted without hesitation, was "a result of Elijah Muhammad's doing." To reconcile this statement with his break from the Nation, he went on to explain that only by establishing himself as an independent force could he implement Muhammad's teachings. With only one exception, he avoided criticism of civil rights leaders. "Martin Luther King must devise a new approach in the coming year," he predicted, "or he will be a man without followers." Once again, he wallowed in the pose of racial avenger: "So far only the Negroes have shed blood, and this is not looked on as bloodshed by the whites. White blood has to be shed before the white man will consider a conflict as a bloody one."

Yet at this moment, Malcolm struggled greatly to come to terms with just how he felt about the Messenger's teachings. Over the years, as his fidelity to the core NOI dogma had waned, he had grown more interested in orthodox Islam. In his role as national minister, he had responded to tens of letters, public and private, written by orthodox Muslims attacking the Nation on its core religious principles, and the steady drumbeat of scorn had not failed to challenge his assumptions about Islam and increase his curiosity. Now, without an organization to define him, he realized that the structure of orthodox Islam could provide a new spiritual framework, and at this moment when almost any direction seemed possible, he saw his chance to fulfill the dream that he had carried since first visiting the Middle East in 1959: making a pilgrimage to Mecca.

Before his suspension the previous year, he had been back in contact with Dr. Mahmoud Shawarbi, the Muslim professor that he had first met in October 1960 at an NOI-sponsored event. They had kept in sporadic touch, but after Malcolm's silencing their meetings became more frequent and intense. Malcolm's expanded interest in orthodox Islam greatly pleased Shawarbi, and upon Malcolm's departure from the Nation Shawarbi immediately began giving him instructional sessions in the proper Islamic rituals. He encouraged Malcolm's trip and used his pull with the Saudis to pave the way for Malcolm through diplomatic channels; he also alerted his friends and associates in the Middle East about Malcolm's upcoming visit to the region, requesting that they assist him.

Shawarbi was crucial to Malcolm's development in other ways. Persistently, but without confrontation, he challenged Malcolm to rethink his race-based worldview, admitting that many orthodox Muslims also fell short of the color-blind ideals they professed. He finally convinced Malcolm that the Qur'an, as conceived in the recitations of the Prophet Muhammad, was racially egalitarian—which meant that whites, through their submission to Allah, would become spiritual brothers and sisters to blacks.

By the time of his recruitment trip to Boston, Malcolm had made his decision to undertake the pilgrimage to Mecca. The chance for spiritual purification at this juncture of great change and uncertainty seemed too important to pass up. It was likely during his time in Boston that Malcolm visited Ella and asked her to loan him the money, some thirteen hundred dollars, that he would need to make the pilgrimage. Despite all the trouble they had given each other since he had moved in with her as a teenager, she agreed.

———

On March 26, Martin Luther King, Jr., was on Capitol Hill with plans to discuss the stalled 1964 civil rights bill with Senators Hubert Humphrey, Jacob Javits, and others. The moment caught King at a difficult time, when even close aides like James Bevel were warning that "people are losing faith . . . in the nonviolent movement." When King moved to a conference room off the Senate floor to discuss developments with the press, Malcolm, who was also visiting that day, slipped in to listen. After the conference, the men left through separate doors, but as King was walking along the crowded Senate gallery observing the filibuster of pro-segregationist senators, he encountered Malcolm and several aides. Malcolm probably was not eager for an informal encounter, much less a staged photograph. It was James 67X who had cleverly set up the entire affair, pushing his boss around a marble column until he and King suddenly stood facing each other. A photographer in the gallery took a photo of them shaking hands, which would come to symbolize the two great streams of black consciousness that flourished in the 1960s and beyond. It was the only time the two men ever met.

Yet the handshake also marked a transition for Malcolm, crystallizing as it did a movement away from the revolutionary rhetoric that defined "Message to the Grassroots" toward something akin to what King had worked his entire adult life to achieve: improvement in the black condition through changing the American system. Three days after the meeting, Malcolm gave a speech at the Audubon Ballroom before six hundred people that served as a foundation for a more famous address he would give a week later. Though the announced topic, "The Ballot or the Bullet," seemed incendiary, at its core the speech actually contained a far more conventional message, one that had defined the civil rights movement as far back as 1962: the importance of voting rights. In the speech, Malcolm emphasized that all Harlemites, and by extension blacks everywhere, had to register as voters. Gone was the old Nation of Islam claim that participation in the system could have little effect. Now Malcolm called for a united black front that would seek to wrest control of blacks' economic and political future. "Unity is the right religion," he insisted. "Black people must forget their differences and discuss the points on which they can agree." He also questioned the ability of the civil rights movement to compensate blacks for "three hundred ten years of unpaid slave labor." What was most significant was his shift from the use of violence to achieve blacks' objectives to the exercising of the electoral franchise. By embracing the ballot, he was implicitly rejecting violence, even if this was at times difficult to discern in the heat of his rhetoric.

The next day he sat down for an interview with the *Militant*, the newspaper of the Socialist Workers Party. For decades, the SWP had promoted revolutionary black nationalism. Leon Trotsky himself had believed that Negro Americans would be the vanguard for the inevitable socialist revolution in the United States. Malcolm's separation from the Nation of Islam and his endorsement of voter registration and mass protest by African Americans seemed to Trotskyists a move toward socialism.

By the time Malcolm arrived at the Cory Methodist Church in Cleveland on April 3 to address a major public rally hosted by the local CORE chapter, he had refined "The Ballot or the Bullet" into a formidable piece of oratory. Much of the Cleveland CORE group had embraced Malcolm as a movement leader, and a crowd of between two and three thousand people, including many whites, packed the church. The format of the evening's program was a dialogue between Malcolm and his old friend Louis Lomax. Lomax spoke first, presenting a pro-integrationist civil rights message that won respectful applause from the audience. Malcolm's talk drew from his recent Audubon addresses, yet ultimately cohered into something greater, a fierce commentary on the lay of the land. On the one hand, the speech caught the mood of black America as it slowly shifted from a belief in the efficacy of nonviolence into a general state of dissatisfaction and impatience with the civil rights movement. In early 1964, as SNCC and CORE began to take more militant positions, the atmosphere of race politics grew heavier with the possibility of violence; indeed, within six months race riots would break out in black neighborhoods throughout the Northeast. "Now we have the type of black man on the scene in America today," Malcolm told the crowd, "who just doesn't intend to turn the other cheek any longer." In raising the specter of the "bullet," he acknowledged that it would take great effort to pull the country from the path to catastrophe. Yet in discussing the "ballot," he held out hope that such a change was possible.

The first part of Malcolm's lecture made an appeal for black unity despite ideological quarrels. "If we have differences," Malcolm argued, "let us differ in the closet; when we come out in front, let us not have anything to argue about until we get finished arguing with the man." This sentiment directly contradicted the "Message to the Grassroots," which had ridiculed King and other civil rights activists. For Malcolm, a precondition for unity was finding a secular basis for common ground, which is why he also strove to decouple his identity as a Muslim cleric from his political engagements. "Just as Adam Clayton Powell is a Christian minister," Malcolm observed, he himself was a Muslim minister who was committed to black liberation "by whatever means necessary." Malcolm then pivoted to denounce both major political parties as well as the U.S. power structure, which continued to deny most blacks a real chance at voting. Malcolm had come to see the vote as a necessary tool if black Americans were to take control of the institutions in their communities. He reminded his audience of the power that a black voting bloc could have in a divided country, claiming that "it was the black man's vote" that secured the Kennedy-Johnson ticket victory in the previous presidential election. But he impressed on the crowd that of voting or violence, the United States was sure to get at least one. The writing was on the wall, with young black boys in Jacksonville throwing Molotov cocktails in the streets. "It'll be Molotov cocktails this month, hand grenades next month, something else next month," he assured the crowd. "It'll be ballots, or it'll be bullets." Yet as ominous as this message sounded, it still represented a step back from the brink of inevitable violence suggested in "Message to the Grassroots." The ballot offered a way out: Malcolm was suggesting that if the federal government guaranteed full voting rights for African Americans nationwide, it could avoid a bloody conflagration. What was also significant about the address was what was now missing: no longer did Malcolm claim that Elijah Muhammad possessed the best program addressing blacks' interests.

The small cadre of Trotskyists at the Cory Methodist Church were thrilled with Malcolm's presentation, which seemed to confirm their own theory that revolutionary black nationalism could be the spark for igniting a socialist revolution in the United States. The *Militant*'s coverage of the Cleveland event highlighted approvingly Malcolm's castigation of "the Democratic party; the 'con game they call the filibuster,' and the 'white political crooks' who keep the black man from control of his own community." At times in the talk, Malcolm appeared to move away from a race-based analysis toward a class perspective. "I am not antiwhite," Malcolm insisted. "I am antiexploitation, antioppression." The *Militant* mentioned Malcolm's support for the creation of a black nationalist party and his call for a "black nationalist convention by August [1964], with delegates from all over the country."

Malcolm's lecture was tape recorded, and soon thousands of record copies were being distributed. Second only to "Message to the Grassroots," "The Ballot or the Bullet" would become one of Malcolm's most widely quoted talks. The FBI monitored the lecture, and appeared to recognize Malcolm's new appeal to a growing number of whites. The Bureau focused on two of his central arguments: that the civil rights bill being filibustered before the Senate either would not be passed or, if signed by President Johnson, would not be implemented; and that African Americans should initiate gun clubs. "It is lawful for anyone to own a rifle or a shotgun and it is everyone's right to protect themselves from anyone who stands in their way to prevent them from obtaining what is rightfully theirs," Malcolm was reported to have said.

By the beginning of April 1964, Malcolm eagerly looked forward to leaving the country; several days after the Cleveland speech, he purchased a plane ticket to travel throughout the Middle East and Africa, with tentative stops including Lagos, Accra, Algiers, Cairo, Jeddah, and Khartoum. If the trip promised spiritual restoration, it also offered a practical respite, giving him at least a month away from his increasingly combative relationship with the Nation and its representatives. The break was much needed. After his March 9 split, he had spent the rest of the month watching tensions escalate. Elijah Muhammad had pressured two of Malcolm's brothers, Philbert and Wilfred, ministers of the mosques in Lansing and Detroit respectively, to publicly denounce him as a hypocrite and a traitor. Worse, the Nation soon took aim at Malcolm's refuge. The day after Handler's *Times* article appeared announcing the split, Captain Joseph had turned up at the Elmhurst home demanding the Mosque's incorporation papers and other valuables, which Malcolm reluctantly turned over. On the last day of March, attorney Joseph Williams, on behalf of Mosque No. 7 secretary Maceo X Owens, filed papers in Queens County demanding the eviction of Malcolm and his family from the house. Outraged, Malcolm secured Harlem civil rights attorney Percy Sutton to oppose the suit, but the squabbling soon left him drained and dispirited. His heart was not in the fight. As April unfolded, he seemed disconnected from these legal proceedings, and he focused on the journey that lay ahead.

A little more than a week before his scheduled departure, the MMI held an evening forum at the Audubon, featuring Malcolm and North Carolina civil rights leader Willie Mae Mallory. Mallory's participation directly associated Malcolm with the incendiary exile Robert Williams, author of *Negroes with Guns* and an early proponent of black armed self-defense. Malcolm insisted that the Black Freedom Movement had to refocus from a quest for "civil rights" to a demand for "human rights," as defined by international law. Again, he stressed the necessity of the vote. The New York FBI office estimated the audience at five hundred. "He cited past lynchings of Negroes in America in accusing the government of genocide," it reported.

On April 8, at New York's Palm Gardens, Malcolm delivered a lecture that sharply broke with the NOI mold. The public lecture had been sponsored by the Militant Labor Forum, the nonpartisan outreach group of the SWP. In theory he was speaking to an eclectic group of nonaligned activists, independent Marxists, and black nationalists, but in reality it was a mostly Marxist audience with many of Malcolm's core followers also in attendance.

Malcolm was also preparing his associates for his extended leave, authorizing James 67X to serve as the MMI's acting chairman and to answer all communications and correspondence. Despite all the last-minute arrangements that needed his attention, he agreed to fly to Detroit once again to address a GOAL (Group on Advanced Leadership) rally. The speech would pressure his already tight schedule, but he recognized that Detroit offered a fertile ground for the message he had been cultivating in "The Ballot or the Bullet." In the years since he had delivered his monthlong series of sermons at Mosque No. 1 in 1957, the city had continued to develop as a national center for black working-class militancy. Black membership in the city's chapter of the United Auto Workers union had exploded, and as in many other Midwestern cities, the heavy industrial base and de facto segregation produced a mass of militant workers living in impoverished, rundown ghettos. Already the seeds had been planted for the violent discontent that would seize the city by the end of the decade. Malcolm had registered the broad impact of Detroit in his "Message to the Grassroots" address in November 1963, but now his renewed emphasis on class exploitation and the plight of the black working class made for an even more natural fit with the mood of the city's black community. As he sought a larger national constituency, he could ill afford to pass up a high-profile speaking engagement before such a promising audience.

GOAL booked the King Solomon Baptist Church in the Northwest Goldberg neighborhood for Malcolm's speech, but when the church leaders discovered that Malcolm would be the featured speaker, an ad hoc coalition of black ministers tried in vain to block his appearance. Despite their efforts, more than two thousand people came out to listen. Drawing on many ideas from the speeches in New York and Cleveland, Malcolm offered perhaps the most refined version of "Ballot" he would ever give; the audio recording that has survived of this speech shows Malcolm at the height of his powers as an orator. In this version, he moved the section on black nationalism front and center, giving one of the most trenchant exegesis of this political philosophy ever set down. Speaking in the urgent tones and pulsing rhythms of a jazz musician, Malcolm told the crowd that he was "a black nationalist freedom fighter." Again he urged his supporters "to leave their religion at home in the closet," because the goal was to unite all African Americans regardless of their religious views behind the politics of black nationalism. As in his Cleveland address, Malcolm placed great importance on blacks' electoral empowerment. "[If] Negroes voted together," he insisted, "they could turn every election, as the white vote is usually divided."

Beneath the rhetoric, there was a glaring inconsistency in his logic. Malcolm was encouraging African Americans to vote, even to throw their weight behind either major party; yet simultaneously he accused both major parties of racism, incapable of delivering fairness to blacks. "I'm one of the twenty-two million victims of the Democrats—the Republicans—of Americanism," he declared. The African American who habitually voted for the Democrats "is not only a chump but a traitor to his race." Malcolm, in effect, was promoting electoralism but in practical terms gave blacks no effective means to exercise their power. Who were they supposed to vote for if no one on the ballot could bring any real relief?

————

Home from Detroit the morning of April 13, Malcolm barely had time to bid his wife and followers good-bye before catching a flight to Cairo that evening. He flew under the name Malik el-Shabazz. When Malcolm disembarked in Cairo the following night, he noticed several dark-complexioned airline staff at the terminal; they would have "fit right into Harlem," he noted in his diary.

During the next two days in Cairo, Malcolm relished life as a tourist, as he had in 1959. Free from the ever present worries about the Nation, his fragile housing status, and the pressures of organization building, he allowed himself to evaporate into a state of rest, though the journey ahead would present its own challenges. On Thursday, April 16, he happened to meet and befriend a group of hajjis about to set off on their pilgrimage to Mecca. Since that was also his intended destination, they agreed to accompany each other to Jeddah, Saudi Arabia, the official center of embarkation for the hajj. Malcolm knew that to enter the Holy City of Mecca he would have to establish his religious credentials as an orthodox Muslim before the tribunal known as the "Hajj Court." Arriving late Friday, a day when the Hajj Court was closed, Malcolm secured a bed in a dormitory housing hundreds of international hajjis. Throughout most of the following day, he was unsuccessful in securing a firm date and time for his Hajj Court appearance. The failure put him in a difficult position. To be considered official, the hajj must be completed within a set range of dates, beginning on the eighth day of the Dhu al-Hijjah, the twelfth month of the Islamic calendar; in 1964, this fell on April 20. To delay much longer in Jeddah would mean missing the start, which would technically make his completion of the rituals an *umrah* instead of an official hajj, as had happened with Elijah Muhammad's pilgrimage years earlier. Frustrated, Malcolm then remembered something that might be of help. While he had prepared for his trip, Dr. Shawarbi had given him a book, *The Eternal Message of Muhammad* by Abd al-Rahman Azzam. Inside, Shawarbi had written the name and telephone number of the author's son, who lived in Jeddah. Malcolm asked someone to dial the number for him, and shortly afterward Dr. Omar Azzam showed up at Malcolm's dormitory. Within minutes Malcolm's personal items were packed and the two men were driven to the residence of Azzam's father. The elder Azzam allowed Malcolm to stay in his own well-appointed suite at the Jeddah Palace hotel. That night, Malcolm dined with the Azzams, explaining his situation, and they agreed to assist him in securing permission to participate in the hajj.

The next day, Malcolm, accompanied by Abd al-Rahman Azzam, stood before Sheikh Muhammad Harkon of the Hajj Court, humbly petitioning the body to allow him access to Mecca. Malcolm had already been introduced to Sheikh Harkon during his 1959 visit and had even enjoyed tea in the judge's home, yet to gain approval he would have to convince him that he had left behind the heretical ideas of the Nation of Islam. Azzam spoke on his behalf, assuring the sheikh that Malcolm was a widely known and respected Muslim in the United States and that he was a sincere proponent of Islam. What proved to be even more persuasive was the supportive intervention of Muhammad Abdul Azziz Maged, the deputy chief of protocol to Saudi prince Muhammad Faisal. Malcolm's acquaintanceship with the Azzams had tipped him into royal circles, as Abd al-Rahman's daughter was married to Prince Faisal's son. Maged's endorsement of Malcolm meant the case was immediately approved, and soon Prince Faisal himself sent word to Malcolm that he had "decreed that I be a guest of the state."

Malcolm's undertaking of the hajj marked his formal entrance into the community of orthodox Islam, placing him in a tradition of pilgrims that stretched back thirteen hundred years, linking him with fellow sojourners of every nationality, ethnicity, and class background imaginable. As the hajj is one of Islam's five pillars, all Muslims are obligated to complete it if able to do so; the essence of this pilgrimage ritual is a representation of episodes from the lives of Abraham (also Ibrahim), Hagar, and Ishmael (also Ismail). The most dramatic event is the *tawaf*, in which thousands of pilgrims circumambulate the Kaaba, the ritual site that symbolizes the spiritual center of the Islamic faith. As they circle the Kaaba, pilgrims attempt to touch or kiss it as a sign indicating the renewal of their covenant with Allah. The hajj also includes the *say*, the running of pilgrims between two small hills,

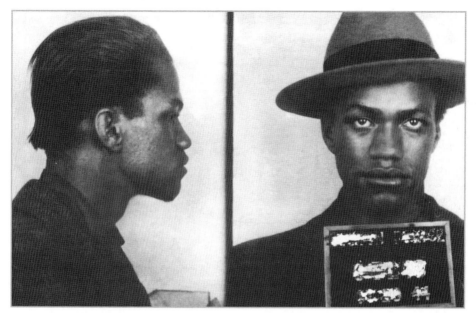

The Detroit Red years: a mug shot following Malcolm's arrest in Boston, 1944.

Throughout his life, Malcolm's half-sister, Ella Collins, would be a source of both comfort and aggravation. Here, she speaks after his assassination in February 1965.

Elijah Muhammad became for Malcolm not just a divine messenger but a trusted mentor; their close relationship sped Malcolm's rise in the Nation of Islam. Above, the two men together in 1961.

The crown prince of the NOI, Malcolm addresses Saviour's Day, 1961. Seated from left to right are Louis Farrakhan, Chicago assistant minister James Shabazz, Elijah Muhammad, Wallace Muhammad, John Ali, and Clara Muhammad.

Malcolm points to an image of Ronald Stokes's murder at rally, 1962. The NOI's anemic response to Stokes's killing would further alienate Malcolm from the Chicago headquarters.

Malcolm, Benjamin Goodman (left in black hat), and Newark minister James 3X Shabazz (right, in glasses) protest police brutality at New York County Criminal Court building, 1963.

The NOI brain trust: Elijah Muhammad (seated) the day after Malcolm X's assassination. Standing from left to right are Herbert Muhammad, John Ali, and Chicago assistant minister James Shabazz.

As Malcolm grew in prominence, he attracted two very different audiences. Here, he speaks to a mostly white crowd at the University of Hartford in Connecticut, October 29, 1963.

Back in Harlem, however, he continued to draw large crowds of urban blacks, as at this NOI rally at 115th Street and Lenox Avenue in 1963.

Elijah Muhammad greets a new convert. His taste for young NOI secretaries would eventually become an open secret that Malcolm struggled to come to terms with.

After splitting with the Nation, Malcolm's travels took him to the Middle East and Africa to find his spiritual and political center. Here, he meets with Sheik Abdel Rahman Tag (far right), soon to be the rector of Al-Azhar University, in Cairo, 1964.

As Malcolm worked to identify African-American struggles with those of blacks worldwide, he found himself embraced by Third World revolutionaries; these included General Abdulrahman Muhammad Babu, leader of the Zanzibar Revolution, shown here with Malcolm in 1964.

As his political thought developed, Malcolm came to believe that blacks could work within the system to improve their lives. In 1965, he observed a joint session of the New York State Legislature at the Assembly Chamber gallery in Albany.

Malcolm's fight with the NOI grew more contentious when the sect claimed ownership of his home and demanded he move out. Here, Fruit of Islam captain Joseph X Gravitt shows a police officer Malcolm's court-ordered eviction notice in February 1965.

Malcolm at his East Elmhurst home after the firebombing, February 15, 1965.

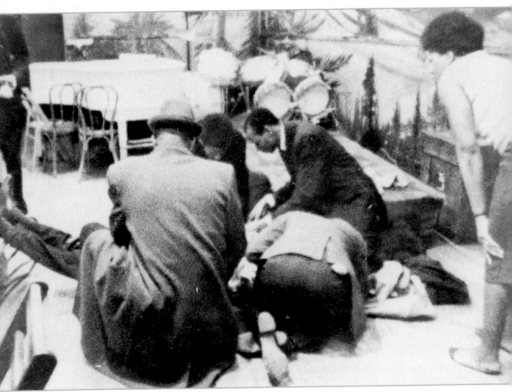

Moments after the assassination, NYPD undercover agent
Gene Roberts attempts to revive Malcolm X.

Thomas 15X Johnson, Malcolm's former driver in the NOI, is booked for his murder on March 3, 1965.

Another Harlem-based NOI enforcer, Norman 3X Butler, is escorted to jail as a second suspect on February 26, 1965.

Malcolm's MMI security chief Reuben Francis leaves a New York City jail the day after the assassination.

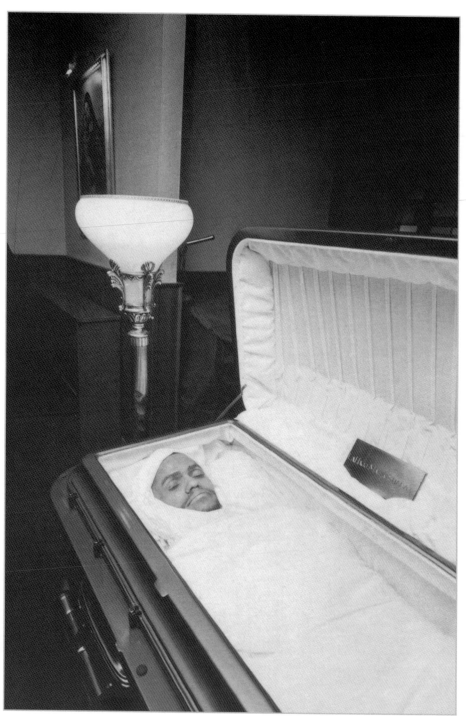

Malcolm lies in state at Faith Temple Church of God in Christ in West Harlem.

Mosque No. 7 is devoured in flames on February 23, 1965, two days after Malcolm's murder.

replaying Hagar's desperate search for water for her son, Ismail; drinking water from the well of Zamzam; prayer on the plains of Arafat; and then walking to the valley of Mina to replay Ibrahim's ordeal of nearly sacrificing his son Ismail. The hajj purges all previous sins of the pilgrim, and often coincides with major changes in an individual Muslim's life, such as marriage or retirement. To Malcolm, his departure from the Nation of Islam was an ideal moment for spiritual reexamination and renewal, fitting well with the purpose of the hajj.

As the beneficiary of Saudi nepotism, Malcolm was given his own private car, which allowed him to cover much of the 120-mile hajj route without worry of falling behind. He was up well before dawn on Tuesday, April 21, and after morning prayers and breakfast he was off to Mount Arafat. The sight before him on the road to Arafat moved him deeply, as he watched thousands of pilgrims of many races jostle and bump their way along, some walking, others packed into buses or riding camels or donkeys. He had not thought possible the egalitarianism he was now witnessing. "Islam brings together in unity all colors and classes," he observed in his diary. "Everyone shares what he has, those who have share with those who have not, those who know teach those who don't know." The common faith shared by all participants appeared to eradicate class divisions, at least as Malcolm could perceive them.

The next morning, Malcolm and other pilgrims awoke around two a.m. and traveled to Mina, where they each "cast seven stones at the devil," a white monument. They then traveled to Mecca, where Malcolm did two rounds of circling the Kaaba seven times each; he attempted but was never able to touch the sacred site. "One look at the fervor of those crowded around it made me see it was hopeless to try," he wrote. Again he was struck by the tremendous diversity of the hajjis. During the hajj rituals, "everyone was in white, the two-piece horum, with right shoulder bare," he observed. At the end of the hajj, "everyone is wearing their own national colors (costumes) and it is really a beauty to behold. It seems every nation and form of culture on earth is represented here. . . ."

Yet as much as Malcolm saw race and class distinctions dissolved in the uniting experience of the hajj, his own pilgrimage was anything but representative. The diplomatic difficulties that had almost kept him from the hajj had been sliced through by accommodating white Arabs with connections to the Saudi royal family, and he himself had been made a guest of state. Then, on one of the last days of the hajj, he joined a caravan led by "his excellency, Crown Prince Faisal . . . which included dignitaries from all over the world." Across the hall from Malcolm's hotel room was the Grand Mufti of Jerusalem, Hajj Amin el-Husseini, a cousin of Yasser Arafat's. In his diary, Malcolm observed that Husseini "seems well loved. He's well up on world affairs and even the latest events in America." Then, without a hint of irony, Malcolm added that the Grand Mufti "referred to New York as Jew York."

Still, the powerful sight of thousands of people of different nationalities and ethnicities praying in unison to the same God deeply moved Malcolm, as he struggled to reconcile the few remaining fragments of NOI dogma he still believed in with the universalism he saw embodied in the hajj. Like many tourists, Malcolm purchased dozens of postcards and sent them to acquaintances back home. These letters revealed the profound shift in his attitudes about white people. Writing to Alex Haley on April 25, Malcolm confessed, "I began to perceive that 'white man,' as commonly used, means complexion only secondarily; primarily it describes attitudes and actions." In the Muslim world he had witnessed individuals who in the United States would be classified as white but who "were more genuinely brotherly than anyone else had ever been." Malcolm was quick to credit Islam with the power to transform whites into nonracists. This revelation reinforced Malcolm's newfound decision to separate himself completely from the Nation of Islam, not simply from its leadership, but from its theology.

If Malcolm found much to rejoice over in his travels through the Middle East, he also wished for a more active role for Islam on the world stage. Here the seeds of his role as a kind of evangelist for true Islam were planted, but he saw in the Arabs' unwillingness to proselytize a problem that could hinder the religion's spread. "The Arabs are poor at public relations," he wrote. "They say insha Allah [if God wills it] and then wait; and while they are waiting the world passes them by." Malcolm hoped that one day Muslims would understand "the necessity of modernizing the methods to propagate Islam, and project an image that the mind of the modern world can understand." But his thoughts of returning home with a new knowledge of the religious rituals filled him with genuine pride and excitement. "America's Black Muslims would fit right into the best of the earth's Muslim[s] anywhere in the world if they would first be encouraged to learn the true prayer ritual and how to say their prayers in Arabic," he wrote.

Upon his arrival in Jeddah, Malcolm encountered an "outspoken" African, a cabinet minister of Nigerian prime minister Ahmadu Bello. The minister informed Malcolm about recent civil disobedience demonstrations by blacks at the 1964 New York World's Fair, and recounted his own unhappy experiences with American racism. "He had suffered many indignities that he could now describe with intense passion, but could not understand why Negroes had not established some degree of business economic independence," Malcolm observed.

Malcolm then flew to Medina, Saudi Arabia, on April 25, and en route he continued to make detailed notes in his travel diary. He was convinced that on the pilgrimage "everyone forgets Self and turns to God and out of this submission to the One God comes a brotherhood in which all are equals." He embraced an inner peace he had not known since the years he was incarcerated in Massachusetts. "There is no greater serenity of mind," Malcolm reflected, "than when one can shut the hectic noise and pace of the materialistic outside world, and seek inner peace within oneself." Later that evening Malcolm wrote, "The very essences of the Islam religion in teaching the Oneness of God, gives the Believer genuine, voluntary obligations towards his fellow man (all of whom are One Human Family, brothers and sisters to each other) . . . the True Believer recognizes the Oneness of all Humanity."

Returning to Jeddah the next day, he toured the local bazaar and purchased an attractive head scarf for Betty. His eyes were drawn to a beautiful necklace, but he could not afford it. Although Malcolm had prepared to depart Saudi Arabia for a quick visit to Beirut, Lebanon, Prince Faisal contacted him at his hotel, requesting to meet him at about noon the next day. Malcolm delayed his trip, and when the two men met, the prince explained "that he had no ulterior motive in the excellent hospitality I had received . . . than the true hospitality shown all Muslims by all Muslims." Faisal also questioned Malcolm about the theological beliefs of the Nation of Islam, suggesting that "from what he had been reading, written by Egyptian writers, they had the wrong Islam"—in other words, their understanding and rituals were alien to orthodox Islam, beyond the boundaries of the community of the faithful. After his experience at Mecca and the hajj, Malcolm could not contest or deny this. In taking the necessary steps to become a true Muslim he had regained the certainty that had abandoned him with each new revelation of Elijah Muhammad's perfidy or infidelity. He could also now see the role Islam would play not just in his spiritual life, but in his work. As Malcolm reflected on his hajj experiences, he concluded that "our success in America will involve two circles, Black Nationalism and Islam." Nationalism was necessary to connect African Americans with

Africa, he reasoned. "And Islam will link us spiritually to Africa, Arabia and Asia."

Malcolm flew from Jeddah's crowded airport and arrived in Beirut in the middle of the night of April 29; he secured a room at the Palm Beach Hotel upon the advice of his cab driver from the airport. Part of his agenda in Beirut was to become acquainted with Lebanon's Muslim Brotherhood organization, which was dedicated to directing the tenets of Islam to political ends. The Brotherhood was originally established in Egypt in 1928, and it spread to other Arab countries, including Syria, Lebanon, Yemen, and Sudan, during and after World War II. Advocating national independence against European colonialists, social reform, charity, and political change in harmony with Islamic practices, by the 1950s it had developed a strong base among middle-class professionals, many workers and intellectuals. In Egypt, the most prominent theoretician in this regard was Sayyid Qutb, who advocated the expansive use of jihad.

Malcolm's attraction to the Brotherhood was probably due to its Islamic foundations, grounding real-world politics in a spiritual basis. Ironically, it was exactly the opposite position he had reached in the United States, having concluded that he would need to keep separate his religious and political groups. In Beirut, he visited the home of Dr. Malik Badri, a professor at American University, whom he had previously met in Sudan in 1959. Badri informed Malcolm that he was scheduled to give a lecture the following day. Later that evening Malcolm met with a group of Sudanese students, who "were well informed on the Black Muslims," Malcolm wrote, "and asked many questions on it and the American race problem in general."

On April 30, after a lunch at the home of Dr. Badri, Malcolm gave a talk at the Sudanese Cultural Center in Beirut. The local Beirut *Daily Star* covered the speech, printing a front-page article about it the next day. The *New York Times* also briefly reported on Malcolm's lecture, characterizing it largely as an attack on King. According to the *Times*, Malcolm "told students at the Sudanese Cultural Center that Negroes in the United States had made no practical gains toward achieving civil rights." He also declared that "only a minority of Negroes believed in nonviolence."

That evening, Malcolm mentioned in his diary that he visited "the offices of the Muslim brothers"—that is, the Brotherhood. Early the next morning, as Malcolm made his way to fly to Cairo, Dr. Malik "and others of the M. B. [Muslim Brotherhood] gave me a very touching send-off." Arriving in Cairo the next morning, he met up with his local contact, Hussein el-Borai, an

Egyptian diplomat who had accompanied Malcolm around Cairo in 1959 and would play the same role during Malcolm's 1964 visit. The two men traveled by train to nearby Alexandria, reaching the ancient seaport city in the evening.

Malcolm spent several days as a tourist in Alexandria, where he soon discovered that photographs taken of himself with heavyweight boxing champion Muhammad Ali had been widely circulated in the Egyptian press; consequently Malcolm was treated like a "VIP," he noted, being besieged by autograph seekers. "Just saying I was an American Muslim who just returned from hajj was enough," Malcolm wrote in his diary. "Then mentioning Clay caused a real 'landslide.'" Most of Malcolm's day was spent at Alexandria's harbor, "trying to unravel red tape and get imported items through customs." After a late afternoon nap, that evening he returned to Cairo, and over several days reacquainted himself with local Muslim contacts, most of whom he had previously met in the United States or on his 1959 trip. Malcolm also kept encountering Egyptians who refused to believe that he could possibly be both an American and a Muslim. One waiter dismissed his assertions, telling el-Borai that Malcolm "was probably from Habachi (Abyssinia)."

On Tuesday morning, May 5, the nineteen-year-old son of Dr. Shawarbi, Muhammad Shawarbi, came by Malcolm's hotel to accompany him around the city and later out to the airport to catch a flight to Lagos, Nigeria. After some delays, on May 6 he arrived in Lagos. A Nigerian official at the airport recognized Malcolm and escorted him to the Federal Palace hotel.

For the next few days Malcolm visited Nigeria, but due to his limited schedule he essentially toured only two major cities, Lagos and Ibadan. Unlike in Cairo, his arrival in Nigeria amid a sea of black faces informed him that he had landed in the center of the long historical struggle that had increasingly found expression in his rhetoric back in Harlem. Yet the situation on the ground hardly matched the idealization promised by his speeches. Here in West Africa he found a land battered by the effects of fierce internecine political battles; the political promises made when Nigeria had gained its independence in 1960 had not been fulfilled, and two years after Malcolm's trip the country would descend into a nightmare of military dictatorship from which it would not emerge for decades.

On Thursday, May 7, he met with several reporters at his hotel, and in the late afternoon toured Lagos by car. Waiting at the hotel for him upon his return were several local contacts, including scholar E. U. Essien-Udom.

The group departed for Ibadan by car, a trip Malcolm described as "frightening." That night Malcolm delivered a powerful address at Ibadan University, sponsored by the National Union of Nigerian Students, to an enthusiastic audience of about five hundred. Malcolm would later note that a riot had barely been averted there when angry students mobbed a West Indian lecturer who had criticized Malcolm's address. Most memorable for Malcolm, however, was the honor bestowed upon him by the Muslim Students' Society of Nigeria: a membership card in their society with the name "Omowale," which in the Yoruba language means "the son (or child) who has returned."

———

With the exception of Mecca, the high point of Malcolm's trip in April–May 1964 was his visit to Ghana, where he arrived on May 10. He came at the invitation of the small African-American expatriate community in the capital city of Accra, which was informally led by the writer/actor Julian Mayfield. Best known for the racially charged novels he wrote during the 1950s, Mayfield had fled to Ghana in 1961 following the kidnapping incident in North Carolina that had also sent Robert F. Williams into exile in Cuba. He was joined in Accra by a number of fellow African-American radicals, which included his wife Ana Livia Cordero, Maya Angelou, Alice Windom, Preston King, and W. E. B. and Shirley Du Bois.

Malcolm had first met Mayfield a few years before his arrival, at the home of Ruby Dee and Ossie Davis, and they had kept in touch as Malcolm's interest in postcolonial politics grew. When Malcolm informed him of his African tour, Mayfield and the other expats grew excited at the chance to bring America's strongest voice for black nationalism to the country that had long epitomized African hopes of a better future. Since becoming the first black African nation to gain its independence from colonialism in 1957, Ghana had come to symbolize possibility for many different groups. The rise to power of Kwame Nkrumah and his Convention People's Party provided a template for African self-rule for other colonized countries throughout the continent, while the peaceful transfer of power from the British colonial government, celebrated by blacks around the globe, gave further validation to American advocates of nonviolence, who saw in the transition clear proof of the efficacy of their methods. The nonviolent strategy also found support within the U.S. State Department, which was eager to limit Soviet influence in Africa.

Yet as in Nigeria, by the time of Malcolm's arrival the bloom had come off the rose of Ghana's celebratory moment. The controversial murder of Congo's Patrice Lumumba in 1961 had marked for many a terrible turn in the continent's affairs, as the policies of Western nations toward Africa complicated the already strained politics of new nations struggling with civil unrest and governmental chaos. The use of violence by the enemies of the African independence movement—and similarly by white supremacists in the United States—increasingly made nonviolence seem like an anemic response, and bolstered the influence of those in favor of a more revolutionary approach. By Malcolm's visit, Ghana was suffering from many of the same political difficulties that he had seen in Nigeria, and his appearance had the dual effect of exciting a population hungry for the ideals he represented while making government officials uneasy about embracing him.

All this did little to dampen the enthusiasm of Accra's African-American expat community, which had been anticipating Malcolm's arrival for several weeks. When he arrived at Mayfield's home early in the morning of Monday, May 11, Mayfield told Malcolm that he had already arranged two major speaking events for him. One was a lecture at the University of Ghana organized by Leslie Lacy, who had been radicalized during his student years at Berkeley and upon moving to Ghana had worked to set up the popular Marxist Study Group at the university. After Malcolm settled in, Mayfield took him to a lunch at Lacy's home, where Alice Windom also joined them. Having first encountered Malcolm when he gave a talk at Chicago's Mosque No. 2 in the early 1960s, she was happy to be reunited with him abroad.

Over lunch, Malcolm explained that he intended "to lend his talents to the building of unity among the various rights groups in America," recalled Windom. "[I]n his view," she wrote, "no useful purpose could be served by exposing all the roots of dissension." This left open the question of Malcolm's quite public struggle with the Nation, leading him to explain his departure from the NOI "in terms of the disagreement on political direction and involvement in the extra-religious struggle for human rights in America." His first day in Ghana in the company of the expats left him feeling welcomed and contented, and late that same night back at his hotel, writing in his diary, Malcolm pondered the possibility of relocating to Africa: "Moving my family out of America may be good for me personally but bad for me politically."

In a May 11 letter to the MMI updating his followers on his travels, Malcolm recounted his triumphal lecture at Ibadan University, where he had given "the true picture of our plight in America, and of the necessity of the independent African Nations helping us bring our case before the United Nations." Politically, the highest priority was building "unity between the Africans of the West and the Africans of the fatherland [which] will well change the course of history." This letter marks Malcolm's final break with the NOI concept of the "Asiatic" black man and the beginning of his identification with Pan-Africanism similar to that espoused by Nkrumah.

By now the *Ghanaian Times* had been alerted of Malcolm's presence, and a short announcement, "X is here," appeared on the front page on May 12. The following day the paper covered his press conference, in which he emphasized "the establishment of good relationship between Afro-Americans and Africans at home [which] is bound to have far reaching results for the common good." The next few days were a whirl of celebrity activity: escorted by Julian Mayfield to the Cuban embassy to meet their young ambassador, Armando Entralgo Gonzalez, "who immediately offered to give a party in my honor"; an intimate lunch at the home of a young Maya Angelou, then a dancer who was also employed as a teacher, whom he recalled fondly from their meeting several years before; meetings with the ambassadors of Nigeria and Mali; and a private conversation with Ghana's minister of defense Kofi Boaka and other ministers at Boaka's home.

On the evening of May 14, Malcolm delivered the lecture that Leslie Lacy had arranged for him, addressing a capacity crowd in the Great Hall of the University of Ghana. Alice Windom, observing the scene, commented that "many of the whites had come to be 'amused.' They were in for a rude surprise." The speech forced Malcolm to be at his most politically adroit, and he warmly praised Nkrumah as one of the African continent's "most progressive leaders." The litmus test he proposed for African heads of state was based on how they were treated by the U.S. media, and thus the U.S. government: "[T]hese leaders over here who are receiving the praise and pats on the back from the Americans, you can just flush the toilet and let them go right down the drain," he told the crowd, which roared with laughter and applause.

Yet in its appreciation of Nkrumah the speech masked the great divisiveness that had emerged in Ghanaian politics. Though Nkrumah had been revered as a national hero during independence, by the mid-1960s his government had degenerated into an authoritarian regime characterized by rigged elections, the loss of an independent judiciary, the decline of the Convention People's Party as a popular democratic force, the expansion of corruption and graft, and a cult of personality surrounding Nkrumah.

Although Nkrumah employed Marxist rhetoric, his regime could be best described as Bonapartist: deeply hostile to the existence of a free civil society and ruled from above by a bureaucracy estranged from the nation's population. In 1964, C. L. R. James, Nkrumah's former mentor, publicly broke with the African president over his suppression of democratic rights in the country. Malcolm undoubtedly heard these criticisms from some of the African-American expatriates, but he wisely used his remarks to emphasize the Pan-Africanist common ground that black Americans continued to share with the Ghanaian president. At times, he even seemed to endorse the authoritarian measures Nkrumah had established over economic and social policies, explaining that only when the "colonial mentality has been destroyed" will the masses of citizens "know what they are voting for, then you give them a chance to vote on this and vote on that."

Malcolm also used his speech to characterize the United States as a "colonial power" like Portugal, France, and Britain. And he predicted that Harlem was "about to explode." The *Ghanaian Times* reported that Malcolm called for Third World unity: "Only a concerted attack by the black, the yellow, the red and the brown races which outnumber the white race would end segregation in the U.S., and the world."

The next morning, Malcolm had been scheduled to speak before Ghana's national parliament, but because of transportation delays, he arrived shortly after the formal session ended. However, members of parliament were still there, and most gathered in the building's Members Room, where Malcolm addressed the group and engaged legislators in a lively discussion. At noon, Malcolm was taken to Christiansborg Castle, the seat of the Ghanaian government, for a private hourlong meeting with President Nkrumah. The fact of the meeting itself was somewhat extraordinary, given that Nkrumah was reluctant to associate with Malcolm; only the appeal of W. E. B. Du Bois's widow, Shirley, who continued to be a friend to Nkrumah after her husband's death in 1963, convinced him to give Malcolm an audience. Later Malcolm spoke before two hundred students at the Kwame Nkrumah Ideological Institute in Winneba, about forty miles from Accra. He even found time to dine with other American expatriates at the Chinese embassy, where they viewed three Chinese documentary films, including one proclaiming Maoist China's support for African-American liberation.

It was a thoroughly triumphal visit. As Alice Windom observed, Malcolm X's "name was almost as familiar to Ghanaians as the Southern dogs, fire hoses, cattle prods, people sticks and ugly hate-contorted white faces, and his decision to enter the mainstream of the struggle was heralded as a hopeful sign." Only two sour events blemished a near perfect week. The first was a negative encounter with Muhammad Ali, who was touring West Africa. As Malcolm was departing from his hotel on the way to the airport, the two men bumped into each other and Ali snubbed him. Later Ali eagerly expressed his unconditional loyalty to Elijah Muhammad, ridiculing Malcolm to a *New York Times* correspondent and laughing at the "funny white robe" his onetime friend wore and his newly grown beard. "Man, he's gone. He's gone so far out he's out completely." With words he would later regret, the boxer added, "Nobody listens to that Malcolm anymore."

Then, within hours of leaving Ghana, Malcolm was attacked in the *Ghanaian Times* by Nkrumah's ideological lieutenant, H. M. Basner. A communist, Basner accused Malcolm of failing to comprehend the "class function of all racial oppression." Malcolm's emphasis on black liberation instead of class struggle would only serve the interests of "American imperialists. . . . If Malcolm X believes what he says, then both Karl Marx and John Brown are excluded by their racial origin from being regarded as human liberators." Julian Mayfield immediately responded to Basner's critique. Mayfield argued that what was so upsetting to Basner was Malcolm's rejection of the classical communist strategy telling blacks to unite with white workers to achieve meaningful change. "The black American has been down that road before," Mayfield observed. "No single factor has so retarded his struggle as his attempt to unite with liberal or progressive whites." The average black American worker "has no more in common with the white worker in America than he has in South Africa." Leslie Lacy later recalled that what truly appalled the African-American expatriate group was that Basner's criticisms of Malcolm had "appeared in a black, revolutionary, government-controlled newspaper. . . . No criticism, however objective, could have appeared attacking Nkrumah."

Malcolm's experiences in Ghana strengthened his commitment to Pan-Africanism. Writing to the MMI, Malcolm praised Ghana as "the fountainhead of Pan-Africanism. . . . Just as the American Jew is in harmony (politically, economically and culturally) with World Jewry, it is time for all African-Americans to become an integral part of the world's Pan-Africanists." He called for a return to Africa "philosophically and culturally." Before he departed on May 17, the American expatriates in Ghana organized a "V.I.P. send off," Malcolm wrote in his diary, adding that an enthusiastic "Maya [Angelou] took the bus right up to the plane." When the airplane stopped briefly in Dakar, the French airport manager escorted Malcolm around the facility. "I signed many autographs," Malcolm wrote, and he prayed with many others.

He arrived in Casablanca, Morocco, well after dark, where he would spend the next day quietly. After touring Casablanca by taxi, Malcolm joined his local contact, a man named Ibrahim Maki, and a friend. The three ended up in the Muslim district, the Medina, where they chatted and dined until late. "They were very race-conscious, proud of the Black Muslims, and thirsting for faster 'progress.'"

Malcolm celebrated what would be his final birthday, turning thirty-nine on May 19, 1964. Part of that day was spent flying from Casablanca to Algiers, where he arrived in the afternoon, before surveying the city by foot and eating a late dinner. This city, his last on the African journey, however, did not yield much. Malcolm was disappointed to find few people who could speak English; plus his calls to the Ghanaian embassy were fruitless and his contact in the Algerian foreign ministry wasn't at his office when Malcolm stopped by. On the twentieth, Malcolm toured the city by taxi, leaning out the car window to take photographs. Meanwhile, that same day back in the United States, he would later learn, a warrant was issued for his arrest for failing to appear at a trial to respond to the speeding ticket he had been given in the hectic days surrounding Cassius Clay's visit to New York.

On departure day, May 21, Malcolm was briefly detained by police at the Algiers airport, who believed that the photos he'd taken were a security risk. It was only by providing evidence of his status as a Muslim that he was released, with apologies. Malcolm arrived home to JFK airport in the late afternoon to a crowd of about sixty, mostly family and friends. A press conference was arranged for that evening at the Hotel Theresa, where, as he would in the days that immediately followed, Malcolm emphasized his desire to create a new "organization which will be open for the participation of all Negroes, and we will be willing to accept the support of people of other races." Malcolm candidly admitted that his "racial philosophy" had been altered after all he had seen—"thousands of people of different races and colors who treated me as a human being."

Malcolm was ready to enter the international political stage, leaving the parochialism and backwardness of Yacub and the Nation far behind him. Yet in returning to the world he had left a month before, he would find that the profound transformation he'd experienced in the Middle East and Africa had not similarly taken root in his MMI brothers. At the airport greeting, despite their break from the sect, they were still wearing the standard Nation of Islam uniform, the "dark blue suits, white shirts and distinctive red or grey bow ties." Malcolm may have traveled to a different world, spiritually and politically, but his followers would not be so easily transported.

CHAPTER 12

"Do Something About Malcolm X"

May 21–July 11, 1964

Malcolm's growing fame in the wake of his split from the Nation of Islam attracted interest from people of many stripes, and throughout March and April secular activists, writers, and even celebrities tried to make personal contact with him. Hundreds of people craved his time and attention at a moment when he desperately needed to find peace. The hajj to Mecca was not unlike a journey to some undiscovered country to learn what a spiritual commitment to Islam would mean in his life. Yet thousands of miles distant from the site of this spiritual pilgrimage, a whirlwind of political activity continued to spiral around Malcolm X.

Within several weeks after Malcolm's break, Muslim Mosque, Inc., had established a regular routine at its Hotel Theresa headquarters. In these early, often chaotic days, stability came at a premium. MMI business meetings were held on Monday nights. On Wednesday evenings, an Islamic religious service was held. On Thursday nights, the MMI office was turned over to MMI women, who were still referred to as MGT. On Sunday nights, if Malcolm was in the city, a public rally or event was scheduled at the Audubon. An FBI informant reported that at the March 26, 1964, MMI gathering about seventy-five people attended the "open meeting," which was followed by a closed session restricted to about forty-five "registered Muslims." James 67X ran the private meeting, focusing on security matters and warning the sisters and brothers "to be careful of the NOI."

As Malcolm traveled and gave speeches throughout the country during this time, he encountered many young African Americans with no prior membership or contacts with the Nation who wanted to devote themselves to his cause. One of these idealistic young people who greatly impressed him was Lynne Carol Shifflett. Born January 26, 1940, Shifflett was raised in an upper-middle-class family, her childhood and teenage years in California filled with the elite social activities of the black bourgeoisie, such as membership in the Jack and Jill organization. Enrolling in Los Angeles City College in the fall of 1956, Shifflett was soon elected student body vice president. A three-month trip to Africa in 1958, in which she met Prime Minister Kwame Nkrumah of Ghana, dramatically expanded her political and social outlook. Her parents, in solidarity with their activist daughter, staged a Freedom Gala to raise funds for Freedom Riders in the South.

By 1963, Shifflett had relocated to New York City, where she was among a handful of blacks then employed at NBC television in Rockefeller Center, and it appears to have been around this time that Malcolm met her. The confident young woman impressed him, and he entrusted her to identify young secular activists like herself who would help him start a new black nationalist group. One of her initial recruits was Peter Bailey, an aspiring young African American who also worked in Rockefeller Center, at Time, Inc. Two years her elder, Bailey was largely raised by his grandparents in Tuskegee, Alabama, and had served as an army medic before enrolling in Howard University in 1959. By the time of his first meeting with Shifflett, Bailey had already grown familiar with Malcolm through NOI rallies in Harlem. "Every Saturday we'd make it down to 116th and listen to him speak," Bailey recalled. "I was fascinated by what he was saying intellectually because of my whole integrationist background." Bailey did not join the Nation of Islam, but continued to attend public events featuring Malcolm as a speaker. After Malcolm's silencing in December 1963, Bailey counted himself among many who felt that the minister's "chickens" remark was fully justified: "All he was saying was that because the situation in this country allowed what happen to black people, that white people would also begin to feel the effects of this."

In early 1964, Shifflett met with Bailey at breakfast, where she asked, "How would you like to be a part of the founding of a new black nationalist organization?" Although Shifflett was extremely secretive, Bailey agreed to help. "I'm going to call you Saturday morning at eight a.m. and tell you where to meet and what time," Shifflett told him. "And don't ask no questions, just be there." When she rang him the next Saturday, she instructed him to go to a Harlem hotel on West 153rd Street, where he arrived to find a small gathering of about fifteen people. Moments later, he was stunned to see Malcolm walk in. These Saturday morning meetings, geared toward the creation of an independent, secular organization that supported Malcolm's goals, soon became a regular event, though mostly without Malcolm's personal direction. Knowing the danger posed by the Nation, Malcolm made sure that his people had no illusions about what they were getting into. Bailey explained, "Malcolm is telling us, 'You know if you get involved with me that you might get harassed by the police and the FBI.' . . . Everyone knew this already and it didn't bother us." It was among this small cadre of young followers that Bailey became, as he described it, a "true believer" completely dedicated to Malcolm. "Somehow this man could absorb the ideas. . . . He was very relaxed and he laughed and he'd joke." Bailey claims the Saturday meetings started in January or February 1964, weeks prior to Malcolm's break with the Nation. If true, this would explain the highly secretive character of these clandestine meetings, suggesting that perhaps Malcolm was pursuing a dual-track strategy: continuing to appeal to rejoin the Nation while simultaneously building an independent base loyal to himself.

Herman Ferguson, the Queens educator, soon became part of this new group. In Ferguson's view, Malcolm had outgrown the Nation. "Long before I'd met Malcolm, [I felt] that he needed to break with the Nation of Islam because [it] held him back, his development." What black nationalists like Ferguson were seeking was an "alternative to integration" and to Dr. King. "I didn't know what would happen when he [Malcolm] left, but I had made up my mind if he left the Nation of Islam . . . that I would join up with anything that Malcolm did," Ferguson said.

From the beginning, there were tensions and rivalries between the former Black Muslims in Muslim Mosque, Inc., and the secular activist newcomers like Shifflett and Ferguson. The MMI brothers and sisters "felt they owned him," Ferguson complained. James 67X, Benjamin 2X Goodman, and the others had joined MMI "with the knowledge that the Nation of Islam would not be friendly toward them," Ferguson went on. "So they felt, to a great extent, responsible for Malcolm and his safety." In the weeks following the split, rallies at the Audubon featured MMI brothers who carried weapons while protecting Malcolm. "Their rifles and shotguns were carried openly," Ferguson remembered. At the time, he convinced himself that this display of force was necessary: "I felt very proud that these were black men . . . escorting our leader out of the building, that he was safe, he had these weapons. . . . As far as I was concerned, [this] is the way that the movement would have to go." Yet this aggressive stance ultimately provoked greater ire from the Nation and increased its members' desire for retaliation. Nation members were not permitted to carry firearms; despite the small size of Muslim Mosque, Inc., three dozen well-armed men constituted a genuine threat to the much larger Mosque No. 7.

As Malcolm's secular organization took shape, it drew in members, like Ferguson, who had been waiting for Malcolm to form a group distinct from the Nation. One of the recruits was, in fact, one of his oldest supporters. In Boston, it had been nearly five years since Ella had bitterly broken with Louis X and the local NOI mosque. She probably felt vindicated by her brother's decision to leave the sect, and their relationship grew closer during this time. Her immediate concerns were to help Malcolm overcome his financial fears and personal doubts through this transition. When Doubleday's promised advances fell behind due to the slow progress of the book, Ella subsidized her brother and his family. The money she lent him for his hajj had been intended to finance her own pilgrimage, but evidently the sacrifice made sense to her. Ella would later insist that, far from desiring the opportunity to experience the hajj, her brother initially resisted going. Supposedly, in an emotional midnight conversation she forced a tearful Malcolm to concede that the Nation of Islam would never readmit him.

A number of progressive African-American artists, playwrights, and writers also welcomed Malcolm's departure from the Nation and anticipated his entry into civil rights causes. Actor and playwright Ossie Davis was one of the most prominent. Davis occupied a peculiar position within the Black Freedom Movement, not unlike that of James Baldwin—an artist who had credentials among integrationists and black separatists alike. Davis had served as master of ceremonies at the 1963 March on Washington, but in Malcolm he saw a proponent of the black class struggle, an advocate "for connecting with people out in the street, drug addicts, criminals, and hustlers—these were folks outside the middle class, people that Dr. King certainly couldn't relate to."

> I remember walking on the street with Malcolm, and people would come up to him and he'd respond to them, and I would respond to them in a different way. While some would be chastising him, Malcolm always had something positive to say. Malcolm was an expert on the damage that slavery and racism had done to the black man's image of himself. He was equally expert in what had to be done to remedy that egregious lack of self-esteem. He knew it would take more than civil rights legislation, jobs, and education to really save the

black man. And he knew that none of the traditional organizations that serviced black folk, such as black churches, colleges, sororities and fraternities, the NAACP, the Urban League, were capable of doing what needed to be done. He felt, as did some of us, that to ask a man who had already been beaten up and beaten down to be nonviolent was only to change black pathology into another religion.

For his part, Malcolm had loved Davis's 1960 play *Purlie Victorious*, which used comic stereotypes to make sharp criticisms of racism, and over the next few years the two men continued to run into each other at demonstrations. By 1964 Malcolm was on a first-name basis with Davis and his actor activist wife, Ruby Dee. Ruby's brother, Tom Wallace, was so influenced by Malcolm that he joined the Nation of Islam, and later Muslim Mosque, Inc.

Writers and journalists who knew Malcolm also generally welcomed his latest move. Peter Goldman continued to maintain close contact and came away impressed with the "complexity and sophistication of [his] political thought." Like many observers during the months of Malcolm's silencing, the writer had been unaware of any impending split. "I'd been hearing rumors about jealousy of Malcolm's prominence," Goldman recalled, "but I didn't know it had come to any kind of crisis." After the fact, though, he came to see the break as necessary to Malcolm's intellectual evolution; leaving the Nation, combined with his excursions in Africa, had prompted him to think "black politically. I think his nationalism had been enriched by his travels." The earlier Malcolm had preached a simplistic, "mom-and-pop . . . economic model." By 1964, he had transformed himself, "moving, I think, probably closer to Pan-Africanism, certainly to a connection with the nonwhite majority of the world."

———

Malcolm's departure from the Nation changed much about his life, but it also affected the Nation in interesting ways. For some key players, the departure of Malcolm and his supporters expanded opportunities. Twenty-six-year-old Norman Butler, a veteran of the navy, for example, had been an NOI member for barely a year, but during that brief tenure he had established a reputation as a tough security man. Mosque No. 7 normally ran two weekly training sessions, including martial arts, for the Fruit of Islam. When one of Malcolm's men left, Butler assumed control of the Tuesday morning session, with dramatic results. From a modest group of three to five, word of mouth grew the group to "seventy to eighty brothers [who] were coming out, because of how we were doing." Soon, Butler recalled, the Tuesday morning Fruit group "got to selling over five thousand papers" per week. Though Malcolm had promoted him to the rank of lieutenant, Butler made no bones about choosing sides during the split. "[Malcolm] made himself large," he remembered years later with resentment. "He kept himself in front of the *New York Times*." This, to Butler, was the crux of the problem that led to Malcolm's expulsion. "He was trying to be bigger than all the other ministers" and was guilty of going "outside of or beyond the teaching that the Messenger wanted taught, say[ing] things that the Messenger didn't want said. That's what the rub was."

Yet for all those who developed negative opinions of Malcolm, many Nation members who had sided with Elijah Muhammad in the split nevertheless retained strong feelings of affection for their former national minister. "I was really a student of his," said Larry 4X Prescott. "I loved him. I admired him. I wanted to be able to do what he was doing. And that's what he encouraged." Larry considered the silencing a kind of moral "test." Both he and other assistant ministers "hoped and prayed that Malcolm would pass whatever trial that the leader had put on him." It was only in late February when Malcolm returned from Florida and "talked about the fight and Muhammad Ali" that Larry realized that the minister had gone too far. His interview at JFK airport "was a violation of the silence imposed on him by the Honorable Elijah Muhammad." For Larry, the subsequent break was Malcolm's fault.

Larry vigorously contested the idea that Malcolm simply "outgrew" the Nation and that his departure was inevitable. As Larry recalled, the truly negative rumors began only in the days directly prior to Malcolm's departure. Referring to young women Elijah Muhammad had bedded, Larry explained that Malcolm had known "about the wives" long before the silencing controversy. "Malcolm [could] see [that the NOI recruited] those dedicated young men, who came out of the streets of America, out of the prisons of America," who benefited most from the Nation's teachings. More educated converts, Larry conceded, may have "felt that the Nation was too confining, that they couldn't make decisions for themselves." When Malcolm formed Muslim Mosque but initially continued to praise Muhammad's social program, Larry believed "that Malcolm felt he could direct people to the Nation . . . better from this [outside] position, because most people didn't want some of the restrictions of the Nation. . . . That's the way I saw it."

The great changes in Malcolm's life also landed hard on Betty, who now found herself forced to negotiate Malcolm's five-week absence overseas with lieutenants in Muslim Mosque for whom she had little love. Before his departure Malcolm had instructed the leaders of MMI to provide security for his wife and children, knowing that while the Nation had yet to hurt the families of dissidents, they could not be trusted at this point to leave them alone. Charles 37X Kenyatta was designated to guard Betty and the children in their house, and no one else was permitted inside the home. Kenyatta would later claim that, at first, Betty resented his constant presence. "She hated me with a passion," he recalled. "She didn't like the role I was playing." Betty similarly disliked James 67X, yet she knew that he represented Malcolm's most likely point of contact in MMI, and she phoned him nearly every night during the weeks her husband was out of the country. In her efforts to keep tabs on him, she canvassed anyone likely to hear from him. Almost on a daily basis she phoned Haley, Malcolm's attorney, Percy Sutton, and others who might have received letters or telegrams. Malcolm himself made an earnest effort to keep Betty informed through letters about the locations he was visiting, and he periodically phoned her as well. At home, she taped a world map on the living room wall so the children could chart the countries Malcolm had visited. Betty correctly sensed that her husband's extensive new contacts with Muslims and others in the Middle East and Africa might liberate him from the Nation's powerful influence. Attallah, the eldest daughter, would later express this sentiment: "The more he traveled, the freer he became, the freer we all became."

Yet this freedom came at a cost, especially when Malcolm's subsequent actions further fueled anger within the Nation's ranks. On May 8, *Muhammad Speaks* featured the first of a two-part editorial attacking Malcolm by the "Minister Who Knew Him Best." The editorial argued that the reasons Malcolm had given the white media for his "defection" were "filled with lies, slander and filth designed to cast aspersions upon Mr. Muhammad and his family." Although Louis X was presented as the author of the polemic, the piece was likely ghostwritten by a Chicago NOI editor, a suggestion that gains credence from the misspelling of Louis's name in the column as "Minister Lewis."

In late April James 67X received a letter Malcolm had written just after his hajj experience, outlining his new views about race. Given the trend in Malcolm's recent statements, James 67X was scared to open the envelope, knowing that the revelations contained in Malcolm's communication could pose major problems with the MMI rank and file. Even James himself was hardly ready to embrace such a radical change. "I had come out of an organization that says Mecca is the only place in the world where a white man can't go . . . ," he explained. Malcolm's affirmation that whites also could be Muslims meant a wholesale rejection of the Nation's theology, which may have fit his own emerging outlook but remained deeply problematic for a group that had only recently departed the Nation and still found much to speak for in its views on race. At first, James 67X didn't know what to do. "I'm walking around with this letter, saying, how am I gonna tell this to [these] people? . . . What do you mean by 'white'? What did Malcolm mean by 'white'?" After several days, James 67X circulated the letter to the MMI. However, he refused to believe that Malcolm "had embraced Sunni Islam."

The ambiguity and confusion that surrounded the letter probably inadvertently helped keep Muslim Mosque together during Malcolm's absence, as members were free to read their own interpretations of Malcolm's feelings into the letter's message. Though Malcolm would go on to make his ideas more concrete upon his return, the question of his true, deep-seated beliefs continued to be debated by his followers. Herman Ferguson thought that Malcolm "had offered to white people the possibility of Islam correcting their sense of values," but that, deep in his soul, he knew "they could never accept the teachings of Islam." Even after Malcolm returned to the United States and personally spoke to MMI and OAAU members about his new views, Ferguson remained adamant that Malcolm's inner politics were still race based. "Because if I had for a moment even suspected that Malcolm was changing his thinking," Ferguson swore, "I would have walked away." Over several decades, Betty gave inconsistent answers to questions about what impact the hajj, Islam, and travels to the Third World had on her husband's racial views. In 1989, however, when Haley biographer Anne Romaine interviewed her and asked, "Do you think that your husband changed his views?" Betty curtly replied, "No."

Despite the intransigence of many of his followers, the notion that Malcolm was undergoing some sort of transformation began to spread in the mainstream and black presses. On May 8, the *New York Times* published an article by M. S. Handler with a surprising title: "Malcolm X Pleased by Whites' Attitude on Trip to Mecca." Quoting an April 25 letter Malcolm had written in Saudi Arabia, Handler wrote that the black leader would soon return to the United States "with new, positive insights on race relations." Throughout his hajj, Malcolm wrote in words that would be much quoted in years to come: "I have eaten from the same plate, drank from the same glass, slept on the same bed or rug, while praying to the same God . . . with fellow Muslims whose skins was the whitest of white, whose eyes were the bluest of blue . . . [for] the first time in my life. . . . I didn't see them as 'white' men." What he had witnessed was so profound, Malcolm admitted, that it had "forced me to 'rearrange' much of my own thought-pattern, and to toss aside some of my previous conclusions." Yet if Malcolm expressed optimism that America could transform itself on racial matters, he also professed to see Islam as the key to that transformation. "I do believe," Malcolm wrote, "that whites of the younger generation, in colleges and universities, through their own young, less hampered intellect, will see the 'handwriting on the wall' and turn for spiritual salvation to the religion of Islam, and force the older generation of American whites to turn with them."

Several weeks after the *Times* article, James Booker of the *Amsterdam News* posed the provocative question "Has the visit of Malcolm X, now El-Hajj Malik El-Shabazz, to Mecca and with Muslim leaders in Africa changed him to become soft in his anti-white feelings and to become more religious?" A clue to this apparent "change in his militant racial attitudes" was contained in a letter he had sent to the newspaper about one week earlier, in which he had written that the proponents of Islam were obligated "to take a firm stand on the side of anyone whose human rights are being violated, no matter what the religious persuasion of the victims may be." Malcolm now understood that "Islam recognizes everyone as part of one human family."

———

The increasing difficulties and uncertainties in Malcolm's life were mirrored in the progress of his autobiography. When Malcolm was silenced by Elijah Muhammad in December 1963, Alex Haley panicked. Without consulting with Malcolm, Haley contacted Chicago to secure a meeting with the Messenger, who assured him that the suspension "wasn't permanent." Haley reported to his agent, Paul Reynolds, that the "real purpose" of Muhammad's action was to underscore his supremacy and authority over the sect. "I assured him that the publisher, you and I, were concerned not to incur his displeasure," Haley wrote to Reynolds. Muhammad "was interested in hearing about the book, and I sketched its pattern, chapter by chapter, which pleased him." Like Peter Goldman, Haley did not at first see how deep ran the fissure, and neither Malcolm nor Elijah Muhammad found it prudent to illuminate it for him. Haley's first priority remained publishing a profitable book, which he still thought required the blessing of Elijah Muhammad.

Haley finally had a lengthy working session with Malcolm just before Christmas 1963. Malcolm read the latest version of the chapter "Laura" and objected to the use of slang in the book, complaining that he no longer spoke that way. Haley consented but complained to his editors and agent, "Somebody said that becoming celebrated always will ruin a good demagogue." And Malcolm was not the only one with money troubles during this time; Haley's relocation to upstate New York left him strapped for cash. Doubleday agreed to give him additional advance payments of $750 upon the submission and approval of each of two new chapters. Deeply grateful, Haley stated, "I can write now for the first time not harassed by intermittent money pressures." In early January, during a heavy snowstorm, Haley managed to drive down to the city to spend time with Malcolm, but found him distressed as his suspension unfolded. Reporting back to his agent and editors, Haley observed that his subject was "tense as the length of his inactivity grows." Malcolm read several of Haley's draft "strips," or sections of narrative text that were the basis for each chapter. Haley was most excited, however, by the essays planned at the end of the book, which presented Malcolm's social program and political agenda. "The most impact material of the book, some of it rather lava-like, is what I have from Malcolm for the three essay chapters, 'The Negro,' 'The End of Christianity,' and 'Twenty Million Black Muslims,'" Haley observed. These three chapters represented a blueprint for where Malcolm at that moment believed black America should be moving, and his conviction that Muslims should take a leading role in the construction of a united front among all black people.

Yet for all his work, Haley was still months away from submitting a finished manuscript, which displeased Wolcott Gibbs, Jr., and other Doubleday executives when they were informed of it. Gibbs asked Haley to "please bear in mind that the more rewriting you do, the further we are away from having a finished book." He pressed for a best estimate of the final manuscript date. Even before Gibbs's request, Haley shipped off yet another rewritten chapter, "Detroit Red," on January 28, but Reynolds didn't like this version and sent off suggestions for revision. On February 6, Haley agreed to "come back to 'Detroit Red' and any other chapters and improve them in whatever ways you are good enough to point out to me." He desperately wanted to finish a whole draft before revising and rearranging chapters, yet Reynolds's displeasure with his recent work kept him busy fixing chapters he had already tweaked or rewritten. On February 7, Reynolds contacted Gibbs, explaining, "I'm worried about interfering with your function [as editor] but I do want to get a really good book on Malcolm X and I don't believe you and Ken would quarrel with what I'm saying to him."

Even by February 1964, Haley remained confused over Malcolm's problems with the Nation, believing that the suspension was only temporary and that he would soon rejoin the group. On February 11, in a letter to Gibbs, he suggested "that the ban will . . . be lifted" sometime that month. He still envisioned the book's climax as revolving around Malcolm's embrace of Elijah, the subject turning "his life . . . around and he becomes arch—'puritan' so to speak, and blasts everything that went before." Haley was not above enhancing the material when discussing it with his editors, partly because of the story's real commercial possibilities, but also probably to justify the many extensions he required to complete it. On February 18, as he submitted his latest chapter, "Hustler," he wrote to his editors, "We have here the book that, when it gets to the public, is going to run away from everything else. Because it has so much. . . . Exciting as is Malcolm's criminal life that we're now seeing, I tell you that it's nothing compared with the front seat. We are going to hear of his in-prison subjective turnabout." Haley anticipated that the book would be done by late March, with a brief afterword, which he would write to represent his own reflections about Malcolm, to be submitted the next month. Because Malcolm had not yet rejected the separatist vision of Muhammad, Haley felt that he had to insert himself into the text, reassuring white readers that the mainstream Negro truly did desire integration. As he explained to his editor and agents, "I plan to hit very hard, speaking from the point of the Negro who has tried to do all of the things that are held up as the pathway to enjoy the American Dream, and who . . . so often gets disillusioned and disappointed. . . . I am going to give some courses that every American and every Christian needs to wrestle with."

When Malcolm left the Nation, it soon became clear that the book could not remain as written, prompting further work from Haley and a necessary reevaluation of his timetable for finishing. On March 21, Haley forwarded a letter to Reynolds and Doubleday editor Kenneth McCormick, explaining why "there has been, over the past couple of weeks, more time-gap than usual between chapters," due to Malcolm's recent moves, which he emphasized would "add, add, add to the book's drama." Once again Haley followed up a request for more time with boasts about the potential of the *Autobiography*: "Gentlemen, not in a decade, and maybe longer, [has there been] a book that is going to sweep the market like wildfire to equal this one." But his primary objective in the letter was to explain how Malcolm's break with the Nation might affect the book's reception. He now envisioned a new chapter, "Iconoclast," in which Malcolm was suspended by "the man he had come to revere (and says he still does)." He would explain Malcolm's new organization and examine his relationship with Cassius Clay. He related Captain Joseph's plot to bomb Malcolm's car and suggested that the recent death threats, and the uncertainty of where Malcolm might turn next, made the whole story a tabloid dream. "For this man is *so* hot, so HOT, a subject, I know you agree . . . this book is *so* pregnant with millions or more sales potential, including to make foreign rights hotly bid for!"

At the end of March, Reynolds contacted Gibbs, informing him that Malcolm had asked for all future royalty payments to him to be paid to Muslim Mosque, Inc. Reynolds also enclosed a document signed by Malcolm approving of all chapters that had been completed. Malcolm pressed Doubleday for more money, asking for an advance of $2,500 on the outstanding $7,500 in advance payment he was to receive with the submission of the completed manuscript. McCormick approved Malcolm's request, but it was not until mid-June, when Malcolm had again left the country, that Gibbs finally forwarded the check.

When Malcolm finally returned to the United States on May 21, 1964, his first priority was to reinvent his public image—and urgently. The appearance of celebrating violence—whether through allusions to the likelihood of black unrest or through his urging blacks to arm themselves—alienated blacks and whites alike and undermined his efforts with the civil rights establishment. It was equally important to claim the support of leaders from the Middle East and Africa for his new cause. Newly energized, he resumed speaking and traveling at a breakneck pace. Accompanied by James 67X, on May 22 he flew to Chicago and held a press conference covering a broad range of topics, from Africa's resources to U.S. police brutality. The next night, before an audience of fifteen hundred at Chicago's Civic Opera House, he unveiled his new views in a debate with Louis Lomax. "Separation is not the goal of the Afro-American," he told the crowd—an announcement that must have created a stir among his black nationalist followers—"nor is integration his goal. They are merely methods toward his real end—respect as a human being."

Lomax and others there that night recognized that they were hearing something new. But what were the political implications, especially as related to the Black Freedom Movement? Sounding remarkably like Martin Luther King, Malcolm appealed for a politics that explicitly rejected racial hatred. There was a "universal law of justice," he declared, that was "sufficient to bring judgment upon those whites who are guilty of racism." He insisted that "it is not necessary for the victims—the Afro-American—to be vengeful. . . . [We] will do better to spend our time removing the scars from our people." Yet he also wanted to communicate the spirit of revolution he believed he had witnessed, especially in Cairo and Accra. According to the *Los Angeles Times*, the "greatest applause came when he said that 'unless the race issue is quickly settled, the 22 million American Negroes could easily adopt the guerrilla tactics of other deprived revolutionaries.'"

Malcolm's dilemma was that virtually all his enemies—and friends— perceived him as the high priest of black social revolution, and despite his letters from Mecca and abroad, and his dramatic address in Chicago, he continued to be perceived as an antiwhite demagogue. While the exhaustion of the civil rights movement had brought many activists around to his old way of thinking, his new ideas made for if not quite a reversal, then a major shift that caught them off guard. As Malcolm made his race-neutral views clear in Chicago, comedian and social critic Dick Gregory characterized him in a newspaper interview as a "necessary evil." Gregory's own position reflected the leftward shift away from the tactics of King. "I'm committed to nonviolence, but I'm sort of embarrassed by it," he said. Black militancy was growing, and if the struggle for civil rights "lasts six months longer, Malcolm X is the man you're all going to have to deal with." Gregory further warned *Los Angeles Times* columnist Drew Pearson, "This is a revolution and a good many Negroes have guns. . . . Out of 22 million Negroes, only one million are with Malcolm X. But a lot of them are saying, 'I'm tired of King.'" In Gregory's mind, "Malcolm X is getting to be about the only man who can stop a race riot." Yet most striking about these remarks was that Gregory and Malcolm were already largely in agreement. They had worked together on civil rights issues, and both men, despite real or imaginary differences on nonviolence, were members of ACT, the civil rights network established earlier that year that also included leaders as diverse as Congressman Adam Clayton Powell, Jr., and SNCC chairman John Lewis. If Malcolm's allies still perceived him as Gregory did, it was not surprising that others doubted the sincerity of his new views.

Malcolm's struggle to establish where he stood also had internal consequences. By late May, Muslim Mosque, Inc.'s core membership was about 125 strong; to James's dismay, however, the majority were not fresh from Mosque No. 7 but an eclectic bunch, most of whom had cut their ties to the Nation several years before. Malcolm's discontent with the Nation was only one of many varieties, and many MMI members had departed the Nation for reasons that had little to do with his new agenda. Some, remembered James, "were brothers who wanted to go and set things right about Ronald Stokes," in Los Angeles. They had quit the Nation back in 1962 "based upon Captain Joseph's throwing cold water on their aspirations" to punish Los Angeles police. Others had fallen away due to the Nation of Islam's rigor: "People who thought of [the NOI] as a good idea said, 'Yeah, but I can't make these moral adjustments in my life.' Some former Muslims could not go back to Mosque No. 7 because they were living, as we say down South, common law. And they were supposed to get married."

These MMI members would require a clear vision to direct their energies, but Malcolm had not fully defined the group's purpose. James assumed that hostilities with the Nation would be inevitable because it would view Muslim Mosque as a competitive sect, but he himself was not so clear on what exactly MMI was as a religious organization, "because Brother Malcolm wasn't specific." Despite the regular meetings, things were so disorganized that he was already tempted to resign as MMI coordinator. Worse yet, many of the lapsed Muslims flocking to the MMI still believed in the Nation's old theology. At a May 20 meeting, one questioner asked Malcolm whether "he had seen W. D. Fard" during his hajj to Mecca—receiving the reply that MMI members must reject "the old notions" of what constituted the Islamic faith and must embrace "reality."

One of the few newspaper articles that presented Malcolm's conversion in a positive light had appeared in the *Washington Post* on May 18. Dr. Mahmoud Shawarbi, by this time the director of the Islamic Center in New York City, was credited with being the "man who tamed Malcolm." He informed the *Post* that some Arab Muslims living in the United States had voiced "opposition to his tutelage of Malcolm X" stemming "from fears that [he] is not sincere and may use the religion and pilgrimage as a device to improve his public image." Shawarbi gave a full-throated defense. "I have no doubt of his sincerity," he said, recalling of Malcolm that "sometimes he would even cry while passages of the Holy Koran were being read." He accurately predicted that Malcolm would soon disavow his call for Negroes to form rifle clubs, and that his political efforts would reach beyond blacks. "If he admits all people . . . and goes about things quietly and Islamically, I am sure it will be a very big movement," he declared. The *Post* story noted, however, that the majority of civil rights observers in New York City were "adopting a wait and see attitude."

The FBI had also not forgotten Malcolm. Early on May 29, Malcolm received a call from its New York office, requesting an interview at his home. He consented, but before the FBI agents arrived he set up a tape recorder hidden under his couch. The agents were investigating a federal case based in Rochester, in which a man awaiting trial had given an incriminating statement about Malcolm. The agents wanted to know if Malcolm had attended an evening meeting of Muslims in that city on January 14 to plan the assassination of President Johnson. Fortunately, he could prove that on that date and time he was with Alex Haley, working on his autobiography; the statement given to the FBI was "so ridiculous," he later wrote, "that it sounds like to me that it was something that was invented even though it would be denied, it would still serve as a propaganda thing." The FBI agents asked him to provide "any information you want to give us about the Muslims." Yet the most curious part of the interview came when the agents questioned him on his current status in the NOI. Malcolm replied that he was still under the suspension ordered by Elijah Muhammad. "He is the only one who can give out any information. I couldn't say nothing behind what he would say." Far from revealing his break from the Nation, he instead vigorously defended its efforts in "cleaning up crime," and said, "I frankly believe that what Mr. Muhammad teaches is 1,000 percent true. . . . I believe it more strongly today than I did ten years ago." Why he should present himself as a faithful follower is puzzling, as he might have already guessed, or anticipated, that the Bureau would have infiltrated Muslim Mosque, Inc., and by this time would know something about the split. The most likely reason for his obfuscation is simpler. By going on record in support of the Nation, he may have been trying to lay the groundwork for his upcoming court case over the ownership of his home. Since Percy Sutton had contested legality of the Nation's attempt at forcing Malcolm out of his East Elmhurst, Queens, parsonage, Malcolm's legal strategy was to argue that the NOI had only suspended him; he was still the minister of Mosque No. 7 as well as the NOI's national minister. If he could establish a working relationship with the sect, then they might have success in arguing the right to the house in Queens.

Later that same day, Malcolm spoke at a public panel sponsored by the Trotskyist Militant Labor Forum. The forum was prompted by a series of newspaper articles about the supposed existence of a Harlem-based "hate gang" of young blacks who had been organized to kill whites. Malcolm took the opportunity to draw parallels between the legacies of European colonial rule he had seen in Africa with the system of institutional racism in the United States. Algeria under French colonial rule, he said, "was a police state; and this is what Harlem is. . . . The police in Harlem, their presence is like occupation forces, like an occupying army." He also linked the African-American struggle to the Chinese and Cuban revolutions. "The people of China grew tired of their oppressors and . . . rose up. They didn't rise up nonviolently. When Castro was up in the mountains in Cuba, they told him the odds were against him. Today he's sitting in Havana and all the power this country has can't remove him."

Of even greater significance was the way in which the speech indicated a profound change in Malcolm's economic program. For years, he had preached the Garvey-endorsed virtues of entrepreneurial capitalism, but here, when asked what kind of political and economic system he wanted, he observed that "all of the countries that are emerging today from under colonialism are turning toward socialism. I don't think it's an accident." For the first time, he publicly made the connection between racial oppression and capitalism, saying, "It's impossible for a white person to believe in capitalism and not believe in racism." Conversely, he noted, those who had a strong personal commitment to racial equality were usually "socialist or their political philosophy is socialism." What Malcolm seemed to be saying was that the Black Freedom Movement, which up to that point had focused on legal rights and legislative reforms, would ultimately have to take aim at America's private enterprise system. He drew an analogy to farm fowls to make his point: "It's impossible for the chicken to produce a duck egg—even though they both belong to the same family of fowl. . . . The system in this country cannot produce freedom for an Afro-American. . . . And if ever a chicken did produce a duck egg, I'm quite sure you would say it was certainly a revolutionary chicken!"

The pro-socialist remarks were strikingly different from anything Malcolm had said before. While traveling through Africa, he had mentioned nothing about socialism and little about economic development. However, Nkrumah's authoritarian regime in Ghana, the country that had most impressed him, was then embracing an economic alliance with the Soviet Union, and both Algeria and Egypt were already committed to versions of Arab socialism. These factors influenced his thinking, but perhaps weighing even more heavily was the Socialist Workers Party's enthusiastic support for Malcolm himself. The Trotskyists perceived him as potentially the leader of an entirely new movement among Negroes, one that would ultimately radicalize the entire American working class. Malcolm must have been aware of this, and would have seen the value of moving toward embracing parts of a socialist perspective. Besides, there were elements of the Trotskyist agenda, such as opposition to both the Democratic and Republican parties, with which he agreed. So while this new economic direction seemed to contradict his previous views, more accurately it represented a gradual evolution and not a sharp rejection. He remained a black nationalist and continued to emphasize the development of black-owned businesses in black communities.

He also recognized that while Muslim Mosque, Inc., needed to be expanded to other cities to consolidate his followers among Muslims, his priority had to be the secular political organization that Lynne Shifflett and Peter Bailey had been quietly working to build for him. "Within the next eight days," he promised in a May 30 interview, he would "launch an organization which will be open for the participation of all Negroes, and we will be willing to accept the support of people of all races." The first goal of this new group would be to submit "the case of the American Negro before the United Nations." What Malcolm envisioned with the United Nations was a strategic shift in civil rights activism within the United States. Instead of passing legislation reforms through Congress, he sought to present blacks' grievances to international bodies in hopes of global intervention. Under the banner of human rights, issues that had long been perceived as domestic or parochial would be presented on a world stage.

He also appeared to offer an olive branch to the Nation of Islam over the issue of his Elmhurst home. A hearing on the case had been scheduled in Queens Civil Court for June 3, but now he told the *Amsterdam News* that if the officers of Mosque No. 7 allowed him to address their members and to defend himself against the charges, he was prepared to abide by the sentiments of the majority. If the NOI members asked him to move, "I'll give the house up," he vowed. "I want to settle this situation quietly, privately, and peacefully, not in the white man's court, whom the Muslims preach is the devil." But better than anyone else, he knew that the Nation was not a debating society with democratic procedures. He issued the appeal not because he expected reconciliation, but for public relations purposes: to illustrate a reasonable position to blacks outside the Nation of Islam.

Several days later, the Queens Civil Court postponed his eviction trial, and Malcolm once again complained to a reporter that this "should be brought before a Muslim court. . . . They are deviating from our religious principles by bringing me here." Malcolm surely knew that the NOI, viewing him as a "heretic," would never consent to resolve the dispute in a Muslim court. The fact alone that Malcolm had not purchased the property with his own funds made it extremely unlikely that he would prevail in court.

Meanwhile he continued to mobilize supporters for his new secular organization. Several weeks after returning from Africa, he assigned the task of drafting a founding document, the "Statement of Basic Aims and Objectives," to a coterie of political activists, intellectuals, and celebrities, including novelist John Oliver Killens and historian John Henrik Clarke. Some of the working sessions of the group were held at a motel on West 153rd Street and Eighth Avenue, the northern boundary of Harlem. On June 4, Malcolm traveled to Philadelphia with Benjamin 2X Goodman, a guard named Lafayette Burton, and one other individual—probably James 67X—to attend several meetings, including one at a private home with seven other people, and another at a Philadelphia barbershop. His primary purpose was to consolidate his supporters in the city, with the immediate goal of starting a Muslim Mosque, Inc., branch there. But he also launched what could later be seen as the first salvo in a battle with the Nation of Islam that would soon grow into an all-out war. During these meetings he voiced for the first time his suspicion that NOI national secretary John Ali was an FBI informant; he said the same of prominent minister Lonnie X Cross.

In Washington, J. Edgar Hoover had grown similarly frustrated with the march of events. False reports concerning the Harlem "hate gang" had reached him, and his suspicion fell on Malcolm, whose rising popularity as a black leader had grown unexpectedly despite his expulsion from the Nation. On Friday, June 5, an irate Hoover sent a Western Union telegram to the Bureau's New York office, with blunt orders: "Do something about Malcolm X enough of this black violence in New York."

—

Malcolm could have chosen a different path, but something within him sought a final resolution between himself and the Nation of Islam. On a personal level, he was lashing out in anger and grief at the father figure who had betrayed him in the basest way. Yet he had become convinced that the successful propagation of orthodox Islam in the United States would not be possible until Elijah Muhammad's infidelities and the internal corruption of the Nation were thoroughly exposed. What may have also prompted Malcolm was his recognition that the racial separatism he had preached as an NOI minister was counterproductive and that African Americans had to reach out, especially to Third World people, to achieve meaningful social change.

The Nation of Islam had not shied from making its stance plain. Throughout the month of May, Nation leaders and ministers continued to whip up antagonism toward Malcolm at every opportunity. In every NOI mosque, the faithful were obligated to swear fealty to Elijah Muhammad and to denounce Malcolm as a heretic. On May 15 the members of Mosque No. 7 were told that Malcolm was "a hypocrite and a liar." They were reminded that their former minister himself "used to say that he would punch in the mouth anyone saying the wrong thing about Muhammad." In Buffalo, at New York's Mosque No. 23, members were read a letter from Chicago headquarters indicating that back in 1959 Elijah Muhammad had warned Malcolm not to appear on Mike Wallace's program. "The wrath of Allah would be brought down on Malcolm X," the letter predicted, "for his actions in first believing and then not believing in the words of Allah." At Mosque No. 17 in Joliet, Illinois, on May 31, members were warned that Malcolm had advocated gun clubs; therefore, they were advised not to keep firearms around their homes "because the 'devil' [white man] is watching."

In a sense, Malcolm's departure in itself represented a threat to the Nation, and his formation of a new organization that was likely to siphon members prompted a firm response. In May, Raymond Sharrieff had put the Fruit of Islam on guard against any attempt by Malcolm to gain a foothold. At one FOI meeting in Chicago Sharrieff informed members that Malcolm's men were "drafting brothers" into the MMI. If any Fruit were approached, they were required to report back. "We want to discover what Malcolm is up to. If his men say they are Muslims and start trouble, they can make us look bad. Find out everything you can and report it to me right away." The next month, Sharrieff addressed the Mosque No. 7 Fruit membership, telling the crowd that "Elijah Muhammad used to like former minister Malcolm X more than he did his own son, but Malcolm X hurt Elijah Muhammad deeply." Sharrieff then predicted, "Malcolm will soon die out." An FBI informant told the Bureau that Sharrieff had made clear how Malcolm was to be treated: "Big Red is the worst of the lot as a defector. He is a hypocrite and a snake in the grass. . . . If anyone misuses the name of Elijah Muhammad the Muslims should put their fist in the mouth of the infamy to the elbow."

Whether motivated by strategy, expedience, or something deeper and more personal, in the early days of June Malcolm began to air publicly his grievances against the Nation of Islam. Occasionally, he drew back from this kind of criticism, as if he knew that he was provoking a response he would not be able to contain, but these moments were—like the FBI interview— probably intended to provide himself reasonable cover in his legal quest to keep his home. Yet the attacks, which cut deeply at the Messenger's claim of divinity, forced the Nation to a place where retaliation seemed necessary for survival. During the month of June the fight between Malcolm and the Nation of Islam arrived at a point of no return.

On June 6, Malcolm had the opportunity to engage in a Third World dialogue when three Japanese writers, representing the Hiroshima/Nagasaki World Peace Study Mission, visited Harlem. All three were *hibakusha*, atomic bomb survivors, and familiar with Malcolm's activities. A reception was held at the Harlem apartment of Japanese-American activist Yuri (Mary) Nakahara Kochiyama, who soon joined the OAAU; Malcolm was invited to attend but never responded. A few minutes after the formal program began at two thirty p.m., however, Malcolm showed up, bringing James 67X, who spoke fluent Japanese, and several security people. Following the formal presentation, scores of friendly people surrounded him, wanting to shake his hand. Kochiyama recalled that Malcolm said to the Japanese delegation, "You have been scarred by the atom bomb. . . . We have also been scarred. The bomb that hit us was racism." Several Japanese journalists also attended the event, giving Malcolm a platform. He praised the leadership of Mao Zedong and the government of the People's Republic of China, noting that Mao had been correct to pursue policies favoring the peasantry over the working class, because the peasants were responsible for feeding the whole country. He also expressed his opposition to the growing U.S. military engagement in Asia, saying, "The struggle of Vietnam is the struggle of the whole Third World—the struggle against colonialism, neocolonialism, and imperialism."

Several hours later, James 67X boarded a plane bound for the West Coast. His assignment was to obtain the signatures on legal documents of several women impregnated by Elijah Muhammad, arranging photographs of the women and setting up interviews with the *Los Angeles Herald-Dispatch*. James completed the assignment; although the women were prepared to file legal charges against Muhammad, they were extremely reluctant to set forth their accusations in the national media.

The next night Malcolm was scheduled to speak at an MMI rally at the Audubon Ballroom; the event had been advertised as a "Special Report from Africa to the People of Harlem." In the hours before he was to appear, he made many phone calls to female Muslims in an attempt to find others who would corroborate the stories of Muhammad's illicit lovers. Once onstage, prompted by a question from the audience, he declared that the Nation of Islam would commit murder in order to suppress the exposure of Elijah Muhammad's serial infidelities and out-of-wedlock children, and he told the crowd that he knew of the infidelities from the Messenger's very own son, Wallace Muhammad. The rally marked the first time that Malcolm set forth, in a detailed manner, the sexual misconduct of Muhammad before a Harlem audience. Given the size of the crowd—about 450 people—several loyal members of Mosque No. 7 were sure to have been present. One can only imagine the fury of Captain Joseph and his enforcers. News of the comments quickly made its way back to Phoenix and Chicago. The next morning, Betty received an anonymous phone call, the first of what would be hundreds of death threats against Malcolm.

The following day Malcolm contacted CBS News, urging the network to air a nationally televised exposé of Muhammad. That evening he appeared on the *Barry Gray Show* on New York radio, yet during a fifty-minute-long appearance, he chose not to mention either the out-of-wedlock children or the infidelities. Instead, Malcolm talked about his African tour, describing the continent as the "greatest place on Earth"; he also insisted that there was no difference politically between segregationist governor George Wallace of Alabama and President Lyndon Johnson.

While he leveled his criticisms against the Nation of Islam, he continued to push his new organization. On June 9 the first decisive organizational meeting of Malcolm's secular political advisers was held at the Riverside Drive apartment of Lynne Shifflett. Unlike previous clandestine discussions, it finally brought together the idealistic young activists and the seasoned Harlem veterans. In the latter group were the historian John Henrik Clarke, the photographer Robert Haggins, the novelist John Oliver Killens, and the journalist Sylvester Leeks. It was Clarke's suggestion to give themselves the name Organization of Afro-American Unity, modeled after the Organization of African Unity, founded on May 25 the previous year. He thought that the OAU's charter might provide a blueprint for the OAAU. This may have been a little ambitious. First, the OAU was a bloc of African nations joining together to achieve strategic objectives, not an ad hoc coalition of individuals. The OAAU was not even a united front of black American groups but resembled more a top-down sect, with Malcolm as charismatic headman. Second, there was little consideration about how decisions would be made and who would be responsible for organizing—and paying for—public events.

Malcolm handled these difficult questions in characteristic manner: by dumping them into James 67X's lap. Driving over to Shifflett's apartment, he curtly explained to James that "he didn't form" this group, but "he wanted it formed. He told me that I was responsible for it being formed." James immediately sensed trouble, and when he reached Shifflett's his suspicions were quickly confirmed. "I went up to [Shifflett's] apartment there thinking the thing is being formed," he recalled, "and they're sitting around talking about what great organizers each of them is." Malcolm later made Shifflett the OAAU's organizing secretary, a role equivalent to James's for the MMI. Their competitive positions fostered an animosity so deep that even decades later James 67X could barely utter her name. From the beginning, James recalled, "Malcolm treated them in an entirely different manner than he treated us." The OAAU people never contributed funds "in charity" to help support Betty and the household. MMI loyalists "were accustomed to be told what to do and doing it. We didn't quarrel with Brother Malcolm. If he said such and such, if he *hinted* at something, I was on it and I told the brothers to do it."

On the same day as the OAAU meeting, Malcolm was the featured guest on a Mike Wallace news program, broadcast by NBC in New York City, on which he emphasized his new position on race—and blamed his "previous antiwhite statements" on his former membership in the Nation of Islam. As the weekend approached, Malcolm prepared to depart for Boston, where that Sunday at Ella's house he was to speak to a large number of potential supporters, including representatives from the National Urban League and CORE. By Friday the public campaign against the Nation had reached fever pitch, and when he appeared on the radio to blame his departure on "a moral problem" within the sect, the show's host told listeners that Malcolm had arrived at the studio under armed guard for fear of attack. Malcolm went into detail on Muhammad's misconduct and reported that Wallace Muhammad had confirmed the behavior that "was still going on." He estimated that Muhammad had at least six out-of-wedlock children. That evening he went on to repeat these charges on the Jerry Williams program, aired in Boston on WMEX radio, and claimed that Louis X had known about them first.

The appearances ratcheted tensions in Boston, but the next morning Malcolm quietly departed the city ahead of schedule; a hastily organized meeting of civil rights insiders and prominent black entertainers at Sidney Poitier's home in upstate New York on June 13 called him away. This meeting was unprecedented in several respects. First, it brought together individuals, or their representatives, who reflected major currents within the Black Freedom Movement. Dr. King, at that moment in a Saint Augustine, Florida, jail for leading desegregation protests in that city, was represented by attorney Clarence Jones, the general counsel for the Gandhi Society for Human Rights; Jones had been "authorized to speak for King." Also in attendance were Whitney Young of the National Urban League, representatives of A. Philip Randolph and CORE, Benjamin Davis of the Communist Party, and artists Ossie Davis, Ruby Dee, and Sidney Poitier. Their conversation was probably focused on ways to build a common agenda between divergent groups within the Black Freedom Movement. It was Malcolm, however, who presented the most attractive proposal: his plan, as Ossie Davis put it, was "to bring the Negro question before the United Nations to internationalize the whole question and bring it before the whole world." The tactic was similar to that of the black communist leader William Patterson, who in the late 1940s sought to present evidence of lynchings and racial discrimination in the United States before the UN. Clarence Jones was taken with this approach, suggesting that they should present their case to the United Nations that September. Malcolm was given the task of contacting those governments in Africa and the Middle East that might be expected to endorse the initiative. His subsequent activities abroad in the second half of 1964 were an attempt to implement this strategy.

Through illegal wiretaps and informants, the FBI was intensely aware of this clandestine meeting. On June 13 the Bureau's New York office teletyped the director that it "consisted of a discussion of [the] general future of [the] civil rights movement in US . . . the best idea presented was subject's idea to internationalize the civil rights movement by taking it to the United Nations." A note attached to this report from the Domestic Intelligence Division dated June 14 indicated that it was being disseminated "to the Department, State, CIA and military intelligence agencies."

In Boston the following day, a crowd of 120 people packed Ella's home to hear Benjamin 2X, whom Malcolm had assigned to replace him. After the meeting, Benjamin set out to fly back to New York. He was accompanied by seven local supporters, who drove a convoy of three automobiles, with Benjamin in the first car. En route, a white Lincoln attempted to crash into the lead car, nearly forcing it off the road. Minutes later, as the convoy entered the Callahan Tunnel, which connects the downtown center to Logan airport, a Chevrolet packed with NOI members sped past Benjamin's car and then attempted to force it into the tunnel's concrete wall. One of the passengers in Benjamin's car brandished a shotgun at the would-be assailants, who then eased back. Still carrying the shotgun for protection, the group entered the airport, where they were promptly arrested before the ticket counter. All eight men were arraigned in East Boston District Court on June 15 and released on one thousand dollars bail each.

The attempted ambush marked the first time that an NOI crew made a serious attempt to wound or kill Malcolm or his key lieutenants in a public setting. Moreover, the Nation recognized that most police departments held such animosity toward Malcolm that they would not aggressively investigate assaults against him or those associated with him.

News of the arrests quickly reached Malcolm in New York as he prepared for a Sunday rally at the Audubon. Onstage that night, eight MMI brothers with rifles flanked him as he bluntly laid out the case of Muhammad's sexual misconduct. He also indicated that while he was still in the Nation, he had consulted with Louis X, Captain Joseph, Maceo X, and several others to resolve the scandal privately. Between 1956 and 1962, Elijah Muhammad had "fathered six to seven" out-of-wedlock children, he explained. The Messenger justified his actions by claiming that "Allah told him to do it." Those Malcolm had consulted then "conspired" to expel him from the Nation. By expanding his grievance from Muhammad and the Chicago headquarters to include Louis X and other prominent ministers, Malcolm was declaring war on the entire leadership group of the Nation of Islam.

It was in this toxic atmosphere that the civil suit filed by the Nation was finally heard, the next morning, June 15, in Queens County Civil Court. The trial, which lasted two days, was heard by Judge Maurice Wahl; the Nation was represented by Joseph Williams and Malcolm's attorney was Percy Sutton. Several local newspapers revealed that Malcolm's life recently had been threatened; the NYPD responded by placing thirty-two officers at the trial for his protection. Muslim Mosque, Inc., sent a modest group of ten to the trial, while Mosque No. 7 was represented by a phalanx of fifty Fruit, who stared angrily at Malcolm's people. One of Malcolm's supporters was observed outside the crowded courtroom carrying a rifle. When questioned, he was found to be carrying two unloaded rifles and no ammunition, so no arrest was made.

Malcolm's game plan at the trial was to take advantage of the general lack of interest in Muslim affairs on the part of the white media by suggesting that, contrary to much evidence, he was still a loyal follower of Elijah Muhammad, but his faith had been rewarded with perfidy and betrayal. The Queens house—which he had done nothing to lose—was bought for him and should remain his. At the beginning of his two-hour-long testimony, Malcolm noted that Mosque No. 7 had been incorporated in the state of New York in 1956, that he was one of "the original incorporators," and that his services to that organization had "never been terminated." His central argument was that not only had he not resigned from the Nation of

Islam, but "no Muslim minister has ever resigned." He described to the court his relatively recent appointment as acting minister of the Washington, D.C., mosque. The mosque's former minister had been removed from his post, but had been permitted to defend himself in a hearing before the entire congregation, which Malcolm had chaired.

Under cross-examination by NOI attorney Williams, Malcolm argued that Muhammad's involvement in the matter disqualified him from chairing such a committee over his own case. He blamed Captain Joseph for "poisoning the community here to the point where there could not be a hearing. They just put me in limbo until they had a chance to solidify their position with false information and this is why they could never give me a hearing in front of the Muslim[s]."

But Williams was unsatisfied with Malcolm's arguments. "Isn't it a fact," he asked Malcolm, "that the Honorable Elijah Muhammad can remove any minister he wants to?" Malcolm reluctantly agreed, explaining that Muhammad "is a divine man. . . . He always follows the divine religious procedure. He is a stickler . . . it has always been his policy never to handle a person in any way that a person could accuse him of an injustice."

Williams countered "that the Honorable Elijah Muhammad removes ministers with or without cause and that has been the custom since the movement started." Malcolm vigorously disagreed. "No. The Honorable Elijah Muhammad has never removed a minister without cause."

Williams then took a different tack. "When this suspension without cause was taken," he asked, "did you ever seek any legal remedy to restore you to your position?"

"I tried to keep it private," Malcolm replied. "I tried to keep it out of the court and I tried to keep it out of the public and I asked for a hearing in private . . . because there were facts that I thought would be destructive to the Muslim movement."

"You are making it public now," Williams replied.

"Yes," Malcolm acknowledged, "only because they have driven me to the point where I have to tell it in order to protect myself."

"Isn't it a fact that you have organized another mosque?" Williams asked.

Malcolm at first dodged the question, but finally admitted that he had started Muslim Mosque, Inc., "to spread the Honorable Elijah Muhammad's teaching among the twenty-two million non-Muslims."

As Williams continued to hammer away, the framework of Malcolm's argument—that he continued to be a faithful follower of Elijah Muhammad—fell apart. The evidence against him was simply all too plain for anyone willing to look closely. Williams noted, for example, that many MMI members were former NOI members. He pointed out that Malcolm had announced to the press that he was "no longer affiliated" with Mosque No. 7, and that he had renounced the leadership and spiritual authority of Muhammad. Therefore, he concluded, the East Elmhurst duplex rightfully belonged to the Nation of Islam.

But Malcolm wasn't yet ready to concede. He pointed out that he actually held two formal positions within the NOI: minister of Mosque No. 7 and national minister. He had been suspended, technically, as Mosque No. 7's head, but Muhammad had never abolished the national minister's office. He argued that the East Elmhurst residence agreement was exclusively "between me and the Honorable Elijah Muhammad," that the place had been "purchased for me," and that the Messenger "told me the house should be mine." Elijah himself had emphasized that this was truly a gift to him personally: "He told me over and over that it should be in my name, that it was for me because of the work I was doing and had been doing."

Williams tried to undercut this argument by implying that Malcolm had been skimming money from the Nation for years—much of his public speaking honoraria surely had gone into his pocket. He tried to present Malcolm's life in the Nation as a long, cushy ride on the organization's dime, asking, "Isn't it also a fact that every mosque you go to, that the mosque themself [*sic*] takes care of your expenses?" Malcolm fought back, denying such claims as slanderous, and asserting that the real reason for his "suspension" in December 1963 was due to a "very private" matter. "I never sought to gain anything personally from the Nation of Islam. This is why I lived [at the beginning of his ministry] in a room and then lived in three rooms." But Williams continued to question Malcolm's motives. "Now, sir, when this house was being purchased," he noted, "you were not even around when they met to buy this house. When they had the first discussion in the mosque about the house, you weren't around, were you?" He was astutely using Malcolm's proselytizing travels to establish his lack of interest in the acquisition of the property.

Malcolm must have been in anguish, sitting before a white judge, listening to himself being accused of theft and corruption in an organization for which he once would have gladly sacrificed his life. He could accept many things, but not dishonor. And the legal maneuvering was merely a way of avoiding the central issue, the real reason for the split, which he remained hesitant to bring up on the record. He told Williams that the funds purchasing the residence never came from the incorporated Mosque No. 7; no mosque trustees met to issue a check covering the home's down payment. "It came from the spiritual body from the Muslims."

Then, after nearly two hours, he finally told the court that "the Honorable Elijah Muhammad had taken on nine wives besides the one that he had. . . . This is the reason for my suspension." He emphasized that he had been prepared to keep "the whole thing secret and private if they would give me a hearing. . . . They would rather take the public court than keep it quiet among Muslims."

What Malcolm may not have fully appreciated until the trial was that the ideological campaign against him was turning into a religious jihad, and the issues raised by the Queens trial only increased the tensions between the two camps. On the first day of courtroom proceedings, 180 men attended Mosque No. 7's regular FOI meeting, whose topic was "So What if He [Elijah Muhammad] Is Not All Pure, Look What He Did for You and I [*sic*]." During this lecture, the speaker asserted, "We should destroy Malcolm." An FOI captain at the meeting—probably Joseph—instructed the Fruit, saying, "Malcolm is not to be touched, the rest is okay"—a statement that amounted to a declaration of open season on any Malcolm loyalist.

The next evening, shortly after eleven p.m., six of Malcolm's followers, believing rumors that their leader had been either kidnapped or murdered, drove to Mosque No. 7, at 102 West 116th Street. The man instigating the confrontation was William George, who was armed with a .30 caliber M-1 carbine rifle containing a clip with thirty rounds of ammunition. Fifty-one-year-old Herbert Dudley, another Malcolmite, brought a 6.75 Beretta rifle. About thirty to thirty-five Nation members rushed out into the street to confront the attackers with improvised weapons of self-defense, such as broom handles. For a few minutes there was a tense standoff, since neither side was prepared to start the hostilities. The NYPD raced to the street scene and largely concurred with the NOI group that Malcolm's people had provoked the incident. The Malcolmites were arrested and their firearms seized. A day later, at Mosque No. 24 in Richmond, Virginia, Minister Nicholas of Washington, D.C., declared that "Malcolm X really should be killed for teaching against Elijah Muhammad."

———

For as much as the trial and the increasing threats on his life consumed Malcolm, they did not keep him from maintaining a hectic schedule of speeches and organization building. Already he sensed that his days were numbered—"I'm probably a dead man already," he'd candidly told Mike Wallace—and as the summer progressed he pushed through events with great speed, straining to accomplish his goals. He accepted many speaking invitations, including one from Henry Kissinger at Harvard, and continued to work at simultaneously building the size and credibility of both Muslim Mosque, Inc., and the Organization of Afro-American Unity. Chairing an MMI business meeting in Harlem, he announced that he was considering asking MMI members to tithe ten dollars weekly, for a period of six months. A report would then be circulated on "all the money taken in" along with all expenditures. His plan was to establish a newspaper similar to *Muhammad Speaks*. MMI branch organizations were also to be established in Boston and Philadelphia, then in other cities. It was finally clear that Malcolm envisioned a national Islamic network that one day could be truly competitive with the Nation of Islam. At an MMI rally in late June he praised Islam as "the only true faith" for black people and promoted the OAAU, which would develop "an educational program" to highlight blacks' contributions to history. This new formation would not engage in sit-ins, he promised, but instead "they will take what is rightfully theirs."

He also returned to his correspondence with a renewed sense of urgency. News of a workers' strike in Nigeria had reached Malcolm, so he wrote to his friend Joseph Iffeorah, of the Ministry of Works and Surveys, asking for information. Malcolm was also highly attentive in efforts to recruit new followers. A letter he wrote on June 22 to a young, single African-American woman working at the *New Yorker* magazine displayed charm and flattery. "Your recent correspondence is really one of the best written letters that I've ever received," she replied. It was "very poetic, but at the same time your thoughts were very clear." The young woman told Malcolm that she did not want to join any organization because she wanted to feel "free." Malcolm reminded her that it takes "organization to coordinate the talents of various people." He urged her to come to the OAAU's founding public gathering at the Audubon on June 28: "Even if you have no desire to become an active participant, I do wish you would come out Sunday as a spectator." The young woman, Sara Mitchell, not only attended that rally, but within several months became an invaluable leader of the OAAU.

The progress Malcolm made in these weeks was constantly under threat of being undone by the growing violence of his increasing public feud with the Nation. In the streets, things were getting out of control. In the Corona neighborhood of Queens, assistant minister Larry 4X Prescott had recently established a Muslim restaurant on Northern Boulevard. On June 22 seventeen-year-old Bryan Kingsley, a Malcolm supporter, was loitering at the restaurant's entrance, talking tough. Larry went outside and smacked the boy hard across the head before—along with other NOI members—he chased Kingsley down the street. The boy telephoned Tom Wallace, Ruby Dee's brother and a strong advocate of Malcolm's. Wallace drove his station wagon to the restaurant, pulled out a rifle, and confronted Larry and another NOI member. "Thomas and I [had] worked together, and I knew something about [his] character," Larry 4X recalled in a 2006 interview. "I said, 'Well, go ahead and shoot if you're going to shoot me.'" Wallace warned him not to approach him, but Larry walked toward him, convinced he would not pull the trigger. When he got close enough, Larry grabbed the rifle and, turning the weapon butt-first, "beat him with it. And then I broke out all of his car windows." His face shattered and bloody, Wallace filed charges with the NYPD, which arrested Larry; Larry in return filed assault charges against Wallace, who was also arrested. Both men were charged five hundred dollars bail, with their cases remanded to the Queens Criminal Court.

Malcolm was extremely disturbed by Wallace's beating. From a personal perspective, it was a deep betrayal: Larry 4X had been one of his trusted protégés. Perhaps worse, the incident threatened to damage connections he needed for his political work, as Ossie Davis and Ruby Dee had become pivotal to his access to the black arts and entertainment community. To the *Amsterdam News*, Malcolm asserted that Muhammad was responsible for the escalating violence. "The followers of Elijah Muhammad," Malcolm explained, "will not do anything unless he tells them to."

Larry 4X clearly recalled his Queens Criminal Court appearance because he had "my suit on, and bow tie." All the other prisoners began to laugh. "They said, 'Look at this guy, and he's clean as a pimp, and he has assaulted somebody!'" Soon after Larry was taken to court, Malcolm entered the chamber: "He came over to me," Larry recalled. "He said—and this is the part where I have lost my respect for him—he said, 'Larry, you're dead.'" The court dismissed the charges against both men, but the damage was done. "That was the last time I had any words with Malcolm," Larry stated. "Then things just got progressively worse."

The beating of Tom Wallace and similar incidents in these weeks prompted Malcolm to issue an "open letter" of conciliation to Elijah Muhammad. Both groups, Malcolm wrote, needed to address the civil rights issues confronting Southern blacks. "Instead of wasting all this energy fighting each other we should be working in unity . . . with other leaders and organizations."

On the surface, it was an appeal for the feuding sides to end the violence, but to those in the Nation who could read between the lines, Malcolm's letter was yet another provocation. The appeal asked Muhammad how, since the Nation had refused to use violence in response to "white racists" in Los Angeles and Rochester, it could employ violence against another Black Muslim group. Muhammad's earlier failure to authorize retaliatory violence against excessive police force was still a sore point for many of Malcolm's followers.

In the midst of the feuding, Malcolm managed to steer the Organization of Afro-American Unity to its triumphant public birth. At a major rally on June 28, a thousand people gathered at the Audubon Ballroom to celebrate the group's official founding. Just over twenty blocks away, the Nation of Islam was holding its own rally before a crowd at least six times as large, but at the Audubon a pivotal event in black American history was unfolding, with the emergence of a militant black nationalist political group that had the potential for redefining both the civil rights mainstream and black electoral politics. And unlike the Nation of Islam or even Muslim Mosque, Inc., the Organization of Afro-American Unity was purely secular, which vastly expanded its potential reach. As Herman Ferguson recalled, "I felt that if Malcolm could . . . present his politics minus the religious side of it, that would remove a lot of the concerns that many black people had." This sentiment could be felt deeply among the group's early organizers. Even before the founding rally, the "nonreligious people" like Shifflett, Ferguson, and others had long felt "they were not a part of the old guard. There was tension and resentment." Finally, though, it was their moment, as Malcolm publicly reached out to the mainstream of the civil rights struggle and the most progressive elements of the black middle class. Present at the rally to acknowledge Malcolm's turn were attorney Conrad Lynn, writer Paule Marshall, newspaper editor William Tatum, and Juanita Poitier, Sidney Poitier's wife.

The high point of the rally was Malcolm's reading of the OAAU's "Statement of Basic Aims and Objectives," in which the new group dedicated itself "to unify[ing] the Americans of African descent in their fight for Human Rights and Dignity" and promised to "dedicate ourselves to the building of a political, economic, and social system of justice and peace" in the United States. The statement praised, among other historic documents, the Declaration of Independence and the U.S. Constitution, which "are the principles in which we believe and these documents if put into practice represent the essence of mankind's hopes and good intentions." Central to the OAAU's program was Malcolm's campaign to bring the United States before the United Nations, where "we can indict Uncle Sam for the continued criminal injustices that our people experience in this government." The bold statement placed the OAAU firmly within the rich protest traditions of black America going back to Frederick Douglass in the nineteenth century.

Instead of demonizing whites, Malcolm now offered them a role in his human rights initiative. White allies could contribute financially to the OAAU, and they were encouraged to work for racial justice within white communities. Black liberation, however, came with a price: OAAU membership cost two dollars, and members were expected to donate one dollar each week to the organization. The group also promised to mobilize the entire African-American community "block by block to make the community aware of its power and potential." Taken in the broad view, the OAAU's founding marked the first major attempt to consolidate black revolutionary nationalism since the age of Garvey.

In June, Paul Reynolds negotiated a "one-shot sale" of excerpts from the *Autobiography* that would appear in the *Saturday Evening Post* prior to the book's publication. To obtain Doubleday's consent, Reynolds volunteered to cut the authors' advances to $15,000. Since Haley and Malcolm together had already been paid a total of $17,769.75, the authors had to agree to pay back $2,500, plus not to request any additional advance money from Doubleday until after the book was published. Unfortunately Haley was still hard-pressed for money, and the new Doubleday agreement provided no material incentive to finish the book project.

Although Malcolm's schedule had become too hectic to accommodate new interviews with Haley, the two men continued to communicate. On June 8, Haley confessed that, after getting a postcard from Malcolm, he had submitted it to "one of the ranking grapho-analysts in the country" and wanted to include "such objective findings" in his afterword of the autobiography. The analyst described Malcolm as an outgoing personality, broadminded and possessing "a definite feeling of purpose, a calling. His goals are practical." But the subject was also "not a deep thinker" and showed "a lack of decisiveness in his makeup." Despite the questionable basis of the report, Haley wrote confidently that "it comes very close to you, I feel, from my own personal appraisals."

Less than two weeks later, Haley again wrote to Malcolm, as well as to Paul Reynolds. In his seven-page typed letter to Malcolm, he urged him to exercise caution: "I sometimes think that you do not really understand what will be the effect of this book. There has never been, at least not in our time, any other book like it. Do you realize that to do these things you will have to be *alive*?" He pleaded with his subject to consider Betty's predicament if he should die—"and for the rest of her life, trying to explain to your and her four children what a man you were." To Reynolds, Haley revealed an entirely different agenda. Reviewing the "wealth of material" in the still unfinished manuscript, he wrote that the book could benefit from "careful, successive rewritings, distilling, aligning, [and] balancing . . . to get it right." Its conclusion, he now recognized, was "all important," because it placed his subject "on the world stage." He cited an article by Malcolm, "Why I Am for Goldwater," and the existence of his recent tour diary, a "soupçon of even fissionable international religious and political concerns." Haley said that he wanted to edit and expand both, asserting that the texts would "keep [Malcolm] on-stage, while providing him with more funds." (These extraordinary materials would not be seen by scholars or the general public until 2008. Malcolm never had the time, or opportunity, to develop his travel diaries into a second book.) Within the severe limitations of his schedule, he read through Haley's *Autobiography* drafts as they were produced. The final essay chapters that had been prepared earlier were cut, a decision that may have been Haley's alone; these are what today are called the book's "missing chapters." Malcolm probably sensed that the *Autobiography* might become a crucial part of his political legacy, and he became more determined to complete the project. Ironically, his extended absence from the United States beginning in July gave Haley an excuse for not working vigorously on the manuscript. As the summer began, Haley moved his attention to more potentially lucrative writing projects. He was already pitching to Kenneth McCormick a book manuscript idea called *Before This Anger*, which a decade later would become the best seller *Roots*.

In the meantime, Malcolm was besieged—by writers, by other activists seeking favors and alliances, and by people who just wanted to have a piece of history. Most met him only once or twice but were changed by these encounters; some were transformed by his rhetoric or writings, still others by his message.

Robert Penn Warren, one of America's most respected Southern writers in the sixties, met Malcolm at the Hotel Theresa on June 2, where they engaged in a mutually revealing conversation. Warren was at first surprised at how animated Malcolm was: "I discovered that the pale, dull yellowish face that had seemed so veiled, so stony, as though beyond all feeling, had flashed into its merciless, leering life—the sudden wolfish grin, the pale pink lips drawn hard back to show the strong teeth." Both intimidated and fascinated, Warren presented Malcolm with a series of scenarios in which white liberals had provided assistance to blacks. When Warren mentioned that "the white man" had been willing to go to jail to oppose segregation, Malcolm retorted, "My personal attitude is that he has done nothing to solve the problem." Malcolm went on to emphasize the necessity to transform institutional arrangements in the U.S. political economy, if blacks were ever to exercise power. Stunned, Warren asked for another chance for liberalism: "You don't see in the American system the possibility of self-regeneration?" "No," Malcolm replied.

Malcolm was clearly toying with Warren—it was several weeks later that he would affirm precisely Warren's point, in his appeal to the country's founding documents at the opening conference of the OAAU, a claim on democracy he could not have advanced had he judged U.S. political institutions incapable of reform. Warren nervously went on to inquire about the new movement's political objectives. In practical terms, what Malcolm sought was not fundamentally different from what waves of European immigrants—the Irish, Italians, and Jews—fought to achieve: equitable representation of their ethnic groups within all levels of government. "Once the black man becomes the political master of his own community, it means the politicians will also be black, which means that he will be sending black representatives even at the federal level." Malcolm's strategy was hardly a Leninist recipe for social revolution, but Warren, a guilty white liberal, could not understand his objectives. He gave far too much weight to Malcolm's incendiary rhetoric and insufficient commentary on the social program he was advancing. At one tense moment Warren inquired if Malcolm believed in political assassination, "and [he] turns the hard, impassive face and veiled eyes upon me, and says, 'I wouldn't know anything about that.'"

At the other end of the political spectrum was a series of meetings between Malcolm and the political activist Max Stanford (later known as Muhammad Ahmed). The two had first met in 1962, when Stanford, then twenty-one, had sought out Malcolm to ask if he should join the Nation of Islam. Malcolm had shocked him by replying, "You can do more for the Honorable Elijah Muhammad by working on the outside." The young man had taken Malcolm's words to heart, and that same year he and Cleveland activist Donald Freeman created a small, militant nationalist group, the Revolutionary Action Movement (RAM). Based originally at Central State University in Ohio, the network developed a presence in Philadelphia in the 1960s and soon had relationships with CORE chapters in Brooklyn and Cleveland. Ideologically, they were influenced by black militants like the exiled Robert Williams and the independent Marxists Grace Lee and James Boggs. The Revolutionary Action Movement perceived itself as an underground organization, "a third force," Stanford later explained, "between the Nation of Islam and SNCC." In late May 1964, Stanford arrived in Harlem asking to see Malcolm. The two met at the Harlem restaurant 22 West, Malcolm's favorite, where Stanford made an outrageously bold request: Would Malcolm consent to be RAM's international spokesman? Robert Williams had already agreed to be their international chairman.

At that time, the proposal likely appealed to Malcolm. For some time he had felt that the absence of clear objectives and a united front within the Black Freedom Movement was attributable, in part, to organizational deficiencies. The NAACP, CORE, SCLC, and other groups were like feuding factions at the national level; worse, the parochialism and personal jealousies of their leaders frequently disrupted cooperation at the grassroots level. Stanford argued that what was required was a more clandestine, cadrelike structure that could operate beyond the gaze of the media. "RAM would be the underground cadre organization," Stanford explained, while "the OAAU would be the public front, united front." At 22 West, Malcolm looked over RAM's organizational chart and said, "I see that you have studied the Nation of Islam's structure." He was correct: the model did draw from the Nation of Islam, as well as from the Communist Party.

Stanford remained in New York City for several months, and at OAAU meetings he was struck by Malcolm's finely honed ethnographic skills and powers of observation. He recalled:

It would be at times twenty to thirty people in our apartment, and Malcolm and John Henrik [Clarke] would be there. Malcolm would not chair the meeting. It would be somebody else chairing. And the discussion on the issue would go around the room. And people would be arguing different points of view. Malcolm would be the last person to say anything. He'd let people air out what they had to say. And then he'd say, "Can I say something?" You could hear a pin drop. And he said, "Sister so-and-so has a good point, and she thinks she's in opposition to Brother so-and-so. And Brother so-and-so has a good argument. But—" And he would synthesize the whole argument. He would show everybody their strong points and everybody their weak points and how everything interrelated. . . . It was amazing. Here's a man with an international reputation. [Yet he also] could have that [relationship] with brothers on the street [and] had that relation with sisters and brothers who graduated from college.

Stanford was also keenly tuned to Malcolm's emotional state at the time. "The only time I ever saw Malcolm emotional, and in a sense irrational," the younger man recalled, "was in his public actions against the NOI in June–July 1964." These moves threatened to destroy a potential relationship with Stanford's group. When Malcolm "accused Elijah of fornicating with his secretaries, [and] put it out in the street that he had illegitimate children," RAM sharply dissented with his tactics. "Malcolm was very disturbed," Stanford said, because, spiritually and personally, "he had not only misled people, but he had physically abused people for their violation of what he thought was Elijah's policy. So he felt like the biggest fool on planet earth."

Stanford claims that Malcolm finally agreed to some kind of association with RAM, and he ordered James 67X to serve as his liaison. However, Stanford was less successful in convincing him to relocate the OAAU. Malcolm was determined to "build a base" in New York, even though James and Grace Lee Boggs were urging him to relocate to Detroit, a city where he had thousands of enthusiastic supporters and where there was "more of the radical base." RAM, Stanford explained, "wanted him to expand the OAAU all over the country because we felt that they couldn't attack him if he had a national base." But Malcolm would not budge. Perhaps he feared that if he moved his operations out of Harlem, the thousands of loyal Mosque No. 7 members would never allow him to reestablish a foothold there. By the 1960s Malcolm no longer lived in the Harlem community, yet Harlem remained the central metaphor for black urban America, and he understood that this sometimes magical, often tragic neighborhood's fortunes were intertwined with his own.

By now, Malcolm had spent years under surveillance by both federal and local officials, but in the summer of 1964 the man listening on the other end of his wiretapped telephone would come to play an important, if hidden, role in Malcolm's life. Gerry Fulcher had graduated from the city police academy less than two years earlier, and as a young Harlem-born cop he had internalized many of the racist, conservative views his father had held about blacks. "I was going to stop all crime in New York City . . . ," he remembered about his attitude in the days fresh out of the academy. "I was going to be the supercop." On his first day as a rookie officer, Fulcher and his partner were confronted by an African American who seriously injured Fulcher's fellow officer when the man hurled a chair at him. Fulcher managed to handcuff the suspect, and when his sergeant arrived at the scene, he gave a clear order: "I don't want that nigger walking by the time you get back to the station house." Fulcher may have been raw, but he wasn't about to disobey. "So I, with the guy handcuffed, with his arms around his back, I beat the crap out of him," he said. "And I was a hero."

After one year on the streets, Fulcher advanced to detective and was transferred into the BOSS unit. By early 1964, he was given his first important assignment, the covert surveillance of Malcolm X. Fulcher had already decided that Malcolm was "one of the bad guys," an opinion shared by many of his fellow cops. "The whole civil rights movement," he would say later, "was considered a brand of communism in the cops' mind back in those days." Fulcher had Malcolm down as a "former junkie and a pusher, when he was called Big Red . . . we knew all that." With his break from the Nation, Malcolm had become an even greater threat, the possible leader of civil unrest and black protest. From BOSS's perspective, all of Malcolm's activities had to be closely monitored, which included the recruitment of black cops to join both Malcolm's group and Mosque No. 7. Fulcher's assignment was no less invasive. A small room had been set up in the 28th Precinct station house with tape recording equipment connected to the bugs that operatives had placed in Malcolm's phone at the Hotel Theresa. The listening devices could pick up any conversations in the room where the telephone was. Fulcher's task was twofold: to wiretap Malcolm, hand-delivering the tapes to police authorities on a daily basis; and to attend OAAU events, doing general surveillance.

Fulcher soon learned that wiretapping required diligence and an attention to detail that made the job difficult. "You had to listen to the bug all the time, and the minute you heard the phone ring you almost had to time with him picking it up," Fulcher recalled. "And then I had to record, decide what I was putting on the [tape] reels." At first, he proudly carried out his duties, believing that Malcolm hated whites and wanted to overthrow the U.S. government. "They are the enemies of police," Fulcher stated, recalling his views in 1964 and 1965. "They [the police] would kill them every chance they have." As far as the cops were concerned, Malcolm and his followers should be targeted.

Within a few weeks, as he listened to Malcolm's telephone conversations, office meetings, and public speeches, "what I heard was nothing like I expected." The officer was impressed by his subject's political analysis and arguments. "I remember saying to myself, 'Let's see, he's right about that. . . . He wants [blacks] to get jobs. He wants them to get education. Wants them to get into the system. What's wrong with that?'" Fulcher soon concluded that Malcolm was not "the enemy of white people in general" after all, which led him to the further realization that the NYPD's entire approach to Malcolm, and more broadly the Black Freedom Movement, required rethinking. He raised his concerns with his superior officers but got nowhere. Inside BOSS, "all black organizations were suspect." From then on, he kept his opinions to himself, while continuing his wiretaps and tape recordings. BOSS even placed a recording device under the stage at the Audubon, to ensure that law enforcement could transcribe and analyze Malcolm's speeches.

The day after the OAAU's founding rally, Malcolm met with some members to take stock of the event and to begin planning for his second excursion abroad that year. That Sunday about ninety individuals filled out forms to join the OAAU, far fewer than anticipated. The *New York Times* had estimated the rally's attendance at only six hundred. Malcolm was quick to attribute the low number of new members to the fact that most Harlemites did not have the initial two-dollar membership fee.

If the OAAU lacked for early members, it was not on account of any lull in the charge for civil rights. For the two weeks prior to the rally, news of the disappearance of three volunteers in Mississippi on the first day of the Freedom Summer project had gripped the nation, as activists across the country demanded a full investigation. King himself was still in Saint Augustine, in and out of jail and under tremendous strain. Early on the morning of June 30 Malcolm sent King a telegram expressing his concern about racist attacks against civil rights demonstrators in Saint Augustine. He indicated that if federal authorities were not willing to protect civil rights workers, then he was prepared to deploy his people in the South to organize self-defense units capable of fighting the Klan. To reporters, he characterized these groups as "guerilla squads. . . . The Klan elements in the South are well known. We believe that whenever they strike against the Negro, the Negro has a chance to strike back."

Later that day he flew to Omaha, Nebraska, upon the invitation of the city's Citizens Coordinating Committee for Civil Liberties. Upon arrival, he kept up his provocative banter, charging that "in Omaha, as in other places, the Ku Klux Klan has just changed its bedsheets for policemen's uniforms." After addressing a local audience at Omaha's City Auditorium, he checked out of his hotel, at three a.m., and later that morning was in downtown Chicago. He was a call-in guest on a local radio program, which alerted thousands of angry NOI members that he was in the city. Although he'd confirmed he would appear on the Chicago television show *Off the Cuff*, he never made it to the station; threats on his life, now openly expressed on the streets, forced him to return immediately to New York.

———

At the beginning of July, Malcolm's former fiancée, Evelyn Williams, and Lucille Rosary filed paternity suits against Elijah Muhammad. The formal legal charge brought the fighting in the Black Muslim world to a boil, with death threats against Malcolm now seeming to come from everywhere. That same day, James 3X Shabazz, the powerful minister of Newark's mosque and active leader of Mosque No. 7, released a broadside against Malcolm, describing him as "the number one hypocrite of all time" and "a dog returning to his own vomit." One night in early July, either the third or fourth, Malcolm contacted the NYPD, alerting them that he was returning alone to his home at eleven thirty p.m. and that their presence might be necessary. When he pulled up in front of his home, he saw no NYPD officers present, but what he could see was two unfamiliar black men approach his car on foot. He quickly accelerated, driving around the block and waiting before going home. Malcolm complained to the police and an officer was eventually placed in front of the residence, but only for twenty-four hours.

Despite this intimidation, Malcolm was not about to become a political fugitive in his own city. The next evening, the OAAU sponsored its second public rally, again at the Audubon. Although most MMI members did not belong to the OAAU, Benjamin 2X Goodman was handed the assignment of introducing Malcolm to the audience. Malcolm informed his audience, "Right now, things are pretty hot for me, you know. Oh, yes, I may sound like I'm cracking, but I'm facting."

On July 8 Malcolm appeared again on the *Barry Gray Show* in New York. On July 9 he carried on correspondence with Hassan Sharrieff, the dissident son of Ethel and Raymond Sharrieff, who had recently broken with and denounced the Nation. Malcolm wrote to him saying he was unable to send Sharrieff funds, but pledged he would assist him in organizing "the believers" in Philadelphia, Chicago, and other cities "behind Brother Wallace" Muhammad.

Malcolm had reached a point where his own physical safety was secondary to the realization of his political objectives. Chief among them were, first, forging a Pan-Africanist alliance between the newly independent African states and black America; and, next, consolidating the MMI's relationships with officials in Saudi Arabia, Egypt, and the entire Muslim world—both goals requiring him to head overseas. This second trip abroad that year would also remove him from the Nation's direct line of fire. Perhaps, he figured, the vicious jihad the Nation had waged against him might abate after a long absence outside the United States.

On the evening of July 9, traveling as Malik el-Shabazz, Malcolm boarded TWA Flight 700 for London. Arriving the next morning, Malcolm held an impromptu press conference in which he charged that the U.S. government "is violating the UN charter by violating our basic human rights." He also predicted that in the summer of 1964 America "will see a bloodbath."

Malcolm deeply believed in the power of prophecy, and only days after his departure from New York, the violence he had long warned of in his speeches finally erupted on the streets of Harlem. On July 18 the police shooting of a black fifteen-year-old sparked an angry march that ended with the crowd surrounding the 123rd Street NYPD station, the same station where Malcolm had led the Johnson Hinton protest in 1957. Only this time, when the police started making arrests, the people fought back; others ran through Harlem's business district, smashing windows and stealing everything they could carry.

In London, though, ready for a momentous trip, he could not have imagined such particulars. After renting a hotel room for the night, Malcolm rang one of his contacts, who provided him with telephone numbers and other contact information for some African leaders. In his hotel lobby, Malcolm managed to attract three British journalists to do a twenty-minute interview. The next day, July 11, he was off to Cairo.

Malcolm's great strength was his ability to speak on behalf of those to whom society and state had denied a voice due to racial prejudice. He understood their yearnings and anticipated their actions. He could now see the possibility of a future without racism for his people, but what he could not anticipate were the terrible dangers closest to him, in the forms of both betrayal and death. Just days prior to Malcolm's return to Africa, Max Stanford recalled forty-five years later, Malcolm had introduced Max to Charles 37X Kenyatta, a member of his inner circle, at a private reception. Stanford quickly explained that Charles "had been in the penitentiary, and in the Nation, and that he trusted Charles more than any man in the world." Malcolm assured both men "that the three of us would meet when he came back from Africa," Stanford remembered. "And the last thing he said to Charles was 'Take care of Betty for me.'"

CHAPTER 13

"In the Struggle for Dignity"

July 11–November 24, 1964

M alcolm's return to Cairo marked the beginning of a nineteen-week sojourn to the Middle East and Africa. In departing New York, he left behind two fledgling organizations whose success depended almost entirely on his personal involvement, and the toll his absence took on both the MMI and OAAU was considerable. Yet several important factors conspired to keep him away. For as much as he wished to lay a foundation for his ideas, he continued during this time to undergo dramatic life changes, completing a transformation that had begun with his departure from the Nation of Islam and accelerated with his recent trip to the Middle East. Now, charged with bringing to Africa his plan to put the U.S. government before the United Nations over human rights violations, he experienced for the first time the fullness and profundity of his own African heritage. If the hajj had brought Malcolm to full realization of his Muslim life, the second trip to Africa immersed him in a broad-based Pan-Africanism that cast into relief his role as a black citizen of the world.

In a whirlwind nearly five months, he would become an honored guest of several heads of state and a beloved figure among ordinary Africans of many countries. Though not every moment of the trip was easy, it presented a stark contrast to the difficult slog of building the OAAU amid constant threats of violence from the Nation of Islam. Indeed, another reason why Malcolm ultimately stayed in Africa so long was safety: he was convinced that the Nation would try to kill him as soon as he returned home.

He had planned his visit to Egypt to coincide with an OAU conference (July 17–21) in Cairo, but eventually stayed in the city longer than originally planned, believing that the friendships he was forming would yield dividends in the long run. During the first two months, he threw himself into a detailed course of study prepared by Muslim clerics, associated with the Cairo-based Supreme Council on Islamic Affairs (SCIA). According to Dr. Mahmoud Shawarbi, the SCIA was also largely responsible for subsidizing Malcolm's expenses in the Middle East, Africa, and Europe during his second tour. He was also in frequent communication with the Mecca-based Muslim World League (Rabitat al-Alam al-Islami) founded in Saudi Arabia in 1962 to promulgate religion and oppose the threats represented by communism. By seeking recognition from such organizations, he hoped to destroy the NOI's access to the orthodox Muslim world, as well as elevate his own position as the most prominent Muslim leader in the United States.

Most important of all to Malcolm, this was also a journey of self-discovery. As an NOI minister, he had preached a theology grounded in hatred. Only now, as his separation from the Nation of Islam grew wider, did he feel the urgent need to reexamine his life. If he packed away the starched white shirts, bow ties, and dark suits, how would he now convey his identity?

Malcolm arrived in Cairo after midnight on July 12, and stayed initially at the Semiramis Hotel. In the days that followed, as he waited for his clearance to attend the OAU conference as an observer, he occupied his time by getting settled in and making contact with key leaders. The evening after his arrival he contacted Dr. Shawarbi, who was so eager to engage him in political conversation that he and a small entourage of mostly African Americans drove over to his hotel lobby, where they talked together until three in the morning. Malcolm also met with a number of dignitaries, including the Kenyan political leader Tom Mboya as well as Hassan Sabn al-Kholy, director of Nasser's Bureau of General Affairs, and he dined with Shirley Graham Du Bois, whom he had previously met in Ghana. He visited Cairo University, the pyramids, and other sites (with an ABC cameraman in tow), and he gave interviews to the London *Observer* and UPI.

Once at the conference, he immediately began to circulate a memorandum, calling upon newly independent African nations to condemn the United States for its violations of black human rights. "Racism in America is the same that it is in South Africa," he argued. He urged African leaders to embrace Pan-Africanist politics by endorsing the struggles of African Americans. "We pray that our African brothers" have not escaped the domination of Europe, Malcolm observed, only to fall victim to "American dollarism."

In the end, Malcolm failed to persuade, though not for any great flaw in his argument or ebbing of his passion; his rhetoric simply could not overcome the cold logic of international politics. In the bipolar political world of the 1960s, backing a formal resolution that sharply condemned the United States for its domestic human rights violations would have been seen by the American government as an act of partnership with the Soviet Union or the communist Chinese. The OAU did pass a tepid resolution applauding the passage of civil rights legislation, but criticizing the lack of racial progress. By late July, media analysis of the meeting had filtered back to the United States, where Malcolm was generally described as having failed. A sympathetic *New York Times* analysis by M. S. Handler did, however, appear; after examining Malcolm's eight-page memorandum, U.S. government officials said that had Malcolm "succeeded in convincing just one African Government to bring up the charge at the United Nations, the United States Government would be faced with a touchy problem." The United States could be held in the same category as South Africa as a violator of human rights.

After the conference ended, Malcolm paused, deciding what to do next. The refusal by African governments to back him could only be overcome, he must have reasoned, by his visiting key countries to lobby for their support. Arranging the tour's logistics and connecting with dozens of local contacts throughout Africa in advance would take at least one month to accomplish. The list was long, including: in Ghana, Maya Angelou, *Ghanaian Times* editor T. D. Baffoe, writer Julian Mayfield, and Alice Windom, recently appointed as administrative assistant for the UN Economic Commission for Africa; in Nigeria, scholar E. U. Essien-Udom; in Saudi Arabia, Prince Faisal, Muhammad Abdul Azziz Maged, and Omar Azzam; in Tanzania, Abdulrahman Muhammad Babu, minister of economic planning and foreign affairs; and in Paris, Alioune Diop, publisher and editor of *Présence Africaine*, the preeminent journal of Francophone black culture. Then there was the planning of accommodations and travel.

In a letter to Betty dated August 4, beginning, "My Dear Wife," Malcolm instructed her to tell Lynne Shifflett to cooperate with attorney Clarence Jones and others in helping to bring racial issues before the United Nations. He indicated he would probably return to the United States sometime in September. Malcolm asked Betty to tell Charles Kenyatta that he recognized the difficulties in remaining abroad for so long, but "the gains outweigh the risks."

He wanted to use his remaining time in Cairo to reexamine his identity and practices as a Muslim and as a person of African descent. During his twelve-year stint in the Nation, obeying the strict dietary instructions of Muhammad, he had eaten only one meal each day, surviving on countless cups of coffee. What if, he now asked himself, these rules in running one's life and body were broken down, made less rigid? Egypt's unique blend of Arabic, Islamic, and African cultures also created an environment very different from that of the United States. Meetings advertised to begin at six p.m. might not start until an hour and half later, if not beyond that; many people usually took midday naps and ate a late dinner. Social and public life had their own, slower pace.

Malcolm's travel diary entries reveal that within several weeks he was experiencing a cultural metamorphosis. For example, he began eating lunch daily, a radical break from NOI orthodoxy. He started taking midday naps, usually between two and five p.m., and would generally dine with local contacts and friends at nine p.m. or later, returning to his hotel usually after midnight. He put away his starched white shirts and purchased Arabic- and African-style tunics and pants, which also underscored his appearance as a Pan-Africanist and Muslim. And he seized the opportunity to immerse himself in the culture, viewing many movies and plays—anathema to the NOI—including one, *The Suez and the Revolution*, at an outdoor theater. This is not to suggest that Malcolm withdrew from active political life; to the contrary, despite his changing habits he kept extremely busy—writing essays for the Egyptian press; giving interviews to newspapers, television networks, and wire services around the world; monitoring the activities of the OAAU and MMI and forwarding orders; meeting with African and Arab educators, political leaders, and government representatives; and studying the Qur'an. He met frequently with Elijah Muhammad's youngest son, Akbar, who was enrolled in Cairo's Al-Azhar University and had just resigned from the Nation of Islam over his father's failure to address the charges of immorality. What was new in his life, however, was the release he granted himself—his short trip to Alexandria to see the city's aquarium, say, or his tourist junket to the Aswan Dam and Luxor at the end of August.

Malcolm's public presence at the OAU conference also generated critical scrutiny back in the United States. One example of this was a *Los Angeles Times* column by Victor Riesel, with the provocative title "African Intrigues of Malcolm X." Riesel, who claimed to have been an observer at the Cairo conference, insisted Malcolm was not there: "He prepared a series of inflammatory anti-U.S. documents here . . . [giving the impression] that he attended the conference. This is nonsense. He did not get near the parley.

He was not accredited to it." Riesel believed that Malcolm was in league with the Chinese communists, whose "broadcasts have been featuring him and his splinter sect." He had also observed Malcolm having dinner with Shirley Graham Du Bois, whom he accused of having been "long active in world communist circles." A fervent anticommunist, Riesel probably drafted his columns using information taken directly from the surveillance of Malcolm that only the CIA would have had. He characterized Malcolm as an even greater menace to U.S. national security than he had been in the Nation of Islam: "I ran into his trail in several cities—especially in Ibadan, Nigeria, where he delivered speeches so anti-U.S., so incendiary, that they could be printed only on asbestos."

A high point for Malcolm during his Egyptian stay was a reception in his honor in Alexandria, hosted by the Supreme Council on Islamic Affairs on August 2. More than eight hundred Muslim students representing ninety-three countries were present to hear the SCIA announce that it would award Malcolm's organization twenty tuition-free scholarships to attend Al-Azhar University. Malcolm was overwhelmed, writing to Betty that the event was "the biggest and warmest reception of my life." The fact that Elijah Muhammad had been able to send only one African American to study at Al-Azhar—his son Akbar—while the MMI would soon be sending twenty students to enroll was certainly a "wonderful blessing." A low point came several days later, on August 6, when at an Alexandria restaurant he ate an exotic dish called "spanish." By midnight he was vomiting, with diarrhea and colic fits. In his diary, he admitted being "so miserable I thought I was really dying." A physician finally arrived the next morning to give him a painful injection and some pills, but as if to prove his indestructibility, he did not scale back his schedule. Weeks later he would come to suspect he might have been poisoned deliberately.

By the second week of August Malcolm's life had begun to settle into a routine. This included travels to the ancient port city of Alexandria, which held a special fascination for Malcolm. He enjoyed frequently taking the train there, eating at its restaurants, and making new contacts with scholars and local leaders.

On August 11 he leisurely munched watermelon at the Hilton restaurant with David Du Bois, Shirley's son. Du Bois interviewed Malcolm for the *Egyptian Gazette*, along with another lengthy interview by a different *Gazette* reporter, and he did not return home until midnight. The next day, Malcolm began writing an article for the *Gazette*.

In the afternoon on August 15, Malcolm met with Sheikh Akbar Hassan, the rector of Al-Azhar University. Sheikh Hassan handed Malcolm a certificate granting him the authority to teach Islam. Soon, Malcolm would learn what the friendship of the Nasser government could mean, when he was moved to a luxurious suite at the Shepherd Hotel as a guest of state. Overwhelmed, Malcolm declared in his diary, "Allah has really blessed me."

On August 19, Malcolm spent part of the day touring the Egyptian Museum and once more visited the pyramids, but he also discussed the U.S. political situation and the OAAU with local contacts Nasir al-Din and Kalid Mahmoud. Once again Malcolm met with David Du Bois. On August 21 he released a press statement in the name of the OAAU, summarizing the recent OAU summit.

First, his intended audience was, as he put it, "the well-meaning element in the American public." Echoing Kwame Nkrumah, he called for continental Pan-Africanism, some kind of federation that could unite all countries. He praised President Nasser's role in laying the foundations for a United States of Africa, and he was impressed by the African delegations' commitment to overthrowing the apartheid regime of South Africa, as well as the African guerrillas battling European colonialism in countries like Angola and Mozambique. He also acknowledged that many summit participants "recognized that Israel is nothing but a base here on the northeast tip of the mother continent for the twentieth-century form of 'benevolent colonialism.'"

But the most interesting features of the statement were Malcolm's justifications for his presence at the conference, and the connections he drew between a united Africa and the interests of black Americans. "My coming to the Summit Conference was not in vain, as some elements in the American press have tried to 'suggest,' but instead . . . proved to be very fruitful." He emphasized the political solidarity African delegates expressed to him: "*I found no doors closed to me.*"

Malcolm's article for the *Egyptian Gazette*, "Racism: The Cancer That Is Destroying America," was duly published, to his pleasure. "I am not a racist," the essay began, "and I do not subscribe to any of the tenets of racism. . . . My religious pilgrimage to Mecca has given me a new insight into the true brotherhood of Islam, which encompasses all of the races of mankind." He went on to separate himself from any black nationalist agenda, insisting that all Negroes desired the same goals. "The common goal of 22 million Afro Americans is respect and HUMAN RIGHTS. . . . We can never get civil rights in America until our HUMAN RIGHTS are first restored." He also characterized the differences among civil rights organizations as merely over "methods of attaining these common objectives" and employed an argument made several years earlier by Frantz Fanon, about the destructive psychological impact of racism on the oppressed: "The denial of HUMAN RIGHTS psychologically castrates the victim and makes him a mental and physical slave of the system. . . ."

From August 26 to August 29, he again became the eager tourist, visiting Aswan and Luxor by plane and spending the night in Luxor in some luxury at the New Winter Palace hotel before moving on to Tutankhamen's tomb and other ancient temples in the Valley of the Kings. It was while sightseeing at Luxor that Malcolm expressed his fears in his diary that he may have "overplay[ed] my hand" by remaining abroad for so long.

Back in Cairo, a letter from Reuben Francis informed Malcolm that Muslim Mosque, Inc., had been admitted to the Islamic Federation of the United States and Canada, and that Malcolm was also named to the federation's board of directors, two important stamps of legitimacy. MMI was now in the position of being the conduit for Arab financial aid and, indirectly, political support to African Americans. The federation's actions would have the effect of isolating the Nation of Islam, making it difficult for Elijah Muhammad to develop major initiatives in, or even send delegations to, the orthodox Muslim world. Such success may also have sealed Malcolm's fate among NOI leaders.

But the mail also contained troubling news. On September 1, Judge Maurice Wahl issued an order in favor of the Nation of Islam over Malcolm's house; he and his family were ordered to vacate their Queens home by January 31, 1965. Meanwhile acting attorney general Nicholas Katzenbach wrote to J. Edgar Hoover suggesting that the FBI explore whether during his stay in Cairo Malcolm had violated the Logan Act, which made it illegal for citizens to enter into unauthorized agreements with foreign governments. Katzenbach's letter establishes that both the FBI and the CIA were monitoring Malcolm in Africa. What is most remarkable about this was the David versus Goliath dimension. Malcolm had few resources and was traveling without bodyguards, yet the attorney general and the FBI director were so fearful of what he alone might accomplish that they searched for any plausible grounds to arrest and prosecute him upon his return to the United States.

With the onset of fall, the 1964 U.S. presidential election drew nearer, and

President Johnson and the Democratic Party courted the civil rights movement, hoping to secure the black vote. As Malcolm watched from Africa, he may have factored the election into his plans to remain abroad until November. Nearly alone among prominent black leaders, he continued to support Barry Goldwater as the better candidate to address blacks' interests. Yet Goldwater's opposition to the Civil Rights Act made him the de facto candidate of Southern white supremacists, and the overwhelming majority of African Americans embraced the Democratic Party. Dr. King and other mainstream civil rights leaders had even decided to call a moratorium on demonstrations throughout the fall, in order to help Lyndon Johnson win. Malcolm must have recognized that his argument for Goldwater would have garnered little support. It was better to avoid the debate and not criticize civil rights leaders. The extra weeks abroad would give Malcolm even greater opportunities to make contacts with African political elites.

When on the evening of September 11 hundreds of Cairo students in the African Association met to protest U.S. intervention in Congo, Malcolm was pleased to speak. Later that night, he phoned Betty. "All is well, including 67X," he wrote of the conversation, "and that upped my low spirits." Four days later, he met with Shawarbi, who informed him that in his upcoming visit to Kuwait he would be the guest of the local governor. In early September Malcolm took a two-day trip to Gaza, meeting a number of local government officials and visiting several Palestinian refugee camps near the Israeli border. He prayed at a local *masjid*, accompanied by several religious leaders, before holding a press conference in Gaza's parliament building. The Nation had admired the state of Israel as a concrete expression of Jewish Zionism; henceforth Malcolm would view Israel as a neocolonial proxy for U.S. imperialism.

Malcolm also attended a press conference featuring Ahmed al-Shukairy, the first president of the Palestinian Liberation Organization. After the conference, the two men met privately. This meeting became the context for Malcolm's controversial essay in the *Egyptian Gazette*, "Zionist Logic," in which he denounced Israeli Zionism as a "new form of colonialism," designed to "deceive the African masses into submitting willingly into their 'divine' authority and guidance." Malcolm noted that the Israeli government had made a series of "benevolent" overtures to African states, "with friendly offers of economic aid, and other tempting gifts that they dangle in front of the newly independent African nations, whose economies are experiencing great difficulties." This combination of U.S. imperialism and

Israeli interference in Africans' affairs constituted "Zionist dollarism," which had led to the military occupation of Arab Palestine, an act of aggression for which there existed "no intelligent or legal basis in history—not even in their own religion."

Malcolm's newfound hostility toward Israel can be explained not only by his obligations to Nasser but also by the shifting currents of one particular African state. In the 1950s, under the anticommunist influence of Pan-Africanist George Padmore, newly independent Ghana had been hostile to the Soviet Union and friendly toward Israel. Padmore died in 1959, and by 1962 Ghana was seriously considering becoming a Soviet client state on the model of Cuba. Trade between Egypt, a Soviet ally, and Ghana nearly doubled between 1961 and 1962, and Nkrumah displayed solidarity with Nasser by announcing his own plan for the establishment of a "separate state for Arab refugees from Palestine." Malcolm's anti-Israeli thesis reflected the political interests of both these allies.

This calculated view reflected the broader balancing act he performed throughout his time in the Middle East. Egypt's secular government stood forcefully at odds with religious groups like the Muslim Brotherhood, which had been implicated in a 1954 plot to kill Nasser and subsequently banned from the country. Malcolm, indebted to both sides, could not afford to take positions that might offend either. During his stay in Cairo, his Islamic studies were directed by Sheikh Muhammad Surur al-Sabban, the secretary-general of the Muslim World League. This group was financed by the Saudi government and it reflected conservative political views, so Malcolm had to exercise considerable tact and political discretion. Simultaneously, he was also corresponding with Dr. Said Ramadan, the son-in-law of Hassan al-Banna, founder of the Muslim Brotherhood. Expelled from Egypt, Ramadan had also founded the World Islamic League, and in 1961 established the Islamic Center in Switzerland. Throughout their correspondence, Malcolm pressed Ramadan about race and Islam. At one point Ramadan appealed to him: "How could a man of your spirit, intellect, and worldwide outlook fail to see in Islam . . . a message that confirms . . . the ethnological oneness and equality of all races, thus striking at the very root of racial discrimination?" Malcolm responded that regardless of Islam's universality, he was obligated to struggle on behalf of African Americans. "As a black American," he explained, "I do feel that my first responsibility is to my twenty-two million fellow black Americans." The cordial dialogue displays Malcolm's deepening interest in the Muslim Brotherhood's faith-based politics—an interest that he knew he had to keep from Nasser's government.

On September 16, Malcolm returned to Al-Azhar University, where he was given a certificate establishing his credentials as an orthodox Muslim. He posed for photographs. Later that day he celebrated with Shawarbi and other friends. Leaving for Jeddah two days later, he was overwhelmed by the "touching farewells" and generosity of his Arab friends, but he also pondered the crux of one friend's words of advice: "the importance of not being sidetracked by needless fights with Elijah Muhammad." On September 21, Prince Faisal designated Malcolm an official state visitor of Saudi Arabia, a status that covered all his local expenses and provided a chauffeured car.

At a meeting with Seyyid Omar el-Saghaf, the vice minister of Saudi Arabia's foreign affairs department, Malcolm presented his proposal and request for funds to establish a mosque, or Islamic center, in Harlem, to promote orthodox Islam. On September 22, writing to M. S. Handler, Malcolm praised the "quiet, sane, and strongly spiritual atmosphere" of Saudi Arabia, a place where "objective thinking" was possible. Under the Nation of Islam, "I lived within the narrow-minded confines of the 'straightjacketed world' . . . I represented and defended [Elijah Muhammad] beyond the level of intellect and reason." He vowed that he would "never rest until I have undone the harm I did to so many innocent Negroes" and affirmed that he was now "a Muslim in the most orthodox sense; my religion is Islam as it is believed in and practiced by the Muslims here in the Holy City of Mecca."

His new political goals, he went on, were firmly within the civil rights mainstream. "I am not anti-American, un-American, seditious nor subversive. I don't buy the anti-capitalist propaganda of the communist, nor do I buy the anti-communist propaganda of capitalists." He was trying hard to establish for himself a relatively objective Third World position of nonalignment. Unlike his earlier endorsements of socialism over capitalism, in these comments to Handler he appears to retreat toward a more pragmatic economic philosophy. "I'm for whoever and whatever benefits humanity (human beings) as a whole whether they are capitalist, communists or socialists, all have assets as well as liabilities. . . ." Then, in a remarkable passage, he seems to repudiate not just Yacub's History but the fascist-like concept that all blacks, as blacks, had to exhibit certain cultural traits or adhere to sets of rigid beliefs, in order to justify their racial identity:

I am a Muslim who believes whole heartily that there is no God but Allah and that Muhammad ibn Abdullah . . . is the Last Messenger of Allah—yet some of my very dearest friends are Christians, Jews, Buddhists, Hindus, agnostics and even atheists—some are capitalists, socialists, conservatives, extremists . . . some are even Uncle Toms—some are black, brown, red, yellow and some are even white. It takes all these religious, political, economic, psychological and racial ingredients (characteristics) to make the Human Family and the Human Society complete.

In a second letter to Handler, dated the following day, he criticized his former belief in Elijah Muhammad "as a divine leader who had no human faults." What had prompted the letter, however, was the news that Surur al-Sabban had named Malcolm as the World Islamic League's representative in the United States, with the authority to start an official center in New York City. The league offered fifteen scholarships to American Muslims to attend the Islamic University of Madinah (Medina). This gift, combined with the twenty scholarships offered in Cairo, gave Malcolm thirty-five fully funded fellowships.

In the final week of September he was back on the move. After a brief stop in Kuwait, where he tried unsuccessfully to obtain financial support for the MMI from the foreign secretary, Malcolm traveled to Beirut on September 29. He was welcomed at the Lebanese airport by a student leader named Azizah and about ten white American students, who informed him that the American University dean had extended permission for him to speak in one of the lecture halls. Malcolm, Azizah, and several other students had lunch at the apartment home of an African-American expatriate named Mrs. Brown. One of the white students there, Marian Faye Novak, reconstructed their brief encounter, and what is obvious is that even those friendly to Malcolm's cause still viewed him by the policies of the Nation of Islam rather than by his new beliefs. Another white student, Sara, said, "I think you were absolutely right, Malcolm, . . . when you accused the white man of having the devil in him." Upset by the remark, Novak replied defensively, "I didn't choose this skin, but it's the only one I have." Sara quickly apologized, Novak remembered, "not just for herself and her particular ancestors, but for me and mine, too, while Malcolm X nodded and smiled." Novak stereotypes Malcolm's response even though he did not utter a word during the exchange.

Though the group had only a few hours to advertise Malcolm's address that afternoon, American University students had not forgotten his stellar speaking performance from earlier in the year, and an overflow crowd turned out. Later that day Malcolm flew from Beirut to Khartoum, then traveled overnight directly to Addis Ababa, arriving on September 30. The major event in Addis Ababa was a lecture to an audience of more than five hundred students and faculty at the University College student union on October 2, which was remarkable for the amount of detail in the FBI's account of the event. The Bureau (and the CIA) had not curtailed its efforts to track Malcolm after his departure from Cairo, and it appears to have followed him closely for most of his time abroad. The intelligence report from Addis Ababa suggested that "another goal of Malcolm's visit was to permit direct contact between the black people of the U.S. and Africa."

On October 5, Malcolm flew to Nairobi, and after some time off to visit a national park, contacted vice president Oginga Odinga and set up a meeting for three days hence. When they met, Odinga seemed "attentive, alert, and sympathetic," and Malcolm subsequently received an invitation to address the Kenyan parliament on October 15. In the interim, he decided to visit Zanzibar and Tanzania, with the hope of solidifying the Pan-African political relationships with Tanzanian leaders he had met at the Cairo conference. Most prominent among those he'd hoped to meet with was Abdul-rahman Muhammad Babu, a Zanzibaran revolutionary Marxist who had helped engineer his island nation's 1964 social revolution and subsequent merger with then Tanganyika.

Over several days, Malcolm met a number of African-American expatriates living in Tanzania's capital city of Dar es Salaam, and he conducted several media interviews. He met with Minister Babu on October 12, although the high point of his Tanzanian excursion was a brief encounter with President Julius K. Nyerere the next day. Like Kwame Nkrumah, Nyerere had risen to power in the wave of colonial uprisings that swept through Africa in the late 1950s and early 1960s, and unlike many leaders who fell as quickly as they rose during those tumultuous years, he would remain popular and in power until 1985. Accompanied by Babu, Malcolm assessed the man called by his citizens as *mwalimu*, or "teacher." He is a "very shrew[d], intelligent, disarming man who laughs and jokes much (but deadly serious)."

As Malcolm's travels brought him into more prominent power circles in African politics, he seemed to meet important figures wherever he turned. And as his presence in Dar es Salaam became more widely known, his schedule became more packed. On October 14 he visited the Cuban embassy to converse with the ambassador, who was an Afro-Cuban. That evening

Malcolm was the guest of honor at a dinner that included a number of prominent Tanzanians. He delayed his return to Nairobi for several days, and when he flew back to Nairobi a few days later, he found himself on the same plane as both the Kenyan president Jomo Kenyatta and the Ugandan prime minister Milton Obote. During the flight, which stopped first in Mombasa, one of Kenyatta's ministers informed the president who Malcolm was, and soon Malcolm was requested to move forward to a seat between the two leaders. Arriving late in Mombasa, Kenyatta decided to spend the night, but Malcolm continued to talk with Obote during the flight to Nairobi. After going through Kenyan customs, Tom Mboya, Kenya's second most powerful politician after Kenyatta, picked up Malcolm "and put me back with the VIPs."

As his stay in Kenya unfolded, famous faces mingled with familiar ones. On Sunday morning, October 18, Malcolm ran into two SNCC leaders, chairman John Lewis and Don Harris, who were on their way to Zambia. During the day, a formal invitation was delivered at Malcolm's hotel on behalf of Mboya, requesting his presence that evening at the gala premiere of Uhuru Films (*uhuru* means "freedom" in Kiswahili). Malcolm attended the event, and at the intermission enjoyed chatting with both Mboya and his wife. Malcolm described Mboya, who would also later be assassinated, as the personification of "perpetual motion." After returning late to his hotel, Malcolm spoke with SNCC's Don Harris about "future cooperation."

On October 20, Mboya and his wife picked Malcolm up at his hotel, and they drove to meet President Kenyatta. Taken to a parade's reviewing stand, he relished joining the VIPs who sat with the president for tea and coffee. Malcolm was seated next to Kenyatta's daughter Jane, and continued the conversation with her back at his hotel, the Equator Inn. That afternoon Malcolm had lunch with Mrs. Mboya, the president's family, and a white head of police. "I had wine with my dinner," Malcolm admitted to his diary. After lunch, Malcolm listened to Kenyatta's public address, in which he boldly assumed "complete responsibility for organizing the Mau Mau," the indigenous revolt against British rule in Kenya in the 1950s. At every step, Malcolm was treated like a visiting dignitary, and his prominence over the course of several days at social and public events must have stunned the CIA and FBI. The Bureau had spent years trying to split Malcolm from Elijah Muhammad, with the expectation that the NOI schism would weaken the organization and discredit its leaders. After Malcolm's supposed failure at the Cairo conference, he should have been greatly weakened. Yet with each stop in his itinerary, the FBI received fresh reports about Malcolm's expansive social calendar and his growing credibility among African heads of state. His media profile also continued to grow. The FBI's New York office reported to the director that while in Nairobi Malcolm "appeared prominently at social functions." On October 21, Malcolm was interviewed on local TV, where he explained that at every opportunity—in Dar es Salaam, Nairobi, and other cities—he had urged leaders "to condemn the United States in the United Nations for racism."

His popularity forced the U.S. government to step up its efforts. Several black Americans living in Nairobi were contacted by the U.S. embassy, Malcolm learned, warning them to stay away from him. A party that had been planned had to be canceled, as pressure was applied in an attempt to discredit him. U.S. authorities by now of course knew all about Malcolm's spiritual epiphany in Mecca, his break with the Nation, and even his overtures to the civil rights movement. But neither the State Department nor the intelligence agencies had any intention of telling the "truth" about Malcolm.

Despite the covert opposition of the U.S. embassy, Malcolm achieved one of his greatest triumphs on October 15, when he spoke before Kenya's parliament. After his talk, the parliament proposed, and then passed, what Malcolm called "a *resolution of support for our human rights struggle.*" His plan, hatched in the wake of defeat in Cairo, had finally yielded results. For a sovereign African state to endorse his human rights formulation was a tremendous political breakthrough.

The resolution brought an immediate response from American authorities. Within hours, Malcolm met with the U.S. ambassador and several aides, who grilled him on his relationships with Kenyan officials and demanded details of all his recent interactions. To Malcolm's face, the ambassador stated that he regarded him as a racist, but Malcolm kept his cool. He vigorously presented his positions and objectives, challenging the authorities to show he had done anything illegal.

From Nairobi, Malcolm flew back briefly to Addis Ababa before departing on October 28 for Nigeria, where his friend the scholar Essien-Udom had arranged several events. Malcolm arrived in Lagos two days later and had settled in for dinner alone before a phone call interrupted him: it was Nigerian president Nnamdi Azikiwe's secretary, seeking to arrange a private meeting the next morning. Writing later of the meeting, Malcolm found

Azikiwe not lacking in humility, and noted that he had a good grasp of the key players in the U.S. civil rights struggle. Later that day, Malcolm went to a party attended by members of the press, the diplomatic corps, and Nigerian officials. "A great deal of soul-searching was being done," he recalled, about the difficult state of Nigerian politics. Malcolm must have shuddered in drafting this prediction, which regrettably would come all too true, with the Biafran War only several years away: "It will take much bloodshed to straighten this country out and I don't believe it can be avoided."

It was only during this trip that he fully grasped the profound divisions among Africans in the postindependence era. On November 1, for example, he was confronted by two young reporters for several hours, much to his surprise, who disagreed with the positive comments he had made about their president at a public event. The mood among young Nigerians, he pondered, "is mostly impatient and explosive."

During the twenty-four weeks from April through November 1964 when Malcolm was out of the United States, his followers were responsible for fashioning his image and message. It did not go well. "Malcolm was aware of the fact that we were having problems," Herman Ferguson later admitted. "There was [MMI] resentment against the members of the OAAU because they didn't go through the struggle in the Nation of Islam." Another source of conflict was the role of women in the organization. Former Black Muslims believed that "women played a secondary role to the men. The men were out front, the protectors, the warriors," Ferguson observed. Malcolm tried to break this patriarchy, insisting that in the OAAU "women [should have an] equal position to the men." His new commitment to gender equality confused and even outraged many members. "A couple of brothers came to me," Ferguson recalled. "They wanted me to approach [Malcolm] about their concerns about the role of the women and how it was not sitting well with many of the brothers." Ferguson decided against carrying the appeal directly to Malcolm. "The women that Malcolm seemed to place a lot of confidence in, they were responsible, they were well educated."

By midsummer the tensions between MMI and OAAU occasionally sparked into verbal combat. James 67X made no secret of his bitter hostility toward Shifflett. The two fought each other constantly, over everything from the content of the OAAU's public rallies and speakers' invitations to the OAAU's struggling efforts to recruit new members. "The Muslim Mosque, Inc. and the OAAU . . . drifted apart," Ferguson explained. "Some people came in and were not a part of the MMI, and all of the MMI people were not part of OAAU. So there was a gap." Even inside the OAAU, there were growing divisions between the pragmatists like Shifflett, who wanted OAAU to join forces with black elected officials and civil rights groups, and Ferguson, who considered himself a revolutionary nationalist and Pan-Africanist. What evolved was a core of "dedicated people," who performed the lion's share of all work without salaries, and the great majority of OAAU members, who came out only for the rallies.

As a result, by late July some of the OAAU committees that had been created a month earlier began falling apart. South Carolina activist James Campbell and Ferguson did establish the Liberation School, which held classes and attracted a dozen or so students. Peter Bailey started the OAAU's newsletter, *Blacklash*, and Muriel Gray led a very productive cultural arts committee. However, the factional discord upset many OAAU people, who felt discouraged and disoriented without their leader's presence. Most had joined after being inspired by Malcolm, but in his long absence members had to assume greater responsibilities. "We sort of hoped [Malcolm] would be like the magnet that would draw the people in," Ferguson explained. Hundreds would regularly turn out for OAAU events but refuse to pay the two-dollar membership fee. Paradoxically, Ferguson attributed the recruitment problems directly to Malcolm. "When you became a known member of Malcolm's organization, you stuck out like a sore thumb. It was easier to be a Black Panther than a Malcomite." Ferguson also blamed the OAAU's problems on the MMI, which was increasingly detached from providing any assistance. "Malcolm recognized the limitations of the brothers," he observed. "They . . . would lay down their lives for him, and he knew that." But "in terms of building and developing and bringing people in, they would tend to frighten people." Early one Saturday morning at their Hotel Theresa office just before his second trip abroad, Malcolm became irate when he saw an MMI brother lounging in a comfortable chair. "Don't you have anything to do?" he snapped. "Go out and deliver some leaflets!" Ferguson narrated the story's bitter conclusion: "The guy left and we didn't see him for several weeks. And then when we saw him next, he was all bandaged up. He went down in the subway, and Nation of Islam guys jumped him, and they put him in the hospital."

Throughout this difficult time three individuals played key roles: James 67X Warden (Shabazz), Benjamin 2X Goodman (Karin), and Charles 37X Morris (Kenyatta). These close associates of Malcolm's had all served in the military and had all joined the NOI; Benjamin and James had both risen to positions of authority in the NOI. When the split occurred, all of them placed their lives on hold to follow Malcolm even without knowing where he was going. The activities of this triumvirate largely defined how Malcolm was presented to the public during the second half of 1964.

James's power rested partially on the fact that he was the only person who could act, or write, on Malcolm's behalf. "I paid the bills, I rented the Audubon Ballroom, [I wrote] every press release that he made." He even purchased "books on how to have press conferences, and advised Malcolm how to engage the media." He also had the authority to send on behalf of Malcolm correspondence and press releases he wrote himself. For all his labors, James was paid a total of one hundred dollars during nearly a year. Despite all these sacrifices, Malcolm occasionally questioned his loyalty.

He got little thanks either from any of his fellow members, who viewed him as notoriously secretive and argumentative. He was constantly receiving a stream of orders from Malcolm, but though he could speak freely on his leader's behalf, he was rarely given full authority to render truly important decisions. On one occasion when he attended an OAAU business meeting, he became so frustrated by the group's disorganization and hopelessness at "getting anything done" that he stood up and slammed his Samsonite briefcase on a nearby table. "Brother Malcolm is holding *me* responsible for the formation of this organization," he warned. "Now, I'm going to leave with these parting words: either *you* organize it or *I'll* organize it." After this stern rebuke, "things started happening."

Benjamin 2X had an easier time ingratiating himself. His primary role kept him busy with MMI; unlike James, he was not tasked with an organization-building role in the OAAU, which made it easier for him to go out of his way to support its development. On July 18, when New York City police shot James Powell, the event that would precipitate the Harlem riot, Benjamin spoke as the OAAU representative at a protest rally that was hastily organized by CORE in Harlem. Though he did not take part in the riots, NYPD and FBI interest in him subsequently increased sharply. According to agents at the rally, Benjamin "stirred them up by stating that Negroes should arm themselves for self-protection and that Negroes must be willing to spill blood for freedom." Looking for someone to blame, especially with

Malcolm out of the country, the FBI and Justice Department focused on Benjamin, though they eventually decided that there was insufficient evidence to arrest him.

Throughout the summer, James and Benjamin tried gamely to fill the hole left by their absent leader. On July 5 Benjamin spoke at the second public rally of the OAAU, held at the Audubon; then, on July 12, he presided over an OAAU rally that attracted 125 people and featured guest speakers Percy Sutton and Charles Rangel, who urged the audience to promote voter registration. Almost by default, James became Malcolm's emissary to the United States left. He addressed a meeting at Columbia University sponsored by the Trotskyist DeBerry-Shaw presidential campaign committee on July 23. About one week later he lectured at the Socialist Workers Party's Militant Labor Forum in Manhattan, charging that the recent Harlem riot was being used as a pretext to "set down" the black community. As Malcolm's absence grew longer, by late summer James finally began making major political and financial decisions without his input. In early August, when a cluster of supporters wanted to initiate an MMI branch in Philadelphia, he promised that any funds collected locally should remain there until the group "got on its feet." James's decision not only represented a sharp break from the Nation's autocratic centralism, but it also fragmented the potential resources of pro-Malcolm forces.

As the summer rolled on, James found himself left with relatively few allies within the MMI because, ironically, members felt he had been excessively accommodating to the OAAU, allowing that group to usurp resources and space at MMI headquarters. James recalled, "We had a space, and men tend to be territorial. . . . And they came in and wanted to do things their way, or spoke to the brothers in a way that brothers were not accustomed to." James believed that OAAU members saw themselves "as intellectually capable individuals who were taking over from these ex-criminals, these . . . nincompoops, and it caused resentment." But if James bore the brunt of their anger, he was not the source of it. For that, the responsibility fell to Malcolm himself, and the changes he had made to his platform, by will or by concession, in order to broaden the appeal of his message. In separating his politics from religion, he had inadvertently undermined the political authority of the MMI. His determination to play a major role in the civil rights movement meant denouncing much of his old past and Nation of Islam beliefs, especially the forceful emphasis on class divisions within the black community. But the MMI was an embodiment of that past, and its members resented those middle-class, better-educated blacks who now pushed to encircle their minister. "The OAAU seemed to be treating us as last year's news," James reflected bitterly. "'We are replacing them,' see?"

James's own Marxist take on the black community left him deeply skeptical of the OAAU's mission, a sentiment at odds with his responsibility to help the group get off the ground. For him, the OAAU's artists like Ossie Davis and Ruby Dee, and its intellectuals like John Oliver Killens, represented the black petite bourgeoisie that Malcolm had once portrayed as part of the problem. "Their bread was buttered on the integrationist side," he complained. "These were not people that were on welfare. They were middle class for America and upper middle class for black America. They didn't have to wonder whether there was milk in the refrigerator." James believed that Malcolm had created the OAAU primarily to serve as a platform to carry out his international objectives. "An African diplomat or African politician could see it and accept it [the OAAU] and understand that . . . what was good for the African-American people would be good for his group." During his April–May visit to Africa, Malcolm had been surprised that "some of the most revolutionary people over there said, 'Well, how does Martin Luther King stand on this?' And they felt that if Martin Luther King wasn't in it, who was this Johnny-come-lately Malcolm?" James continued. "So [Malcolm] made adjustments." Among them was to pursue a recruitment strategy bringing middle-class blacks, liberal celebrities, and intellectuals into the OAAU. "Besides," added James, Malcolm's views were "changing so rapidly that almost as soon as he reached a particular level [they would become] obsolete, because he was at another place." This was pragmatic, self-interested politics: "He needed people of stature and substance that would allow him to have that kind of dialogue with Africa, or with the UN, or international bodies. And people like Ossie Davis or Ruby Dee or Sidney Poitier are people who are well known."

The tug-of-war between the OAAU and MMI finally surfaced into open conflict when several MMI brothers were arrested on weapons possession charges. Though the brothers were also OAAU members, the OAAU made no effort to post their bail. "When they came out," James recalled, "they were behind in their annual [OAAU] dues. So they . . . went to go to [an OAAU] meeting, and the sisters said, 'No, you can't come to the meeting because you're behind in your dues.'" The brothers were stunned, and over the next few months many MMI members with dual membership would quit the OAAU, or simply drift away from both organizations. One furious MMI member named Talfiq brought his grievances to James, who explained that Malcolm had given him the responsibility to build the OAAU. "[This brother] had enough respect for me to abide his plans for revolution." The fragmentation grew still worse when Betty initiated her own group of supporters. "Betty had a group going on at her house, who thought they should [take over] the OAAU, because Lynne Shifflett wasn't moving fast enough." Betty also had a special dislike for Shifflett, who she feared might be sexually involved with her husband. According to Max Stanford, at an OAAU meeting, an irate Betty charged in and accused Shifflett and an OAAU secretary of sleeping with Malcolm.

Betty felt particularly vulnerable as an unhappy wife in a strained marriage. She had been left behind by Malcolm under the guard of Charles 37X Kenyatta, who held a position of some significance within the MMI. During Malcolm's absence the relationship between protector and protected grew more complicated, and more intimate, than Malcolm could have imagined. Kenyatta, still one of Malcolm's favorites thanks to his silky charm and easy nature, had never ingratiated himself with James 67X or some of the other former Nation stalwarts who had come over in the split. In the new era of the MMI their suspicion of him had not abated. Yet Malcolm had designated Kenyatta to be the sole bodyguard of his wife and children while he was out of the country, giving him the authority to control access to the Shabazz residence.

Kenyatta found himself presiding over a household on the verge of a breakdown as Betty struggled to shoulder the burden of Malcolm's absence. She had given birth to their fourth child, Gamilah Lumumba, three days after the OAAU's founding, and it was just eight days later that Malcolm, with his old habit of disappearing whenever a new baby appeared, departed for Africa. Raising four children alone would have been hard enough, given the household's meager income, at this point coming only from Malcolm's book advances, lecture honoraria, and small donations from dedicated MMI members. Now, however, she had become the most accessible target of the Nation's intimidation campaign. The telephoned death threats that Malcolm had left behind continued to ring with unbearable frequency in his home, wearing down his wife, who could not avoid them. Captain Joseph had devised a harassment strategy to instill further fear in the household. Fruit of Islam members were instructed to ring Malcolm's home once every five minutes. If anyone picked up, the FOI member might say something threatening—or say nothing at all—and after a long silence would simply hang up. "You'll never see your husband again," one caller promised Betty.

"We got him. We cut his throat." The constant stream of such calls sapped Betty of her strength and patience during Malcolm's long absence.

Although Kenyatta had been assigned to protect her, Betty must have felt utterly abandoned. With four children age five and under, without adequate finances, and caring for a newborn infant by herself, she could hardly have believed that her husband's political responsibilities should take precedence over her personal needs. She came to dislike most of his key lieutenants, including James and Benjamin, for taking her husband away from her. Yet she soon grew closer to Kenyatta in ways that attracted the notice of the FBI and caused great consternation among Malcolm's loyal lieutenants.

James 67X had seen troubling omens in what he considered Betty's inappropriate behavior at her home when Malcolm was away. She seemed coquettish, almost inviting male guests to make sexual advances toward her. On one occasion, James experienced her amorous overtures himself. "This woman took my glasses off," he recalled, "and put them behind her back and told me, 'Come and get them.' That's why I would never go to that house again." He soon found that Kenyatta was also giving him cause to be suspicious.

Malcolm frequently sent his instructions from abroad to his home address, and James discovered that Kenyatta had been withholding vital communications from him for days or even weeks. It marked the beginning of a power play: Kenyatta believed James to be his most important rival for Malcolm's attention, and so he severely restricted his access to Betty.

In September 1964, the FBI observed that Kenyatta had been frequently traveling by car outside the city in the company of a woman who was identified as "Malcolm X's [redacted]." This was indeed Betty Shabazz, who enjoyed going out on the town with the handsome man. Within weeks rumors were rife within the OAAU, MMI, and Mosque No. 7 that Betty and Kenyatta were sexually involved, and even planned to marry. The actual extent of their relationship is difficult to discern, but it set off alarms with James 67X and other leaders who heard about their liaisons. By the standards of orthodox Islam—and even by Nation of Islam standards—the relationship was highly inappropriate and threatened to bring shame upon everyone involved. Moreover, both parties were being extraordinarily conspicuous, given that both of them should have known that they were under FBI surveillance.

Yet Malcolm, clueless about what was transpiring in his absence, came to depend increasingly on Betty while he was away. For months, he corresponded with her through telegrams, letters, and phone calls. One letter, dated July 26, affirmed that he missed Betty and the children "much and I do pray that you are well and secure." Much of his early correspondence described his activities in Cairo and at the OAU conference. "I realize many there in the States may think I'm shirking my duties as a leader . . . by being way over here," he confessed. "But what I am doing here will be more helpful to the *whole* [Malcolm's emphasis] in the long run."

In another letter, dated August 4, he wrote, "It looks like another month at least may pass before I see you," placing his return at that point in mid to late September. He also described his conversations with Akbar Muhammad, telling Betty that Akbar "says he knows his father is wrong and doesn't go along with his father's claim of being a divine messenger. But I'm still watching him." He continued, "I've learned to trust no one."

Even during the period when Betty grew close to Kenyatta, she was sending letters and magazines to Malcolm, carrying out political tasks on his behalf, and trying to keep him at least partially informed. Late in his trip, she traveled to Philadelphia to attend a meeting of Wallace Muhammad's followers, but was disappointed by what she heard. While Wallace had broken with his father and the Nation of Islam, he did not call for a merger with Malcolm's groups, instead characterizing Malcolm as having a "violent image." Betty reported back that Wallace was "just like his father" and she believed that "everyone" was trying to use Malcolm "as a stepping stone."

It was also during this time that Betty became directly involved in the schisms inside both the OAAU and MMI. Along with the group that met at her home and schemed to take over the OAAU, she also met secretly with MMI security head Reuben X Francis, who was planning to start a new youth group. The FBI picked up a phone call between Francis and Betty during which he explained that the group, the Organization of Afro-American Cadets, would function separately from the MMI because, he said, "I don't want the officials to know too much about it." MMI leaders were "corrupt," and this new group had to be kept at arm's length from them "to avoid contamination." Perhaps playing to Betty's favor, Francis also defended Charles 37X Kenyatta, claiming that MMI leaders "are trying to set him up to make him look bad in our eyes"; she agreed to meet him later that week. The fact that a dissident MMI member had the confidence to confide in her probably indicates that she was perceived as an influential political force in her own right. It also implies that her displeasure with James, and with how the MMI was run, was public knowledge.

In the fall of 1964, probably because of his relationship with Betty, Charles Kenyatta felt bold enough to publicly challenge James 67X's leadership. The basic criticisms leveled against James were that he was secretive, dictatorial, and a closet communist—a Marxist who dishonestly presented himself as a black nationalist. Because of his administrative responsibilities, he had alienated many members; his unambiguous dislike of Shifflett and the OAAU guaranteed that he would have few allies in that organization. By contrast, Kenyatta maintained cordial relations with OAAU members and attended some of their events. As the power struggle between the two men became public, MMI members were divided. But old habits die hard. The NOI tradition of allowing the minister, or supreme leader, to make important decisions led the majority of MMI members to defer any judgments about the leadership until Malcolm's return. Still, the long summer of disunity had left members of both groups with frazzled nerves and little sense of direction. Adding to their anxiety were the continuing conflicts with the Nation of Islam. Malcolm's departure from the United States had done little to reduce the Nation's vitriolic campaign against him and his defenders. Everyone craved Malcolm's return, but feared that it would trigger a new escalation of violence.

———

By the beginning of November 1964, Malcolm had been away from the United States for four months. He was aware of the dissension and near collapse of his fledgling organizations. Undoubtedly, he missed his wife and children. Yet he had successfully fashioned a new image, another reinvention, on the African continent. No other private citizen from America, devoid of title or official status, had been welcomed and honored as Malcolm had been. Instead of being projected as a racist zealot, as was still too often the case in the American press, he was identified by African media as a freedom fighter and Pan-Africanist. But it was not the flattery that affected Malcolm; it was the romance with Africa itself, its beauty, diversity, and complexity. It was the African people who had embraced Malcolm as their own long-lost son. It must have been difficult to leave all of this behind, by returning to the United States and facing the death threats and escalating violence he knew was sure to come.

The final leg of his African tour brought him back to Ghana, and to the expat community for whom he had only grown in stature in the months since his last visit. Maya Angelou, Julian Mayfield, and others met him at the Accra airport on November 2, and soon various expats were once again competing with one another for his time and attention. The next day Malcolm enjoyed seeing Angelou, spending the morning together and dining at the home of the intellectual Nana Nketsia with about half a dozen artists and writers. He also spent several hours with Shirley Du Bois, by then the executive director of Ghanaian television, and together they toured Ghana's national television and radio stations. Perhaps his looming return to the United States had made him restless, because during this time he found himself unable to sleep through the night, turning to sleeping pills for relief. Yet he was also exhausted, worn down from weeks of grinding international travel. He had loosened his rules about alcohol despite the Muslim restrictions against it; after a newspaper interview, he had grown tired, and noted in his diary that he'd had a rum and Coke in an attempt to wake up. He would have more to keep his thoughts filled soon enough, when news reached him that Lyndon Johnson had buried Goldwater in a landslide victory in the U.S. presidential election, capturing 96 percent of the black vote.

Shirley Du Bois, Julian Mayfield, and Malcolm sat down for a quick lunch with the Chinese ambassador before meeting with President Nkrumah in the early afternoon on November 5. Their talk once again went unrecorded, but its content might be gleaned from Malcolm's speeches about the United Nations during the rest of his trip. Part of Malcolm's agenda for returning to Accra was to promote the development of the OAAU on the African continent, and in the expat community his ideas, especially that of bringing U.S. race issues before the UN, were met with great excitement. "The idea was so stimulating to the community of African-American residents," recalled Angelou, "that I persuaded myself I should return to the States to help establish the organization." Maya's decision to return home to help Malcolm won her immediate status among the expatriates. "My friends," Maya remembered, "began to treat me as if I had suddenly became special. . . . My stature had definitely increased."

On Friday, November 6, a delegation of admirers, including Shirley Du Bois, Nana Nketsia, Maya Angelou, and others, bid Malcolm a bon voyage. As his plane departed for Liberia, the reality of leaving Ghana sank in and he grew sad as he reflected on how much he had come to cherish the community there. As he watched Maya and another African-American female expatriate "waving 'sadly' from the rail," he characterized Maya and her friend as "two very lonely women." Arriving in Monrovia, Liberia, at about noon, Malcolm attended a dance held at city hall, then went out to a country club. After some sightseeing and a cocktail party the next day, Malcolm spent several hours being wined and dined—and being challenged in vigorous debate with expatriates and others about the role of Israel in Africa. Members of the Liberian elite made the case that African-American "technicians and of other skills" needed to migrate to Liberia, yet, like any other ruling class, they were candid about their determination to hold on to power. Black Americans would be welcomed to Liberia, "but we don't want them to interfere with our internal political structure. Our fear is that they may get into politics."

On the morning of November 9 Malcolm visited the Liberian executive mansion, where he was introduced to members of the cabinet; however, President William Tubman was "too busy" to meet him. Malcolm then headed to the airport to depart—after three packed days he was off to Conakry, Guinea. Arriving in the early evening, he was driven much to his amazement to President Sékou Touré's "private home, where I will reside while in Conakory [sic]. *I'm speechless!* All praise is due Allah!" He was allocated three personal servants, a driver, and one army officer.

As Malcolm sought to process this extraordinary recognition of status, he reflected on how he had changed in the past few months: "My mind seems to be more at peace, since I left Mecca in September. My thoughts come strong and clear and it is easier to express myself." Paradoxically, he then added, "My mind has been almost incapable of producing words and phrases lately and it has worried me." What he appears to be saying is that his Middle East and Africa experiences had greatly broadened his mind, yet his limited vocabulary of black nationalism was insufficient to address the challenges he so clearly saw confronting Africa. Malcolm sensed that he needed to create new theoretical tools and a different frame of reference beyond race.

Malcolm was chauffeured around Conakry like a visiting head of state the morning after his arrival there. A quick visit at the Algerian embassy caused him brief embarrassment, due to the enthusiastic reception he received there. "It is difficult to believe that I could be so widely known (and respected) here on this continent," Malcolm later reflected. "The negative image the Western press has tried to paint of me certainly hasn't succeeded." That evening he was finally introduced to President Touré, who enthusiastically embraced him. "He congratulated me for my firmness in the struggle for dignity." They agreed to meet for lunch the next afternoon. That night Malcolm went to a nightclub, but perhaps because Guinea was an overwhelmingly Muslim country, he wisely stuck with coffee and orange juice.

At his lunch with President Touré and several other international guests the next day, Malcolm noted that Touré "ate fast, but politely, and several times added food to my plate." After several guests had left, Touré returned to the topic that had animated him at their encounter the night before, the quest for "dignity." Malcolm knew about the president's extraordinary history—as a trade union militant and anti-French revolutionary, the sole leader in Francophone Africa to defy De Gaulle by rejecting union with metropolitan France in 1958. To Touré dignity meant African self-determination, concepts very close to his own new lexicon of Pan-Africanism. "We are aware of your reputation as a freedom fighter," Touré told Malcolm, "so I talk frankly, a fighting language to you."

Over the next several days Malcolm experienced a series of travel mishaps; unbeknownst to him his flight out of Conakry had been rescheduled, and he had to spend an extra night there. On his flight to Dakar on November 13 one brother recognized Malcolm, "and it was all over the airport" that the black American Muslim was present once he'd arrived. Travelers came up requesting autographs. He continued on, with a brief transfer stop in Geneva and then Paris, where he spent the night at the Hôtel Terminus St. Lazare. Malcolm flew to Algiers the next morning, but the visit was not productive. The French language barrier, Malcolm lamented, was so "tremendous" that it was almost impossible to communicate effectively. With his crisscross flight pattern continuing, Malcolm arrived in Geneva on the morning of November 16. His objective was to make contact with the city's Islamic Center and to deepen his links to the Muslim Brotherhood. That afternoon, he had a surprise encounter with a young woman named Fifi, a United Nations secretary and Swiss national who had worked with Malcolm in Cairo. She met him at his hotel, chatting with him for hours and truly surprising him by saying that she "is madly in love with me and seems willing to do *anything* to prove it." Malcolm slept late the next day, then went shopping, buying a new overcoat and suit. Dr. Said Ramadan of the Islamic Center came by, taking Malcolm first to his mosque, then to dinner with several guests. When Malcolm returned to his hotel at about nine p.m., "Fifi was knocking on my door as I came up the stairs." She joined him in his room and left a couple hours later. Uncharacteristically, Malcolm did not record in his diary what transpired between the two of them; based on the diary, Fifi appears to be the only female he admitted to his private space during his entire time abroad. After her departure, Malcolm subsequently left the hotel and took a brief walk in the rain, "alone and feeling lonely . . . thinking of Betty."

He arrived in Paris on November 18, checking in to the Hôtel Delavine, where he would stay for a week (despite receiving an invitation to visit London) to address a crowd at the Maison de la Mutualité five days later. His international reputation preceded him, and though his appearance at the Mutualité was not widely covered by the U.S. press, one reporter recalled, "There wasn't a square inch of unoccupied space in the meeting room." Those who arrived late stood or sat on the floor. Malcolm's formal remarks were supposed to address the theme "The Black Struggle in the United States," but as he confessed in his diary, he seemed to lack mental focus in the formulation of new political ideas, especially in the aftermath of Johnson's presidential victory. Instead, the substance of his remarks consisted of responses to questions. From the beginning, he veered ideologically to the left. When asked, "How is it possible that some people are still preaching nonviolence?" he responded with an attack on King, saying, "That's easy to understand—shows you the power of dollarism." It was the "imperialists" who "give out another peace prize to again try and strengthen the image of nonviolence." His trip to Africa and the Middle East also seemed to have revived his inflammatory anti-Semitic views. "The American Negroes especially have been maneuvered into doing more crying for the Jews than they cry for themselves," he complained, going on to present a fictive history of progressive Jews and claiming, incorrectly, that they had not participated as Freedom Riders. "If they were barred from hotels they bought the hotel. But when they join us, they don't show us how to solve our problem that way."

Yet in other ways Malcolm had become more tolerant. He announced his new views about interracial romance and marriage: "How can anyone be against love? Whoever a person wants to love, that's their business." And he presciently speculated that in a multicultural future it was conceivable that "the black culture will be the dominant culture." The day after his speech in Paris, November 24, 1964, Malcolm X finally arrived home in New York City; but his homecoming this day coincided with the killing of sixty white hostages during a joint Belgian-American rescue attempt staged against Congolese rebels in Stanleyville. As he disembarked at John F. Kennedy airport, about sixty supporters displaying signs reading "Welcome Back, Brother Malcolm" greeted him. He wasted no time in accusing both the U.S. government and the Congolese regime of Moise Tshombe for their responsibility in the Stanleyville slaughter. It was "Johnson's financing of Tshombe's mercenaries," Malcolm declared, that had produced such "disastrous results." Once more tempting fate, he described the U.S. involvement in the Congo as "the chickens coming home to roost."

CHAPTER 14

"Such a Man Is Worthy of Death"

November 24, 1964–February 14, 1965

At the OAAU Homecoming Rally for Malcolm on November 29 at the Audubon Ballroom, Charles 37X mingled in the modest crowd of three hundred, shaking hands and displaying his usual charm and good cheer. No one had yet told Malcolm, still freshly arrived, about the rumors concerning Betty and his duplicitous lieutenant. James 67X, however, did know. In October, hoping to ease tensions over leadership of the MMI in Malcolm's absence, he had traveled to Boston and spent several days as a houseguest of Ella Collins, where he met with MMI supporters. During his stay, Ella told him about the gossip. In its way, the news of Charles and Betty's liaisons helped settle him, perhaps because it gave him something he could use to his advantage if the power struggle escalated further. As it was, he took the opportunity to reassert his leadership through magnanimity. On October 18 he and Benjamin 2X held an MMI meeting in Harlem, where they encouraged members to attend an OAAU rally scheduled for later that day. Two nights later, he held a further meeting at his West 113th Street apartment, to discuss the formation of an MMI judo program. The participants, who included Reuben Francis, had been some of his staunchest critics; this overture to his opponents may have quelled their worries. Toward Kenyatta himself, James displayed generosity, inviting his rival to speak at events. By the time of the Audubon rally, James had largely reestablished his leadership role in the MMI.

Even so, members of the OAAU and MMI were excited about having Malcolm back. Arguments and feuds that had threatened to destroy both organizations could now be resolved. Both groups had closely followed

Malcolm's itinerary and adventures from abroad, the honors bestowed upon him by such worthies as Kwame Nkrumah, Jomo Kenyatta, Julius Nyerere, Sékou Touré, and Prince Faisal, all of which was in part a recognition of their efforts. Yet the changes he had clearly undergone during the trip produced conflicting reactions among his followers. The OAAU had approved of Malcolm's political evolution and of the frequent comments he had sent to M. S. Handler for publication in the *Times*. For the MMI, however, the question to be answered was whether Malcolm X was still *their* Malcolm—a committed black separatist who espoused the core ideas he had promoted as a Nation of Islam minister. Many had agreed with Herman Ferguson in seeing Malcolm's May press conference comments offering an olive branch to whites as a kind of necessary smoke screen, but the news of him from Africa conveyed only further movement in a more inclusive direction. The MMI, its heels dug in on race issues, saw little to approve of in the deeper change in their leader's philosophical outlook. James 67X, for one, was glad that Malcolm "had not changed his position one whit" after his second African sojourn. And even after he came back, James said with relief, "he would refer to certain people as devils."

Yet his separatism-minded supporters could not have been pleased with the undercurrent of his speech at his Audubon homecoming. He was introduced there by Clifton DeBerry, the Socialist Workers Party 1964 presidential candidate. After touching briefly on current events in Stanleyville, Malcolm spent the bulk of the talk recounting his trip, going country by country and focusing on the African continent's unprecedented social change. "This is the era of revolution," he proudly announced, taking the opportunity to draw negative contrasts between the nonviolent civil rights leaders in the United States and the African revolutionaries who were seeking to overthrow colonial dictatorships. "Whenever you hear a man saying he wants freedom, but in the next breath he is going to tell you what he won't do to get it . . . he doesn't believe in freedom." Yet in espousing the necessity for a Pan-Africanist approach, Malcolm once again made an important distinction between whites who "don't act all right" compared to antiracist whites. "When I say white man, I'm not saying all of you," he explained, "because some of you might be all right. And whichever one of you acts all right with me, you're all right with me." His point left little room for interpretation of his changing values: all whites weren't "devils"; many were antiracist and sympathetic to the black struggle, while African leaders like Tshombe may have been black but were a threat to blacks' interests. The message cost him further support among those who wished for a hard line when it came to race.

From Africa, Malcolm had contacted James 67X to help arrange a brief lecture tour in Britain, for which he would depart on November 30 and return on December 6—once again setting off abroad after he had barely settled back in the United States. Early on his day of departure he set aside time to contact patrons and colleagues in the Muslim world, where he was involved in a delicate balancing act. During his trip he had courted and received sponsorship from both the Muslim World League in Mecca and the Supreme Council for Islamic Affairs in Cairo, an arm of Nasser's government. These groups shared a deep commitment to Muslim ideals but otherwise could not have been more different, with the Saudi Muslim World League's conservatism and staunch anticommunism putting them at odds with Nasser, who by then had made Egypt practically a client state of the Soviet Union. The schism required Malcolm to become a pluralist in the Muslim world, an approach that had produced real breakthroughs during his travels. While he had been in Mecca, the Muslim World League had agreed to assign Sheikh Ahmed Hassoun to the New York Muslim community, and now Malcolm wrote the league's secretary-general, Muhammad Surur al-Sabban, to express his appreciation. His letter, however, was actually a cover under which to bring up a delicate issue. Malcolm had returned home to find the MMI virtually broke, with no funds to pay Hassoun's salary or to cover the cost of his lodgings. He blamed the lack of resources on the split with Elijah Muhammad: "We represent the Afro-American Muslims who have broken away from the Black Muslim Movement. We had to leave all our treasures behind." Estimating that it would cost four hundred to five hundred dollars for Hassoun's monthly living expenses, he did not ask for funds directly, but obliquely requested "instructions on how to solve this problem."

That same morning, perhaps anticipating the problems that might be caused in Egypt by news of his involvement with the Muslim World League, Malcolm also contacted Muhammad Taufik Oweida of the Supreme Council for Islamic Affairs. Since the SCIA had granted Malcolm twenty scholarships, he recognized the importance of presenting an organized official front for his groups, noting that "there is much reorganization to be done here." The immediate task was "to separate our religious activities from our nonreligious," which implied increasing the division between MMI and OAAU. Then, in a revealing comment, Malcolm explained his motives for cultivating the more conservative Muslims in Saudi Arabia:

I have gone quite far in establishing myself and the Muslim Mosque Inc., also with the Muslim World League which is headquartered at Mecca. I am hoping that you understand my strategy in cementing good relations with them. My heart is in Cairo and I believe the mose [*sic*] progressive relations forces in the Muslim world are in Cairo. I think that I can be more helpful and of more value to these progressive relation forces at Cairo by solidifying myself also with the more moderate or conservative forces that are headquartered in Mecca.

Touching down in London on December 1, he spent some of the next few days preparing for his most significant UK appearance, an event at Oxford University on the third. The student union had invited him to defend, in a formal debate, Barry Goldwater's statement that "extremism in the defense of liberty is no vice, and moderation in the pursuit of justice is no virtue." The BBC televised the event, which featured three speakers for the motion and three against it. In his presentation, Malcolm once again carefully separated himself from his Black Muslim past, emphasizing his commitment to orthodox Islam. He argued that since the U.S. government had failed to safeguard the lives and property of African Americans over several centuries, it was not unreasonable for blacks to use extreme measures to defend their liberties. Yet he also tried to ground this sentiment in a multiracial approach. "I firmly believe in my heart," he declared, that when the black man acts "to use any means necessary to bring about his freedom or put a halt to that injustice, I don't think he'll be by himself. . . . I for one will join in with anyone, I don't care what color you are, as long as you want to change this miserable condition." A few days later he lectured before a mostly Muslim audience of three hundred people, at the University of London. The British press registered the change in his outlook. The *Manchester Guardian* declared, "At one time whites in the United States called him a racialist, an extremist, and a Communist," but based on his university presentation, there was noted the appearance of a new Malcolm X: "relaxed, mellifluous and reasonable. He has the assurance of Dr. Billy Graham and details are swamped by the powerful generalities of his message. And no one should doubt the power."

Malcolm returned to the United States on December 6, and that same day he met privately with Wallace Muhammad. If the two men had followed the same arc in fleeing the ideas of the Nation and earning its enmity in the process, their journeys had ultimately left them in different circumstances. For all their disagreement with Elijah Muhammad and what they perceived as his heretical version of Islam, Wallace remained the heir apparent and had much more to lose than Malcolm. And while Malcolm had risen in stature and continued to make headlines, Wallace was toiling practically in obscurity in Philadelphia and Chicago, where he led Muslim groups so small they seemed under threat of dissolving at any moment. In fact, by the end of 1964, he was weeks away from giving up his leadership role altogether and taking up a carpet cleaning business in Chicago. He, too, had suffered through months of death threats from his father's men, yet for him, unlike Malcolm, standing down and staying alive remained an option, and an appealing one.

Despite the obstacles, Malcolm continued to ponder the idea of a merger with Wallace, perhaps because he believed the two of them standing together at the head of a major Muslim organization would present the most powerful repudiation possible of the Nation of Islam. At their meeting, Malcolm told Wallace that he was now truly an orthodox Muslim and that he did not consider the MMI or OAAU as permanent organizations—either could be disbanded. This made a certain kind of sense; Malcolm likely already saw that the MMI's overlap with the Nation left it ill equipped to grow into the kind of religious organization that could have the reach he wanted. The OAAU was still young and inchoate enough to be morphed into something more politically effective without discarding too many sunk costs. He may even have proposed that Wallace become the imam of a restructured MMI, so becoming the chief beneficiary of the extensive contacts Malcolm had forged in the Middle East. Wallace expressed interest, but remained noncommittal. Malcolm's incendiary rhetoric made him uncomfortable, and his interest in such a joint project ended where Malcolm's political passions began. He also knew as well as anyone the unpleasantness likely to be visited on Malcolm by the Nation at any time. Throwing in his lot so publicly would mean crossing the same threshold Malcolm had, and he had little desire to join his spiritual kinsman as marked man in his father's eyes. Ever perceptive, Malcolm sensed the roots of this reluctance, and a few weeks after their meeting he wrote Wallace (by then calling himself Walith) urging him to focus attention on his followers in Philadelphia, and to "forget Chicago . . . I would ignore the Black Muslim Movement completely." Pointedly he tried to keep Wallace clear of his own continuing war with Elijah Muhammad. "You are not ruthless enough to deal with a man like your father and his bloodthirsty henchmen. This is one reason why he doesn't molest you but he knows I can be just as ruthless and cold-blooded."

Around the time Malcolm returned from London, he learned about the romantic relationship between his wife and Charles Kenyatta. James 67X had been dreading the moment when his boss would finally ask him about it, and when Malcolm did broach the subject he was careful to be deliberately vague. Alone together in the office, Malcolm turned to James and said sadly, "I understand that my wife has been 'tripping the light fantastic' while I've been gone."

James kept his eyes glued to the papers on his desk and said nothing, but Malcolm pushed the issue. "Brother, they say that my wife is going with Charles 37."

James did not relish confirming this, nor did he wish to reveal that he had heard the rumors from Ella, so he lied, hoping to leave enough room in his response to suggest various interpretations of Charles's behavior. "I don't know anything about that," he told Malcolm. "But take this into consideration: Charles 37 is a street man, and he's very egotistical. So he could do things to make it seem like something is going on between him and your wife."

Malcolm thought for a moment and said, "If such a thing is going on, I'm not going to allow any of my personal problems to interfere with what I have to do."

At a meeting soon thereafter, Malcolm put a permanent end to the conflict between James and Charles by reaffirming that James was his number two man. In the black-and-white world of the MMI, this decision quickly made Charles persona non grata and put him in considerable danger of retaliation. The old pipe-squad instincts of the MMI brothers, ready to punish dissenters and betrayers at a moment's notice, were never far from the surface. But Malcolm quickly stepped in to calm the storm. He put out the word that absolutely no harm should come to Charles, and that he would not be barred from participation in any MMI or OAAU meetings. "The word was out to kill [Kenyatta]," James said. "And it was Malcolm who kept him from being 'terminated with extreme prejudice.'"

Malcolm's skillful defusing of the Betty situation lent the impression that cooler heads had prevailed, yet inwardly the news of infidelity seems to have loosened Malcolm's own marital bonds. What is difficult to know is whether the first such transgressions on his part occurred even earlier. Betty's speculation as to the nature of Malcolm's close relationship with Lynne Shifflett may have been paranoid, but it may also have been grounded in truth. And Malcolm's hesitant diary entries about the night spent with Fifi in Switzerland suggest the possibility of a more intimate involvement. Of these, no certainty can be had, but after his return from Africa, Malcolm appears to have begun an illicit sexual affair with an eighteen-year-old OAAU secretary named Sharon 6X Poole. Little is known about her or about their relationship except that it appears to have continued up to Malcolm's death. She joined Mosque No. 7 only months before Malcolm's silencing. Knowledge of the affair did not spread widely like the gossip of Betty's involvement with Kenyatta, but stayed close within Malcolm's core circle, for whom his protection was a paramount concern.

Though the specter of internal violence had been quelled, external threats continued to make their grim presence known. On December 12, Malcolm addressed a local group, the Domestic Peace Corps, as part of its Cultural Enrichment Lecture Series. Before an audience of two hundred on West 137th Street, Malcolm urged blacks to remain in the United States, but to "migrate to Africa culturally, philosophically, and spiritually." Emphasizing that he rejected violence "despite what the press may tell you," he also affirmed his opposition to "any form of racism." Black Americans needed to construct a coalition with emerging, independent African nations. He spoke again about the bombings of Congolese villages carried out by Belgian mercenaries and "American-trained, anti-Castro Cuban pilots" as acts of mass murder. But some of his most interesting commentary had to do with the capacity of the U.S. government to reform itself. "United States history is that of a country that does whatever it wants to by any means necessary . . . but when it comes to your and my interest, then all of this means become limited," he argued. "We are dealing with a powerful enemy, and again, I am not anti-American or un-American. I think there are plenty of good people in America, but there are also plenty of bad people in America and the bad ones are the ones who seem to have all the power." What he was conceding was that the solution to America's racial dilemma would not be found by African Americans alone. Also attending the lecture were several dozen NOI members, all dressed in dark suits and wearing "I am with Muhammad" red and white buttons, a reminder of the ever-present threat. Six police officers were assigned to the event, and no trouble erupted.

That same week, to Malcolm's excitement, Ernesto "Che" Guevara, the former guerrilla leader of the Cuban revolution, swept into town to address the General Assembly of the UN on December 11. At that moment, Guevara was perhaps Malcolm's closest analogue on the world stage, a relentless supporter of the struggles of oppressed people and a committed revolutionary. Like Malcolm he was deeply concerned about ongoing and recent events in Africa. In making broad connections between the Cuban revolution and other struggles around the globe, he gave special mention to "the painful case of the Congo, unique in modern history, that shows how the rights of the peoples can be thwarted with the utmost impunity." He insisted that the root of the Congo's misery was that nation's "immense wealth, which the imperialist nations want to keep under their control." In a language markedly similar to Malcolm's, he described the dynamics of neocolonialism as forms of military and economic collaboration between Western powers: "Who committed those crimes? Belgian paratroopers, brought in by U.S. planes, which left from English bases. . . . All free men in the world should prepare to avenge the crime in the Congo."

Malcolm invited Guevara to address his OAAU rally at the Audubon on December 13, but the Argentine declined to attend, concerned that his presence might be seen as a provocative foray into internal U.S. politics. Still, many of the themes Guevara had addressed at the UN were central to the discussion that evening, especially when Malcolm took the stage to fill time after Tanzanian minister Abdulrahman Muhammad Babu, who also happened to be in New York for the General Assembly, was late in arriving. "We're living in a revolutionary world and in a revolutionary age," Malcolm told the overflowing crowd, numbering at least five hundred and, by some reports, many more. We must realize, he said, "the direct connection between the struggle of the Afro-American in this country and the struggle of our people all over the world." For those who might suggest resolving the racial crisis in Mississippi before worrying about the Congo, he warned, "You'll never get Mississippi straightened out. Not until you start realizing your connection with the Congo." His argument defined Pan-Africanist logic, but also ran deeper in light of the "imperialist" connections that Guevara had drawn at the UN. Underlying Malcolm's main argument about the unity of the black struggle was an important point about exploitation. The "connection with the Congo" for black Americans had as much to do with the commonality of economic oppression as it did with race. It was this leap from race-specific ideas to broader ones about class, politics, and economics that pushed Malcolm's thinking forward in late 1964, a lesson that his travels in Africa had brought into focus.

Yet he continued to have difficulty conveying the change in his thinking to Harlem audiences, often because of his reliance on an older, cumbersome political language that lumped nearly all whites into one hostile group. He also defined the enemy as "the man" rather than in the more nuanced terms of class and politics. Indeed, at one point when he was calling for "a firm, uncompromising stand against the man," Malcolm was forced to stop in midsentence to explain that by "the man" he meant "the segregationist, lyncher, and exploiter." These speaking efforts found his mind in transition, and still struggling to find a new terminology to translate increasingly complex ideas into crowd-friendly language.

Babu finally arrived at the Audubon nearly two hours late, but before he took the stage, Malcolm presented the crowd with a delicious surprise: a statement of solidarity from Che Guevara, which Malcolm read aloud with pride: "Dear brothers and sisters of Harlem, I would have liked to have been with you and Brother Babu, but the actual conditions are not good for this meeting. Receive the warm salutations of the Cuban people and especially those of Fidel, who remembers enthusiastically his visit to Harlem a few years ago. United we will win." As the audience applauded, Malcolm relished the moment. The man, Malcolm said, "was in no position anymore to tell blacks who we should applaud for and who we shouldn't applaud for. And you don't see any anti-Castro Cubans around here—we eat them up."

Circumstantial evidence provided by James 67X suggests that Malcolm and Guevara briefly met that week in December. Although there is no direct evidence, Guevara's subsequent actions in 1965 can be accurately described as carrying out Malcolm's revolutionary agenda for the continent. The two men were kindred spirits politically, a bond revealed not only by the similarity of their worldviews but by Guevara's subsequent travels. Days after his UN speech, Guevara flew to Africa and literally traced Malcolm's steps from Algiers; on January 8 he was in Guinea; and from January 14 to 24 he visited Accra. He met with Julius Nyerere, and it was through Tanzania that Cuban guerrillas gained safe passage into the eastern provinces of Congo. And only days following Malcolm's assassination, Guevara met Nasser in Cairo, where he obtained the Egyptian government's support for the guerrilla war. That both men eventually met such a violent fate in the name of their struggles and found in death iconic stature as revolutionaries seems only to further bind their legacies.

———

During his final two months in Africa and the Middle East, Malcolm had said relatively little publicly about his feud with the Nation of Islam. After his return, he tried to remain silent about his dispute, but the gears set in motion within the Nation could no longer be stopped. There would be no more negotiation. The charismatic minister who had whipped members into a frenzy now became the object of that violent energy, and Malcolm's outspokenness about the Nation through 1964 had given its leaders more than enough fuel to keep the fires burning. NOI membership had stagnated without Malcolm's recruitment appeal, and as the paternity suit against Elijah Muhammad wended its way through the court system, it continued to produce damning public revelations, which could only be refuted as lies spread by their former national minister.

And though Malcolm had mostly kept quiet about the Nation during his time abroad, his political actions had been all too provocative. Muhammad and the Chicago headquarters bristled at Malcolm's successful negotiations with Islamic organizations in Cairo and Mecca, which had the effect of furthering perceptions of the Nation in the United States and the Middle East as beyond the boundaries of true Islam. This especially infuriated Muhammad, who had worked hard to Islamify the Nation in recent years, though always around the central, heretical idea of his own divinity. Hiring teachers of Arabic, cultivating relations with Islamic states abroad—all this had been done to strengthen the Nation's religious bona fides, yet by embracing orthodox Islam under his own program, Malcolm had marginalized the Nation in one fell swoop, circumscribing its membership growth at the most critical moment. This move, and its continuing ramifications as Malcolm broadened his reach, had made his murder all the more necessary from an institutional standpoint.

Throughout Malcolm's long absence in the summer and fall, the Nation had waged what might be called a one-sided jihad against him. On July 15, John Ali informed a meeting of Mosque No. 7 that the X had been stripped from Malcolm's name. He reminded the faithful that Malcolm had after all been a "thief, dope addict, and a pimp." Such vitriolic speeches found their complement in the slanderous campaign unfolding in the pages of *Muhammad Speaks*. On September 25, Captain Joseph and Atlanta leader Jeremiah X published an article entitled "Biography of a Hypocrite," aimed at characterizing Malcolm's entire career within the Nation as a record of opportunism. Since Malcolm had personally opened or had a hand in developing nearly every NOI mosque between 1953 and 1962, their task was difficult. Nevertheless, they constantly denigrated Malcom and managed to identify scores of transgressions that supposedly had undermined the Nation of Islam. In the same issue, Minister Carl of Wilmington, Delaware, described Malcolm as a "shift-with-the-wind WEATHERCOCK." Captain Clarence 2X Gill of Boston also denounced Malcolm and all other hypocrites, adding, "May Allah burn them in hell." On Malcolm's return to the United States he was met with another *Muhammad Speaks* broadside, dated November 26, by Edwina X of the Newark mosque. For Edwina X, the struggle to defeat everything Malcolm represented was vital: "As in all great struggles for truth and freedom, there are the envious, the insincere and the hypocritical who will attempt to smear and wreck the work of a Divine leader. We have had such a hypocrite in the NOI in the form of one Malcolm X Little." She then warned, "For one who has heard the truth and still wants to go astray—there is nothing but total destruction for such a defector." Probably the single most influential attack appeared in *Muhammad Speaks* under the name Louis X on December 4. "The die is set, and Malcolm shall not escape, especially after such evil, foolish talk," Farrakhan declared. "Such a man as Malcolm is worthy of death." This code phrase was a call to arms within the sect.

On the street, safety soon proved elusive for Malcolm's people in the MMI. In late October, Kenneth Morton, who had quit the mosque at the time of Malcolm's departure, was ambushed by members of the Fruit in front of his Bronx home. He was so severely beaten in the head that he subsequently died from his wounds. Captain Joseph denied that Mosque No. 7 and its officers had had any involvement in Morton's death, but no one in the MMI needed proof to convince them to keep a low profile. Benjamin 2X narrowly escaped a beating or worse at the hands of Malcolm's former driver Thomas 15X Johnson and a group of Nation thugs who chased him for several blocks. Almost as much a target as Malcolm himself, James 67X avoided sleeping in the same place for more than a night, rotating between four apartments, including one kept by his former roommate Anas Luqman.

Despite this gathering storm, Malcolm did not curtail his public activities. In mid-December he took off several days to speak at Harvard Law School. His talk, "The African Revolution and Its Impact on the American Negro," explained his ideas about Islam, drawing connections with Judaism and Christianity. He embraced the "brotherhood of all men," he said, "but I don't believe in wasting brotherhood on anyone who doesn't want to practice it with me." He drew again on a theme developed by Frantz Fanon, suggesting a link between the self-reinvention of black identity with the dismantling of racism. "Victims of racism are created in the image of the racists," Malcolm argued. "When the victims struggle vigorously to protect themselves from violence of others, they are made to appear in the image of criminals, as the criminal image is projected onto the victim." Liberation, he implied, was not simply political but cultural. His central point, however, was the necessity for blacks to transform their struggle from "civil rights" to "human rights," redefining racism as "a problem for all humanity." The OAAU favored getting "our problem before the United Nations," but it also supported black voting and voter education.

As Christmas drew near, Malcolm was invited to appear at the Williams Institutional Christian Methodist Episcopal Church in Harlem, where the principal speaker was the Mississippi freedom fighter Fannie Lou Hamer. The crowd at the Williams was somewhat small, about 175 people, but Malcolm gave a spirited and provocative presentation. His explorations in the philosophy of social movements in recent months had brought him face-to-face with an old debate within the Western left over how human beings come to perceive themselves as social actors, asking whether an external force, such as a tightly organized party, is necessary to bring oppressed people to full political consciousness, or if the oppressed by themselves have the ability to transform their own situations. Addressing this question, Malcolm came down strongly on the side of what has often been called spontaneity. "I, for one, believe that if you give people a thorough understanding of what it is that confronts them, and the basic causes that produce it, they'll create their own program," he remarked. "And when the people create a program, you get action." In effect, Malcolm's remarks implicitly rejected the Marxist-Leninist theory of a cadre-style revolutionary party and embraced C. L. R. James's belief that the oppressed possessed the power to transform their own existence.

If ordinary people possess the intelligence and potential for changing their conditions, around what economic principles should that take place? Here again Malcolm returned to socialism, but explained it in a new, geopolitical context. In his judgment, the basic geopolitical division of the world was not between the United States and the Soviet Union, but America versus communist China. "Among Asian countries, whether they are communist, socialist . . . almost every one . . . that has gotten independence has devised some kind of socialistic system, and this is no accident." Although Malcolm had visited neither China nor Cuba, it was clear that the socialist societies he admired most drew from the models of Mao and Castro.

That he should have looked to Asia, and specifically China, for examples made sense given the direction of his recent investigations into the history of global politics, and could also be placed in a much older context of black interest in China as a model for the struggle of oppressed peoples. As early as the turn of the century, W. E. B. Du Bois had made reference to the "color line" in *The Souls of Black Folk*, with the implication that "colored" people included Africans, Asians, Jews, and other minorities around the world engaged in a struggle against Western imperialism. Based on this argument, some blacks had entertained great sympathy for the Japanese empire in the 1930s. A generation later, many black leftists saw Mao Zedong as a triumphant leader of nonwhite people. The idea of black identification with Asia had even been reflected in the ideology of the Nation of Islam, which had viewed African Americans as genealogically "Asiatic," a classification that Malcolm had abandoned before eventually coming to see the connection differently, in global-political terms. He was encouraged in this direction by his relationship with Shirley Graham Du Bois and her son, David, who enthusiastically picked up the torch their patriarch had long carried. Indeed, by the end of his life, W. E. B. Du Bois had come to be a revered figure in Asia, celebrated both by the Chinese and by Nehru in India. He had perceived revolutionary China as a triumph for all colored people.

In the Williams church speech, Malcolm drew on the triumph of Asian socialism to return to the notion that capitalism as an economic system was inherently exploitative: "You can't operate a capitalistic system unless you are vulturistic; you have to have someone else's blood to suck to be a capitalist." The tide of history for people of African descent was moving inextricably toward the East: "When we look at the African continent, when we look at the trouble that's going on between East and West, we find that the nations in Africa are developing socialistic systems to solve their problems."

At the event, Malcolm invited Fannie Lou Hamer and the SNCC Freedom Singers, traveling with her, to attend the OAAU's rally at the Audubon that evening. The successful rally with Hamer opened for Malcolm and the OAAU a long-desired conduit for political work with a progressive organization in the South. Attention in the civil rights movement was directed at this moment at Selma, Alabama, where various groups hoped to launch a major voting rights initiative in the new year. Malcolm found Selma intriguing, and continued his efforts to redefine his image within the civil rights community. On Christmas Eve, accompanied by James 67X, he visited the home of James Farmer. Malcolm had learned that the CORE leader was soon embarking on a six-week tour of Africa, and he wanted to suggest local contacts. Farmer was oddly offended by James's presence. "Why did you bring the bodyguard?" he asked. "Do you think I'm going to kill you?"

Malcolm explained that James's presence was necessary because "there are a lot of people after me . . . they're bound to get me." During the visit, Farmer retrieved two postcards he had received from Malcolm when he was in Mecca, and he asked if Malcolm's inscriptions on the cards reflected a new racial outlook. Malcolm confirmed that his thinking had profoundly changed and that the distance between the two leaders, while still considerable, had been narrowed.

Yet Malcolm's progress on so many fronts was increasingly impeded by the Nation of Islam, which had begun to draw tight the net around him. By year's end, he was not safe in any city with an NOI presence, and when he traveled he was subjected to direct physical intimidation and threats. On December 23, when he appeared on the Joe Rainey program in Philadelphia, the station received a message that an attempt on his life would be made; Philadelphia police were called to protect Malcolm as he left the station. Two days later, on Christmas, the Nation sent Malcolm a clear message, brutal in its particulars, when four Boston Fruit led by mosque captain Clarence Gill ambushed Malcolm associate Leon 4X Ameer in the lobby of Boston's Sherry Biltmore hotel. Ameer, a former NOI officer who had been assigned to be a press representative of Muhammad Ali, had fallen from Ali's favor after Malcolm's split with the Nation, and took to laying low at the Biltmore. He suffered mightily at the hands of Gill and his men until the beating was broken up at gunpoint by a police officer. Yet this was not the worst of it. Later that night, after Gill had retreated to his hotel room to recover, a second Nation pipe squad broke into his room to finish what their brothers had started. Ameer was so severely injured that he was hospitalized for more than two weeks, yet Gill and his men, arrested after the first incident, were fined a mere hundred dollars each.

The day after Ameer's beatings, Malcolm returned to Philadelphia to be a guest on WPEN's Red Benson show. The program was broadcast from an auditorium open to the general public, and it soon became clear that without the presence of MMI security personnel and on a public stage or podium, Malcolm would be completely vulnerable. At least four NOI members were in the audience throughout the program. Returning to Philadelphia four days later, at two p.m. on December 30, Malcolm held a press conference at the Sheraton hotel, criticizing both black and white newspapers on their distorted coverage of the Congo crisis, and of Africa generally. Five hours later he attended the International Muslim Brotherhood dinner, where he delivered a talk of thirty to forty minutes. A significant number, perhaps more than thirty of those in attendance, were anti-Malcolm NOI members from Philadelphia. By nine p.m. Malcolm and a cordon of MMI security and MMI and OAAU supporters had returned to the Sheraton. An hour and a half later, approximately fifteen NOI members entered the hotel and began a frontal assault of MMI members. The brawling stopped when a police officer appeared. Malcolm immediately phoned Betty, instructing her not to let anyone into their house. One of his final acts of 1964 was to write to Akbar Muhammad, warning him that NOI leaders were trying "to destroy your image in the sight of the Black Muslims in the same way they did mine." He urged him to hold a press conference denouncing "these vicious people." Recent events had made him understand that international religious bodies of the Islamic world did not consider the Nation of Islam "as authentical [sic] . . . it is time [for them] to speak out and verify what I am saying. I am going to send letters to religious officials there in the Muslim world, enclosing your father's statements against you, claiming himself to be the Messenger of Allah and I am going to insist that they take a stand on your side." Malcolm's intervention was probably too manipulative, getting in the middle of the long-standing conflict between Akbar and his father. However, his basic threat—mobilizing international Islamic organizations to boycott the Nation of Islam—was no bluff. Nation headquarters genuinely feared that Malcolm could lead an international campaign that could effectively exclude it from being part of the *ummah*. Akbar and Wallace had been petulant in their criticisms of Elijah Muhammad, and little they had said actually threatened to damage the Nation. That was not true for Malcolm. The fatwa, or death warrant, may or may not have been signed by Elijah Muhammad; there is no way of knowing. It is far more likely that Muhammad, like the fabled King Henry II, announced no decision but made his feelings all too clear, allowing his underlings to take their own murderous initiative.

Despite his many other obligations, Malcolm continued to make time available for Alex Haley. The journalist now understood the importance of Malcolm's most recent reinvention, and it required him to expand the length of the *Autobiography*. In an October 1964 letter to Paul Reynolds, Haley had estimated that the book would be ready to hand over to Doubleday by late January 1965. "I am a little put-out," Haley pouted, that Malcolm "has rather crossed up the project by, one, staying away so long and, two, his new conversion." But Haley recognized that Malcolm's embrace of Islamic orthodoxy might, after all, be beneficial to increased book sales and "intense interest in the Moslem countries where he is viewed as the most famous Orthodox Brother in America." On November 19, Haley contacted Reynolds again, "happy to report" that Malcolm would be returning to the United States within the week. "So I am going to be on a plane Monday, to be awaiting him, to get the information I'll need to write new final chapters." Haley thus met with Malcolm several times in December 1964 and January 1965, incorporating his new views into the final chapters of the *Autobiography*.

Surprisingly little about the OAAU was mentioned in the new material, however. On February 14, Haley reported to Reynolds that he was "deep into winding up Malcolm X's book. . . . You'll have it prior [to] March . . . it's a powerful book."

———

Malcolm was increasingly a magnet for representatives of the freedom struggle, who no longer viewed him as a racial separatist. The end of 1964 marked a moment of convergence, when Malcolm's move away from stark separatism brought him into alignment with elements of the civil rights movement that were growing increasingly radicalized. Had Malcolm continued to mainstream his views, it is unclear how he would have negotiated relations a few years later with the Black Panthers, a group born of much of the intellectual framework Malcolm had assembled in the early to mid-1960s. Yet in this moment, Malcolm found himself able to straddle both the most leftist elements of the struggle and the mainstream. Early in 1965, the Malcolm-minded Floyd McKissick took control of CORE from James Farmer, continuing the group's decisive shift away from King's nonviolent integrationist model. And in the months after Freedom Summer, SNCC, too, had splintered along similar lines, with the pacifist Bob Moses set against the increasingly radicalized Stokely Carmichael, who would subsequently join the Black Panthers and later form the All-African People's Revolutionary Party. Near the end of 1964, a letter and attached money order had arrived at the OAAU's offices from future Panthers cofounder Bobby Seale, requesting a subscription to *Blacklash*.

Yet this period also saw Malcolm's most concerted and successful effort to court the civil rights mainstream. Just before the new year, he received a delegation of thirty-seven teenagers from McComb, Mississippi, who had traveled to New York City on the sponsorship of the SNCC. Greeting the young people at his Hotel Theresa office, Malcolm urged them to think for themselves, applauding those who were committed to nonviolence but also insisting that "if black people alone are going to be the ones who are nonviolent, then it's not fair." He presented the OAAU as "a new approach," rejecting traditional integrationist and separatist strategies in favor of "making our problem a world problem." The plight of Mississippi could not be overcome by focusing narrowly just on its problems. "It is important for you to know that when you're in Mississippi, you're not alone. . . . You've got as much power on your side as the Ku Klux Klan has on its side." Malcolm promised to send some of his militant followers to aid the freedom fighters. "We will organize brothers here in New York who know how to handle these kind of affairs," he vowed, "and they'll slip into Mississippi like Jesus slipped into Jerusalem."

On Sunday, January 3, the OAAU's evening program at the Audubon Ballroom featured color films taken by Malcolm during his travels. Despite freezing weather, the program attracted a crowd of seven hundred. Two days later Malcolm visited Montreal for an unusual reason: he was to appear on the CBC television program *Front Page Challenge*. With a format similar to the 1950s U.S. television show *What's My Line?*, guests answered questions from masked panelists, who attempted to guess their identities. Malcolm's panelists were Gordon Sinclair, Betty Kennedy, and Charles Templeton. Why would he go on a television game show? Perhaps it was another means to generate funds for his family. Or perhaps it was a way to display his softer personality to a mass audience.

He also continued to expand his rhetoric on the internationalist connections between Asia, Africa, and black America. As the featured speaker at the Militant Labor Forum at Palm Gardens on January 7, he noted that Vietnamese rice farmers had successfully fought "against all the highly mechanized weapons of warfare" of the United States. China's explosion of a nuclear bomb, he declared, "was a scientific breakthrough for the oppressed people of China." The communist Chinese displayed "their advanced knowledge of science to the point where a country which is as backward as *this* country keeps saying China is, and so behind everybody, and so poor, could come up with an atomic bomb. I had to marvel at that." He tied these developments to the legacies of imperialism and colonialism. Moise Tshombe, Malcolm explained, was an "agent of Western imperialism" in Africa, and he pointed out that in 1964 both Northern Rhodesia and Nyasaland, after years of effort, had successfully overthrown colonial powers, becoming independent Zambia and Malawi respectively. Taken together, these international events were all driven by the same global political forces, and African Americans' issues had to be addressed within that same dynamic context.

Over the next few days, Malcolm wrote a series of letters to consolidate the OAAU as an international movement. From Carlos Moore, an anti-Castro black Cuban who had nevertheless assisted Malcolm during the week he was in Paris, Malcolm solicited help in starting an office there. In a friendly letter to Maya Angelou, Malcolm praised her critique against talking "over the head of the masses," telling her that she was able to communicate with "plenty of [soul] and you always keep your feet firmly on the ground. This is what makes you, *you*." Without overt appeals, Malcolm's letter so flattered Angelou that it accelerated her decision to give up her teaching position in Ghana immediately to join this man in whom she had placed her faith and hopes.

On January 17, Malcolm showed up at a Harlem public vigil of one thousand people, standing in heavy snow, demanding school desegregation. Though he was constantly on the watch for NOI attacks, he seems to have decided that significantly large crowds presented a stronger deterrent to violence. In this case, he may have also been persuaded by the fact that most of the protesters were white, which made an attack even more unlikely. Organized by EQUAL, a parents group, the protest began at four p.m. on Saturday afternoon and ended twenty-four hours later. Among those participating were the Reverend Milton Galamison and Dr. Arthur Logan of the advocacy group HARYOU (Harlem Youth Opportunities Unlimited), two black liberals whose favor Malcolm sought.

Yet although he had braved the cold and potential threats to be there, Malcolm's comments about the effort reported by the *Times* were neither supportive nor encouraging. "Whites should spend more time influencing whites," he advised. "These people have good intentions, but they are misdirected." His complaint—that "Harlem doesn't need to be told about integration"—largely missed the point.

Malcolm frequently ran into trouble like this in his speeches and remarks in early 1965, partly because he was trying to appeal to so many different constituencies. He took different tones and attitudes depending on which group he was speaking to, and often presented contradictory opinions only days apart. That he was not caught up in these contradictions more often owed to the fact that news traveled slowly across the country, that black politics were underreported, and that speeches were not regularly recorded. In his later speeches outside the United States, he was at his most revolutionary. There the Malcolm who sometimes advocated armed violence would appear, generating significant controversy, as would soon be the case in England. At home, he was more subdued, more conciliatory, yet on many occasions he would alternately praise King and other civil rights leaders one day and ridicule them and liberal Democrats the next. He also counted on the support of the Trotskyists, making overt appeals to them in speeches that seemed to be in support of a socialist system, often at the expense of building alliances to his ideological right. But Malcolm could not restrain himself, because he sincerely believed that blacks and other oppressed Americans had to break from the existing two-party system.

This balancing act partly explains his contradictions, but when it came to his ambivalence about King and movement liberals, Malcolm's political beliefs may have led him to misunderstand the fundamental importance of the mainstream civil rights struggle to the large majority of black Americans. Whereas he, along with an increasingly large faction of the black left, criticized the flaws in the nonviolent approach, they did not acknowledge how rewarding even incremental progress was. In several speeches, Malcolm explained away Lyndon Johnson's massive electoral mandate from millions of black voters by claiming that African Americans had been duped and "controlled by Uncle Tom leaders." It apparently did not occur to him that great social change usually occurs through small transformations in individual behavior; that for blacks who had been denied voting rights for three generations, casting their ballots for reformist candidates wasn't betraying the cause or being "held on the plantation by overseers." To them, King was an emancipating figure, not an Uncle Tom.

He similarly misread the sentiment behind the EQUAL school desegregation rally. By 1965, the masses of black parents and children were fed up with substandard schools and the racial tracking of black and Latino children into remedial education. The vigil was part of a citywide struggle for educational reform. Social change that matters to most people occurs around practical issues they see every day, yet Malcolm still failed to appreciate the necessary connection between gradual reforms and revolutionary change.

That same weekend, Jack Barnes and Barry Sheppard of the Trotskyist Young Socialist Alliance interviewed Malcolm for the group's publication, *Young Socialist*. In the resulting article, Malcolm explained why in recent months he had dropped the phrase "black nationalism" to describe his politics. During his first visit to Ghana the previous May, he had been impressed by the Algerian ambassador, "a revolutionary in the true sense of the word." When told that Malcolm's philosophy was "black nationalism," the Algerian asked, "Where does that leave him? Where does that leave the revolutionaries of Morocco, Egypt, Iraq, Mauritania?" The phrase "black nationalism" was highly problematic in a global context, because it excluded too many "true revolutionaries." This was the main reason that Malcolm increasingly sought refuge under the political rubric of Pan-Africanism. But he may also have recognized that there were enormous difficulties with this theoretical category as well, which ranged from the anticommunism of George Padmore to the angry Marxism-Leninism of Nkrumah in exile after 1966.

Despite his newfound reluctance at being described as a black nationalist, Malcolm still perceived political action in distinctly racial categories, which may further explain why he made no moves to integrate his groups. For example, when Barnes and Sheppard asked what contributions antiracist young whites and especially students could make, he urged them not to join Negro organizations. "Whites who are sincere should organize among themselves and figure out some strategy to break down the prejudice that exists in white communities." In the year ahead, Malcolm predicted more blood in the streets, as white liberals and Negro moderates would fail to divert the social unrest brewing. "Negro leaders have lost their control over the people. So that when the people begin to explode—and their explosion is fully justified, not unjustified—the Negro leaders can't contain it."

The next day Malcolm flew to Toronto, to be the guest on the *Pierre Berton Show* on CFTO television. He resisted discussing Muhammad's out-of-wedlock children, but still managed to castigate him as a false prophet. "When I ceased to respect him as a man," he told Berton, "I could see that he was also not divine. There was no God with him at all." Malcolm now claimed that God embraced Jews, Christians, and Muslims alike—"We all believe in the same God"—and denied that whites were "devils," insisting "this is what Elijah Muhammad teaches. . . . A man should not be judged by the color of his skin but rather by his conscious behavior, by his actions." Malcolm explicitly rejected the separatist political demand for a black state or nation, stating, "I believe in a society in which people can live like human beings on the basis of equality." When Berton asked whether his guest still believed in the Nation of Islam's eschatology of "an Armageddon," Malcolm artfully turned this NOI theory into the language of revolution and Marxist class struggle:

I do believe that there will be a clash between East and West. I believe that there will ultimately be a clash between the oppressed and those that do the oppressing. I believe that there will be a clash between those who want freedom, justice, and equality for everyone, and those who want to continue the systems of exploitation. I believe that there will be that kind of clash, but I don't think that it will be based upon the color of the skin, as Elijah Muhammad has taught it.

At the next OAAU public rally, held on January 24, he spoke on African and African-American history, from ancient black civilizations and slavery

up to the present era. The OAAU leadership planned for Malcolm to follow this lecture with two others: a second analyzing current conditions,
and a third about the future, presenting the organization's program to the
public.

Malcolm extensively read history, but he was not a historian. His interpretation of enslavement in the United States cast black culture as utterly
decimated by the institution of slavery and framed slavery's consequences
in America as the very worst forms of racial oppression. As historical analysis, this approach did not adequately measure the myriad forms of resistance mounted by enslaved blacks. But in political terms, his emphasis on
American exceptionalism and its unrelenting oppression of blacks was a
brilliant motivating tool for African Americans. Peter Goldman explained
that Malcolm "differentiated between America and the rest of the world. . . .
I don't think he romanticized Western Europe, but I think he probably
thought they were doing a little better than we were." Placing the United
States on the last level of racial oppression, even below South Africa, in a
curious way recognized the importance of the African-American struggle.

Two days after his history lecture at the OAAU rally, Malcolm gave an
address at Dartmouth College, in Hanover, New Hampshire. The talk was
arranged by a Muslim undergraduate student, Omar Osman, who was affiliated with the Islamic Center in Geneva. Demand for admission was so
great that while fifteen hundred attended, five hundred more were unable
to get in. Malcolm's lecture built upon his new image as a human rights advocate. Barriers like religion, race, and color could no longer be used as excuses
for inaction against injustice. "We must approach the problem as humans
first," he stated, "and whatever else we are second."

Bold lectures like this before large crowds stood in stark contrast to the
scrambling he often took to avoid altercations with the Nation, though he
continued even at this late date, and despite all warnings from those who
cared about him, to provoke his former brothers. He had not let go of his
involvement in the paternity lawsuit pending against Elijah Muhammad in
Los Angeles, which was now on the verge of proceeding. The case had been
delayed until a hearing was finally set on January 11, 1965. However, on the
day of the hearing neither Evelyn Williams nor Lucille Rosary showed up.
The judge consequently removed the case from the calendar until an explanation was given, and when it came it was hardly surprising: the women
had been so intimidated by the NOI that they had become frightened for
their own safety. They were living together in Los Angeles, but had moved

twice out of fear. When contacted by Los Angeles attorney Gladys Towles Root, Malcolm encouraged her to speed up her efforts, saying, "If the case doesn't get to trial soon, I won't be alive to testify."

His prophecy gained credence almost immediately. At approximately eleven fifteen p.m. on January 22, Malcolm opened the front door of his home and took several steps outside when suddenly several Muslims who had been hiding rushed toward him. "They came at me three seconds too soon," Malcolm later recounted. He ran back inside, secured the door, and called the police. But the Nation had made its point: once he left his home, Malcolm would be safe nowhere. The police arrived, searched the surrounding blocks, but unsurprisingly failed to find the attackers. Malcolm denied allegations in the press that he traveled only with a bodyguard. He retorted, "My alertness is my bodyguard." In truth, he routinely traveled with James 67X or Reuben Francis or both, and had recently taken to carrying a tear gas pen for self-defense.

Undeterred by the attack, Malcolm flew out to the West Coast, where on January 28 he met with Evelyn, Lucille, and Gladys Root to secure their continued commitment to the lawsuit. Malcolm promised personally to testify at the hearing. Then, by coincidence, a group of NOI loyalists ran into Malcolm in the lobby of his hotel. Over the next two days they closely tracked his movements, always staying close enough to let Malcolm know he was being watched and that they might strike at any moment. Root attested later that Malcolm seemed truly frightened throughout this trip. On the day he was to leave town, two carloads of Fruit tailed Malcolm's automobile on the highway to the airport. Without any weapon to defend himself, Malcolm found a cane in the car, poked it out a side window, and aimed it like a rifle. It was convincing enough; the would-be attackers quickly pulled back. At the airport, though, there were several more Muslims waiting. The LAPD responded by taking Malcolm through an underground tunnel to reach his plane. Prior to embarking, the captain of the flight ordered all the passengers off and had the plane thoroughly searched for bombs. As soon as he arrived in Chicago, Malcolm was placed under close police guard.

The stop in Chicago was itself a bold provocation. Malcolm had come to the Nation's base for the very purpose of further undermining its reach. He was there to be interviewed by the Illinois attorney general's office, which was considering him as a witness in a legal case, *Thomas Cooper v. State of Illinois*. Cooper, a prisoner and follower of Elijah Muhammad at the Illinois state penitentiary, was suing the state on constitutional grounds, claiming that while incarcerated he had been restricted from obtaining a copy of the Qur'an and other reading materials related to the Nation of Islam. As a witness, Malcolm was prepared to argue that the Nation was not a legitimately Islamic religious organization, and that therefore it did not merit access to penal institutions. His newfound hostility to the Nation's religious activities inside prisons directly contradicted his extensive efforts to convert prisoners, going back to his own incarceration in the 1940s. But his opposition to the Nation was now so intense that he was willing to support the efforts of the Illinois attorney general to ban the Nation from access to those in the penal system. This purpose alone would have raised the Nation's hackles, but Malcolm did not pass quietly through town. Instead, he devoted nearly ten full hours to television, radio, and newspaper interviews, including a taped appearance on the popular *Kup's Show* on WBKB.

Though Malcolm returned safely to New York City on January 31, the incident in Los Angeles had left him shaken. That night he seemed subdued addressing an OAAU rally at the Audubon before a crowd of 550, an unusually large draw for the group. The next day, he gave a revealing interview to the *Amsterdam News.* "My death has been ordered by higher-ups in the movement," he said of the NOI. He had become convinced that the greater the negative publicity concerning the Nation's attempts to kill him, the safer he would be; if any harm came to him, he figured, law enforcement would immediately place members of the Nation under arrest. The statement, however, had no immediate effect. Two days later, after he appeared as a panelist on the TV show *Hotline,* on WPIX in New York City, with Ossie Davis, Jimmy Breslin, and others, Nation thugs swarmed Malcolm's men outside the television studio, precipitating a violent brawl. Malcolm again escaped unharmed.

During these final days, many of Malcolm's closest associates detected disturbing changes in his behavior and physical appearance. For years, Malcolm had come to public meetings and lectures impeccably dressed, always wearing a clean white shirt and tie. But now, he always seemed to be tired, even exhausted and depressed. His shoes weren't shined; his clothing was frequently wrinkled. There was even "a kind of fatalism" in his conversations, observes Malcolm X researcher Abdur-Rahman Muhammad. In his personal exchanges with Anas Luqman during this time, Malcolm ruminated that "the males in his family didn't die a natural death." To Luqman, just before the assassination, the leader seemed to resign himself to his fate: "Whatever's going to happen, is going to happen." The disenchantment of Malcolm loyalists in their leader was also directly related to the confusion and alienation they felt about the new political directions they had been given. In practical terms, as Abdur-Rahman Muhammad explains, the ex–Black Muslims who had followed Malcolm into the MMI "didn't sign up for orthodox Islam. They didn't sign up for this OAAU thing. And they positively resented the fact that the OAAU seemed to be where Malcolm was putting all of his energy."

Despite his growing uncertainty and bouts with depression, Malcolm steeled himself to press forward. On February 3 he took an early-morning flight from New York City, arriving in Montgomery, Alabama, around noon. An hour and a half later he was addressing three thousand students at Tuskegee Institute's Logan Hall. The auditorium was so crowded that even before the formal program began hundreds had to be turned away. Malcolm's title for the lecture, "Spectrum on Political Ideologies," did not reflect its content, which covered much of the same ground as his other recent addresses. He condemned the Tshombe regime, the Johnson administration's links to it, and the growing U.S. involvement in Vietnam, suggesting the United States was "trapped" there. When asked about his disputes with Elijah Muhammad, he responded with a soft, theological argument: "Elijah believes that God is going to come and straighten things out. . . . I'm not willing to sit and wait on God to come. . . . I believe in religion, but a religion that includes political, economic, and social action designed to eliminate some of these things, and make a paradise here on earth while we're waiting for the other."

The students affiliated with SNCC who attended his lecture invited him to visit Selma, then the headquarters of the national campaign for black voting rights, and only one hundred miles west in the heart of the Black Belt. Malcolm could not refuse. The beauty of the Selma struggle was its brutal simplicity: hundreds of local blacks lined up at Selma's Dallas County building daily, demanding the right to register to vote; white county and city police beat and arrested them. By the first week in February thirty-four hundred people had been jailed, including Dr. King. Under cover of darkness, terrorist groups like the Ku Klux Klan harassed civil rights workers, black families, and households. On February 4, Malcolm addressed an audience of three hundred at the Brown's Chapel African Methodist Episcopal Church. Significantly, while the event had been arranged through SNCC, after some negotiations it was formally cosponsored by King's SCLC. Malcolm's sermon praised King's dedication to nonviolence, but he advised that should white America refuse to accept the nonviolent model of social change, his own example of armed "self-defense" was an alternative. After the talk he met with Coretta Scott King, stating that in the future he would work in concert with her husband. Before leaving, he informed SNCC workers that he planned to start an OAAU recruitment drive in the South within a few weeks. In this one visit, he had significantly expanded the OAAU's purpose and mission, from lobbying the UN to playing an activist role in the grassroots trenches of voting rights and community organizing.

Back in New York, he purchased air tickets for London, with stops in Paris and Geneva, for what would be his final trip out of the country. He planned to attend the first Congress of the Council of African Organizations, held in London on February 6–8, and then to move on to Paris to work with Carlos Moore in consolidating the OAAU's presence there. Arriving in London, he gave interviews to the New China news agency and the *Ghanaian Times*. As had happened so many times before, the good rapport he had developed with movement activists in Selma and Tuskegee quickly disappeared in favor of more radical sentiments. He told the Chinese media that "the greatest event in 1964 was China's explosion of an atom bomb, because this is a great contribution to the struggle of the oppressed people in the world." He deplored the 1964 Civil Rights Act as "nothing but a device to deceive the African people," and characterized U.S. racism as being "an inseparable part of the entire political and social system." And his opposition to the Vietnam War was escalating: the basic choice America had was "to die there or pull out. . . . Time is against the U.S., and the American people do not support the U.S. war."

In his interview with the *Ghanaian Times*, he promoted the call by Nkrumah for the establishment of an African union government. Those leaders who reject the creation of a union, he declared, "will be doing a greater service to the imperialists than Moise Tshombe." Once again Malcolm the visionary anticipated the future contours of history, with the creation of the African Union a half century later. Addressing the conference on February 8, he encouraged the African press to challenge the racist stereotypes and distortions of Africans in the Western media. In the Western press, he noted, the African freedom fighter was made to look "like a criminal."

On February 9 he flew on to Paris, yet at customs the authorities detained him and refused to allow him to enter the country. During a subsequent two-hour delay, he learned that the government of Charles de Gaulle had determined that his presence was "undesirable," and that a talk he had scheduled with the Federation of African Students might "provoke demonstrations." Returning to London, he quickly organized a press conference, challenging the French decision. "I did not even get as far as immigration control," he complained. "I might as well have been locked up."

A telephone interview was arranged in London that was audiotaped and later played on speakers for a crowd of three hundred in Paris. The incident seemed to have pulled him back for the moment, and he once again returned to the language of unity and racial harmony. "I do not advocate violence," he explained. "In fact, the violence that exists in the United States is the violence that the Negro in America has been a victim of." On the issues of black nationalism and the Southern civil rights movement, he once again channeled King. "I believe in taking an uncompromising stand against any forms of segregation and discrimination that are based on race. I myself do not judge a man by the color of his skin."

Already he suspected that the restriction on his travel went deeper than mere concern on the part of the French government, and the next day he forwarded a letter of protest to U.S. secretary of state Dean Rusk. "While in possession of an American passport, I was denied entry to France with no explanation." He called for "an investigation being made to determine why this incident took place." The enforced change of schedule allowed Malcolm to explore the racial politics of Great Britain for several additional days, and during this time he was interviewed by *Flamingo* magazine, a London-based publication read primarily by blacks in Great Britain. What is surprising is the harshness Malcolm displayed to distinguish himself from civil rights moderates in the States. "King and his kind believe in turning the other cheek," he stated, almost in contempt. "Their freedom fighters follow the rules of the game laid down by the big bosses in Washington, D.C., the citadel of imperialism." He once more disavowed any identification as a "racialist": "I adopt a judgment of deeds, not of color." He appeared to call not for voting rights and electoral change, but Guevara-inspired insurrection. "Mau Mau I love," he stated, applauding the Kenyan guerrilla struggle of the 1950s. "When you put a fire under a pot, you learn what's in it." He added, "Anger produces action." When asked about his reasons for leaving the Nation, he focused on politics, not personalities or religion. "The original brotherhood [of the NOI] became too lax and conservative." He accused some NOI leaders of greed, in response to which "I formed the Muslim Mosque, which is not limited by civil rights in America, but rather worldwide human rights for the black man."

On February 11 he delivered a lecture at the London School of Economics, a frank and lively assessment of the politics of race in the United States. Racial stigmatization, he explained, projects negative images of nonwhites as criminals; as a consequence, "it makes it possible for the power structure to set up a police state." He then drew parallels between the U.S. treatment of African Americans with the conditions of the West Indian and Asian populations in Great Britain, where racist stereotypes promoted political apathy among minorities, making them believe that change was impossible. "Police state methods are used . . . to suppress the people's honest and just struggle against discrimination and other forms of segregation," he insisted.

Malcolm described a generational change that separated the older African leaders from the rising generation of young revolutionaries. The older "generation of Africans . . . have believed that they could negotiate . . . and eventually get some kind of independence." The new generation rejected gradualism: "If something is yours by right, then you fight for it or shut up." Next he addressed the problem of black cultural identity. "We in the West were made to hate Africa and to hate Africans." West Indians in Britain, he said, "don't want to accept their origin; they have no origin, they have no identity . . . they want to be Englishmen." The same process of identity confusion occurred among African Americans. "By skillfully making us hate Africa . . . our color became a chain. It became a prison." An appreciation of black culture would liberate blacks to advocate their own interests.

Finally, he returned to the concept of a two-stage African revolution—first gradual reform, then revolution. The same social process, he implied, might be at work in the United States. "The Black Muslim movement was one of the main ingredients in the civil rights struggle," he claimed, remarkably, without referencing the massive evidence to the contrary. "[Whites] should say thank you for Martin Luther King, because Martin Luther King has held Negroes in check up to recently. But he's losing his grip; he's losing his control."

For Malcolm, the strategic pursuit of Pan-African and Third World empowerment meant addressing new constituencies who looked to him for inspiration and leadership. South Asians and West Indians who experienced ethnic and religious discrimination in the English working-class town of Smethwick, for example, contacted him to solicit his support. The BBC, which at that time was filming a documentary on Smethwick, followed Malcolm around with a camera crew—although it was unsuccessful in its attempts to arrange a meeting between Malcolm and the right-wing Conservative Party member Peter Griffiths, who represented Smethwick's parliamentary seat. After meeting with local minority leaders, Malcolm determined that town authorities were buying up vacant houses and selling them only to whites, thus restricting what houses were available for Asians and blacks. At a press conference in nearby Birmingham, he denounced the schemes to limit home sales and rentals in the town to non-Europeans. "I have heard that the blacks of Smethwick are being treated in the same way as the Negroes were treated in Birmingham, Alabama—like Hitler treated the Jews," he charged. This was inflammatory enough, but as so often he took the argument even further, toward a call for violent revolution. "If colored people here continue to be oppressed," he warned, "it will start off a bloody battle."

A major national debate erupted, with the BBC roundly condemned for assisting Malcolm's investigations. Even the *Sun*, at that time a liberal newspaper, editorialized that Malcolm's visit had been a "deplorable mistake." Cedric Taylor, the chairman of the Standing Conference of West Indian Organizations for the Birmingham district, condemned his visit. "Conditions here are entirely different from Alabama," he told a *Los Angeles Times* reporter. The West Indians in his town, he judged, were "not the sort of people who would want to follow Malcolm X."

Before leaving the UK, Malcolm was interviewed by a correspondent for the liberal South African newspaper *Sunday Express*. His rhetoric grew even more heated, as he urged blacks in Angola and South Africa to employ violence "all the way. . . . I don't give the [South African] blacks credit in any way . . . for restraining themselves or confining themselves to ground rules that limit the scope of their activity." He dismissed the Nobel Peace Prize recipient Chief Albert Luthuli as "just another Martin Luther King, used to keep the oppressed people in check." To Malcolm, South Africa's "real leaders" were Nelson Mandela of the African National Congress and Robert Sobukwe, founder of the Pan-African Congress. He then entertained the possibility of the OAAU taking up the cause of Australian aborigines. "Just as racism has become an international thing, the fight against it is also becoming international. . . . [Racism's] victims were kept apart from each other." The larger point for him was to make the case for Pan-Africanism— that blacks regardless of nationality and language had a common destiny. "We believe," he explained, "that it is one struggle in South Africa, Angola, Mozambique, and Alabama. They are all the same."

Malcolm arrived back at John F. Kennedy airport on February 13 to grim news. Several weeks before, he had submitted to the Queens court a request for a "show cause" order aimed at staying his family's scheduled eviction. It was now obvious, however, that his family would lose their home and would have to begin looking for temporary housing. Malcolm had also just learned that Betty was again pregnant, this time with twins. What had been an extremely difficult financial situation—supporting four children—would soon be even more challenging with six.

But his thoughts soon returned to politics. He had not been able to shake off the larger implication of his incident at French customs. As he entered his Hotel Theresa office, he admitted to his associates that he had been making a "serious mistake" by focusing attention on the NOI Chicago headquarters, "thinking all of my problems were coming from Chicago, and they're not." Colleagues asked where the "trouble" was coming from. "From Washington," Malcolm replied.

After a few hours of conversation with staff at his office, he drove to his East Elmhurst home. This time, it was without incident. Malcolm was scheduled to wake up early to fly to Detroit to deliver an important public address that day. As on so many other nights, he fell asleep upstairs while working late into the night in his study.

At two forty-five a.m., the Shabazz family's sleep was shattered by the crack of a window downstairs, and seconds later a Molotov cocktail exploded, quickly filling the entire house with black smoke. As Malcolm raced downstairs to the children's room, a second bomb landed. A third struck a rear window but glanced off, without combusting. Malcolm helped Betty escape through the rear door, then gathered the children together and led them into the backyard. A few seconds later he dashed back into the now blazing house to retrieve important property and clothing. "I was almost frightened by his courage and efficiency in a time of terror," Betty would later reflect. "I always knew he was strong. But at that hour I learned how great his strength was." By the time firefighters arrived to put out the blaze, the house was engulfed in flames.

For decades there has been intense speculation regarding the firebombing of Malcolm's home on February 14, 1965. The actions of three parties have been questioned: Malcolm himself, the Nation of Islam, and law enforcement. Since the Shabazz family faced imminent eviction, some thought that Malcolm firebombed the house out of malice. The argument placing the blame on the Nation was evident, based on the escalating violence aimed against Malcolm. Firebombing his home, endangering his wife and four small children, was a logical next step. There was also speculation that either BOSS or the FBI, or perhaps their informants, committed the bombing, which was the view held by OAAU stalwarts like Herman Ferguson and Peter Bailey. The most persuasive evidence pointed to the Nation of Islam. Almost forty years after the firebombing, NOI member Thomas 15X Johnson acknowledged that the Nation "definitely did it." One participant, he recalled, was Edward X—"a close friend of mine, and I didn't know until after it happened that he was a part of that." Edward was "just a dedicated follower. Him and two other brothers did that firebombing [of the] house."

Malcolm's supporters had quickly gathered outside the burning house, where it was decided that Betty and the four girls would be taken to the home of Tom Wallace, who also lived in Queens. Standing outside in the freezing cold, Betty learned that Malcolm still intended to travel to Detroit that day, and she erupted into an almost uncontrollable rage. But his mind was made up. The firebombing would not frighten him into canceling his speaking commitments. Death had missed him and his family that night; he would not run from it tomorrow.

CHAPTER 15

Death Comes on Time

February 14–February 21, 1965

When a bleary-eyed Malcolm disembarked at Detroit airport at nine thirty a.m. and checked in at the Statler Hilton hotel, his friends were worried for his safety and his sanity. His home had just been firebombed, and his wife and children were in hiding. His coat jacket stank of smoke; he had grabbed the clothing from the half-burned residence. Since being shaken from sleep by the firebombs, he had not slept. One Detroit friend gave him a sedative; Malcolm napped briefly, yet he had a schedule to keep, and soon he was awakened to be interviewed by WXYZ-TV at four p.m. He was then taken to the Ford Auditorium, where he delivered the keynote address at the first annual Dignity Projection and Scholarship Award, where Sidney Poitier and the opera star Marian Anderson also received honors. The program was sponsored by the Afro-American Broadcasting Company, and chaired by a good friend of Malcolm's, attorney Milton Henry, who was also a leader of the Freedom Now Party in Michigan.

The Reverend Albert Cleage remembered Malcolm's troubled condition backstage before the event, tired and irritable from the effects of smoke inhalation, and when he took the podium his usual sharpness had abandoned him. At first he rambled through stories of his African and Middle Eastern travels, but eventually found surer footing on the theme of cultural identity that had recently traced its way through his speeches. He characterized the decade 1955–65 as "the era in which we witnessed the emerging of Africa. The spirit of Bandung created a working unity that made it possible for the Asians, who were oppressed, and the Africans, who were oppressed . . . to work together toward gaining independence." In the United States, the civil rights movement and the Black Muslims emerged. The

Nation of Islam "frightened the white man so much he began to say, 'Thank God for old Uncle Roy [Wilkins] and Uncle Whitney and Uncle A. Philip.'" The audience laughed; Malcolm not only ridiculed the moderates, he tried to paint the Nation of Islam's role in the most favorable light. Black Muslims, he said, "made the whole civil rights movement become more militant, and more acceptable to the white power structure. . . . We forced many of the civil rights leaders to be even more militant than they intended." But in 1965, the situation calls for "new methods. . . . It takes power to talk to power. It takes madness almost to deal with a power structure that's so corrupt."

Back in New York, a media circus had gathered outside the charred wreckage of his home. The Molotov cocktails had totally destroyed two of the rooms and left three others severely damaged. In a bold move, Captain Joseph drove to the house and met with reporters standing outside. "We own this place, man," he protested. "We have money tied up here. . . . He didn't even give us the courtesy of a phone call." Allegations swirled suggesting the Nation's involvement, but Newark minister James Shabazz told reporters that the Nation "was unlikely to bomb a house which it was about to repossess. Of course, we would rather have had our property than a burned-out building. . . . We sure didn't bomb it." Speculation was also rife that Malcolm had been responsible after detectives found a small bottle containing gasoline on a child's dresser, and the Nation amplified these rumors in the press. For his part, Malcolm threw the blame back at them. "I have no compassion or mercy or forgiveness for anyone who attacks sleeping babies," he told the press. "The only thing I regret is that two black groups have to fight and kill each other off." Yet to confidants, he broached more conspiratorial possibilities. "The Nation of Islam does not attack women and children," Herman Ferguson recalled him saying. "The Nation would not have burned my house with my wife and children in that house. That was the government." He could not have known what Thomas 15X later confirmed, that the NOI had in fact been responsible.

He arrived back in New York on February 15, and spent part of the day checking on damage to the house and conducting interviews. The OAAU had planned to unveil its program that evening, but the firebombing had changed the agenda, bringing out a large crowd of seven hundred to hear what Malcolm had to say about it. Benjamin 2X opened up the evening meeting with a short talk. Malcolm's speech, "There's a Worldwide Revolution Going On," was not his final public lecture, but it was certainly the most significant of those he gave in the last two weeks of his life. He began by mentioning the firebombing, and how stunned he was to see the Nation "using the same tactic that's used by the Ku Klux Klan." After bouncing through a few other topics, he circled back to offer his interpretation about how the Nation of Islam had lost its way. Before 1960, he explained, "there was not a better organization among black people in this country than the Muslim movement. It was militant. It made the whole strength of the black man in this country pick up momentum." But after Muhammad's return from Mecca in early 1960, things changed. Muhammad began to be "more interested in wealth. And, yes, more interested in girls." The audience erupted with laughter. According to Malcolm, a conspiracy existed to "suppress news that would open the eyes" of NOI members about their leader. As long as Elijah Muhammad ran the Nation of Islam, "it will not do anything in the struggle that the black man is confronted with in this country." One proof of this was the Nation's failure to challenge the terrorist activities of the Ku Klux Klan. "They know how to do it. Only to another brother." As the audience applauded, Malcolm added soberly, "I am well aware of what I'm setting into motion. . . . But I have never said or done anything in my life that I wasn't prepared to suffer the consequences for."

After a one-night trip to Rochester to deliver a speech, he returned to New York City to face the ugly business of emptying his ruined home. The court order to evict the Shabazz household was to be enforced on the morning of February 18, so just after one a.m. he and about fifteen MMI and OAAU members drove out to the house in advance of the city marshal's arrival. In four hours they cleared the building of all items—furniture, clothing, files, desks, photographs, correspondence—and placed everything in a small moving van and three station wagons. When the marshal pulled up a few hours later along with several assistants, they discovered the house completely vacant.

For a second day, Malcolm was working without sleep, compelled forward through a whirlwind of activity by nerves and sheer will. Several weeks earlier, he had planned to travel to Jackson on February 19, to address a rally of Hamer's Mississippi Freedom Democratic Party. The firebombing forced him to reschedule, and instead of traveling, he gave more interviews. That morning he spoke with the *New York Times*, telling the paper that he lived "like a man who's already dead." The remarks he had been making for months about his own demise took on new gravity in light of the firebombing. "This thing with me," he said plainly, "will be resolved by death and violence."

Later that morning he was interviewed by an ABC camera crew. In the afternoon, Malcolm delivered his final public address, before fifteen hundred students at the Barnard College gymnasium, explaining that the black revolt in the United States "is part of the rebellion against the oppression and colonialism which has characterized this era." His speech cast a wide net and suggested a breadth of reading in its echoes of Du Bois and even Lenin. "We are today seeing a global rebellion of the oppressed against the oppressor," he declared, "the exploited against the exploiter." Malcolm condemned Western industrialized nations for "deliberately subjugating the Negro for economic reasons. These international criminals raped the African continent to feed their factories, and are themselves responsible for the low standards of living prevalent throughout Africa."

The day then took him to the home of his friend Gordon Parks, the great photographer and writer whom he had first met and come to trust in 1963 when *Life* magazine assigned Parks to cover the Nation of Islam. For the last year, Malcolm had been sending Parks postcards from abroad, and Parks, intrigued by his friend's evolving beliefs, had asked Malcolm to sit for an interview. Their tone was friendly, the discussion serious. "Brother, nobody can protect you from a Muslim but a Muslim—or someone trained in Muslim tactics," Malcolm explained when Parks asked how he was keeping safe. "I know. I invented many of those tactics." As the interview progressed, Malcolm seemed almost wistful, and his words brimmed with regret for what he perceived as the damage done by the racial intolerance in his past. "Brother, remember the time that white college girl came into the restaurant—the one who wanted to help the Muslims and the whites get together—and I told her there wasn't a ghost of a chance and she went away crying?" Parks nodded. Malcolm continued, "I've lived to regret that incident." He had seen many white students working to assist people throughout Africa. "I did many things as a Muslim that I'm sorry for now."

During this same week, about sixty MMI and OAAU members met to discuss the firebombing and its security implications. "We said that from that day forward every person that came to one of our rallies was going to be searched," recalled Peter Bailey, "and this [is] where we made a crucial error—[Malcolm] overruled this because he wanted to break away from this image of searching people before they came to rallies." Malcolm insisted not only that no one should be searched, but that all MMI security personnel should be unarmed at the event coming up that Sunday, February 21. The sole exception to this rule would be Malcolm's bodyguard and security chief, Reuben X Francis. Nearly everyone argued against Malcolm's position, but there was no tradition or practice of democratic decision making inside the MMI and OAAU. When Malcolm demanded something, he received it.

The fact that his guards would be unarmed was surely communicated to the NYPD through its MMI and OAAU informants and undercover police officers. The most important police operative inside the MMI and OAAU was Gene Roberts. A four-year veteran of the U.S. Navy, Roberts was admitted to the NYPD academy, and after induction as an officer was transferred to BOSS as a detective. His first assignment was to infiltrate the newly formed MMI; his NYPD code name was "Adam." BOSS supervisors took steps to ensure Roberts's safety and anonymity, even from fellow officers. Along with other undercover cops, his ID photo was kept separately in BOSS headquarters. Roberts was given a cover job as a clothing salesman in the Bronx. By late 1964 Roberts had become an integral member of the MMI security team, standing guard at public events as one of Malcolm's bodyguards. Throughout his assignment Roberts feared he would be revealed as a cop. Roberts and his wife, Joan, even sent their daughter away to Joan's parents' home in Virginia for her safety. Through Roberts, all of MMI's and OAAU's major decisions and plans would be promptly revealed to the NYPD.

On Saturday, February 20, Malcolm and Betty went looking for a new place to live. A real estate agent escorted them to look at a property in a predominantly Jewish but racially integrated community on Long Island. The house was attractive and to their liking, but the three-thousand-dollar down payment was well beyond their reach. The estimated moving cost for their furniture, clothing, and other personal items was one thousand dollars. Once again, Malcolm looked to Ella to solve his financial problems. Either before or just after the firebombing, when it became clear that Malcolm would have to find a new place to live, he had spoken to her and she agreed to purchase a new home for him under her name; after a short period of time, the title would be transferred to either Betty or Attallah (then age six). All agreed that Malcolm's name was so controversial that it would have been impossible for him to purchase a home in an integrated neighborhood.

That afternoon, Malcolm called Alex Haley to check in on the state of the manuscript. In a strange and timely coincidence, Haley told him that the completed autobiography would be mailed off to Doubleday by the end of the following week. As night fell, Malcolm dropped Betty off at the home of Tom Wallace, where he stayed and talked for several hours before leaving to check in to the midtown New York Hilton, paying eighteen dollars for a single room on the twelfth floor. He ate dinner at the hotel's restaurant, the Old Bourbon Steak House, and returned to his room, remaining there until the next day. That evening, Sharon 6X may have joined him in his hotel room.

Later that night, several African-American men entered the Hilton lobby asking for Malcolm's room number. Someone contacted the hotel's head of security, who confronted the men. They promptly left.

———

The plans to murder Malcolm X had been discussed within the Nation of Islam for nearly a year before the morning of February 21, 1965. The delay in carrying out the crime had occurred for several reasons. First, up to the final days prior to the assassination Elijah Muhammad had not given an explicit order that his former national spokesman be killed, and for as much anger as had been stirred up against Malcolm in the preceding months, no one would actually take action without clear orders from on high. Second, although Malcolm was being pilloried as a heretic, he retained the respect and even love of a significant minority of NOI members. Some still recognized the contributions he had made to the sect, despite his errors. The best proof of his lasting legacy was the fierce jihad his enemies waged against him in every NOI mosque, month after month. Third, Malcolm made himself an elusive and difficult target by being out of the United States for twenty-four weeks from April to November 1964. An assassination attempt in an Islamic or African nation would have been unthinkable, even for the Nation of Islam. As long as he was abroad, he was safe.

From where the Nation stood in late 1964, the benefits of killing Malcolm outweighed the potentially significant costs. His involvement in publicizing the individual paternity cases of Evelyn Williams and Lucille Rosary, and his success in establishing MMI's connections with international Islamic organizations, had created a new and threatening situation. Some NOI officials fretted that the very legitimacy of the sect might be called into question; the defections of Wallace and Akbar Muhammad only reinforced these fears. They were now convinced that only Malcolm's death would void the inroads he had made and allow them to once again grow membership and continue business unmolested.

Still, Elijah Muhammad knew that if Malcolm were to suffer a violent death, the Nation of Islam would immediately become the primary suspect.

Killing him would almost certainly bring a local and perhaps even federal investigation down on the group, so the assassination's architects within the Nation would need to devise a plan that could deflect attention from national headquarters such that it might plausibly deny any involvement. From this perspective, the year spent ginning up anger with the membership carried an added benefit: it would be easier to cast the killing as rogue members taking matters into their own hands.

They were helped in creating distance by the punishment structure that had developed within the organization, which had grown into a well-oiled machine as the Nation of Islam came to be dominated by fear and violence in the months after Malcolm's departure. Most NOI members knew that disciplinary units and hit crews almost never carried out extreme actions in the cities where their mosques were located. In other words, Captain Joseph might authorize Harlem crews to attack Malcolm's people, or to harass him, but not to commit homicide. Such extreme measures would first have to be authorized by Chicago officials, then carried out by a crew from Newark, Boston, or Philadelphia. The Newark group would have been deployed against Malcolm in New York City, but only on the direct orders of Captain Joseph, Raymond Sharrieff, and John Ali. Other assassination crews may have been organized on both the West and East Coasts.

Finally, the convergence of interests between law enforcement, national security institutions, and the Nation of Islam undoubtedly made Malcolm's murder easier to carry out. Both the FBI and BOSS placed informants inside the OAAU, MMI, and NOI, making all three organizations virtual rats' nests of conflicting loyalties. John Ali was named by several parties as an FBI informant, and there is good reason to believe that both James Shabazz of Newark and Captain Joseph fed information to their local police departments as well as the FBI; BOSS carried out extensive wiretapping and/or surveillance against all three organizations, while the CIA had kept up surveillance of Malcolm throughout his Middle Eastern and African travels. Yet while the channels of information remained open among various organizations interested in Malcolm's silencing, it remains difficult to determine what the FBI and the police authorized—whether, for instance, either subtly suggested certain crimes could be committed by their nonpolice operatives. Circumstantial evidence that they may have done so is both BOSS's and the FBI's refusal nearly a half century after Malcolm's murder to make available thousands of pages of evidence connected with the crime.

What has been established is that around the time Malcolm returned from Africa in May 1964, two members of the Newark mosque began planning how to carry out his murder, almost certainly at the direct order of minister James Shabazz, whose control of the mosque necessitated his involvement. The older of the two members was mosque assistant secretary Benjamin X Thomas, a twenty-nine-year-old father of four employed at a Hackensack envelope manufacturing company. His younger partner was electronics plant employee Leon X Davis, of Paterson, New Jersey, about twenty years of age. Both men were active in the Fruit of Islam. Probably while driving Ben's black Chrysler, the two men spotted young Talmadge Hayer, another Newark mosque member in his early twenties, on a street in downtown Paterson. They invited Hayer into the car, and drove around for a while. Ben and Leon fished for Hayer's attitudes about Malcolm and his split from the NOI. Within weeks Hayer became the third member committed to participating in the murder. "I had a bit of love and admiration for the Honorable Elijah Muhammad," he later wrote, "and I just felt that like this is something that I have to stand up for."

In short order, two more NOI members joined the Newark conspiracy. Willie X Bradley was twenty-six years old, tall, dark in complexion, and heavyset, with a history of violence. Wilbur X McKinley, by contrast, was over thirty-five years old, thin, and like three other men in the conspiracy, only about five feet, nine inches tall. The proprietor of a small construction business, Wilbur X had worked at the Newark mosque.

While beatings like the one carried out against Leon Ameer in Boston had become disturbingly common for the Nation, executions of members or dissidents remained extremely rare. Yet as the Nation seemed to flounder in the wake of Malcolm's defection, brutal disciplinary measures were taken with greater frequency. In the Bronx in late 1964, for example, NOI member Benjamin Brown started his own "Universal Peace" mosque, which featured a large photograph of Muhammad in its storefront window. Since Brown had not requested the prior approval of Mosque No. 7 or the Chicago headquarters, his actions were judged insurrectionary. In the early evening of January 6, 1965, three Muslims dropped by Brown's mosque, complained about the display of Muhammad's portrait, and departed. Several hours later, as Brown left the mosque, he was killed by a shot in the back by a .22 caliber rifle. The NYPD investigated the death and arrested three men, all NOI members, two of them Mosque No. 7 lieutenants: Thomas 15X Johnson and Norman 3X Butler. The police found a .22 caliber Winchester repeating rifle in Johnson's home. It had been fired once, then jammed. Butler and

Johnson were subsequently bailed out of jail, but police were convinced that both men were involved in Brown's shooting, because they were well-known "enforcers."

Thomas 15X presented a curious case in the Nation's crusade to poison its members' opinions. Malcolm's driver for years, Johnson had abandoned his boss during the schism with the Nation. However, at first, he had not shared the obsession to destroy Malcolm that had infected other FOI members. When in December 1963 Malcolm had been silenced, Johnson stated that like all mosque members he was surprised, but had assumed that the minister soon would be reinstated. Yet after Malcolm established the MMI and OAAU, Johnson firmly sided with the Nation against him. Thomas 15X's hardening of purpose began with the Queens court hearing over the disputed ownership of the Shabazz home. "Malcolm wasn't just a minister; he was top minister," Johnson stated, going on to explain that, because of his status, NOI members had agreed to purchase a house for him and his family. "But if you leave, you can't have that house. We bought you a brand-new car and everything. . . . As long as you are correct, you've got that."

Johnson claimed that the order to assassinate Malcolm came directly from national secretary John Ali, who while visiting New York City gathered Mosque No. 7's lieutenants separately from Captain Joseph and gave a series of reasons why Malcolm had to die. In the more than four decades that have passed, however, nothing has emerged that could definitively prove or disprove Johnson's claim of Ali's involvement. Johnson had great difficulty accepting some of the national secretary's reasoning, and noted that "the other lieutenants didn't [buy Ali's arguments] either." Several weeks later new instructions came down from Chicago: "Elijah Muhammad sent specific orders. He said, 'Don't touch [Malcolm].'" Consequently Johnson and his crew beat up and harassed Malcolm's people, but no active plan was set in motion to murder him. Johnson claimed, "I used to see Malcolm every day in the Theresa Hotel." Malcolm would walk over and say, "How you doing?" That his intended victim maintained a degree of civility impressed Johnson.

By the fall of 1964, though, as the rage against Malcolm infected every part of the Nation, Johnson was finally persuaded that Malcolm had to be killed. He received instructions with four other lieutenants "that we had to go to Philly. He was speaking over there . . . and we were supposed to hit him then." The crew drove to Malcolm's lecture site (probably on December 26), but Malcolm had anticipated such an assault. "He sent a brother out that sort of favored him." The would-be assassins chased after the decoy, and Malcolm escaped. Johnson may have also participated in at least one other failed attempt to assassinate Malcolm in Philadelphia. Had he been present at the Audubon Ballroom on February 21, 1965, Thomas would have eagerly participated in the assassination. The fact that he was absent that afternoon, but was subsequently sentenced to life imprisonment for the crime, raises profound questions about both U.S. law enforcement and the courts.

——

During the final weeks of Malcolm's life, there were two topics that preoccupied his followers. First, the obvious political, ideological, and religious changes Malcolm was experiencing disoriented both his critics and supporters. His evolution seemed to keep unfolding toward tolerance and pluralism along racial and religious lines. In Rochester on February 19, Malcolm had told his audience, "I believe in one God, and I believe that God had one religion. . . . God taught all of the prophets the same religion. . . . Moses, Jesus, Muhammad, or some of the others. . . . They all had one doctrine and that doctrine was designed to give clarification of humanity." This, along with his increasing statements about not judging men by the color of their skin, produced deep concern among followers who clung to the belief that Malcolm's new pronouncements were merely cosmetic changes designed to increase his public appeal. Some die-hards like James 67X simply refused to believe that their boss had changed. Betty, for her own reasons, took the same position. But in the Harlem audience that had loyally turned out for Audubon rallies, there was tremendous uneasiness.

After Betty publicly accused Lynne Shifflett of sleeping with Malcolm, Shifflett resigned from her position as general secretary of the OAAU in late 1964. Weeks later, after Malcolm returned home from Africa, he replaced Shifflett with another articulate, intelligent black woman, Sara Mitchell, the young woman from the *New Yorker* who had written him in June. Although Mitchell shared some of Shifflett's middle-class views about politics, at heart she was a progressive black nationalist who viewed Malcolm from that vantage point. Describing Malcolm's 1965 activities years later, for instance, Mitchell argued that "underlying [his] efforts was his still unfulfilled and paramount ambition: the redemption of the 'disgraced' manhood of the American Blackman. That was the spur piercing him; it would not let him stop or even rest." To Mitchell, the two new organizations Malcolm had established performed distinctly different functions. Muslim Mosque, Inc. "was set up to encourage study and consideration of a religious alternative" while the Organization of Afro-American Unity had been designed "for eventual correlation and unification of varied aspects of the black struggle." She recognized the limitations of both groups, lacking resources and permanent, full-time staff. "Consequently," she recalled, "deadlines were not met and postponements were inevitable. During the lagging interim, dissatisfied fingers shook in his face from all directions."

Mitchell could sense that broad elements of the black nationalist community outside the Nation were displeased with Malcolm's new orientation. Many African Americans had "experienced discreet self-pride" when Malcolm had promoted "black supremacy," but as his change progressed "they were disappointed and annoyed; for he was no longer providing the bold, caustic, chastising voice." She also thought that Malcolm's preoccupation with lecturing at elite universities had a negative effect among sectors of the black dispossessed. "Grassroots black people began wondering if his participation on Ivy League type forums meant that 'their' Malcolm was abandoning them for the 'good life' and higher stakes." From an organizational standpoint, Mitchell found this effect highly problematic. Virtually alone within Malcolm's inner administrative circle, Mitchell worried that her leader's ideological leaps in new directions alienated many old core supporters, while not converting enough new followers. As a result, "isolation and loneliness were prices paid for his radical pioneering."

James 67X was relieved to be rid of Lynne Shifflett and quickly found a much better working relationship with Mitchell. But the tensions and disaffections that Mitchell described created an atmosphere of uncertainty that benefited opportunists like Charles 37X Kenyatta. During December and part of January, after Malcolm had discovered his involvement with Betty, Kenyatta had disappeared from MMI and OAAU events. On January 24 he finally showed up at an OAAU rally, voicing complaints. He bitterly announced to several members that he was now "finished" with both the MMI and the OAAU. He hinted that James was responsible for financial irregularities. The "best way to get money is to go out and work for it," Charles advised.

Yet the worries over Malcolm's positions were trumped by fears about his safety. By early 1965 most of Malcolm's closest associates believed that without a change of course he would soon be dead, and they grew preoccupied with exploring ways to save their leader's life. They knew that various African governments had offered him positions; Ethiopia had been willing to grant sanctuary; the Saudis would have permitted both him and his family to live in the kingdom as guests of the state. The entire African-

American expatriate community in Ghana urged him to bring Betty and the children to Accra. Even Malcolm's celebrity friends had offered their summer homes and second houses, where the family could live in anonymity. A nervous Ruby Dee had even suggested hiding Malcolm behind a secret wall in her home, a plan vetoed by her husband, Ossie Davis.

On Friday, February 19, Maya Angelou arrived from Ghana, ready to volunteer for the OAAU's staff. She had heard about the firebombing and was so shaken that she phoned Malcolm while still at JFK airport. "They almost caught me," he admitted to her. Malcolm offered to pick up Angelou at the airport, but she informed him that she planned to travel straight to San Francisco to see her family first. However, when she returned home, her mother cautioned her not to work with that "rabble-rouser." "If you feel you have to do that—work for no money—go back to Martin Luther King," her mother advised.

Although most Malcolmites thought the Nation of Islam was actively conspiring to kill their leader, many also suspected the U.S. government as being behind the murder attempts. "We all knew what was happening to black people, and [Malcolm] always talked about the government being involved in the problems we were having," Herman Ferguson recalled. Malcolm supposedly had been worried that "the CIA was out to kill him" when he was abroad, and his rejection at French customs made him further suspect government meddling in his affairs. Ferguson felt that during the final weeks OAAU members did too little to protect Malcolm: "We didn't pick up on the signs that we should have picked up on. . . . Like cannon fodder, people sat around and talked about the danger that Malcolm was in. It was just like, 'The brother should be more careful.'" Several OAAU members had places in Manhattan that Malcolm could use as safe houses to spend the night. There was some discussion about assigning him drivers, but nothing was done about it. The drift toward disaster continued.

It is difficult to know what Malcolm may have contemplated as he pondered the likelihood of impending murder. For decades after the assassination, James 67X struggled privately with the question of whether his leader truly wanted to die. He had lived for over a year with death threats coming from the Nation, and in his final days he seemed of two minds, partly accepting of what he believed to be his fate and partly wishing or hoping that the problems might disappear and allow him to go back to a normal life. In his last week, he spent much of his time away from his family, so as not to put them in danger. He also appears to have traveled around without bodyguards, though he had long had either James 67X or Reuben X accompanying him wherever he went. He communicated infrequently, and sometimes it was impossible for MMI and OAAU members to reach him with information. As the world closed in on him, Malcolm, always an extremely private individual, kept his own counsel. He fought desperately to shield others' doubts and fears.

That he continued to harangue the Nation even when he knew that doing so would leave little choice but to strike at him seems to suggest that on some level he may have been inviting death. As Malcolm became more aware of Islamic tradition in his last years, he probably learned about the third Shiite imam, Husayn ibn Ali, and his tragic murder. Husayn was the grandson of the Prophet Muhammad, and the son of Ali ibn Abi Talib and Fatima, the daughter of Muhammad. After the murder of Ali and the abdication of his older brother, Hasan, Husayn became the object of allegiance for many Muslims. At Karbala in 680 CE in what today is Iraq, Husayn and a small band of supporters were attacked by religious opponents; nearly all of them were killed or captured. Husayn died bravely and gloriously, so much so that his murder became central to the Shiite ethos of martyrdom, suffering, and resistance to oppression. The Shiite mourning observance of Ashura reenacts the tragedy as a passion play, in which participants engage in remorse and self-punishment over Husayn's assassination, and rededicate themselves to the struggle for freedom and justice.

Like Husayn, Malcolm made the conscious decision not to avoid or escape death. This he could have accomplished easily; had he remained in Africa for several years, the level of the Nation of Islam's animosity surely would have diminished. That he chose to return to the United States meant he recognized the real possibility of being killed at any moment, even while asleep inside his home. If he did not desire death, he still seemed prepared to embrace it as an inevitable part of his personal destiny. Such an interpretation would help explain why Malcolm was so insistent that no one at the Audubon be searched and that none of his men except Reuben X carry weapons. By not checking for guns, Malcolm made the assassination more likely; by disarming his security personnel, he protected them from being targets in an exchange of gunfire as Malcolm's murderers probably would not shoot unarmed security personnel. If anyone should die, Malcolm may have reasoned, let it be him.

Law enforcement agencies acted with equal reticence when it came to intervening with Malcolm's fate. Rather than investigate the threats on his life, they stood back, almost waiting for a crime to happen. "They had the mentality of wanting an assassination," said Gerry Fulcher of the NYPD brass, though it is unlikely that NYPD officers were directly involved in the murder. "They would want to keep their hands clean from the actual thing." Fulcher knew that the NYPD and BOSS had placed Gene Roberts inside the MMI and OAAU, but they had also recruited other informants who provided the police with internal information. By early 1965, Fulcher had been taping conversations at the MMI and OAAU office for over nine months. After Malcolm's return from abroad, Fulcher listened carefully to his arguments and became even more convinced that the police were making a big mistake about him. "This is a guy we should be supporting," he concluded. One of the favorite topics for cops was "'them niggers on welfare.' [Malcolm] wants them off, too," he argued. Malcolm "should have been a companion, not an enemy" of law enforcement, Fulcher insisted. "But they always viewed him like the enemy."

By that time, however, Malcolm and the NYPD had already reached a practical détente. Even before leaving the Nation, Malcolm had developed what Peter Goldman called "distant cooperation" with the police, hoping to avoid the confrontations and shootings that had occurred in Los Angeles. He consequently informed the police whenever he was having public rallies, and ordered Reuben X Francis and other subordinates to share information with them. In 1964 and 1965, the NYPD regularly assigned between one and two dozen officers to the MMI and OAAU rallies held at the Audubon. Several would be stationed inside the building but rarely the Grand Ballroom, where the rallies were held. Most were positioned outside the building, either clustered around the entrance or standing across the street in the small neighborhood park. The detail's commander and one or two other policemen sat in a glassed-in booth on the second floor, overlooking the entrances to the building's two ballrooms, the Rose and the larger Grand.

Across the Hudson in Newark, the small assassination crew that had been formed in the spring of 1964 had fallen apart when Malcolm was out of the country. But after his return, the question of whether, and how, to commit the murder became active once again. Talmadge Hayer had several conversations with Ben Thomas and Leon Davis. Hayer later told Goldman that, since Ben was a mosque administrator, he naturally assumed from the outset that senior NOI officials had authorized the mission. "I didn't ask a whole lot of questions," Hayer explained. "I thought that somebody was giving instructions: 'Brother, you got to move on this situation.' But I felt we was in accord."

As the group began exploring how to go about the killing, they contemplated gunning Malcolm down outside of his East Elmhurst home; however, when they drove out one day to case the house, they found it heavily protected by armed guards. For a time they considered just following Malcolm around Harlem and striking at some public event where he was scheduled to talk, but, according to Hayer, practical considerations got in the way. All of the Newark conspirators worked full-time, and they couldn't take off work to spend hours driving around Harlem. The group finally settled on a simple but bold tactical approach: shooting Malcolm at an Audubon rally, in front of hundreds of supporters and several dozen probably armed security people. The plan's advantage was the element of surprise. Malcolm's people believed he was safe at the rallies; they never considered a direct, frontal assault, because it would be suicidal. Yet every member of the assassination team was a devoted follower of Elijah Muhammad, prepared to sacrifice his life to kill Malcolm. If a would-be assassin is willing to die, anyone can be killed.

The likelihood of success was "a long shot," Hayer remembered. "But we just felt we would have to move on it . . . and that's what we did. Why there? . . . It was the only place we knew he'd be." Hayer was familiar with weapons, so he was assigned to purchase the guns, using his own money. He and several others in the assassination crew attended an OAAU rally, probably in January 1965, where they were surprised to discover that no one was being searched at the main entrance. They sat down and studied where guards were positioned and when they were relieved. On the night of February 20, the group paid to enter a dance in the Audubon Ballroom, checking out all possible exits.

The conspirators then drove back to Ben Thomas's home. It was decided that the initial round aimed at Malcolm, the decisive kill shot, would be fired by William Bradley. "Willie" had been a star athlete in high school, excelling in baseball. By his mid-twenties, however, he had grown fat, weighing over 220 pounds. But he was still athletic in his movements and he had learned how to handle a shotgun. Everyone agreed that the assassination would take place the next afternoon, Sunday, February 21.

On the morning of the twenty-first, a phone call awakened Malcolm in his room at the Hilton. A voice over the receiver menacingly said, "Wake up, brother." He checked the time; it was eight o'clock on a winter morning, but the day would not be frigid. Still, Malcolm wasn't taking chances with the weather. He put on long underwear beneath his suit—the same suit coat he had worn during his tour through Great Britain.

At about nine a.m., he phoned Betty, asking her to come to the afternoon rally, and to bring the children with her. His request surprised and pleased her. Since his return from Africa Malcolm had again discouraged her involvement in MMI and OAAU affairs, and earlier that week had strictly ordered her not to come on Sunday because of the threat of violence. He failed to explain why he had changed his mind. Betty and her daughters were still staying with the Wallaces, and around one p.m. she began getting ready. All of the little girls were stuffed into attractive children's snowsuits. The children were thrilled. As Attallah Shabazz recalled, "It was still an exciting adventure to get ready and go see Daddy." If Malcolm expected a day of reckoning, why would he ask Betty to bring the children to witness his possible murder? One reason might be that, despite his observations about the dangers surrounding his daily life, he still wasn't absolutely sure. Or it might have been ambivalence as a kind of defense mechanism, a way of not thinking about something terrifying and inevitable. Perhaps, like Husayn, he wanted his death to be symbolic, a passion play representing his beliefs.

At one p.m. Malcolm checked out of the Hilton and drove uptown in his Oldsmobile. When he reached West 146th Street and Broadway in West Harlem, he pulled over and parked. He had made it a habit not to park his car at speaking venues, where he might be vulnerable to attack. As he waited for the uptown bus, an automobile with New Jersey plates slowed and stopped where he was standing. Malcolm did not recognize the driver, a young African American named Fred Williams, but he did know MMI member Charles X Blackwell in the backseat. Thus reassured, Malcolm slipped into the rear to join him. The car quickly covered the twenty blocks north to the Audubon Ballroom. It was by now just after two in the afternoon, but people were still standing about, indicating that no formal program had started on the main ballroom's stage.

As Malcolm walked into the Audubon, he might have noticed the absence of the usual police presence stationed in front of the building. According to Peter Goldman, one of Malcolm's "senior people had talked with the duty captain, requesting that the police leave the building and station themselves in a less public place." Given the firebombing and the restrictions Malcolm had placed on the MMI's security—the lack of weapons, and no frisking at the main door—it is difficult to imagine the rationale for such an odd request, or why the police would grant it. In any event, about eighteen officers were relocated several blocks away, up Broadway, at Columbia Presbyterian Hospital.

When Malcolm entered the Grand Ballroom on the second floor, he was immediately encountered by Peter Bailey, holding a bundle of copies of *Blacklash*. There was something in the OAAU's publication that wasn't quite right, and Malcolm ordered him not to distribute copies of the issue. "For the first time," remembered Bailey, Malcolm appeared "harried, not fearful . . . but just [like] somebody who had a lot on their mind." Malcolm asked Bailey if he recognized the Reverend Galamison, and Bailey said that he could. Malcolm further asked him to wait near the main entrance downstairs for Galamison; when he arrived, the civil rights leader should be escorted to the rear room behind the Grand Ballroom's main stage.

From its entrance to the far end of its plywood stage, the ballroom stretched 180 feet. Behind the stage, waiting in the small room for Malcolm to arrive, was his core MMI and OAAU staff: Sara Mitchell, James 67X, and Benjamin 2X. They immediately sensed that their leader was in a terrible mood. He flopped down on a metal folding chair, but a few minutes later was up, nervously pacing the floor. Benjamin recalled, "He was more tense than I'd ever seen him. . . . He just lost control of himself completely." When James explained that Galamison's secretary had contacted him hours before, saying that the minister's schedule was so crowded that afternoon that it would be impossible for him to drive uptown to address the Audubon audience, Malcolm demanded to know why he had not been informed earlier. James cautiously reminded Malcolm that he had neglected to notify him the previous day where he would be spending the night, so he had no idea where to contact him. Several hours ago, he explained, he had phoned Betty with this information and asked her to pass it on. Malcolm exploded: "You gave that message to a *woman*! . . . You should know better than that!" He continued to lash out at anyone near him. When Sheikh Hassoun tried to embrace him, he yelled, "Get out of here!" Both Benjamin and Hassoun left the rear room together, and Benjamin walked up to the podium to start the program.

Within a few minutes Malcolm quietly apologized to those still left in the room. "Something felt *wrong* out there," he told them. He added that he felt almost at his "wit's end." The OAAU program that was to have been announced at the rally, already postponed once because of the firebombing, was still not ready; Galamison and several other invited speakers would not be present. A successful event now all depended on his giving a suitably spirited speech. "When he came backstage, Malcolm was trying to brush aside his own problems," Mitchell observed. "When someone suggested that he should let the people worry about *him* for a change, he answered with some irritation, 'No matter what has happened to me, I can't go out there complaining about it. What I say has to be said with their problems in mind.'"

Rattled by Malcolm's anger, Benjamin spent the first few minutes of his remarks trying to find focus. Repeatedly he implored audience members to "remain seated" and to "keep the aisles clear." It took about five minutes before he finally found his footing on familiar rhetorical terrain, and having established his rhythm, he reminded the audience that for more than a year, Malcolm had spoken frequently against the U.S. invasion of Southeast Asia. "So tonight, when Brother Minister Malcolm comes before you, I hope you will open your minds, open your ears," he told the crowd. "He'll try to do anything for us without the approval of the power structure that controls the policy systems that you and I live under." Without mentioning the recent firebombing and the growing death threats, Benjamin underscored the leader's personal courage and many sacrifices for their common cause. Any time such a person is "in our midst, he does not care anything about personal consequences, but only cares about the welfare of the people, this is a good man. A man like this," Benjamin emphasized, "should be supported. A man like this should be successful. Because men like this don't come every day. Few men will risk their lives for somebody else." A person in the audience shouted with approval, "That's right!" Most people would be "running away from death, even if they're in the right," Benjamin continued. Malcolm X was without question a leader who "cares nothing about the consequences, cares only for the people . . . I hope you understand." At this, the Audubon audience burst into applause.

As Benjamin 2X continued his address, the Audubon's main entrance and second-floor lobby became packed with late arrivals. At about 2:50 p.m., Betty arrived at the Audubon. For some of Malcolm's followers, Sister Betty's attendance was a pleasant surprise, as she had made few if any public appearances since his return from Africa. MMI member Jessie 8X Ryan left his seat beside his wife and escorted Betty and her children to a booth close to the stage. Betty's prominent appearance undoubtedly told the audience that Malcolm would soon emerge onstage. There were now approximately four hundred people seated in the ballroom.

At 2:55 p.m., the MMI's security detail made its third and final change of assignments. A few minutes before three p.m., without advance warning

Malcolm walked briskly out onto the stage with a portfolio in his hand and sat down next to Benjamin 2X. "Without further ado, I bring before you Minister Malcolm," Benjamin hastily announced. As the applause began, Benjamin dutifully turned from the speaker's platform and moved to sit down on the stage, but Malcolm stopped him from sitting down and, leaning over slightly, asked him to look out for Galamison's arrival. Since Galamison had canceled his appearance, the order made no sense, but Benjamin obediently left the stage and Malcolm walked up to the podium.

The enthusiastic applause lasted almost a full minute as Malcolm surveyed his admiring audience. To his immediate left, bodyguard Gene X Roberts quietly left box two and walked swiftly to the rear of the ballroom, only a few feet from Reuben X Francis. By doing so, whether by coincidence or design, he would escape being near the primary line of fire that ensued seconds later. "*As-salaam alaikum,*" Malcolm declared in Arabic, extending the traditional Muslim words of greeting. "*Walaikum salaam,*" hundreds in the audience responded. Before he could utter another sentence, a disruption broke out in the front center of the ballroom, approximately six or seven rows from the stage. "Get your hands out of my pockets!" Wilbur McKinley exclaimed to another conspirator seated next to him. As both pretended to tussle, the pushing and shoving distracted the entire audience, including the MMI security team. From the rostrum, Malcolm shouted repeatedly: "Hold it! Hold it! Hold it! Hold it!"

The principal rostrum guards that afternoon were Charles X Blackwell and Robert 35X Smith, unusual choices as they did not usually serve in this role and had little experience guarding Malcolm. William 64X George had guarded Malcolm at the rostrum many times, yet on this day he had been stationed outside. When the commotion broke out, Blackwell and Smith made a tactical blunder: they moved from their posts and began walking toward the two bickering men. Gene Roberts, George Whitney, and several other security personnel approached the men from the rear. Malcolm was now completely alone and unguarded onstage. At that precise moment, an incendiary smoke bomb ignited at the extreme rear of the ballroom, instantly creating panic, screams, and confusion. It was only then that Willie Bradley, sitting in the front row, got to his feet and walked briskly toward the rostrum. When he was fifteen feet away, he elevated his sawed-off shotgun from under his coat, took careful aim, and fired. The shotgun pellets ripped squarely into Malcolm's left side, cutting a seven-inch-wide circle around his heart and left chest. This was the kill shot, the blow that executed Malcolm X; the other bullets caused terrible damage but were not decisive.

This single shotgun blast oddly failed to topple Malcolm. As Herman Ferguson recalled, "There was a loud blast, a boom that filled the auditorium with the sound of a weapon going off." On cue, two men—Hayer in the first row, with a .45 next to his stomach, and Leon X Davis sitting next to him, also holding a handgun—stood up, ran to the stage, and emptied their guns into Malcolm. Ferguson, still sitting only feet from the stage, took in everything that happened next:

> Malcolm straightened up momentarily . . . his hand came up and he stiffened. The shotgun blast [had been fired] at him by one of the assassins, who fired from the crook of his elbow. . . . He hit Malcolm point-blank in his left chest. . . . Then a fusillade of shots rang out. . . . This kept up for several seconds. And I remember saying, "If they would just stop firing, maybe he could survive. . . ." And when they did, Malcolm toppled over backwards . . . and the back of his head hit the floor with a crash.

Ferguson was perhaps the only eyewitness who had not fallen to the floor to escape the line of fire. He continued his account:

> After so much noise, shooting and so on and the screaming of people, there was this sudden silence. . . . I could see all of the chairs and the people lying on the floor. There were three men standing in the center aisle, facing the door. And one of them appeared to have some sort of weapon in his hand. They [were] standing in a row, one behind the other. And they stood frozen in time [and] space for another few seconds, and then they took off, running and hopping over chairs and people's bodies.

Most of the MMI security force had also scrambled for cover at the first shot, making no effort to protect Malcolm or to apprehend his murderers. Rostrum guards Charles X Blackwell and Robert 35X Smith both had pulled out of position and had rolled to the floor seeking their own safety. John X Davis, nominally the chief of MMI's rostrum detail, subsequently admitted to police that when the shooting started, he, too, "fell to the ground." Charles 37X Kenyatta had also flopped to the floor and later claimed that he "did not see anything."

Several eyewitness accounts suggest that Bradley then pivoted to his left and may have fired a second blast above the heads of the audience, narrowly missing Ferguson. He then ran down the right corridor of the ballroom and quickly ducked into the women's lavatory, located barely sixty feet from the stage. Discarding his shotgun, he and perhaps a second conspirator descended a narrow, seldom-used flight of stairs leading down to the street, making an easy escape. The other two gunmen, Hayer and Leon X Davis, inexplicably chose to run a virtual gauntlet, leaping over chairs and people, attempting to escape through the ballroom's main entrance on West 166th Street, 180 feet away. Adding to the confusion, the homemade incendiary device, composed of a bundle of matches and film stuffed in a sock, was still smoking up the ballroom.

The two shooters, trying to escape through the main entrance, hoped to conceal themselves within the large, panicking audience, but even before they were halfway across the ballroom, Gene Roberts intercepted them. One assailant, probably Hayer, fired at him at point-blank range. The bullet tore through Roberts's coat but did not hit him. Roberts grabbed a folding chair and hurled it into Hayer's legs, causing him to stumble and fall, after which Hayer tried to scramble up toward the now packed exit. As he did so, Reuben X Francis took aim and fired at him from eight feet away, pulling off three shots. Hayer was struck just once, in the left thigh; in pain, he stumbled and continued running down the stairwell, where he was immediately surrounded by Malcolm's enraged followers and viciously beaten. In the confusion, Leon X and the other conspirators managed to escape.

From his lone security outpost at the front door, William 64X George had heard the gunfire and immediately ran down the street to tell police, who within a minute were outside the Audubon. Turning back to the main entrance and front stairwell, William saw Hayer being grabbed by two MMI and OAAU brothers, Alvin Johnson and George 44X, who dragged the wounded shooter to the ground. "The crowd started to beat him," William would later recount. At that moment, police patrolman Thomas Hoy arrived at the scene and attempted to pull Hayer into the rear of his squad car. Seconds later Sergeant Alvin Aronoff and patrolman Louis Angelos drove up in a squad car and assisted Hoy in dispersing the angry crowd. Aronoff fired his revolver into the air and the officers were finally able to secure Hayer into a squad car.

The most detailed eyewitness account by a journalist was that of freelance writer Welton Smith, whose story appeared in the *New York Herald Tribune*. Smith first observed a man wearing "a black overcoat in the middle of the hall" rise to his feet and "[yell] at the man next to him, 'Get your hand out of my pockets!'" Gunshots then erupted from the front stage as Smith found himself violently pushed to the ballroom floor by others. All the shots took place "within fifteen seconds." By the time Smith rose to his feet, he saw two men chase the man in the black overcoat, who turned and fired at his pursuers as he ran toward the main entrance. Smith located the smoke bomb at the back of the ballroom, smothered the fuse, and looked for water to douse it. Several minutes later, he could see that about eight people were bending over Malcolm. As several MMI security personnel attempted to keep others from crowding onto the stage, Smith saw Yuri Kochiyama, an OAAU member, bend over Malcolm and heard her shout, "He's still alive! His heart's still beating!"

Mercifully, Betty had witnessed only the first terrible seconds of her husband's murder. When she first heard the boom of the shotgun blast, she instinctively turned her body toward the stage. "There was no one else in there they'd be shooting at," she recalled later. Two more killers with handguns stepped forward, firing into Malcolm. Betty would later claim that she had seen her husband collapse onstage under this withering fire. Observers, however, saw her quickly gathering her terrified children, pushing them to the floor, shielded partially by a wooden bench and her own body. As the shooting continued, Betty screamed out, "They're killing my husband!" While the assassins fled the scene, the Shabazz children began to cry and to speak up. "Are they going to kill everyone?" one daughter asked. Betty could see people running up to the stage, overwhelmed by the terrible damage that Malcolm had sustained. Finally rising to her feet, she began to run toward the body, sobbing and screaming; friends tried to hold her back because she was clearly hysterical. After Gene Roberts checked on the safety of his wife, Joan, who had been seated in the front near several reporters, he rushed to the stage. Immediately he sensed that Malcolm was dead, yet he desperately attempted to revive him with mouth-to-mouth resuscitation. Joan Roberts was deeply traumatized by Malcolm's assassination and her husband's near death. She wept uncontrollably in the taxi as she went home with her husband. Forty years later, Gene Roberts observed that "the horror of the incident stayed with her for years."

As the smoke still wafted overhead, MMI and OAAU members stumbled around the ballroom aimlessly, in stunned disbelief at what they had just witnessed. The journalist and OAAU member Earl Grant had been using the pay telephone near the front entrance, making a follow-up call to solicit funds at Malcolm's request, when the first shot rang out. He tried to reenter the ballroom but was pushed aside by the stampede of people fleeing the building. When he finally reached the stage, Malcolm's shirt had been opened and blood covered his torso. Grant retrieved his reporter's camera and began taking photographs. His photos would become the main images of the death of Malcolm X.

When Herman Ferguson finally managed to reach the Audubon's main entrance, he saw to his immediate right "a big commotion going on in the street. . . . A crowd of people had a man up in the air and they were pulling and tugging on him." Wandering in shock, Ferguson found himself on the corner of Broadway and West 166th Street brooding over "what I had just seen—Malcolm's death." A few minutes later he recognized several MMI and OAAU brothers rushing by with a hospital gurney, which they wheeled into the building. Soon a group of policemen and the brothers returned with the gurney bearing a familiar figure: "I looked down at Malcolm. I could already see the pallor, the grayish pallor of his face. . . . His shirt was opened and his collar and tie were pulled down. You could see his chest . . . [and] a pattern of about seven bullet holes, holes large enough to fit your little finger. And I [thought] to myself that he was gone."

Ferguson stood disoriented at the corner for several minutes, trying to decide what to do next. Just then a police car, traveling north up Broadway, turned sharply and stopped only a few feet from him. The squad car held two policemen, one of whom he judged to be "police brass," due to "the scrambled eggs on his hat." The officer left the car and entered the Audubon, returning moments later with a man with an olive complexion who was "obviously in great pain." As the man was assisted into the backseat, Ferguson walked to the car. "He was slumped over, holding his midsection, and I had to bend down and look into his face." Ferguson figured the man had been shot; thinking that the wounded man was "one of our guys," he asked what was happening. The squad car sped away—only instead of making a right turn across Broadway toward Columbia Presbyterian, the nearest hospital, "they kept going down towards the [Hudson] river, across the street, down that incline, and disappeared out of sight."

When the frantic MMI and OAAU members and police carrying Malcolm's body reached Columbia Presbyterian's emergency room, one physician immediately performed a stab tracheotomy in an effort to revive him. Malcolm was then taken to the hospital's third floor, where other physicians set to work. The doctors knew Malcolm was almost certainly dead by the time he was brought into the emergency room, but they continued to try to revive him for fifteen minutes before giving up. At three thirty p.m., in a small office overflowing with Malcolm's supporters and a growing cluster of journalists, a doctor announced in an oddly detached manner: "The gentleman you knew as Malcolm X is dead."

Malcolm's principal lieutenants did not personally witness the shooting. Mitchell, Benjamin 2X, and James 67X were all together backstage. "I heard a sound like firecrackers," Benjamin recalled. "I heard blasts of gunfire. . . . The perspiration broke out of every pore of my body. I knew that he was gone." He had tried to get up but physically couldn't. "I just sat there, stunned, staring through the open doorway at the body on the stage. . . . Then, all at once, it left me, the weight on my shoulders, and I felt a great relief come over me, Malcolm's relief from all his suffering. Death ends a thing on time. Whatever may be the instruments to bring it about, when it comes, it comes on time."

Sara Mitchell was struck by the actions of Malcolm's disciples, who clustered around his body: "'Maybe he can still make it,' they told each other and his wife, Betty. And together, they tried to beg him, pray him, will him back to life." Mitchell later complained, "After the gunfire ceased, terrible minutes passed and still there were no policemen on the scene." Although one of the city's major medical centers was only several blocks away, no ambulance arrived at the Audubon, which is why Malcolm's own men had to run to the emergency room to pick up a gurney. Several women "steered [Malcolm's] dazed wife outside and gathered his four little girls to be taken home. Only then did policemen come inside." MMI and OAAU members were outraged when the police finally showed up. "Their appearance was so ridiculously late," Mitchell recalled, "that one tearful woman yelled and waved them aside, saying, 'Don't hurry; come tomorrow!'"

"When the shots rang out," James 67X recalled, "Benjamin . . . dived down to the floor. I then walked out. . . . People were up on the stage, Malcolm was laying down, and I saw the life go out of his body." A film taken of the assassination's aftermath shows James kneeling over Malcolm and apparently removing something from the body. Then, inexplicably, without giving orders to subordinates or assuming command, he promptly walked through what remained of the disoriented crowd, passed by several police officers who were just arriving, and left the building. James 67X would claim years later that his immediate intention was "to shoot [Captain] Joseph" in retaliation.

———

Patrolmen Gilbert Henry and John Carroll had been assigned to the smaller Rose Ballroom, the farthest distance from the shooting site. When the sounds of gunfire erupted, Henry frantically attempted to call for police backup, but "couldn't get an answer" on his walkie-talkie. Both officers scrambled toward the Audubon's entrance, the only direct route into the main ballroom, but they were blocked by hundreds of screaming, jostling people fleeing down the main stairwell into the street. In the chaos and confusion, it was impossible for the two officers to identify a fleeing assailant.

At approximately 3:05 p.m., less than two minutes after the shooting, Lieutenant Bernard Mulligan of BOSS learned that Malcolm had been shot. NYPD detectives Henry Suarez and Kenneth Egan were immediately dispatched to the crime scene.

Several minutes later, the two men arrived at the Audubon, where they were met by several other officers desperately attempting to restore order. Informed that Malcolm had been taken to Columbia Presbyterian, Suarez and Egan promptly went over to the hospital, where they consulted with NYPD detectives Ferdinand "Rocky" Cavallaro and Thomas Cusmano of the 34th Precinct. The officers jotted down the names of all those who had gone to the hospital from the ballroom; they also learned that although the assassination had occurred only ten minutes earlier, a wounded suspect, "Tommy Hagan," was already being interrogated at the 34th Precinct. At 3:14 p.m., doctors told them that Malcolm had been "dead on arrival" upon reaching the emergency room.

At the hospital, Egan and Suarez secured the personal items found in Malcolm's clothing. They carefully cataloged them: "One 1965 Red Diary which had been in his breast pocket, had 3 bullet holes; one tear gas pen devise [sic] 'Penguin' with two TG-4 cartridges for same, one of which was in the pen for immediate use."

By 3:35 p.m., Cavallaro and Cusmano had returned to the Audubon, where they learned that one of the probable murder weapons, a sawed-off J.C. Higgins shotgun "wrapped in a man's suit jacket," had been found lying on a table in the left rear of the stage. Together with other officers they proceeded to comb the vacant ballrooms for additional physical evidence related to the crime. Locations of bullet holes and other ballistics debris were duly marked off, and the NYPD's photo unit was called up. Investigators also learned that several others had been wounded during the assassination, all of whom were relocated to the hospital, and proceeded to interrogate them. The fifty-one-year-old OAAU member Willie Harris had been sitting three rows from the back of the ballroom when the trouble started. After the barrage of gunshots, he had tried to flee through the ballroom's main entrance. As he explained to detective James Rushin, "I was hit by a bullet. I then left the hall and went to a patrolman . . . and told him I had been hit."

NYPD detective James O'Connell took the statement of another man receiving medical attention, thirty-six-year-old William Parker, a building superintendent in Astoria, Queens. Parker had taken his six-year-old son Nathaniel to the rally just "to see what the meeting was all about." Sitting three rows back from the stage near the middle aisle, he had grabbed his son and dropped to the floor when the first shot was fired. As the fusillade continued, Parker felt a sharp pain in his left foot. It was only after he and the boy walked down the crowded stairwell that he realized that he had been shot. Given the number of bullets fired in an enclosed space, it was remarkable that, apart from minor wounds such as this, Malcolm's was the sole fatality.

As the remaining MMI and OAAU members still inside the Audubon surveyed the initial stages of the NYPD's investigation, most officers at the crime scene appeared apathetic about the shooting. Earl Grant recalled that the first police officers who entered the Audubon were "strolling at about the pace one would expect of them if they were patrolling a quiet park. . . . Not one of them had his gun out!" A few cops "even had their hands in their pockets." As many as 150 members of the audience who had initially fled into the street by now had returned to the Grand Ballroom. One frustrated black man cried out, "There ain't no goddamn hope for our people in this lousy country. You got to fight them lousy whites and fight the stupid niggahs too." An elderly West Indian woman confronted reporter Welton Smith: "Don't you menfolk let them get away with it. They done hurt Malcolm and don't you let them get away with it. They can't stop us. And the white man can't stop us. We know the white man put them up to it." Another man angrily declared to Smith, "I know the cops had a hand in it. . . . [L]ook how long it took the cops to get up to the hall after this happened. It must have been ten minutes, and it took the ambulance almost half an hour to come from the hospital right across the street. Now you tell me that this wasn't nothing but coincidence."

The deep skepticism about the NYPD's unprofessional behavior was not without merit. Most street cops were contemptuous of Malcolm, whom they considered a dangerous racist demagogue. Many believed that Malcolm had firebombed his own house in some kind of publicity stunt. Besides, they thought, given Malcolm's incendiary rhetoric, it was inevitable that the black leader would be struck down by the very violence he had promoted. Most police officers generally treated his murder case not as a significant political assassination, but as a neighborhood shooting in the dark ghetto, a casualty from two rival black gangs feuding against each other.

Shortly before four p.m., James 67X returned to the Audubon, where police officers demanded to know where he had been. He replied, "I was going up . . ." Then James asked himself, "How do they know that I left? . . . They must have photographed this whole thing." Days later the police showed him "a seating plan . . . where everybody was seated in the Audubon Ballroom." The police demanded that both James and Reuben X accompany them to the 34th Precinct, where they were driven by a detective named Kitchman. Apparently, either Reuben or James left some ammunition in the rear seat of Kitchman's car, for the following day the detective found five .32 caliber bullets there. Reuben was charged with felonious assault and possession of a deadly weapon in the shooting of Hayer. At 8:20 p.m., New York County assistant district attorney Herbert Stern and police detective William Confrey began James's interview, which yielded little. At 8:32 p.m., the police report noted, "Mr. Warden stopped talking." James was released, going immediately to the Hotel Theresa, where he met with some MMI and OAAU members.

Two hours later, Stern interrogated Reuben X; police detectives John J. Keeley and William Confrey witnessed this interview. Reuben's story was only slightly less obscure than James's. He asserted that he had "arrived at the ballroom before Malcolm, and stood in the rear of the hall." After the gunfire had stopped, he said, he "saw two men running back towards the exit." He "ran after them and saw that one had been captured by the police." Reuben claimed that he then had just "returned to the ballroom" and that "he could offer nothing of any further value." Several days later, Reuben was released on bail. "Brother Reuben" was immediately hailed as a "hero" by MMI and OAAU members and other black activists as the sole bodyguard who had displayed the courage to return fire at Malcolm's killers.

Meanwhile, back at the Audubon, the NYPD photo unit was well into its forensic work. The detectives caucused informally to evaluate the evidence they had obtained so far, concluding that the open hostilities between two "black hate groups" could spark a riot throughout Harlem—and the possibility of having to quell such a major uprising was something they feared far more than the public slaying of a single black man. To forestall any act of vengeance by Malcolm's followers, officers promptly ordered the Nation's Harlem restaurant to close.

For the detectives working the case, too many facts didn't make sense. The request from Malcolm's team that the usual police detail be pulled back several blocks from the Audubon seemed strange, as did the police's agreement to do so in light of the recent firebombing. The detectives were also suspicious when they learned that nearly all of the MMI and OAAU security personnel had been unarmed and that none of the audience had been checked for weapons. Yet time would not be on the side of justice. As the forensic team continued its work, the Audubon's management asked that the police vacate the building as quickly as possible. A dance sponsored by a local black church had been scheduled for later that evening. Remarkably, the police never completed a full forensic analysis of the crime scene: the back wall of the stage was literally pockmarked with bullet holes of different calibers; Malcolm's blood still covered part of the shattered stage—yet the officers agreed to leave. By six p.m. three women workers were mopping up Malcolm's blood, moving chairs, and cleaning the ballroom floor. The festive George Washington Birthday Party dance was held at the Audubon Ballroom, as advertised, at seven p.m., only four hours after the assassination.

Meanwhile, the FBI was trying to piece together its own interpretation of what had happened. At least five undercover informants had been in the ballroom at the time of the shooting. One of them reported that the first assailant had been a man standing near or at the front row. He "put his left hand in his left pocket of his jacket and removed something. He then extended his arm toward Malcolm X." According to this informant, Malcolm "said, excitedly, 'Don't do it,' and stepped further to his left." This first gunman then fired four or five shots.

Another informant, Jasper Davis, placed the initial disturbance in the seventh or eighth row back from the stage. Others seated around the two quarreling men also stood up "and added to the confusion." Only then, reported Davis, did he hear "a shot coming from the front of the room." A third informant estimated that four to five individuals had been involved in the shooting. Two of the gunmen ran "past him," and two others ran "out [through] the ballroom." An FBI memo dated February 22 describes Reuben X Francis as having "shot one of the quote decoys unquote," which suggests that the FBI believed Hayer was one of the two men involved in the initial altercation, just before the first shot. The same memorandum reports that four other individuals had also been hit. Several hours after the shootings, one informant reported, "trusted members of the MMI met at the Hotel Theresa," where James 67X "stated that he had never headed an organization but would do all he could to preserve the idea and keep the program alive. He stated that a lesson had been learned by the group in that now they must tighten up the security of both members and leaders, and stated, 'We are at war.'"

Other important FBI evidence was connected with OAAU member and FBI informant Ronald Timberlake. Several hours after the shooting, Timberlake telephoned the Bureau's New York office to report that he had picked up one of the murder weapons. He specified that he would turn over the gun only to the FBI, not to the NYPD. The next day, however, February 22, he gave an account of the murder to the NYPD, specifying that he had arrived at the Audubon at approximately 2:10 the previous afternoon, where he had "hung out at the rear of the hall." When the audience disruption began, Malcolm had instructed the audience to "keep your seats." Shots were fired at Malcolm from four or five assailants, who then attempted to flee. Timberlake claimed that he had thrown a "body block" at the gunman closest to him. His general description of the man he had attempted to block was detailed: black, six feet in height, wearing a dark gray tweed coat and blue pants. Timberlake had tripped him and both of them had tumbled to the floor. A second assailant, whom Timberlake described as also black, approximately twenty years old and five feet, seven inches tall, wearing a dark brown three-quarter-length jacket, jumped over them and fled down the central stairway and out the main door. Seconds later, as the stairway was clogged with people, Timberlake pulled out his gun but found it impossible to locate the other shooters, or even to exit the front door. He put his handgun back in his pocket and returned to the ballroom to look for his coat. After waiting a few minutes, he simply returned home. Timberlake subsequently identified "Tommy Hagen [Hayer]" as one of the two shooters he had seen.

———

The news of Malcolm's murder was broadcast by the media within minutes, nationally and internationally. At the Nation of Islam Chicago headquarters, Elijah Muhammad was stunned, according to an account provided by a grandson. "Oh my God! . . . Um, um, um!" Muhammad reportedly murmured. The emotional split with his "lost-found" disciple had finally come to a tragic end. "You know, I really want to go home now," Muhammad told his grandson and other NOI subordinates. It was a wise decision. Undoubtedly, Muhammad's dedicated security force, the Fruit of Islam, realized that Malcolm's murder would almost certainly trigger an act of retaliatory violence against their leader. The Chicago office, while protected by a corps of highly trained men, could still be difficult to defend from a frontal assault, but Muhammad's Hyde Park mansion had been carefully constructed to be virtually impregnable. Several family members and other devoted followers owned residences adjacent to Muhammad's mansion, and NOI security men routinely prowled the sidewalks surrounding the property. Muhammad and his advisers retreated to his fortress and waited.

The terrible news of Malcolm's murder quickly reached Alex Haley at his home in upstate New York. Less than two hours later, his grief was pushed aside by practical concerns. Haley typed a letter to Paul Reynolds, fearing their lucrative deal might now be in jeopardy. "None of us would have had it be this way," Haley wrote, "but since this book represent's [*sic*] Malcolm's sole financial legacy to his widow and four little daughters . . . I'm just glad that it's ready for the press now at a peak of interest for what will be international large sales, and paperback, and all." He also advised Reynolds that Doubleday should be alerted to a potential financial problem:

> I am almost certain that within the next two or three days Malcolm's widow, Sister Betty, will contact me asking for some advance money from Doubleday or some other would be possible for her, to tide her through the immediate weeks. She hasn't a home since last week they moved in the middle of the night, just ahead of the next day's legal eviction to return the home to the Muslims. And Malcolm, talking with me yesterday, said that he had "two or three hundred dollars," which would be the total extent of Sister Betty's funds.

A few days later, Haley had another thought. Again writing to Reynolds, he suggested, "Maybe some magazine might wish to pay well enough for a probing interview of Elijah Muhammad. I could accomplish this." Haley proposed something along the lines of his earlier personal interviews with Malcolm and Martin Luther King, Jr., featured in *Playboy*. Haley assured Reynolds that he would not be at any personal risk from such an assignment. "I know there would be no danger from the Muhammad faction side of the fence; they would want me to do it. They associate me with major publicity done with dignity, which they desperately want." Some of Malcolm's friends might "feel nettled that I was in Chicago with Muhammad," but they could be handled. Get the contract first, Haley advised; he would then "contact Sister Betty and also a couple of Malcolm's close lieutenants and tell them that I had the order, which is a professional job." Another benefit for Haley would be to maintain his line of communications with the Nation's leadership. "It would give me a chance to say to Muhammad some things I'd like to regarding the book—that he isn't attacked as he might think, that he actually is praised by Malcolm." Haley insisted that "some other writers might presently have bigger 'names' (Baldwin, Lomax, Lincoln) . . . [but] actually I have the very best inside track to the Muslims' confidence." Nothing came of these overtures, and Haley and Reynolds's fears were fully justified. Within two weeks, in a terribly shortsighted move, Doubleday's owner, Nelson Doubleday, abruptly canceled the contract.

On the day of the assassination, NOI enforcer Norman Butler was still out on bail for the Benjamin Brown killing. That morning he'd visited a doctor to obtain treatment for leg injuries, which had come from his violent beating by the police during his recent arrest. Butler had spent most of Sunday watching television at home. When he saw the news reports about Malcolm's murder, he phoned Mosque No. 7 and finally reached Captain Joseph, who strongly advised him to get himself seen by others as soon as possible—to walk to the corner store and "buy a quart of milk," to speak to several neighbors in his building, and so on. Butler decided not to follow Joseph's advice; after all, he had not attended the event at the Audubon. He slumped back in his chair and continued watching television. That decision would cost him two decades of his life.

Thomas 15X Johnson, like Butler, had not known that Malcolm "was going to get hit that Sunday." At the time, he lived in a top-floor apartment across from the Bronx Zoo. A neighbor called up to Johnson and yelled, "Turn your TV on . . . Big Red just got hit!" Since the Benjamin Brown shooting and Johnson's arrest, Captain Joseph had forbidden Johnson from attending Mosque No. 7 functions. For weeks Joseph had met with him privately, giving him orders. Johnson was not at all surprised by Malcolm's murder: "I already knew—John Ali made it known." He found himself pleased that Malcolm was finally dead.

In Detroit, at Nation of Islam Mosque No. 1, Malcolm's oldest brother, Wilfred X Little, was conducting a service that Sunday afternoon when he received word of the murder. The news shook him terribly, but he went on with the service. At its conclusion, he solemnly announced to the congregation that Malcolm had been assassinated. Some in the audience had known his brother many years earlier, when he was their energetic assistant minister. "No sense in getting emotional," Minister Wilfred cautioned his flock. "This is the kind of times we are living in. Once you are dead your troubles are over. It's those living that're in trouble."

And in northern California that Sunday afternoon, Maya Angelou was chatting on the telephone with her girlfriend Ivonne. Angelou recalled that there "was no cheer in [Ivonne's] voice" when she said, "These Negroes are crazy here. I mean, really crazy. Otherwise why would they have just killed that man in New York?" In disbelief, Angelou managed to place the phone receiver down on a table. She walked into a bedroom and locked the door behind her. "I didn't have to ask," she remembered. "I knew 'that man in New York' was Malcolm X and that someone had just killed him." The next morning in bed, her first thought was that she "had returned from Africa to give my energies and wit to the OAAU, and Malcolm was dead."

CHAPTER 16

Life After Death

The shattered remains of Malcolm Little were in the hands of Dr. Milton Helpern on the morning of Monday, February 22, 1965. A veteran medical examiner, Helpern had previously directed more than twelve thousand autopsies and had participated in fifty thousand others. As stenographer Frank Smith transcribed Helpern's forensic remarks, the autopsy examination proceeded: "The body is that of an adult colored male, six foot three inches tall, scale weight 178 lbs. There is slight frontal baldness. There is a wide mustache brown in color, also a goatee of brown hair with a few gray hairs." Physically, Malcolm had been in good condition: slender, but muscular. "The hands are well developed. The fingernails are neatly trimmed." Examining the head, Helpern determined that there were no hemorrhages to the scalp. Malcolm's brain was "heavy, weighs 1700 grams." A brain section was taken, which revealed "no abnormalities."

Helpern surveyed the evidence provided from the multiple gunshot wounds. Much of the damage had been caused by the initial shotgun blast, including two wounds on the right forearm, two more in the right hand. The full force of the blast perforated the chest, cutting into "the thoracic cavity, the left lung, pericardium, heart, aorta, right lung." Handgun bullet wounds pockmarked the rest of the body: several in the left leg, a slug shattering the left index and middle fingers, a slug fragment embedded into the right side of his chin, a "bullet wound of [the] left thigh" that extended "through the innominate bone into the peritoneal cavity, penetrating the intestines and the mesentery and aorta." Helpern methodically counted twenty-one separate wounds, ten of which had been from the initial blast. The forensic evidence indicated that three different guns had been used—a sawed-off shotgun, a 9mm automatic, and a .45 caliber handgun, probably a Luger. Helpern set aside a number of slugs and bullets for further testing by the NYPD's ballistics bureau.

The NYPD's narrative about Malcolm's murder was simple. The slaying was the culmination of an almost yearlong feud between two black hate groups. The NYPD had two priorities in conducting its investigation: first, to protect the identities of its undercover police officers and informants, like Gene Roberts; and second, to make successful cases against NOI members with histories of violence. Its hasty and haphazard treatment of forensic evidence at the crime scene suggested that it had little interest in solving the actual homicide.

From the outset, the NYPD focused its attention on Norman 3X Butler and Thomas 15X Johnson, the two NOI lieutenants they believed had participated in the shooting of Benjamin Brown in the Bronx. The department's hypothesis in the Malcolm killing was that Butler was the second gunman along with Hayer. Johnson was supposedly the shotgun shooter, despite that he was about four inches taller and fairer complexioned than the very dark, stocky Willie Bradley. Still, the police's suspicions were not entirely without merit. Several OAAU and MMI members placed either Butler or Johnson in the Audubon on the day of the shooting. George Matthews, a member of both groups, informed an NYPD detective that "Butler looks like one of the men who had been engaged in the argument but that he would not swear to this." An "unspecified number" of other eyewitnesses viewed Butler in lineups, and two claimed that he had been inside the Grand Ballroom on the day of the shooting.

Yet the most intriguing piece of evidence against Butler came from Sharon 6X Poole, the eighteen-year-old OAAU secretary with whom Malcolm had been secretly involved in the previous weeks. Only minutes after the shooting, she told a news interviewer that one of the assassins was definitely a member of Harlem Mosque No. 7. Sharon had been sitting in the first row when the shooting began, and had fallen to the floor like nearly everyone else. She was still able to identify one of the assassins, she claimed, as a man wearing a brown suit who was an NOI member from Harlem.

On February 26 police arrested Butler at his home and drove him to a station house to be questioned, prompting the *Times* and newspapers across the country to assert that the NYPD was solving the case. The next day, without being contacted by the police first, Sharon 6X phoned the NYPD and presented what appeared to be a convincing story. Again, she explained that she had been seated in the front row when the shooting started. She "observed Malcolm get shot, place his hands across his chest, and then fall backwards." One of the shooters who sprinted past her with a gun in his hand looked like "the pictures of Norman Butler" she had seen in newspapers. She described Butler as "thirty-five years, five foot eleven inches, or six foot, medium build, 170 pounds, brown skin. . . . [The] subject was firing his gun in all directions in an attempt to get out of the premises." Sharon 6X also told the police that MMI "guards were all ordered not to have any guns, that is all except Reuben Francis."

Her statements focused attention on Harlem Mosque No. 7, yet police never examined Sharon's possible connections with Newark mosque members. After entering the Grand Ballroom on the afternoon of the assassination, Sharon 6X had sat in the front row next to Linwood X Cathcart, an NOI member from New Jersey whose presence perturbed the MMI members who recognized him. The seating arrangement may have been a coincidence, but subsequent evidence concerning Sharon and Cathcart makes this hard to believe. More than forty years after the assassination, Cathcart and Sharon 6X Poole Shabazz live together in the same New Jersey residence, and Shabazz has maintained absolute silence about her relationships with both Malcolm X and Cathcart.

A grand jury was impaneled on March 1, and the New York district attorney's office vigorously presented its theory that only three men—Hayer, Johnson, and Butler—had committed the murder. Johnson was arrested on March 3. He, too, was placed in the Audubon by eyewitnesses. Photojournalist Earl Grant divulged important details to the NYPD about the murder that had been confided in him by a fellow MMI member, Charles X Blackwell, one of the rostrum guards during the assassination. On March 8, Grant told police that Blackwell observed one assassin "fleeing from the chair area to the ladies room located on the east side of the ballroom." Blackwell "feels that this person [Thomas Johnson] was arrested for this crime—he knows Johnson from previous meetings." Blackwell also identified "another person who he knows as Benjamin from Paterson or Newark seated about the third row on the left side." Although the police were pleased that Johnson was placed at the crime scene, the fact that Blackwell had identified Ben X Thomas of the Newark mosque, one of the actual assassins, was not further investigated. On March 10 the grand jury ruled that Hayer, Butler, and Johnson had "willfully, feloniously and of malice aforethought" killed Malcolm X.

The police were well aware that New Jersey Muslims might have been involved in the murder. MMI guards had mentioned the presence of Linwood Cathcart in the Grand Ballroom, and he was interviewed by the NYPD on March 25, 1965; Robert 16X Gray, a member of the Newark mosque, had already been interviewed three days earlier. However, the police did not systematically investigate Hayer's ties to the Newark mosque, or endeavor to explain how he might have hooked up with Butler and Johnson, two Harlem-based NOI officers more senior than himself. They apparently did not consider that NOI protocol would never have allowed enforcers from the Harlem mosque to murder Malcolm in broad daylight, because such men almost certainly would have been recognized by many in the crowd. The NYPD file for Joseph Gravitt is empty, indicating perhaps that any evidence obtained from the Mosque No. 7 captain had been destroyed years ago.

Within Malcolm's organizations, suspicion quickly rose over the truth of the NYPD's assertion, and murmurs could be heard about the possibility of an inside job. Since the day of the murder, some inside the MMI had started to revise their estimation of Reuben X Francis as the day's hero, for shooting Talmadge Hayer. If the NYPD had been asked to relocate their detail outside the Audubon to a location several blocks away, there were only two individuals, other than Malcolm, who had the authority to negotiate a pullback: James 67X and Reuben. In addition, many began to wonder why Charles X Blackwell and Robert 35X Smith had been assigned to guard Malcolm that day when neither man had much experience in a forward defensive position, and when a usual rostrum guard, William 64X George, was present but assigned to guard the door. Reuben's position as Malcolm's head of security, responsible for both communicating with the police and arranging Malcolm's guard detail, had some brothers believing that he might have been involved in the killing.

Gerry Fulcher was convinced that Reuben Francis "was *the* guy. He organized it. And he wanted to get out of Dodge when he knew things were going to get hot. It would come back to him." The key question for Fulcher was whether Francis was an informant for either the FBI or the NYPD. If Francis had been involved, Fulcher believes, "he had to have contacts within the agency [FBI], or with our office." But Francis's role remains uncertain; even the police records are unclear because BOSS and the FBI rarely shared important information about undercover operatives. "The last thing the FBI would ever tell BOSS," Fulcher said, "is that Francis was an informant."

Francis began telling others that things were too hot to stay in New York. Released for bail of $10,000, he began expressing fears that New York district attorneys intended to prosecute him for the Hayer shooting, so he decided to flee the country. Anas Luqman, who had also been dragged in by police and then released, thought this made sense, and the two men hatched a plot to drive to the Mexican border and hide out in the desert. Francis recruited three other men with NOI connections who, for different reasons, also wanted to leave the United States. Luqman insisted that one of them, a seventeen-year-old boy, be left behind. "So we started driving," Luqman recalled more than forty years later, and after several days on the road the group crossed the border.

Whether or not Malcolm's own men played a role in his death, nearly all Malcolmites were convinced that law enforcement and the U.S. government were extensively involved in the murder. Peter Bailey, for example, charged in a 1968 interview that the NYPD and the FBI "knew that brother Malcolm's destiny was assigned for assassination." Bailey believed that both Thomas Johnson and Norman Butler were innocent. Although he himself did not witness the shooting—he was waiting downstairs for the arrival of Reverend Galamison—he developed a strong theory on how the assassination had occurred. "I think that brother Malcolm was killed by trained killers," he said, not "amateurs." Bailey doubted that "the Muslims were capable of doing it." Consequently, most OAAU and MMI members decided not to be cooperative with the police. What they failed to understand was that there was intense competition and mistrust between the NYPD and the FBI. Even within the NYPD itself, BOSS operated largely above the law, shielding its own operatives and paid informants from the rest of the police force. Consequently there was no unified law enforcement strategy in place to suppress the investigation of Malcolm's death. In the end, cooperation with police detectives might have increased the likelihood that Malcolm's real killers would have been brought to justice.

Ultimately, the police's version of events gained credibility from the media's sensationalizing of Malcolm's antiwhite image. A *New York Times* news article, for example, was headlined "Malcolm X Lived in Two Worlds, White and Black, Both Bitter." In its editorial, the *Times* described Malcolm as "an extraordinary and twisted man, turning many true gifts to evil purpose. . . . Malcolm X had the ingredients for leadership, but his ruthless and fanatical belief in violence not only set him apart from the responsible leaders of the civil rights movement and the overwhelming majority of Negroes. It also marked him for notoriety, and for a violent end." The editorial implied that Malcolm's break from the NOI was due to jealousy rather than political or ethical differences. It also suggested that black nationalist extremists, whether in the Nation or in some other group, had been responsible for the murder. "The world he saw through those horn-rimmed glasses of his was distorted and dark," the editorial concluded. "But he made it darker still with his exaltation of fanaticism. Yesterday someone came out of that darkness that he spawned, and killed him."

Several days later, *Time* magazine left no doubt regarding its interpretation: "Malcolm X had been a pimp, a cocaine addict and a thief. He was an unashamed demagogue. His gospel was hatred." The magazine also concurred with the NYPD's theory of the assassination. "Malcolm's murder [was] almost certainly at the hands of the Black Muslims from whom he had defected." But it was not enough just to condemn Malcolm on ideological grounds; *Time* went on to invent a story to ridicule his character. The Sunday afternoon program at the Audubon had started late, the magazine declared, because "characteristically [Malcolm] had kept his followers waiting for nearly an hour while he lingered over tea and a banana split at a nearby Harlem restaurant."

Other publications expressed similar sentiments. The *Saturday Evening Post*'s obituary was more sensitive than most, but expressed frustration and confusion over the murdered black leader. "The ugly killing of Malcolm X prompted many people to attempt an assessment of this violent and baffling young demagogue. Was his death an inevitable part of the struggle for Negro equality?" the obituary asked. "His death resembled a martyrdom less than a gangland execution. But Americans have had too much of assassination, too much of the settlement of conflict by violence."

The *New York Herald Tribune*'s initial headline story on Malcolm, printed that Sunday evening but dated as the first edition of February 22, read "Malcolm X Slain by Gunmen as 400 in Ballroom Watch: Police Rescue Two Suspects." An accompanying article stated that Hayer had been "taken to the Bellevue Prison Ward and was sealed off by a dozen policemen. The other suspect was taken to the Wadsworth Avenue precinct, where the city's top policemen immediately converged." Several hours later, in the *Herald Tribune*'s late edition, the subhead of the article was changed: "Police Rescue One Suspect." References to a second suspect being taken to the Wadsworth Avenue police precinct were deleted. Black nationalists and Trotskyists would subsequently charge that the NYPD "covered up" its own involvement in the assassination by suppressing evidence and witnesses, including the capture of one assailant who may have been a BOSS operative. The NYPD and mainstream journalists such as Peter Goldman ridiculed such speculations. Goldman attributed the confusion to the fact that reporters debriefed Officer Thomas Hoy "at the scene and Aronoff at the station house," not realizing they "were talking about the same man. . . . [T]he confusion lasted long enough to create a whole folklore around the 'arrest' of a mysterious second suspect—a mythology that endures to this day." However, Herman Ferguson's 2004 account of a second man who had been shot being taken away by the police lends some credence to the "second suspect" theory. If an informant or undercover operative of the FBI or BOSS had been shot, or was part of the assassination team, the police almost certainly never would have permitted his role to become public. Another possibility was the presence of more than one assassination team in the Grand Ballroom that Sunday. Although Ferguson and many eyewitnesses saw three shooters, some observers, including FBI informants, claimed that there were four or even five.

Within twenty-four hours of the assassination, nearly every national civil rights organization had distanced itself from both Malcolm and the bloody events at the Audubon. To Dr. Martin Luther King, Jr., for example, Malcolm's assassination "revealed that our society is still sick enough to express dissent through murder. We have not learned to disagree without being violently disagreeable." The NAACP leader Roy Wilkins deplored Malcolm's "gunning down" as a "shocking and ghastly demonstration of the futility of resorting to violence as a means of settling differences." Speaking on behalf of SNCC, the young desegregation activist Julian Bond informed the *New York Times*, "I don't think Malcolm's death or any man's death could influence our deep-seated belief in nonviolence."

From London, James Baldwin responded by linking the crime to the involvement of the U.S. government. "Whoever did it," he speculated, "was formed in the crucible of the Western world, of the American Republic." Much more explicit was CORE's James Farmer, who was well aware of Malcolm's metamorphosis and had expressed doubts that the leader's murder was the product of a feud with the Nation of Islam. "I believe that his killing was a political killing," he declared. It was hardly "accidental that his death came at a time when his views were changing [toward] the mainstream of the civil rights movement." Farmer's demand for a "federal inquiry into the murder," however, found virtually no support. To the public, the Nation of Islam was evidently responsible for the shooting.

———

Malcolm's death set off a chain reaction of violence and intimidation that kept his supporters in fear and left his organizations crumbling. On the night of the murder, a fire ignited in Muhammad Ali's Chicago apartment, but the fire was later determined to have been accidental. Ali informed the press that Malcolm had been his friend "as long as he was a member of [the Nation of] Islam. Now I don't want to talk about him." Perhaps still suspicious about his apartment fire, Ali protested, "All of us were shocked at the way [Malcolm] was killed." Ali denied that Elijah Muhammad, or others in the NOI, had any involvement in the murder.

Two days later, early in the morning on February 23, unknown parties ascended to the roof of a building next door to Mosque No. 7 and tossed Molotov cocktails into the mosque's fourth floor, igniting a fire that soon raged out of control, with flames soaring as high as thirty feet. The fire quickly spread next door to the Gethsemane Church of God in Christ, and soon seventy-five firemen were working frantically to put it out. As a section of the mosque's wall collapsed, five firefighters and a civilian were injured. Within an hour the entire building was gutted. The Fruit of Islam was mustered, and soon about three hundred people were watching the fire blaze away. As the crowd grew and emotions surged, the police became worried and called in reinforcements. In the frigid night air, Larry 4X Prescott huddled next to Captain Joseph, who had begun to weep. Larry was shocked to see the almost stoic, deeply private Joseph now overwhelmed with grief.

The destruction of the mosque greatly increased public perceptions that an open gang war was imminent. The NYPD policed the Nation's Brooklyn mosque and the ten businesses it owned in the surrounding neighborhood; the mosque in Queens was similarly protected. In Chicago, squads stood an around-the-clock vigil to protect the life of Muhammad, still cloistered in his Hyde Park mansion. Captain Joseph characterized the Harlem firebombing as "a vicious sneak attack. . . . The worst thing a man can do is tamper with your religious sanctuary."

The Nation would exact its revenge not in Harlem's streets, but in Chicago at the Saviour's Day convention. In preparation, administrators worked closely with the Chicago police to carry out extraordinary security measures around the convention hall. A police bomb squad thoroughly checked the facility; attendees were processed through police barricades before entering. Elijah Muhammad himself "will not make a move unless accompanied by at least six members of his security force, the Fruit of Islam brigade," reported the *Chicago Tribune*. Twenty-five hundred members were present as the convention began on February 26. The event was orchestrated as a triumph of the victors. "Malcolm was a hypocrite who got what he was preaching," Elijah Muhammad proclaimed. "Just weeks ago he came to this city to blast away with his hate and mudslinging. He didn't stop here, either, but then went around the country trying to slander me."

The audience was treated to the spectacle of Wallace Muhammad and Malcolm's brothers, Wilfred X and Philbert X, walking out onstage to ask forgiveness and to pledge fidelity to the Messenger. Wallace claimed that he had been confused, that it had been wrong to leave the Nation and his father. In tears, he announced that "only God was in a position to judge a figure so exalted" as Elijah Muhammad. Reading texts that had been prepared for them, both Wilfred and Philbert denounced their dead brother for "his mistakes" and made it clear they would not attend his funeral. Wilfred declared to the convention, "We must not let our natural enemy, the white man, come between us [to] get us to kill each other. I was shocked to hear the news of my brother's death but from my heart I ask Allah to strengthen me as a follower of Elijah Muhammad."

Back in New York, there were by now serious questions about how Malcolm was to be buried. By Islamic standards, the autopsy itself had represented a desecration of his body. Muslim tradition also requires the prompt burial of the deceased, and on the opening day of the Saviour's Day convention Malcolm's corpse was lying in state for the fourth day at Harlem's Unity Funeral Home, dressed in a Western-style business suit. Since Tuesday, about thirty thousand people had come to pay their respects. During the week Betty and others close to her had contacted more than a dozen Harlem churches, including Adam Clayton Powell's Abyssinian Baptist, to host Malcolm's last rites; all declined, fearing Nation of Islam retaliation. Finally, the Faith Temple Church of God in Christ, on Amsterdam Avenue in West Harlem, agreed to make its auditorium available. Within hours, the church received a series of bomb threats, but the ceremony went forward without incident. Just before the funeral, Sheikh Ahmed Hassoun prepared and wrapped Malcolm's body in a *kafan*, a traditional Muslim burial sheet.

More than a thousand people packed the Faith Temple Church on Saturday, February 27, to bear witness to Malcolm's funeral. There were a small number of movement leaders—Bayard Rustin, James Farmer, Dick Gregory, and SNCC's John Lewis and James Forman—but the majority stayed away, probably fearing violence. Adam Clayton Powell, Jr., was not present, nor were most of Harlem's civic leaders. Betty had asked Ossie Davis and Ruby Dee to preside over the program, and the two read out dozens of notes of condolence from a range of dignitaries, including King, Whitney Young, and Kwame Nkrumah. But it was Davis's soliloquy on the meaning of Malcolm's life to the black people of Harlem that captured the public's imagination, and in subsequent decades would dwarf everything else that occurred that day. Using notes scribbled at his kitchen table, Davis spoke these words:

> Many will ask what Harlem finds to honor in this stormy, controversial, and bold young captain—and we will smile. . . . And we will answer and say unto them: Did you ever talk to Brother Malcolm? Did you ever touch him, or have him smile at you? . . . And if you knew him you would know why we must honor him: Malcolm was our manhood, our living black manhood! . . . And we will know him then for what he was and is—a prince—our own black shining prince—who didn't hesitate to die, because he loved us so.

Following Davis's eulogy, Betty walked to the coffin to view her husband a final time. Accompanied by two plainclothes police officers, she bent down and kissed the glass cover that had been placed over his body. She then collapsed in tears. The funeral cortege, which included three family cars, twelve police vehicles, and eighteen mourners' cars, headed north to Westchester County. About twenty-five thousand people braved the freezing weather along the route to the cemetery. Only two hundred people, including media representatives, were allowed at the gravesite. After the last prayers, the coffin was lowered into the grave. There was still time for a final moment of controversy, one that in many respects illustrates the dilemma Malcolm faced at the end of his life. Several MMI and OAAU brothers noticed that the cemetery workers waiting to bury the coffin were all white. No white men, they complained, should be allowed to throw dirt on Malcolm's body. The workers were persuaded to surrender their shovels, and under a drizzling rain the brothers proceeded to bury Malcolm themselves.

During the weeks after the mosque firebombing and the funeral, Malcolm loyalists feared for their lives. The Nation was convinced that die-hard Malcolmites were responsible for the fire, and that their actions merited fierce retribution. On March 12, Leon 4X Ameer, mostly recovered from the savage beating he had suffered at the hands of Clarence Gill and his men back in December, spoke to a meeting of Boston Trotskyists, claiming he had evidence that the U.S. government was involved in Malcolm's death. The next day his body was found in his room at the Sherry Biltmore hotel. A medical examiner ruled that Ameer's death was caused by a coma from a sleeping pill overdose. Another victim was Robert 35X Smith, one of Malcolm's rostrum guards at the assassination. "Karate Bob," as he was called, died when he either jumped or was pushed in front of a speeding subway car. When questioned years later about the death, Larry 4X Prescott curtly explained, "He got killed in the subway. They claimed that we pushed him off the subway [platform] or something, which I don't believe."

Neither the OAAU nor MMI had cultivated procedures of collective decision making, and without Malcolm, the weak bonds that had held the groups together came apart. Leaders worked on a volunteer basis out of personal devotion to Malcolm, and his death did more than deny them his physical presence: it froze their universe. He had become the cutting edge for rethinking black nationalism, Pan-Africanism, and their own home-grown version of Islam, and often his devotees stumbled behind him—even at times suppressing his letters because his shifts in ideology were too disturbing. Without the architecture of his expanding social vision, they found it almost impossible to build upon his legacy. Trust soon evaporated between most members, as people renounced their ties.

In retrospect, Max Stanford said, "the OAAU was trying to put [itself] together too fast." Collective leadership was the desired goal, but in reality "most people were mesmerized by Malcolm." Even when Stanford expressed disagreements with Malcolm, he admitted, "Malcolm would mesmerize me. He was further developed" politically and intellectually than nearly all his followers. Consequently, when Malcolm became "a mass spokesman who's world-acclaimed," there was no one after the assassination prepared to assume his leadership mantle. At first, James 67X thought he might be up to the task. Several days after the assassination, he met with Revolutionary Action Movement members Max Stanford and Larry Neal. According to Stanford, James said that "Malcolm had formed a RAM cell somewhere in Muslim Mosque, Inc. and had said that if anything happened to him, I would know what to do." RAM's representatives agreed to work with James and other MMI activists. "The agreement was for [James] to continue to go internationally and around the country like Malcolm," Stanford recalled, "because he could sound like Malcolm." Yet James soon had his hands full simply trying to keep both groups alive. Because of the long-troublesome divisions between the MMI and the OAAU, there was no one in either group who could inspire the trust and confidence of members in the other group. The secular-oriented activists, moreover, had little interest in the MMI's Islamic spiritual agenda. Given the absence of administrative resources or even a permanent office, neither organization could be sustained.

As the core of Malcolm's supporters disappeared or fell away, James alone was left to deal with Betty Shabazz. Even within hours of Malcolm's murder, her relationship with the MMI and the OAAU had become confrontational. She blamed Malcolm's supporters for his death; in her bitterness and anger, she instructed several OAAU members to dump into the garbage many of her husband's important papers, all of which had been moved for safety to the Wallaces' home. She demanded that James forward to her all MMI correspondence unopened, including letters addressed to Malcolm, allowing her to review everything first. James refused. "She was a grieving widow, a hero's widow," he explained, but one who had at best a limited comprehension of the MMI and OAAU's work.

The care and security of Betty and the children were largely assumed by Ruby Dee, Juanita Poitier, and other female friends, most of them celebrities. These women established the Committee of Concerned Mothers to provide support. Percy Sutton, James Baldwin, and John Oliver Killens also became actively involved. Within several weeks, over six thousand dollars was raised, including a five-hundred-dollar contribution from Shirley Graham Du Bois. In August, the committee organized a benefit concert that attracted a thousand people and generated another five thousand dollars for the purchase of a home. Malcolm's core constituency, the black poor and working class, never abandoned Betty. She received many envelopes with small amounts of cash, sent either to the Hotel Theresa or to the MMI's post office box. James 67X wrote to many of Malcolm's international contacts requesting funds. Advertisements were placed on New York radio stations. Several aggressive MMI brothers even visited Harlem merchants and demanded cash and merchandise "contributions" for Betty and the children. Yet some Malcolm loyalists found Betty's behavior at this time disturbing. To them, she seemed to be rejecting her husband's poor and working-class black constituency, favoring instead overtures to the black bourgeoisie. Ferguson put Betty's elitist politics in the context of Malcolm's "Message to the Grassroots" speech: "She moved from the field slaves to the house slaves."

As James 67X's most trusted allies dissipated, and the difficulties of working with Betty grew more apparent, he recalled his promise to Malcolm to work for him for twelve months. Mid-March 1965 marked the end of that obligation, and he now began considering other options. He was exhausted, and Charles Kenyatta's scurrilous rumors also had a poisonous effect; some MMI members wondered why James had left the Audubon for nearly an hour following the shooting, and questioned his cordial relations with the Marxists in RAM. So when Ella Collins contacted James, demanding the right to take over the MMI and OAAU based on her blood tie with Malcolm, he at first resisted, but soon agreed to resign his post. Ella was also given the incorporation papers for Muslim Mosque, Inc., becoming the effective leader of both groups.

On March 15, Ella held a press conference at OAAU and MMI headquarters. Described in the *New York Times* as "an ample figure in black skirt and large-buttoned blouse," Collins was "terse and cryptic in speech," a far cry from her charismatic brother. Collins's claim to leadership was based on her questionable assertion that she had been executive director of Boston's OAAU chapter since June 1964. She also asserted that Malcolm himself had appointed her as "his successor" on February 20, 1965. Collins generally expressed conservative views. She said that she had "no desire to fight against" Muhammad or the Nation of Islam; she attributed the firebombing of Malcolm's Queens home to forces "much bigger than the Black Muslims"; and when asked whether the OAAU would reject "leftist or communist" support, Collins responded, "I believe so." Within days, Collins's reactionary politics—when compared to Malcolm's—and her belligerent behavior drove out the few remaining veteran activists. Soon after, James 67X informed RAM that he planned to abandon all future political activity. At perhaps their final meeting, James announced mysteriously "that he was going to disappear, and that the initial cadre that was with Malcolm were going to go under[ground]." When RAM representatives suggested that youth organizing might offer new possibilities, James laughed, saying that they "were crazy" and "the youth were crazy." And then, recalled Max Stanford, "he disappeared."

James had decided to go underground because both the OAAU and MMI quickly fell apart without Malcolm. The best—and worst—example was Charles Kenyatta. Within days of the assassination, he insinuated to the press that the killing was an inside job, carried out by Marxists and the Revolutionary Action Movement. He talked extensively with the NYPD, and on March 15 was interviewed by the FBI. He pointed out that it was "very odd that Malcolm X's bodyguards were not beside him on the stage." Nor had he recognized any of Malcolm's bodyguards in the rear of the hall. He further claimed that he and Malcolm "were very close friends" and that they had frequently discussed "certain matters pertaining to the NOI and the MMI." Kenyatta then proceeded to trash Malcolm's most faithful supporters. Although the FBI report is redacted, it is clear that he told the FBI that James 67X was "not a Negro nationalist but a Marxist Communist," and that Malcolm had deliberately lied in claiming that scholarships would be made available for MMI members to study in Cairo; this was "only stated by Malcolm to make him look important." In summary, Kenyatta warned FBI agents he "may be next in line to be assassinated."

———

The trial of Hayer, Butler, and Johnson began the following winter, on January 12, 1966. The district attorney's office was represented by veteran prosecutor Vincent J. Dermody. The judge was seventy-one-year-old Charles Marks, a law-and-order jurist who was personally responsible for sentencing one-fourth of all the prisoners on New York State's death row. The case against Hayer was open and shut, because he had been shot attempting to flee the murder scene; in his pocket had been found an ammunition clip that matched the .45 caliber bullets taken from Malcolm's body. In the cases of Butler and Johnson, however, there was of course no physical evidence connecting them with the murder. Both men had alibis for that Sunday afternoon, and there was no tangible connection between them and Hayer, beyond their NOI membership. There was also the problem of the chain of command: the police had no clue who had actually given the order to kill.

The prosecution's star witness was Cary 2X Thomas (also known as Abdul Malik). Born in New York City in 1930, by his mid-twenties he had become a heroin addict and narcotics dealer. For years he was in and out of jail on drug charges, and in early 1963 was assigned to Bellevue Hospital after a nervous breakdown. In December of that year he joined Mosque No. 7, but soon left, siding with Malcolm in the split. Thomas's extremely short tenure in the Nation meant that he knew relatively little about the organization, or the reasons for Malcolm's separation. After detectives interviewed him, the district attorney's office decided to arrest him as a material witness. For almost a year he was held in protective custody. On one occasion, highly disturbed, he set fire to his jail mattress.

In his original testimony to the grand jury, Thomas was one of the few OAAU members who claimed to have seen all three men—Hayer, Butler, and Johnson—at the murder. He explained that Butler and Johnson were the two who had tussled with each other while Hayer attacked Malcolm with the sawed-off shotgun. Since Hayer bore absolutely no physical resemblance to the shooter, the prosecutors and police persuaded Thomas to revise his testimony. At the 1966 trial, he was better prepared, insisting that Johnson, not Hayer, had wielded the shotgun; Hayer and Butler were the two handgun attackers. But he continued to make minor mistakes that undermined his testimony, for example, identifying Hayer as a member of

Mosque No. 7; he also admitted to the jury that he had not actually seen guns in the hands of Butler or Hayer.

Butler struggled to understand how the assassination had actually occurred, and why he ended up being tried for the murder. He didn't know Hayer, indeed had never met him. After his arrest, Butler sadly discovered that the Nation's promises to him were empty. "Nobody took care of my children, nobody looked after my wife," he complained. "I think that the people—the city, the state, the feds, whoever—they wanted this case closed, and they got somebody to say I was there and that I did it." Butler, now out of prison, having served his sentence, insists "everybody know[s] there was four or five people involved. They didn't go look for nobody else."

As Johnson and Butler listened to the prosecution's weak case being presented, they were brimming with confidence. There was no way, they believed, that the jury would convict them. Indeed, as the trial progressed, Hayer informed the court that Johnson and Butler were not involved in the assassination; he and three other men had committed the crime. Hayer even provided some accurate details. But Johnson correctly feared that these last-minute confessions would be used against him and Butler. Dermody effectively argued that Hayer was merely under orders by NOI bosses to sacrifice himself, in order to free his coassassins. Johnson's attorneys also made things worse by putting up Charles Kenyatta as a defense witness. Johnson had extreme misgivings: "When they wanted to put Kenyatta on the stand to testify for me, I was against it. I never trusted Kenyatta—never." Kenyatta had agreed to tell the jury that it would have been impossible for Butler and Johnson to enter the Grand Ballroom that afternoon, because both were well known as militant NOI members. Kenyatta also wanted to get into the public record his belief that an "internal left plot" was possibly responsible for Malcolm's murder. However, under Dermody's cross-examination, he also identified both Johnson and Butler as members of an NOI "hundred-man enforcing squad."

Any chance for Johnson and Butler to be acquitted disintegrated with the appearance of Betty Shabazz. Betty had only briefly witnessed the actual shooting, so her testimony added only limited information. She described the chaos: "Everyone had fallen to the floor, chairs were on the floor, people were crawling around . . ." She'd pushed all her children under a bench and covered it with her body until things appeared to have settled down. A few minutes later she found Malcolm on his back on the stage. Dermody asked only a few questions, and the defense attorneys passed on cross-examining her. But as she walked slowly away from the witness stand, anger over-whelmed her and she clenched her fists in rage. Standing near the defense table, Betty cried out, "They killed my husband! They killed him!" As two court attendants quickly escorted the widow out, she continued murmuring her charges. Defense attorneys demanded a mistrial, but Judge Marks blandly instructed the jury to disregard Betty's off-stand statements. As Johnson remembered the scene, Betty halted in front of the defense table "and started screaming and pointing at me: 'They killed my husband!' And that's when the jury convicted me."

Johnson was right. Hayer, Butler, and Johnson were all convicted of first-degree murder. On April 14, Judge Marks told each man that he would be incarcerated in a New York state prison for the remainder of his natural life. Peter L. F. Sabbatino, one of the defense attorneys, responded prophetically, "I don't think that you have a solution here that history will support."

——

The initial remaking of Malcolm's posthumous image began, interestingly enough, with jazz musicians. John Coltrane, the most influential saxophone artist of the 1960s, was deeply influenced by Malcolm's style of rhetoric and by his political philosophy of black nationalism. The new breed of musicians, emerging a generation after bebop, rejected political modera-tion and nonviolence; the anger and militancy identified with Malcolm captured their mood. For musician Archie Shepp, Malcolm inspired "inno-vations" in African-American music, making jazz an "extension of the black nationalist movement." Amiri Baraka (LeRoi Jones), recognizing the con-nections between black art and political protest, described Coltrane as the "Malcolm in the New Super Bop Fire." Malcolm's effective public presen-tations, his use of timing and the cadence of his speaking voice, were strik-ingly like jazz. As John Oliver Killens explained, "I have always thought of Malcolm X as an artist . . . but an artist of the spoken word."

Malcolm's popularity among millions of white Americans, however, began only with the publication, in late 1965, of *The Autobiography of Mal-colm X*. After Doubleday's cancellation of the book, Paul Reynolds had shopped the manuscript to other publishers, eventually securing a contract for Haley with the radical house Grove Press. The reviews of the narrative of Malcolm's life were overwhelmingly positive. Eliot Fremont-Smith of the *New York Times* praised the *Autobiography* as a "brilliant, painful, impor-tant book. . . . As a document for our time, its insights may be crucial; its relevance cannot be doubted." In the *Nation*, Truman Nelson declared, "its dead-level honesty, its passion, its exalted purpose, even its manifold unsolved ambiguities will make it stand as a monument to the most painful of truths." But the most insightful commentary on Malcolm's memoir was written by his former debating partner, Bayard Rustin. In the *Washington Post*, Rustin powerfully characterized the book as "the odyssey of an American Negro in search of his identity and place in society." Rustin sharply disputed the notion that Malcolm was simply the product of the "Harlem ghetto"; the book's initial chapters on Malcolm's Midwestern childhood "are essential reading for anyone who wants to understand the plight of the American Negro." There was much to criticize in Malcolm's politics, and Rustin did not mince words. The black nationalism of groups like the Nation of Islam, he said, offers "an arena for struggle, for power and status-denied lower-class Negroes in the outside world." It was here that Malcolm brought his intelligence and "his burning ambition to succeed."

Rustin remained sharply critical of Malcolm's "anti-Semitic comments" and former black nationalist views, but acknowledged that he was attempting to "turn a corner," to assimilate into the civil rights mainstream. Had he been successful, Rustin observed, "he would have made an enormous contribution to the struggle for equal rights. As it was, his contribution was substantial. He brought hope and a measure of dignity to thousands of despairing ghetto Negroes." Rustin, like Alex Haley, discounted the effectiveness of black nationalism as a potential force in challenging racial inequality. Both men misinterpreted Malcolm's last frenetic year as an effort to gain respectability as an integrationist and liberal reformer, which was not an accurate or complete reading of him. Rustin's characterization of Malcolm was designed to deny the militancy and radical potential of "field Negroes," the black ghetto masses. Rustin wanted to make the point that Malcolm would have inevitably turned his back to the ghetto. "Malcolm's life was tragic on a heroic scale. He had choices, but never took the easy or comfortable ones," Rustin observed. Malcolm could have been "a successful lawyer, sipping cocktails with other members of the black bourgeoisie." Rustin's image of a transformed Malcolm was that of a pragmatic liberal, not a revolutionary. It was a vision that Haley shared, which is why the *Autobiography* does not read like a manifesto for black insurrection, but much more in the tradition of Benjamin Franklin's autobiography. This may help to explain the enormous popularity of the *Autobiography* and its adoption into the curricula in hundreds of colleges and thousands of high schools. Between 1965 and 1977, the number of copies of the *Autobiography* sold worldwide exceeded six million.

––––

During the next few years, the FBI would continue its surveillance of Charles Kenyatta, believing him to be a security risk. BOSS and the NYPD, however, considered him a reliable informant and developed a close working relationship with him. By late April 1965, Kenyatta was observed giving rambling speeches along 125th Street. And by early 1966 he had rejoined the Nation of Islam, probably to provide inside information about the sect to the police. In the late 1960s he started his own organization in Harlem, which proclaimed identification with Kenya's Mau Mau revolt and the necessity to bring that level of black revolution to the United States. Simultaneously, Kenyatta continued to work closely and cordially as a BOSS informant. In fact, Kenyatta was so highly prized by the police that the NYPD urged the FBI to back off from its continuing surveillance of him. Kenyatta's strength was in manipulating his own image as Malcolm's right-hand man while collecting damaging information about other black groups. His true role as a disrupter became evident only with the availability of his FBI file in 2007. Financially, he also cashed in on his political kinship with Malcolm X for decades.

Benjamin 2X Goodman's response to the assassination was, oddly, to blame the largely secular black audience for panicking, so allowing the killers to escape. "A Muslim audience," he believed, "would not have panicked. It would have responded to the situation with military discipline, not like a herd of cattle in a thunderstorm." He was convinced that, without the "stampede," the "Muslim brothers . . . [would] probably have taken all five assassins." He decided to retreat from political life, getting work with children's educational programs through HARYOU, the Harlem-based federally funded advocacy program. Agreeing to meet with FBI agents on April 22, 1966, Goodman indicated that "on many occasions individuals [in NOI Mosque No. 7] have invited [him] to return to the faith as a teacher." Benjamin admitted that he "truthfully has given it much consideration." Rewriting history, he denied that Muslim Mosque, Inc., had ever opposed "the basic aims and objectives" of the Nation of Islam. During the interview, he promised naively that he would always be "a brother" to one FBI agent, but that he would not exchange information for money. New York's FBI special agent in charge, reporting to Hoover, observed, "This indicates that Goodman, if properly and delicately handled, can be influenced to return to the NOI, assuming his Assistant Ministership and possibly move up to the minister capacity and be of extremely valuable assistance to the Bureau." Unfortunately for the FBI, Benjamin never rejoined the Nation, and he eventually, like Malcolm, embraced orthodox Islam.

It did not take many days of hiding out in the Mexican desert for Reuben Francis and Anas Luqman to become intensely suspicious of the two ex-NOI members with whom they had gone south to escape police attention after the assassination. Yet Luqman was deliberately vague about what actually happened next, when tensions spiraled out of control and violence flared. Luqman admitted only that when the group decided to split up, things fell apart. There was an altercation and the dead body of an ex-NOI member was left in the desert. One ex-NOI member named John, according to Luqman, "went off, got broke, and couldn't handle it." Luqman said he subsequently purchased a fishing boat, and he and Reuben managed to live for a time from the proceeds from their catches. Eventually they parted company; Luqman believes Reuben eventually went back to New York City. The story is a strange one from the start, as Francis's denunciations of James 67X were well known, and Luqman was James's best friend and roommate. Was Francis the man who was murdered in the Mexican desert? Since 1965, rumors of his appearance have popped up occasionally, but no credible evidence placing him in the United States—or anywhere else—has emerged.

Ella Collins purchased an attractive Harlem town house that would become the OAAU's headquarters. Peter Goldman, who visited Collins in the early 1970s, observed that "the OAAU's active membership had dwindled to a handful, and its most visible activities in Harlem were the annual commemorations of Malcolm's birth and death."

Meanwhile, James 67X simply slipped into obscurity. From 1976 until 1988 he lived in Guyana. When he came back to the United States, he became a nurse; in his sixties he remarried and started a new family. His earlier life as Malcolm's chief aide became as remote as another world.

Muhammad Ali once again met Sonny Liston, in Lewiston, Maine, on May 25, 1965, for their second heavyweight championship bout. Although Ali quickly knocked out Liston, the fight was secondary to the swirl of police activity surrounding the event. Prompted by bomb threats, two hundred Maine police were stationed in the arena. FBI agents and state troopers were also present. The mood was so tense that the event's singer, entertainer Robert Goulet, forgot the words to the national anthem.

Over the next two years Ali achieved a spectacular boxing record. In

November 1965, he humiliated former heavyweight champion Floyd Patterson. Several months later Ali was reclassified by his draft board as 1-A, and was soon notified that he would be inducted into the U.S. military. Ali's response in opposition to the Vietnam War—"I ain't got no quarrel with them Vietcong"—placed the Black Muslim, paradoxically, in the identical political posture as Malcolm X. When Ali refused to be inducted, his championship was stripped from him and he was barred from fighting for more than three years. He became a hero to the antiwar generation that rejected both the war and the military-industrial complex. To millions of Muslims throughout the world, Ali became a symbol of resistance to American imperialism. There would be many more twists and ironic turns in the magnificent but flawed journey of Ali, from his 1974 recapturing of the heavyweight championship by defeating George Foreman in Zaire to his 1996 surprise appearance at the Atlanta Olympics, holding a torch in his hands to mark the opening event. Like Malcolm before him, Ali also evolved in his beliefs from the Nation of Islam to orthodox Islam. Despite his physical infirmities, he has found peace within his life.

It would be left to Wallace Muhammad to complete Malcolm's posthumous rehabilitation. His 1965 capitulation to his father was so transparently contrived that his ouster from the sect several years later was predictable. However, by 1974 he was back in the Nation, preaching orthodox Islam and challenging prominent ministers like Farrakhan. When Elijah Muhammad died, on February 25, 1975, Wallace quickly outmaneuvered his siblings to seize control of nearly all the Nation's operations. Within a year, he had carried out an orthodox Islamic revolution within the sect. Farrakhan was stripped of his Harlem ministry and sentenced to serve at a minor mosque in the Chicago suburbs. Yacub's History, the demonization of whites, the advocacy of strict racial separatism—these were all discarded. In June 1975, the Nation of Islam announced that it would accept white followers, and a few whites actually joined. The organization's archival heritage—its thousands of publications and newspapers, audiotaped recordings, internal records, and photographs—were largely destroyed, and a new memory, branded by orthodoxy, was imposed. Wallace later changed his name to W. Deen Mohammed, to distinguish himself from his father.

As the group's new imam, W. Deen Mohammed opened the financial records of the Nation for the first time to its members. Its fish import enterprises alone grossed $22 million in income annually. The Nation employed more than a thousand people and owned over $6 million worth of farmland—yet it also carried a $4.5 million debt, due in part to financial mismanagement. But Imam Mohammed's most shocking move for diehards was the restoration of Malcolm X. On February 2, 1976, Mohammed announced that Harlem Mosque No. 7 was to be renamed in honor of El-Hajj Malik El-Shabazz, and praised Malcolm as "the greatest minister the Nation of Islam ever had, except for the Honorable Elijah Muhammad." As the name Nation of Islam was jettisoned in favor of World Community of Al-Islam in the West, Farrakhan had enough, and began to reconstitute the old Nation of Islam around himself. Imam Mohammed's response, in 1977, was to excommunicate him. Fidelity to Elijah Muhammad's teachings now meant being expelled from the Islamic faith community.

And even years after the Messenger's death, embarrassing episodes generated by his sexual infidelities continued to surface. In 1981, for example, three individuals claiming to be Muhammad's illegitimate children filed a $5 million lawsuit charging that Muhammad's children, relatives, and two banks had converted millions of dollars of Muhammad's assets for themselves. The children suing were the son and daughter of June Muhammad—Abdulla Yasin Muhammad (born December 30, 1960) and Ayesha Muhammad (born September 4, 1962), and the daughter of Evelyn Williams, Marie Muhammad (born March 30, 1960).

Larry 4X Prescott at first supported Wallace's efforts to reform the Nation of Islam. However, when Farrakhan broke with Wallace to reestablish the old NOI, Prescott joined him. Now, as Akbar Muhammad, looking back four decades, he identifies errors of judgment that he believes were made on both sides. After the firebombing of Malcolm's home, for instance, James 3X Shabazz was among those who had accused Malcolm of burning his own house. "And Malcolm responded, 'Do you think that I would burn a house down with my babies in there?' . . . And it made us look like we were really out to lunch." But Shabazz's rhetoric had the effect of intensifying anti-Malcolm sentiment among "the brothers in the mosque, the bean soup eaters and the black coffee drinkers, they start to say, 'Yeah, he went so far as to burn his own house down.' That's the way it started going." Prescott suggested that the MMI was too small to represent "a challenge to the Nation." What truly motivated Malcolm, he believed, was "wanting to get in the front of the civil rights movement." His blanket repudiations of the Nation of Islam and the revelations of Elijah Muhammad's infidelities all advanced Malcolm's objectives. A last-minute rapprochement between the factions was never going to be possible.

Some of those who had a hand in Malcolm's murder began disappearing from the scene as early as the 1970s. The body of James 3X Shabazz, fifty-two and the boss of the Newark mosque, was discovered on September 4, 1973, next to his Cadillac, which was parked in his driveway. In a mob-style hit reminiscent of that of Bugsy Siegel, James had been shot just above his left eye, with another bullet wound through the forehead into his brain. He left behind a wife and thirteen children. Apparently, James 3X's death was not in belated retribution for Malcolm X, but the result of a war between the corrupt Newark mosque and a local criminal gang, the New World of Islam, for control of extortion and murders for hire. Three thousand people attended Shabazz's funeral, including Newark mayor Kenneth Gibson and Farrakhan. The Newark murders continued. On September 18, 1973, two Muslims were shot to death, their bodies found in an automobile near an auto plant. A copy of *Muhammad Speaks* was spread out over the dead men's faces. One month later, the heads of Newark mosque members Michael X Huff and Warren X Marcello were found in a lot near James 3X Shabazz's home. Their bodies were subsequently found four miles distant.

There were also attempts on the life of Raymond Sharrieff. On one occasion in October 1971, someone pumped five shotgun rounds into Sharrieff's Chicago mansion from outside; Sharrieff was wounded by several pellets. In late December 1971 an assailant shot into his downtown office window, just barely missing his secretary. Sharrieff died, peacefully, of natural causes on December 18, 2003.

Members of Elijah Muhammad's family also began disappearing from the scene. Elijah's third son and former manager of Muhammad Ali, Herbert Muhammad, spent years in litigation fighting his younger brother, Wallace, in the 1990s. On August 26, 2008, Herbert died from complications after heart surgery, leaving a wife, Aminah Antonia Muhammad, six sons, and eight daughters. About two weeks later, on September 9, 2008, Wallace Mohammed died. At the time of his death, Muhammad was the spiritual leader of 185 mosques with an estimated fifty thousand congregants. In death he was proclaimed as "America's imam" by Ahmed Rehab of the Council on American-Islamic Relations.

In the final years of their lives, Ella and Betty were locked even more intensely in conflict. In the early 1990s, when Spike Lee proposed a Hollywood-style biographical film on Malcolm X, Ella was outraged to find out Betty was retained as a paid consultant. "Spike Lee's after the money, the prestige," Ella contemptuously complained to a reporter. "He doesn't know any facts." Ella protested that Betty "doesn't know enough about Malcolm to consult on anything pertaining to his life. Her activities [with him] were very limited." Betty had her revenge by eliminating any references to Ella in Lee's movie. "I don't have any respect for the lady," Betty coolly explained to the *Boston Globe*. "She was not a good influence on him." As the renaissance of interest in Malcolm exploded across American popular culture, Ella's personal situation became much worse. No longer able to maintain the OAAU headquarters in Harlem, she relocated to Boston. Her health soon declined as she fell ill with diabetes; in 1990 she was discovered in her apartment lying in her own waste. One of her legs, swollen with a gangrenous ulcer, was filled with maggots. Both of her legs were soon amputated. Ella painfully passed away on August 6, 1996.

Following Malcolm's death, Betty Shabazz appeared to live a successful and rewarding life. In 1972 she enrolled in a doctoral program in education at the University of Massachusetts Amherst, receiving her Ph.D. three years later. Subsequently she served as an academic administrator at Medgar Evers College in Brooklyn, becoming a sort of celebrity among black middle-class and professional groups. But she could never escape Malcolm's shadow, his terrible death, and the desire to punish those who were responsible. Her animus largely focused on Farrakhan, who she felt had betrayed Malcolm, and she believed he had directly participated in the conspiracy to murder him. Betty's attacks on Farrakhan probably inspired her daughter Qubilah to attempt to hire a hit man to murder him in 1995. The would-be assassin, Michael Fitzpatrick, was an FBI informer, and Qubilah was quickly arrested and charged in federal court. In an astute move, Farrakhan rallied to Qubilah's defense, claiming the young woman had been entrapped by the FBI. The government's case fell apart at trial. Betty was forced to praise Farrakhan publicly for his "kindness in wanting to help my daughter."

Tragically, barely a year after Qubilah's legal ordeal, her disturbed twelve-year-old son, called "Little Malcolm" by the family, set fire one night to his grandmother's apartment. Betty, sleeping in her bedroom, was horrifically burned. She struggled in the hospital for more than three weeks, with severe burns covering more than 80 percent of her body. Physicians took aggressive action, operating five times to remove layers of charred skin and replacing it with artificial skin. But the damage was too great and Betty Shabazz died on June 23, 1997. President William Jefferson Clinton noted her passing, applauding her for her commitments to "education and to uplifting women and children." Like Malcolm X, noted District of Columbia representative Eleanor Holmes Norton, Shabazz "will be remembered not for her death, but for the principled life she lived and the tower of strength she became." Her public memorial gathering, held at the prestigious Riverside Church in Manhattan, included testimonials by Republican governor George Pataki of New York and New York City's Republican mayor, Rudolph Giuliani. The mayor, widely unpopular among many working-class and poor black New Yorkers, was roundly booed when he began to address the audience. It was significant that the eldest daughter, Attallah Shabazz, rushed to the podium in defense of Giuliani, praising the conservative mayor's gestures of kindness toward her mother and criticizing the mostly black crowd for its rudeness. Her defense of Giuliani may have reflected Betty's black bourgeois politics, but not those of her father.

From the beginning of the criminal investigation following Malcolm's murder, BOSS detective Gerry Fulcher had been troubled by what he considered major mistakes. The problems began at the crime scene. The first priority, Fulcher later recounted, should have been to "protect the whole area. You get rid of everybody who's not going to be a witness." Any evidence must be preserved. "You don't want people finding things. . . ." In Fulcher's judgment, the NYPD's treatment of the murder scene was "totally contrary to what should be standard operating procedure. That thing should have been covered all night long." In high-profile cases, it is not unusual to find "crime scenes stay[ing] locked up for days." Fulcher expressed his misgivings to his police colleagues at the time of the assassination. Perhaps as a consequence, he found himself shut out of the investigation. Fulcher recalled:

> I should have been an indispensable part of finding out what went on and so on, because they should have been grilling me. . . . I was flat out told, you know, "Stay out, you're not involved." Made me think that they could have been getting their stories straight, so to speak, without the interference of this young guy who didn't know anything. . . . All they wanted to know is "Did you hear anything on the phone?" To me that was just a show. They knew I wouldn't hear anything on the phone, because there'd be nobody there [at the Hotel Theresa office]. They knew the schedule. . . . So I think they were playing their roles. I think that was all bullshit. And when I went up and tried to join them, you know—"No, no, this is where we get our stories straight. You're out, kid."

Several months after the assassination, Fulcher was transferred from BOSS headquarters to one of the city's most dangerous precincts, Fort Apache in the Bronx. He lasted there less than three years, before resigning from the force.

In early 1978, radical attorney William Kunstler took up the cases of Thomas 15X Johnson and Norman 3X Butler, petitioning to the appellate division of the New York State Supreme Court for a new trial. His principal new evidence was a signed affidavit by Talmadge Hayer that identified four other men, "torpedoes from New Jersey," who had been responsible for the killing of Malcolm X. Kunstler informed the supreme court that "the FBI knew all along that there were four [other] men involved in the killing and that two of the men convicted were innocent." The FBI refused to release its findings about Malcolm's assassination to the court. Kunstler also noted rumors, never confirmed, that Reuben Francis had recently resurfaced "around his old haunts spending large sums of money he allegedly received from the FBI." Another affidavit was also submitted by Benjamin Goodman (then Ben Karim), who affirmed that "at no time did I see the faces of Butler or Johnson whom I knew well, and would have been sure to notice."

On November 1, 1978, Justice Harold J. Rothwax of the state supreme court denied the motion to set aside the 1966 convictions of Butler and Johnson. The information in the affidavit might have exonerated those two men while identifying four others who, Hayer said, were guilty. However, the judge deemed the document insufficient to grant a new trial. Throughout 1978 and 1979 civil rights groups took up the Butler-Johnson case, first petitioning the U.S. House Select Committee on Assassinations, requesting an investigation into Malcolm X's death. The petition charged, "The 'official version' has it that Malcolm X was the victim of a Muslim vendetta. Many unanswered questions and unexplained events that predate the assassination . . . do not support the 'official version' at all." Signatories of the petition included Ossie Davis, African Methodist Episcopal bishop H. H. Brookins, California state assemblywoman Maxine Waters, and Huey P. Newton of the Black Panther Party. Despite the campaign's efforts, no congressional hearings were held.

Norman Butler was paroled in 1985 and Thomas Johnson received parole in 1987. For decades both men agitated to clear their names. Johnson, who had changed his name to Khalil Islam, died on August 4, 2009. Butler changed his name to Muhammad Abdul Aziz, and in the early 1990s was employed as a supportive services counselor at a Harlem drug rehabilitation clinic. In 1998, Aziz briefly served as security chief for Harlem Mosque No. 7. Beginning in 1990, Hayer was incarcerated part-time at the Lincoln Correctional Facility in Manhattan, where he was confined for a total of twelve hours per week on weekends. After seventeen unsuccessful attempts,

Hayer was finally granted full parole in April 2010. Hayer told the parole board, "I've had a lot of time . . . to think about [Malcolm X's murder] . . . I understand a lot better the dynamics of movements . . . and conflicts that can come up, but I have deep regrets about my participation in that." It was an oddly impersonal mea culpa, an apology without actually articulating the crime he had committed. Hayer's parole provoked a negative response from the Malcolm X Commemoration Committee, which announced at a press conference that Hayer's crimes were too serious to permit his release.

Other than Talmadge Hayer, the alleged assassins of Malcolm X, according to Hayer's affidavit, continued their lives in the Nation of Islam as before. The senior member of the crew, Newark mosque administrator Benjamin Thomas, was killed in 1986, at age forty-eight. Leon Davis lived on in Paterson, New Jersey, employed at an electronics factory there; he continued his affiliation with the Nation and the FOI for decades. Businessman Wilbur McKinley also continued to be associated with the Newark mosque.

Alleged murderer Willie Bradley went into a life of crime. On April 11, 1968, the Livingston National Bank of Livingston, New Jersey, was robbed by three masked men brandishing three handguns and one sawed-off shotgun. They escaped with over $12,500. The following year Bradley and a second man, James Moore, were charged with the bank robbery and were brought to trial. Bradley, however, received privileged treatment, and he retained his own attorney separate from Moore. The charges against him were ultimately dismissed; meanwhile, after a first trial ending in a hung jury, Moore was convicted in a second trial.

Bradley's special treatment by the criminal justice system in 1969–70 raises the question of whether he was an FBI informant, either after the assassination of Malcolm X or very possibly even before. It would perhaps explain why Bradley took a different exit from the murder scene than the two other shooters, shielding him from the crowd's retaliation. It suggests that Bradley and possibly other Newark mosque members may have actively collaborated on the shooting with local law enforcement and/or the FBI. The existing evidence raises the question of whether the murder of Malcolm X was not the initiative of the Nation of Islam alone. In *The Death and Life of Malcolm X*, Goldman does not identify Bradley by name but seems to be referring to him when he notes that one of the assassins "was tracked to a New Jersey state prison, where he was serving seven and a half to fifteen years for an unrelated felony."

Bradley continued to experience legal problems into the 1980s. In 1983, he was indicted on twelve counts, including robbery, "terroristic threat," aggravated assault, and possession of a controlled substance. He first pled not guilty to the charges, but was eventually convicted of several of them and was incarcerated. His life was turned around through a romantic relationship with Carolyn F. Kelly. A longtime leader of Newark's black community, Kelly, a Republican, led the defense for boxer Rubin "Hurricane" Carter in the 1970s, which helped overturn his murder conviction. The owner of First Class Championship Center, a boxing establishment in Newark, Kelly was the first black woman in the state to promote lucrative prize fights. By the 2000s, Bradley could usually be found on Friday afternoons at his wife's boxing gymnasium. In October 2009, he was inducted into the Newark Athletic Hall of Fame for his baseball achivements in high school.

In 2010, Bradley even appeared briefly in a campaign video, promoting the reelection of Newark's charismatic mayor, Cory Booker. Bradley's metamorphosis from criminality to respectability seemed complete.

But things began falling apart in May 2010, with the Internet publication of an investigative article on Bradley by journalist Richard Prince. In the article, journalist Abdur-Rahman Muhammad directly accused Bradley of being "the man who fired the first and deadliest shot" killing Malcolm X. Journalist Karl Evanzz, the author of several studies on the Nation of Islam, called for Bradley's exposure and prosecution "for depriving Malcolm X of his civil rights in the same way that the Klansmen who killed black activists were prosecuted. . . . Bradley killed Malcolm X to stop him from exercising his freedom of speech, freedom of religion, and freedom of assembly." Weeks later, filmmaker Omar Shabazz released a documentary film naming Bradley, Hayer, and the other Newark NOI members as the real killers of Malcolm X. The goal of these critics appears to be Bradley's indictment by federal or local authorities.

The chief beneficiary of Malcolm's assassination was Louis Farrakhan. Indeed, the transition from Minister Louis X of Boston to Louis Farrakhan was made possible only through the leadership model that Malcolm had established years earlier. For a decade Malcolm had spread the salvation message of Elijah Muhammad throughout the United States, and for another decade, 1965 to 1975, Farrakhan assumed the identical role as the Nation of Islam's national minister. Just as Malcolm predicted, most of those inside the Nation who had criticized him and sought to undermine his influence were equally opposed to Farrakhan. Elijah Muhammad's family was jealous and fearful of him, because as the patriarch approached death it seemed possible that Farrakhan might usurp the mantle of leadership.

But he never managed to escape the shadow of speculation and rumor regarding his possible role in Malcolm's murder. Farrakhan's vivid description of Malcolm as a man "worthy of death" may have sealed his reputation. In an interview with Mike Wallace decades after the killing, Farrakhan conceded, "In one sense I may have been complicit in the murder of Brother Malcolm in that when Malcolm spoke against the Messenger, I spoke against him, and this helped to create an atmosphere [in which] Malcolm was assassinated." But that admission has never satisfied latter-day Malcolmites, many of whom continue to demand a reopening of the case. Farrakhan is fully aware that "even now there are some black people calling for a grand jury because there's no statute of limitations on murder to bring me into a grand jury to question me."

Even in his dreams, Farrakhan cannot escape his link to Malcolm. In a 2007 oral history interview, he shared this nocturnal revelation:

> As God is my witness, I had a vision of Brother Malcolm. He came to me in like a dream vision. . . . And gray is in his hair. You know he had this little hair, that knot sometime, you know, and I saw the gray in his hair. And he comes to me and he said, "Brother Louis, what went wrong?" And I said to him, "Brother, you were slated to sit in [Elijah Muhammad's] seat. He had to try you, to see what was in you. And you failed the test. It wasn't that he was against you, but he wanted to see what was really in you." . . . I am here because my brother died that I might live. It's very difficult for me not to just beat him down, because I walked in his shoes. And I know what pain is when you love people, and you work for people, and they turn against you and seek to destroy you. I understand that.

Today, Farrakhan still seeks to demonstrate his continuing filial devotion to Malcolm, despite his central role in advocating his death. His dream, however, places the cause of the murder in Malcolm's own failures. Farrakhan suggests that Elijah Muhammad intended to make Malcolm his spiritual heir, setting aside the claims of Wallace and his other children. Muhammad was simply testing Malcolm, to determine if he had the leadership qualities necessary to direct the Nation. While it is true that Malcolm, after being silenced, at first desperately attempted to remain inside the Nation of Islam, once the break occurred he was liberated from the restrictions that had been imposed on him. What Farrakhan has difficulty admitting is that it was only when Malcolm accepted the universalism and humanism of orthodox Islam, explicitly rejecting racial separatism, that he could reach a truly global audience. Had he lived, Malcolm could have led an international campaign for human rights for blacks, but he could have accomplished this only by divorcing himself from the Nation of Islam's sectarian creed.

Several weeks after the firebombing and destruction of Mosque No. 7 in February 1965, Louis was asked to visit and speak to the Nation's congregation in New York. It was only months later that Elijah Muhammad telephoned to say that he would be transferred to serve as minister of Mosque No. 7 in Harlem. Under Louis's supervision, the destroyed mosque would be reconstructed; he would move into Malcolm's rebuilt home in Elmhurst. In August 1965, Muhammad announced Louis's appointment before six thousand members in Detroit's Cobo Center.

Upon being told about his new position, an overwhelmed Farrakhan jumped into his car and drove to a park on the outskirts of Boston. Years before, as a high school distance runner, it had been a place of solitude, where he would run and exercise. He recounts how he jogged out into the middle of a grassy field, tears streaming down his face, dropped to his knees, looking up into the sky, and confessed to Malcolm: "I didn't mean to take your mosque—I didn't mean to take your home!" As Farrakhan relates this story, it is powerful and it may even be plausible. But is it true?

Only three hours after the assassination of Malcolm X, Louis Farrakhan delivered the guest sermon at Newark Mosque No. 25—the very mosque where the assassins had been recruited and organized. Was his presence in Newark on that fateful day simply coincidence, or something more?

Years from now, when thousands of pages of FBI and BOSS surveillance are finally accessible, more definitive judgments will be made about the connections between Elijah Muhammad, Malcolm X, Louis Farrakhan, and various law enforcement agencies. It would not be entirely surprising if an FBI transcript surfaced documenting a telephone call from Elijah Muhammad to a subordinate, authorizing Malcolm's murder. At present, the evidence suggests that Farrakhan, for one, was not personally involved and had no prior knowledge of the plot; however, he surely understood the consequences of his fiery condemnation of Malcolm, as well as of the forces within the Nation of Islam that would rid Elijah Muhammad of the turbulent priest. He may have suspected that his order to speak at the Newark mosque that February 21, 1965, was not a wholly innocent pursuit. It was ambition, not direct involvement in the crime, that blinded Farrakhan to what was going on around him.

Reflections on a Revolutionary Vision

A biography maps the social architecture of an individual's life. The biographer charts the evolution of a subject over time, and the various challenges and tests that the individual endures provide insights into the person's character. But the biographer has an additional burden: to explain events and the perspectives and actions of others that the subject could not possibly know, that nevertheless had a direct bearing on the individual's life.

Malcolm X today has iconic status, in the pantheon of multicultural American heroes. But at the time of his death he was widely reviled and dismissed as an irresponsible demagogue. Malcolm deliberately sought to stand at the margins, challenging the United States government and American institutions. There was a cost to all this. The state branded him as a subversive and a security risk. J. Edgar Hoover's animus toward Malcolm X, for example, set into motion acts of illegal wiretapping, surveillance, and disruption by law enforcement officers that probably surpassed anything Malcolm could have imagined. Malcolm was not fully aware, until too late, of the deep hostilities he had provoked inside the Nation of Islam that led a coterie of officials around Muhammad to call for his murder. He placed his trust in a bodyguard who may have planned and helped to carry out his public execution. Leaders like Malcolm have enormous confidence in themselves and in their ability to persuade others. It was extremely difficult for him to anticipate betrayal, or even to acknowledge it.

Malcolm's strength was his ability to reinvent himself, in order to function and even thrive in a wide variety of environments. He carefully crafted his physical presentation, the manner in which he approached others, drawing upon the past experiences from his own life as well as from African-American folklore and culture. He wove a narrative of suffering and resistance, of tragedy and triumph, that captured the imaginations of black people throughout the world. He lived the existence of an itinerant musician, traveling constantly from city to city, standing night after night on the stage, manipulating his melodic tenor voice as an instrument. He was consciously a performer, who presented himself as the vessel for conveying the anger and impatience the black masses felt. Impoverished African Americans could admire Dr. King, but Malcolm not only spoke their language, he had lived their experiences—in foster homes, in prisons, in unemployment lines. Malcolm was loved because he could present himself as one of them.

One great gift of such remarkable individuals is the ability to seize their time, to speak to their unique moment in history. Both Martin and Malcolm were such leaders, but they expressed their pragmatic visions in different ways. King embodied the historic struggles waged by generations of African Americans for full equality. He established predominantly black political organizations, such as the Montgomery Improvement Association in 1955 and the Southern Christian Leadership Conference in 1957, but their emphasis was the achievement of desegregation and interracial cooperation. King never pitted blacks against whites, or used the atrocities committed by white extremists as a justification for condemning all whites. By contrast, throughout most of his public career Malcolm sought to place whites on the defensive in their relationship with African Americans. He keenly felt, and expressed, the varied emotions and frustrations of the black poor and working class. His constant message was black pride, self-respect, and an awareness of one's heritage. At a time when American society stigmatized or excluded people of African descent, Malcolm's militant advocacy was stunning. He gave millions of younger African Americans newfound confidence. These expressions were at the foundation of what in 1966 became Black Power, and Malcolm was its fountainhead.

Malcolm came to occupy a central space in the rich folk tradition of black outlaws and dissidents, fighting against the established social hierarchy. In the antebellum era, such men of resistance were Gabriel Prosser and Nat Turner. In African-American music, this tradition includes the notorious folklore of Stagger Lee, the inventive blues guitarist Robert Johnson, and the charismatic hip-hop artist Tupac Shakur. What these black outlaws all had in common was a cool contempt for the bourgeois status quo, the system of white supremacy and its law and courts. More significantly, the tradition of the black outlaw was to transgress the established moral order. In this respect, Detroit Red as Malcolm constructed him was the antihero, the hepcat who laughed at conventional mores, who used illegal drugs and engaged in illicit sex, who broke all the rules. A close examination of the *Autobiography* illustrates that many of the elements of Detroit Red's narrative are fictive; despite this, the character's experiences resonate with black audiences because the contexts of racism, crime, and violence are integral aspects of ghetto life.

The other dimension of Malcolm's appearance was his identity as a righteous preacher, the man who dedicated his life to Allah. Again, this was a role that resonated deeply with African-American culture. Through his powerful language, Malcolm inspired blacks to see themselves not as victims, but possessing the agency to transform themselves and their lives. Like Marcus Garvey, Malcolm boldly insisted to blacks that racism would not define their futures; that, instead, people of African descent were destined for greatness. He developed a profound love for black history, and he integrated into many of his lectures insights taken from the heritage of African-American and African people. Malcolm encouraged blacks to celebrate their culture and the tales of black resistance to European colonialism and white domination. And despite his genuine conversion to orthodox Islam, his spiritual journey was linked to his black consciousness. Only weeks following the assassination, the poet Amiri Baraka proclaimed, "Malcolm's greatest contribution was to preach Black Consciousness to the Black Man. Now we must find the flesh of our spiritual creation." To Baraka, Malcolm represented a black aesthetic, a set of values and criteria for cultural representations that affirmed the genius and creativity of people of African descent. Malcolm provided the template for what black artists should aspire to achieve. "The Black artist is needed to change the images his people identify with, by asserting Black feeling, Black mind, Black judgment," Baraka asserted. In March 1965, Baraka left Greenwich Village and migrated to Harlem, where he established the Black Arts Repertory Theatre/ School (BARTS). This became the foundation for the flowering of the modern black arts movement, involving thousands of poets, playwrights, dancers, and other cultural producers. Malcolm became their muse, the ideal expression of blackness. Even the *New York Times*, measuring his continuing influence in Harlem, observed that "the central idea of Malcolm's that has taken hold since his death is that Negroes must hold fast to and nurture their own black culture, and not have it 'integrated out of existence.'"

Stokely Carmichael, perhaps Black Power's most important architect, traced his own development directly back to Malcolm. In his autobiography, Carmichael explains that as an undergraduate at Howard University in the early 1960s he had first viewed Bayard Rustin as his political mentor. He attended the public debate between Rustin and Malcolm in Washington, D.C., on October 30, 1961, expecting Bayard "to win the debate hands down." But like others there he was overwhelmed by Malcolm's advocacy. "What Malcolm demonstrated that night . . . was the raw power, the visceral potency, of the grip our unarticulated collective blackness held over us. I'll never forget it." Three decades after Malcolm's triumph over Rustin, Carmichael was still inspired by the proud man who personified blackness: "A spotlight picked him out as he strode, slim, erect, immaculately tailored, to the mike on an otherwise darkened stage."

There is now a tendency of historical revisionism, to interpret Malcolm X through the powerful lens of Dr. Martin Luther King, Jr.: that Malcolm was ultimately evolving into an integrationist, liberal reformer. This view is not only wrong, but unfair to both Malcolm and Martin. King saw himself, like Frederick Douglass, first and foremost as an American, who pursued the civil rights and civic privileges enjoyed by other Americans. King struggled to erase the color bar of stigmatization and exclusion that had relegated racial minorities to second-class citizenship. As in the successful 2008 presidential campaign of Barack Obama, King wanted to convince white Americans that "race doesn't matter"—in other words, the physical and color differences that appear to distinguish blacks from whites should be meaningless in the application of justice and equal rights.

In striking contrast, Malcolm perceived himself first and foremost as a black man, a person of African descent who happened to be a United States citizen. This was a crucial difference from King and other civil rights leaders. When he was a member of the Nation of Islam, Malcolm saw himself as a member of the tribe of Shabazz, the fictive Asiatic black clan invented by W. D. Fard. But by the final phases of his career, and especially in 1964–65, Malcolm linked his black consciousness to the ideological imperative of self-determination, the concept that all people have a natural right to decide for themselves their own destiny. Malcolm perceived black Americans as an oppressed nation-within-a-nation, with its own culture, social institutions, and group psychology. Its memories of struggles for freedom were starkly different from those of white Americans. At the end of his life he realized that blacks indeed could achieve representation and even power under America's constitutional system. But he always thought first and foremost about blacks' interests. Many blacks instinctively sensed this, and loved him for it.

King presented a narrative to white Americans that suggested that Negroes were prepared to protest nonviolently, and even die, to realize the promise of the nation's Founding Fathers. By contrast, Malcolm proposed that the oppressed had a natural right to armed self-defense. His narrative was that of the history of structural racism—from the transatlantic slave trade to ghettoization—and his remedy was black reparations, compensation for the years of exploitation blacks had endured. This is why Malcolm, had he survived to the 1990s, would not have been an enthusiastic defender of affirmative action as a centerpiece for civil rights reforms. Affirmative action was never designed to promote full employment or to transfer wealth to African Americans. What Malcolm sought was a fundamental restructuring of wealth and power in the United States—not a violent social revolution, but radical and meaningful change nevertheless.

Another critical difference between the two leaders was their relationship to the African-American middle class. King was the product of Atlanta's well-educated, affluent black petite bourgeoisie. He was a graduate of Morehouse College and Boston University; Malcolm had left school without completing the ninth grade. His "university" was Norfolk Prison Colony. More than any other twentieth-century black leader, Malcolm demanded that blacks in the professional and managerial classes should be more accountable to the masses of poor and working-class African Americans. In speeches like "Message to the Grassroots," he sharply condemned middle-class black leaders for their compromises with white power brokers. He demanded greater integrity and accountability from privileged blacks, as an essential element in the strategy for achieving black freedom.

In his 2003 oral history, Ossie Davis was asked why, in his famous eulogy, he had referred to Malcolm as a "black shining prince." "Because a prince," Davis said, "is not a king." He implied that Malcolm's premature death cut short his maturity and full potential as a leader. Another way of examining Davis's insight is asking whether Malcolm's vision of racial justice was fully realized or achieved. Again, a comparison between Martin and Malcolm is illuminating. Following his assassination, King's image evolved from an anti-Vietnam protester and controversial civil rights advocate into a defender of a color-blind America. His birthday was celebrated by the U.S. government as a national holiday dedicated to public service. Politicians of all ideological stripes praise King's nonviolence but rarely examine his fierce impatience with racial injustice and its relevance to our times. By contrast for several decades Malcolm was pilloried and stereotyped for his racial extremism. However, to most black Americans he became an icon of black encouragement, who fearlessly challenged racism wherever he found it and inspired black youth to take pride in their history and culture. These aspects of Malcolm's public personality were indelibly stamped into the Black Power movement; they were present in the cry "It's our turn!" by black proponents of Harold Washington in the Democrat's successful 1983 mayoral race in Chicago. It was partially expressed in the unprecedented voter turnouts in black neighborhoods in Jesse Jackson's presidential campaigns of 1984 and 1988 and in the successful electoral bid of Barack Obama in 2008. Malcolm truly anticipated that the black electorate could potentially be the balance of power in a divided white republic.

Malcolm's revolutionary vision also challenged white America to think and talk differently about race. In an era when some white entertainers still blackened their faces to perform, Malcolm challenged whites to examine the policies and practices of racial discrimination. Before postmodernists wrote about "white privilege," Malcolm spoke about the destructive effects of racism upon both its victims and its promulgators. Toward the end of his life he could imagine the destruction of racism itself, and the possibility of creating a humane social order devoid of racial injustice. He offered hope that whites could overcome centuries of negative socialization toward blacks, and that a racially just society was achievable. He did not embrace "color blindness" but, like Frantz Fanon, believed that racial hierarchies within society could be dismantled.

Malcolm also changed the discourse and politics of race internationally. During a period when many African-American leaders were preoccupied with efforts to change federal and state policies about race relations, Malcolm saw that for the domestic struggle for civil rights to succeed, it had to be expanded into an international campaign for human rights. The United Nations, not the U.S. Congress or the White House, had to be the central forum. Equally important were the distinctions he made between black politics inside the United States versus liberation politics in Africa and the Caribbean.

Despite his radical rhetoric, as "The Ballot or the Bullet" makes clear, the mature Malcolm believed that African Americans could use the electoral system and voting rights to achieve meaningful change. His position calling for massive black voter education and mobilization was virtually identical to SNCC's, and would later be embraced by the Black Panther Party in Oakland in the 1970s. But outside of the United States, despite his respect for Nkrumah, he did not see electoral politics and gradual social change as a viable approach for transforming postcolonial societies. He endorsed revolutionary violence against the apartheid regime in South Africa, and guerrilla warfare against the neocolonial regime in Congo and in the Portuguese colonies of Guinea-Bissau, Angola, and Mozambique. Nelson Mandela, who in 1961 founded Umkhonto we Sizwe (the Spear of the Nation), the secret armed wing of the African National Congress, was a hero to Malcolm because of his identification with guerrilla attacks against white South Africa. Although today Mandela is perceived as a racial reconciliator, much like King, a half century ago the future president of South Africa largely shared Malcolm's views about the necessity of armed struggle in Africa. So the view that there were "two Malcolm Xs"—one who advocated violence when he was a Black Muslim, and a second who espoused nonviolent change—is absolutely wrong. To Malcolm, armed self-defense was never equated with violence for its own sake.

Malcolm envisioned a modern version of Pan-Africanism, based on a global antiracism. The United Nations World Conference Against Racism, held in Durban, South Africa, in 2001, was in many ways a fulfillment of Malcolm's international vision. Hundreds of religious, social justice, and civil rights nongovernmental organizations engaged in transnational dialogues, examining racism from a truly global perspective. Of the 11,500 delegates and observers, about three thousand were Americans, and nearly two-thirds of that number were black Americans. Malcolm believed that black freedom in the United States depended on internationalist geopolitical strategy.

The unrealized dimension of Malcolm's racial vision was that of black nationalism. A political ideology that originated before the Civil War, black nationalism was based on the assumption that racial pluralism leading to assimilation was impossible in the United States. So cynical were many nationalists about the incapacity of whites to overcome their own racism that they occasionally negotiated with white terrorist groups like the Ku Klux Klan, in the mistaken belief that they were more honest about their racial attitudes than liberals. Yet as Malcolm's international experiences became more varied and extensive, his social vision expanded. He became less intolerant and more open to multiethnic and interfaith coalitions. By the final months of his life he resisted identification as a "black nationalist," seeking ideological shelter under the race-neutral concepts of Pan-Africanism and Third World revolution. He had also come to reject violence for its own sake, but he never abandoned the nationalists' ideal of "self-determnation," the right of oppressed nations or minorities to decide for themselves their own political futures. Given the election of Barack Obama, it now raises the question of whether blacks have a separate political destiny from their white fellow citizens. If legal racial segregation was permanently in America's past, Malcolm's vision today would have to radically redefine self-determination and the meaning of black power in a political environment that appeared to many to be "post-racial."

Finally, and perhaps most important, Malcolm X represents the most important bridge between the American people and more than one billion Muslims throughout the world. Before immigration law reform in 1965, the most prominent group of self-identified American Muslims was the heretical Nation of Islam. As Malcolm learned more about orthodox Islam, he became determined to propagate the meaning of that faith to audiences regardless of race. Even before his death, Malcolm became widely known and well respected across the Islamic and Arab diasporas. He reached out to Islamic sects and organizations reflecting widely divergent opinions and theological tenets—Wahhabi Muslims in Saudi Arabia, Nasserite socialists in Egypt, African Sufis in Senegal, the Muslim Brotherhood in Lebanon, the Palestine Liberation Organization. He avoided arguments that pitted Muslims against one another; he emphasized Islam's capacity to transform the believer from hatred and intolerance toward love. His own remarkable life story personified this reinvention.

And what of Malcolm X's future life after death? As hip-hop culture was decisive in promoting his second renaissance in the 1990s, it seems probable that Islam will influence his future legacy.

The process of jihadist reinvention began with the Iranian revolution. The government of Ayatollah Khomeini was the first to issue a postage stamp featuring a likeness of Malcolm, which was released in 1984 to promote the Universal Day of Struggle Against Race Discrimination. Less than two decades later, his influence was discovered in the mountain caves of Afghanistan, in the radicalism of Islamic convert and Talibanist John Walker Lindh. An upper-middle-class white American from affluent Marin County, California, Lindh was introduced to Malcolm when his mother took him to Spike Lee's film. After reading the *Autobiography*, Lindh's fascination grew into fierce dedication. In October 2001, as American forces stormed into Afghanistan, Lindh was captured among the Taliban combatants and is now serving a twenty-year sentence. Lindh's religious adviser, Shakeel Syed, is convinced that Lindh could "become the new Malcolm X."

The al-Qaeda terrorist network is also sufficiently aware of American racial politics to make sharp distinctions between mainstream African-American leaders and black revolutionaries like Malcolm. An al-Qaeda video released following the election of Barack Obama in November 2008 described the president-elect as a "race traitor" and "hypocrite" when compared to Malcolm X. "And in [Barack Obama] and Colin Powell, [Condoleezza] Rice and your likes, the words of Malcolm X (may Allah have mercy on him) concerning 'house Negroes' are confirmed," declared al-Qaeda deputy Ayman al-Zawahiri. Malcolm was described as central to the political traditions of "honorable black Americans." What is truly ironic is that Malcolm would certainly have condemned the terrorist attacks on September 11, 2001, as representing the negation of Islam's core tenets. A religion based on universal compassion and respect for the teachings of the Torah and the Gospels, Malcolm would have known, holds no common ground with those who employ terror as a tool for politics. Malcolm's personal journey of self-discovery, the quest for God, led him toward peace and away from violence.

But there is one more legacy that may shape the memory of Malcolm: the politics of radical humanism. James Baldwin's first real encounter with Malcolm occurred in 1961, when he was asked to moderate a radio program panel that included the Nation of Islam leader. Malcolm had been invited to debate a young civil rights activist who had just returned from desegregation protests in the South. Baldwin feared that the celebrated firebrand would take the young protester apart. Baldwin later wrote that he had come "to throw out the lifeline whenever Malcolm should seem to be carrying the child beyond his depth." To Baldwin's amazement, Malcolm "understood that child and talked to him as though he was talking to a younger brother." Baldwin was profoundly moved. "I will never forget Malcolm and that child facing each other, and Malcolm's extraordinary gentleness. And that's the truth about Malcolm: he was one of the gentlest people I have ever met."

A deep respect for, and a belief in, black humanity was at the heart of this revolutionary visionary's faith. And as his social vision expanded to include people of divergent nationalities and racial identities, his gentle humanism and antiracism could have become a platform for a new kind of radical, global ethnic politics. Instead of the fiery symbol of ethnic violence and religious hatred, as al-Qaeda might project him, Malcolm X should become a representative for hope and human dignity. At least for the African-American people, he has already come to embody those loftier aspirations.

The origins of this book date back to the winter of 1969, my freshman year at Earlham College in Indiana, when I first read *The Autobiography of Malcolm X*. Malcolm had become the icon of the Black Power movement, and I eagerly devoured the edited volumes of his speeches and interviews. Like others, I did not question the inconsistencies between some parts of his speeches and recordings and the printed texts of these same speeches in publications. Nearly all of the scholarly work on Malcolm was based on a very narrow selection of primary sources, his transcribed speeches, and secondary sources, such as newspapers articles.

Nearly two decades later, in 1988, I was teaching a course in African-American politics that included *The Autobiography of Malcolm X* as part of the required reading, at Ohio State University. A close reading of the text revealed numerous inconsistencies, errors, and fictive characters at odds with Malcolm's actual life history. There also seemed to be missing sections of analysis. Chief among them was the absence of any detailed discussion of Malcolm's two groups formed in 1964—Muslim Mosque, Incorporated, and the Organization of Afro-American Unity. *The Autobiography* had been long accepted as Malcolm's political testament, yet it was largely silent on major political issues. There was also a strange yet unmistakable fissure within the body of the text, separating chapters one through fifteen from a second "book" consisting of chapters sixteen through nineteen. About two-fifths of the book focused exclusively on Malcolm's childhood and juvenile years, describing the criminal exploits of the teenage Malcolm, "Detroit Red." It was only years later that I would learn that much of Detroit Red was fictive, that Malcolm's actual involvement in burglaries and hard-core crime was short-lived.

At the University of Colorado at Boulder, where I taught from 1989 to 1993, I began work on what I thought would be a modest political biography of Malcolm X. The study was first designed to map the evolution of his political and social thought. I hired a team of student researchers, led by then Ph.D. candidate Eleanor Hubbard, and we began to construct a bibliography of nearly one thousand works about the black leader.

Opportunities rarely come in life without a certain cost. In 1993, I accepted the appointment as director of the newly established Institute for Research in African-American Studies at Columbia University. For the next ten years my primary focus was building the Institute; the Malcolm X biography project was placed on hold. It was only in 1999–2000, after meeting on several occasions with one of Malcolm's children, Ilyasah Shabazz, that I decided to return to the biography. But in reading nearly all of the literature about Malcolm produced in the 1990s, I was struck by its shallow character and lack of original sources. Many Malcolmites had constructed a mythic legend to surround their leader that erased all blemishes and any mistakes he had made. Another version of "Malcolmology" simplistically equated Martin Luther King, Jr., with Malcolm, both advocating multicultural harmony and universal understanding. I decided to write a full, comprehensive study of Malcolm's life.

The historical Malcolm, the man with all his strengths and flaws, was being strangled by the iconic legend that had been constructed around him. There were several reasons for this. Inexplicably, Betty Shabazz, and later the Shabazz estate, did not make available to the public hundreds of documents—personal correspondence, photographs, texts of speeches—by Malcolm X until 2008. Following Malcolm's 1965 assassination, many of his closest associates went underground, fled the country, or simply refused to speak to scholars. The Nation of Islam, accused of murdering Malcolm, obviously had no incentive to go on the record explaining its reasons for opposing the former Black Muslim leader. NOI leader Louis Farrakhan had made speeches and statements about his relationship with Malcolm, but had never given a detailed life history of himself related to the subject. And finally, both the Federal Bureau of Investigation and the New York Police Department continued to suppress thousands of pages of surveillance and wiretapping related to Malcolm. At times these multiple roadblocks were so difficult to navigate around that it seemed no serious life history could be written.

My initial breakthrough came when I finally realized that critical deconstruction of the *Autobiography* held the key to reinterpreting Malcolm's life. In this process, I was aided tremendously by Jonathan Cole, then Columbia University's provost, and Vice Provost Michael Crow, who provided the financial support in 2001–2004 to fund the development of a multimedia version of the *Autobiography*. At one point more than twenty graduate and undergraduate students were employed by the Malcolm X Project, writing hundreds of profiles and abstracts of important individuals, institutions, and groups that were mentioned in the *Autobiography*. The Columbia Center for New Media Teaching and Learning, directed by Frank Moretti, produced our extraordinary website, http://ccnmtl.columbia.edu/projects/mmt/malcolmx/, which greatly accelerated the early development of the biography. A more recent multimedia resource presenting materials on Malcolm X is available at http://mxp.manningmarable.com.

As we deconstructed the *Autobiography*, I came to appreciate the book as a brilliant literary work, but more of a memoir than a factual and objective reconstruction of a man's life. Consequently, the book focused largely on personalities rather than on deeper ideological or political differences that increasingly divided Malcolm from the Nation. It also said little about Malcolm's extensive travels across the Middle East and Africa, in July–November 1964.

Another important element in the making of this biography was the critical advice of Clayborne Carson, the director of the Martin Luther King, Jr., Papers Project at Stanford University. I visited the Stanford campus in 2001 to observe how Clay had organized his project, and assigned specific responsibilities to student researchers. Clay suggested that the key to writing a full biography of Malcolm X would be the construction of an extremely detailed chronological grid of his life; in covering his last two years, 1963 to 1965, there would be almost daily entries. Each entry would indicate where the information came from and, whenever possible, would contain multiple sources of documentation. Over a six-year period, a massive chronology was developed, which became the foundation for this biography.

One additional detail in reading this work is the issue of names. Most of the central figures in Malcolm's life changed their names two or three times, or even more. Malcolm's invaluable and crusty chief of staff, James Warden, was usually called James 67X when he belonged to Mosque No. 7, and was often referred to as James Shabazz in 1964–65. However, there was at the same time another James Shabazz, James 3X McGregor, head of the Newark mosque, a deadly opponent of Malcolm's. Consequently, Warden is referred to throughout the text as James 67X. There are similar problems with others' names: Malcolm's trusted assistant minister, Benjamin 2X Goodman, was also Benjamin Karim after embracing orthodox Islam; Thomas 15X Johnson, who was unjustly convicted of Malcolm's murder, was later Khalil Islam; Louis Walcott, also named Louis X, the minister of Boston's NOI mosque, is known throughout the world today as Louis Farrakhan. Wallace Muhammad, Elijah Muhammad's son who inherited the leadership of the Nation of Islam in 1975, changed the spelling of his name to Warith Mohammed. With the partial exception of Farrakhan, I have tried to be consistent in the identification of key personalities throughout the text. This guideline also extends to individuals such as Maya Angelou, who was for several years in the 1960s known as Maya Maké.

Any work of this type is the product of many individuals. One of my Columbia University doctoral assistants, Zaheer Ali, made many important contributions as the Malcolm X Project's associate director for four years, especially during the development of the multimedia version of the *Autobiography*. Zaheer's extensive knowledge of the Nation of Islam as well as orthodox Islam expanded our study to include the voices of Black Muslims like Louis Farrakhan. Zaheer's successor, Elizabeth Mazucci, was largely responsible for building the Malcolm X chronology and organizing thousands of pages of FBI surveillance. This was the chronological core that made the construction of the biography possible, and I am deeply grateful to Elizabeth for her years of tireless effort. Doctoral student Elizabeth Hinton was critical in cross-checking multiple sources, from archives to newspapers, to fully document important events in Malcolm's life. Russell Rickford, now a history professor at Dartmouth College, was instrumental in setting up many oral histories and interviews with individuals who were Malcolm's contemporaries. Since 2008 the Malcolm X Project has been expertly coordinated by Garrett Felber, who is an extraordinary researcher and young scholar of twentieth-century black America. Garrett has the uncanny ability to locate the rarest and most obscure documents connected with Malcolm's life. In the past year our newest researcher, Kevin Loughran, has also made important contributions to the project.

Earlier drafts or various chapters in this biography were read by Ira Katznelson, Renate Bridenthal, Hishaam Aidi, Samuel Roberts, and Bill Fletcher, Jr. Their comments and criticisms were extremely helpful. Richard Cohen, my superb editor, worked closely with me in the development of each chapter. My editors at Viking Penguin, particularly Wendy Wolf and Kevin Doughten, have been extremely supportive throughout the evolution of this manuscript. For nearly eighteen months, Kevin and I communicated almost daily, discussing various versions of chapters, in the effort to build an effective narrative to reach the broadest possible audience. Thanks are also richly due to my agent, Elyse Cheney, and my attorney, Lisa Davis, who have both worked closely with me on this book project for nearly a decade.

Sara Crafts has been my primary manuscript typist for many previous book projects, and she has done a superb job of processing the many different versions of each chapter and keeping the corrected manuscripts on track. I have always valued her friendship and advice. Courtney Teague, my secretary at Columbia's Center for Contemporary Black History, has been instrumental in coordinating my Malcolm X seminar, and also typing manuscripts. Both have been invaluable in keeping the project on track.

A final, unanticipated roadblock in completing this work came in the form of a serious health challenge. For a quarter century I have had sarcoidosis, an illness that gradually destroyed my pulmonary functions. In the last year in researching this book, I could not travel and I carried oxygen tanks in order to breathe. In July 2010, I received a double lung transplant, and following two months' hospitalization, managed a full recovery. Throughout this ordeal, the writing, editing, and research on the Malcolm X biography continued. For this, I am deeply grateful to my pulmonologists, Dr. David Lederer and Dr. Doreen Addrizzo-Harris; my surgeon, Dr. Frank D'Ovidio; and the entire lung transplant team—the coordinators, nurses, and physical and occupational therapists at New York Presbyterian Hospital, all of whom were instrumental in my successful surgery and recovery. Equally important in my recovery were my family members—including Sandra Mullings, Alia Tyner, Michael Tyner, Pansy Mullings, Pauline Mullings, Paul Mullings, Malaika Marable Serrano, Sojourner Marable Grimmett, Joshua Marable, Adriana Nova, and Chris Nova—who stayed up night after night at the hospital and were so supportive during my difficult weeks of recovery.

My greatest debt of gratitude is owed to my intellectual partner and companion, Leith Mullings. For years, she patiently listened to, or read, countless chapters from Malcolm's life. She critiqued the final drafts of the entire book, line by line, making important suggestions along the way. Leith also put her own life on hold for more than two years as I struggled with my pulmonary crisis, surgery, and recovery. Without her constant encouragement and unfailing support, I would not have survived.

And finally, I am deeply grateful to the real Malcolm X, the man behind the myth, who courageously challenged and transformed himself, seeking to achieve a vision of a world without racism. Without erasing his mistakes and contradictions, Malcolm embodies a definitive yardstick by which all other Americans who aspire to a mantle of leadership should be measured.

Manning Marable
September 25, 2010

Key to Notes

MANY—Municipal Archives in the City of New York

RWL—Robert W. Woodruff Library Special Collections Department

MX FBI—Malcolm X FBI file

MXC-S—Malcolm X Collection, Schomburg Center for Research in Black Culture

BOSS—Bureau of Special Services

UTLSC—University of Tennessee Library Special Collection

KMC—The Ken McCormick Collection of the Records of Doubleday and Company

Prologue: Life Beyond The Legend

1 *larger Grand Ballroom, holding up to fifteen hundred.* See Eric William Allison, "Audubon Theatre and Ballroom," in Kenneth T. Jackson, ed., *The Encyclopedia of New York City* (New Haven, CT: Yale University Press, 1995), p. 66.

1 *accompanied by the occasional violent confrontation.* Letter to the editor, Shirley G. Quill, *New York Times*, April 1, 1990. Quill observed that "long before the gruesome assassination of Malcolm X, the Audubon Ballroom was known as the cradle of the T.W.U., the first union of municipal transit workers in modern labor history."

1 *Two people were badly wounded.* "Girl and Man Shot in Dance Hall," *New York Times*, September 22, 1929.

3 *"The Negroes at the mass level are ready to act."* M. S. Handler, "Malcolm X Splits with Muhammad," *New York Times*, March 9, 1964; and M. S. Handler, "Malcolm X Sees Rise in Violence," *New York Times*, March 13, 1964.

3 *"who are responsible to white authorities—Negro Uncle Toms."* Emanuel Perlmutter, "Murphy Says City Will Not Permit Rights Violence," *New York Times*, March 16, 1964.

4 *and only one, briefly, was stationed.* Herman Ferguson interview, OAAU member and eyewitness to Malcolm X's assassination, June 27, 2003.

4 *at a considerable distance from the featured event.* Peter Goldman, *The Death and Life of Malcolm X*, revised edition (Urbana: University of Illinois Press, 1979), pp. 269, 274.

4 *an easy escape to New Jersey.* Ibid., pp. 416–19.

4 *about as far as he could have been from the stage.* William 64X George statement with New York County District Attorney's office, March 18, 1965. The police interviews related to the Malcolm X murder investigation are available in Case File 871-65, Series I, New York Department of Records and Information Services, Municipal Archives in the City of New York (MANY). The district attorney's case file on the assassination of Malcolm X is divided into three series, according to chronological periods corresponding with the murder case. Series I includes materials from the police investigation and indictment; Series II includes the 1966 murder trial; Series III encompasses the appeals of the convicted assailants, Norman Butler, Thomas Johnson, and Talmadge Hayer (aka Thomas Hagan). Of great significance is the availability of unredacted FBI internal documents and a copy of the full grand jury

transcript of the Malcolm X murder trial, in Series I. The district attorney's files were closed to the public until 1993, at which point they were transferred to the New York City Municipal Archives. For a comprehensive analysis of the case file, see Elizabeth Mazucci, "St. Malcolm's Relics: A Study of the Artifacts Shaped by the Assassination of Malcolm X," M.A. thesis, Columbia University, 2005.

5 *Cathcart complied and returned to his seat.* In his NYPD interview, Linwood X Cathcart was shown photographs of Norman Butler and Thomas Johnson, two NOI members who by then had been arrested for Malcolm X's murder. Linwood X denied knowing the identities of Johnson and Butler from their photographs. He stated that neither man was in attendance at the Audubon Ballroom rally. Then, provocatively, according to police records, "Mr. Cathcart went on to say that Malcolm X could be compared to Benedict Arnold as he was also a traitor and that Allah takes care of us all." See Augurs Linwood C. Cathcart interview with NYPD, March 22, 1965. Case File 871-65, Series I, MANY.

5 *security people, he returned to his seat.* Langston Savage grand jury testimony and NYPD interview with Langston Savage, March 22, 1965. Case File 871-65, Series I, MANY.

5 *"We're dealing with an entirely different group."* James 67X Warden (also known as Abdullah Abdur Razzaq and James Shabazz) interview, July 21, 2003.

5 *to pay the manager that afternoon's $150 fee.* Officer William E. Confrey, "Interview of Mr. William Fogel, Manager of Audubon Ballroom, February 21, 1965." Case File 871-65, Series I, MANY.

6 *one of them was going to ignite a smoke bomb.* Goldman, *The Death and Life of Malcolm X,* pp. 418–19.

6 *podium immediately following Benjamin's introductions.* Transcript of address by Benjamin 2X Goodman (also known as Benjamin Karim), delivered at the Audubon Ballroom, February 21, 1965. Copy and audiotape recording in possession of author.

6 *Benjamin stepped down and returned to the backstage room.* Ibid. Also see Goldman, *The Death and Life of Malcolm X,* pp. 271–73.

6 *Malcolm yelled out, "Hold it! Hold it!"* Transcript of address by Benjamin 2X Goodman. Malcolm X's initial remarks can be heard on the tape recording.

8 *"our manhood, our living, black manhood."* Malcolm X and Alex Haley, *The Autobiography of Malcolm X* (New York: Ballantine, 1999), p. 462.

8 *formed a Malcolm X Democrat Club.* Goldman, *The Death and Life of Malcolm X,* p. 378.

8 *"any black cat in this curious place and time."* See James Baldwin, *One Day, When I Was Lost: A Scenario Based on Alex Haley's The Autobiography of Malcolm X* (New York: Dell, 1972); David Leeming, *James Baldwin: A Biography* (New York: Henry Holt, 1994), pp. 297–99; and Brian Norman, "Reading a Closet Screenplay: Hollywood, James Baldwin's Malcolm X and the Threat of Historical Irrelevance," *African American Review,* vol. 39, no. 2 (Spring 2005), pp. 103–18.

8 *promoting the reelection of Richard Nixon.* Paul Deloney, "Black Parlays in Capital Hail Nixon and Thurmond," *New York Times,* June 12, 1972.

8 *a portrait of Malcolm on the cover of one of its CDs.* William T. Strickland and Cheryll Y. Greene, eds., *Malcolm X: Make It Plain* (New York: Viking, 1994), p. 225.

8 *"Quayle should think he's talking about him."* Sam Roberts, "Dan Quayle, Malcolm X and American Values," *New York Times,* June 15, 1992.

8 *"a hero for black Americans today."* "Will the Real Malcolm X Please Stand Up?" *Los Angeles Sentinel,* January 7, 1993.

8 *"undergirded his bond with blacks."* Gerald Horne, "'Myth' and the Making of 'Malcolm X,'" *American Historical Review,* vol. 98, no. 2 (April 1993), p. 448.

8 *"integrationist solution to racial problems."* Manning Marable, *Living Black History: How Reimagining the African-American Past Can Remake America's Racial Future* (New York: Basic Civitas, 2006), p. 147.

10 *"to the cause of liberating the black man."* Malcolm X and Haley, *Autobiography,* p. xxv.

10 *"cellblock had a name for me: 'Satan.'"* Ibid., p. 256.

11 *"it was like having tea with a black panther."* Ibid., p. xxv.

11 *his autobiography is highly exaggerated.* See the analysis of Detroit Red's criminal career

in Rodnell P. Collins and Peter Bailey, *Seventh Child: A Family Memoir of Malcolm X* (New York: Kensington, 1998).

Chapter 1: "Up, You Mighty Race!"

15 *on July 29, 1890.* Early (Earl) Little's death certificate, March 30, 1931, Michigan Department of Community Health, Division of Vital Statistics, State Official Number 1338243. Copy in possession of author. There is some uncertainty about the precise birth date of Earl Little. According to the 1930 census, E. Little was born in 1891–92. However, in his 1959 passport application Malcolm placed the birth of his father, "J. Early Little," in 1889. See MX FBI, Memorandum, July 27, 1959; and MX FBI, Summary Report, New York Office, November 17, 1959, p. 31.

15 *eight thousand bales each year.* "Reynolds," *The Butler Herald* (Georgia), June 20, 1911.

15 *second only to Mississippi in lynching deaths.* Walter White, *Rope and Faggot* (New York: Arno, 1969), pp. 254–56.

15 *especially in masonry, carpentry, and the mechanical trades.* Sarah A. Soule, "Populism and Black Lynching in Georgia, 1890–1900," *Social Forces*, vol. 71, no. 2 (December 1992), pp. 431–49.

16 *before finally settling in Montreal.* Ira Berlin, *The Making of African America* (New York: Viking, 2010), p. 172.

16 *He did not bother to get a legal divorce.* The early years of Earl Little, Sr., and Louise Norton are described in Strickland and Greene, eds., *Malcolm X: Make It Plain.* A literary treatment of the complex and often tense relationship between Malcolm's parents is provided in Jan Carew, *Ghosts in Our Blood: With Malcolm X in Africa, England, and the Caribbean* (Westport, CT: Lawrence Hill, 1994). Also see Mary G. Rolinson, *Grassroots Garveyism* (Chapel Hill: University of North Carolina Press, 2007), pp. 193–94.

16 *small island homeland could provide.* Louis A. DeCaro, Jr., *On the Side of My People: A Religious Life of Malcolm X* (New York: New York University Press, 1996), pp. 41–42. The 1930 census places Louise Little's birth in 1898–99. On his 1959 passport application Malcolm states that his mother was born in 1896. See MX FBI, Summary Report, New York Office, November 17, 1959.

16 *even sending delegations to international conventions.* See Leo W. Bertley, "The Universal Negro Improvement Association of Montreal, 1917–1974," Ph.D. dissertation, Concordia University, California, 1980.

17 *advanced the national leadership of the reformers over their conservative rivals.* There is a substantial body of scholarship on the conflict between Booker T. Washington and W. E. B. Du Bois. The place to begin is with August Meier's *Negro Thought in America, 1880–1915* (Ann Arbor: University of Michigan Press, 1963). Other sources on Washington and Du Bois include Louis R. Harlan, *Booker T. Washington: The Making of a Black Leader, 1856–1901* (New York: Oxford University Press, 1972); Louis R. Harlan, *Booker T. Washington: The Wizard of Tuskegee, 1901–1915* (New York: Oxford University Press, 1983); Kevin Gaines, *Uplifting the Race: Black Leadership, Politics and Culture in the Twentieth Century* (Chapel Hill: University of North Carolina Press, 1996); Michael Rudolph West, *The Education of Booker T. Washington* (New York: Columbia University Press, 2006); Raymond Walters, *W. E. B. Du Bois and His Rivals* (Columbia: University of Missouri Press, 2002), and Manning Marable, *W. E. B. Du Bois: Black Radical Democrat*, second edition (Boulder, CO: Paradigm, 2005).

17 *religious and cultural institutions that nurtured black families.* DeCaro, *On the Side of My People*, pp. 13–15.

17 *naming their building Liberty Hall.* Robert A. Hill and Barbara Blair, eds., *Marcus Garvey: Life and Lessons* (Berkeley: University of California Press, 1987), p. lxiv.

17 *"is liberty, is real human rights."* *Black Man*, vol. 1 (July 1935), p. 5.

18 *movement's growing list of businesses.* Marcus Garvey, "Autobiography," in Hill and Blair, eds., *Marcus Garvey: Life and Lessons*, pp. 92–93.

18 *"the backward tribes of Africa."* Richard Brent Turner, *Islam in the African-American Experience* (Bloomington: Indiana University Press, 1997), p. 81.

19 "Of the red, the black, and the green." Garvey, "Autobiography," in Hill and Blair, eds., Marcus Garvey: Life and Lessons, pp. 49–50.

19 "Order of Ethiopia and Dukes of Niger and of Uganda." Kelly Miller, "After Marcus Garvey—What of the Negro?" Contemporary Review, vol. 131 (April 1927), pp. 492–500.

19 "religion to the Negroes of the world." DeCaro, On the Side of My People, p. 15.

19 "is fundamentally a religious institution." Hill and Blair, eds., Marcus Garvey: Life and Lessons, p. xxxvii. There are numerous studies on Garvey and Garveyism. Several important works are: Robert A. Hill, ed., The Marcus Garvey and Universal Negro Improvement Association Papers (Berkeley: University of California Press, 1983–present); Rupert Lewis, Marcus Garvey: Anti-Colonial Champion (Trenton, NJ: Africa World Press, 1988); Claudrena N. Harold, The Rise and Fall of the Garvey Movement in the Urban South, 1918–1942 (London: Routledge, 2007); and Emory J. Tolbert, The UNIA and Black Los Angeles (Los Angeles: Center for Afro-American Studies, University of California Press, 1980).

20 putting Philadelphia behind only New York City in total membership. Peter Cole, Wobblies on the Waterfront: Interracial Unionism in Progressive-Era Philadelphia (Champaign: University of Illinois Press, 2007), pp. 138–39.

20 presidential candidate in the 1920 elections. Robert Gregg, Sparks from the Anvil of Oppression: Philadelphia's African Methodists and Southern Migrants, 1840–1940 (Philadelphia: Temple University Press, 1993), pp. 189–90; and Hill, ed., The Marcus Garvey and Universal Negro Improvement Association Papers, vol. 1, 1826–August 1919, p. 515. Eason's sale of his church building backfired, as congregants filed a civil suit against him. The majority of church members subsequently moved to replace Eason with the Reverend B. J. Bolding. In the wake of the controversy Eason relocated most of his activities for Garvey to Harlem, where he remained wildly popular. See Gregg, Sparks from the Anvil of Oppression, p. 190.

20 "French Negro . . . we represent all Negroes." James Walker Hood Eason, "Declaration of Aims," in Robert A. Hill, ed., Marcus Garvey and the Universal Negro Improvement Association Papers, vol. 2, August 1919–August 31, 1920 (Berkeley: University of California Press, 1983), pp. 502–7.

20 in more than eight hundred branch organizations or chapters. Turner, Islam in the African-American Experience, p. 80.

20 one of the largest mass movements in black history. See Tony Martin, Race First: The Ideological and Organizational Strategies of Marcus Garvey and the Universal Negro Improvement Association (New York: Dover, 1976); and E. U. Essien-Udom, Black Nationalism: A Search for an Identity in America (Chicago: University of Chicago Press, 1962).

21 and by 1923 membership totaled forty-five thousand. See Michael W. Schuyler, "The Ku Klux Klan in Nebraska, 1920–1930," Nebraska History, vol. 66, no. 3 (1985), pp. 234–56; and Eldora F. Hess, "The Negro in Nebraska," M.A. thesis, University of Nebraska at Lincoln, 1932.

21 "frequently carrying American flags; others rode horses." Schuyler, "The Ku Klux Klan in Nebraska, 1920–1930," pp. 235–36.

21 "will drive the common allies together." Ibid., p. 247.

21 where Klan supporters ensured its failure. Ibid., pp. 247–48.

22 and it had become a force in national politics. Hugo Black formally joined the Ku Klux Klan in Birmingham in 1923. His induction was in front of seventeen hundred Klansmen in the Robert E. Lee chapter. See Howard Ball, Hugo Black: Cold Steel Warrior (Oxford: Oxford University Press, 1996), p. 61. Robert Byrd joined the KKK in 1942, when he was twenty-four years old. See Eric Pianin, "A Senator's Shame," Washington Post, June 19, 2005.

22 "the feelings of every real white American." "Hon. Marcus Garvey Tells of Interview with the Ku Klux Klan," in The Negro World, July 15, 1922, from Robert A. Hill, ed., The Marcus Garvey and Universal Negro Improvement Association Papers, vol. 4, September 1921–September 1922 (Berkeley: University of California Press, 1985), pp. 707–15.

22 were far more ruthless than their leader. Colin Grant, Negro with a Hat: The Rise and Fall

of Marcus Garvey (Oxford: Oxford University Press, 2008), pp. 360–61; and Hill, ed., *The Marcus Garvey and Universal Negro Improvement Association Papers, vol. 1,* p. 515.

22 *led local blacks to fear KKK reprisals.* According to Rodnell P. Collins, the son of Malcolm X's paternal half sister Ella Collins, Omaha's black population feared that Little's activities would "bring down the white folks on us." See Collins, *Seventh Child,* p. 15. Collins's book contains much valuable information about the relationship between Ella and Malcolm. However, Collins and his ghostwriter, Peter Bailey, embellished the narrative with their own speculations.

23 *"as suddenly as they had come."* Malcolm X and Haley, *Autobiography,* p. 1.

23 *and a public picnic drew twenty-five thousand followers.* Schuyler, "The Ku Klux Klan in Nebraska, 1920–1930," pp. 236, 237–39.

23 *The boy, Earl's seventh child, was christened Malcolm.* Goldman, *The Death and Life of Malcolm X,* p. 26. Malcolm later recalled, "I was born in a segregated hospital of a segregated mother and a segregated father."

23 *"much alive to its part in carrying on the great work."* *Negro World,* March 27, 1926. Louise Little's report in the *Negro World* of July 3, 1926, noted that the Omaha division of the UNIA's meeting of that day featured a poetry reading, prayer, a musical selection, and a discussion "about matters of the organization." See Louise Little, "Omaha, Neb. Report," *Negro World,* July 3, 1926.

23 *Black Star Line and given a five-year sentence.* Hill and Blair, eds., *Marcus Garvey: Life and Lessons,* p. lxv.

24 *to reverse Garvey's conviction.* Rolinson, *Grassroots Garveyism,* p. 158.

24 *higher than in many other cities.* Joe William Trotter, Jr., *Black Milwaukee: The Making of an Industrial Proletariat, 1915–45,* second edition (Urbana: University of Illinois Press, 2007), p. 60.

24 *"black city within the city."* Ibid., pp. 87, 90, 93.

24 *preventing racial strife between striking workers.* Ibid., p. 57.

24 *to elevate African Americans to elective office.* Ibid., pp. 125, 135–36. Also see "News of Divisions," *Negro World,* January 29, 1927, February 5, 1927, and February 19, 1927.

24 *June 8, 1927, asking for Garvey to be released.* Earl Little, W. M. Townsend, and Robert Finney, Officers, International Industrial Club of Milwaukee, to President Calvin Coolidge, June 8, 1927, in Hill, ed., *The Marcus Garvey and Universal Negro Improvement Association Papers, vol. 6, September 1924–December 1927* (Berkeley: University of California Press, 1989), pp. 561–62. Two years earlier, on April 27, 1925, the Milwaukee UNIA Division No. 207 had appealed to President Coolidge to grant executive clemency to Garvey. The UNIA branch's appeal noted that "Mr. Garvey is suffering, and has for some years been suffering, from chronic bronchial asthma and is subject to attacks of vertigo." In ibid., p. 204.

24 *delayed only by the birth of yet another son, Reginald.* Actually, the Little family may have moved from Milwaukee earlier. According to the *Negro World* issue of May 27, 1927, Earl Little is reported to have been the leader of the Indiana Harbor (East Chicago, Indiana) UNIA branch organization.

25 *a lawyer, who filed an appeal.* DeCaro, *On the Side of My People,* pp. 44–45.

25 *"and they knew where the baby was."* Wilfred Little (Wilfred Shabazz) interview, in Strickland and Greene, eds., *Malcolm X: Make It Plain,* p. 21.

25 *"away from the house,"* Wilfred recalled. Ibid.

26 *February 26, 1930, when it was quickly dismissed.* G. W. Waterman, Special Report, Case 2155, "Suspected Arson," *People of the State of Michigan v. Earl Little (colored),* November 8, 1929, in Department of State Police, State of Michigan, Lansing, Michigan; and information on George W. Waterman in 1910 and 1920 censuses.

26 *would surely have made the late payment first.* DeCaro, *On the Side of My People,* pp. 45–46.

27 *and ultimately the Sweets were freed.* See Joseph Tumini, "Sweet Justice," *Michigan History Magazine,* vol. 83, no. 4 (July/August 1999), pp. 23–27; and Kevin Boyle, *Arc of Justice: A Saga of Race, Civil Rights, and Murder in the Jazz Age* (New York: Henry Holt, 2004). Gladys Sweet contracted tuberculosis during her incarceration and died

at the age of twenty-seven. Dr. Ossian Sweet moved back into the Garland Avenue residence in 1928. Financial problems forced Dr. Sweet to sell the house in the 1950s; he committed suicide in 1960.

27 *but to forfeit the disputed land.* Bruce Perry, *Malcolm: The Life of a Man Who Changed America* (Barrytown, NY: Station Hill Press, 1991), p. 11.

27 *'Up, you mighty race, you can accomplish what you will!'* Malcolm X and Haley, *Autobiography*, pp. 6–7.

28 *a poor neighborhood in west central Lansing.* Douglas K. Meyer, "Evolution of a Permanent Negro Community in Lansing," *Michigan History Magazine*, vol. 55, no. 2 (1971), pp. 141–54.

28 *"it was the same as being down South."* Wilfred Little interview, in Strickland and Greene, eds., *Malcolm X: Make It Plain*, p. 20.

28 *he was considered just such a troublemaker.* Ibid., p. 21.

28 *"and the shoeshine boys at the state capitol."* Malcolm X and Haley, *Autobiography*, pp. 5–6.

29 *and started a daily newspaper, Blackman.* Hill and Blair, eds., *Marcus Garvey: Life and Lessons*, p. lxvi.

29 *estimated membership in the city at seven thousand.* See Ronald J. Stephens, "Garveyism in Idlewild, 1927 to 1936," *Journal of Black Studies*, vol. 34, no. 4 (March 2004), pp. 462–88.

29 *dangerous jobs in the foundries.* See Thomas N. Maloney and Warren C. Whatley, "Making the Effort: The Contours of Racial Discrimination in Detroit's Labor Markets," *Journal of Economic History*, vol. 55, no. 3 (September 1995), pp. 456–93. In 1930, Ford Motor Company employed 25 percent of all black workers in Detroit. Also see Joyce Shaw Peterson, "Black Automobile Workers in Detroit, 1910–1930," *Journal of Negro History*, vol. 64, no. 3 (Summer 1979), pp. 177–90.

29 *or branch organizations were established there.* See Stephens, "Garveyism in Idlewild, 1927 to 1936"; and "Concentration of UNIA Divisions by Regions, 1921–1933," in Robert Hill, ed., *The Marcus Garvey and Universal Negro Improvement Association Papers*, vol. 5, *1826–August 1919* (Berkeley: University of California Press,1991), pp. 751–52.

29 *news of the movement from around the country.* DeCaro, *On the Side of My People*, p. 43.

29 *become so crucial for Malcolm later in life.* Ibid.

30 *"It wasn't the way they wanted things to go."* Wilfred Little interview, in Strickland and Greene, eds., *Malcolm X: Make It Plain*, p. 19.

30 *reputation as Garveyite oddballs took its toll.* DeCaro, *On the Side of My People*, p. 46.

30 *as a kind of shield from Earl's beatings.* Perry, *Malcolm*, p. 6.

30 *as a boy came from his mother.* Malcolm X and Haley, *Autobiography*, p. 4.

30 *"noontime parades down Main Street were out."* Peter H. Amann, "Vigilante Fascism: The Black Legion as an American Hybrid," *Contemporary Studies in Society and History*, vol. 25, no. 3 (July 1983), pp. 490–524; quotation from p. 406.

30 *tarred and feathered, or just being run out of town.* See Kenneth R. Dvorak, "Terror in Detroit: The Rise and Fall of Michigan's Black Legion," Ph.D. dissertation, Bowling Green State University, 1990; quotation from p. 106. Also see Michael S. Clinansmith, "The Black Legion: Hooded Americanism in Michigan," *Michigan History Magazine*, vol. 55, no. 3 (1971), pp. 243–62.

30 *"two . . . the accident was quite violent."* Florentina Baril interview, in Strickland and Greene, eds., *Malcolm X: Make It Plain*, pp. 14–25.

31 *have been the victim of racist violence.* Perry, *Malcolm*, pp. 12–13.

31 *Louise reached him, he was dead.* Strickland and Greene, eds., *Malcolm X: Make It Plain*, p. 25.

31 *"He ended up bleeding to death."* Ibid.

31 *Early Little's death better than Louise did.* Malcolm X and Haley, *Autobiography*, p. 10.

31 *"somebody had shoved him under that car."* Philbert Little interview, in Strickland and Greene, eds., *Malcolm X: Make It Plain*, p. 25.

31 *Few blacks lived in the area.* "Man Run Over by Street Car," *State Journal* (Lansing, Michigan), September 28, 1931.

32 *the policy payout was almost exhausted.* Louise Little, "Petition for Widow's Allow-

ance," Ingham County Probate Court, State of Michigan, February 24, 1932; U. S. Begley, M.D., petition to Judge of Ingham County Probate Court, State of Michigan, January 26, 1932; J. Wilson, dentist, petition to Ingham County Probate Court, State of Michigan, January 14, 1932; and John L. Leighton, petition to Ingham County Probate Court, State of Michigan, January 16, 1932, all in the Estate of Earl Little, File A-4053, Ingham County Probate Court, State of Michigan.

32   *"she rented that out."* Yvonne Little Woodward interview, in Strickland and Greene, eds., *Malcolm X: Make It Plain*, p. 26.

32   *as Philbert later admitted.* Philbert Little interview, in ibid., p. 27.

32   *"the hole that they had prepared."* Cyril McGuine interview, in ibid., p. 27.

33   *"so happy to be around him that we worked."* Yvonne Little Woodward interview, in ibid., p. 28.

33   *"go along with it—a Black Robin Hood!"* Wilfred Little interview, in ibid., p. 28.

33   *marital status, race, and other factors was widespread.* See Susan Stein-Roggenbuck, "'Wholly Within the Discretion of the Probate Court': Judicial Authority and Mothers' Pensions in Michigan, 1913–1940," *Social Service Review*, vol. 79, no. 2 (June 2005), pp. 294–321. Michigan's system of "mothers' pensions" was not fully integrated into the federal government's Aid to Dependent Children program until 1940.

33   *"weren't enough, as many as there were."* Malcolm X and Haley, *Autobiography*, pp. 12–13.

33   *victims of the state's bureaucracy.* Ibid., pp. 18–19.

34   *"would tell us stories about our ancestry."* Wilfred Little interview, in Strickland and Greene, eds., *Malcolm X: Make It Plain*, pp. 15–16.

34   *take him in as a foster child.* Malcolm X and Haley, *Autobiography*, pp. 14–15.

34   *"mother threw a fit, though,"* Malcolm related. Ibid., pp. 15–18; and Thaddeus M. Smith, "Gohanna Family," in Robert L. Jenkins, ed., *The Malcolm X Encyclopedia* (Westport, CT: Greenwood, 2002), p. 240.

34   *"look what they put my mother through."* Yvonne Little Woodward interview, in Strickland and Greene, eds., *Malcolm X: Make It Plain*, p. 29.

35   *"to kneel . . . because she was independent."* Wilfred Little interview, in ibid., p. 28.

35   *he "jilted my mother suddenly."* Malcolm X and Haley, *Autobiography*, p. 21; and Perry, *Malcolm*, pp. 30–32.

35   *"watched our anchor giving way."* Ibid., p. 19; and Thaddeus M. Smith, "Gohanna Family," in Jenkins, ed., *Malcolm X Encyclopedia*, p. 240.

35   *for welcoming ex-convicts into their home.* Malcolm X's maternal half brother, Robert Little, discussed Malcolm's experiences with the Gohanna family and Michigan's foster care system, in Clara Hemphill, "Keep Children," *Newsday* (New York), May 13, 1991.

35   *did not know who or where she was.* Malcolm X and Haley, *Autobiography*, p. 21; and Perry, *Malcolm*, pp. 30–32.

35   *"an insane person . . . care and treatment in an institution."* Physician's certificate of Louise Little's institutionalization, January 3, 1939, in Strickland and Greene, eds., *Malcolm X: Make It Plain*, p. 32.

36   *for the next twenty-four years.* Mental Health File of Louise Little (B-4398), Ingham County Probate Court.

36   *which contributed to neglect and improper diagnoses.* See Catherine Jean Whitaker, "Almshouses and Mental Institutions in Michigan, 1871–1930," Ph.D. dissertation, University of Michigan, 1986; and "Kalamazoo Psychiatric Hospital," Clarence L. Miller Local History Room, Kalamazoo Public Library, Kalamazoo, Michigan.

36   *likely to have included electroconvulsive therapy.* William A. Decker, *Asylum for the Insane: History of the Kalamazoo State Hospital* (Traverse City, MI: Arbutus, 2007), pp. 34, 195, 196, 199.

36   *Mason, ten miles south of Lansing.* Hemphill, "Keep Children." Also see FBI surveillance report of Malcolm X, NY 105-8999, May 23, 1955. The report's number indicates that the file was prepared by the FBI's New York City office.

37   *"Red," due to the color of his hair.* Malcolm X and Haley, *Autobiography*, pp. 34–35.

37   *"I jumped at the chance,"* Malcolm recalled. Ibid., p. 36.

37 Massachusetts Avenue between Columbus and Huntington avenues. Ibid., pp. 37–38.
38 "white race as he is doing today." Photograph of Mason's 1940 football team, reprinted in Strickland and Greene, eds., Malcolm X: Make It Plain, p. 34.
38 "in other words, keep him in his place." Ibid., p. 39.
38 "Why don't you plan on carpentry?" Collins, Seventh Child, pp. 209–10.
38 "could you pay all your bills? Let me know real soon." Ibid.

Chapter 2: The Legend of Detroit Red

39 promptly walked out, never to return to a classroom. DeCaro, On the Side of My People, p. 54.
39 refusal to be dominated, led to divorce in 1934. Collins, Seventh Child, pp. 51–52.
39 as Ella scrambled to assist her relatives. Ibid., pp. 50–51.
40 "could be considered a dangerous individual." FBI—Ella X Collins, Memo, Elvin V. Semrad, M.D., to Daniel Lynch, Clerk, Boston Municipal Court, June 9, 1960.
40 and the two became involved. Collins, Seventh Child, pp. 60–61.
41 Boston was multiethnic and expanding. Violet Showers Johnson, The Other Black Bostonians: West Indians in Boston, 1900–1950 (Bloomington and Indianapolis: Indiana State University Press, 2006), pp. 38, 84.
41 extended family living in greater Boston. Collins, Seventh Child, pp. 42–43.
41 seek out better housing in places like the Hill. Johnson, The Other Black Bostonians, pp. 36–37, 121–22.
42 time as a "destructive detour" in an otherwise purpose-driven life. See Robin D. G. Kelley, "The Riddle of the Zoot: Malcolm Little and Black Cultural Politics During World War II," in Joe Wood, ed., Malcolm X: In Our Own Image (New York: St. Martin's, 1992), pp. 155–82.
42 Shorty immediately dubbed his new friend "Homeboy." Malcolm X and Haley, Autobiography, pp. 45–47.
43 "in the Boston street life and nightclub scene." Collins, Seventh Child, p. 42.
43 well informed whether pointing out gamblers or pimps. Malcolm X and Haley, Autobiography, pp. 45–47.
43 redistributing the remainder as daily winnings. See Jessa Drucker, "Numbers," in Jackson, ed., Encyclopedia of New York City, p. 856.
43 "Stomping at the Savoy," were crafted for the Lindy Hop. The Lindy Hop dance began in the late 1920s and was the most popular swing dance for two decades. Its name derived from famous aviator Charles Lindbergh, following his 1927 solo flight across the Atlantic Ocean. See Marshall and Jean Stearns, Jazz Dance: The Story of American Vernacular Dance, second revised edition (New York: Da Capo, 1994); and L. F. Emery, Black Dance in the U.S. from 1619 to 1970 (Palo Alto: National Press Books, 1972).
43 watch the dancers go through their paces. Malcolm X and Haley, Autobiography, pp. 52–53.
44 docile yet loyal, obese and hardworking. See "Motion Pictures," in Augustus Low and Virgil A. Cliff, eds., Encyclopedia of Black America (New York: Da Capo, 1984), pp. 277–79.
44 Nellie LaFleur, the numbers queen. Ibid., p. 277.
44 the Fair Employment Practices Committee. "Labor Unions" and "A. Philip Randolph," in ibid., pp. 493, 727.
44 latest gossip at Mason High School. Christine Hoyt to Malcolm Little, February 7, 1941, in "Malcolm X Collection, 1941–1955," Manuscript Collection No. 827, Robert W. Woodruff Library (RWL) Special Collections Department, Emory University, Atlanta, Georgia.
44 some former sweethearts also kept in touch. Peter Hawryleiw to Malcolm Little, March 2, 1941, ibid.
44 to write more clearly in the future. Philbert Little to Malcolm Little, March 6, 1941, ibid.
45 relationships with several Lansing girls. Reginald Little to Malcolm Little, March 22, 1941, ibid.
45 his first colorful "zoot suit" on credit. Malcolm X and Haley, Autobiography, p. 54.

45 *"after a lifetime of kinks, is staggering."* Ibid., pp. 55–56.
45 *life as the ultimate act of self-debasement.* Ibid., pp. 56–57.
45 *wavy-haired Latinos, whom blacks sought to emulate.* DeCaro, *On the Side of My People*, p. 55.
45 *to declare the wearing of a zoot suit a misdemeanor.* Kelley, "The Riddle of the Zoot," pp. 159–60. Also see Chester B. Himes, "Zoot Riots Are Race Riots," *Crisis*, vol. 50 (July 1943), pp. 200–201.
45 *place in Baltimore, Detroit, San Diego, and New York City.* See Eric Lott, "Double V, Double-Time: Bebop's Politics of Style," *Callaloo*, no. 36 (Summer 1988), pp. 597–605; and Douglas Henry Daniels, "Los Angeles Zoot Race 'Riot': The Pachuco and Black Culture Music," *Journal of Negro History*, vol. 82, no. 2 (Spring 1997), pp. 201–20.
46 *inquiring about his intentions, but to no avail.* Eleanor L. Matthews to Malcolm Little, October 9, 1941; and Matthews to Little, October 21, 1941, "Malcolm X Collection, 1941–1955," RWL.
46 *after Malcolm had moved to Harlem in early 1942.* Gloria Strother to Malcolm Little, October 29, 1941, ibid.
46 *as a blonde Armenian named Bea Caragulian.* DeCaro, *On the Side of My People*, p. 64.
46 *discussion of Bea, who is referred to as "Sophia."* Malcolm X and Haley, *Autobiography*, p. 72.
46 *the far less glamorous Tick Tock Club.* Robert L. Jenkins, "Beatrice Caragulian Bazarian," in Jenkins, ed., *Malcolm X Encyclopedia*, pp. 94–95.
47 *"the young ones and the old ones both."* Malcolm X and Haley, *Autobiography*, pp. 62–63.
47 *working in the dining room as a waiter.* Kofi Natambu, *Malcolm X* (Indianapolis: Alpha, 2002), pp. 57–58.
47 *that he hoped to travel to California soon.* Malcolm Little to Zolma Holman, November 18, 1941. The letter is in the possession of the Wright Museum, Detroit, Michigan, and was displayed with the Malcolm X exhibit, Schomburg Center, New York Public Library, 2005.
47 *Martha's Vineyard, describing her boredom.* Catherine Haines to Malcolm Little, June 25, 1942, "Malcolm X Collection, 1941–1955," RWL.
47 *"not have wanted to hear it in the first place."* Malcolm X and Haley, *Autobiography*, p. 71.
47 *sixty thousand blacks from New York City had served their country.* "Members of Nine Harlem Draft Boards Praised by Gen. Davis as They Get Medals," *New York Times*, June 13, 1946. Also see Bernard C. Nalty, *Strength for the Fight: A History of Black Americans in the Military* (New York: Free Press, 1986); and Arthur E. Barbeau and Florette Henri, *The Unknown Soldiers: Black American Troops in World War I* (Philadelphia: Temple University Press, 1974).
48 *on a railroad line as a fourth-class cook.* Malcolm X and Haley, *Autobiography*, p. 74.
48 *"as laborers, janitors, guards, taxi-drivers and the like."* Ibid., p. 75.
48 *coworkers began to call him "Sandwich Red."* Ibid.
48 *"And Harlem was Seventh Heaven!"* Ibid., p. 80.
49 *along with the Cotton Club and Connie's Inn.* See Marc Ferris, "Small's Paradise," in Jackson, ed., *Encyclopedia of New York City*, p. 1079; Wallace Thurman, *Negro Life in New York's Harlem* (Girard, KS: Haldeman-Julius, 1928); and Carl Van Vechten, *Nigger Heaven* (New York: Harper and Row, 1977).
49 *"mostly men, drinking and talking."* Malcolm X and Haley, *Autobiography*, p. 75.
49 *an entertainment center featuring black performers.* See Beth L. Savage, ed., *African American Historic Places* (Washington, D.C.: Preservation Press, 1994).
49 *after winning the heavyweight championship.* See Sondra Kathryn Wilson, *Meet Me at the Theresa: The Story of Harlem's Most Famous Hotel* (New York: Simon and Schuster, 2004); Amanda Aaron, "Hotel Theresa," in Jackson, ed., *Encyclopedia of New York City*, p. 364; and Malcolm X and Haley, *Autobiography*, p. 76.
49 *"I had left Boston and Roxbury forever."* Malcolm X and Haley, *Autobiography*, p. 76.
49 *a hangout for the Apollo's entertainers.* Ibid., p. 80.
50 *with customers, and especially with servicemen.* Ibid.

50 *"but they would pay him a thousand dollars a trip."* Wilfred Little, quoted in DeCaro, *On the Side of My People*, p. 68.

50 *the conditions in which blacks lived and worked.* Malcolm X and Haley, *Autobiography*, p. 108. Also see Albert Murray, *The Blue Devils of Nada* (New York: Pantheon, 1996), pp. 99–102.

50 *on credit, but he had no intention of paying.* See "Personal Business Records," O.K. Tailoring Company, March 24, 1942, "Order received and owes $28.45"; and Empire Credit Clothing Company, July 14, 1942, "Owes $25.00," in "Malcolm X Collection, 1941–1955," RWL.

50 *Boyle Brothers collection agency, which threatened legal action.* Boyle Brothers Collection Service, no date, "Threatening court action"; Boyle Brothers Collection Service, no date, "Threatening court action if Little does not pay," ibid.

50 *his dues to the Dining Car Employees Union.* "Dining Car Employees Union Bill," no date, "Owes five dollars in union dues," ibid.

51 *"might have been taken as a man from Mars,"* he recalled. Malcolm X and Haley, *Autobiography*, p. 82.

51 *with the bold signature "Harlem Red."* Ibid., pp. 82–83.

51 *were spent pursuing a number of different women.* Natambu, *Malcolm X*, p. 63.

51 *fired seventeen days later for insubordination.* Ibid., p. 64; and Collins, *Seventh Child*, p. 42.

51 *prompting arrest for solicitation, and another firing.* Malcolm X and Haley, *Autobiography*, pp. 83, 99–101.

51 *"over the place where he could sleep."* DeCaro, *On the Side of My People*, p. 68.

52 *become famous as the comedian Redd Foxx.* Ibid., pp. 66–67.

52 *"how they could benefit us as a people."* Ibid., p. 67.

52 *"'fought the hardest to help free those Scottsboro boys?'"* Malcolm X and Haley, *Autobiography*, p. 79.

52 *"Harlem was like it still is today—virtually all black."* Ibid., p. 85.

53 *to Negroes who followed them north.* Gilbert Osofsky, *Harlem: The Making of a Ghetto: Negro New York, 1890–1930* (New York: Harper and Row, 1966), pp. 115–17.

53 *part of the cultural bedrock of black Harlem.* David Levering Lewis, *When Harlem Was in Vogue* (New York: Alfred A. Knopf, 1981), pp. 28, 104–5, 217–18.

54 *global expression for youth culture.* Osofsky, *Harlem*, pp. 3, 28, 128–31, 137.

54 *the neighborhood in the New York State Assembly in 1940.* Hulan Jack was elected Manhattan borough president in 1953, making him at the time the highest-ranking black official in the United States. Following his reelection in 1957, Jack was convicted for accepting an illegal gift of $4,500, and was forced to resign. See Calvin B. Holder, "Hulan Jack," in Jackson, ed., *Encyclopedia of New York City*, p. 607.

54 *employees were black, and all held low-wage jobs.* Herman D. Bloch, "The Employment Status of the New York Negro in Retrospect," *Phylon*, vol. 20, no. 4 (1959), pp. 327–44; quotations from pp. 333 and 327.

54 *period was estimated well above 50 percent.* Ibid., p. 337.

54 *estimated the average black family's income at $1,025.* Cheryl Greenberg, "The Politics of Disorder: Reexamining Harlem's Riots of 1935 and 1943," *Journal of Urban History*, vol. 18, no. 4 (August 1992), pp. 395–441; quotation from p. 399.

55 *inciting to riot and malicious mischief to felonious assault and burglary.* Ibid., pp. 403–8.

55 *"to arrest an unarmed drunk, hit the drunk so hard that he died."* Ibid., p. 414.

55 *white-collar positions at Consolidated Edison.* Ibid., pp. 418–19.

56 *two liberals campaigned together—and both won.* Dominic J. Capeci, "From Different Liberal Perspectives: Fiorello H. LaGuardia, Adam Clayton Powell, Jr., and Civil Rights in New York City, 1941–1943," *Journal of Negro History*, vol. 62, no. 2 (April 1977), pp. 160–73; quotations from pp. 160–63.

56 *Walton High School, Powell denounced the action.* Ibid., p. 164.

56 *over fascism abroad and racial discrimination at home.* See "The Courier's Double 'V' for Double Victory Campaign Gets Country-Wide Support," *Pittsburgh Courier*, Feb-

ruary 14, 1942; and Lee Finkle, *Forum for Protest* (Cranbury, NJ: Associated University Presses, 1975).

57 *executive order placing the streetcar company under army control.* Philip S. Foner, *Organized Labor and the Black Worker, 1619–1981*, second edition (New York: International Publishers, 1981), p. 265.

57 *"a certain respect for white Americans faded."* James Baldwin, *The Fire Next Time* (New York: Dell, 1970), p. 76.

57 *even the rising Republican star Thomas E. Dewey.* Ibid., pp. 50, 52. Sources on the Savoy Ballroom include: Jervis Anderson, *This Was Harlem, 1900–1950* (New York: Farrar, Straus and Giroux, 1982); Morgan Smith and Marvin Smith, *Harlem: The Vision of Morgan and Marvin Smith* (Lexington, KY: University Press of Kentucky, 1997); and Stearns, *Jazz Dance.*

57 *stop the ballroom from being closed down.* Russell Gold, "Guilty of Syncopation, Joy, and Animation: The Closing of Harlem's Savoy Ballroom," *Studies in Dance History*, vol. 5, no. 1 (1994), pp. 50–64; quotation from pp. 54, 56.

58 *"actions that didn't help Harlem to love the white man any."* Malcolm X and Haley, *Autobiography*, p. 116.

58 *Powell demanded LaGuardia be impeached.* Capeci, "From Different Liberal Perspectives," p. 166.

58 *housing projects constructed under the city's authority.* Ibid., p. 167.

58 *assigned to escort trolley cars and buses.* Harvard Sitkoff, "The Detroit Race Riot of 1943," *Michigan History*, vol. 53, no. 3 (1969), pp. 183–206; quotation from pp. 195–96.

59 *"physical disturbances, aided and abetted indirectly."* Greenberg, "The Politics of Disorder," pp. 426–27.

59 *to blacks to "please go home and stay inside."* Malcolm X and Haley, *Autobiography*, pp. 116–17.

59 *black soldiers were simply going AWOL.* See Harvard Sitkoff, "Racial Militancy and Interracial Violence in the Second World War," *Journal of American History*, vol. 58, no. 3 (December 1971), pp. 661–81; and Paul T. Murray, "Blacks and the Draft: A History of Institutional Racism," *Journal of Black Studies*, vol. 2, no. 1 (September 1971), pp. 57–76.

59 *"to go and bleed for him? Let him fight."* Malcolm X and Haley, *Autobiography*, p. 74.

60 *"and I never heard from the Army anymore."* Ibid., pp. 108–10.

60 *"sexual perversion, psychiatric rejection."* MX FBI, Memo, New York Office, January 28, 1955.

60 *robberies and burglaries outside New York City.* Malcolm X and Haley, *Autobiography*, p. 112.

60 *"We just barely escaped."* Ibid., p. 118.

61 *the filth and hypocrisy of the white man.* Ibid., p. 122.

61 *failed to turn up any criminal charges or arrests.* Goldman, *The Death and Life of Malcolm X*, pp. 30–31.

61 *"no big-time racketeer or thug."* DeCaro, *On the Side of My People*, p. 69.

61 *and subsequently "divide[d] the spoils."* Ibid.

61 *New York City's nearly all-white suburbs.* Malcolm X and Haley, *Autobiography*, p. 112.

61 *and sales receipts from the purchase of the goods.* Ibid., p. 115.

62 *the margins of musical taste and commercialism.* There is an impressive literature on the impact of bebop during World War II. For example, see Lott, "Double V, Double-Time: Bebop's Politics of Style"; Scott DeVeaux, "Bebop and the Recording Industry: The 1942 AFM Recording Ban Reconsidered," *Journal of the American Musicological Society*, vol. 41, no. 1 (Spring 1988), pp. 126–65; Ira Gitler, ed., *Swing to Bop: An Oral History of the Transition of Jazz in the 1940s* (Oxford: Oxford University Press, 1985); and Scott DeVeaux, *The Birth of Bebop: A Social and Musical History* (Berkeley: University of California Press, 1997).

62 *could not be so easily exploited and commodified.* Frank Kofsky, *Black Nationalism and the Revolution in Music* (New York: Pathfinder, 1970), p. 56.

63 he had observed in Harlem as "the Zoot Effect." Eric Lott, "Double V, Double-Time," pp. 597–605.
63 "for the expression of outraged protest." Kofsky, Black Nationalism and the Revolution in Music, pp. 64–65.
63 spirit of rebellion and artistic nonconformity. Ibid.
64 "usually to those spruced-up bars which he had sold to someone." Malcolm X and Haley, Autobiography, pp. 126–27.
64 "but under proper guidance, a good boy." John T. Herstrom, July 23, 1946, Prison File of Malcolm Little, Office of Public Safety and Security, Department of Corrections, Commonwealth of Massachusetts.
64 He was nineteen years old. "Malcolm Little Criminal Record," ibid.; and MX FBI, Memo, Boston Office, February 17, 1953.
65 a warrant was issued for his arrest. Malcolm Little, "Out-State Progress Report," February 14, 1953, Division of Pardons, Paroles, and Probation, State of Michigan, in Prison File of Malcolm Little.
65 speculation in the years following Malcolm's death. Bruce Perry's Malcolm asserts that on several occasions in 1944–45 Malcolm engaged in homosexual acts for payment. These "male-to-male encounters," Perry observes, "afforded him an opportunity for sexual release. . . ." Perry also cites sexual encounters in Boston in 1945 where a wealthy white man named William Paul Lennon paid Malcolm "to disrobe him, place him on his bed, sprinkle him with talcum powder, and massage him until he reached his climax. . . . Like a prostitute, he sold himself as if the best he had to offer was his body." Perry adds that Malcolm would later excuse his actions by insisting that another man actually gave his white male client "satisfaction." Perry's claims, when published in 1991, generated a firestorm of criticism from those devoted to Malcolm's iconic image, who pointed out that his only credible source for these escapades was "Shorty" Jarvis. See Perry, Malcolm, pp. 75–77, 82–83. Since the publication of Perry's book, other evidence has surfaced that supports his general assertions. For example, according to Rodnell Collins, Malcolm revealed details to Ella Collins about "a business deal he and Malcolm Jarvis had with an elderly, wealthy white millionaire, named Paul Lennon, who would pay them to rub powder over his body." See Collins, Seventh Child, p. 76.
65 to Bernard and Nellie F. Lennon. Federal United States Census (1910), Rhode Island, Providence County.
65 active in local Democratic Party politics. Robert Grieve, An Illustrated History of Pawtucket, Central Falls, and Vicinity: A Narrative of the Growth and Evolution of the Community (Pawtucket, RI: Pawtucket Gazette and Chronicle, 1897), p. 368. Also see Federal United States Census (1900), Rhode Island, Providence County; and Edward Field, State of Rhode Island and Providence Plantations at the End of the Century: A History (Boston: Mason Publishing, 1902), p. 598.
65 "have had the requisite preliminary training." The Catalogue of Brown University (Providence, RI: Brown University Press, 1960), p. 33.
65 his discharge he lived briefly with his parents. In the 1920 census, thirty-one-year-old William Paul Lennon appears residing in his parents' household in Rhode Island. See Federal United States Census (1920), Rhode Island, Providence County.
65 to employ male secretaries in his home. Classified Ad 5, no title, New York Times, October 2, 1942; and Classified Ad 23, no title, New York Times, October 4, 1942.
66 as a "butler and occasional house worker." "Employment History," Prison File of Malcolm Little.
66 an affluent stretch of Arlington Street overlooking the Public Garden. Herstrom, July 23, 1946, Prison File of Malcolm Little.
66 "the old man would actually reach his climax from that." Malcolm X and Haley, Autobiography, p. 143.
66 "send to his brothers and sisters in Lansing." Collins, Seventh Child, pp. 68–69.
67 a mistake no veteran burglar would ever have made. Herstrom, July 23, 1946, Prison File of Malcolm Little; DeCaro, On the Side of My People, pp. 72–73; and Natambu, Malcolm X, pp. 100–101.

67 *additional merchandise, with a total value estimated by police at $6,275.* Malcolm Little, "Out-State Progress Report," February 14, 1953, Division of Pardons, Paroles, and Probation, State of Michigan, Prison File of Malcolm Little.

67 *everyone in the gang was promptly arrested.* Ibid.; and DeCaro, *On the Side of My People,* p. 73.

68 *"a fifteen-to-twenty-year sentence or life in prison."* Malcolm L. Jarvis, *Myself and I* (New Haven, CT: Yale University Press, 1995), pp. 33–35.

68 *"I had had no business associating with white women."* Ibid., p. 42.

68 *"friendless, scared lost girls.'"* Collins, *Seventh Child,* p. 46.

68 *"I would rather be dead than do ten years."* Jarvis, *Myself and I,* p. 34.

68 *"constant fear,"* she told the court with emotion. DeCaro, *On the Side of My People,* pp. 73–74; Natambu, *Malcolm X,* pp. 113–14; and Malcolm X and Haley, *Autobiography,* p. 153.

68 *seven months of a five-year sentence.* Jenkins, "Beatrice Caragulian Bazarian," in Jenkins, ed., *Malcolm X Encyclopedia,* p. 95; and Natambu, *Malcolm X,* p. 119.

68 *as a steerer for Harlem prostitutes.* Malcolm X and Haley, *Autobiography,* p. 96.

69 *"best possible source, from his own women."* Ibid., p. 94.

Chapter 3: Becoming "X"

70 *"physically miserable and as evil-tempered as a snake."* Malcolm X and Haley, *Autobiography,* p. 155.

70 *"which seems to be affected because of his sensitiveness to color."* "Massachusetts State Prison Psychometric Report (of Malcolm Little)," May 1, 1946, Prison File of Malcolm Little.

71 *"It grew stenciled on your brain."* Malcolm X and Haley, *Autobiography,* p. 155.

71 *"institution life at Charlestown [prison]."* John F. Rockett, May 7, 1946, Prison File of Malcolm Little.

71 *forced to eat in their cells.*"Bay State Prison Started: Governor Calls Old Charlestown Institution 'a Disgrace,'" *New York Times,* May 14, 1952; and Albert Morris, "Massachusetts: The Aftermath of the Prison Riots of 1952," *The Prison Journal,* vol. 34, no. 1 (April 1954), pp. 35–37. Michael Stephen Hindus has examined the terrible conditions of Charlestown prisoners in the nineteenth century, equating them with slavery in South Carolina. See Michael Stephen Hindus, *Prison and Plantation: Crime, Justice and Authority in Massachusetts and South Carolina, 1767–1878* (Chapel Hill: University of North Carolina Press, 1980).

71 *1920 robbery and double homicide.* "Sacco and Vanzetti," in Paul Finkelman, ed., *Encyclopedia of American Civil Liberties,* vol. 2 (New York: Routledge, 2006), pp. 1395–96; "End of Seven Years of Legal Fight," *Chicago Daily Tribune,* August 23, 1927; and "Sacco and Vanzetti Pay Death-Chair Penalty," *Los Angeles Times,* August 23, 1927. Sacco and Vanzetti were found guilty in 1921, in a trial characterized by anti-immigrant bias and hostility toward their political views.

71 *"any current prison in the United States."* "Bay State Prison Started," *New York Times,* May 14, 1952.

71 *calling him the "Green-Eyed Monster."* Natambu, *Malcolm X,* p. 118.

71 *"further nickname for him: 'Satan.'"* Malcolm X and Haley, *Autobiography,* p. 156.

72 *but can also suffer mental breakdown.* Ivan Fras and Joseph Joel Friedman, "Hallucinogenic Effects of Nutmeg in Adolescents," *New York State Journal of Medicine,* February 1, 1969, pp. 463–65; R. B. Payne, "Nutmeg Intoxication," *New England Journal of Medicine,* vol. 269 (1963), p. 36; and G. Weiss, "Hallucinogenic and Narcotic-Like Effects of Powdered Myristica (nutmeg)," *Psychiatric Quarterly,* vol. 34, no. 1 (1960), pp. 346–56. Weiss notes that "doses of two to three tablespoonfuls of powdered nutmeg tended to narcotize the subjects against the unpleasant experience of incarceration, without a blurring of the boundaries between the self and the outer world."

72 *"wished she hadn't come at all."* Malcolm X and Haley, *Autobiography,* p. 155.

72 *fallen deeply in love with Malcolm.* Collins, *Seventh Child*, pp. 74–75.

72 *"adventurous, highly impressionable" boy.* Ibid., pp. 75–76.

73 *those decadent whites whom he had been hustling.* Ibid., p. 71.

73 *"poor in skill, and average to poor in effort."* "Institution History of Malcolm Little," May 1951, Prison File of Malcolm Little.

74 *to "study English and penmanship."* Malcolm X and Haley, *Autobiography*, pp. 156–57.

74 *"So, feeling I had time on my hands, I did."* Ibid., p. 157.

74 *English and elementary Latin and German.* DeCaro, *On the Side of My People*, p. 79.

74 *of both commonly used and obscure words.* Frantz Fanon, *Black Skin, White Masks* (New York: Grove, 1967), p. 38.

74 *including betting on baseball.* DeCaro, *On the Side of My People*, p. 79.

74 *conditions of work and supervision.* Morris, "Massachusetts: The Aftermath of the Prison Riots of 1952," pp. 35–37.

75 *and possibly William Paul Lennon.* "Transfer Summary," March 31, 1948, Prison File of Malcolm Little.

75 *"of use to me when I regain my freedom."* Malcolm Little to Mr. Dwyer, Norfolk Prison Colony Transportation Board, July 28, 1947, ibid.

75 *performance sufficiently so as to avoid severe discipline.* "Institution History of Malcolm Little," May 1951, ibid.

75 *proper English, was completely dismissive.* Malcolm X and Haley, *Autobiography*, p. 158; and DeCaro, *On the Side of My People*, p. 80.

75 *"And they had the best program going."* Wilfred Little Shabazz interview with Louis DeCaro, Jr., August 14, 1992, in DeCaro, *On the Side of My People*, pp. 80–81.

75 *"I'll show you how to get out of prison."* Malcolm X and Haley, *Autobiography*, p. 158. In the *Autobiography*, Malcolm places the time of Philbert's and Reginald's letters after his transfer to the Concord prison, in January 1947. However, Wilfred Little, in his 1992 interview with Louis DeCaro, Jr., stated that this correspondence arrived while Malcolm was still at Charlestown.

76 *all with windows and doors.* Carl R. Doering, ed., *A Report on the Development of Penological Treatment at Norfolk Prison Colony in Massachusetts* (New York: Bureau of Social Hygiene, 1940), pp. 33–34, 42–44, 73, 111.

76 *observances were permitted for "Hebrews."* Ibid., pp. 35–44. Also see George B. Vold, "A Report on the Development of Penological Treatment at Norfolk Prison Colony in Massachusetts," *American Journal of Sociology*, vol. 46, no. 6 (May 1941), p. 917. Vold observed that "criminologists will welcome this account of an effort in penology that was unique in many ways."

76 *reading agenda to include works on Buddhism.* DeCaro, *On the Side of My People*, p. 313.

77 *stopped cursing the guards and fellow prisoners.* "Institution History of Malcolm Little," May 1951, Prison File of Malcolm Little.

77 *held a deep animus toward blacks.* Malcolm X and Haley, *Autobiography*, pp. 161–63.

77 *and Reginald all to become members.* Karl Evanzz, *The Messenger: The Rise and Fall of Elijah Muhammad* (New York: Pantheon, 1999), p. 161.

77 *"we were black and should be proud or anything like that."* Strickland and Greene, eds., *Malcolm X: Make It Plain*, pp. 59–60.

78 *"to open my mouth and say goodbye."* Malcolm X and Haley, *Autobiography*, pp. 167–71.

78 *and Philbert had been married for several years.* Malcolm Little to Henrietta Little, October 16, 1950, Malcolm X Collection, Schomburg Center for Research in Black Culture (MXC-S), box 3, folder 1. Writing to Henrietta, Malcolm related how happy he was that "Allah has given both Philbert and me a wonderful Sister."

78 *and the couple had relocated to Grand Rapids.* Malcolm Little to Philbert Little, December 18, 1949, MXC-S, box 3, folder 1.

79 *together with a five-dollar bill.* Malcolm X and Haley, *Autobiography*, p. 172.

79 *against those who oppose Muhammad's message.* See Reza Aslan, *No God but God: The Origins, Evolution and Future of Islam* (New York: Random House, 2003), pp. 43, 60, 79–81, 84–44; and Robert Dannin, *Black Pilgrimage to Islam* (New York: Oxford University Press, 2002), p. 8.

79 *followers to marry Jews, as he himself did.* Aslan, *No God but God*, p. 100.

80 *was an Ethiopian former slave named Bilal.* Turner, *Islam in the African-American Experience*, p. 13.

80 *Muslims made up about 7 or 8 percent.* Ibid., pp. 22–25, 27–32, 36–37.

81 *uniting black humanity throughout the world.* Wilson Jeremiah Moses, *The Golden Age of Black Nationalism* (New York: Oxford University Press, 1976), p. 21.

81 *aesthetics drawing upon Africa and the black diaspora.* Turner, *Islam in the African-American Experience*, p. 50.

82 *and their genealogy extended back to Christ.* Ibid., pp. 92–93.

82 *temples were investigated for sedition.* Ibid., pp. 94–104.

83 *who supported rapprochement with orthodox Islam.* Ibid., pp. 109–28.

83 *does away with all distinctions of race, color and creed.* Mufti Muhammad Sadiq, article in *Moslem Sunrise*, January 1923, quoted in ibid., p. 129.

84 *Pittsburgh, Cleveland, Chicago, and Kansas City (Missouri).* Ibid., pp. 129–34. Literature documenting the history and evolution of the global Ahmadiyya movement includes: Humphrey J. Fisher, *The Ahmadiyya Movement* (London: Oxford University Press, 1963); and Yohannon Friedman, *Prophecy Continuous: Aspects of Ahmadi Religious Thought and Its Medieval Background* (Berkeley: University of California Press, 1989).

84 *those of the Moorish Science Temple.* Turner, *Islam in the African-American Experience*, p. 127.

84 *antiwhite views of the staunch Garveyite.* Louis A. DeCaro, Jr., *Malcolm and the Cross: The Nation of Islam, Malcolm X, and Christianity* (New York: New York University Press, 1998), pp. 11–12.

84 *which connected in ancestry to Muhammad.* Erdmann Doane Beynon, "The Voodoo Cult Among Negro Migrants in Detroit," *American Journal of Sociology*, vol. 43, no. 6 (May 1938), p. 897.

84 *"and higher mathematics, especially calculus."* Ibid., p. 900.

85 *"I was turned around completely."* Ibid., p. 896.

85 *"also a free transportation to the Holy City of Mecca."* Gardell, *In the Name of Elijah Muhammad: Louis Farrakhan and the Nation of Islam* (Durham, NC: Duke University Press, 1996), p. 56.

86 *Asiatic black man from his centuries-long slumber.* Ibid., pp. 151–53.

86 *"yet time for me to be known."* Turner, *Islam in the African-American Experience*, p. 151; and DeCaro, *Malcolm and the Cross*, pp. 29–30.

86 *realize the shattered dreams of Garveyites.* Turner, *Islam in the African-American Experience*, pp. 152–55; and DeCaro, *Malcolm and the Cross*, pp. 22–31.

87 *instructed them in their roles as Muslim wives.* Carlos D. Morrison, "The Rhetoric of the Nation of Islam, 1930–1975: A Functional Approach," Ph.D. dissertation, Howard University, 1996, pp. 73–74; and Gardell, *In the Name of Elijah Muhammad*, pp. 60–61.

87 *missionary efforts had been particularly well received.* Gardell, *In the Name of Elijah Muhammad*, p. 56.

87 *Then, in 1934, Fard simply vanished.* Malcolm X and Haley, *Autobiography*, pp. 212–13.

87 *citing his arrest for disorderly conduct.* Gardell, *In the Name of Elijah Muhammad*, p. 58.

87 *black American organization, Development of Our Own.* Ibid., pp. 58–59; and Turner, *Islam in the African-American Experience*, pp. 166–67.

88 *622 CE and Elijah Muhammad's wanderings.* Turner, *Islam in the African-American Experience*, pp. 167–68.

88 *his followers to resist military service.* Ibid., p. 168.

88 *her husband and visiting him in prison.* Malu Halasa, *Elijah Muhammad: Religious Leader* (New York: Chelsea House, 1990), p. 60.

88 *"Holy City of Mecca, Arabia, in 1930."* Elijah Muhammad, *The Supreme Wisdom: Solution to the So-Called Negroes' Problem*, vol. 1 (Newport News, VA: The National Newport News and Commentator, 1957), pp. 12–13.

88 *"through its devilish nature, destroying itself."* Malcolm X and Haley, *Autobiography*, p. 170.

89 *"in the destruction of this world."* Elijah Muhammad, *The Message to the Blackman in America* (Newport News, VA: United Brothers Communication Systems, 1965), chapter 125, pp. 1–6.

90   *and at his headquarters in Chicago.* Turner, *Islam in the African-American Experience,*
     p. 169.
90   *"and give a focus to my inner life."* Quintin Hoare and Geoffrey Nowell Smith, eds.,
     Selections from the Prison Notebooks of Antonio Gramsci (New York: International Pub-
     lishers, 1971), pp. xcii–xciii.
91   *"wet, I was gone on debating."* Malcolm X and Haley, *Autobiography,* p. 187.
91   *which helped him attract listeners.* Robin D. G. Kelley interview, July 26, 2001. Kelly
     argues that there existed an "important intersection between the great preachers"
     like Malcolm and the great jazz performers, who frequently talked about playing as
     "preaching." In jazz, Kelley explains, "there are shout choruses that are called preach-
     er's choruses, in which you have a call-and-response. Someone like Ben Webster
     would play a measure, and then not play the next measure. . . . When Malcolm would
     speak, he would speak and leave a space for response, a space for congregations of
     people—whether it's on the street or inside a mosque—to say, 'Amen, Preach.'"
91   *speaking style borrowed its cadences.* Ibid. There is a growing scholarly literature on
     the rhetoric and effective use of language by Malcolm X. See John Franklin Gay,
     "The Rhetorical Strategies and Tactics of Malcolm X (Movement Theory, Neo-
     Aristotelian, Black Muslims, Persuasion)," Ph.D. dissertation, Indiana University,
     1985; Andrew Ann Dinkins, "Malcolm X and the Rhetoric of Transformation: 1948–
     1965," Ph.D. dissertation, University of Pittsburgh, 1995; Archie Epps, "The Rheto-
     ric of Malcolm X," *Harvard Review,* no. 3 (Winter 1993), pp. 64–75; Celeste Michelle
     Condit and John Louis Lucaites, "Malcolm X and the Limits of the Rhetoric of
     Revolutionary Dissent," *Journal of Black Studies,* vol. 23, no. 3 (March 1993),
     pp. 291–313; and Scott Joseph Varda, "A Rhetorical History of Malcolm X," Ph.D.
     dissertation, University of Iowa, 2007.
91   *"ever got more out of going to prison than I did."* Malcolm X and Haley, *Autobiography,*
     pp. 178–83.
92   *"no circumstances don't ever preach to me,"* he warned. Malcolm Little to Philbert Little,
     no date (approximately mid-1948), MXC-S, box 3, folder 1.
92   *"rid the planet of these wretched devils."* Malcolm to Philbert, November 28, 1948, ibid.
92   *"vast emptiness created by men."* Malcolm to Philbert, February 4, 1949, ibid.
92   *"I certainly woke up the hard way, hmm?"* Malcolm to Philbert, February 1949, ibid.
92   *a new appreciation for their mother.* Malcolm to Philbert, December 12, 1949, ibid.
92   *"as he had come, he was gone."* Malcolm X and Haley, *Autobiography,* p. 190.
93   *of "Master W. D. Fard, the Messiah."* Ibid., p. 192.
93   *"truth in the first place,"* he charged. Ibid., p. 190.
93   *"ocean of blackness where I was to save me."* Ibid., p. 192.
94   *of "his dislike for the white race."* "Transfer Summary for Malcolm Little," March 23,
     1950, Prison File of Malcolm Little.
94   *"Saturday I told her to do whatever she can."* Malcolm to Philbert, March 26, 1950,
     MXC-S, box 3, folder 1.
94   *"Cells to Facilitate 'Prayers to Allah.'"* See "Four Convicts Turn Moslems, Get Calls
     Looking to Mecca," *Boston Herald,* April 20, 1950; and "Local Criminals in Prison,
     Claim Moslem Faith Now: Grow Beards, Won't Eat Pork; Demand East-Facing Cells
     to Facilitate 'Prayer to Mecca,'" *Springfield Union* (Massachusetts), April 21, 1950.
95   *"Peace to cease,"* Malcolm predicted, *"peace will cease!"* Malcolm Little to Commissioner
     MacDowell, June 6, 1950, Prison File of Malcolm Little.
95   *"isn't hard to convince people that I am."* Malcolm Little to Harry S. Truman, June 29,
     1950, in MX FBI, Summary Report, Detroit Office, March 16, 1954, p. 6. Also see Karl
     Evanzz, *The Judas Factor: The Plot to Kill Malcolm X* (New York: Thunder's Mouth,
     1992), p. 11.
96   *"of the wicked accidental world."* DeCaro, *On the Side of My People,* pp. 57–58.
96   *his name "Malcolm X (surprised?)."* Malcolm to Philbert, December 11, 1950, MXC-S,
     box 3, folder 1.
96   *"However he can give me a home and a job."* Malcolm to Philbert, December 19, 1951,
     ibid.
97   *"Just in all that I think, speak and do."* Malcolm Little letter, January 9, 1951, in MX FBI,

Summary Report, Boston Office, May 4, 1953, pp. 5–6; and MX FBI, Memo, Boston Office, February 17, 1953. This report indicates that Malcolm "has been the subject of a Communist Index Card" by the FBI.

97 *become targets of harassment by prison guards.* Evanzz, *The Judas Factor,* p. 10.

97 *composed primarily of bread and cheese.* DeCaro, *On the Side of My People,* p. 92.

97 *had "read so much by the lights-out glow in my room."* Malcolm X and Haley, *Autobiography,* p. 193.

98 *the petition be denied. Not surprisingly, Dever agreed.* Ralph E. Johnson, Executive Secretary, Council Chamber, State House, to Elliott E. MacDowell, Commissioner, Department of Corrections, December 6, 1950; George E. Thompson, District Attorney for the Northern District, Commonwealth of Massachusetts, to Governor Paul A. Dever, December 13, 1950; and MacDowell to Dever, December 19, 1950, all in Prison File of Malcolm Little.

98 *countries throughout the world.* Malcolm Little to Commissioner MacDowell, December 13, 1950, ibid. Also see DeCaro, *On the Side of My People,* p. 94.

98 *he go to Detroit to live with Wilfred.* Philip J. Flynn, Massachusetts Supervisor of Parole, to Gus Harrison, State Supervisor of Parole, Division of Pardons, Paroles and Probation, State of Michigan, Lansing, Michigan, June 27, 1952, in Prison File of Malcolm Little.

98 *date for his release was set for August 7.* P. J. Flynn, Massachusetts Supervisor of Parole, to Parole Board, August 4, 1952; Flynn to Harrison, August 6, 1952; and Flynn to Harrison, August 12, 1952, ibid.

98 *younger brother on as a salesman.* DeCaro, *On the Side of My People,* p. 95.

98 *with the warden to resolve grievances.* Morris, "Massachusetts: The Aftermath of the Prison Riots of 1952," pp. 36–37.

99 *"my life was about to become."* Malcolm X and Haley, *Autobiography,* pp. 195–96.

Chapter 4: "They Don't Come Like the Minister"

100 *it was ready for morning prayers.* Malcolm X and Haley, *Autobiography,* pp. 197–98.

100 *Mecca for their prayers.* Dannin, *Black Pilgrimage to Mecca,* p. 170.

101 *"the fine print that never was read."* Malcolm X and Haley, *Autobiography,* pp. 196–97.

101 *but Wilfred advised patience.* Ibid., pp. 198–200.

101 *accompanied by three of his brothers.* MX FBI, Memo, Detroit Office, March 16, 1954.

101 *such peerless example recalled Job.* Malcolm X and Haley, *Autobiography,* pp. 201–2.

102 *The point went home.* Ibid., pp. 203–4.

102 *Ismail al-Faruqi termed "Islamicity."* Ismail al-Faruqi quoted in Larry Poston, *Islamic Da'wah in the West: Muslim Missionaries and the Dynamics of Conversion to Islam* (New York: Oxford University Press, 1992), p. 6.

102 *metamorphosis adding to Malcolm's reputation.* FBI—Joseph Gravitt (also known as Captain Joseph and Yusuf Shah) file, St. Louis, Missouri Office, January 17, 1955; Robert L. Jenkins, "(Captain) Joseph X Gravitt (Yusuf Shah)," in Jenkins, ed., *Malcolm X Encyclopedia,* pp. 243–46. Also see Karl Evanzz, *The Judas Factor;* Collins, *Seventh Child,* p. 137.

103 *United Auto Workers Local 900.* Ferruccio Gambino, "The Transgression of a Laborer: Malcolm X in the Wilderness of America," *Radical History,* vol. 55 (Winter 1993), pp. 7–31.

103 *truck equipment, cranes, and road machinery.* MX FBI, Memo, Detroit Office, March 16, 1954; and "Wood Workers," *Time,* July, 20, 1936.

103 *"material or grinds surface objects."* Gambino, "The Transgression of a Laborer," p. 22.

103 *"serve Mr. Muhammad in the lowliest capacity."* Malcolm X and Haley, *Autobiography,* p. 204.

103 *the beginnings of his life as a minister.* Ibid., p. 205.

103 *Michigan's discharge followed shortly thereafter.* "The Commonwealth of Massachusetts Parole Board Certification of Discharge, Malcolm Little #8077," Prison File of Malcolm Little; and MX FBI, Summary Report, Detroit Office, March 16, 1954, p. 4.

103 *claiming conscientious objector status.* Malcolm X and Haley, *Autobiography,* pp. 206–7.

104 *"asocial personality with paranoid trends."* MX FBI, Memo, New York Office, January 24, 1955.

104 *Detroit Temple No. 1's assistant minister.* Malcolm X and Haley, *Autobiography*, p. 205.

104 *he was preparing for the ministry.* MX FBI, Memo, Philadelphia Office, April 30, 1954.

104 *"spreading his wisdom to his students."* Malcolm X and Haley, *Autobiography*, pp. 208–9.

104 *delivered to one such gathering in early January 1954.* Ibid, p. 216.

104 *dangerous the sect was believed to be.* MX FBI, Summary Report, New York Office, September 7, 1954, cover page.

105 *"the cult towards the white race."* Ibid., p. 3.

105 *"to have been able to convert Ella."* Malcolm X and Haley, *Autobiography*, pp. 217–18.

106 *throughout the last three weeks of March.* MX FBI, Memo, Philadelphia Office, April 30, 1954; and MX FBI, Memo, Philadelphia Office, August 23, 1954.

106 *and commercial ventures in Chicago.* Sharron Y. Herron, "Raymond Sharrieff," in Jenkins, ed., *Malcolm X Encyclopedia*, pp. 503–4. Also see Claude Andrew Clegg III, *An Original Man: The Life and Times of Elijah Muhammad* (New York: St. Martin's, 1997).

106 *most of the Nation of Islam's ruling elite in Chicago.* Evanzz, *The Messenger*, p. 162.

106 *"cutting off a devil's head."* FBI—Gravitt, Summary Report, Philadelphia Office, November 19, 1954.

107 *Fruit of Islam and as a substitute minister.* Ibid.; and MX FBI, Memo, Philadelphia Office, August 23, 1954.

107 *"contained over a million black people."* Malcolm X and Haley, *Autobiography*, p. 219.

107 *Temple No. 7 as its FOI boss.* MX FBI, Memo, Philadelphia Office, April 30, 1954; and MX FBI, Memo, Philadelphia Office, August 23, 1955.

108 *"sometimes not that many."* Malcolm X and Haley, *Autobiography*, pp. 221–22.

108 *their garbage into the streets.* For example, see "50 Called on Rubbish: Harlem Tenants Summoned for Tossing Refuse from Windows," *New York Times*, May 1, 1954; and "93 Face Rubbish Charges," *New York Times*, May 12, 1954.

108 *for nearly all-white Flushing, Queens.* "Tuberculosis Death Rate Here Declines 12 Percent from the Level of a Year Ago," *New York Times*, June 10, 1954.

108 *the Bronx, Queens, and Brooklyn.* Alphonso Pinkney and Roger Woock, *Poverty and Politics in Harlem* (New Haven, CT: College and University Press Services, 1970), p. 27.

108 *symbolized that growing clout.* Layhmond Robinson, Jr., "Our Changing City: Harlem Now on the Upswing," *New York Times*, July 8, 1955.

108 *Tri-State Bank, in Memphis, Tennessee.* "Boycott of Banks Slated in Harlem," *New York Times*, March 5, 1955.

109 *"themselves and voting as independents."* "G.O.P. Appeal in Harlem," *New York Times*, October 18, 1956; and "Powell Sees Shift of Negroes to G.O.P.," *New York Times*, November 7, 1956.

109 *address racial discrimination in the city.* "10,000 in Harlem Protest Verdict," *New York Times*, September 26, 1955.

109 *"white-skinned people in free America."* Turner, *Islam in the African-American Experience*, p. 135.

110 *1,331 of them had any nonwhite members.* Ibid.

110 *drummer Kenny Clarke's (Liaqat Ali Salaam).* Dannin, *Black Pilgrimage to Islam*, p. 58.

110 *visa for a pilgrimage to Mecca, in 1957.* Ibid., pp. 61, 112.

110 *by a black couple, Curtis and Susie Kenner.* MX FBI, Memo, New York Office, January 28, 1955.

110 *Cincinnati, Ohio, to support local initiatives.* MX FBI, Summary Report, May 23, 1955, p. 25; and MX FBI, Summary Report, New York Office, April 23, 1957, p. 22.

111 *but sharply reminded the faithful that he (Joseph) "was not."* FBI—Gravitt, Summary Report, New York Office, June 9, 1955.

111 *the Shabazz restaurant on Fifth Avenue.* FBI—Gravitt, Memo, New York Office, January 7, 1955.

111 *it was announced that he would be remaining in New York.* FBI—Gravitt, Summary Report, New York Office, June 9, 1955.

112 *ever having been a member of the Communist Party.* MX FBI, Memo, New York Office, date illegible (around mid-1955). Based on its expanded surveillance of Malcolm X in the first five months of 1955, the New York FBI office advised the office of Director J. Edgar Hoover: "In view of the subject's long active membership in the MCI and his position as minister of the MCI as well as his speeches and statements against the U.S. government, it is believed that he could possibly commit acts inimical to the national defense and public safety in a time of emergency."

112 *with FBI agents who might contact them.* MX FBI, Summary Report, New York Office, January 31, 1956, pp. 33–34.

112 *"of the white man by the 'black man.'"* MX FBI, Summary Report, New York Office, May 23, 1955, pp. 23–24.

112 *New York City on May 11, 1933.* Curtis Austin, "Louis Farrakhan," in Jenkins, ed., *Malcolm X Encyclopedia,* pp. 218–19.

112 *"in my mind, and in my spirit."* Louis Farrakhan, "The Murder of Malcolm X and Its Effects on Black America—Twenty-five Years Later," lecture delivered at Malcolm X College, Chicago, Illinois, February 21, 1990. Text of speech in possession of author.

113 *first as Louis X, and then as Louis Farrakhan.* Evanzz, *The Messenger,* p. 168.

113 *"I was scared of him."* Louis Farrakhan (also known as Louis X Walcott) interview, December 27, 2007; and Farrakhan, "The Murder of Malcolm X and Its Effects on Black America."

113 *They heard nothing for five months.* Louis Farrakhan interview, December 27, 2007.

113 *"talk the way this brother talked,"* Farrakhan recalled. Ibid.

113 *"nook and cranny in the United States of America."* Ibid.

114 *"the father I never had."* Farrakhan, "The Murder of Malcolm X and Its Effects on Black America."

114 *Within a year Louis was elevated to minister.* Louis Farrakhan interview, December 27, 2007.

114 *that became wildly popular among temple members.* Evanzz, *The Messenger,* pp. 168–69.

115 *"has always been to be good at both,"* he said. James 67X Warden interviews, July 24, 2007, and August 1, 2007.

115 *"the other dog in the streets."* MX FBI, Summary Report, New York Office, January 31, 1956, p. 18.

115 *"whether you want to survive the war of Armageddon."* Ibid., pp. 6–7.

116 *"to frighten the black men who are still dead."* Ibid., p. 7.

116 *"very wrong that sisters are not coming in."* Ibid., p. 10.

116 *"who has any chance to save himself."* Ibid., p. 22.

116 *"so if you are not white you must be black."* Ibid., p. 11.

117 *"many members . . . as he possibly can."* Ibid., pp. 33–34.

117 *commitment to the international Islamic community.* See Yvonne Haddad and Jane Smith, *Mission to America: Five Islamic Sectarian Communities in North America* (Gainesville: University Press of Florida, 1993), pp. 49–78.

117 *"Black Muslims" to describe the Nation of Islam.* Ibid., p. 252.

117 *"required precision and order of the service."* Frederick Mathewson Denny, *An Introduction to Islam* (New York: Macmillan, 1985), p. 105.

118 *"intercessors between humans and God."* Ibid., p. 237.

118 *generally have not participated in politics.* Hamid Enayat, *Modern Islamic Political Thought* (London: I. B. Taurus, 1982), pp. 22, 26–27.

118 *religious knowledge and truth over time.* Ibid., p. 23.

118 *but who also practices spiritual self-discipline.* Dannin, *Black Pilgrimage to Islam,* pp. 274–75.

119 *transnational conference of colored peoples in history.* George McTurnan Kahin, *The Asian-African Conference: Bandung, Indonesia, April 1955* (Ithaca: Cornell University Press, 1956), p. 39.

120 decline and fall of European and U.S. power. Ibid., p. 81. See Liz Mazucci, "Going Back to Our Own: Interpreting Malcolm X's Transition from 'Black Asiatic' to 'Afro-American,'" Souls, vol. 7, no. 1 (Winter 2005), pp. 66–83.

120 "are united all over the world to fight the 'devils.'" MX FBI, Memo, New York Office, May 23, 1955.

120 Pan-Africanism, Pan-Islam, and Third World liberation. Melani McAlister, "One Black Allah: The Middle East in the Cultural Politics of African American Liberation, 1955–1970," American Quarterly, vol. 51, no. 3 (1999), p. 631.

121 because he was hardest on himself. James 67X Warden interview, July 24, 2007.

121 "late for an appointment. Malcolm was like a clock." Farrakhan, "The Murder of Malcolm X and Its Effects on Black America."

121 "lost-founds" was sufficient compensation. James 67X Warden interview, July 24, 2007.

122 "you would have gotten out of the temple." MX FBI, Summary Report, New York Office, January 31, 1956, p. 10.

122 his self-destructive opposition to Elijah Muhammad. DeCaro, On the Side of My People, p. 88. DeCaro interviewed Jeremiah Shabazz in Philadelphia on May 17, 1993.

122 while both were serving time in prison. DeCaro, On the Side of My People, p. 109.

122 more than forty new converts had been won. Malcolm X and Haley, Autobiography, p. 226.

123 highly paid skilled workers and trade unionists. Ibid., p. 229.

123 "than in every place in the world." MX FBI, Memo, New York Office to the Director, no date.

124 "the destruction of the 'devil.'" Ibid.

124 he would be criticized on some point or other. Malcolm X and Haley, Autobiography, pp. 226–27.

125 Joseph's advancement as the Nation's supreme captain. Collins, Seventh Child, p. 137.

125 damaging rumor about Elijah Muhammad that was circulating. See Evanzz, The Judas Factor, pp. 184–85.

125 "or anything, because you should know better." Transcript of audiotaped recording. Disciplinary trials supervised by Malcolm X at NOI Temple No. 7, Harlem, mid-September 1956. Audiotape provided by the Nation of Islam and Akbar Muhammad.

126 "good work for Allah and his Messenger in the Nation." Ibid.

126 "all of those Muslims that follow him are outcasts." Ibid.

126 to hold a job as a night cook at the temple's restaurant. FBI—Gravitt, Memo, New York Office, December 12, 1956.

126 had been fully restored to his rank. FBI—Gravitt, Memo, New York Office, October 23, 1956.

126 whose members were working-class blacks. Collins, Seventh Child, p. 104.

127 frequent examples of police brutality toward blacks. Tillman Durdin, "Barriers for Negro Here Still High Despite Gains," New York Times, April 23, 1956.

127 the NOI's restaurant several blocks away with the news. James Hicks, "Riot Threat as Cops Beat Muslim: 'God's Angry Men' Tangle with Police," Amsterdam News, May 4, 1957; and Evelyn Cunningham, "Moslems, Cops Battle in Harlem," Pittsburgh Courier, May 4, 1957.

128 Hinton was transported in an ambulance to Harlem Hospital. Hicks, "Riot Threat as Cops Beat Muslim."

128 down the busiest thoroughfare in Harlem. Malcolm X and Haley, Autobiography, pp. 238–39.

128 A confrontation appeared inevitable. Hicks, "Riot Threat as Cops Beat Muslim"; and DeCaro, On the Side of My People, pp. 112–13.

128 "No one man should have that much power." Hicks, "Riot Threat as Cops Beat Muslim."

129 "as orderly as a battalion of Marines." Ibid.; and "400 March to Score Police in Harlem," New York Times, April 29, 1957.

129 judgment that a New York jury had ever awarded. Malcolm X and Haley, Autobiography, p. 239; and "Moslem Announces $Million NY Suit," Pittsburgh Courier, November

9, 1957. A large silver plate was inserted in Hinton's skull to replace the bone that the police beating had shattered. Hinton was permanently disabled.
129 *or to be "on the side of my people."* DeCaro, *On the Side of My People,* p. 113.

Chapter 5: "Brother, a Minister *Has* to Be Married"

130 *"with plagues of cancer, polio, [and] heart disease."* Malcolm X, "God's Angry Men," *Amsterdam News,* June 1, 1957.
130 *he rarely failed to deliver a command performance.* See "Mr. X Tells What Islan [*sic*] Means," *Amsterdam News,* April 20, 1957; and Malcolm X, "God's Angry Men," *Amsterdam News,* April 27, 1957.
131 *"beginning to realize that there is strength in numbers."* MX FBI, Memo, New York Office, April 30, 1958.
131 *and Ahmad Zaki el-Barail, the Egyptian attaché.* "2,000 at Moslem Feast in Harlem," *Amsterdam News,* July 20, 1957.
131 *an impressive lineup of speakers was present.* "New Yorkers to Honor Marcus Garvey," *Chicago Defender,* August 2, 1957.
131 *"being nothing but 'puppets for the white man.'"* "Moslem Speaker Electrifies Garvey Crowd," *Amsterdam News,* August 19, 1957.
132 *"information with photo showing full description."* Thomas A. Nielson, Chief Inspector, to Paul R. Taylor, Police Chief, Lansing, Michigan; Nielson to John W. Whearty, Chief of Police, Milton, Massachusetts; Nielson to Edward S. Piggins, Police Commissioner, Detroit, Michigan; Nielson to Michigan Parole Commission, Inkster, Michigan; Nielson to Walter Carroll, Chief of Police, Dedham, Massachusetts; Nielson to Superintendent of State Prison, Charlesten [*sic*], Massachusetts; and Nielson to Superintendent, Massachusetts State Reformatory, Concord Massachusetts, all May 15, 1957 in Malcolm X Bureau of Special Services (BOSS) file, New York Police Department.
132 *"does speak out, he is always too late."* "Malcolm X Will Lecture Four Weeks at Detroit Spot," *Pittsburgh Courier,* August 17, 1957.
133 *begin to take matters into his own hands.* "'Negroes, No Compromise on Civil Rights' Malcolm X," *Los Angeles Herald Dispatch,* August 22, 1957.
133 *They were hardly "revolutionaries."* W. Haywood Burns, "The Black Muslims in America: A Reinterpretation," *Race,* vol. 5, no. 1 (July 1963), pp. 29–31.
134 *would become head minister of Temple No. 1.* MX FBI, Memo, New York Office, April 30, 1958.
134 *in that city were "packed to capacity."* "Malcolm X Making Hit in Detroit," *Amsterdam News,* September 7, 1957.
134 *produced major gains for the Nation.* "Malcolm X Returns; Detroit Moslems Grow," *Amsterdam News,* October 26, 1957.
134 *advised that he take time off, but he adamantly refused.* DeCaro, *On the Side of My People,* p. 117; and "Malcolm Shabazz Speaker at DC Brotherhood Feast," *Amsterdam News,* November 30, 1959.
134 *for his protégé Louis X, the Boston temple minister.* "Malcolm X in Boston," *Amsterdam News,* November 9, 1957; and DeCaro, *On the Side of My People,* p. 117.
134 *he argued, "but a Jew can."* MX FBI, Memo, New York Office, June 22, 1961.
135 *"menace to society, but to world peace."* Telegram, Malcolm X to Stephen Kennedy, NYPD Commissioner, November 2, 1957, BOSS.
135 *name and address of his private physician.* Memorandum, Walter Upshur to the BOSS Commanding Officer, November 7, 1957, ibid.
135 *in Detroit, and soon after departed.* MX FBI, Correlation Summary, New York Office, August 22, 1961, p. 20.
135 *"uniting Negroes where it is heard."* "Malcolm X Speaks in Detroit Again," *Amsterdam News,* December 14, 1957.
135 *he was using this name widely by 1957.* DeCaro, *On the Side of My People,* p. 117.

136 *"hard-working, Christian-believing black woman."* Malcolm X and Haley, *Autobiography*, p. 274.
136 *Atlanta temple had doubled its membership.* DeCaro, *On the Side of My People*, p. 118.
136 *secure their release with only minor fines.* Ibid., p. 120; and "Moslem Fight R.R. Station Bias, Jailed," *Pittsburgh Courier*, March 7, 1957. The county solicitor hearing the case levied fines of $226 on each of the two Muslim men. Considering that the Muslims had severely beaten the white police officer who initially tried to arrest them, it was a remarkably lenient fine.
137 *"creation of the Northern white man."* Malcolm X and Haley, *Autobiography*, pp. 276–77.
137 *Columbia University's East Asian Institute.* James 67X Warden interview, July 24, 2007.
138 *"being arrested, I will never come back."* James 67X Warden interview, June 18, 2003.
138 *"This was not the case."* Ibid.
139 *at the Bronx's Montefiore Hospital.* Russell J. Rickford, *Betty Shabazz: A Life Before and After Malcolm X* (Naperville, IL: Sourcebooks, 2003), pp. 2–11, 23, 27, 31.
139 *"This man is totally malnourished!" she thought.* Ibid., p. 39.
139 *"nor drinks and is of high moral character."* MX FBI, Summary Report, New York Office, May 19, 1959, p. 20.
140 *Sundays reserved for the week's main religious service.* Malcolm X and Haley, *Autobiography*, pp. 231–32.
141 *"that if she complains she is justified."* Malcolm X to Elijah Muhammad, March 25, 1959. Copy in possession of author.
141 *"carry a gun, or telling a hen not to cackle."* Malcolm X and Haley, *Autobiography*, pp. 231–32.
142 *"control her if he expects to get her respect."* Ibid.
142 *chaos, or* fitna, *if not tightly controlled.* Robert Dannin observes that "most Muslim commentators regard sexuality as a purely carnal activity that will wreak chaos and confusion in the social body if it is not systematically controlled." See Dannin, *Black Pilgrimage to Islam*, p. 217.
142 *commitment toward an Islamic lifestyle.* Denny, *An Introduction to Islam*, pp. 300–301.
142 *reveal what they hide of their adornment.* Holy Qur'an, surah XXIV, verse 31.
143 *"wants a sterile wom[a]n?" he asked rhetorically.* See Muhammad, *Message to the Blackman in America*, especially chapter 35.
143 *"[and] that there will be economic stability."* Farah Jasmine Griffin interview, August 6, 2001.
143 *as well as other community concerns.* See Cynthia S'thembile West, "Revisiting Female Activism in the 1960s: The Newark Branch Nation of Islam," *Black Scholar*, vol. 26, nos. 3–4 (Fall 1996/Winter 1997), pp. 41–48.
144 *romantically attracted to her she might reject him.* Malcolm X and Haley *Autobiography*, pp. 231–34.
144 *that he thought Betty X was "a fine sister."* Ibid., p. 234.
145 *chief instigator of his lieutenant's marriage.* Rickford, *Betty Shabazz*, pp. 62–65, 66.
145 *deeply in love with Evelyn Williams.* Louis Farrakhan interview, December 27, 2007.
145 *pursued her "persistently and correctly."* Rickford, *Betty Shabazz*, pp. 62–66.
145 *packed her suitcase and made plans to fly to Detroit.* Ibid., pp. 66–70; and Malcolm X and Haley, *Autobiography*, pp. 234–35.
145 *but she was determined to have her way.* Rickford, *Betty Shabazz*, pp. 71–73.
145 *Malloys "were very friendly, and happily surprised."* Malcolm X and Haley, *Autobiography*, p. 235.
146 *"kissing and hugging . . . like Cinderella."* Ibid., pp. 235–36.
146 *"all the time. Maybe she did get me!"* Ibid., p. 236.
146 *ran from the building screaming.* Evanzz, *The Messenger*, p. 261.
147 *"who has been brought up under the devil can accept this."* Rickford, *Betty Shabazz*, p. 103; and James 67X Warden interview, July 24, 2007.
147 *"the greatest thing in my life."* Rickford, *Betty Shabazz*, p. 78.
148 *only name he had come up with was a boy's.* Ibid., p. 109.
148 *he virtually disappeared following the birth.* Malcolm X and Haley, *Autobiography*, p. 232; and MX FBI, Summary Report, New York Office, May 19, 1959, pp. 31–32.

148 *to speak at an NOI gathering.* MX FBI, Summary Report, New York Office, May 19, 1958, p. 6.
148 *before moving along to Newark, New Jersey.* Ibid., pp. 18, 22.
148 *he allowed her to continue working to clear these debts.* Malcolm X to Elijah Muhammad, March 25, 1959.
149 *at meetings held at the Normandie Hall in Los Angeles.* MX FBI, Summary Report, New York Office, November 19, 1958, pp. 6–10; "Build Heaven on Earth," *Los Angeles Herald Dispatch*, March 27, 1958.
149 *gala reception honoring the Republic of Pakistan.* "Moslems Celebrate Third Pakistan Republic Day in L.A.," *Los Angeles Herald Dispatch*, March 27, 1957.
149 *media "since it is controlled by the Zionists."* "Sees Aggressive Zionism as Threat to World Peace," *Los Angeles Herald Dispatch*, April 10, 1958; and "Arab Director, Malcolm X Hit U.S. Press, Radio, TV," *Amsterdam News*, May 3, 1958. At the April 7, 1958, press conference, Mendi denied that there was any conflict between "Arabs and Jews"; the only real difficulty existed between Arabs and "aggressive Zionists."
149 *African-American churches and the poverty of their worshippers.* "Christians Walk Out on Moslems," *Amsterdam News*, April 26, 1958.
149 *find among those standing his sister Ella.* Malcolm X and Haley, *Autobiography*, pp. 237–38.
149 *"she married and of being pregnant, and she cursed me too."* Malcolm X to Elijah Muhammad, March 25, 1959.
150 *"you and her were no longer equals."* Rickford, *Betty Shabazz*, p. 144.
150 *"(not able to engage in the act long enough to satisfy her)."* Malcolm X to Elijah Muhammad, March 25, 1959.
150 *on the ground floor of the Littles' duplex.* The 1958 police raid on Malcolm X's East Elmhurst, Queens, home is recounted in detail in "Three Moslems Seized as Police Fighters: Home of 'X' Group's Leader Site of Battle," *Amsterdam News*, May 24, 1958; "Moslems Await 'D-Day' in N.Y. Court," *Pittsburgh Courier*, May 24, 1958; and "Moslems Freed, Cry for Arrest of Cops," *Pittsburgh Courier*, March 28, 1959.
151 *(either in the ground-floor living quarters or in the basement.)* Memorandum, Detective William K. DeFossett to BOSS Commanding Officer, May 27, 1958, BOSS.
151 *all were eventually released on bail.* "Three Moslems Seized as Police Fighters," *Amsterdam News*; "Moslems Await 'D-Day' in N.Y. Court," *Pittsburgh Courier*; and "Moslems Freed, Cry for Arrest of Cops," *Pittsburgh Courier*, March 28, 1959.
152 *one press account, utterly amazed the police.* "Moslems Await 'D-Day' in N.Y. Court," *Pittsburgh Courier.*
152 *1958 Saviour's Day festivities in Chicago.* FBI—Betty Sanders (also known as Betty Shabazz and Betty X) file, Summary Report, New York Office, June 30, 1958.
152 *and another for $742.42 to Sacks Quality Stores, Inc.* FBI—Sanders, Summary Report, New York Office, December 9, 1964.
152 *so they can help their own people.* FBI—Sanders, Summary Report, New York Office, June 2, 1959. Betty Shabazz also gave a speech at the NOI meeting in Hartford, Connecticut, on September 13, 1959.
153 *speeches primarily based on the event.* MX FBI, Correlation Summary, New York Office, August 22, 1961, pp. 55–56.
153 *"key points that forced the jury into a deadlock."* "Moslems Freed, Cry for Arrest of Cops," *Pittsburgh Courier*; and Report of Little-Molette-Simmons Trial, Memorandum, March 27, 1959, BOSS.
154 *a surveillance update every six months.* MX FBI, Memo, New York Office, July 2, 1958.
154 *Jim Crow segregation and Northern discrimination.* As Oliver Jones, Jr., has observed, the Nation of Islam drew upon the traditional demands of black nationalism, but it was not primarily concerned with constructing an agenda and political strategy to achieve these objectives. The Muslims' "belief in a nation of their own never produced a political program for the establishment of such a national home," Jones noted. "Indeed, the Muslims looked to Allah instead of Washington for the ultimate solution." See Oliver Jones, Jr., "The Black Muslim Movement and the American Constitutional System," *Journal of Black Studies*, vol. 13, no. 4 (June 1983), pp. 417–37.

Chapter 6: "The Hate That Hate Produced"

156 *protesters by declaring racial gerrymandering illegal.* A good general reference is August Meier and Elliott Rudwick, *From Plantation to Ghetto,* third edition (New York: Hill and Wang, 1976), pp. 267–79.

156 *to investigating and publicizing racist crimes.* Myrlie Evers-Williams and Manning Marable, eds., *The Autobiography of Medgar Evers: A Hero's Life and Legacy Revealed Through His Writings, Letters and Speeches* (New York: Basic Civitas, 2005), pp. 14–15.

156 *of the new Southern Christian Leadership Conference (SCLC).* Devon W. Carbada and Donald Weise, eds., *Time on Two Crosses: The Collected Writings of Bayard Rustin* (San Francisco: Cleis, 2003), pp. x–xxv.

156 *American Committee for the Protection of the Foreign Born.* Martha Biondi, *To Stand and Fight: The Struggle for Civil Rights in Postwar New York City* (Cambridge: Harvard University Press, 2003), p. 162.

157 *to endear Robeson to white authorities.* Martin Bauml Duberman, *Paul Robeson* (New York: Ballantine, 1989), pp. 454–55, 460.

157 *to pressure his government to cancel the event.* Ibid., pp. 461–62.

157 *promptly charged him with kidnapping.* See Timothy B. Tyson, *Radio Free Dixie: Robert F. Williams and the Roots of Black Power* (Chapel Hill: University of North Carolina Press, 1999).

157 *conferences and rallies in more than two dozen cities.* Barbara Ransby, *Ella Baker and the Black Freedom Movement: A Radical Democratic Vision* (Chapel Hill: University of North Carolina Press, 2003), pp. 178–83.

158 *won more Harlem votes than in his previous elections.* See Charles Rosenberg, "Davis, Benjamin J., Jr.," in Paul Finkelman, ed., *Encyclopedia of African American History, 1896 to the Present: From the Age of Segregation to the Twenty-first Century,* vol. 2 (New York: Oxford University Press, 2009), pp. 14–15.

158 *the NAACP, also ran for the council.* Ransby, *Ella Baker and the Black Freedom Movement,* pp. 153–55, 157–58.

158 *assembly members; and ten of its 189 judges.* Biondi, *To Stand and Fight,* pp. 215–19.

158 *"couched in left-wing phraseology."* Harold Cruse, *The Crisis of the Negro Intellectual: From Its Origins to the Present* (New York: William Morrow, 1967), p. 227.

158 *its associations with the Marxist Left.* Ibid., p. 245.

159 *such notable intellectuals as Allen Ginsberg, C. Wright Mills, and I. F. Stone.* Jon Lee Anderson, *Che Guevara: A Revolutionary Life* (New York: Grove, 1997), pp. 399, 416, 409.

159 *sponsored Williams's first trip to Cuba.* Peniel E. Joseph, *Waiting 'Til the Midnight Hour* (New York: Henry Holt, 2006), pp. 29–30.

159 *"violence to successful revolutions."* Cruse, *The Crisis of the Negro Intellectual,* pp. 356–57.

160 *"know that the devil has no Justice for you."* Elijah Muhammad to Minister James 3X Shabazz, April 28, 1959. Copy in possession of author.

160 *presented the Nation of Islam in a favorable light.* See Al Nall, "Moslem Trial Begins," *Amsterdam News,* March 7, 1959; Al Nall, "Moslems Accuse Cops," *Amsterdam News,* March 14, 1959; and Al Nall, "Moslems Go Free," *Amsterdam News,* March 21, 1959.

160 *for a crusading African-American press.* "Say Paper Helped Free 5 Moslems," *Amsterdam News,* April 11, 1959.

160 *a familiar presence on New York–area television.* Val Adams, "Wallace May Get New TV Programs," *New York Times,* February 11, 1959.

160 *from American University and Yale (in 1944 and 1947 respectively).* See "Louis Lomax, 47, Dies in Car Crash," *New York Times,* August 1, 1970; David Shaw, "Louis Lomax, Black Author, Killed in Crash," *Los Angeles Times,* August 1, 1970; and "Author Lomax Killed When His Auto Overturns," *Chicago Tribune,* August 1, 1970.

160 *"skits over the air in the District of Columbia."* FBI—Louis E. Lomax file, Memo, M. A. Jones to Louis B. Nichols, February 2, 1956.

161 *during which time his wife had divorced him.* FBI—Lomax, Memo, Chicago Office, February 7, 1956.

161 *the Associated Negro Press in Washington.* Ibid.

161 *in magazines such as* Pageant, Coronet, *and* The Nation. FBI—Lomax, Memo, G. C. Moore to W. C. Sullivan, February 23, 1969. This memo states, "Bureau files reflect that Lomax is an unscrupulous charlatan who has been extremely critical of the FBI and the Director." The FBI also noted that Lomax's 1968 book, *To Kill a Black Man*, attributed the assassination to "the American Government, particularly the CIA ..."

161 *guests prior to their appearance on his show.* Walt Dutton, "Controversy Is Lomax Forte," *Los Angeles Times*, April 23, 1965.

161 *Elijah Muhammad's approval through Malcolm.* DeCaro, *On the Side of My People*, p. 134.

161 *to film Muhammad at a rally in Washington on May 31.* Louis E. Lomax, "10,000 Muslims Hold Meeting in Washington," *Amsterdam News*, June 6, 1959. Lomax reported in his story that "following the speech, Mr. Muhammad was given a police escort back to the hotel where, for the first time, he submitted to a filmed TV interview.... A reporter and camera crew were flown to Washington from New York for that purpose." In that interview, Muhammad predicted "the pending destruction of the white man will occur before 1970."

161 *"pertinent facts in refutation is not conscientious or constructive reporting."* Jack Gould, "Negro Documentary: Wallace's Guide to the 'Black Supremacy' Movement Challenged by Experts," *New York Times*, July 23, 1959.

162 *"an invasion by 'men from Mars.'"* Malcolm X and Haley, *Autobiography*, pp. 240–42.

162 *longest-running news feature program in television history.* See Mike Wallace with Gary Paul Gates, *Close Encounters* (New York: William Morrow, 1984); Susan King, "Q and A: Mike Wallace: 40 Years of Asking," *Los Angeles Times*, September 23, 1990; and Donna Rosenthal, "Mike Without Malice," *San Francisco Chronicle*, September 23, 1990.

162 *to exploit their connections with the NOI.* See M. S. Handler, "Author Describes Slaying of 3 Rights Workers in Mississippi," *New York Times*, October 26, 1964; Walt Dutton, "Controversy Is Lomax Forte"; and "Louis Lomax, 47, Dies in Car Crash," *New York Times*.

162 *"No enemy wants to see the so-called American Negro free and united."* DeCaro, *On the Side of My People*, pp. 134–35; MX FBI, Memo, New York Office, July 29, 1959; MX FBI, Summary Report, New York Office, November 17, 1959, pp. 34–35; and MX FBI, Correlation Summary, August 22, 1961, p. 55.

163 *under the title* The Black Muslims in America, *became the standard work for decades.* See C. Eric Lincoln, *The Black Muslims in America* (Boston: Beacon, 1961). Lincoln believed that the Nation of Islam, despite its unorthodox beliefs, had some legitimacy in claiming to be part of the larger Islamic faith community. His principal thesis, however, was that the Nation was essentially a black nationalist political movement that used Islam as the pretext for demanding complete separation from white Americans and their religion, Christianity.

163 *"and work at a job that leads only to a dead end."* See Louis E. Lomax, *When the Word Is Given* ... (Cleveland: World Publishing, 1963); and Herb Nipson, "Black Muslims—Promise and Threat," *Chicago Tribune*, November 10, 1963.

163 *"spiritual growth among the Negroes of America."* Advertisement, "Hon. Elijah Muhammad/The Messenger Magazine," in *Amsterdam News*, November 7, 1959.

164 *and distribution also shifted to Chicago.* DeCaro, *On the Side of My People*, pp. 180–81.

164 *"do without our wonderful MGT Sisters? (smile)."* Malcolm to Betty Shabazz, April 1, 1959, MXC-S, box 3, folder 2.

164 *some stamps in the envelope he mailed to her.* Malcolm to Betty Shabazz, April 1, 1959, MXC-S, box 3, folder 2.

165 *"lifting their voices to Allah five times a day."* DeCaro, *On the Side of My People*, p. 135.

165 *"Believers in Allah recognize no such thing as race."* Yusuf Ibrahim, Letter to the Editor, *Pittsburgh Courier*, March 1, 1958.

165 *"all of them, though the polytheists may be adverse."* Elijah Muhammad, *Message to the Blackman in America*, front cover.

165 *Egypt's president, Gamal Abdel Nasser.* "Mister Muhammad's Message to African-Asian Conference," *Pittsburgh Courier*, January 18, 1958.

166 *scheduled from June 9 to June 16.* MX FBI, Memo, Washington Office, July 27, 1959; and MX FBI, Summary Report, New York Office, November 17, 1959, pp. 31–32.

166 *he continued carrying out his duties throughout June.* MX FBI, Summary Report, New York Office, November 17, 1959, pp. 8, 21; and MX FBI, Correlation Summary, New York Office, August 22, 1961, p. 22.

166 *religious leaders at Al-Azhar University.* DeCaro, *On the Side of My People*, p. 139.

166 *"all mortals are equal and brothers."* "Arabs Send Warm Greetings to 'Our Brothers' of Color in U.S.A.," *Pittsburgh Courier*, August 15, 1959.

167 *"are destined to play a key role."* Ibid.

167 *"for administrative jim-crow in the United States."* Ibid.

168 *and by African-American newspapers.* MX FBI, Summary Report, New York Office, November 17, 1959, p. 33.

168 *"and robbed of his name and wisdom."* Ibid., p. 23.

168 *made umrah, a spiritually motivated visit.* DeCaro, *On the Side of My People*, p. 168.

169 *Muhammad arrived back home on January 6, 1960.* "Muhammad Speaks," *Los Angeles Herald Tribune*, January 14, 1960.

169 *in keeping with orthodox Islam.* DeCaro, *On the Side of My People*, p. 23.

169 *"that he would make such charges."* MX FBI, Memo, New York Office, March 18, 1960.

170 *"and their own teachings are filled with it."* Ibid.

170 *exchange went on for more than two hours.* See "Defends Muslim Leader at Meet," *Chicago Defender*, March 15, 1960.

170 *black leader who so sharply opposed its policies.* Ibid.

170 *in the streets and along the sidewalks.* See FBI—Leon 4X Phillips (also known as Leon Ameer) file, Summary Report, New York Office, January 1962; and "Malcolm X on 'Unity,'" in Lomax, *When the Word Is Given*, pp. 128–35. This speech is reproduced in John Bracey, Jr., August Meier, and Elliott Rudwick, eds., *Black Nationalism in America* (New York: Bobbs-Merrill, 1970), pp. 413–20. A typed manuscript of Malcolm's speech is located in MXC-S, box 5, folder 1.

170 *"but have as yet not received."* Lomax, *When the Word Is Given*, p. 129.

171 *significant increase in BOSS's surveillance.* Memorandum, BOSS Detective Ernest B. Latty to the Commanding Officer, May 30, 1960, BOSS.

171 *himself to Mosque No. 7 at all hours.* Ibid., pp. 4–12.

171 *"Elijah Muhammad was a messenger of God."* Louis Farrakhan interview, December 27, 2007.

171 *Malcolm might run for public office.* MX FBI, Summary Report, New York Office, November 17, 1960, pp. 17–18.

171 *selling records featuring "A White Man's Heaven Is a Black Man's Hell."* See *Yale Daily News* (New Haven), October 21, 1960; MX FBI, Summary Report, New York Office, November 17, 1960, pp. 22–23; and MX FBI, Summary Report, New York Office, May 17, 1961, p. 17.

172 *"We are used to sleeping in the open air."* Max Frankel, "Angry Castro Quits Hotel in Row Over Bill; Moves to Harlem," *New York Times*, September 20, 1960; "Castro Moves Out of Hotel in Huff, Takes His Party to One in Harlem," *Washington Post*, September 20, 1960; and Jules Du Bois, "Irate Castro Moves to Harlem Hotel," *Chicago Tribune*, September 20, 1960.

172 *"much propaganda as possible out of his move."* Mel Opotowsky, "Castro Settles Down in Harlem, Paying Double, Minding Manners," *Washington Post*, September 21, 1960; and Philip Benjamin, "Theresa Hotel on 125th St. Is Unruffled by Its Cuban Guests," *New York Times*, September 21, 1960.

172 *"He knows what's hip and bugs the squares."* "Nikita Visits Castro in Harlem," *Chicago Defender*, September 21, 1960; Harrison E. Salisbury, "Russian Goes to Harlem, Then Hugs Cuban at U.N.," *New York Times*, September 21, 1960; and "Police Break Up Harlem Crowd as Groups Mingle," *New York Times*, September 22, 1960.

173 *to "fish" Castro, inviting him to join the NOI.* "Fidel Castro," in Jenkins, ed., *Malcolm X Encyclopedia*, p. 144.

173 *visit Cuba, but made no commitments.* Carlos Moore, *Castro, the Blacks, and Africa* (Los Angeles: University of California Center for Afro-American Studies, 1988), p. 120.

173 *"event of any anti-Castro demonstrations."* MX FBI, Correlation Summary, New York Office, August 22, 1961, p. 27.

173 *about the meeting between Malcolm and Castro.* Moore, *Castro, the Blacks, and Africa,* p. 120.

173 *like Raymond and Ethel Sharrieff.* Ibid., p. 162.

173 *"and Muhammad might do it to save face."* MX FBI, Summary Report, New York Office, November 17, 1959, p. 9.

174 *semiautonomy and flexibility that he himself enjoyed.* The December 1961 issue of *Muhammad Speaks* raised Wallace's refusal "to answer an army draft call because all preachers, priests, ministers and rabbis have been exempt from military duty." Wallace's conviction and imprisonment, like that of his father during the 1940s, was "for teaching the religion of Islam!" See "Courts Jail Muslim Ministers; Taught Negroes in Faith of Islam Religion!" *Muhammad Speaks*, December 1961.

174 *"what the people were saying and correct me."* Louis Farrakhan interview, December 27, 2007.

175 *that Malcolm would sacrifice to his loyalty to the Nation.* Ibid.

176 *coordinators caved in and "disinvited" him.* Corbado and Weise, eds., *Time on Two Crosses*, pp. 164–65.

176 *student protests at City University of New York.* Rosenberg, "Davis, Benjamin J., Jr.," in Finkelman, ed., *Encyclopedia of African American History*, pp. 14–15.

176 *asserting Elijah Muhammad was "not a politician."* Corbado and Weise, eds., *Time on Two Crosses*, pp. 165–66.

177 *"to go, they're going to want to stay."* Ibid., pp. 168–71.

177 *publicized police brutality cases in the state.* Evers-Williams and Marable, eds., *The Autobiography of Medgar Evers*, pp. 181–82.

178 *desegregationist protesters into the Deep South.* Manning Marable, *Race, Reform and Rebellion: The Second Reconstruction and Beyond in Black America, 1945–2006* (Jackson: University Press of Mississippi, 2007), p. 62.

178 *meetings in Tampa, Miami, and Jacksonville.* MX FBI, Summary Report, New York Office, May 17, 1961, pp. 5–8.

178 *to participate in local NOI meetings.* MX FBI, Summary Report, New York Office, May 17, 1961, p. 6.

178 *"traitors who assisted integration leaders."* Ibid., p. 19.

179 *publicly admit his role until years later.* DeCaro, *On the Side of My People*, pp. 180–81.

179 *Ku Klux Klan Imperial Wizard Robert M. Shelton.* Gardell, *In the Name of Elijah Muhammad*, p. 273.

179 *"movement, using the Negro as a tool."* MX FBI, Summary Report, New York Office, May 17, 1961, pp. 5–19.

Chapter 7: "As Sure As God Made Green Apples"

180 *of her birth father, Shelman Sandlin.* Rickford, *Betty Shabazz*, pp. 1, 105.

180 *he even stuffed forty dollars into the envelope.* Malik Shabazz to Mrs. Malik Shabazz, January 25, 1961, MXC-S, box 3, folder 2.

181 *"It looks like she will have to be put down."* Evanzz, *The Messenger*, p. 211.

181 *in Lynwood, California, on March 30, 1960.* Stanley G. Robertson, "Paternity Charge Faces Muhammad: It's Denied," *Los Angeles Sentinel*, July 9, 1964; "Ex-Sweetheart of Malcolm X Accuses Elijah," *Amsterdam News*, July 11, 1964; and Evanzz, *The Messenger*, p. 218.

181 *for him to get what he wanted from them.* Evanzz, *The Messenger*, pp. 238–39.

182 *"I'm sick of being treated like a dog."* Ibid., pp. 215–17.

182 *"under control in his own household."* Ibid., p. 218.

182 *"obtain policy and future plans of Muhammad."* Ibid., pp. 218–19.

183 *take long for the new arrangement to sour.* Ibid., pp. 238–39, 248.

183 *but neither was formally charged.* Ibid., pp. 248–49.

184 *"into a 'diplomatic withdrawal' of his earlier statement."* "Malcolm X Rips JFK Advisor," *Pittsburgh Courier,* February 4, 1961; Robert James Branham, "'I Was Gone on Debating': Malcolm X's Prison Debates and Public Confrontations," *Argumentation and Advocacy,* vol. 31 (Winter 1995), p. 125; and MX FBI, Summary Report, New York Office, May 17, 1961, p. 14.

184 *"Muslims Give the JFK Man a Fit."* "Muslims Give the JFK Man a Fit," *New Jersey Herald News,* February 4, 1961.

185 *to accommodate the anticipated audience.* See "Invited by Campus NAACP," *Pittsburgh Courier,* February 11, 1961; "Muslim Malcolm X Out as Howard U. History Speaker," *Pittsburgh Courier,* February 25, 1961; and "Malcolm May Not Talk at Howard," *Amsterdam News,* February 25, 1961. DeCaro states that an NAACP official intervened to cancel the lecture. See DeCaro, *On the Side of My People,* p. 174.

185 *"on them when we get there."* DeCaro, *On the Side of My People,* p. 174.

186 *was his identity as "A BLACK MAN!"* "1,500 Hear Integration-Non-Segregation Debate," *Chicago Defender,* November 11, 1961; and "Malcolm X's Howard University Lecture," October 30, 1961, MXC-S, box 5, folder 15.

187 *"I feel a reluctance to face my class tomorrow."* "1,500 Hear Integration-Non-Segregation Debate."

187 *"must have some land of our own."* "Harvard Hears Malcolm X, NAACP Speaker," *Amsterdam News,* April 8, 1961; and "The Harvard Law School Forum of March 24, 1961," in Archie Epps, ed., *The Malcolm X Speeches at Harvard* (New York: Paragon House, 1961), pp. 115–31.

188 *would often dictate parts of his speeches.* Louis Farrakhan interview, December 27, 2007.

188 *John Ali could monitor the addresses.* FBI—Gravitt, Summary Report, New York Office, January 23, 1962.

188 *which had to be relocated to the local YMCA.* "UC Forbids," *San Francisco Chronicle,* May 7, 1961; "Malcolm 'X' Raps UC," *San Francisco Chronicle,* May 9, 1961; "West Coast University Bars," *Afro-American* (Baltimore), May 20, 1961; and MX FBI, Memo, San Francisco Office, May 19, 1961.

188 *debate "hate" journalist Louis Lomax.* MX FBI, Summary Report, New York Office, May 17, 1961, p. 18.

188 *Malcolm denied that such a position existed.* MX FBI, Summary Report, New York Office, May 17, 1961, p. 17; and DeCaro, *On the Side of My People,* p. 182.

188 *"house of bondage four thousand years ago."* "A Partial Transcript of a Sermon by Malcolm X at Elder Solomon Lightfoot Michaux's New York Church of God, June 16, 1961," in DeCaro, *Malcolm and the Cross,* pp. 223–35. Michaux was one of the first African-American radio and television evangelists. Michaux's brother Lewis operated a black bookstore on Harlem's 125th Street that was a popular meeting place for black nationalists.

189 *it could very well be "the start of a holy war."* FBI—Gravitt, Summary Report, New York Office, April 14, 1961.

189 *and demanded secretary Dag Hammarskjöld's firing.* Martin Meredith, *The First Dance of Freedom: Black Africa in the Post-War Era* (New York: Harper and Row, 1984), pp. 150–51.

190 *"no one to use me against the nationalists."* "Muslims to Sue Adlai Stevenson," *Amsterdam News,* February 25, 1961; "Muslims Sue Dailies," *Amsterdam News,* March 11, 1961; MX FBI, Summary Report, New York Office, May 17, 1961, pp. 15–16; and MX FBI, Correlation Summary, New York Office, September 25, 1963, pp. 8, 24; "Americans Active in Demonstration at U.N. Meeting," *Atlanta Daily World,* February 16, 1961; "Mob Invades U.N., 21 Hurt!" *Chicago Daily Tribune,* February 16, 1961; "U.S. Blames Reds for Negroes Act," *Chicago Defender,* February 16, 1961.

190 *her acquaintance with him several years later.* Maya Angelou, *The Heart of a Woman* (New York: Random House, 1981), pp. 166–70.

190 *"and will not be a 'spooky war.'"* FBI—Gravitt, Summary Report, New York Office,

January 23, 1962; and MX FBI, Correlation Summary, New York Office, August 25, 1963, pp. 25, 26.

190 *to achieve under the "American flag."* FBI—Gravitt, Summary Report, New York Office, January 23, 1962.

191 *NOI duly sold discounted copies of the book.* Elijah Muhammad to Malcolm X, March 23, 1961, MXC-S, box 3, folder 8.

191 *"August fourteenth, 217 West 125th Street."* Telegram, A. Phillip Randolph to Malcolm X, August 11, 1961, MXC-S, box 3, folder 13.

192 *"with the white man, we must separate."* FBI—Phillips, Summary Report, New York Office, January 1962.

193 *"think this will accomplish anything," he declared.* Harold L. Keith, "Leaders Bury Differences, Merge: New York Group Formed to Uplift Negro Masses," *Pittsburgh Courier*, October 7, 1961.

193 *name, in parentheses, was written "Malik el Shabazz."* Evelyn Cunningham, "Panel Will Continue; Malcolm X and Randolph Spark Rally in Harlem," *Pittsburgh Courier*, September 16, 1961.

194 *"blond hair, and he has a white skin."* FBI—Gravitt, Summary Report, New York Office, January 23, 1962.

194 *at the top of the command structure.* FBI—Raymond X Sharrieff file, Summary Report, Chicago Office, February 8, 1962, and August 8, 1962.

194 *cash register, and resentment began to grow.* James 67X Warden interview, June 18, 2003.

194 *"making jokes about sexual nonperformance."* Ibid.

195 *local captains directly responsible to Malcolm.* Clegg, *An Original Man*, pp. 113, 181. Goldman directly disputes Clegg on this issue. According to Goldman, "A 1961 administrative decree had made the temple captains answerable only to Chicago." See Goldman, *The Death and Life of Malcolm X*, p. 110.

195 *that would have meant for Sharrieff's continued authority.* FBI—Gravitt, Summary Report, New York Office, January 11, 1963.

195 *"among the masses they would lead to a black Utopia."* DeCaro, *On the Side of My People*, p. 177.

196 *of whom 737 were defined as active.* Secretary's Account of Records, Mosque No. 7. Copy in possession of author.

196 *"Everybody got a story."* James 67X Warden interview, July 24, 2007.

196 *at a Seventh Avenue nightclub.* FBI—Charles 37X Morris (also known as Charles Kenyatta) file, Correlation Summary, New York Office, August 4, 2006; FBI—Morris, Memo, Washington Office, November 6, 1968; and FBI—Morris, Memo, New York Office to the Director, March 13, 1968.

196 *was discharged on September 13, 1946.* FBI—Morris, Memo, New York Office, March 13, 1968.

196 *where the latter was assistant minister.* Ibid.; and Charles Kenyatta, Oral History Interview, 1970, Moorland-Spingarn Research Center, Manuscript Division, Howard University Library.

197 *"mixed type, mildly depressed but cooperative."* FBI—Morris, Memo, New York Office, March 13, 1968.

197 *he described as a "really beautiful childhood."* Mark Jacobson, "The Man Who Didn't Shoot Malcolm X," *New York*, October 1, 2007, p. 41.

197 *he was sentenced to twelve months in prison.* Ibid., p. 40.

197 *"rescue, bring relief or salvation."* John L. Esposito, *The Oxford Dictionary of Islam* (New York: Oxford University Press, 2003), p. 138.

197 *adhered rigidly to Muslim dietary laws.* Jacobson, pp. 40–41.

197 *"I would be the first one on the scene."* Thomas 15X Johnson (also known as Khalil Islam) interview, September 29, 2004.

198 *that had also fascinated Frantz Fanon.* Ibid.

198 *"grow to be hated when you become well known."* Malcolm X and Haley, *Autobiography*, p. 270.

199 greatly inflated image of his party's actual number. See William H. Schmaltz, Hate: George Lincoln Rockwell and the American Nazi Party (Washington, D.C.: Batsford Brassey, 1999).

199 "and admirable human beings in spite of their color." On the connections between the American Nazi Party and the Nation of Islam, see Clegg, An Original Man, pp. 152–56; and Schmaltz, Hate, pp. 119–20.

199 and the races dwelled in separate states. Clegg, An Original Man, pp. 154–55.

200 "You got the biggest hand you ever got." Schmaltz, Hate, pp. 120–21; and "Separation—or Death: Muslim Watchword," Amsterdam News, July 1, 1961.

200 "its mishandling of the Black Man." George Lincoln Rockwell, "The Jew: Moment of Lies in the South," The Rockwell Report, January 3, 1962.

201 "Muhammad is right—separation or death!" Schmaltz, Hate, pp. 133–34; and "U.S. Nazi Boss Among 3,000 at Rally," Chicago Tribune, February 26, 1962.

201 "Muhammad used to scare blacks into the NOI." Clegg, An Original Man, p. 154.

201 "be separated to get justice and freedom." "Rockwell and Co.—They Speak for All White," Muhammad Speaks, April 1962.

201 "doesn't necessarily mean we gotta kill each other." Schmaltz, Hate, pp. 159–60, 201. Rockwell continued to cite the views of Malcolm X as a justification for his own racist agenda, up to the time of his death in 1967. During an interview with Alex Haley, published in Playboy magazine in April 1966, for instance, Rockwell declared that "the harder you people push for that [integration], the madder white people are going to get. . . . Malcolm X said the same thing I'm saying." See "Interview with George Lincoln Rockwell," Playboy, vol. 13, no. 4 (April 1966), pp. 71–72, 74, 76–82, 154, 156.

201 should have favored Rustin. FBI—Gravitt, Summary Report, New York Office, January 11, 1963.

201 "'he couldn't be talking about me—I'm the liberal.'" John D'Emilio, Lost Prophet: The Life and Times of Bayard Rustin (New York: Free Press, 2003), p. 324; and Goldman, The Death and Life of Malcolm X, p. 67.

202 Mosque No. 23 in Buffalo, New York. MX FBI, Summary Report, New York Office, May 17, 1962, p. 7; and FBI—Gravitt, Summary Report, New York Office, January 11, 1963.

202 at Harlem's Rockland Palace. FBI—Gravitt, Summary Report, New York Office, October 18, 1962; and FBI—Benjamin 2X Goodman (also known as Benjamin Karim) file, Summary Report, New York Office, January 11, 1963.

202 "when the Government shows interest?" Elijah Muhammad to Malcolm X, February 15, 1962, MXC-S, box 3, folder 8.

203 "made to suffer, morning, noon and night." Malcolm X and James Farmer, "Separation or Integration: A Debate," Dialogue, vol. 2, no. 3 (May 1962), pp. 14–18.

203 the black middle class that opposed desegregation. Ibid.

203 that Farmer was married to a white woman. Ibid.

204 "boycotting, withholding their patronage." Ibid.

204 partnership between the two men in the year to come. "Malcolm X Packs Powell's Church," no date, MXC-S, box 5, folder 17. Also see FBI—Gravitt, Summary Report, New York Office, January 11, 1963; FBI—Phillips, Summary Report, New York Office, March 21, 1963.

204 selling bulk copies of Muhammad Speaks. "Louis Farrakhan," in Jenkins, ed., Malcolm X Encyclopedia, pp. 218–19; and Evanzz, The Messenger, pp. 296–97.

205 "would have liked to [have been] in her position." Rickford, Betty Shabazz, pp. 143–44.

205 certainly provide for Betty and their children. Ibid., pp. 144–45.

206 against racially restrictive housing covenants. See Douglas Flamming, Bound for Freedom: Black Los Angeles in Jim Crow America (Berkeley: University of California Press, 2005), p. 69.

206 continued to be a problem well into the 1960s. Stephen Meyer Grant, As Long as They Don't Move Next Door: Segregation and Racial Conflict in American Neighborhoods (Lanham, MD: Rowman and Littlefield, 2000), pp. 178–83.

206 By 1960, 468,000 blacks resided in Los Angeles County. On the economic conditions of

blacks in Los Angeles, see Josh Sides, *L.A. City Limits: African American Los Angeles from the Great Depression to the Present* (Berkeley: University of California Press, 2003). The best study documenting the socioeconomic and political factors leading up to the 1965 Watts riots in South Central Los Angeles is Gerald Horne, *Fire This Time: The Watts Uprising and the 1960s* (Charlottesville: University of Virginia Press, 1995).

206 *to settle a local factional dispute.* Frederick Knight, "Justifiable Homicide, Police Brutality, or Governmental Repression? The 1962 Los Angeles Police Shooting of Seven Members of the Nation of Islam," *Journal of Negro History*, vol. 79, no. 2 (Spring 1974), pp. 182–96.

206 *"violence or any other means."* Ibid.

206 *acquitted the Muslims on all charges.* Ibid.; and "Study Shows Los Angeles Police Were Investigating Muslims at Time of Riot," *Amsterdam News*, May 12, 1962.

207 *mosque, they approached with suspicion.* Knight, "Justifiable Homicide, Police Brutality, or Governmental Repression?" pp. 12–196; and DeCaro, *On the Side of My People*, p. 184.

207 *"that Stokes's death was 'justifiable.'"* Goldman, *The Death and Life of Malcolm X*, p. 97.

207 *"What the hell are you here for?"* Ibid., pp. 97–98.

207 *"came out of the street with gangster leanings."* Louis Farrakhan interview, December 27, 2007.

208 *"Brothers volunteered for it."* James 67X Warden interview, June 18, 2003.

208 *"rather than go out with the struggle of our people."* Louis Farrakhan interview, December 27, 2007.

208 *"You're black—that's enough."* MX FBI, Summary Report, New York Office, November 16, 1962, pp. 17–18; and "Conduct Rites for California Black Muslim Riot Victim," *Chicago Defender*, May 7, 1962.

209 *"of the followers of the Honorable Elijah."* Louis Farrakhan interview, December 27, 2007.

209 *"an aggressor to come into their mosque."* Clegg, *An Original Man*, p. 171.

209 *Roland Stokes submitted and was killed.* James 67X Warden interview, June 18, 2003.

209 *"It would have been a trap."* Goldman, *The Death and Life of Malcolm X*, p. 98.

Chapter 8: From Prayer to Protest

211 *"any black person anywhere on this earth."* Knight, "Justifiable Homicide, Police Brutality, or Governmental Repression?," p. 190.

211 *in front of the Hotel Theresa.* "Malcolm X Heads Rally Sunday," *Amsterdam News*, May 26, 1962; FBI—Gravitt, Summary Report, New York Office, January 11, 1963; and FBI—Phillips, Summary Report, New York Office, March 21, 1963.

212 *"a religious solution will fit the problem of Police Brutality."* Minister John Shabazz to Brother Minister, June 1, 1962, MXC-S, box 12, folder 1.

212 *"call on our God—He gets rid of 120 of them."* Jack V. Fox, "Negro Leaders Lambaste Malcolm X's Delight in Death of Atlanta Whites," *Chicago Defender*, July 14, 1962. Also see Clegg, *An Original Man*, p. 201.

212 *"developed into a large-scale hatred of whites."* Fox, "Negro Leaders Lambaste Malcolm X's Delight in Death of Atlanta Whites."

212 *"fanatical" and "anti-white organization."* MX FBI, Memo, Director to French Legal Attaché, August 8, 1962.

213 *"word 'freedom' out of your vocabulary."* Wallace Turner, "Militancy Urged on U.S. Negroes," *New York Times*, November 26, 1962.

213 *"would be eliminated from the mosque."* MX FBI, Summary Report, New York Office, November 16, 1962, p. 8; FBI—Gravitt, Summary Report, New York Office, January 11, 1963; and FBI—Sharrieff, Summary Report, Chicago Office, February 12, 1963.

215 *"self-defense is granted throughout the world."* FBI—Gravitt, Summary Report, New York Office, January 11, 1963.

216 *moved toward these ideas long before Chicago.* "Muhammad Asks for Black State, Tax Exemptions," *Chicago Defender*, July 16, 1962; FBI—Gravitt, Summary Report, New York Office, January 11, 1963; and FBI—Sharrieff, Summary Report, Chicago Office, February 12, 1963.

216 *"coming at the cadenced pauses in his oratory."* H. D. Quigg, "2,000 Jam Harlem Square to Hear Muslim Leaders Extol Their Cause," *Chicago Defender*, July 24, 1962; and FBI—Gravitt, Summary Report, New York Office, January 11, 1963.

216 *Malcolm's old sparring partner Bayard Rustin.* "2,500 at Moslem Rally," *Amsterdam News*, July 28, 1962.

217 *the feminized Arabic version of Elijah.* Rickford, *Betty Shabazz*, p. 123; and Clegg, *An Original Man*, pp. 180–81.

217 *Malcolm even briefly addressed the strikers.* MX FBI, Summary Report, New York Office, November 16, 1962, p. 23; and MX FBI, Correlation Summary, New York Office, September 25, 1963, p. 17.

217 *hopes of prompting a federal investigation of the NOI.* Taylor Branch, *Pillar of Fire* (New York: Touchstone, 1998), p. 12.

217 *"be a Nazi than whatever Mr. Yorty is."* "Mayor Yorty Says Cult Backs 'Hate,'" *New York Times*, July 27, 1962.

217 *prominent role in determining the course of the case.* Branch, *Pillar of Fire*, pp. 10–11.

217 *"impaneled jury because of the lack of sufficient numbers of Negroes."* MX FBI, Summary Report, New York Office, November 16, 1962, p. 19.

218 *except to cancel all his remaining college appearances.* Ibid., p. 24.

218 *"and the sort of Ivy League suit (and bald head)."* Peter Goldman interview, July 12, 2004.

218 *it also earned him Malcolm's attention.* See Peter Goldman, "Black Muslims Fail to Flourish Here," *St. Louis Globe-Democrat*, January 2, 1962.

218 *"understand the Nation of Islam?"* Peter Goldman interview, July 12, 2004.

219 *"moment you saw him, [you felt] this incredible presence."* Ibid.

219 *Louis X's "A White Man's Heaven Is a Black Man's Hell."* Goldman, *The Death and Life of Malcolm X*, p. 6.

219 *"device for disarming the blacks and, worse still, unmanning them."* Ibid.

219 *still believing "the threat was useful."* Peter Goldman interview, July 12, 2004.

220 *years of covert surveillance, but all of it unattributed.* Marable, *Living Black History*, p. 150.

221 *"So it began eating away at [my] brother."* Louis Farrakhan interview, December 27, 2007.

221 *University of Bridgeport because of "throat trouble."* MX FBI, Summary Report, New York Office, November 16, 1962, p. 24.

221 *also found employment as a building supervisor.* FBI—Goodman, Summary Report, New York Office, September 8, 1960.

221 *a "specialist in Islamic literature and history."* Ibid., October 27, 1961.

221 *to establish an NOI mosque in Bridgeport, Connecticut.* Ibid., October 17, 1962.

222 *that year was named the mosque's "main speaker."* Ibid.

222 *"Not in the buddy sense. He was always in command."* Goldman, *The Death and Life of Malcolm X*, p. 19.

222 *"If you leave again, I'm not coming after you."* Rickford, *Betty Shabazz*, pp. 105–6.

222 *"that I would defend him. . . . It was a good place for Betty to be."* Louis Farrakhan interview, December 27, 2007.

223 *"get to the grade school level in Mississippi."* Goldman, *The Death and Life of Malcolm X*, pp. 8, 96.

223 *he would punch him "right in the mouth."* FBI—Gravitt, Summary Report, New York Office, January 11, 1963.

224 *among those who "suffer" from a "colonial mentality."* Malcolm X to the Editor, "What *Courier* Readers Think: Muslim vs. Moslem!," *Pittsburgh Courier*, October 6, 1962; and Travel Diaries (Transcription): Middle East and West Africa, April–May 1964, MXC-S, box 5, folder 18.

224 *"that they are being led straight to Hell."* Yahya Hayari to the Editor, "What *Courier* Readers Think: A Blast at Muhammad," *Pittsburgh Courier*, October 27, 1962.

224 *"from the evils of this Christian world overnight."* Malcolm X to the Editor, "*Amsterdam News* Readers Write," *Amsterdam News*, November 24, 1962; and Edward Curtis, IV, "Islamism and Its African American Muslim Critics: Black Muslims in the Era of the Arab Cold War," *American Quarterly*, vol. 59, no. 3 (September 2007), pp. 88–89.

224 *literature and asked Osman for more.* DeCaro, *On the Side of My People*, pp. 201–2; and Curtis, "Islamism and Its African American Critics," p. 90.

224 *"Christians call him Christ, Jews call him Jehovah."* Ibid., p. 159.

225 *Malcolm, upset, left in a waiting automobile.* Ibid., pp. 159–60.

225 *all the way from Louisville to hear Elijah Muhammad speak.* There is a massive literature about Muhammad Ali (Cassius Clay). For a general introduction to the subject, see: David Remnick, *King of the World: Muhammad Ali and the Rise of an American Hero* (New York: Random House, 1998); John Miller and Aaron Kenedi, eds., *Muhammad Ali: Ringside* (Boston: Bullfinch, 1999); Anthony O. Edmonds, *Muhammad Ali: A Biography* (Westport, CT: Greenwood, 2006); and Mike Marqusee, *Redemption Song: Muhammad Ali and the Spirit of the Sixties* (New York: Verso, 1999).

226 *"I said to myself, listen, this man's saying something!"* Interview with Muhammad Ali by Alex Haley, in Miller and Kenedi, eds., *Muhammad Ali: Ringside*, pp. 39, 42.

226 *"the first time I ever felt spiritual in my life."* Edmonds, *Muhammad Ali*, p. 37.

226 *"down-to-earth youngster," as he later related.* Remnick, *King of the World*, p. 165.

227 *"It certainly rubbed off on Ali."* Ibid.

227 *fund-raising drive and teaching classes for two weeks.* MX FBI, Summary Report, New York Office, May 17, 1962, p. 11.

227 *priest of black cultural nationalism, known as Maulana Karenga.* "Racial Militancy and Pride Urged at West Coast Rally," *Chicago Defender*, November 28, 1962.

227 *"punctuated the statements made by Malcolm X."* Wallace Turner, "Militancy Urged on U.S. Negroes," *New York Times*, November 26, 1962.

228 *"the white man. We must solve it for ourselves."* Ibid.; Robin D. G. Kelley and Betsy Esch, "Black Like Mao: Red China and Black Revolution," *Souls*, vol. 1, no. 4 (Fall 1999), pp. 6–41.

228 *while selling* Muhammad Speaks *in Times Square.* DeCaro, *On the Side of My People*, p. 185; and "Jail Term," *Militant* (New York), February 4, 1963.

228 *to court, but he could not condone cowardice.* FBI—Gravitt, Summary Report, New York Office, January 27, 1964.

228 *suppression of press freedom, and "the freedom of religious expression."* Telegram, Malcolm X to Mayor Robert Wagner, New York City, January 2, 1963, MXC-S, box 5, folder 18.

228 *he told the press, before filing formal complaints.* "Muslims Protest Rights Violation by Police," *Chicago Defender*, January 10, 1963; "Rights Violated," *Democrat and Chronicle* (Rochester, NY), January 8, 1963; "Muslim Assails," *Democrat and Chronicle*, February 15, 1963; and DeCaro, *On the Side of My People*, p. 185.

228 *"that the whole Dark World is with them."* DeCaro, *On the Side of My People*, p. 185.

228 *"tired of hearing about Muslims being pistol-whipped."* FBI—Gravitt, Summary Report, New York Office, January 27, 1964.

229 *newspaper salesmen were sentenced to sixty days in jail.* See *Muhammad Speaks*, February 4, 1963; and *Militant*, February 4, 1963.

229 *"for a wind to come along and fan the breeze."* Malcolm X address, "Twenty Million Black People in a Political, Economic and Mental Prison," in Bruce Perry, ed., *Malcolm X: The Last Speeches* (New York: Pathfinder, 1989), pp. 25–57.

229 *or accomplishment that black people want.* Ibid.

229 *"They usually go and use the economic weapon."* Ibid. Also see "Muslim Leader Asks Negro Nation in U.S.," *Chicago Defender*, January 26, 1963.

230 *"if the Negro could 'speak as an American.'"* "Meredith, Gantt Entries 'Hypocritical': Malcolm X," *Chicago Defender*, January 31, 1963.

230 *plan for a separate black state inside the United States.* MX FBI, Memo, New York Office, May 6, 1963.

230 *his responsibility. No one was arrested.* DeCaro, *On the Side of My People*, p. 185; and MX FBI, Summary Report, New York Office, May 16, 1963, p. 19.

231 *for their bail had been forwarded by Elijah Muhammad.* MX FBI, Summary, New York Office, May 16, 1963, pp. 18–20.

231 *hundreds of protesters down affluent midtown Manhattan streets.* Ibid.

231 *"denied the leadership if he wants it."* Alfred Balk and Alex Haley, "Black Merchants of Hate," *Saturday Evening Post*, vol. 236 (January 26, 1963), pp. 67–74.

232 *but the crowd still buzzed with whispers of impropriety.* Natambu, *Malcolm X*, p. 263.

232 *had a "very nasty attitude."* "Negroes: Death, Lost Sheep," February 13, 1964, MXC-S, box 9, folder 1.

232 *find a way around the family's demands.* Branch, *Pillar of Fire*, p. 17.

233 *"attempts to advise and tell the family what to do."* MX FBI, Summary Report, New York Office, May 16, 1963, p. 21.

233 *Muhammad's sexual misconduct in the mid-1950s.* Malcolm X and Haley, *Autobiography*, p. 301.

233 *"he was tearing me apart behind my back."* Ibid., p. 303.

233 *"You are a married man!"* Marable, *Living Black History*, p. 172.

233 *Malcolm "would really hurt Betty."* Louis Farrakhan interview, December 27, 2007.

234 *in early April flew to Phoenix to learn his future.* Malcolm X and Haley, *Autobiography*, pp. 303–4.

Chapter 9: "He Was Developing Too Fast"

235 *"than the positive fact of David's killing Goliath."* Malcolm X and Haley, *Autobiography*, p. 304.

235 *"man's wife, I'm that David,"* he told Malcolm. Ibid., p. 305.

235 *his goal was to "inoculate" the Nation's rank and file.* Ibid. Also see Goldman, *The Death and Life of Malcolm X*, pp. 113–14; Clegg, *An Original Man*, pp. 188, 191–92; and DeCaro, *On the Side of My People*, p. 191.

236 *ease the news of Muhammad's transgressions.* MX FBI, Summary Report, New York Office, November 15, 1963, pp. 6, 9.

236 *Elijah Muhammad, but was reluctant to bring it up with him.* James 67X Warden interview, June 18, 2003.

236 *"doctrine to Muslims, and current events, and politics."* Malcolm X and Haley, *Autobiography*, pp. 300–301.

236 *"and also the devils in that city."* Elijah Muhammad to Malcolm Shabazz, April 25, 1963, MXC-S, box 3, folder 6.

236 *"negative attitude" toward* Muhammad Speaks. FBI—Gravitt, Summary Report, New York Office, January 27, 1964; and MX FBI, Memo, New York Office, May 15, 1963, and May 23, 1963.

237 *contacting Joseph directly on mosque matters.* Branch, *Pillar of Fire*, p. 163.

237 *"our people to our one from the Speaker's Stand!"* Open letter from Elijah Muhammad, April 25, 1963, MXC-S, box 3, folder 8.

237 *"the No. 2 man of the Black Muslim sect."* "Malcolm X Coming Here," *Washington Post*, May 1, 1963.

237 *black street crime in the nation's capital.* "Malcolm X in D.C. with Solution to Crime Rate," *Chicago Defender*, May 13, 1963. The press conference was held on May 9, 1963.

238 *at the invitation of the local minister, Jeremiah X.* MX FBI, Memo, New York Office, May 15, 1963; and MX FBI, Summary Report, New York Office, November 15, 1963, p. 26.

238 *"he is a four-legged dog or a two-legged dog."* "Malcolm X in D.C. with Solution to Crime Rate."

238 *The trial of fourteen Muslims began on April 8, 1964.* "14 Muslims Go on Trial in Fatal Riot," *Los Angeles Times*, April 9, 1963.

238 *"circulated in a dense crowd outside."* Bill Lane, "Jury Selection for Muslim Trial Fair," *Los Angeles Sentinel*, April 12, 1963; and "14 Muslims Go on Trial in Fatal Riot."

238 *all-white jury of eleven women and one man was sworn in.* "Row Flares Over Jurors in Muslim Riot Trial," *Los Angeles Times*, April 25, 1963. Reporter Bill Lane of the *Los Angeles Sentinel* claimed that six of the twelve jurors were black. See Lane, "Jury Selection for Muslim Trial Fair."

238 *separate section was created for the women.* "Negroes Ask Segregated Court Seats," *Los Angeles Times*, May 1, 1963.

238 *would be allotted on a first-come, first-served basis.* "Muslim Riot Described by Officer," *Los Angeles Times,* May 2, 1963.
238 *who had killed Ronald Stokes, and provocatively took several photos of him.* "Top New York Muslim Says L.A. Is on Trial," *Los Angeles Times,* May 4, 1963.
239 *"white people of the country are in agreement with the Nazis."* Gladwin Hill, "Muslims' Defense Opened on Coast," *New York Times,* May 12, 1963; "Use of Word 'Negro' Issue in Muslim Trial," *Chicago Defender,* May 8, 1963; and "Malcolm X Raps L.A. Press as Favoring Cops in Trial," *Chicago Defender,* May 25, 1963.
239 *"I just thought I might lose my temper."* "Muslim Trial Interrupted by Attorney," *Los Angeles Times,* May 7, 1963.
239 *"so they would have a reason to shoot us."* "Muslim Trial to Jury, Malcolm X Is Rousted," *Los Angeles Sentinel,* May 23, 1963.
239 *had made their point, and beat a hasty retreat.* Ben Burns, "First Negro-Owned Station to Hit Airwaves," *Chicago Defender,* May 8, 1963; and "Negro Picket Slugged at Black Muslim Rally," *Los Angeles Times,* May 5, 1963.
239 *failed to reach unanimous verdicts on two others.* "9 Muslims Guilty in Coast Riot," *Los Angeles Times,* June 14, 1963; and "11 Convicted on 37 of 42 Counts in Muslim Trial," *Los Angeles Sentinel,* June 20, 1963.
239 *the prisoners' probation hearing on their behalf.* "Black Muslim Rioters Get Prison Terms," *Chicago Tribune,* August 1, 1963; and "6 Jurors Say Muslims Got Unfair Trial," *Atlanta Daily World,* September 1, 1963.
240 *he met privately with Green for two hours.* C. Portis, "Celebrities and Celebrators Pour into City," *New York Herald Tribune,* May 15, 1963; MX FBI, Memo, New York Office, May 15, 1963; and "Miscellaneous Financial Documents," MXC-S, box 11, folder 15.
240 *"had demonstrated their ability to defend themselves."* "Black Muslim Raps Hearing Postponement," *Washington Post,* May 17, 1963; M. S. Handler, "Malcolm X Scores Kennedy on Racial Policy," *New York Times,* May 17, 1963; and "Malcolm X Denounces JFK on Civil Rights," *Chicago Defender,* May 25, 1963.
240 *"fox will eat you with a smile instead of a scowl."* MX FBI, Memo, Washington Office, May 13, 1963, May 14, 1963, and May 23, 1963; "400 Hear Malcolm X Speak Here," *Washington Post,* May 13, 1963; DeCaro, *On the Side of My People,* p. 163; and Clegg, *An Original Man,* p. 217.
241 *"better with whites than Negroes who are Christians."* "Malcolm X Denies Muslims Preach Hate," *Chicago Defender,* October 18, 1962; "'Rights Violated'—Muslims," *Chicago Defender,* October 20, 1962; and "Muslims Chained in N.Y. Courtroom," *Amsterdam News,* October 27, 1962.
241 *"cheating, stealing . . . all forms of vice."* "Malcolm X in Court," *Amsterdam News,* November 17, 1962.
241 *at the Lorton Reformatory, located in Virginia.* H. D. Quigg, "Debate Muslim Claim to Be Legitimate Religion," *Chicago Defender,* June 18, 1963.
241 *had conducted a service at Lorton back in May.* MX FBI, Memo, Washington Office, June 3, 1963; and MX FBI, Memo, Washington Office, August 6, 1963.
241 *American Civil Liberties Union at once took up the issue.* "D.C. Rejects Malcolm X Prayer Role," *Washington Post,* June 29, 1963; and "Black Muslim Tension Eases," *Washington Post,* August 1, 1963.
241 *Malcolm added, was "just another [prison] warden."* Transcript of Kenneth Clark interview of Malcolm X, aired on WNDT-TV, New York City, and WGBH-TV, Boston, on June 4, 1963, MXC-S, box 5, folder 11.
242 *"If you are caught, you will wish you were dead."* FBI—Sharrieff, Summary Report, Chicago Office, August 19, 1963.
243 *fellow lieutenants, or other FOI "enforcers."* Thomas 15X Johnson (also known as Khalil Islam) interview, September 29, 2004.
243 *"They didn't deserve even to be killed."* Louis Farrakhan interview, December 27, 2007.
243 *"because that puts him in a bad position."* Thomas 15X Johnson interview, September 29, 2004.

243 saying, "Brother, you're just spiritual." Louis Farrakhan interview, December 27, 2007.

243 own group of Fruit for that particular assignment. Thomas 15X Johnson interview, September 29, 2004.

244 "that's unheard of, man, violating like that." Ibid.

244 "This was a law. It was untouchable." Ibid.

245 "'Larry has lost his mind. He's messing with them Muslims!'" Larry 4X Prescott (also known as Akbar Muhammad) interview, November 7, 2007.

245 "Georgia on it, he said, 'Elijah answered our prayers.'" Ibid., June 9, 2006.

245 Malcolm was the "boss of the bosses." Ibid.

246 "That was the signal: close out and bring him on." Ibid., November 7, 2007.

246 millions of non-Islamic African Americans. Alex Haley, "Malcolm X Interview," Playboy, vol. 10, no. 5 (May 1963), pp. 53, 56–60, 62.

246 strategy of integration that was doomed to failure. Ibid., pp. 56–57.

247 "very much taken aback when Playboy kept its word." Malcolm X and Haley, Autobiography, p. 392.

247 "and made me the man that I am today." Ibid., pp. 393–94.

248 the completion of the biography. Alex Haley to Malcolm X, "Author/Collaborator Letter of Agreement," June 1, 1963, MXC-S, box 3, folder 6.

248 with projected total sales of twenty thousand. "Production Information," June 5, 1963, The Ken McCormick Collection of the Records of Doubleday and Company (KMC), Manuscript Division, Library of Congress, box 44, folder 9.

248 "the manuscript that you want in the manuscript." Haley, "Author/Collaborator Letter of Agreement."

248 petty Negro bourgeoisie that he enjoyed ridiculing. Malcolm X and Haley, Autobiography, pp. 393–95.

248 with "As told to Alex Haley." Alex Haley to Oliver Swan, August 5, 1963, Anne Romaine Collection, Special Collections Library, University of Tennessee (UTLSC), Knoxville, Tennessee, series I, box 3, folder 24.

248 "when mine are almost a complete antithesis of his." Ibid.

249 to fly to Chicago for an interview with Elijah Muhammad. Alex Haley to Paul Reynolds, September 5, 1963, ibid.

249 complete the entire work by the end of October 1963. Alex Haley to Paul Reynolds, September 22, 1963, ibid.

249 "such as we had, will be the most productive." Alex Haley to Malcolm X, September 25, 1963, MXC-S, box 3, folder 6.

249 "as neat and attractive as that of her husband." Ann Geracimos, "Mrs. Malcolm X—Her Role as Wife," New York Herald Tribune, June 30, 1963. Although the article was theoretically about Betty, Malcolm peppered the interview with attacks on "Western civilization," which had "destroyed women's femininity. . . . It is oriented to make a woman what she is not. Western society has lost touch with home and family."

249 "no two people should stay together who can't get along." Ibid.

250 climaxing with two days of public activities. D'Emilio, Lost Prophet, p. 328.

250 "unemployment, especially as it related to minority groups." "Preamble to the March on Washington," Carbada and Weise, eds., Time on Two Crosses, pp. 112–15.

250 John Lewis, its national chair, to represent the organization. D'Emilio, Lost Prophet, pp. 340–42, 355.

250 was persuaded to support the Washington march. David J. Garrow, Bearing the Cross: Martin Luther King, Jr., and the Southern Christian Leadership Conference (New York: Vintage, 1986), pp. 265, 268.

250 Kennedy administration to offer its endorsement. D'Emilio, Lost Prophet, pp. 344–45; and Goldman, The Death and Life of Malcolm X, pp. 102–3.

250 in Harlem—on West 130th Street. D'Emilio, Lost Prophet, p. 340.

251 Martin Luther King, Jr., and Adam Clayton Powell, Jr. Mosque No. 7 Press Releases for June 29, 1963, Harlem Rally, MXC-S, box 5, folder 17.

251 *made it impossible for him to address the rally.* Telegram, Adam Clayton Powell, Jr., to Malcolm X, June 28, 1963, MXC-S, box 3, folder 11.

251 *dispatched to the rooftops to observe both crowd and cops.* Thomas P. Ronan, "Malcolm X Tells Rally in Harlem Kennedy Fails to Help Negroes," *New York Times,* June 30, 1963; "Romney Bobs Up and Leads Rights Parade," *Chicago Tribune,* June 30, 1963; FBI—Gravitt, Summary Report, New York Office, January 27, 1964; and FBI—Goodman, Summary Report, New York Office, December 13, 1964.

251 *"a comprehensive united front of African Americans."* "Muhammad Son Calls for Unity," *Muhammad Speaks,* July 20, 1963; "Muhammad's Son at Rally Saturday," *Amsterdam News,* July 13, 1963; and NOI Mosque No. 7 Press Release, "Elijah Muhammad's Son to Speak in Harlem at Outdoor Rally," MXC-S, box 5, folder 17.

251 *"ready to help us win our freedom."* Lomax, *When the Word Is Given,* pp. 84–87.

252 *"'Islamic' and more 'political' in the days just ahead."* Ibid., pp. 87–91. Writing in late 1963, Lomax was convinced that Akbar Muhammad, or "almost certainly" another son of Elijah Muhammad, would inherit the leadership of the NOI; Malcolm X would never lead the Nation, Lomax believed: "I see Malcolm, then, not as the maximum leader, but as prime minister and behind-the-scenes policy maker."

252 *"this message that I have been assigned to."* "Islamic Exports Plan to Microscope Muslims," *Chicago Defender,* July 15, 1963.

253 *"these policemen put us into those paddy wagons."* "Police Haul Off 300 Pickets in Racial Protest," *Los Angeles Times,* July 23, 1963.

253 *"the New York police is that this is 1963."* Homer Bigart, "Building Trades Accused of Snub by Racial Groups," *New York Times,* August 6, 1963.

253 *that brought out more than three hundred people.* MX FBI, Summary Report, New York Office, November 15, 1963, pp. 5, 6, 7, and 12; FBI—Gravitt, Summary Report, New York Office, January 27, 1964; and FBI—Goodman, Summary Report, New York Office, February 13, 1964.

253 *"no real differences" between the various civil rights groups.* Martin Arnold, "Brooklyn Rally Held by Muslims," *New York Times,* July 28, 1963.

253 *"use his teeth" if he had to protect himself.* FBI—Gravitt, Summary Report, New York Office, January 27, 1964.

253 *that increasingly troubled Malcolm.* Evanzz, *The Messenger,* p. 266.

253 *"his brother Malcolm for the next six."* Ben Burns, "JFK Gags About TFX and Malcolm X," *Chicago Defender,* June 5, 1963.

254 *"use U.S.A. or the American Government."* Elijah Muhammad to Malcolm Shabazz, August 1, 1963, MXC-S, box 3, folder 8.

254 *"[the march], he joined it," Malcolm told the crowd.* "Muslim Leader Plans to Join Washington March," *Chicago Defender,* August 10, 1963.

254 *"be wise in your decision when choosing."* FBI—Sharrieff, Summary Report, Chicago Office, February 19, 1964.

254 *in Washington, speaking at a local NOI meeting.* Ibid., p. 11.

255 *"this present Catholic administration."* "Unity Rally," August 18, 1963, MXC-S, box 5, folder 3.

255 *Southern Democrat and taking place within one year.* Ibid.

255 *Fard never claimed, at least not publicly.* DeCaro, *On the Side of My People,* pp. 166–67.

255 *story of Yacub and the white devils.* Branch, *Pillar of Fire,* pp. 130–31.

255 *"to do whatsoever with the March," he insisted.* "NAACP Official Says 250,000 Will March," *Los Angeles Times,* August 26, 1963. Malcolm's statement was taken from a CBS television interview.

255 *"an Emancipation Proclamation a hundred years ago."* William Raspberry, "Rights Leaders Reaffirm Belief That Marchers Will Be Orderly," *Washington Post,* August 26, 1963.

256 *"a part of history that we should be a part of."* Larry 4X Prescott interview, November 7, 2007.

256 *that they were duped by whites in power.* "The Farce on Washington," no date, MXC-S,

box 5, folder 5. Also see "'No Muslims in D.C. March': Malcolm X," *Chicago Defender,* August 26, 1963.

257 *"epicenter of black America on that day."* Peter Goldman interview, July 12, 2004; and Goldman, *The Death and Life of Malcolm X,* pp. 102–6.

257 *association with Malcolm would damage their image.* Goldman, *The Death and Life of Malcolm X,* p. 104.

257 *"You're probably right,"* Rustin replied. Ibid., p. 107.

258 *fully inclusive for the first time in history.* Garrow, *Bearing the Cross,* p. 383.

258 *audience gave its consent for every demand.* Ibid., pp. 284–85.

258 *a shady tree, looking out over the crowd.* Manning Marable comment, in Peter Goldman interview, July 12, 2004.

258 *racial separation, and if not, "they will die."* FBI—Sharrieff, Summary Report, Chicago Office, February 19, 1964; FBI—Goodman, Summary Report, New York Office, February 13, 1964; and FBI—Gravitt, Summary Report, New York Office, January 27, 1964.

259 *"He will follow me until he dies."* Malcolm X and Haley, *Autobiography,* pp. 297–300; and Clegg, *An Original Man,* pp. 181, 324. According to Armiya Nu'man, an assistant minister under Farrakhan at Mosque No. 7 in the early 1970s, the first NOI national minister had been Sultan Muhammad, minister of Milwaukee's Temple No. 3 in the 1930s. Malcolm was only the second national minister to be named in the Nation.

259 *"he went jubilantly lindy-hopping around."* Malcolm X and Haley, *Autobiography,* p. 398.

259 *"Justice to what the book can do for the Muslims needs it."* Alex Haley to Malcolm X, September 25, 1963, MXC-S, box 3, folder 6.

259 *"date before the 1964 election is in full swing."* Wolcott (Tony) Gibbs, Jr., to Alex Haley, October 1, 1963, KMC, box 44, folder 9.

259 *"intrusion by the 'as told to' writer."* Alex Haley to Tony Gibbs, October 11, 1963, Anne Romaine Collection, UTLSC, series I, box 3, folder 24.

260 *"speaking at Harvard Law School."* Wolcott Gibbs, Jr., to Alex Haley, October 24, 1963, KMC, box 44, folder 9.

261 *"and represents, to Negroes, to white people, to America."* Alex Haley to Paul Reynolds, October 24, 1963, Anne Romaine Collection, UTLSC, series I, box 3, folder 1.

261 *including one of a young Malcolm alongside singer Billie Holiday.* Alex Haley to Tony Gibbs, October 27, 1963, KMC, box 44, folder 9.

261 *"command you into what must be done with it."* Alex Haley to Paul Reynolds, Kenneth McCormick, and Tony Gibbs, November 14, 1963, Anne Romaine Collection, UTLSC, series I, box 3, folder 24.

261 *"and, then, the galvanic, absolute conversion."* Alex Haley to Malcolm X, November 14, 1963, MXC-S, box 3, folder 6.

261 *panel discussion at the University of California at Berkeley.* MX FBI, Summary Report, New York Office, June 18, 1964, p. 17.

261 *specific references to "the Honorable Elijah Muhammad."* "America's Gravest Crisis Since the Civil War," University of California at Berkeley, October 11, 1963, in Perry, ed., *Malcolm X: The Last Speeches,* pp. 59–79.

262 *cause "violence and bloodshed."* Ibid., pp. 66–67.

262 *"You look upon him as being a man."* Ibid., pp. 72–73.

262 *"Adam Powell is one of the best examples."* Ibid., pp. 78–79.

262 *on "the condition of Negroes on the West Coast."* "Malcolm X, Back, Will Speak Friday," *Amsterdam News,* October 19, 1963; and MX FBI, Summary Report, New York Office, November 15, 1963, pp. 16–17.

262 *"full time to the truth of Mr. Elijah Muhammad."* "Professor to Direct Black Muslims Here," *Washington Post,* October 21, 1963.

263 *to Philadelphia to address the local NOI mosque.* MX FBI, Summary Report, New York Office, June 18, 1964, p. 9.

263 *Malcolm engaged in a public dialogue with James Baldwin.* MX FBI, Summary Report, New York Office, November 15, 1963, p. 18.

263 *books by and about him, was George Breitman.* George Breitman's works about Malcolm X include: George Breitman, ed., *Malcolm X: The Man and His Ideas* (New York: Path-

finder, 1965); George Breitman, ed., *Malcolm X on Afro-American History* (New York: Pathfinder, 1967); George Breitman, *The Last Year of Malcolm X: The Evolution of a Revolutionary* (New York: Schocken, 1967); George Breitman, ed., *By Any Means Necessary: Speeches, Interviews, and a Letter by Malcolm X* (New York: Pathfinder, 1970); and George Breitman, ed., *Malcolm X Speaks: Selected Speeches and Statements* (New York: Grove, Weidenfield, 1990).

264 *considered themselves more militant than he was.* The letter inviting Malcolm X to attend the conference, dated October 26, 1963, came from GOAL. The letter outlined GOAL's objectives and political philosophy; it also invited Malcolm to join its advisory board. What may be most important about Malcolm X's post-NOI career is that GOAL provided a democratic model of protest organization that may have shaped the subsequent evolution of the Organization of Afro-American Unity (OAAU) in 1964. The OAAU's political statements and objectives clearly paralleled those of GOAL. See Group on Advanced Leadership (GOAL) to Malcolm X, October 26, 1963, MXC-S, box 15, folder 11.

264 *based on nonviolent direct action, was no revolution at all.* "Message to the Grassroots," November 10, 1963, in Breitman, ed., *Malcolm X Speaks*, pp. 3–17.

264 *"love revolution, you love black nationalism."* Ibid., pp. 9–10.

265 *Academy Awards "for the best supporting cast."* Ibid., pp. 12–17.

265 *"Malcolm's going to split with Elijah Muhammad."* Grace Lee Boggs, "Let's Talk About Malcolm and Martin," lecture presented at Brecht Forum, New York, May 4, 2007.

265 *"residing with my brother Philbert in Lansing."* Malcolm is quoted in a letter dated November 1963, Alex Haley to Ken McCormick, Anne Romaine Collection, UTLSC, series I, box 3, folder 24.

265 *until most of the Autobiography was completed.* Alex Haley to Malcolm X, November 14, 1963, MXC-S, box 3, folder 6.

265 *"story, this caliber of a 'happy ending.'"* Alex Haley to Malcolm X, November 19, 1963, ibid.

265 *"There's something that I want to tell you both."* Louis Farrakhan interview, December 27, 2007.

265 *activity was "as bad as it ever was."* DeCaro, *On the Side of My People*, p. 191.

266 *Louis consented to Malcolm's request.* Louis Farrakhan interview, December 27, 2007.

266 *traditional NOI dogma, and classical tenets of Sunni Islam.* "Reminiscences of Malcolm X: A Lecture," Oral History Research Office, Columbia University, New York. An incomplete transcript of Malcolm X's talk is in MXC-S, box 5, folder 12.

267 *"I'll have to say he's the foxiest of the foxy."* Ibid.

267 *"Why, they would upset the entire political picture."* Ibid.

267 *"involved because they were not allowed to."* Herman Ferguson interview, June 27, 2003.

268 *even on the Thanksgiving holiday.* Herman Ferguson interview, June 24, 2004.

268 *"something that was happening around him."* Ibid.

268 *"He was developing too fast."* Herman Ferguson interview, June 27, 2003.

Chapter 10: "The Chickens Coming Home to Roost"

269 *alongside a photo of Kennedy.* Clegg, *An Original Man*, pp. 200–201.

269 *if questioned about the assassination.* Evanzz, *The Messenger*, pp. 271–72.

269 *an NOI leader since the assassination.* Clegg, *An Original Man*, p. 201.

270 *but a significant minority of non-Muslim blacks.* "Malcolm X Scores U.S. and Kennedy: Likens Slaying to 'Chickens Coming Home to Roost,'" *New York Times*, December 2, 1963; and Herman Ferguson interview, June 27, 2003.

271 *"been making [the Mecca pilgrimage] since then."* Ibid.

271 *affirmed Islam as their faith would be saved.* Ibid.

271 *"speaks for the black masses of America"—that is, Elijah Muhammad.* Ibid.

272 *"Revolutions are destructive and bloody."* Ibid.

273 *"never did make me sad; they've always made me glad."* "Malcolm X Scores U.S. and Kennedy."

273 *"he made the statement, I didn't think anything about it."* Larry 4X Prescott interview, June 9, 2006.

273 *"nobody paid any particular attention to it."* Herman Ferguson interview, June 27, 2003.

274 *Marilyn E.X., his secretary, would continue working for him.* Clegg, *An Original Man*, p. 202; and DeCaro, *On the Side of My People*, pp. 191–92. It appears that Malcolm continued to have access to Mosque No. 7's secretary until early 1964. Marilyn E.X., Malcolm's secretary, wrote Frank Quinn of the San Francisco Council for Civic Unity on December 30, 1963, requesting a copy of a television interview featuring Malcolm X on a local program, "Cities and Negroes." See Marilyn E.X. to Frank Quinn, December 30, 1963, MXC-S, box 3, folder 4.

274 *"'very shocked at the assassination of President Kennedy.'"* "Malcolm X Suspended for JFK Remarks," *Amsterdam News*, December 7, 1963.

274 *"I agree I need to withdraw from public appearance."* Ibid.; and "Malcolm X Suspended," *Chicago Defender*, December 5, 1963.

274 *"and even that job reportedly was in doubt."* "X On the Spot," *Newsweek*, December 16, 1963.

275 *"but he would make no public speeches."* Larry 4X Prescott interview, June 9, 2006.

275 *"and I said, 'Oh-oh, something funny is going on.'"* James 67X Warden interview, June 18, 2003.

275 *public fiascos with the American Nazi Party.* Ibid.

275 *otherwise surely heightened the tension between them.* Rickford, *Betty Shabazz*, pp. 164–65. Rickford speculates that Malcolm's "lingering loyalty" to the NOI "might have sparked more feuds at home."

276 *"just exclude public speaking engagements."* "Malcolm X Expected to Be Replaced," *New York Times*, December 6, 1963.

276 *Malcolm never really worked on the project.* DeCaro, *On the Side of My People*, pp. 191–92.

276 *"just as they put it in the back of Medgar Evers."* "Malcolm Answers Jackie Robinson," *Chicago Defender*, December 7, 1963. Also see "Reject Racist Views in Open Retort to Malcolm," *Chicago Defender*, December 14, 1963.

277 *"he will not be permitted to speak in public."* "Malcolm X Maintains Silence," *Amsterdam News*, December 14, 1963.

277 *"people without cultural roots are automatically dead."* Malcolm X to Martin Miller, December 6, 1963, MXC-S, box 3, folder 4.

277 *"the only spokesman for the Black Muslims."* "A Summing Up: Louis Lomax Interviews Malcolm X," in Lomax, *When the Word Is Given*, pp. 169–80.

277 *"sticks out his lip and starts popping off."* Clegg, *An Original Man*, p. 203.

278 *corroborate Malcolm's supposed rumormongering.* Evanzz, *The Messenger*, p. 278.

278 *neither believed that a total split was inevitable.* Clegg, *An Original Man*, pp. 203–5.

278 *he was praying to atone for his errors.* Ibid., pp. 205–6.

278 *Elijah Muhammad, Ali, and Sharrieff were all present.* Ibid., pp. 203–7; and Goldman, *The Death and Life of Malcolm X*, p. 125.

279 *"Go back and put out the fire you started."* Clegg, *An Original Man*, p. 207; and Goldman, *The Death and Life of Malcolm X*, pp. 125–26.

279 *"another, less metaphorical grave in mind."* Goldman, *The Death and Life of Malcolm X*, p. 126.

279 *even by James 3X Shabazz in Malcolm's own former post.* Larry 4X Prescott interview, June 9, 2006.

279 *over seven hours, deep into the night.* MX FBI, Memo, New York Office, February 12, 1964.

280 *having Clay on his side was a plus.* Goldman, *The Death and Life of Malcolm X*, pp. 127–29.

280 *to Washington, D.C., until January 21.* David Remnick, *King of the World*, p. 168.

281 *the couple's youngest daughter, Ilyasah.* Photograph, "Clay Celebrates with Malcolm X," *Chicago Defender*, February 6, 1964.

281 *published in the* Amsterdam News. Photograph, "Malcolm X's Family and Friend," *Amsterdam News*, February 1, 1964.

281 *to Miami and resumed training.* Remnick, *King of the World*, pp. 168–69.

281 *"of heavyweight boxer Cassius Clay."* "Malcolm X in Florida," *Amsterdam News*, January 25, 1964.

281 *"a Muslim meeting I get inspired."* "Cassius Clay Almost Says He's a Muslim," *Amsterdam News*, January 25, 1964.

281 *"what's wrong with the Muslims?"* Remnick, *King of the World*, p. 169.

282 *of about $3,000 per month.* James 67X Warden interview, July 24, 2007.

283 *"without speaking against myself."* "Notebook—Separation from NOI," MXC-S, box 9, folder 2.

283 *"only adds division upon division."* DeCaro, *On the Side of My People*, p. 192.

283 *"in Muslims, but self."* "Notebook—Separation from NOI," MXC-S, box 9, folder 2.

283 *"(two-thirds a cop) same situation everywhere."* Ibid.

284 *coalitions on a case-by-case basis.* Claude Lightfoot, "Negro Nationalism and the Black Muslims," *Political Affairs*, vol. 41, no. 7 (July 1962), pp. 3–20.

285 *"survive the War of Armageddon?"* McAlister, "One Black Allah," pp. 622–56; and Malcolm X and Haley, *Autobiography*, pp. 224–25.

285 *"a worldwide and historic struggle."* McAlister, "One Black Allah," p. 628.

285 *had talked with God personally.* Lomax, *When the Word Is Given*, pp. 177–80.

285 *Allah nor God, Malcolm dissented.* "Notebook—Separation from NOI," MXC-S, box 9, folder 2.

286 *seat 7, his favorite number.* Remnick, *King of the World*, pp. 170–72.

286 *of allowing Malcolm back in.* Goldman, *The Death and Life of Malcolm X*, pp. 128–29.

287 *and led them in prayer.* Remnick, *King of the World*, pp. 186–88.

287 *"I'm the king of the world!"* Ibid., pp. 176, 183–200.

287 *were given bowls of ice cream.* Ibid., pp. 204, 207–8; and Goldman, *The Death and Life of Malcolm X*, p. 129.

287 *"blinded them to his ability."* Remnick, *King of the World*, p. 207.

288 *and an entourage of six.* "Clay Talks with Malcolm Here," *New York Times*, March 2, 1954.

288 *"a mind of his own."* Steve Cady, "Clay, on 2-Hour Tour of U.N., Tells of Plans to Visit Mecca," *New York Times*, March 5, 1964.

288 *near his East Elmhurst home.* Remnick, *King of the World*, p. 213.

288 *"secret conference with Malcolm X."* ". . . and to Complete the Report," *Chicago Tribune*, March 2, 1964.

288 *rival organization to the Nation of Islam.* "Report Clay, Malcolm X Plan New Organization," *Chicago Defender*, March 2, 1964.

289 *"'kill Malcolm, they'll kill me.'"* James 67X Warden interview, August 1, 2007.

289 *"would raise up against them."* James 67X Warden interview, June 18, 2003.

289 *"in the middle of the night."* Ibid.

290 *"'are talking about killing you.'"* James 67X Warden interview, August 1, 2007.

290 *"just don't lie to me."* Ibid.

291 *"that's the way it was."* Langston Hughes Savage (also known as Anas Luqman) interview, September 6, 2008.

291 *"break with all of them."* Ibid.

291 *"'He ain't been removed.'"* James 67X Warden interview, August 1, 2007.

292 *"became more and more political."* Louis Farrakhan interview, December 27, 2007.

292 *"I held with my brother."* Ibid.

292 *"in Allah and follows me."* "Clay Puts Black Muslim X in His Name," *New York Times*, March 7, 1964.

293 *"talk about him no more."* Remnick, *King of the World*, p. 214.

293 *"would not join with Malcolm X."* "Clay to Take Draft Physical," *New York Times*, March 7, 1964.

293 *"champion Cassius X Clay, has completely failed."* "Clay Drops Malcolm X," *Pittsburgh Courier*, March 21, 1964.

293 *Triborough Bridge and given a ticket.* "Order Arrest of Brother Malcolm," *Chicago Defender*, May 21, 1964.

293 *that he was suspended indefinitely.* Malcolm X, "Why I Quit," *Amsterdam News*, March 14, 1964.

294 *"engagements at colleges and universities."* M. S. Handler, "Malcolm X Splits with Muhammad," *New York Times*, March 9, 1964; and "Occasional Statements, Open Letters, Declarations and Letters to the Editor, 1962–1964," MXC-S, box 5, folder 18.
294 *"wherever Negroes ask for my help."* Handler, "Malcolm X Splits with Muhammad."
295 *"and that he should be killed."* William H. George interview with Assistant District Attorney Herbert Stern, March 18, 1964, MANY.
295 *a second election would be held.* MX FBI, Summary Report, New York Office, June 18, 1964, p. 33.
295 *whom had been former NOI members.* James 67X Warden interview, June 18, 2003.
295 *New York's WNDT, Channel 13.* "Malcolm X Charts," *Jet*, April 2, 1964; and MX FBI, Memo, New York Office, March 11, 1964.
295 *with an interview with Malcolm.* "Telegram to Muhammad" and "Malcolm X: Why I Quit," *Amsterdam News*, March 14, 1964.
296 *"while there is still time."* M. S. Handler, "Malcolm X Sees Rise in Violence," *New York Times*, March 12, 1964.
296 *Muhammad only isolated him further.* Ibid.; MX FBI, Memo, New York Office, March 13, 1964; DeCaro, *On the Side of My People*, p. 195; and "Occasional Statements," MXC-S, box 5, folder 18.
296 *Malcolm would later explain.* Rickford, *Betty Shabazz*, p. 163.
296 *"had yet to be broken."* Ibid., p. 171.

Chapter 11: An Epiphany in the Hajj

298 *"within their rights to kill those dogs."* MX FBI, Memo, New York Office, March 13, 1964.
298 *Murphy's condemnation was a "compliment."* "'Get Guns,' Says Malcolm X," *Chicago Defender*, March 14, 1964; "Top New York Cop Vows Fight Against Malcolm X," *Chicago Defender*, March 17, 1964; "Negroes Seek Ouster," *Chicago Defender*, March 19, 1964; and MX FBI, Memo, New York Office, March 26, 1964.
298 *quality of blacks' public education.* MX FBI, Memo, New York Office, March 13, 1964; and MX FBI, Memo, Boston Office, April 3, 1964.
298 *most blacks to dismiss his claims.* "Malcolm X Tells of Death Threat," *Amsterdam News*, March 21, 1964.
298 *room located on the hotel's mezzanine.* MX FBI, Memo, Chicago Office, March 17, 1964; MX FBI, Memo, New York Office, March 13, 1964; and MX FBI, Summary Report, New York Office, June 18, 1964, p. 35.
299 *"the white man himself bleeds a little."* MX FBI, Memo, Boston Office, April 3, 1964.
299 *"anti-Semitic. We are simply against exploitation."* MX FBI, Memo, Paris Office, August 26, 1964.
299 *had requested information on how to join up.* MX FBI, New York Office, June 18, 1964, p. 48.
299 *to form "a black nationalist army."* "Malcolm X May Form Black National Army," *Amsterdam News*, March 25, 1964; "Malcolm X Says Form a New Party," *Chicago Defender*, March 26, 1964; and MX FBI, Summary Report, New York Office, June 18, 1964, p. 36.
300 *"will consider a conflict as a bloody one."* Ibid.
301 *would become spiritual brothers and sisters to blacks.* DeCaro, *On the Side of My People*, pp. 207–8.
301 *"in the nonviolent movement."* Garrow, *Bearing the Cross*, p. 319.
302 *only time the two men ever met.* James 67X Warden interview, August 1, 2007.
302 *compensate blacks for "three hundred ten years of unpaid slave labor."* "Malcolm X to Organize Mass Voter Registration," *Militant*, April 6, 1964.
302 *the inevitable socialist revolution in the United States.* Trotsky's theory of "permanent revolution" suggested that revolutionary societies could "leap" economic stages of development—for example, from feudalism to socialism, bypassing capitalism. In

the United States, this meant that the vanguard of the socialist revolution would not come from the industrial proletariat, but from the most oppressed sectors of the working class and peasantry. This meant that Negroes would be a major force within the vanguard of the American socialist revolution. The Socialist Workers Party, Trotsky advised, should support movements promoting black nationalism and demands for self-determination. See Manning Marable, *Black American Politics: From the Washington Marches to Jesse Jackson* (London: Verso, 1985), p. 52.

304 *best program addressing blacks' interests.* Ibid.; Breitman, ed., *Malcolm X Speaks*, p. 23; and Robert Terrill, *Malcolm X: Inventing Radical Judgment* (Lansing: Michigan State University Press, 2004), pp. 121–33.

304 *"by August [1964], with delegates from all over the country."* "2,000 Hear Malcolm X in Cleveland," *Militant*, June 13, 1964. Provocatively, Malcolm also raised the specter of armed struggle by blacks inside the United States. At the proposed August 1964 convention, Malcolm declared, "If it's necessary to form a black nationalist army, we'll form a black nationalist army."

304 *one of Malcolm's most widely quoted talks.* "The Ballot or the Bullet," Transcript, MXC-S, box 5, folder 8.

304 *"rightfully theirs," Malcolm was reported stating.* MX FBI, Cleveland Office, April 7, 1964; and "Organize Rifle Club in Ohio," *Amsterdam News*, April 11, 1964.

305 *eviction of Malcolm and his family from the house.* James Booker, "Seek to Evict Malcolm X from Home in Queens," *Amsterdam News*, March 31, 1964.

305 *"accusing the government of genocide," it reported.* FBI—Muslim Mosque, Incorporated (MMI) file, Memo, New York Office, April 5, 1964; Travel Diaries (Transcription): Middle East and West Africa, April–May 1964, MXC-S, box 5, folder 13.

305 *Malcolm's core followers also in attendance.* Breitman, ed., *Malcolm X Speaks*, pp. 45–57; and DeCaro, *On the Side of My People*, p. 282.

306 *ministers tried in vain to block his appearance.* "Malcolm X's Detroit Date Sparks Battle of Ministers," *Afro-American*, April 11, 1964.

307 *"a chump but a traitor to his race."* MX FBI, Memo, Detroit Office, April 9, 1964; MX FBI, Memo, Detroit Office, April 14, 1964; and "Leading Dixiecrat in White House," *Chicago Defender*, April 14, 1964.

307 *"fit right into Harlem," he noted in his diary.* Travel Diaries, April 13–14, 1964, MXC-S, box 5, folder 13.

307 *Saudi Arabia, the official center of embarkation for the hajj.* Malcolm X and Haley, *Auto-biography*, pp. 326–31; and DeCaro, *On the Side of My People*, p. 204.

308 *in securing permission to participate in the hajj.* Malcolm X and Haley, *Autobiography*, pp. 328–31, 336–37; DeCaro, *On the Side of My People*, p. 205; and "Malcolm X Gets Religion," *Chicago Defender*, May 14, 1964.

308 *"decreed that I be a guest of the state."* Travel Diaries, April 17–19, 1964, MXC-S, box 5, folder 13; and DeCaro, *On the Side of My People*, p. 205.

309 *and renewal, fitting well with the purpose of the hajj.* Letter from Malcolm X, Jeddah, Saudi Arabia, April 20, 1964, Best Efforts, Inc. Archives, Highland Park, Michigan, in DeCaro, *On the Side of My People*, p. 206; "Malcolm X Gets Religion," *Chicago Defender*; "Malcolm X Has New Name in Arabia," *Amsterdam News*, May 9, 1964; and Esposito, *The Oxford Dictionary of Islam*, pp. 103–4.

309 *"horum, with right shoulder bare." Malcolm observed on April 23.* Travel Diaries, April 22–23, 1964, MXC-S, box 5, folder 13.

310 *who "were more genuinely brotherly than anyone else had ever been."* Rickford, *Betty Shabazz*, p. 179.

310 *"modernizing the methods to propagate Islam."* Travel Diaries, April 22–23, 1964, MXC-S, box 5, folder 13.

311 *unhappy experiences with American racism.* Travel Diaries, April 24, 1964, ibid.

311 *years he was incarcerated in Massachusetts.* Travel Diaries, April 25, 1964, ibid.

311 *"True Believer recognizes the Oneness of all Humanity."* Travel Diaries, April 26–27, 1964, ibid.

312 *"Islam will link us spiritually to Africa, Arabia and Asia."* Travel Diaries, April 23, 1964, MXC-S, box 5, folder 13.

312 *who advocated the expansive use of jihad.* Esposito, *The Oxford Dictionary of Islam,* pp. 217–18. In 1980, Hafez al-Assad mandated death for any Syrian who belonged to the Muslim Brotherhood.

312 *scheduled to give a lecture the following day.* Travel Diaries, April 27–29, 1964, ibid.

312 *a front-page article about it the next day.* Travel Diaries, April 30, 1964, ibid.; and Malcolm X's Itinerary, April 30, 1964, MXC-S, box 13, folder 7.

312 *"only a minority of Negroes believed in nonviolence."* "Negro Moderation Decried by Malcolm X in Lebanon," *New York Times,* May 2, 1964.

312 *"the offices of the Muslim borthers"* — that is, the Brotherhood. Travel Diaries, May 1, 1964, MXC-S, box 5, folder 13.

313 *would play the same role during Malcolm's 1964 visit.* Abdul Basit Naeem statement, August 5, 1959, BOSS; Travel Diaries, MXC-S, box 5, folder 13; and Malcolm X to Hussein el-Borai, June 1, 1964, and January 7, 1965, MXC-S, box 3, folder 4.

313 *reaching the ancient seaport city in the evening.* Ibid.

313 *"get imported items through customs."* Travel Diaries, May 2–3, 1964, MXC-S, box 5, folder 13.

313 *Malcolm "was probably from Habachi (Abyssinia)."* Travel Diaries, May 4, 1964, ibid.

313 *and escorted him to the Federal Palace hotel.* Travel Diaries, May 5, 1964, ibid.

313 *including scholar E. U. Essien-Udom.* Travel Diaries, May 7, 1964, ibid.; E. U. Essien-Udom's *Black Nationalism: The Search for an Identity in America* (Chicago: University of Chicago Press, 1963) presented a sympathetic critique of the Nation of Islam.

314 *"the son (or child) who has returned."* Alice Windom to Christine, May 1964, John Henrik Clarke Papers, Manuscripts, Archives and Rare Books Division, Schomburg Center for Research in Black Culture, box 24, folder 33; Malcolm X's Itinerary, MXC-S, box 13, folder 7; and "Malcolm X Gives Africa Twisted Look," *New York Journal American,* July 25, 1964, which includes excerpts of Malcolm's address.

314 *Maya Angelou, Alice Windom, Preston King and W. E. B. and Shirley Du Bois.* Kevin Gaines, *African Americans in Ghana* (Chapel Hill: University of North Carolina Press, 2006), pp. 198–99; and Jenkins, ed., *Malcolm X Encyclopedia,* "Julian Mayfield," pp. 376–77.

315 *during his student years at Berkeley.* See Leslie Lacy, "Malcolm X in Ghana," in John Henrik Clarke, ed., *Malcolm X: The Man and His Times* (Trenton, NJ: Africa World Press, 1990), pp. 217–25.

315 *he gave a talk at Chicago's Mosque No. 2 in the early 1960s.* "Alice Windom," in Jenkins, ed. *Malcolm X Encyclopedia,* pp. 566–67.

315 *"extra-religious struggle for human rights in America."* Alice Windom to Christine, May 1964, John Henrik Clarke Papers, box 24, folder 33.

315 *"personally but bad for me politically."* Travel Diaries, May 11, 1964, MXC-S, box 5, folder 13.

316 *Pan-Africanism similar to that espoused by Nkrumah.* Malcolm X to Muslim Mosque, Inc., May 11, 1964, MXC-S, box 13, folder 2.

316 *"to have far reaching results for the common good."* "X Is Here," *Ghanaian Times,* May 12, 1964; and "Civil Rights Issue in U.S. Is Mislabeled," *Ghanaian Times,* May 13, 1964.

316 *Ghana's minister of defense Kofi Boaka and other ministers at Boaka's home.* Alice Windom to Christine, May 1964, John Henrik Clarke Papers, box 24, folder 33; Malcolm X's Itinerary, MXC-S, box 13, folders 6–7; and Travel Diaries, May 14–16, 1964, MXC-S, box 5, folder 13.

316 *"to be 'amused.' They were in for a rude surprise."* Alice Windom to Christine, May 1964, John Henrik Clarke Papers, box 24, folder 33.

317 *he predicted that Harlem was "about to explode."* Calvin Smith, ed., *Where To, Black Man?* (Chicago: Quadrangle, 1967), pp. 211–20. The text is a transcript of Malcolm's University of Ghana lecture. See also Manning Marable, *African and Caribbean Politics: From Kwame Nkrumah to the Grenada Revolution* (London: Verso, 1987), pp. 136–43.

317 *"white race would end segregation in the U.S., and the world."* "African States Must Force U.S. for Racial Equality," *Ghanaian Times,* May 15, 1964.

317 *in Winneba, about forty miles from Accra.* Alice Windom to Christine, May 1964, John Henrik Clarke Papers, box 24, folder 33; Travel Diaries, May 15, 1964, MXC-S, box 5, folder 13; and Malcolm X's Itinerary, MXC-S, box 13, folders 6–7.

317 *proclaiming Maoist China's support for African-American liberation.* Alice Windom to Christine, May 1964, John Henrik Clarke Papers, box 24, folder 33; FBI—Revolutionary Action Movement (RAM) file, Memo, W. R. Wannall to W. C. Sullivan, October 1, 1964; and MX FBI Summary Report, New York Office, January 20, 1965, p. 70. Also see William Worthy, "The Red Chinese and the American Negro," *Esquire,* October 1964, pp. 132, 173–79.

318 *"mainstream of the struggle was heralded as a hopeful sign."* Alice Windom to Christine, May 1964, John Henrik Clarke Papers, box 24, folder 33.

318 *"Nobody listens to that Malcolm anymore."* Ali's traveling retinue included Herbert Muhammad. See "Cassius Without His Lip," *Ghanaian Times,* May 18, 1964; "Muhammad Ali Meets His Hero (Nkrumah)," *Ghanaian Times,* May 19, 1964; and Lloyd Garrison, "Clay Makes Malcolm Ex-Friend," *New York Times,* May 18, 1964.

318 *"by their racial origin from being regarded as human liberators."* H. M. Basner, "Malcolm X and the Martyrdom of Rev. Clayton Hewett," *Ghanaian Times,* May 18, 1964.

318 *"white worker in America than he has in South Africa."* Julian Mayfield, "Basner Misses Malcolm X's Point," *Ghanaian Times,* May 19, 1964.

318 *"objective, could have appeared attacking Nkrumah."* Leslie A. Lacy, "African Responses to Malcolm X," in LeRoi Jones and Larry Neal, eds., *Black Fire* (New York: William Morrow, 1968), pp. 32–38.

318 *to Africa "philosophically and culturally."* Malcolm X to Muslim Mosque, Inc., May 11, 1964, MXC-S, box 13, folder 2.

319 *and he prayed with many others.* Travel Diaries, May 18, 1964, MXC-S, box 5, folder 13.

319 *"Black Muslims, and thirsting for faster 'progress.'"* Ibid.

319 *appear at a trial to respond to a speeding ticket.* Travel Diaries, May 19, 1964, ibid.; Malcolm X's Itinerary, MXC-S, box 13, folder 7; "Warrant Issued for Malcolm X," *Chicago Daily News,* May 19, 1964; "Order Arrest of Brother Malcolm," *Chicago Defender,* May 21, 1964; and "Warrant for Malcolm as Speeder to Be Issued," *New York Times,* May 20, 1964. The charge against Malcolm was that he was driving fifty-five miles per hour in a forty-mile-per-hour zone on the Triborough Bridge in New York City on March 6, 1964.

319 *"different races and colors who treated me as a human being."* Travel Diaries, May 21, 1964, MXC-S, box 5, folder 13; Malcolm X's Itinerary, MXC-S, box 13, folder 7; MX FBI, Summary Report, New York Office, January 20, 1965, p. 90; "Malcolm X Makes It In from Mecca," *Chicago Defender,* May 25, 1964; "Malcolm Says He Is Backed Abroad," *New York Times,* May 22, 1964; and "'My Next Move'—Malcolm X: An Exclusive Interview," *Amsterdam News,* May 30, 1964.

320 *"dark blue suits, white shirts and distinctive red or grey bow ties."* "Malcolm Says He Is Backed Abroad," *New York Times,* May 22, 1964.

Chapter 12: "Do Something About Malcolm X"

321 *brothers "to be careful of the NOI."* FBI—MMI, Memo, New York Office, March 26, 1964.

322 *membership in the Jack and Jill organization.* "Lynn Shifflett in 'Big Sister' Contest," *Los Angeles Sentinel,* April 28, 1955; "Marion DeMan Hosts Teenager Party," *Los Angeles Sentinel,* August 25, 1955; "Jack, Jill Conference First for Teen-Agers," *Los Angeles Sentinel,* September 1, 1955; and "Founders Day Noted by Sigma Gamma Rho," *Los Angeles Sentinel,* December 27, 1956.

322 *funds for Freedom Riders in the South.* "The Guest Corner," *Los Angeles Sentinel,* July 11, 1957; "College Girl Relates African Experiences," *Los Angeles Sentinel,* November 13, 1958; "Photo of Shifflett," *Los Angeles Sentinel,* April 30, 1959; "Photo of Shifflett," *Los Angeles Sentinel,* October 22, 1959; and "Photo of Shifflett," *Los Angeles Sentinel,* July 6, 1961.

322 *"white people would also begin to feel the effects of this."* Peter Bailey interview, September 4, 1968, Manuscript Division, Moorland-Spingarn Research Center, Howard University Library.

322 *"And don't ask no questions, just be there."* Peter Bailey interview, June 20, 2003.

323 *"relaxed and he laughed and he'd joke."* Peter Bailey interview, September 4, 1968.

323 *weeks prior to Malcolm's break with the Nation.* Peter Bailey interview, June 20, 2003.

323 *"anything that Malcolm did,"* Ferguson said. Herman Ferguson interview, June 24, 2004.

324 *evidently the sacrifice made sense to her.* Ibid.

324 *the Nation of Islam would never readmit him.* DeCaro, *On the Side of My People*, pp. 199–200.

325 *"change black pathology into another religion."* "A Conversation with Ossie Davis," *Souls*, vol. 2, no. 3 (Summer 2000), pp. 6–16; quotation, p. 15. Davis also predicted that Malcolm X would emerge once again "as a central figure in any effort to unite, to regroup, our forces and to prepare ourselves for the onslaught that is sure to be visited upon us in this new century."

325 · *to run into each other at demonstrations.* See Von Hugo Washington, "An Evaluation of the Play *Purlie Victorious* and Its Impact on the American Theater Scene," Ph.D. dissertation, Wayne State University, 1979.

325 *"with the nonwhite majority of the world."* Peter Goldman interview, July 12, 2004.

326 *"That's what the rub was."* Norman 3X Butler (also known as Muhammad Abdul Aziz) interview, December 22, 2008.

326 *subsequent break was Malcolm's fault.* Larry 4X Prescott interview, June 9, 2006.

326 *"the Nation. . . . That's the way I saw it."* Ibid.

327 *her husband was out of the country.* Rickford, *Betty Shabazz*, pp. 180–81.

327 *"the freer we all became."* Ibid., p. 182.

327 *Louis's name in the column as "Minister Lewis."* Minister Lewis, "Minister Who Knew Him Best—Part I, Rips Malcolm's Treachery, Defection," *Muhammad Speaks*, May 8, 1964. Also see Minister Louis, "Fall of a Minister," *Muhammad Speaks*, June 5, 1964.

328 *Malcolm "had embraced Sunni Islam."* James 67X Warden interview, June 18, 2003.

328 *"I would have walked away."* Herman Ferguson interview, July 24, 2004.

328 *Betty curtly replied, "No."* Betty Shabazz interview, January 27, 1989, Anne Romaine Collection, UTLSC, series I, box 3, folder 24.

329 *"generation of American whites to turn with them."* M. S. Handler, "Malcolm X Pleased by Whites' Attitude on Trip to Mecca," *New York Times*, May 8, 1964.

329 *"everyone as part of one human family."* James Booker, "Is Mecca Trip Changing Malcolm?" *Amsterdam News*, May 23, 1964.

329 *required the blessing of Elijah Muhammad.* Alex Haley to Paul Reynolds, December 11, 1963, KMC, box 44, folder 1.

330 *"harassed by intermittent money pressures."* Alex Haley to Kenneth McCormick, Tony Gibbs, Jr., and Paul Reynolds, December 28, 1963, ibid.

330 *"'Twenty Million Black Muslims,'" Haley observed.* Alex Haley to Kenneth McCormick, Tony Gibbs, Jr., and Paul Reynolds, January 19, 1964, KMC, box 44, folder 2.

330 *best estimate of the final manuscript date.* Wolcott Gibbs, Jr., to Alex Haley, January 29, 1964, ibid.

330 *sent off suggestions for revision.* Alex Haley to Ken McCormick, Wolcott Gibbs, Jr., and Paul Reynolds, January 28, 1964, ibid.

330 *"would quarrel with what I'm saying to him."* Paul Reynolds to Tony Gibbs, Jr., February 7, 1964, ibid.

331 *"blasts everything that went before."* Alex Haley to Tony Gibbs, Jr., February 11, 1964, ibid.

331 *"every Christian needs to wrestle with."* Alex Haley to Ken McCormick, Paul Reynolds, and Tony Gibbs, Jr., February 18, 1964, ibid.

332 *"including to make foreign rights hotly bid for!"* Alex Haley to Ken McCormick and Paul Reynolds, March 21, 1964, ibid.

332 *of all chapters that had been completed.* Paul Reynolds to Anthony Gibbs, Jr., March 30, 1964, ibid.

332 *that Gibbs finally forwarded the check.* Tony Gibbs to Robert Banker, April 7, 1964, ibid.

332 *Africa's resources to U.S. police brutality.* MX FBI, Memo, Chicago Office, May 27, 1964; and "Malcolm Says He Is Backed Abroad," *New York Times.*

332 *"his real end—respect as a human being."* "Goals Changed by Malcolm X," *Los Angeles Times*, May 24, 1964; MX FBI, Summary Report, New York Office, January 20, 1965, pp. 10–11, 15, 98–100; FBI—MMI, Summary Report, New York Office, November 6, 1964, p. 14; and "Photo Standalone," *Chicago Defender*, May 20, 1964.

333 *"'guerrilla tactics of other deprived revolutionaries.'"* "Goals Changed by Malcolm X," *Los Angeles Times*; and Breitman, ed., *By Any Means Necessary*, pp. 178–79.

333 *"man you're all going to have to deal with."* Judith Martin, "Gregory Predicts Social Revolution," *Washington Post*, April 28, 1964.

333 *"the only man who can stop a race riot."* Drew Pearson, "A Comedian Sounds a Warning," *Los Angeles Times*, May 19, 1964. Gregory also drew parallels between Malcolm and the Ku Klux Klan: "The Klan tells the Negro, 'Don't fool with the white woman. Don't live in a white neighborhood.' Malcolm X says the same thing."

333 *and SNCC chairman John Lewis.* "Civil Rights Chiefs Form National Unit," *New York Times*, April 17, 1964.

334 *"And they were supposed to get married."* James 67X Warden interview, August 1, 2007.

334 *tempted to resign as MMI coordinator.* Ibid.

334 *Islamic faith, and must embrace "reality."* DeCaro, *On the Side of My People*, p. 231.

334 *were "adopting a wait and see attitude."* Jesse Lewis, "Man Who 'Tamed' Malcolm Is Hopeful," *Washington Post*, May 18, 1964.

335 *"strongly today than I did ten years ago."* "A Visit from the FBI," in Clarke, ed., *Malcolm X: The Man and His Times*, pp. 182–204.

336 *"all the power this country has can't remove him."* Breitman, ed., *Malcolm X Speaks*, pp. 64–71.

336 *"it was certainly a revolutionary chicken!"* Ibid., pp. 68–69. Malcolm also used the forum to reach out to potential white allies, indicating his break from the racial separatism of the NOI. "We will work with anyone, with any group, no matter what their color is," Malcolm declared, "as long as they are genuinely interested in taking the type of steps necessary to bring an end to the injustices that black people in this country are affected by" (p. 70). Also see MX FBI, Summary Report, New York Office, January 20, 1965, pp. 78–79.

337 *"whom the Muslims preach is the devil."* "'My Next Move'—Malcolm X," *Amsterdam News.*

337 *to resolve the dispute in a Muslim court.* MX FBI, Summary Report, New York Office, January 20, 1965, p. 56; and FBI—Goodman, Summary Report, New York Office, October 16, 1964.

338 *the northern boundary of Harlem.* Robert E. Terrill, *Malcolm X: Inventing Radical Judgment*, p. 138.

338 *same of prominent minister Lonnie X Cross.* FBI—MMI, Memo, Philadelphia Office, June 3, 1964; FBI—MMI, Memo, Philadelphia Office, June 9, 1964; MX FBI, Summary Report, New York Office, January 20, 1965, p. 59; FBI—Goodman, Summary Report, New York Office, October 16, 1964; and "Schedule," June 4–7, 1964, MXC-S, box 13, folder 7.

338 *"enough of this black violence in New York."* MX FBI, Telegram, J. Edgar Hoover to New York Office, June 5, 1964; and "Schedule," June 4–7, 1964, MXC-S, box 13, folder 7.

339 *"and then not believing in the words of Allah."* MX FBI, Summary Report, New York Office, January 20, 1965, p. 55.

339 *"because the 'devil' [white man] is watching."* Ibid.

339 *"you can and report it to me right away."* FBI—Sharrieff, Summary Report, Chicago Office, August 27, 1964.

339 *"in the mouth of the infamy to the elbow."* Ibid.

340 *"against colonialism, neocolonialism, and imperialism."* Marjorie Lee, Akemi Kochiyama-Sardinha, and Audee Kochiyama-Holman, eds., *Passing It On—A Memoir by Yuri Kochiyama* (Los Angeles: UCLA Asian American Studies Center Press, 2004), pp. 67–70; and "Schedule," June 4–7, 1964, MXC-S, box 13, folder 7.

340 *forth their accusations in the national media.* MX FBI, Summary Report, New York Office, January 20, 1965, pp. 20–21.

340 *corroborate the stories of Muhammad's illicit lovers.* Taylor Branch, *Pillar of Fire*, p. 328.

340 *Messenger's very own son, Wallace Muhammad.* FBI—Morris, Summary Report, New York Office, March 1, 1965; and MX FBI, Summary Report, New York Office, January 20, 1965, pp. 3–4, 22.

341 *death threats against Malcolm.* Branch, *Pillar of Fire*, p. 329.

341 *Wallace of Alabama and President Lyndon Johnson.* MX FBI, Memo, New York Office, June 9, 1964; MX FBI, Summary Report, New York Office, January 20, 1965, pp. 16, 21; and DeCaro, *On the Side of My People*, p. 331.

341 *a blueprint for the OAAU.* FBI—Organization of Afro-American Unity (OAAU) file, Memo, New York Office, June 19, 1964.

342 *"what great organizers each of them is."* James 67X Warden interview, June 18, 2003.

342 *"and I told the brothers to do it."* James 67X Warden interview, July 24, 2007.

342 *his former membership in the Nation of Islam.* MX FBI, Summary Report, New York Office, January 20, 1965, p. 15.

342 *armed guard for fear of attack.* Branch, *Pillar of Fire*, p. 346.

342 *had known about them first.* MX FBI, Summary Report, New York Office, January 20, 1965, pp. 22–23, 59; and Branch, *Pillar of Fire*, p. 346.

343 *might be expected to endorse the initiative.* MX FBI, Memo, New York Office, June 16, 1964.

343 *"CIA and military intelligence agencies."* MX FBI, Teletype, New York Office, June 13, 1964.

343 *on one thousand dollars bail each.* FBI—Goodman, Summary Report, New York Office, October 10, 1964; FBI—MMI, Memo, Boston Office, June 15, 1964; and FBI—MMI, Teletype, Boston Office, June 15, 1964. The men accompanying Benjamin were former NOI members Aubrey Barnette, Robert Lee Wise, John Thomas, Frank Terrelongo, Goulbourne Busby, Jr., Larryn Douglas, and Malcolm's nephew Rodnell Collins, then nineteen years old.

344 *"conspired" to expel him from the Nation.* MX FBI, Summary Report, New York Office, January 20, 1965, p. 60.

344 *no ammunition, so no arrest was made.* "Malcolm X Death Threat Brings Heavy Court Guard," *New York Telegraph and Sun*, June 1, 1964; "Muslims Deny Fight Going On within Ranks," *Chicago Defender*, June 18, 1964; and MX FBI, Teletype, New York Office, June 16, 1964.

345 *"a hearing in front of the Muslim[s]."* Transcript of Queens County Civil Court Trial, June 15–16, 1964.

345 *"never removed a minister without cause."* Ibid.

346 *belonged to the Nation of Islam.* Ibid.

346 *"doing and had been doing."* Ibid.

346 *in the acquisition of the property.* Ibid.

347 *"than keep it quiet among Muslims."* Ibid.

347 *of open season on any Malcolm loyalist.* MX FBI, Summary Report, New York Office, January 20, 1965, p. 70.

347 *were arrested and their firearms seized.* MX FBI, Memo, New York Office, June 19, 1964. The men arrested were William George, Herbert Dudley, Jesse Ryans, Vincent Woldan, James Vestal, and George Whitney. Also see FBI—MMI, Teletype, New York Office, June 17, 1964.

347 *"killed for teaching against Elijah Muhammad."* MX FBI, Summary Report, New York Office, January 20, 1965, p. 75.

348 *great speed, straining to accomplish his goals.* Branch, *Pillar of Fire*, p. 332.

348 *and the Organization of Afro-American Unity.* Marilyn E.X. to Henry Kissinger, June 18, 1964, MXC-S, box 3, folder 4.

348 *could be truly competitive with the Nation of Islam.* MX FBI, Summary Report, New York Office, January 20, 1965, pp. 4–5.

348 *"will take what is rightfully theirs."* Ibid., p. 4.

348 *Works and Surveys, asking for information.* Malcolm X to Joseph Iffeorah, June 22, 1964, MXC-S, box 3, folder 4.

348 *"you would come out Sunday as a spectator."* Malcolm X to Sara Mitchell, June 22, 1964, ibid.

349 *remanded to the Queens Criminal Court.* "Muslim Factions Keep Fighting," *Amsterdam News,* June 27, 1964; and Larry 4X Prescott interview, June 9, 2006.

349 *"Then things just got progressively worse."* Larry 4X Prescott interview, June 9, 2006. To this day, Larry 4X is unapologetic about his actions: "I got the gun from him and I beat him with it. And I should have—you know, I didn't have the mind to shoot him. But I definitely whipped his behind real good with it."

350 *a sore point for many of Malcolm's followers.* Malcolm X to Elijah Muhammad, June 23, 1964, MXC-S, box 13, folder 1; and "Malcolm X to Elijah: Let's End the Fighting," *New York Post,* June 26, 1964.

350 *"There was tension and resentment."* Herman Ferguson interview, June 24, 2004.

351 *"that our people experience in this government."* "Organization of Afro-American Unity, A Statement of Basic Aims and Objectives," in Clarke, ed., *Malcolm X: The Man and His Times,* pp. 335–42; and MX FBI, Summary Report, New York Office, January 20, 1965, pp. 25, 29, 76.

351 *"block by block to make the community aware of its power and potential."* "Organization of Afro-American Unity, A Statement of Basic Aims and Objectives"; Terrill, *Malcolm X: Inventing Radical Judgment,* pp. 138–39; William W. Sales, *From Civil Rights to Black Liberation: Malcolm X and the Organization of Afro-American Unity* (Boston: South End, 1994), pp. 104–7; David Herman, "Malcolm X Launches a New Organization," *Militant,* July 13, 1964; and "Program of Organization of Afro-American Unity," *Militant,* July 13, 1964.

351 *no material incentive to finish the book project.* Wolcott Gibbs, Jr., to Robert Banker, July 1, 1964, KMC, box 44, folder 1; and Doubleday and Company, Inc., to Alex Haley and Malcolm X, sometimes called Malik Shabazz, July 8, 1964, KMC, box 44, folder 1. In mid-July 1964, Haley was telling literary agent Paul Reynolds that the *Autobiography* was nearly finished; his afterword could be written in less than one week. "[It] should be wrapped up . . . by the end of the month." See Haley to Reynolds, July 14, 1964, KMC, box 44, folder 1.

351 *"from my own personal appraisals."* Alex Haley to Malcolm X, June 8, 1964, MXC-S, box 3, folder 6.

352 *"and her four children what a man you were."* Alex Haley to Malcolm X, June 21, 1964, ibid.

352 *"while providing him with more funds."* Alex Haley to Paul Reynolds, June 21, 1964, ibid.

353 *"possibility of self-regeneration?" "No,"* Malcolm replied. Robert Penn Warren, *Who Speaks for the Negro?* (New York: Random House, 1965), pp. 251–66.

353 *"'I wouldn't know anything about that.'"* Ibid., p. 260.

354 *agreed to be their international chairman.* Max Stanford (also known as Muhammad Ahmed) interview, January 31, 2003.

354 *"the public front, united front."* Ibid.

355 *"brothers who graduated from college."* Ibid.

355 *"like the biggest fool on planet earth."* Ibid.

355 *"couldn't attack him if he had a national base."* Max Stanford interview, August 28, 2007. In his 2007 interview, Stanford attributed Malcolm's outing of Elijah Muhammad's sexual misconduct to his own humiliation. After the Queens trial, Malcolm justified his attack on Muhammad to Stanford by explaining he was a fool, and that he had

gone around the world saying Elijah Muhammad "is a holy man" when Elijah Muhammad had been messing around with a lot of women. "Well, he was devastated, totally. . . . You know, Malcolm was a street hustler, so he was a player, right? I mean, the player got played."

356 *"And I was a hero."* Gerry Fulcher interview, October 3, 2007.

356 *attend OAAU events, doing general surveillance.* Ibid.

357 *could transcribe and analyze Malcolm's speeches.* Ibid.

357 *join the OAAU, far fewer than anticipated.* "Malcolm X Repeats Call for Negro Unity on Rights," *New York Times*, June 29, 1964.

357 *Harlemites did not have the initial two-dollar membership fee.* MX FBI, Summary Report, New York Office, January 20, 1965, p. 29.

357 *organize self-defense units capable of fighting the Klan.* FBI—OAAU, Teletype, New York Office, June 30, 1964.

357 *"the Negro has a chance to strike back."* "Malcolm Sending Armed Troops to Mississippi," *Chicago Defender*, July 2, 1964.

358 *on the streets, forced him to return immediately to New York.* MX FBI, Memo, Chicago Office, June 26, 1964; and MX FBI, Memo, Chicago Office, July 23, 1964.

358 *filed paternity suits against Elijah Muhammad.* "Two Paternity Suits," *New York Times*, July 4, 1964; "Deny Paternity Suits," *Chicago Defender*, July 6, 1964; and "Ex-Sweetheart of Malcolm X Accuses Elijah," *Amsterdam News*, July 11, 1964. On July 7, Rosemary gave birth in Los Angeles to another child fathered by Muhammad.

358 *but only for twenty-four hours.* "Malcolm X Flees for His Life," *Pittsburgh Courier*, July 11, 1964; "New York Police Put Guard," *Washington Post*, July 5, 1964; and John Shabazz, "Muslim Minister Writes to Malcolm," *Muhammad Speaks*, July 3, 1964.

358 *assignment of introducing Malcolm to the audience.* FBI—Goodman, Summary Report, New York Office, October 16, 1964.

358 *"sound like I'm cracking, but I'm facting."* Goldman, *The Death and Life of Malcolm X*, p. 204.

358 *other cities "behind Brother Wallace" Muhammad.* Malcolm X to Hassan Sharrieff, July 9, 1964, MXC-S, box 3, folder 4.

359 *TWA Flight 700 for London.* MX FBI, Teletype, New York Office, July 10, 1964; and MX FBI, Memo, New York Office, July 10, 1964.

359 *summer of 1964 America "will see a bloodbath."* "Malcolm X Seeks U.N. Aid," *Chicago Defender*, July 13, 1964; and "Malcolm X to Meet Leaders in Africa," *New York Times*, July 10, 1964.

359 *windows and stealing everything they could carry.* Goldman, *The Death and Life of Malcolm X*, pp. 204–5. Goldman correctly viewed Malcolm "as a force against rioting in Harlem," not because America's white power structure did not deserve to be rioted against, but "because he loved Harlem too well" (p. 204).

359 *July 11, he was off to Cairo.* See Travel Diaries (Transcription): Africa and Middle East, July–November 1964, July 9–11, 1964, MXC-S, box 5, folder 14.

359 *said to Charles was 'Take care of Betty for me.'"* Max Stanford interview, August 28, 2007.

Chapter 13: "In the Struggle for Dignity"

361 *Europe during his second tour.* "Malcolm X Reports He Now Represents World Muslim Unit," *New York Times*, October 11, 1964.

361 *they talked together until three in the morning.* MX FBI, Summary Report, New York Office, January 20, 1965, p. 105; "Malcolm X in Cairo," *New York Times*, July 14, 1964; and Travel Diaries (Transcription): Africa and Middle East, July–November 1964, July 12, 1964, MXC-S, box 5, folder 14.

361 *Nasser's Bureau of General Affairs.* Travel Diaries, July 13–17, 1964, MXC-S, box 5, folder 14.

361 *whom he had previously met in Ghana.* Ibid.

361 *only to fall victim to "American dollarism."* Address to the OAU, July 17, 1964, MXC-S, box 14, folder 5; and Travel Diaries, July 17–21, 1964, MXC-S, box 5, folder 14.

362 *criticizing the lack of racial progress.* "Malcolm X Bids Africans Take Negro Issue to U.N.," *New York Times*, July 17, 1964; and DeCaro, *On the Side of My People*, pp. 236–38.

362 *generally described as having failed.* "Malcolm X Fails with Africans," *Chicago Defender*, July 27, 1964.

362 *a violator of human rights.* M. S. Handler, "Malcolm X Seeks U.N. Negro Debate," *New York Times*, August 13, 1964.

362 *"the gains outweigh the risks."* Malcolm to Betty Shabazz, August 4, 1964, MXC-S, box 3, folder 2.

363 *including one,* The Suez and the Revolution, *accompanied by local contacts.* Travel Diaries, August 4, 1964, MXC-S, box 5, folder 14.

363 *anathema to the NOI.* Ibid.

363 *failure to address the charges of immorality.* "Muhammad's Son to Quit, Says Report," *Chicago Defender*, August 17, 1964.

364 *"be printed only on asbestos."* Victor Riesel, "African Intrigues of Malcolm X," *Los Angeles Times*, August 7, 1964.

364 *was certainly a "wonderful blessing."* Malcolm to Betty Shabazz, August 4, 1964, MXC-S, box 3, folder 2.

364 *not scale back his schedule.* Travel Diaries, August 6–7, 1964, MXC-S, box 5, folder 14.

365 *"Allah has really blessed me."* Travel Diaries, August 11–16, 1964, ibid.

365 *summarizing the recent OAU summit.* Ibid.; MX FBI, Memo, New York Office, September 8, 1964; and "The 2nd African Summit Conference," MXC-S, box 5, folder 18.

365 *"twentieth-century form of 'benevolent colonialism.'"* Malcolm X, "The Second African Summit Conference, August 21, 1964," in Clarke, ed., *Malcolm X: The Man and His Times*, pp. 294–98.

365 *"found no doors closed to me."* Ibid., pp. 299–300.

366 *"and physical slave of the system."* "Racism: The Cancer That Is Destroying America," MXC-S, box 5, folder 10. Fanon advanced this argument in *Black Skin, White Masks* (New York: Grove, 1967).

366 *ancient temples in the Valley of the Kings.* Travel Diaries, August 26–29, 1964, MXC-S, box 5, folder 14.

366 *important stamps of legitimacy.* Travel Diaries, August 30, 1964, ibid.

366 *Queens home by January 31, 1965.* MX FBI, Summary Report, New York Office, January 20, 1965, pp. 57–58, 140; and "Order Eviction of Malcolm X," *Amsterdam News*, September 5, 1964.

366 *into unauthorized agreements with foreign governments.* FBI—Goodman, Memo, Nicholas Katzenbach to the Director, September 1964.

367 *would be the guest of the local governor.* Travel Diaries, September 12, 1964, ibid; MX FBI, Memo, New York Office, September 10, 1964; and Advertisement, *Chicago Defender*, September 12, 1964.

367 *press conference in Gaza's parliament building.* Travel Diaries, September 5, 1964, MXC-S, box 5, folder 14.

367 *the two men met privately.* Travel Diaries, September 15, 1964, MXC-S, box 5, folder 14. Al-Shukari was named PLO president at a Jerusalem conference from May 31 to June 4, 1964.

368 *"in their own religion" existed.* Malcolm X, "Zionist Logic," *Egyptian Gazette*, September 17, 1964.

368 *"for Arab refugees from Palestine."* Marable, *African and Caribbean Politics*, p. 134.

368 *considerable tact and political discretion.* Edward E. Curtis, IV, *Islam in Black America* (New York: State University of New York Press, 2002), p. 100.

368 *"twenty-two million fellow black Americans."* Ibid., pp. 104–5; and Antoine Sfier, ed., *The Columbia World Dictionary of Islamism* (New York: Columbia University Press, 2007), pp. 290–91.

369 *with Shawarbi and other friends.* Travel Diaries, September 16, 1964, MXC-S, box 5, folder 14.

369 *provided a chauffeured car.* Travel Diaries, September 18–19 and 21, 1964, ibid.

369 *in Harlem, to promote orthodox Islam.* Travel Diaries, September 22, 1964, ibid.; and MX FBI, Memo, New York Office, October 5, 1964.

369 *"in the Holy City of Mecca."* Malcolm X to M. S. Handler, September 22, 1964, Alex Haley Papers, Manuscripts, Archives and Rare Books Division, Schomburg Center for Research in Black Culture, box 3, folder 1; and M. S. Handler, "Malcolm Rejects Racist Doctrines," *New York Times,* October 4, 1964.

370 *"and the Human Society complete."* Malcolm X to M. S. Handler, September 22, 1964, Alex Haley Papers, box 3, folder 1.

370 *Malcolm thirty-five fully funded fellowships.* Malcolm X to M. S. Handler, September 23, 1964, ibid.; and "Malcolm X Reports He Now Represents World Muslim Unit," *New York Times,* October 11, 1964.

370 *to Beirut on September 29.* Travel Diaries, September 24–25, 1964, MXC-S, box 5, folder 14. According to the FBI, Malcolm called upon the U.S. embassy in Kuwait on September 29, 1964, and obtained a new health certificate. See MX FBI, Memo, Washington Office, October 1, 1964.

370 *a word during the exchange.* Marian Faye Novak, "Meeting Mr. X," *American Heritage,* vol. 46, no. 1 (February/March 1995), pp. 36–39.

370 *and an overflow crowd turned out.* Alex Haley to Malcolm X, October 14, 1964, MXC-S, box 3, folder 6; Travel Diaries, September 29, 1964, MXC-S, box 5, folder 14.

371 *"people of the U.S. and Africa."* MX FBI, Summary Report, New York Office, January 20, 1965, pp. 16–18.

371 *seemed "attentive, alert, and sympathetic."* Travel Diaries, October 8, 1964, MXC-S, box 5, folder 14.

371 *and subsequent merger with then Tanganyika.* On A. M. Babu, see Carole Boyce Davies, ed., *Encyclopedia of the African Diaspora: Origins, Experiences, and Culture* (Santa Barbara: ABC-Clio, 2008), p. 139; and Clarke, ed., *Malcolm X: The Man and His Times,* p. 261.

371 *"jokes much (but deadly serious)."* Travel Diaries, October 12–13, 1964, MXC-S, box 5, folder 14.

372 *"me back with the VIPs."* Travel Diaries, October 16–17, 1964, ibid.

372 *Don Harris about "future cooperation."* Travel Diaries, October 18, 1964, ibid.

372 *"for organizing the Mau Mau."* Travel Diaries, October 19–20, 1964, ibid.

373 *"the United Nations for racism."* MX FBI, Summary Report, New York Office, January 20, 1965, pp. 22–23.

373 *telling the "truth" about Malcolm.* Travel Diaries, October 19–20, 1964, MXC-S, box S, folder 14.

373 *"for our human rights struggle."* Travel Diaries, October 21–22, 1964, ibid.

374 *"believe it can be avoided.* Travel Diaries, October 24–30, 1964, ibid.

374 *"is mostly impatient and explosive."* Travel Diaries, November 1, 1964, ibid.

374 *"responsible, they were well educated."* Herman Ferguson interview, June 24, 2004.

375 *"So there was a gap."* Ibid.

376 *dollars during nearly a year.* James 67X Warden interview, August 1, 2007.

376 *stern rebuke, "things started happening."* Ibid.

377 *was insufficient evidence to arrest him.* FBI—Goodman, Summary Report, New York Office, October 16, 1964.

377 *audience to promote voter registration.* Ibid.; FBI—OAAU, Memo, New York Office, July 13, 1964.

377 *presidential campaign committee on July 23.* FBI—MMI, Summary Report, New York Office, November 6, 1964, p. 28.

377 *"set down" the black community.* Ibid., p. 44.

377 *until the group "got on its feet."* FBI—MMI, Memo, Philadelphia Office, August 5, 1964.

378 *"'We are replacing them,' see?"* James 67X Warden interview, August 1, 2007.

378 *"are people who are well known."* Ibid.

379 *"to abide his plans for revolution."* Ibid.

379 *than Malcolm could have imagined.* FBI—Morris, Summary Report, New York Office, March 1, 1965.

379 *had given birth to their fourth child, Gamilah Lumumba.* Rickford, *Betty Shabazz,* p. 197.

Gamilah's middle name was in honor of Congolese martyr Patrice Lumumba, slain in 1961 with the assistance of the CIA.

379 *baby appeared, departed for Africa.* Ibid.

380 *"We got him. We cut his throat."* Ibid., pp. 200–201.

380 *involved, and even planned to marry.* FBI—Morris, Summary Report, New York Office, March 1, 1965.

381 *"more helpful to the* whole *[Malcolm's emphasis] in the long run."* Malcolm to Betty Shabazz, July 26, 1964, MXC-S, box 3, folder 2.

381 *"I've learned to trust no one."* Malcolm to Betty Shabazz, August 4, 1964, MXC-S, box 3, folder 2.

381 *Malcolm "as a stepping stone."* FBI—Shabazz, Summary Report, New York Office, August 30, 1968; FBI—MMI, Memo, Philadelphia Office, September 29, 1964.

381 *meet him later that week.* FBI—MMI, Memo, New York Office, August 27, 1964.

382 *the leadership until Malcolm's return.* FBI—Morris, Summary Report, New York Office, March 1, 1965.

383 *half a dozen artists and writers.* Travel Diaries, November 1–2, 1964, MXC-S, box 5, folder 14.

383 *executive director of Ghanaian television.* Travel Diaries, November 4, 1964, ibid. See Gerald Horne, *Race Woman: The Lives of Shirley Graham Du Bois* (New York: New York University Press, 2000).

383 *turning to sleeping pills for relief.* Travel Diaries, November 2–3, 1964, MXC-S, box 5, folder 14.

383 *he'd had a rum and Coke in an attempt to wake up.* Travel Diaries, November 4–5, 1964, ibid.

383 *"My stature had definitely increased."* Maya Angelou, *A Song Flung Up to Heaven* (New York: Random House, 2002), p. 3.

384 *her friend as "two very lonely women."* Travel Diaries, November 6, 1964, MXC-S, box 5, folder 14.

384 *"they may get into politics."* Travel Diaries, November 7, 1964, ibid.

384 *"phrases lately and it has worried me."* Travel Diaries, November 8–9, 1964, ibid.

385 *stuck with coffee and orange juice.* Ibid.

385 *"frankly, a fighting language to you."* Travel Diaries, November 11, 1964, MXC-S, box 5, folder 14.

385 *almost impossible to communicate effectively.* Travel Diaries, November 12–14, 1964, ibid.

385 *"willing to do* anything *to prove it."* Travel Diaries, November 15, 1964, ibid.

386 *"feeling lonely . . . thinking of Betty."* Travel Diaries, November 16, 1964, ibid.

386 *checking in to the Hôtel Delavine.* See Nicol Davidson, "Alioune Diop and the African Renaissance," *African Affairs*, vol. 78, no. 310 (January 1979), pp. 3–11.

387 *as "the chickens coming home to roost."* "Malcolm X Accuses U.S. and Tshombe," *Los Angeles Times*, November 25, 1964; "Malcolm X, Back in the U.S., Accuses Johnson on Congo," *New York Times*, November 25, 1964; MX FBI, Memo, New York Office, November 25, 1964; MX FBI, Summary Report, New York Office, January 20, 1965, p. B; and MX FBI, Teletype, New York Office, November 24, 1964.

Chapter 14: "Such a Man Is Worthy of Death"

388 *rally scheduled for later that day.* FBI—MMI Memo, Philadelphia Office, October 22, 1964.

388 *may have quelled their worries.* FBI—MMI Memo, New York Office, October 22, 1964.

388 *leadership role in the MMI.* FBI—Morris Summary Report, New York Office, March 1, 1965; and FBI Memo, New York Office, December 1, 1964.

389 *"to certain people as devils."* James 67X Warden interview, August 1, 2007.

389 *the African continent's unprecedented social change.* "The Homecoming Rally of the OAAU," in Breitman, ed., *By Any Means Necessary*, pp. 132–56.

389 *a threat to blacks' interests.* Ibid.

390 *"how to solve this problem."* Hajj Malik el-Shabazz to Muhammad Sourour el-Sabban, November 30, 1964, MXC-S, box 3, folder 4.

391 *"that are headquartered in Mecca."* Hajj Malik el-Shabazz to Muhammad Taufik Oweida, November 30, 1964, MXC-S, box 3, folder 4; and MX FBI, Teletype, New York Office, December 1, 1964.

391 *"to change this miserable condition."* Ibid., pp. 252–53; MX FBI, Memo, London Office, December 9, 1964; MX FBI, Memo, London Office, January 11, 1965; and "Cheers for Malcolm X at Oxford," *Daily Telegraph*, December 4, 1964.

391 *"no one should doubt the power."* "Militant Muslim," *Manchester Guardian Weekly*, December 10, 1964.

391 *met privately with Wallace Muhammad.* FBI—MMI Summary Report, New York Office, February 21, 1965, p. 40; MX FBI, Teletype, New York Office, December 6, 1964; and a reception invitation from the Tanzanian representative to the United Nations, December 9, 1964, in OAAU Papers, Schomburg Center for Research in Black Culture.

392 *man in his father's eyes.* DeCaro, *On the Side of My People*, p. 236.

392 *"just as ruthless and cold-blooded."* Hajj Malik el-Shabazz (Malcolm X) to Walith Mohammed (Wallace Muhammad), December 21, 1964, MXC-S, box 3, folder 4.

393 *"with what I have to do."* James 67X Warden interview, July 24, 2007.

393 *"being 'terminated with extreme prejudice.'"* Ibid.

394 *"seem to have all the power."* "Communication and Reality," in Clarke, ed., *Malcolm X: The Man and His Times*, pp. 307–20.

395 *"avenge the crime in the Congo."* William Gálves, *Che in Africa: Che Guevara's Congo Diary* (Melbourne, Australia: Ocean, 1999), pp. 27–28.

395 *reports, many more.* The FBI estimated the December 13, 1964, audience at the Audubon Ballroom at two thousand. See MX FBI, Memo, New York Office, January 8, 1965.

395 *"the segregationist, lyncher, and exploiter."* "At the Audubon, December 13, 1964," in Breitman, ed., *Malcolm X Speaks*, pp. 88–104; and MX FBI, Memo, New York Office, January 8, 1965.

396 *"here—we eat them up."* "At the Audubon, December 13, 1964."

396 *support for the guerrilla war.* The best single study of Ernesto Che Guevara's guerrilla activities in Congo in 1965 is Gálvez, *Che in Africa*, especially pp. 29–32, 35–36, 43. An excellent biography of the subject is Anderson, *Che Guevara*.

397 *"thief, dope addict, and a pimp."* MX FBI, Summary Report, New York Office, January 20, 1965, p. 56.

397 *"May Allah burn them in hell."* See *Muhammad Speaks*, September 25, 1964, especially Captain Joseph and Jeremiah X, "Biography of a Hypocrite."

398 *"destruction for such a defector."* Edwina X, "Open Invitation: Come to Muhammad's Mosque," *Muhammad Speaks*, November 26, 1964.

398 *"as Malcolm is worthy of death."* Louis X, "Boston Minister Tells of Malcolm—Muhammad's Biggest Hypocrite," *Muhammad Speaks*, December 4, 1964.

398 *them to keep a low profile.* Clegg, *An Original Man*, pp. 226, 330; and "Muslims Charged," *Amsterdam News*, November 14, 1964.

398 *by his former roommate Anas Luqman.* James 67X Warden interview, August 1, 2007.

399 *"a program, you get action."* "At the Audubon," in Breitman, ed., *Malcolm X Speaks*, pp. 115–36; MX FBI, Memo, New York Office, December 21, 1964, and December 22, 1964; and "Malcolm Favors Mau Mau in U.S.," *New York Times*, December 21, 1964.

400 *triumph for all colored people.* W. E. B. Du Bois's address on his ninety-first birthday (February 21, 1959), from Beijing, advanced similar ideas about China serving as a model for the world's oppressed non-Europeans. Malcolm continued to stay in communication with the Du Bois family; in fact he had just written to David Du Bois on December 15, 1964, urging him to start an OAAU branch in Egypt. See Marable, *W. E. B. Du Bois*, pp. 205–6; and Malcolm X to David Graham, December 15, 1964, MXC-S, box 3, folder 4.

400 *"systems to solve their problems."* "At the Audubon," in Breitman, ed., *Malcolm X Speaks*, pp. 115–36.

401 *still considerable, had been narrowed.* Reminiscences of James Farmer (1979), in the Columbia University Oral History Research Office Collection.

401 *as he left the station.* FBI—MMI Summary Report, New York Office, May 21, 1965, p. 27; MX FBI, Memo, New York Office, December 30, 1964.

401 *a mere hundred dollars each.* "Convict Muslims in Boston," *Amsterdam News*, February 6, 1965; Branch, *Pillar of Fire*, p. 549.

401 *the audience throughout the program.* MX FBI, Memo from [redacted] to W. C. Sullivan, December 29, 1964; and MX FBI, Memo, Philadelphia Office, January 19, 1965.

402 *let anyone into their house.* MX FBI, Memo, Philadelphia Office, January 19, 1965.

402 *"a stand on your side."* Hajj Malik el-Shabazz to Akbar Muhammad, December 30, 1964, MXC-S, box 3, folder 7.

402 *to take their own murderous initiative.* Ibid.

402 *"famous Orthodox Brother in America."* Alex Haley to Paul Reynolds, October 17, 1964, Anne Romaine Collection, UTLSC, series I, box 3, folder 24.

402 *"to write new final chapters."* Alex Haley to Paul Reynolds, November 19, 1964, ibid.

403 *"March . . . it's a powerful book."* Alex Haley to Paul Reynolds, February 14, 1965, ibid.

404 *"like Jesus slipped into Jerusalem."* "To Mississippi Youth," in Breitman, ed., *Malcolm X Speaks*, pp. 137–46.

404 *a crowd of seven hundred.* "Is Malcolm X Clueing In Africans on U.S.?" *Militant*, January 11, 1965.

404 *personality to a mass audience.* MX FBI, Teletype, Washington Office, Director to New York Office, January 6, 1965; MX FBI, Memo, Washington Office, Director to Ottawa, January 3, 1965; and *Front Page Challenge* with Malcolm X, CBC, January 5, 1965 (accessible on www.youtube.com/watch?v=Id98PH7TZb8&feature=related and http://www.youtube.com/watch?v=IUSthrNcgQQ&feature=related).

404 *within that same dynamic context.* "Prospects for Freedom in 1965," in Breitman, ed., *Malcolm X Speaks*, pp. 147–56.

404 *in starting an office there.* Malcolm X to Carlos Moore, January 15, 1965, MXC-S, box 3, folder 4.

405 *placed her faith and hopes.* Malcolm X to Maya Maké, January 15, 1965, ibid.

405 *largely missed the point.* "1,000 in Vigil Defy Cold in Harlem," *New York Times*, January 18, 1965.

406 *"on the plantation by overseers."* Ibid. Malcolm vowed that in 1965 black people "won't be held in check . . . won't be held on the corral, they won't be held back at all."

406 *excluded too many "true revolutionaries."* Ibid.

407 *"Negro leaders can't contain it."* Ibid.

407 *"Elijah Muhammad has taught it."* Malcolm X interview with Pierre Berton in Toronto, January 19, 1965, in David Gallen, ed., *Malcolm X: As They Knew Him* (New York: Carroll and Graf, 1992), pp. 179–87.

408 *"little better than we were."* Peter Goldman interview, July 12, 2004.

408 *"whatever else we are second."* DeCaro, *On the Side of My People*, pp. 201–2, 248.

408 *moved twice out of fear.* Evanzz, *The Messenger*, p. 315.

409 *"My alertness is my bodyguard."* James Booker, "Malcolm X Speaks," *Amsterdam News*, February 6, 1965.

409 *to testify at the hearing.* "Malcolm X Was to Testify Here in Suits," *Los Angeles Times*, February 25, 1965.

409 *tunnel to reach his plane.* MX FBI, Summary Report, New York Office, September 8, 1965, pp. 19–20, 37; and Goldman, *The Death and Life of Malcolm X*, pp. 250–51.

409 *placed under close police guard.* Goldman, *The Death and Life of Malcolm X*, p. 251; "Malcolm X Had Fear of Death While in L.A.," *Los Angeles Times*, February 23, 1965; MX FBI, Memo, Chicago Office, January 29, 1965; MX FBI, Teletype, Chicago Office, January 31, 1965; and MX FBI, Summary Report, New York Office, September 8, 1965, p. 36.

410 *access to penal institutions.* MX FBI, Memo, New York Office, February 17, 1965; FBI—OAAU, Memo, Chicago Office, February 4, 1965, and February 18, 1965; MX FBI, Teletype, Chicago Office, January 31, 1965; MX FBI, Memo, Chicago Office, February 4, 1965, and February 18, 1965.

410 *large draw for the group.* MX FBI, Memo, New York Office, February 2, 1965; and FBI—OAAU, Enclosure, New York Office, February 2, 1965.

410 *of the Nation under arrest.* James Booker, "Malcolm X Speaks," *Amsterdam News*, February 6, 1965; and Steve Clark, ed., *February 1965: The Final Speeches* (New York: Pathfinder, 1992), pp. 17–19.

410 *Malcolm again escaped unharmed.* Booker, "Malcolm X Speaks," *Amsterdam News*, February 6, 1965; and MX FBI, Memo, New York Office, February 9, 1965.

411 *"we're waiting for the other."* Clark, ed., *February 1965*, pp. 20–22.

412 *the South within a few weeks.* "Stop Demonstrations," *Chicago Defender*, February 6, 1965; Clark, ed., *February 1965*, pp. 23–28; and MX FBI, Teletype, New York Office, February 4, 1965. A few weeks later, Malcolm gave a very different interpretation of his experience at Selma. In his February 15, 1965, lecture at the Audubon Ballroom, he criticized "my good friend, the Right Reverend Dr. Martin [laughter] in Alabama, using school children to do what the federal government should do. . . . School children shouldn't have to march." One of King's assistants did not want Malcolm speaking with young people involved in the protest. "The children insisted that I be heard. . . . Many of the students from SNCC also insisted that I be heard. This is the only way I got a chance to talk to them." See Clark, ed., *February 1965*, pp. 138–39.

412 *"do not support the U.S. war."* MX FBI, Memo, New York Office, February 2, 1965; MX FBI, Memo, New York Office, February 8, 1965, and February 9, 1965; and MX FBI, Memo, Tokyo Office, February 19, 1965.

412 *"than Moise Tshombe," he declared.* Clark, ed., *February 1965*, pp. 32–33.

412 *to look "like a criminal."* Ibid., p. 33.

413 *"well have been locked up."* Ibid., pp. 34–41; MX FBI, Cablegram, Paris Office, February 11, 1965; MX FBI, New York Office, February 10, 1965, and February 11, 1965; and "France Bars Malcolm," *Chicago Defender*, February 10, 1965.

413 *"determine why this incident took place."* Malcolm X to Dean Rusk, February 10, 1965, MXC-S, box 3, folder 4.

413 *"human rights for the black man."* Clark, ed., *February 1965*, pp. 42–44.

414 *"forms of segregation," he insisted.* Ibid., pp. 46–65.

414 *"he's losing his control."* Ibid.

415 *"start off a bloody battle."* "Aid to Malcolm X by BBC Assailed," *New York Times*, February 14, 1965; "Malcolm X Pays Smethwick Call," *Washington Post*, February 14, 1965; and "Malcolm X On Tour," *New York Herald Tribune*, February 14, 1965.

415 *"want to follow Malcolm X."* Gene Sherman, "Malcolm X Stirs Up Resentment in Britain," *Los Angeles Times*, February 14, 1965.

415 *"They are all the same."* Clark, ed., *February 1965*, pp. 69–72.

416 *"From Washington," Malcolm replied.* Rickford, *Betty Shabazz*, p. 222.

416 *late into the night in his study.* Ibid.

416 *"how great his strength was."* Ibid., pp. 222–24; "Malcolm X's Home Is Bombed," *Chicago Tribune*, February 15, 1965; "Three Fire Bombs Hit Home of Malcolm X," *Los Angeles Times*, February 15, 1965; "Malcolm X, Kin Flee Bombing," *New York Daily News*, February 15, 1965; "Who Bombed Malcolm X's Home?" *New York Post*, February 15, 1965; "Malcolm X Denies He Is Bomber," *Amsterdam News*, February 20, 1965; and "Malcolm X Accuses Muslims," *New York Times*, February 16, 1965.

417 *"firebombing [of the] house."* Thomas 15X Johnson interview, September 29, 2004. Since Johnson's death, Malcolm X researcher Abdur-Rahman Muhammad has also confirmed that NOI members were responsible for firebombing the Shabazz home.

417 *into an almost uncontrollable rage.* Rickford, *Betty Shabazz*, pp. 222–24.

Chapter 15: Death Comes on Time

418 *Freedom Now Party in Michigan.* MX FBI, Memo, W. C. Sullivan to J. F. Bland, February 1, 1965; MX FBI, Memo, Detroit Office, February 14, 1965, and February 17, 1965; and Clark, ed., *February 1965*, pp. 75–107.
418 *usual sharpness had abandoned him.* Rev. Albert Cleage, "Myths About Malcolm X," *International Socialist Review*, vol. 28, no. 5 (September–October 1967), p. 33.
419 *"power structure that's so corrupt."* Clark, ed., *February 1965*, pp. 75–107.
419 *"We sure didn't bomb it."* "Malcolm X's Home Is Bombed," *Chicago Tribune*; "Three Fire Bombs Hit Home of Malcolm X," *Los Angeles Times*; and "Malcolm X's Home is Fire-Bombed," *Washington Post*, February 15, 1965.
419 *"house. That was the government."* "Malcolm Accused Muslims of Blaze; They Point to Him," *New York Times*, February 18, 1965; "Malcolm X Promises Names of Bombers," *Los Angeles Sentinel*, February 18, 1965; "Malcolm X Denies He Is Bomber," *Amsterdam News*; and "Bottle of Gasoline Found on Dresser in Malcolm X Home," *New York Times*, February 17, 1965.
420 *"by the Ku Klux Klan."* Perry, ed., *Malcolm X: The Last Speeches*, pp. 111–49; "Malcolm Links Klan, Muslims," *New York Post*, February 16, 1965; FBI—Goodman, Summary Report, New York Office, February 17, 1966; and MX FBI, Memo, New York Office, February 16, 1965.
420 *"to suffer the consequences for."* Perry, ed., *Malcolm X: The Last Speeches*, pp. 124–26.
420 *discovered the house completely vacant.* "Malcolm X Averts Writ by Moving Out," *New York Times*, February 19, 1965.
420 *Hamer's Mississippi Freedom Democratic Party.* James Booker, "Malcolm X Speaks," *Amsterdam News*, February 6, 1965.
420 *"resolved by death and violence."* Goldman, *The Death and Life of Malcolm X*, p. 266.
421 *"of living prevalent throughout Africa."* Martin Paris, "Negroes Are Willing to Use Terrorism, Says Malcolm X," *Columbia Daily Spectator*, February 19, 1965.
421 *"that I'm sorry for now."* Clark, ed., *February 1965*, pp. 240–42.
421 *"before they came to rallies."* Peter Bailey interview, September 4, 1968, Manuscript Division, Moorland-Spingarn Research Center, Howard University Library.
422 *would be promptly revealed to the NYPD.* Roger Abel, *The Black Shield* (Bloomington, IN: Author House, 2006), pp. 471–72.
423 *remaining there until the next day.* Rickford, *Betty Shabazz*, p. 225; and Goldman, *The Death and Life of Malcolm X*, pp. 267–68.
423 *Sharon 6X may have joined him.* Oral history with James 67X Warden, June 18, 2003; and interview with Abdur-Rahman Muhammad, October 4, 2010.
423 *confronted the men. They promptly left.* Goldman, *The Death and Life of Malcolm X*, p. 268.
424 *the West and East Coasts.* Ibid.
425 *"I have to stand up for."* Michael Friedly, *Malcolm X: The Assassination* (New York: Carroll and Graf, 1992), p. 104; and Notes of Attorney William Kunstler, Case File 871-65, MANY.
426 *they were well-known "enforcers."* Goldman, *The Death and Life of Malcolm X*, pp. 250–51.
426 *degree of civility impressed Johnson.* Thomas 15X Johnson interview, September 29, 2004.
427 *law enforcement and the courts.* Ibid.
427 *Shifflett resigned . . . as general secretary.* Oral history of Max Stanford, August 28, 2007; and interview with Abdur-Rahman Muhammad, October 4, 2010.
428 *"his face from all directions."* Mitchell, *Shepherd of Black-Sheep*, pp. 15–17.
428 *"paid for his radical pioneering."* Ibid., pp. 17–18.
428 *better working relationship with Mitchell.* James 67X Warden interview, August 1, 2007.
428 *"work for it," Charles advised.* FBI—Morris, Summary Report, New York Office, March 1, 1965.
429 *vetoed by her husband, Ossie Davis.* Rickford, *Betty Shabazz*, p. 215.
429 *"caught me," he admitted to her.* Goldman, *The Death and Life of Malcolm X*, p. 266.
429 *"Martin Luther King," her mother advised.* Angelou, *A Song Flung Up to Heaven*, pp. 8–11, 14.
429 *"'brother should be more careful.'"* Herman Ferguson interview, July 24, 2004.

429 the likelihood of impending murder. Goldman, The Death and Life of Malcolm X, p. 418.
429 leader truly wanted to die. James 67X Warden interviews, June 18, 2003, and August 1, 2007.
430 struggle for freedom and justice. Esposito, ed., The Oxford Dictionary of Islam, pp. 27, 120.
431 "viewed him like the enemy." Gerry Fulcher interview, October 3, 2007.
431 the Rose and the larger Grand. Goldman, The Death and Life of Malcolm X, pp. 261–62.
431 "But I felt we was in accord." Ibid., p. 416; and Notes of Attorney William Kunstler, Case File 871-65, Series I, MANY.
432 his life to kill Malcolm. Goldman, The Death and Life of Malcolm X, pp. 416–17; and Peter Goldman interview, July 12, 2004.
432 "we knew he'd be." Goldman, The Death and Life of Malcolm X, pp. 417–18.
432 next afternoon, Sunday, February 21. Almustafa Shabazz, Offender Details, New Jersey Department of Corrections. Information can be found online using the New Jersey offender search (http://www.state.nj.us/corrections/). In the 1970s and 1980s, Bradley began calling himself Mustafa, or Almustafa Shabazz. His surname Shabazz indicates a continuing relationship to NOI.
432 would not be frigid. Goldman, The Death and Life of Malcolm X, p. 268.
433 "get ready and go see Daddy." Rickford, Betty Shabazz, pp. 226–27.
433 on the main ballroom's stage. Goldman, The Death and Life of Malcolm X, pp. 269–70.
434 at Columbia Presbyterian Hospital. Ibid., p. 269; and Peter Goldman interview, July 12, 2004.
434 rear room behind the Grand Ballroom's main stage. Peter Bailey interview, June 20, 2003.
434 "should know better than that." Goldman, The Death and Life of Malcolm X, p. 271; and James 67X Warden interviews, June 18, 2003, and August 1, 2007.
434 he yelled, "Get out of here!" Goldman, The Death and Life of Malcolm X, p. 271.
434 almost at his "wit's end." Ibid.
435 "'with their problems in mind.'" Mitchell, Shepherd of Black-Sheep, p. 7.
435 Audubon audience burst into applause. Goldman, The Death and Life of Malcolm X, p. 271; Transcript of address by Benjamin 2X Goodman, delivered at the Audubon Ballroom, February 21, 1965. Copy and audiotape recording in possession of author.
435 booth close to the stage. Betty Shabazz interview with NYPD, March 1, 1965, Case File 871-65, Series I, MANY; and Jessie 8X Ryan interview with NYPD, no date, Case File 871-65, Series I, MANY.
435 "Minister Malcolm," Benjamin hastily announced. Transcript of address by Benjamin 2X Goodman. Benjamin's subsequent reconstructions of his final remarks bore faint resemblance to what he actually said on February 21, 1965. To journalist/historian Peter Goldman, Benjamin recounted that he had introduced Malcolm with these stirring words: "I present . . . one who is willing to put himself on the line for you. . . . A man who would give his life for you." See Goldman, The Death and Life of Malcolm X, pp. 271–73.
436 "Hold it! Hold it! Hold it!" Ibid.
436 the men from the rear. Roberts responded to the disruption in the audience by moving forward from the rear of the ballroom. See Goldman, The Death and Life of Malcolm X, p. 273.
437 "hit the floor with a crash." Herman Ferguson interview, June 27, 2003.
437 "over chairs and people's bodies." Ibid.
437 he, too, "fell to the ground." John D. Davis interview with NYPD, March 5, 1965, Case File 871-65, Series I, MANY.
437 he "did not see anything." Charles 37X Morris interview with NYPD, no date, ibid.
438 conspirators managed to escape. Goldman, The Death and Life of Malcolm X, pp. 275–77.
438 William would later recount. William H. George, interview with New York District Attorney's office, March 18, 1965, Case File 871-65, Series I, MANY.
439 "alive! His heart's still beating." Welton Smith, "The 15 Seconds of Murder: Shots, a Bomb, and Despair," New York Herald Tribune, February 22, 1965. Other detailed media accounts of Malcolm X's assassination include: John Mallon, "Gunned Down as He Addresses Rally; 3 Men Wounded," New York Daily News, February 22, 1965; Walter Blitz, "Gunmen Kill Malcolm X: Black Nationalist Is Shot at Rally in NY,"

Chicago Tribune, February 22, 1965; "There Are Three Who Will Remember," New York World-Telegram, February 22, 1965; and Richard Barr, "Malcolm X Slain—The Reason Why," New York Journal-American, February 22, 1965.

439 because she was clearly hysterical. Rickford, Betty Shabazz, pp. 229–30.

439 revive him with mouth-to-mouth resuscitation. Jenkins, ed., Malcolm X Encyclopedia, pp. 471–72.

440 camera and began taking photographs. Earl Grant, "The Last Days of Malcolm X," in Clarke, ed., Malcolm X: The Man and His Times, p. 96.

440 "to myself that he was gone." Herman Ferguson interview, July 24, 2004.

441 "knew as Malcolm X is dead." Goldman, The Death and Life of Malcolm X, p. 278.

441 "when it comes, it comes on time." Benjamin Karim, with Peter Skutches and David Gallen, Remembering Malcolm (New York: Carroll and Graf, 1992), p. 190.

441 "'Don't hurry; come tomorrow!'" Mitchell, Shepherd of Black-Sheep, p. 20.

441 "life go out of his body." Abdullah Abdur-Razaaq interviewed by journalist Gil Noble, Like It Is, ABC, June 7, 1998, New York City.

441 "shoot [Captain] Joseph" in retaliation. Ibid. In this 1998 television interview Abdur-Razaaq insisted, "There's no question in my mind Malcolm was executed. He was not assassinated. When you assassinate someone, you are concerned with the manner and the audience that see this. And you have an authority behind you when someone is executed. . . . There is no question in my mind that the Federal Bureau of Investigation, the Bureau of Special Services of the New York Police Department [were] in cohort with those who pulled the trigger," stated James.

442 main stairwell into the street. Goldman, The Death and Life of Malcolm X, p. 274.

442 dispatched to the crime scene. Investigation Timeline, February 21, 1965, Case File 871-65, Series I, MANY.

442 reaching the emergency room. Ibid.

442 "the pen for immediate use." Ibid.

443 "told him I had been hit." Willie Harris interview with NYPD, February 21, 1965, Case File 871-65, Series I, MANY.

443 Malcolm's was the sole fatality. William Parker interview with NYPD, February 21, 1965, ibid.

443 "their hands in their pockets." Grant, "The Last Days of Malcolm X," p. 96.

443 "this wasn't nothing but coincidence." Smith, "The 15 Seconds of Murder: Shots, a Bomb, and Despair."

444 gangs feuding against each other. In a 2004 interview, Goldman sharply posed the question "What should the police have done? . . . They should have taken the threat very seriously. They should not have said in the press that the firebombing, for instance, was a publicity stunt. They should have been more aggressive in trying" to stop the assassination. To Goldman, the FBI was far more responsible for triggering Malcolm X's murder than the NYPD, because it had "inflamed the civil war" between Malcolm's followers and the NOI. Peter Goldman interview, July 12, 2004.

444 "seated in the Audubon Ballroom." Abdur-Razaaq, Like It Is, June 7, 1998.

444 "Mr. Warden stopped talking." James Warden interview with the New York Assistant District Attorney Herbert Stern and NYPD, February 21, 1965, Case File 871-65, Series I, MANY.

444 "nothing of any further value." Reuben Francis interview with Herbert Stern and NYPD, February 21, 1965, ibid.

445 light of the recent firebombing. Peter Goldman interview, July 12, 2004.

445 as advertised, at seven p.m. DeCaro, On the Side of My People, pp. 271–72.

445 fired four or five shots. FBI "Informant Report," unnamed, February 22, 1965, Case File 871-65, Series I, MANY. Author's note: The FBI maintained numerous open files on Malcolm X, Elijah Muhammad, and other NOI leaders, at FBI headquarters and at different field offices throughout the United States. Each individual document, even relevant newspaper clippings pertaining to the subjects, were individually cataloged. For several relevant FBI documents, both redacted and unredacted, that are available in the New York District Attorney's case file on the murder of Malcolm X, I have simply identified the document by its contents and date.

445 *"the front of the room."* Jasper Davis Report, Teletype, New York Office, February 23, 1965, in District Attorney's Files, ibid.

445 *ran "out [through] the ballroom."* Teletype, New York Office, February 22, 1965, ibid.

446 *"stated, 'We are at war.'"* Ibid.

446 *FBI informant Ronald Timberlake.* Teletype regarding Ronald Timberlake, New York Office, February 22, 1965, ibid.

446 *the two shooters he had seen.* Ronald Timberlake interview with NYPD, February 22, 1965, ibid.

446 *grandson and other NOI subordinates.* Clegg, *An Original Man*, p. 228.

447 *"total extent of Sister Betty's funds."* Alex Haley to Paul Reynolds, February 21, 1965; and Alex Haley to Paul Reynolds, February 27, 1965, Anne Romaine Collection, UTLSC, series I, box 3, folder 24.

448 *abruptly canceled the contract.* Kenneth McCormick to Alex Haley, March 16, 1965; Haley to McCormick, March 22, 1965; McCormick to Bob Banker, April 7, 1965; and McCormick to Haley and the Estate of Malcolm X, sometimes called Malik Shabazz, April 19, 1965, all in Anne Romaine Collection, UTLSC, series I, box 3, folder 23. In early March 1965, Nelson Doubleday, owner of Doubleday and Company, ordered his senior editor Kenneth McCormick to cancel the agreement. Doubleday had paid up to then over $15,000 in royalty advances to Haley and Malcolm X. McCormick would later write Haley that "the hardest thing I ever had to do was to call Paul Reynolds and ask him to show *The Autobiography of Malcolm X* to other publishers. In a policy decision at Doubleday, where I was a minor, contrary vote, it was decided that we could not publish the book." See McCormick to Haley, March 16, 1965.

448 *neighbors in his building, and so on.* Friedly, *Malcolm X: The Assassination*, p. 36; and Norman 3X Butler interview, December 22, 2008.

448 *chair and continued watching television.* Evanzz, *The Judas Factor*, pp. 282, 303.

448 *"John Ali made it known."* Thomas 15X Johnson interview, September 28, 2004.

448 *"those living that're in trouble."* DeCaro, *On the Side of My People*, pp. 274–75.

449 *"the OAAU, and Malcolm was dead."* Angelou, *A Song Flung Up to Heaven*, pp. 24–25.

Chapter 16: Life After Death

450 *participated in fifty thousand others.* Goldman, *The Death and Life of Malcolm X*, p. 287.

450 *was taken, which revealed "no abnormalities."* Autopsy of Malcolm X, Dr. Milton Helpern, February 22, 1965, Case File 871-65, Series I, MANY.

451 *by the NYPD's ballistics bureau.* Ibid.

451 *"he would not swear to this."* George Matthews interview with NYPD, April 8, 1965, Case File 871-65, Series I, MANY.

451 *an NOI member from Harlem.* Sharon 6X Shabazz interview at Audubon Ballroom, February 21, 1965, in documentary film produced by Omar Shabazz, *Inside Job: Betrayal of the Black Messiah*, May 19, 2010.

451 *NYPD was solving the case.* Friedly, *Malcolm X: The Assassination*, pp. 34–37.

452 *"is all except Reuben Francis."* Sharon 6X Shabazz interview with NYPD, February 27, 1965, Case File 871-65, Series I, MANY.

452 *relationship with both Malcolm X and Cathcart.* Abdur-Rahman Muhammad interview, November 4, 2010.

452 *"third row on the left side."* Earl Grant interview with NYPD, March 8, 1965, Case File 871-65, Series I, MANY.

452 *"malice aforethought" killed Malcolm X.* Goldman, *The Death and Life of Malcolm X*, pp. 305–7.

453 *NYPD on March 25, 1965.* Linwood X Cathcart interview with NYPD, March 25, 1965, Case File 871-65, Series I, MANY.

453 *interviewed three days earlier.* Robert 16X Gray interview with NYPD, March 22, 1965, ibid.

453 *captain had been destroyed years ago.* Joseph Gravitt file, empty, no date, ibid.

453   *"that Francis was an informant."* Gerry Fulcher interview, October 3, 2007.

453   *decided to flee the country.* Peter Kihss, "Mosque Fires Stir Fear of Vendetta in Malcolm Case," *New York Times,* February 24, 1965.

454   *"were capable of doing it."* Peter Bailey interview, September 4, 1968.

454   *"White and Black, Both Bitter."* Philip Benjamin, "Malcolm X Lived in Two Worlds, White and Black, Both Bitter," *New York Times,* February 22, 1965.

455   *"he spawned, and killed him."* "Malcolm X," *New York Times,* February 22, 1965. National press coverage and editorials throughout the United States were, with few exceptions, similar to the *Times*. The *Los Angeles Times,* for example, declared that "for a dozen years, the name of Malcolm X has been almost synonymous with hatred of the white race." Even "after the break" with the Nation, "he made it clear that he still hated whites, whom he called 'white devils.'" See "Hatred for Whites Obsessed Malcolm X," *Los Angeles Times,* February 22, 1965.

455   *"at a nearby Harlem restaurant."* "Death and Transfiguration," *Time,* March 5, 1965.

455   *"settlement of conflict by violence."* "Malcolm X (1925–1965)," *Saturday Evening Post,* vol. 238, no. 6 (March 27, 1965), p. 88.

455   *"city's top policemen immediately converged."* Jimmy Breslin, "Malcolm X Slain by Gunmen as 400 in Ballroom Watch: Police Rescue Two Suspects," *New York Herald Tribune,* February 22, 1965 (first edition printed February 21, 1965).

455   *Avenue police precinct were deleted.* Ibid.

455   *have been a BOSS operative.* See George Breitman, Herman Porter, and Baxter Smith, eds., *The Assassination of Malcolm X* (New York: Pathfinder, 1976).

456   *"that endures to this day."* Goldman, *The Death and Life of Malcolm X,* p. 276.

456   *"our deep-seated belief in nonviolence."* Douglas Robinson, "Rights Leaders Decry 'Violence,'" *New York Times,* February 22, 1965.

456   *"world, of the American Republic."* "What They're Saying," *Afro-American,* March 6, 1965.

456   *the Nation of Islam was evidently responsible.* Fred Powledge, "CORE Chief Calls Slaying Political," *New York Times,* February 24, 1965.

457   *any involvement in the murder.* Remnick, *King of the World,* p. 304.

457   *worried and called in reinforcements.* "Muslim Mosque Burns in Harlem; Blast Reported," *New York Times,* February 23, 1965; Walter Bilitz, "See Fire as Reprisal," *Chicago Tribune,* February 23, 1965; and "NYC Mosque Destroyed in Blast," *Chicago Defender,* February 24, 1965.

457   *deeply private Joseph now overwhelmed.* Larry 4X Prescott interview, June 9, 2006.

457   *cloistered in his Hyde Park mansion.* Kihss, "Mosque Fires Stir Fear," *New York Times.* The NOI mosque in San Francisco was also firebombed.

457   *"tamper with your religious sanctuary."* Paul L. Montgomery, "Muslims Enraged by 'Sneak Attack,'" *New York Times,* February 24, 1965.

457   *"brigade," reported the* Chicago Tribune. Thomas Fitzpatrick, "5,000 Muslims Meet Today in Security Vise," *Chicago Tribune,* February 26, 1965; and Thomas Fitzpatrick, "Heavy Guard Readied for Muslim Chief," *Chicago Tribune,* February 25, 1965.

458   *"country trying to slander me."* Thomas Fitzpatrick, "Muslim Sect Hears Chief Hit Malcolm," *Chicago Tribune,* February 27, 1965.

458   *"a follower of Elijah Muhammad."* Ibid.; "Muhammad Passes Up Session of Convention," *Los Angeles Times,* February 28, 1965; and Thomas Fitzpatrick, "Elijah's Men Maul Foe, 30, at Sect Rally," *Chicago Tribune,* March 1, 1965. About 7,500 people attended the three-day convention. Muhammad Ali also took the stage to repledge his loyalty to the patriarch.

458   *a traditional Muslim burial sheet.* Rickford, *Betty Shabazz,* pp. 242–52.

458   *King, Whitney Young, and Kwame Nkrumah.* Ibid., pp. 252–53.

459   *"because he loved us so."* Malcolm X and Haley, *Autobiography,* pp. 461–62; and Ossie Davis interview, June 29, 2003.

459   *the brothers proceeded to bury Malcolm themselves.* Malcolm X and Haley, *Autobiography,* p. 462; and Rickford, *Betty Shabazz,* pp. 254–55.

459   *from a sleeping pill overdose.* Goldman, *The Death and Life of Malcolm X,* p. 308.

460   *"something, which I don't believe."* Larry 4X Prescott interview, June 9, 2006.

460 *to assume his leadership mantle.* Max Stanford interview, August 28, 2007.

461 *for Betty and the children.* Rickford, *Betty Shabazz*, pp. 255–65.

461 *"field slaves to the house slaves."* Ibid., pp. 268–70.

462 *Collins responded, "I believe so."* James 67X Warden interviews, July 24, 2007, and August 1, 2007.

462 *"the youth were crazy."* Max Stanford interview, August 28, 2007.

463 *"in line to be assassinated."* FBI—Morris, Memo, New York Office, June 4, 1965.

463 *New York State's death row.* Goldman, *The Death and Life of Malcolm X*, p. 318.

463 *Hayer, beyond their NOI membership.* Ibid., pp. 310, 318–20, 329–33.

463 *fire to his jail mattress.* Robert L. Jenkins, "Cary Thomas," in Jenkins, ed., *Malcolm X Encyclopedia*, pp. 531–32.

464 *hands of Butler or Hayer.* Friedly, *Malcolm X: The Assassination*, pp. 42–43; and Cary Thomas interview with NYPD, March 3, 1965, and March 12, 1965, Case File 871-65, Series I, MANY.

464 *"go look for nobody else."* Norman 3X Butler interview, December 22, 2008.

464 *order to free his coassassins.* Goldman, *The Death and Life of Malcolm X*, pp. 335–39, 348–53.

464 *I never trusted Kenyatta—never.*" Ibid., pp. 339–40; and Thomas 15X Johnson interview, September 29, 2004.

464 *an NOI "hundred-man enforcing squad."* Goldman, *The Death and Life of Malcolm X*, pp. 339–40.

465 *to disregard Betty's off-stand statements.* Ibid., pp. 333–35.

465 *"when the jury convicted me."* Thomas 15X Johnson interview, September 29, 2004.

465 *"here that history will support."* Goldman, *The Death and Life of Malcolm X*, pp. 357–59, 373–74.

465 *political philosophy of black nationalism.* Marable, *Living Black History*, p. 197; and Kofsky, *Black Nationalism and the Revolution in Music*, p. 155.

465 *"of the black nationalist movement."* Kofsky, *Black Nationalism and the Revolution in Music*, p. 64.

465 *"the New Super Bop Fire."* Amiri Baraka (also known as LeRoi Jones), "Jazz Criticism and Its Effect on the Art Form," in David Baker, ed., *New Perspectives in Jazz* (Washington, D.C.: Smithsonian, 1986), p. 66.

465 *"artist of the spoken word."* Goldman, *The Death and Life of Malcolm X*, p. 383.

465 *"its relevance cannot be doubted."* Eliot Fremont-Smith, "An Eloquent Testament," *New York Times*, November 5, 1965.

466 *"the most painful of truths."* Truman Nelson, "Delinquent's Progress," *Nation*, November 8, 1965, pp. 336–38.

466 *"his burning ambition to succeed."* Bayard Rustin, "Making His Mark," *Washington Post*, November 14, 1965.

466 *"members of the black bourgeoisie."* Ibid.

467 *sold worldwide exceeded six million.* Eric Pace, "Alex Haley, 70, Author of *Roots*, Dies," *New York Times*, February 11, 1992.

467 *with Malcolm X for decades.* See FBI—Morris file.

467 *"have taken all five assassins."* Karim, Skutches, and Gallen, *Remembering Malcolm*, p. 191.

468 *"valuable assistance to the Bureau."* FBI—Goodman, Memo, New York Office, April 27, 1966.

468 *went back to New York City.* Ibid.

468 *or anywhere else—has emerged.* Langston Hughes Savage interview, September 6, 2008.

468 *"of Malcolm's birth and death."* Remnick, *King of the World*, p. 240.

468 *as remote as another world.* Ibid., pp. 253–56.

469 *of nearly all the Nation's operations.* On Wallace Muhammad's rise to power in the NOI, see Clifton E. Marsh, *From Black Muslims to Muslims: The Resurrection, Transformation, and Change of the Lost-Found Nation of Islam in America, 1930–1995*, second edition (London: Scarecrow, 1996), pp. 101–11, 157–71; Clegg, *An Original Man*, pp. 98, 162, 181–83, 206–7, 273–74, 282; "Son Will Succeed Elijah Muhammad," *Amsterdam News*, March 1, 1975; "There Is No Power Struggle Among Black Mus-

lims," *Amsterdam News*, March 22, 1975; and "An Interview with Elijah Muhammad's Successor," *Amsterdam News*, April 9, 1975.

469 *a few whites actually joined.* "New Muslim Leader Invites Contributions from Whites," *Amsterdam News*, April 23, 1975; and "Muslims to Accept White Followers," *Amsterdam News*, June 25, 1975.

469 *distinguish himself from his father.* "W. Deen Mohammed: A Leap of Faith," *Chicago Tribune*, October 20, 2002.

469 *"for the Honorable Elijah Muhammad."* Marsh, *From Black Muslims to Muslims*, pp. 103–6.

470 *in 1977, was to excommunicate him.* Ibid., pp. 107–10.

470 *Marie Muhammad (born March 30, 1960).* "Suit Charges Late Muslim Leader's Estate Misused," *Jet*, March 26, 1981.

470 *"get in the front of the civil rights movement."* Larry 4X Prescott interview, November 7, 2007.

471 *a wife and thirteen children.* "Muslim Slain in Jersey," *Amsterdam News*, September 8, 1973.

471 *subsequently found four miles distant.* Evanzz, *The Messenger*, p. 377.

471 *just barely missing his secretary.* Ibid., p. 364.

471 *causes, on December 18, 2003.* Illinois Deaths, Raymond Sharrieff, U.S. Social Security Death Index, Family Search Internet (www.familysearch.org, June 19, 2010).

471 *six sons, and eight daughters.* Richard Goldstein, "Jabir Herbert Muhammad, Who Managed Muhammad Ali, Dies at 79," *New York Times*, August 27, 2008.

471 *Council on American-Islamic Relations.* Margaret Ramirez, Manya Brachear, and Ron Grossman, "Imam W. Deen Mohammed, 1933–2008," *Chicago Tribune*, September 10, 2008; and Patricia Sullivan, "W. D. Mohammed: Changed Muslim Movement in U.S.," *Washington Post*, September 10, 2008.

472 *"not a good influence on him."* Bill Cunningham and Daniel Golden, "Malcolm: The Boston Years," *Boston Globe*, February 16, 1992.

472 *passed away on August 6, 1996.* Ibid.

472 *"wanting to help my daughter."* Rickford, *Betty Shabazz*, pp. 359–61, 364–66, 437–39, 505–13.

472 *"to uplifting women and children."* Emanuel Parker, "Nation Mourns Loss of Betty Shabazz," *Los Angeles Sentinel*, June 26, 1997.

472 *District of Columbia representative Eleanor Holmes Norton.* Ibid.

473 *not those of her father.* Rickford, *Betty Shabazz*, pp. 536–45.

473 *"stories straight. You're out, kid."* Gerry Fulcher interview, October 3, 2007.

473 *before resigning from the force.* Ibid.

474 *"allegedly received from the FBI."* Les Matthews, "Malcolm X Killer Talks; Names 4," *Amsterdam News*, April 29, 1978.

474 *"have been sure to notice."* Charles Kaiser, "2 Held Not Guilty in Malcolm Case," *New York Times*, July 27, 1978.

474 *to grant a new trial.* "Federal Hearings Asked into Malcolm X Murder," *New York Times*, April 30, 1979.

474 *of the Black Panther Party.* Ibid.; and "Probe Requested in Malcolm Death," *Los Angeles Sentinel*, July 20, 1978.

474 *died on August 4, 2009.* Robert Fleming, "Khalil Islam; Wrongly Convicted of Killing Malcolm X, Dies," *Black Star News*, August 7, 2009.

475 *serious to permit his release.* Jennifer Peltz, "Thomas Hagen, Only Man to Admit Role in Malcolm X Assassination, Is Freed on Parole in NYC," Associated Press, April 27, 2010.

475 *associated with the Newark mosque.* See Zak Kondo, *Conspiracys: Unraveling the Assassination of Malcolm X* (Washington, D.C.: Nubia, 1993).

475 *They escaped with over $12,500. United States of America v. James Henry Moore and William Bradley*, Title 18 U.S.C. Secs. 2113(d) and (D.N.J. 1699); and "Livingston Bank Is Held Up," *New York Times*, April 12, 1968.

475 *charged with the bank robbery. United States of America v. James Henry Moore, appellant, and William Bradley*, 453F. 2d 601 (3d Cir. 1971).

475 *own attorney separate from Moore. United States of America v. William Bradley*, Notice of Appearance, July 18, 1969.

475 *were ultimately dismissed. United States of America v. William Bradley*, Order for Dismissal, August 21, 1970.

475 *"years for an unrelated felony."* Goldman, *The Death and Life of Malcolm X*, p. 428.

476 *baseball achievements in high school.* "Sports Briefs," *Amsterdam News*, February 21, 1981; Collie J. Nicholson, "King Refutes *New York Post* Claim," *Los Angeles Sentinel*, June 24, 1999; and Newark Athletic Hall of Fame (http://www.newarkathletichall offame.org/_fileCabinet/NAHFPastInductees.pdf). Carolyn Kelly-Shabazz was inducted into the Newark Athletic Hall of Fame in 2005.

476 *criminality to respectability seemed complete.* Omar Shabazz, *Inside Job: Betrayal of the Black Messiah*, 2010.

476 *"religion, and freedom of assembly."* Richard Prince, "Malcolm X Scholars Point to a Triggerman," May 24, 2010, Maynard Institute (http://mije.org/richardprince/malcolm-x-scholars-id-triggerman).

476 *real killers of Malcolm X.* Omar Shabazz, *Inside Job: Betrayal of the Black Messiah*, 2010.

477 *"[in which] Malcolm was assassinated."* Louis Farrakhan interview, December 27, 2007; and Mike Wallace interview with Louis Farrakhan, *60 Minutes*, CBS, September 29, 2009.

477 *"grand jury to question me."* Louis Farrakhan interview, December 27, 2007.

477 *destroy you. I understand that.* Ibid.

478 *members in Detroit's Cobo Center.* "Muslims Name Successor to Malcolm X," *Afro-American*, August 28, 1965.

478 *"didn't mean to take your home!"* Louis Farrakhan interview, May 9, 2005.

478 *Farrakhan delivered the guest sermon.* Louis Farrakhan interview, December 27, 2007.

Epilogue: Reflections on a Revolutionary Vision

481 *"mind, Black judgment,"* Baraka *asserted.* LeRoi Jones, *Home: Social Essays* (New York: William Morrow, 1966), pp. 238–50.

481 *"'integrated out of existence.'"* "Malcolm X a Harlem Idol on Eve of Murder Trial," *New York Times*, December 5, 1965.

482 *"on an otherwise darkened stage."* Stokely Carmichael (Kwame Ture) and Ekwueme Michael Thelwell, *Ready for Revolution* (New York: Scribner, 1993), pp. 253, 259. Carmichael added, "It was simply refreshing for young Africans to hear someone stand up and so fearlessly describe the real American black folks knew and experienced daily. Especially in a setting usually so relentlessly cautious, guarded, and overly sensitive to the sensibilities of the same white ruling class responsible for perpetuating our people's oppression" (p. 261).

483 *Davis said, "is not a king."* Ossie Davis interview, June 29, 2003.

485 *necessity of armed struggle in Africa.* William Mervin Gumede, *Thabo Mbeki and the Battle for the Soul of the ANC* (Cape Town, South Africa: Zebra Press, 2007), p. 24.

485 *that number were black Americans.* See Marable, *Race, Reform and Rebellion*, pp. 238–40.

486 *will influence his future legacy.* The sales of *The Autobiography of Malcolm X* rose 300 percent between 1989 and 1992, during the golden age of hip-hop music. See Lewis Lord, Jeannye Thornton, and Alejandro Bodipo-Memba, "The Legacy of Malcolm X," *U.S. News and World Report*, November 15, 1992.

486 *Universal Day of Struggle Against Race Discrimination.* Paul Lee, "Unseen Unity," *Michigan Citizen*, September 30, 2009.

486 *"become the new Malcolm X."* Philip Sherwell, "The New Malcolm X?" *Sunday Telegraph*, April 9, 2006.

487 *traditions of "honorable black Americans."* Mark Mazzetti, "Al-Qaeda Offers Obama Insults and a Warning," *New York Times*, November 20, 2008.

487 *"people I have ever met."* James Baldwin, "Malcolm and Martin," *Esquire*, vol. 77, no. 4 (April 1972), pp. 94–97, 195–202.

A GLOSSARY OF TERMS

As-salaam alaikum—An Arabic spoken greeting; the term *salaam* means "peace" and the greeting can be translated as "Peace be upon you."

Black Legion—A hate group related to the Ku Klux Klan which numbered nearly thirty thousand and was centered on Detroit and other Midwestern cities. The Black Legion was responsible for numerous crimes against immigrants, minorities, and suspected communists; the group was allegedly responsible for the death of Malcolm X's father, Earl Little.

Fishing—The searching for new converts to the Nation of Islam.

Fitna—From the Arabic verb meaning "to seduce, tempt, or lure," *fitna* can refer to the temptation believers must face or the period of chaos and disorder prior to salvation. It can also describe fracturing or civil war within the Muslim community.

Five Pillars of Islam—The five duties of every Sunni Muslim, including *shahada, salat, zakat, sawm,* and *hajj.*

Fruit of Islam—The "Fruit," as it is often called, is a male-only paramilitary group of the Nation of Islam, which is in charge of security and whose membership is drawn from the various mosques. Members are characterized by distinct blue or white uniforms and caps bearing a star and crescent or the abbreviation FOI.

Hajj—The fifth pillar of Islam, the hajj is the largest annual pilgrimage in the world and must be performed at least once by every Muslim who is physically or financially able. It occurs from the seventh to the thirteenth day during the twelfth month of the Islamic calendar.

Imam—Muslim spiritual or community leader, and the person who leads prayer during a religious gathering.

Jihad—Religious duty meaning "struggle," jihad is the striving for perfection in Islam; it can also refer to a holy war against infidels. Some Sunni scholars categorize this as the unofficial sixth pillar of Islam.

Kaaba—A cuboidal building built by Abraham, according to Islamic tradition, it is enclosed within the Masjid al-Haram in Mecca and is the point toward which all Muslims pray. The *Kaaba* is circled during the hajj, a process called *tawaf.*

Kafan—Clean white cloth that the body is wrapped in during a traditional Islamic funeral.

Mecca—The holiest city in Islam, Mecca is closed to non-Muslims and is the site of the hajj festivities.

Medina—The second holiest city in Islam, Medina is the burial place of the Prophet Muhammad and was the place of his migration from Mecca in 622 CE.

The Mother Plane—A cylindrical spaceship believed to carry fifteen hundred smaller ships, which would destroy America and England during the judgment, according to NOI eschatology.

Muhammad Speaks—Official newspaper of the Nation of Islam, *Muhammad Speaks* was started by Malcolm X as a small New York pamphlet in 1960; editorial control was quickly transferred to Herbert Muhammad, and the newspaper eventually rose to become the most widely published black weekly, with a circulation estimated between six hundred thousand and nine hundred thousand in the early 1970s.

Muslim Girls Training (MGT) and General Civilization Class—A weekly class for women within the Nation which stressed domestic skills such as keeping house, rearing children, sewing, cooking, and hygiene. It also offered a social space for women within the movement to organize and meet others with shared religious or political views.

Orgena—A play written by Louis Farrakhan in the late 1950s, *Orgena*—"A Negro" spelled in reverse—depicted a history in which the black man is estranged from his original culture and then enslaved, before becoming a second-class citizen and eventually rediscovering his cultural heritage. The play was performed most notably at Carnegie Hall and Town Hall in New York City.

Original Man—Term used by the Nation of Islam to emphasize that black people were the first humans on earth and thus the originators of human civilization.

The Royal Family—Name referring to the immediate family of Elijah Muhammad, specifically his wife, Clara, daughters Ethel and Lottie, and sons Nathaniel, Herbert, Elijah Jr., Akbar, and Wallace. Son-in-law Raymond Sharrieff was also close to the family and shared a large portion of power.

Salat—One of the five pillars, *salat* refers to formal prayer, which is to be practiced five times a day: dawn, noon, afternoon, sunset, and nightfall.

Saviour's Day Convention—The Nation's annual gathering, held in Chicago around February 26 to honor the birth of founder W. D. Fard.

Sawm—An Arabic word for fasting, it means "to abstain from eating, drinking, and intercourse," under the terms of Islamic law. The observance of *sawm* during Ramadan is one of the five pillars.

Shahada—The recitation of the *shahada*, meaning "witnessing," is the most important of the five pillars of Islam. The recitation translates as "There is no god but Allah, and Muhammad is the Messenger of Allah."

Shi'a—Second largest denomination of Muslims, Shi'as regard Ali (Muhammad's cousin and son-in-law) and his lineage as the legitimate heirs to the Prophet.

Sunni—Refers to those who accept the Sunna, or words and actions of the Prophet Muhammad; it is the largest Muslim community, comprising nearly 90 percent of all Muslims worldwide.

Tawaf—An Islamic ritual of the hajj and *umrah*, meant to demonstrate the unity of believers, in which Muslims circumambulate the Kaaba seven times counterclockwise.

Tribe of Shabazz—According to NOI theology, the Tribe of Shabazz was the lone survivor of thirteen tribes that lived sixty-six trillion years ago. Led by a scientist of the same name, it was believed that members of the Nation were descendants of the tribe, which eventually settled in present-day Mecca.

Ummah—Arabic word meaning "community" or "nation," it refers to the Arab world or, in Islam, the diaspora of believers throughout the world.

Umrah—Lesser pilgrimage compared to the hajj, it refers to travel to the holy sites out of season.

Walaikum salaam—The typical response to *As-salaam alaikum*, meaning "And upon you be peace."

Well of Zamzam—A well located within the Masjid al-Haram, not far from the *Kaaba*. Pilgrims drink from the well each year during hajj or *umrah*.

"A White Man's Heaven Is a Black Man's Hell"—Song composed by calypso singer and future national minister Louis Farrakhan for the Nation of Islam.

X—Each Nation of Islam member was required to drop his or her surname and replace it with an X, representing the unknown ancestral surname that had been stripped away through slavery. Numbers preceded the X if more than one member of a mosque shared the same first name, progressing in order of membership.

Yacub's History—According to NOI theology, Dr. Yacub (often spelled Yakub) was an evil scientist who lived in Mecca in 8400 BCE. After he and his followers were exiled to an island in the Aegean Sea, Dr. Yacub sought revenge by genetically grafting the black gene from the Original Man until the white race was eventually created, long after his death at the age of 152.

Zakat—Another of the five pillars, *zakat* is the calculated percentage of one's possessions or earnings to be given to the needy and community.

Government Documents

Federal Bureau of Investigation, U.S. Department of Justice
(listed by numerical file number)

62-102926	Louis E. Lomax
100-399321	Malcolm X Little
100-410846	James 3X Shabazz
100-430081	Leon 4X Phillips
100-433888	Benjamin 2X Goodman
100-436766	Ethel Sharrieff
100-441765	Muslim Mosque, Incorporated (MMI)
100-442684	Revolutionary Action Movement (RAM)
100-442735	Organization of Afro-American Unity (OAAU)
100-443409	Charles 37X Morris
105-141877	Ella X Collins
105-24822	Elijah Muhammad
105-24951	Raymond X Sharrieff
105-32655	Joseph X Gravitt
105-41637	Wilfred X Little
105-54106	John Hassan
105-54773	Herbert Jabir Muhammad
105-71196	Betty Shabazz
157-2209	Nation of Islam (NOI)

Freedom of Information Act (FOIA) releases

Earl Little Arson Special Report (#2155), Department of State Police, Lansing, Michigan
Estate of Earl Little (File A-4053), Ingham County Probate Court, State of Michigan
Louise Little Mental Health Record (File B-4398), Ingham County Probate Court, State of Michigan
Malcolm Little, Office of Public Safety and Security, Department of Corrections, State of Michigan
Malcolm X Bureau of Special Services and Investigation file, New York Police Department
Malcolm X Central Intelligence Agency file
Malcolm X Secret Service file
Malcolm X State Department file
New York City Department of Records and Information Services, Municipal Archives in the City of New York
Prison File of Malcolm Little (#22843), Department of Corrections, Commonwealth of Massachusetts

Archival Collections

A. Peter Bailey/OAAU Papers, Manuscripts, Archives and Rare Books Division, Schomburg Center for Research in Black Culture, New York Public Library, New York, New York

563

Alex Haley Papers, Manuscripts, Archives and Rare Books Division, Schomburg Center for Research in Black Culture, New York Public Library, New York, New York

Aliya Hassen Papers, Bentley Historical Library, University of Michigan, Ann Arbor, Michigan

Anne Romaine Collection, Special Collections Library, University of Tennessee, Knoxville, Tennessee

C. Eric Lincoln Collection, Robert W. Woodruff Library, Special Collections Department, Emory University, Atlanta, Georgia

Earl Little Death Certificate, Michigan Department of Community Health, Division for Vital Records and Health Statistics

George Breitman Papers, Tamiment Library and Robert F. Wagner Labor Archives, New York University

Howard K. Smith Papers, Archives Division, Wisconsin Historical Society

J. B. Matthews Papers, Rare Book, Manuscript, and Special Collections Library, Duke University, Durham, North Carolina

James Haughton Papers, Manuscripts, Archives and Rare Books Division, Schomburg Center for Research in Black Culture, New York Public Library, New York, New York

John Henrik Clarke Papers, Manuscripts, Archives and Rare Books Division, Schomburg Center for Research in Black Culture, New York Public Library, New York, New York

Julian Mayfield Papers, Manuscripts, Archives and Rare Books Division, Schomburg Center for Research in Black Culture, New York Public Library, New York, New York

Kalamazoo State Hospital, Clarence L. Miller Local History Room, Kalamazoo Public Library, Kalamazoo, Michigan

Ken McCormick Collection of the Records of Doubleday and Company, Manuscript Division, Library of Congress

Malcolm X Assassination Trial Transcripts, Union Theological Seminary, New York, New York

Malcolm X Collection, 1941–1955, Robert W. Woodruff Library, Special Collections Department, Emory University, Atlanta, Georgia

Malcolm X Collection, Manuscripts, Archives and Rare Books Division, Schomburg Center for Research in Black Culture, New York Public Library, New York, New York

Malcolm X Debate with Willoughby Abner, 1962, Archives Division, Wisconsin Historical Society

Milton A. Galamison Papers, Manuscripts, Archives and Rare Books Division, Schomburg Center for Research in Black Culture, New York Public Library, New York, New York

National Union of Hospital and Health Care Employees Record, Division of Rare and Manuscript Collections, Cornell University, Ithaca, New York

Oral History of Charles Kenyatta, 1970, Manuscript Division, Moorland-Spingarn Research Center, Howard University Library, Washington, D.C.

Oral History of Peter Bailey, 1968, Manuscript Division, Moorland-Spingarn Research Center, Howard University Library, Washington, D.C.

Papers of Jackie Robinson, Manuscript Division, Library of Congress

Paul Revere Reynolds Papers, Rare Book and Manuscript Library, Columbia University, New York, New York

Percival Leroy Prattis Papers, Manuscript Division, Moorland-Spingarn Research Center, Howard University Library, Washington, D.C.

Reminiscences of Bayard Rustin, 1987, Oral History Research Office, Columbia University, New York, New York

Reminiscences of Ed Edwin, 1967, Oral History Research Office, Columbia University, New York, New York

Reminiscences of James Farmer, 1979, Oral History Research Office, Columbia University, New York, New York

Reminiscences of Kenneth B. Clark, 1976, Oral History Research Office, Columbia University, New York, New York

Reminiscences of Malcolm X: A Lecture, 1963, Oral History Research Office, Columbia University, New York, New York
Reminiscences of Mamie Clark, 1976, Oral History Research Office, Columbia University, New York, New York
Willoughby Abner Collection, Walter P. Reuther Library, Wayne State University, Detroit, Michigan

Oral Histories

Bailey, A. Peter. June 20, 2003
Baraka, Amiri. June 11, 2001
Brown, Dr. William Neal. May 10, 2005
Butler, Norman 3X. December 22, 2008
Davis, Ossie. June 29, 2003
Farrakhan, Louis. May 9, 2005; December 27, 2007
Feelings, Muriel. October 10, 2003
Ferguson, Herman. June 27, 2003; June 24, 2004; July 31, 2007; August 28, 2007
Fulcher, Gerry. October 3, 2007
Johnson, Thomas 15X. September 29, 2004
McCallum, Dr. Leo X. December 26, 2005
Prescott, Larry 4X. March 10, 2006; June 9, 2006; November 7, 2007
Reynolds, Jeanne. June 25, 2003
Savage, Langston Hughes. September 6, 2008
Stanford, Max. January 31, 2003; August 28, 2007
Warden, James 67X. June 18, 2003; July 24, 2007; August 1, 2007

Interviews

DeCaro, Louis A., Jr. July 16, 2001
Goldman, Peter. July 12, 2004
Griffin, Farah Jasmine. August 6, 2001
Hussey, Dermot. May 7, 2005
Kelley, Robin D. G. July 13, 2001
Muhammad, Najee. September 5, 2003
Powell, Kevin. June 22, 2001
Sherwood, Marika. December 6, 2002

Newspapers and Periodicals

Afro-American (Baltimore)
American Heritage
Amsterdam News
Atlanta Daily World
The Atlantic (Washington, D.C.)
Baltimore Sun
The Black Panther
Black Scholar
Black World
Boston Herald
The Butler Herald (Butler, GA)
The Catalogue of Brown University
The Challenger
The Charleston Chronicle (Charleston, SC)
Chicago Daily News
Chicago Defender
Chicago Tribune
Chicago's American

Christian Century
Christianity and Crisis
City Sun (New York)
Columbia Daily Spectator
Daily Graphic (Ghana)
Daily Telegraph
Democrat and Chronicle (Rochester, NY)
The Detroit News
Dialogue Magazine
Ebony
Egyptian Gazette
Emerge
Esquire
Essence
Ghanaian Times
Guardian (London)
Hartford Courant
The Harvard Crimson
Herald Tribune (New York)
International Socialist Review
Jet
Journal American
Journal and Guide (Norfolk, VA)
The Liberator
Look
Los Angeles Herald-Dispatch
Los Angeles Sentinel
Los Angeles Times
Manchester Guardian Weekly
Michigan Chronicle
Michigan Citizen
The Militant (New York)
Monthly Review
Moslem Sunrise
Muhammad Speaks
Muslim World
Negro Digest
Negro World
New Crusader (Chicago)
New Jersey Herald News (Newark)
The New Leader
New Statesman (London)
New York magazine
New York Herald Tribune
New York Journal American
New York Post
New York Telegraph and Sun
New York Times
The New York Times Book Review
New York World Telegram and the Sun
Newsday (New York)
Newsweek
Oakland Tribune
Pittsburgh Courier
Playboy
Readers Digest
The Rockwell Report

Rutgers Observer
Sacramento Observer
San Francisco Chronicle
Saturday Evening Post
The Source
Springfield Union (Springfield, MA)
St. Louis Globe-Democrat
State Journal (Lansing, MI)
The Sunday Telegraph (London)
Time
Tri-State Defender (Memphis, TN)
U.S. News and World Report
Village Voice
Wall Street Journal
Washington Post
Yale Daily News
Young Socialist

Dissertations and Theses

Bertley, Leo W. "The Universal Negro Improvement Association of Montreal, 1917–1974." Ph.D. dissertation, Concordia University, California, 1980.

Brooks, Stacy Lamar. "Celebrating Martin and Forgetting Malcolm: The Punishment of Black Leadership Purpose Agency." M.A. thesis, University of Louisville, 2004.

Burrows, Cedric Dewayne. "The Contemporary Rhetoric About Martin Luther King, Jr., and Malcolm X in the Post-Reagan Era." M.A. thesis, Miami University, 2005.

DeCaro, Louis Anthony, Jr. "Malcolm X and the Nation of Islam: Two Moments in His Religious Sojourn." Ph.D. dissertation, New York University, 1994.

Dinkins, Andrew Ann. "Malcolm X and the Rhetoric of Transformation: 1948–1965." Ph.D. dissertation, University of Pittsburgh, 1995.

Dvorak, Kenneth R. "Terror in Detroit: The Rise and Fall of Michigan's Black Legion." Ph.D. dissertation, Bowling Green State University, 1990.

Dyson, Michael Eric. "Uses of Heroes: Celebration and Criticism in the Interpretation of Malcolm X and Martin Luther King, Jr." Ph.D. dissertation, Princeton University, 1993.

Farrah, Daryl. "Re-examining Malcolm X." M.A. thesis San Jose State University, 2000.

Gay, John Franklin. "The Rhetorical Strategies and Tactics of Malcolm X (Movement Theory, Neo-Aristotelian, Black Muslims, Persuasion)." Ph.D. dissertation, Indiana University, 1985.

Hess, Eldora F. "The Negro in Nebraska." M.A. thesis, University of Nebraska, 1932.

Hodges, John Oliver. "The Quest for Selfhood in the Autobiographies of W. E. B. Du Bois, Richard Wright, and Malcolm X." Ph.D. dissertation, University of Chicago, 1980.

Lee, Andrew Ann Dinkins. "Malcolm X and the Rhetoric of Transformation: 1948–1965." Ph.D. dissertation, University of Pittsburgh, 1995.

Leullen, David Elmer. "Ministers and Martyrs: Malcolm X and Martin Luther King, Jr." Ph.D. dissertation, Ball State University, 1972.

Mazucci, Elizabeth. "St. Martin's Relics: A Study of the Artifacts Shaped by the Assassination of Malcolm X." M.A. thesis, Columbia University, 2005.

Moore, William Henry. "On Identity and Consciousness of El-Hajj Malik El-Shabazz (Malcolm X): An Application of the Theory of Identity to the History of Black Consciousness." Ph.D. dissertation, University of California, Santa Cruz, 1974.

Morrison, Carlos D. "The Rhetoric of the Nation of Islam, 1930–1975: A Functional Approach." Ph.D. dissertation, Howard University, 1996.

Muhammad, Najee Emerson. "The Transformational Leadership and Educational Philosophic Legacy of Malcolm X." Ed.D. dissertation, University of Cincinnati, 1999.

Namphy, Mychel Josef. "Malcolm's Mood Indigo: A Theodicy of Literary Contests." Ph.D. dissertation, Princeton University, 2003.

Norman, Barbara Ann. "The Black Muslims: A Rhetorical Analysis (Malcolm X, Nation of Islam, Elijah Muhammad)." Ph.D. dissertation, University of Oklahoma, 1985.

Onwubu, Chukwuemeka. "Black Ideologies and the Sociology of Knowledge: The Public Response to the Protest Thoughts and Teachings of Martin Luther King, Jr., and Malcolm X." Ph.D. dissertation, Michigan State University, 1975.

Polizzi, David. "The Experience of Antiblack Racism: A Phenomenological Hermeneutic of *The Autobiography of Malcolm X.*" Ph.D. dissertation, Duquesne University, 2002.

Pugh, Maurice. "Black Theology: Cone, King, and Malcolm X." Ph.D. dissertation, Dallas Theological Seminary, 2006.

Sales, William W., Jr. "Malcolm X and the Organization of Afro-American Unity: A Case Study in Afro-American Nationalism." Ph.D. dissertation, Columbia University, 1991.

Smallwood, Andrew Peter. "Malcolm X: An Intellectual Aesthetic for Black Adult Education. Ed.D. dissertation, Northern Illinois University, 1998.

Terrill, Robert Edward. "Symbolic Emancipation in the Rhetoric of Malcolm X." Ph.D. dissertation, Northwestern University, 1996.

Varda, Scott Joseph. "A Rhetorical History of Malcolm X." Ph.D. dissertation, University of Iowa, 2007.

Washington, Von Hugo. "An Evaluation of the Play *Purlie Victorious* and Its Impact on the American Theater Scene." Ph.D. dissertation, Wayne State University, 1979.

Whitaker, Catherine Jean. "Almshouses and Mental Institutions in Michigan, 1871–1930." Ph.D. dissertation, University of Michigan, 1986.

Woods, Ventris. "Political Communication and the Social Construction of Malcolm X." Ph.D. dissertation, Northern Arizona University, 1998.

Woodyard, Jeffrey Lynn. "Africalogical Rhetorical Theory and Criticism: Afrocentric Approaches to the Rhetoric of Malcolm X." Ph.D. dissertation, Temple University, 1996.

Journal Articles

"A Conversation with Ossie Davis." *Souls*, vol. 2, no. 3 (Summer 2000): 6–16.

Amann, Peter H. "Vigilante Fascism: The Black Legion as an American Hybrid." *Contemporary Studies in Society and History*, vol. 25, no. 3 (July 1983): 490–524.

Baraka, Amiri (aka LeRoi Jones). "Jazz Criticism and Its effects on the Art Form," pp. 55–70, in Baker, David, ed. *New Perspectives in Jazz*. Washington, D.C.: Smithsonian, 1986.

Beynon, Erdmann Doane. "The Voodoo Cult Among Negro Migrants in Detroit." *American Journal of Sociology*, vol. 43, no. 6 (May 1938): 894–907.

Bloch, Herman D. "The Employment Status of the New York Negro in Retrospect." *Phylon*, vol. 20, no. 4 (1959): 327–344.

Branham, Robert James. "'I Was Gone on Debating' Malcolm X's Prison Debates and Public Confrontations." *Argumentation and Advocacy*, vol. 31 (Winter 1995): 117–137.

Burns, W. Haywood. "The Black Muslims in America: a Reinterpretation." *Race*, vol. 5, no. 1 (July 1963): 26–37.

Capeci, Dominic J. "From Different Liberal Perspectives: Fiorello H. LaGuardia, Adam Clayton Powell, Jr., and Civil Rights in New York City, 1941–1943." *Journal of Negro History*, vol. 62, no. 2 (April 1977): 160–173.

Clinonsmith, Michael S. "The Black Legion: Hooded Americanism in Michigan." *Michigan History Magazine*, vol. 55, no. 3 (1971): 243–262.

Condit, Celeste Michelle, and John Louis Lucaites. "Malcolm X and the Limits of the Rhetoric of Revolutionary Dissent." *Journal of Black Studies*, vol. 23, no. 3 (March 1993): 291–313.

Curtis, IV, Edward. "Islamism and Its African American Muslim Critics: Black Muslims in the Era of the Arab Cold War." *American Quarterly*, vol. 59, no. 3 (September 2007): 683–709.

Daniels, Douglas Henry. "Los Angeles Zoot Race 'Riot': The Pachuco and Black Culture Music." *Journal of Negro History*, vol. 82, issue 2 (Spring 1997): 201–220.

Davidson, Nicol. "Alioune Diop and the African Renaissance." *African Affairs*, vol. 78, no. 310 (January 1979): 3–11.

Demarest, David P., Jr. "The Autobiography of Malcolm X: Beyond Didacticism." *CLA Journal*, vol. 16, no. 2 (December 1972): 179–187.

DeVeaux, Scott. "Bebop and the Recording Industry: The 1942 AFM Recording Ban Reconsidered." *Journal of the American Musicological Society*, vol. 41, no. 1 (Spring 1988): 126–165.

El-Beshti, Bashir M. "The Semiotics of Salvation: Malcolm X and the Autobiographical Self." *The Journal of Negro History*, vol. 82, no. 4 (Autumn 1997): 359–367.

Epps, Archie. "The Rhetoric of Malcolm X." *Harvard Review*, no. 3 (Winter 1993): 64–75.

Fras, Ivan, and Joseph Joel Friedman. "Hallucinogenic Effects of Nutmeg in Adolescent." *New York State Journal of Medicine*, vol. 69, no. 3 (February 1, 1969): 463–465.

Gambino, Ferruccio. "The Transgression of a Laborer: Malcolm X in the Wilderness of America." *Radical History*, vol. 55 (Winter 1993): 7–31.

Gold, Russell. "Guilty of Syncopation, Joy, and Animation: The Closing of Harlem's Savoy Ballroom." *Studies in Dance History*, vol. 5, no. 1 (1994): 50–64.

Greenberg, Cheryl. "The Politics of Disorder: Reexamining Harlem's Riots of 1935 and 1943." *Journal of Urban History*, vol. 18, no. 4 (August 1992): 395–441.

Himes, Chester B. "Zoot Riots Are Race Riots." *Crisis*, vol. 50 (July 1943): 200–201.

Horne, Gerald. "'Myth' and the Making of 'Malcolm X.'" *American Historical Review*, vol. 98, no. 2 (April 1993): 440–450.

Jones, Oliver, Jr. "The Black Muslim Movement and the American Constitutional System." *Journal of Black Studies*, vol. 13, no. 4 (June 1983): 417–437.

Kelley, Robin D. G., "The Riddle of the Zoot: Malcolm Little and Black Cultural Politics During World War II," pp. 155–182, in Wood, Joe, ed. *Malcolm X: In Our Own Image.* New York: St. Martin's, 1992.

Kelley, Robin D. G., and Betsy Esch. "Black Like Mao: Red China and Black Revolution." *Souls*, vol. 1, no. 4 (Fall 1999): 6–41.

Knight, Frederick. "Justifiable Homicide, Police Brutality, or Governmental Repression? The 1962 Los Angeles Police Shooting of Seven Members of the Nation of Islam." *Journal of Negro History*, vol. 79, no. 2 (Spring 1974): 182–196.

Laremont, Ricardo René. "Race, Islam, and Politics: Differing Visions Among Black American Muslims." *Journal of Islamic Studies*, vol. 10, no. 1 (1999): 33–49.

Lightfoot, Claude. "Negro Nationalism and the Black Muslims." *Political Affairs*, vol. 41, no. 7 (July 1962): 3–20.

Lott, Eric. "Double V, Double-Time: Bebop's Politics of Style." *Callaloo*, no. 36 (Summer 1988): 597–605.

Maloney, Thomas N., and Warren C. Whatley. "Making the Effort: The Contours of Racial Discrimination in Detroit's Labor Markets." *Journal of Economic History*, vol. 55, no. 3 (September 1995): 456–493.

Mazucci, Liz. "Going Back to Our Own: Interpreting Malcolm X's Transition from 'Black Asiatic' to 'Afro-American.'" *Souls*, vol. 7, no. 1 (Winter 2005): 66–83.

McAlister, Melani. "One Black Allah: The Middle East in the Cultural Politics of African American Liberation, 1955–1970." *American Quarterly*, vol. 51, no. 3 (September 1999): 622–656.

Meyer, Douglas K. "Evolution of a Permanent Negro Community in Lansing." *Michigan History Magazine*, vol. 55, no. 2 (1971): 141–154.

Miller, Kelly. "After Marcus Garvey—What of the Negro?" *Contemporary Review*, vol. 131 (April 1927): 492–500.

Morris, Albert. "Massachusetts: The Aftermath of the Prison Riots of 1952." *The Prison Journal 1954*, vol. 34, no. 1 (April 1954): 35–37.

Murray, Paul T. "Blacks and the Draft: A History of Institutional Racism." *Journal of Black Studies*, vol. 2, no. 1 (September 1971): 57–76.

Norman, Brian. "Reading a Closet Screenplay: Hollywood, James Baldwin's Malcolm X and the Threat of Historical Irrelevance." *African American Review*, vol. 39, no. 2 (Spring 2005): 103–118.

Ohmann, Carol. "The Autobiography of Malcolm X: A Revolutionary Use of the Franklin Tradition." *American Quarterly*, vol. 22, no. 2 (1970): 131–149.

Payne, R. B. "Nutmeg Intoxication." *New England Journal of Medicine*, vol. 269 (1963): 36–38.

Peterson, Joyce Shaw. "Black Automobile Workers in Detroit, 1910–1930." *Journal of Negro History*, vol. 64, no. 3 (Summer 1979): 177–190.

Schuyler, Michael W. "The Ku Klux Klan in Nebraska, 1920–1930." *Nebraska History*, vol. 66, no. 3 (1985): 234–256.

Sitkoff, Harvard. "Racial Militancy and Interracial Violence in the Second World War." *Journal of American History*, vol. 58, no. 3 (December 1971): 661–681.

Sitkoff, Harvard. "The Detroit Race Riot of 1943." *Michigan History*, vol. 53, no. 3 (1969): 183–206.

Soule, Sarah A. "Populism and Black Lynching in Georgia, 1890–1900." *Social Forces*, vol. 71, no. 2 (December 1992): pp. 431–449.

Stein-Roggenbuck, Susan. "'Wholly Within the Discretion of the Probate Court': Judicial Authority and Mothers' Pensions in Michigan, 1913–1940." *Social Service Review*, vol. 79, no. 2 (June 2005): 294–321.

Stephens, Ronald J. "Garveyism in Idlewild, 1927 to 1936." *Journal of Black Studies*, vol. 34, no. 4 (March 2004): 462–488.

Taylor, Wayne. "Premillennium Tension: Malcolm X and the Eschatology of the Nation of Islam." *Souls*, vol. 7, no. 1 (Winter 2007): 52–65.

Tumini, Joseph. "Sweet Justice." *Michigan History Magazine*, vol. 83, no. 4 (July/August 1999): 23–27.

Vold, George B. "A Report on the Development of Penological Treatment at Norfolk Prison Colony in Massachusetts." *American Journal of Sociology*, vol. 46, no. 6 (May 1941): 917.

Weiss, G. "Hallucinogenic and Narcotic-Like Effects of Powdered Myristica (nutmeg)." *Psychiatric Quarterly*, vol. 34, no. 1 (1960): 346–356.

West, Cynthia S'thembile. "Revisiting Female Activism in the 1960s: The Newark Branch Nation of Islam." *Black Scholar*, vol. 26, nos. 3–4 (Fall 1996/Winter 1997): 41–48.

Books

Abel, Roger. *The Black Shield*. Bloomington, IN: Author House, 2006.

Anderson, Jervis. *This Was Harlem, 1900–1950*. New York: Farrar, Straus and Giroux, 1982.

Anderson, Jon Lee. *Che Guevara: A Revolutionary Life*. New York: Grove, 1997.

Angelou, Maya. *The Heart of a Woman*. New York: Random House, 1981.

Angelou, Maya. *A Song Flung Up to Heaven*. New York: Random House, 2002.

Appiah, Kwame Anthony, and Henry Louis Gates, Jr., eds. *Africana Encyclopedia of the African American Experience*. New York: Oxford University Press, 2005.

Aslan, Reza. *No God but God: The Origins, Evolution and Future of Islam*. New York: Random House, 2003.

Baldwin, James. *One Day When I Was Lost: A Scenario Based on Alex Haley's 'The Autobiography of Malcolm X.'* New York: Dell, 1972.

Baldwin, James. *The Fire Next Time*. New York: Dell, 1970.

Ball, Howard. *Hugo Black: Cold Steel Warrior*. Oxford: Oxford University Press, 1996.

Barbeau, Arthur E, and Florette Henri. *The Unknown Soldiers: Black American Troops in World War I*. Philadelphia: Temple University Press, 1974.

Berlin, Ira. *The Making of African America*. New York: Viking, 2010.

Biondi, Martha. *To Stand and Fight: The Struggle for Civil Rights in Postwar New York City*. Cambridge: Harvard University Press, 2003.

Boyle, Kevin. *Arc of Justice: A Saga of Race, Civil Rights, and Murder in the Jazz Age*. New York: Henry Holt, 2004.

Bracey, John, Jr., August Meier, and Elliott Rudwick, eds. *Black Nationalism in America*. New York: Bobbs-Merrill, 1970.

Branch, Taylor. *Pillar of Fire*. New York: Touchstone, 1998.

Breitman, George. *The Last Year of Malcolm X: The Evolution of a Revolutionary*. New York: Schocken, 1967.

Breitman, George, ed. *By Any Means Necessary: Speeches, Interviews, and a Letter by Malcolm X*. New York: Pathfinder, 1970.

Breitman, George, ed. *Malcolm X on Afro-American History*. New York: Pathfinder, 1967.

Breitman, George, ed. *Malcolm X Speaks: Selected Speeches and Statements*. New York: Grove, Weidenfield, 1990.

Breitman, George, ed. *Malcolm X: The Man and His Ideas*. New York: Pathfinder, 1965.

Breitman, George, Herman Porter, and Baxter Smith, eds. *The Assassination of Malcolm X*. New York: Pathfinder, 1976.

Carbada, Devon W., and Donald Weise, eds. *Time on Two Crosses: The Collected Writings of Bayard Rustin*. San Francisco: Cleis, 2003.

Carew, Jan. *Ghosts in Our Blood: With Malcolm X in Africa, England, and the Caribbean*. Westport, CT: Laurence Hill, 1994.

Carmichael, Stokely, and Ekwueme Michael Thelwell. *Ready for Revolution*. New York: Scribner, 1993.

Carson, Clayborne, ed. *Malcolm X: The FBI File*. New York: Carroll and Graf, 1991.

Clark, Kenneth B. *The Negro Protest: James Baldwin, Malcolm X and Martin Luther King*. Boston: Beacon, 1963.

Clark, Steve, ed. *February 1965: The Final Speeches*. New York: Pathfinder, 1992.

Clark, Steve, ed. *Malcolm X Talks to Young People: Speeches in the U.S., Britain, and Africa*. New York: Pathfinder, 1991.

Clarke, John Henrik, ed. *Malcolm X: The Man and His Times*. Trenton, NJ: Africa World Press, 1990.

Clegg III, Claude Andrew. *An Original Man: The Life and Times of Elijah Muhammad*. New York: St. Martin's, 1997.

Cole, Peter. *Wobblies on the Waterfront: Interracial Unionism in Progressive-Era Philadelphia*. Illinois: University of Illinois Press, 2007.

Collins, Rodnell P., with A. Peter Bailey. *Seventh Child: A Family Memoir of Malcolm X*. New York: Kensington, 1998.

Cone, James. *Martin and Malcolm and America: A Dream or a Nightmare*. Maryknoll, NY: Orbis, 1992.

Cruse, Harold. *The Crisis of the Negro Intellectual: From Its Origins to the Present*. New York: William Morrow, 1967.

Curtis, IV, Edward. *Islam in Black America*. New York: State University of New York Press, 2002.

Dannin, Robert. *Black Pilgrimage to Islam*. New York: Oxford University Press, 2002.

Davies, Carole Boyce, ed. *Encyclopedia of the African Diaspora: Origins, Experiences, and Culture*. Santa Barbara: ABC-Clio, 2008.

DeCaro, Louis A., Jr. *Malcolm and the Cross: The Nation of Islam, Malcolm X, and Christianity*. New York: New York University Press, 1998.

DeCaro, Louis A., Jr. *On the Side of My People: A Religious Life of Malcolm X*. New York: New York University Press, 1996.

Decker, William A. *Asylum for the Insane: History of the Kalamazoo State Hospital*. Traverse City, MI: Arbutus, 2007.

D'Emilio, John. *Lost Prophet: The Life and Times of Bayard Rustin*. New York: Free Press, 2003.

Denny, Frederick Mathewson. *An Introduction to Islam*. New York: Macmillan, 1985.

Deutsch, Nathaniel, ed. *Black Zion*. New York: Oxford University Press, 2000.

DeVeaux, Scott. *The Birth of Bebop: A Social and Musical History*. Berkeley: University of California Press, 1997.

Doering, Carl R., ed. *A Report on the Development of Peneological Treatment at Norfolk Prison Colony in Massachusetts*. New York: Bureau of Social Hygiene, 1940.

Du Bois, David Graham. . . . *And Bid Him Sing*. Palo Alto: Ramparts, 1975.

Duberman, Martin Bauml. *Paul Robeson*. New York: Ballantine, 1989.

Dyson, Michael Eric. *Making Malcolm: The Myth and Meaning of Malcolm X*. New York: Oxford University Press, 1995.

Edmonds, Anthony O. *Muhammad Ali: A Biography*. Westport, CT: Greenwood, 2006.

Emery, L. F. *Black Dance in the U.S. from 1619 to 1970*. Palo Alto: National Press Books, 1972.

Enayat, Hamid. *Modern Islamic Political Thought*. London: I. B. Taurus, 1982.

Epps, Archie, ed. *The Malcolm X Speeches at Harvard*. New York: Paragon House, 1961.

Esposito, John L. *The Oxford Dictionary of Islam*. New York: Oxford University Press, 2003.

Essien-Udom, E. U. *Black Nationalism: A Search for an Identity in America*. Chicago: University of Chicago Press, 1962.

Evanzz, Karl. *The Judas Factor: The Plot to Kill Malcolm X*. New York: Thunder's Mouth, 1992.

Evanzz, Karl. *The Messenger: The Rise and Fall of Elijah Muhammad*. New York: Pantheon, 1999.

Evers-Williams, Myrlie, and Manning Marable, eds. *The Autobiography of Medgar Evers: A Hero's Life and Legacy Revealed Through His Writings, Letters and Speeches*. New York: Basic Civitas, 2005.

Fanon, Frantz. *Black Skin, White Masks*. New York: Grove, 1967.

Field, Edward. *State of Rhode Island and Providence Plantations at the End of the Century: A History*. Boston: Mason, 1902.

Finkelman, Paul, ed. *Encyclopedia of African American History, 1896 to the Present: From the Age of Segregation to the Twenty-first Century*, vol. 2. New York: Oxford University Press, 2009.

Finkelman, Paul, ed. *Encyclopedia of American Civil Liberties*, vol. 2. New York: Routledge, 2006.

Finkle, Lee. *Forum for Protest*. Cranbury, NJ: Associated University Presses, 1975.

Fisher, Humphrey J. *The Ahmadiyya Movement*. London: Oxford University Press, 1963.

Flamming, Douglas. *Bound for Freedom: Black Los Angeles in Jim Crow America*. Berkeley: University of California Press, 2005.

Foner, Philip S. *Organized Labor and the Black Worker, 1619–1981*, second edition. New York: International Publishers, 1981.

Friedly, Michael. *Malcolm X: The Assassination*. New York: Carroll and Graf, 1992.

Friedman, Yohannon. *Prophecy Continuous: Aspects of Ahmadi Religious Thought and Its Medieval Background*. Berkeley: University of California Press, 1989.

Gaines, Kevin. *African Americans in Ghana: Black Expatriates and the Civil Rights Era*. Chapel Hill: University of North Carolina Press, 2007.

Gaines, Kevin. *Uplifting the Race: Black Leadership, Politics and Culture in the Twentieth Century*. Chapel Hill: University of North Carolina Press, 1996.

Gallen, David, ed. *Malcolm X: As They Knew Him*. New York: Carroll and Graf, 1992.

Gálves, William. *Ché in Africa: Ché Guevara's Congo Diary*. Melbourne, Australia: Ocean, 1999.

Gardell, Mattias. *In the Name of Elijah Muhammad: Louis Farrakhan and the Nation of Islam*. Durham: Duke University Press, 1996.

Garrow, David J. *Bearing the Cross: Martin Luther King, Jr., and the Southern Christian Leadership Conference*. New York: Vintage, 1986.

Gitler, Ira., ed. *Swing to Bop: An Oral History of the Transition of Jazz in the 1940s*. Oxford: Oxford University Press, 1985.

Goldman, Peter. *The Death and Life of Malcolm X*, revised edition. Urbana: University of Illinois Press, 1979.

Grant, Colin. *Negro with a Hat: The Rise and Fall of Marcus Garvey*. Oxford: Oxford University Press, 2008.

Grant, Stephen Meyer. *As Long as They Don't Move Next Door: Segregation and Racial Conflict in American Neighborhoods*. Lanham, MD: Rowman and Littlefield, 2000.

Gregg, Robert. *Sparks from the Anvil of Oppression: Philadelphia's African Methodists and Southern Migrants, 1840–1940*. Philadelphia: Temple University Press, 1993.

Grieve, Robert. *An Illustrated History of Pawtucket, Central Falls, and Vicinity: A Narrative of the Growth and Evolution of the Community*. Pawtucket, RI: Pawtucket Gazette and Chronicle, 1897.

Haddad, Yvonne, and Jane Smith. *Mission to America: Five Islamic Sectarian Communities in North America*. Gainesville: University Press of Florida, 1993.

Halasa, Malu. *Elijah Muhammad: Religious Leader*. New York: Chelsea House, 1990.

Harlan, Louis R. *Booker T. Washington: The Making of a Black Leader, 1856–1901*. New York: Oxford University Press, 1972.

Harlan, Louis R. *Booker T. Washington: The Wizard of Tuskegee, 1901–1915*. New York: Oxford University Press, 1983.

Harold, Claudrena N. *The Rise and Fall of the Garvey Movement in the Urban South, 1918–1942*. London: Routledge, 2007.

Hill, Robert A., ed. *The Marcus Garvey and Universal Negro Improvement Association Papers, Volume 1: 1826–August 1919*. Berkeley: University of California Press, 1983.

Hill, Robert A., ed. *The Marcus Garvey and Universal Negro Improvement Association Papers, Volume 2: August 1919–August 31, 1920*. Berkeley: University of California Press, 1983.

Hill Robert A., ed. *The Marcus Garvey and Universal Negro Improvement Association Papers, Volume 4: September 1921–September 1922*. Berkeley: University of California, 1985.

Hill, Robert A., ed. *The Marcus Garvey and Universal Negro Improvement Association Papers, Volume 5: September 1922–August 1924*. Berkeley: University of California Press, 1991.

Hill, Robert A., ed. *The Marcus Garvey and Universal Negro Improvement Association Papers, Volume 6: September 1924–December 1927*. Berkeley: University of California Press, 1989.

Hill, Robert A., and Barbara Blair, eds. *Marcus Garvey: Life and Lessons*. Berkeley: University of California Press, 1987.

Hindus, Michael Stephen. *Prison and Plantation: Crime, Justice and Authority in Massachusetts and South Carolina, 1767–1878*. Chapel Hill: University of North Carolina Press, 1980.

Hoare, Quintin, and Geoffrey Nowell Smith, eds. *Selections from the Prison Notebooks of Antonio Gramsci*. New York: International Publishers, 1971.

Horne, Gerald. *Fire This Time: The Watts Uprising and the 1960s*. Charlottesville, VA: University of Virginia Press, 1995.

Horne, Gerald. *Race Woman: The Lives of Shirley Graham Du Bois*. New York: New York University Press, 2000.

Jackson, Kenneth T., ed. *The Encyclopedia of New York City*, first edition. New Haven, CT: Yale University Press, 1995.

Jamal, Hakim. *From the Dead Level: Malcolm X and Me*. London: Andre Deutsch, 1971.

Jarvis, Malcolm L. *Myself and I: Malcolm L. Jarvis*, first edition. No location: Printed by Rice Offset Printing, December 1979.

Jenkins, Robert L., ed. *The Malcolm X Encyclopedia*. Westport, CT: Greenwood Press, 2002.

Johnson, Violet Showers. *The Other Black Bostonians: West Indians in Boston, 1900–1950*. Bloomington and Indianapolis: Indiana State University Press, 2006.

Jones, LeRoi. *Home: Social Essays*. New York: William Morrow, 1966.

Jones, LeRoi, and Larry Neal, eds. *Black Fire*. New York: William Morrow, 1968.

Joseph, Peniel E. *Waiting 'Til the Midnight Hour*. New York: Henry Holt, 2006.

Kahin, George McTurnan. *The Asian-African Conference: Bandung, Indonesia, April, 1955*. Ithaca: Cornell University Press, 1956.

Karim, Benjamin, with Peter Skutches and David Gallen. *Remembering Malcolm*. New York: Carroll and Graf, 1992.

Karim, Benjamin, ed. *The End of White World Supremacy: Four Speeches by Malcolm X*. New York: Seaver, 1971.

Knight, Michael Muhammad. *The Five Percenters: Islam, Hip-Hop and the Gods of New York.* Oxford: Oneworld, 2007.

Kofsky, Frank. *Black Nationalism and the Revolution in Music.* New York: Pathfinder, 1970.

Kondo, Zak. *Conspiracys: Unraveling the Assassination of Malcolm X.* Washington, D.C.: Nubia, 1993.

Leader, Edward Roland. *Understanding Malcolm X: The Controversial Changes in His Political Philosophy.* New York: Vantage, 1993.

Lee, Marjorie, Akemi Kochiyama-Sardinha, and Audee Kochiyama-Holman, eds. *Passing It On—A Memoir By Yuri Kochiyama.* Los Angeles: UCLA Asian American Studies Center Press, 2004.

Leeming, David. *James Baldwin: A Biography.* New York: Henry Holt, 1994.

Lewis, David Levering. *When Harlem Was in Vogue.* New York: Knopf, 1981.

Lewis, Rupert. *Marcus Garvey: Anti-Colonial Champion.* Trenton, NJ: Africa World Press, 1988.

Lincoln, C. Eric. *The Black Muslims in America.* Boston: Beacon, 1961.

Lomax, Louis E. *The Negro Revolt.* New York: Signet, 1964.

Lomax, Louis E. *To Kill a Black Man.* Los Angeles: Holloway House, 1987.

Lomax, Louis E. *When the Word Is Given . . .* Cleveland: World Publishing, 1963.

Low, Augustus, and Virgil A. Cliff, eds. *Encyclopedia of Black America.* New York: Da Capo, 1984.

Lynch, Hollis. *Edward Wilmot Blyden: Pan-Negro Patriot.* London: Oxford University Press, 1967.

Marable, Manning. *African and Caribbean Politics: From Kwame Nkrumah to the Grenada Revolution.* London: Verso, 1987.

Marable, Manning. *Black American Politics: From the Washington Marches to Jesse Jackson.* London: Verso, 1985.

Marable, Manning. *Living Black History: How Reimagining the African-American Past Can Remake America's Racial Future.* New York: Basic Civitas, 2006.

Marable, Manning. *Race, Reform and Rebellion: The Second Reconstruction and Beyond in Black America, 1945–2006.* Jackson: University Press of Mississippi, 2007.

Marable, Manning. *W. E. B. Du Bois: Black Radical Democrat,* second edition. Boulder, CO: Paradigm, 2005.

Marqusee, Mike. *Redemption Song: Muhammad Ali and the Spirit of the Sixties.* New York: Verso, 1999.

Marsh, Clifton E. *From Black Muslims to Muslims: The Resurrection, Transformation, and Change of the Lost-Found Nation of Islam in America, 1930–1995,* second edition. London: Scarecrow, 1996.

Martin, Tony. *Race First: The Ideological and Organizational Strategies of Marcus Garvey and the Universal Negro Improvement Association.* New York: Dover, 1976.

Meier, August, and Elliott Rudwick. *From Plantation to Ghetto,* third edition. New York: Hill and Wang, 1976.

Meier, August. *Negro Thought in America, 1880–1915.* Ann Arbor: University of Michigan Press, 1963.

Meredith, Martin. *The First Dance of Freedom: Black Africa in the Post-War Era.* New York: Harper and Row, 1984.

Miller, John, and Aaron Kenedi, eds. *Muhammad Ali: Ringside.* Boston: Bullfinch, 1999.

Mitchell, Sara. *Shepherd of Black-Sheep: A Commentary on the Life of Malcolm X with an On the Scene Account of His Assassination.* Macon, GA: Harriet Tubman Foundation, 1981.

Moore, Carlos. *Castro, the Blacks, and Africa.* Los Angeles: Center for Afro-American Studies, University of California, Los Angeles, 1988.

Moses, Wilson Jeremiah. *The Golden Age of Black Nationalism.* New York: Oxford University Press, 1976.

Mudimbe, V. Y. *The Invention of Africa.* Bloomington: Indiana University Press, 1988.

Muhammad, Elijah. *The Message to the Black Man in America.* Newport News, VA: United Brothers Communication Systems, 1965.

Muhammad, Elijah. *The Supreme Wisdom: Solution to the So-Called Negroes' Problem,* vol. 1. Newport News, VA: The National Newport News and Commentator, 1957.

Murray, Albert. *The Blue Devils of Nada*. New York: Pantheon, 1996.

Nalty, Bernard C. *Strength for the Fight: A History of Black Americans in the Military*. New York: Free Press, 1986.

Natambu, Kofi. *Malcolm X*. Indianapolis: Alpha, 2002.

Osofsky, Gilbert. *Harlem: The Making of a Ghetto: Negro New York, 1890–1930*. New York: Harper and Row, 1966.

Perry, Bruce, ed. *Malcolm X: The Last Speeches*. New York: Pathfinder, 1989.

Perry, Bruce. *Malcolm: The Life of a Man Who Changed Black America*. Barrytown, NY: Station Hill, 1991.

Pinkney, Alphonso, and Roger Woock. *Poverty and Politics in Harlem*. New Haven, CT.: College and University Press Services, 1970.

Poston, Larry. *Islamic Da'wah in the West: Muslim Missionaries and the Dynamics of Conversion to Islam*. New York: Oxford University Press, 1992.

Ransby, Barbara. *Ella Baker and the Black Freedom Movement: A Radical Democratic Vision*. Chapel Hill: University of North Carolina Press, 2003.

Remnick, David. *King of the World: Muhammad Ali and the Rise of an American Hero*. New York: Random House, 1998.

Rickford, Russell J. *Betty Shabazz: A Life Before and After Malcolm X*. Naperville, IL: Sourcebooks, 2003.

Rolinson, Mary G. *Grassroots Garveyism*. Chapel Hill: University of North Carolina Press, 2007.

Sales, William W., Jr. *From Civil Rights to Black Liberation: Malcolm X and the Organization of Afro-American Unity*. Boston: South End, 1994.

Savage, Beth L., ed. *African American Historic Places*. Washington, D.C.: Preservation, 1994.

Schmaltz, William H. *Hate: George Lincoln Rockwell and the American Nazi Party*. Washington, D.C.: Batsford Brassey, 1999.

Sfier, Antoine, ed. *The Columbia World Dictionary of Islamism*. New York: Columbia University Press, 2007.

Shukri, Sabih M., ed. *The International Who's Who of the Arab World*, third edition. London: The International Who's Who of the Arab World LTD, 1978.

Sides, Josh. *L.A. City Limits: African American Los Angeles from the Great Depression to the Present*. Berkeley: University of California Press, 2003.

Smallwood, Andrew P. *An Afrocentric Study of the Intellectual Development, Leadership Praxis and Pedagogy of Malcolm X*. Lewiston, NY: Edwin Mellen, 2001.

Smith, Ed Calvin, ed. *Where To, Black Man?* Chicago: Quadrangle, 1967.

Smith, Morgan, and Marvin Smith. *Harlem: The Vision of Morgan and Marvin Smith*. Lexington, KY: University Press of Kentucky, 1997.

Stearns, Marshall and Jean. *Jazz Dance: The Story of American Vernacular Dance*, second revised edition. New York: Da Capo, 1994.

Strickland, William T., and Cheryll Y. Greene, eds. *Malcolm X: Make It Plain*. New York: Viking, 1994.

Terrill, Robert E. *Malcolm X: Inventing Radical Judgment*. Lansing, MI: Michigan State University Press, 2004.

Thurman, Wallace. *Negro Life in New York's Harlem*. Girard, KS: Haldeman-Julius, 1928.

Tolbert, Emory J. *The UNIA and Black Los Angeles*. Los Angeles: Center for Afro-American Studies, University of California Press, 1980.

Trotter, Joe William, Jr. *Black Milwaukee: The Making of an Industrial Proletariat, 1915–45*, second edition. Urbana: University of Illinois Press, 2007.

Turner, Richard Brent. *Islam in the African-American Experience*. Bloomington: Indiana University Press, 1997.

Tyner, James A. *The Geography of Malcolm X: Black Radicalism and the Remaking of American Space*. New York: Routledge, 2005.

Tyson, Timothy B. *Radio Free Dixie: Robert F. Williams and the Roots of Black Power*. Chapel Hill: University of North Carolina Press, 1999.

Vechten, Carl Van. *Nigger Heaven*. New York: Harper and Row, 1977.

Wallace, Mike, with Gary Paul Gates. *Close Encounters*. New York: William Morrow, 1984.

Walters, Raymond. *W. E. B. Du Bois and His Rivals*. Columbia: University of Missouri Press, 2002.

Warren, Robert Penn. *Who Speaks for the Negro?* New York: Random House, 1965.

West, Michael Rudolph. *The Education of Booker T. Washington*. New York: Columbia University Press, 2006.

White, Walter. *Rope and Faggot*. New York: Arno, 1969.

Wilmot Blyden, Edward. *Christianity, Islam and the Negro Race*. Originally published 1888; reprinted Edinburgh: University of Edinburgh Press, 1967.

Wilson, Sandra Kathryn. *Meet Me at the Theresa: The Story of Harlem's Most Famous Hotel*. New York: Simon and Schuster, 2004.

Wolfenstein, Eugene V. *Victims of Democracy*. London: Free Association, 1989.

Wood, Joe., ed. *Malcolm X: In Our Own Image*. New York: St. Martin's, 1992.

X, Malcolm, and Alex Haley. *The Autobiography of Malcolm X*. New York: Ballantine, 1999.

X, Malcolm. *Malcolm X on Afro-American History*. New York: Pathfinder, 1988.

Abernathy, Ralph, 297
ACT, 333
Africa, 29, 81, 167, 187, 189, 229, 264, 272, 315, 327, 332, 343, 365, 389–90, 404, 408, 412, 414, 415, 421, 484–85
  Garvey and, 18, 19
  Islam in, 80
  Malcolm's travels in, 159, 305, 313–20, 325, 336, 341, 359, 360–74, 382–85, 389, 395, 396
  see also Pan-Africanism
African National Congress, 415, 485
Afro-American Association, 227, 228
Afro-Asian Solidarity Conference, 165
Ahmad, Hazrat Mirza Ghulam, 83
Ahmadiyya, 83–84, 87–88, 90, 109–10, 117
Akram, Wali, 110
Al-Azhar University, 363, 364, 365, 369
Alexandria, 313, 363, 364
Algeria, 120, 167, 264, 319, 336, 384–85, 406
Ali, John, 164, 183, 188, 195, 218, 220, 221, 232, 237, 269, 270, 273, 274, 278–79, 283, 289, 298, 338, 397, 424, 426, 448
Ali, Muhammad (Cassius Clay), 225–27, 280–81, 286–89, 292–93, 313, 318, 319, 326, 332, 401, 457, 468–69, 471
Ali, Noble Drew, 81–82, 85–86
Allen, Joe, 136
al-Qaeda, 487
Ameer, Leon 4X, 401, 425, 459
American Nazi Party, 199–201, 267, 275
Amsterdam News, 128, 130, 134, 160, 163, 174, 195, 224, 274, 276, 281, 289, 295, 298, 329, 337, 349, 410
Angelos, Louis, 438
Angelou, Maya, 189, 190, 314, 316, 319, 362, 383–84, 404–5, 429, 448–49
Apollo Theater, 9, 49
Armstrong, Wallace, 56
Aronoff, Alvin, 438, 455
Asha, Rafik, 131
Asia, 119, 120, 124, 130

Atkins, Clarence, 51, 52, 61
Atlanta, Ga., 136–37, 178
Audubon Ballroom, 1–2, 323, 340, 344, 348, 376
  OAAU rallies at, 2, 3–6, 350, 358, 377, 388, 395–96, 400, 404, 410, 431–35
Autobiography of Malcolm X, The (Malcolm X and Alex Haley), 7, 8–9, 28, 43, 46, 51, 52, 59–61, 63, 65, 66, 74, 77, 93, 100, 107, 137, 143, 168, 236, 276, 293, 324, 329–32, 351–52, 402, 422–23, 481, 486
  chapters deleted from, 9, 352
  excerpts published, 351
  Malcolm's assassination and, 447
  and Malcolm's suspension and split from Nation of Islam, 329, 330–32
  publication of, 465–67
  writing of, 247–49, 259–61, 265, 279, 335, 352, 402–3
Azikiwe, Nnamdi, 373–74
Aziz, Rashid Abdul, 367
Azzam, Abd al-Rahman, 308
Azzam, Omar, 308, 362

Babu, Abdulrahman Muhammad, 362, 371, 395, 396
Badri, Malik, 312
Baffoe, T. D., 362
Bailey, Peter, 322–23, 337, 375, 416, 434, 454
Baker, Ella, 156, 157, 158, 175
Baldwin, James, 7, 8, 57, 159, 163, 188, 263, 324, 456, 461, 487
Bailey, Peter, 421
Balk, Alfred, 220, 231
Bandung Conference, 119, 120, 124, 130, 264, 418
Banna, Hassan al-, 368
Barail, Ahmad Zaki el-, 131
Baraka, Amiri, 159, 465, 481
Baril, Florentina, 30
Baril, Lawrence G., 30
Barnes, Jack, 406–7
Barnette, Aubrey, 213–15

Barnette, Ruth, 213
Barry, Marion, 175–76
Barry Gray Show, 341, 358
Basner, H. M., 318
Bazarian, Mehan, 66
Beavers, Charles J., 128
Bee, Eugene X, 106
Beirut, 312, 370, 371
Bello, Ahmadu, 310–11
Bembry, John Elton, 73–74, 91
Bengalee, Sufi, 83–84
Berkeley, University of California at, 188
Berton, Pierre, 407
Bethune, Mary McLeod, 156
Bevel, James, 301
Bey, Kirkman, 82
Birmingham, Ala., 237–38, 240, 250, 297
Black, Hugo, 21
Black Freedom Movement, 176, 203, 227,
    230, 237, 256, 263, 305, 324, 332,
    336, 342–43, 354, 357
Blacklash, 375, 403, 434
Black Legion, 30, 31
"Black Merchants of Hate" (Haley and
    Balk), 231–32
Black Muslims in America, The (Lincoln),
    163, 190–91, 207, 218
black nationalism, 81, 83, 107, 161, 199,
    201, 204, 228, 284, 293–94, 298, 299,
    304, 306, 311–12, 314, 322, 332, 337,
    351, 366, 384, 406–7, 413, 454, 460,
    465, 466, 485–86
Black Panther Party, 227, 403, 484
Black Power, 163, 299, 480, 484
Black Star Line, 18, 20, 22, 23
Blackwell, Charles X, 6, 433, 436, 437,
    452, 453
Bland, Ernest, 24
Blyden, Edward Wilmot, 80–81, 82, 120
Boaka, Kofi, 316
Boggs, Grace Lee, 263, 265, 354, 355
Boggs, James, 263, 354, 355
Bond, Julian, 456
Bonura, Michael, 150–51
Booker, James, 329
Borai, Hussein el-, 312
Boston, Mass., 37, 40–42, 106, 111, 114,
    149, 213–14, 342, 343
    Malcolm in, 38, 39–47, 49, 64, 65, 67,
    104, 105, 107
Boston Globe, 471
Boston Herald, 94
Bradley, Willie X, 425, 432, 436–38, 451,
    475–76

Breitman, George, 263
Broady, Earl, 217, 239
Brown, Benjamin, 425–26, 448, 451
Brown, Francis E. "Sonny," 67
Brown, Lucius X, 173
Buffalo, N.Y., 202, 339
Burton, Lafayette, 338
buses, 123, 136, 156, 175, 178, 202
Butler, Norman 3X, 325–26, 425–26, 448,
    451–54, 463–65, 473–74
Byrd, Robert, 21–22

Cairo, 307, 312–13, 333, 359, 360–63,
    365–67, 371, 373, 390, 391, 396, 397,
    462
Campbell, James, 375
Caragulian, Bea, 46, 47, 50, 66–69, 70, 71,
    72, 147
Caragulian, Joyce, 67
Carmichael, Stokely, 403, 481–82
Carrington, Walter C., 187, 218
Carroll, John, 441
Castro, Fidel, 158–59, 172–73, 177, 262,
    336, 394, 396, 399
Cathcart, Linwood X, 5, 452–53
Cavallaro, Ferdinand, 442
Charlestown State Prison, 71, 97–98
    Malcolm in, 70–74, 93–99
Chicago, Ill., 104, 105, 106, 113, 117,
    215, 221, 232–34, 237, 238, 288–89,
    409–10, 457
Chicago Defender, 186, 195, 216, 252, 276,
    281, 288
Chicago Tribune, 288, 457
China, 119, 264, 317, 336, 340, 362, 364,
    399, 404, 412
Christianity, Islam and the Negro Race
    (Blyden), 81
Christians, Christianity, 19, 79, 80–81,
    83, 103, 109–10, 116, 177, 178, 188,
    285
    Malcolm and, 188–89, 212, 223, 224,
    236, 240, 370, 398, 407
Christian Science Monitor, 367
CIA, 343, 364, 367, 371, 372, 424, 429
civil rights legislation, 237–38, 241, 250,
    255, 258, 260, 267, 297, 301, 304,
    367, 412
civil rights movement, 44, 57, 109, 123,
    133, 155–59, 169, 176–79, 202, 204,
    215, 237–38, 255, 258, 267, 297, 305,
    333, 343, 356, 357, 367, 378, 400,
    411
    Elijah Muhammad and, 208–9, 227

Malcolm and, 127–29, 153–54, 155, 159, 177, 189, 208–10, 211, 212, 227–28, 242, 252–53, 255–56, 264, 293–96, 298, 300, 302, 303, 312, 324, 332, 334, 350, 366, 369, 372, 389, 403–4, 406, 413, 414, 418–19, 456, 466, 470, 482, 486
    Nation of Islam and, 153–54, 159, 208–9, 215–17, 255–56, 260, 267, 284
Clark, Kenneth, 241
Clarke, Edward Young, 22
Clarke, John Henrik, 159, 338, 341
Clarke, Kenneth, 63
Clay, Cassius, *see* Ali, Muhammad
Cleage, Albert B., Jr., 263, 264, 265, 418
Clegg, Claude Andrew, 201
Clement, Rufus, 212
Coleman, David, 238, 239
Collins, Ella Little (half-sister), 15, 37, 38, 39–43, 46, 47, 59, 64, 66, 67, 68, 72–73, 75, 76, 78, 94, 98, 204–5, 300, 301, 342, 343, 388, 393, 422, 461–62, 468, 471–72
    Nation of Islam and, 105, 149, 174–75, 324
Collins, Kenneth, 40, 42
Collins, Rodnell P., 39, 41, 42, 46, 66, 68, 72
Coltrane, John, 465
Communist Party, 54, 56, 95, 112, 119, 158–59, 162, 175, 206, 264, 284, 343, 354, 364, 369
    McCarthyism and, 155, 156, 175, 264
Concord, Massachusetts Reformatory at, 74–76, 98, 132
Confrey, William, 444
Congo, 172, 189, 223, 315, 367, 386–87, 394–95, 396, 401, 485
Congress of Racial Equality (CORE), 156, 177, 178, 202, 203–4, 209–10, 215, 218, 227–28, 229, 250, 257, 263, 303, 343, 354, 354, 376, 400, 403, 456
Congress of the Council of African Organizations, 412
Connor, Bull, 237
Coolidge, Calvin, 24, 29
Cooper, Thomas, 409–10
Crosby, Alvin, 151
Cross, Lonnie X, 262, 338
Cruse, Harold, 158, 159
Cuba, 158–59, 172–73, 262, 336, 394–96, 399
Cusmano, Thomas, 442

Darrow, Clarence, 27
Davis, Benjamin, Jr., 54, 158, 176, 343, 431
Davis, Jasper, 445
Davis, John X, 437
Davis, Leon X, 425, 431, 437, 438, 475
Davis, Ossie, 8, 253, 314, 324–25, 343, 349, 378, 410, 429, 458–59, 474, 483
Deanar, Tynetta, 165
DeBerry, Clifton, 389
Dee, Ruby, 314, 325, 343, 349, 378, 429, 458, 461
Delaney, Martin R., 191
De Loach, Cartha, 182
Dermody, Vincent J., 463, 464
Detroit, Mich., 29, 98, 106, 305, 306–7, 417, 418
    Malcolm in, 100–104
    Mosque No. 1 in, 101, 102, 103, 104, 106, 132, 134, 306, 448
    radical constituencies in, 263–64
    riot in (1943), 58, 109
Dever, Paul A., 71, 97
Diop, Alioune, 362
Domestic Peace Corps, 394
Dorsey, Margaret, 150–51
Douglass, Frederick, 17, 18, 351, 482
Du Bois, David, 364, 367, 400
Du Bois, Shirley, 314, 317, 361, 364, 383, 400, 461
Du Bois, W. E. B., 7, 17, 81, 91, 314, 317, 399–400, 421
Dudar, Helen, 219
Dudley, Herbert, 347
Dunbar Apartments, 53
Dundee, Angelo, 281, 287
Durso, Joe, 295

Eason, James Walker Hood, 20, 22
Edwards, Isaiah X, 105
Edwards, Quinton X Roosevelt, 241
Egan, Kenneth, 442
Egypt, 120, 165–66, 252, 312, 336, 359, 360–69, 364, 390, 396, 406, 486
Egyptian Gazette, 364, 365–66, 367
Eisenhower, Dwight D., 109, 120, 132, 158–59, 240
Emergency Committee, 191–93, 216
English, Josephine, 148
EQUAL, 405, 406
Essien-Udom, E. U., 313, 362, 373
Evanzz, Karl, 476
Everett, Ron, 227

Evers, Medgar, 13, 156, 177, 241–42, 272, 276
Ezekiel's Wheel, 89

Faisal of Saudi Arabia, 308, 309, 311, 362, 369, 389
Fanon, Frantz, 187, 198, 366, 398, 484
Fard, Wallace D., 84–90, 93, 105, 118, 135, 255, 285, 334, 482
Farmer, James, 178, 202–4, 227–28, 229, 230, 251, 253, 264, 400, 403, 456, 458
Farrakhan, Louis (Louis Walcott; Louis X), 12, 112–14, 121, 134, 149, 170, 171, 174–75, 187, 204, 207–9, 213, 214, 216, 219, 221, 222, 233, 242–43, 265, 266, 277, 291–92, 300, 324, 327, 342, 344, 469–71, 476–78
    assassination plot against, 472
    attack on Malcolm in *Muhammad Speaks*, 398, 476–77
    introduction to Nation of Islam, 113, 114
    Malcolm's assassination and, 476–77, 478
    Malcolm's meeting of, 113
    on Malcolm's relationship with Williams, 145, 146
    as national minister, 292, 476
Farrell, Peter T., 153
Faruqi, Ismail al-, 102
FBI, 82, 155, 156, 217, 376–77, 381, 424, 453, 468, 472
    Clay and, 280
    Elijah Muhammad and, 88, 182, 183
    Goodman and, 467
    Kenyatta and, 380, 467
    Malcolm and, 12, 95, 96–97, 103–5, 111–12, 116, 124, 134, 139–40, 154, 155, 171, 173, 178, 212, 218, 273, 299, 304, 305, 323, 334, 338, 339, 343, 366–67, 371, 372, 416, 479
    Malcolm's assassination and, 13, 445–46, 453, 454, 456, 462, 474, 475, 478
    Muslim Mosque and, 321
    Nation of Islam and, 104, 111, 126, 139–40, 154, 173, 212, 214, 218, 220, 222, 231, 233, 243, 273, 277–78
    Betty Shabazz and, 152
Ferguson, Herman, 267–68, 273, 323, 324, 328, 350, 374–76, 389, 416, 419, 429, 437, 440, 456
Fitzpatrick, Michael, 472

Florida, 137
Flynn, Philip J., 98
Forman, James, 157, 458
Forster, Arnold, 161
Fox, William, 1
Foxx, Redd, 52
France, 385, 412–13, 416, 429
Francis, Reuben X, 4, 5–6, 289, 294, 366, 381–82, 388, 422, 429–30, 431, 436, 438, 444, 445, 452–54, 468, 474
Frazier, E. Franklin, 156, 185, 186
Freedom, 158
Freedom Now Party, 267
Freedom Rides, 202, 203, 211, 215, 228, 260, 322, 386
Freedomways, 158
Freeman, Donald, 353
Fremont-Smith, Eliot, 465
Fruit of Islam (FOI), 86, 101, 102, 104–7, 111, 114, 123, 124, 128, 138, 140, 150, 153, 164, 173, 194, 195, 205, 207–8, 213, 214, 216, 217, 238, 242–44, 251, 253, 275, 279, 284, 290–91, 295, 298, 325–26, 339, 347, 379, 398, 401, 426, 446
Fulcher, Gerry, 355–57, 430–41, 453, 473
Fulwood, William T. X, 241

Galamison, Milton, 3, 298, 405, 434, 436
Gandhi, Mahatma, 91
Gang Starr, 8
Garvey, Amy Jacques, 22, 29
Garvey, Marcus, 16–20, 22–24, 39, 41, 42, 44, 52, 54, 81, 85, 89, 137, 191, 336, 351, 481
    Clay and, 225, 226
    festival in honor of, 131
    imprisonment and exile of, 23–24, 29, 86
Garveyism, 16, 18–20, 22, 28, 29, 30, 33, 34, 41, 54–55, 77, 82, 83, 84, 86, 89, 107, 112, 135, 177
Gar Wood Industries, 103, 104, 107
George, William 64X, 4, 294–95, 347, 436, 438, 453
Georgia, 15
Ghana, 314–19, 336, 362, 368, 382–83, 406, 428–29
Ghanaian Times, 316, 317, 318, 362, 412
Gibbs, Wolcott (Tony), Jr., 259, 260, 261, 330, 331, 332
Gibson, Richard, 159
Gill, Clarence 2X, 204, 213–14, 397, 401, 459

Giuliani, Rudolph, 473
Givens-El, John, 82
GOAL (Group on Advanced Leadership), 306
Gohanna, Thornton and Mabel, 34, 35, 36
Goldman, Eric, 188
Goldman, Peter, 218–19, 257, 279, 325, 329, 408, 431, 433, 455, 468, 475
Goldstein, Abe, 63–64
Goldwater, Barry, 3, 11, 213, 352, 367, 383, 391
Gonzalez, Armando Entralgo, 316
Goodman, Benjamin 2X, 6, 173, 193, 209, 221–22, 323, 338, 343, 358, 376–77, 380, 388, 398, 419, 434, 435, 436, 441, 467–68
Gould, Jack, 161–62
Gramsci, Antonio, 90
Grant, Earl, 439–40, 443, 452
Gravitt, Joseph X, 102, 106–7, 110–11, 112, 114, 121, 125, 127, 150, 193, 195–98, 202, 215, 237, 242, 243, 245, 270, 273, 275, 276, 278, 279, 283, 284, 292, 295, 305, 344, 345, 379, 397, 419, 426, 448, 453, 457
    charges against, 125–26, 196
    Malcolm's assassination plotted by, 290–91, 298, 332
Gray, Barry, 223
Gray, Muriel, 375
Gray, Robert 16X, 453
Great Britain, 390, 391, 413, 414–15
Green, Edith, 240
Greene, Claude, 82
Gregory, Dick, 298, 333, 458
Griffiths, Peter, 414
Guevara, Che, 12, 394–95, 396, 413

Haggins, Robert, 341
Haley, Alex, 7, 9, 219–20, 226, 231–32, 246–47, 259–61, 265, 279, 293, 310, 327, 329–32, 335, 351–52, 402–3, 422–23, 447–48, 465, 466
Halls, Herbert, 151
Hamer, Fannie Lou, 399, 400, 420
Hammarskjöld, Dag, 172, 189
Handler, M. S., 9, 10–11, 293–94, 296, 305, 328, 362, 369–70, 389
Harkon, Sheikh Muhammad, 308
Harlem, 46–49, 51–64, 108–10, 127, 158, 202, 216, 231, 237, 250, 336, 355, 369, 405, 481
    Abyssinian Baptist Church in, 204
    Cuban delegation in, 172–73

Emergency Committee and, 191–93, 216
    Freedom Rally in, 170–71
    Hotel Theresa in, 49, 172, 192, 211, 216, 288, 292, 295, 298, 319, 321, 356
    Mosque No. 7 in, *see* Mosque No. 7
    riots in, 54–55, 58–59, 60, 62, 359, 376–77
Harris, Don, 372
Harris, Robert, 87
Harris, Willie, 442
Harvard Law School Forum, 187–88
Hassan, Lemuel (Lemuel Anderson), 101, 103, 106
Hassan, Sheikh Akbar, 365
Hassoun, Sheikh Ahmed, 390, 434, 458
Hate That Hate Produced, The, 160–64, 168, 169, 212, 220
Hayari, Yahya, 223–24
Hayer, Talmadge, 425, 431–32, 437, 438, 444, 446, 452, 453, 455, 463–65, 473–76
Haynes, Douglas, 64
Helpern, Milton, 450
Hemby, "Red," 136
Henry, Gilbert, 441–42
Henry, Milton, 418
Hicks, James, 128, 129
Hill, Norman, 250
Hinton, Johnson X, 127–29, 130, 131, 134–35, 151, 152, 177, 209, 231
Hogan, Frank, 228
Holman, Zolma, 47
Home, Gerald, 8
Hoover, J. Edgar, 212, 291, 338, 366, 479
Hotel Theresa, 49, 172, 192, 211, 216, 288, 292, 295, 298, 319, 321, 356
housing restrictions, 26–27, 28, 206
Howard University, 185–87
Hoy, Thomas, 438, 455
Huff, Michael X, 471
Hughes, Ola, 232
Husayn ibn Ali, 430, 433
Husseini, Hajj Amin el-, 310

Ibrahim, Yasuf, 165
Iffeorah, Joseph, 348
Ingham County Juvenile Home, 36–38
Islam, 12, 79–86, 100, 110, 117–19, 486–87
    Ahmadiyya, 83–84, 87–88, 90, 109–10, 117
    evangelical work in, 102

Islam (*cont.*)
  five pillars of, 79, 81, 100, 167, 271,
    308
  imams in, 117–18
  Moorish Science Temple of America,
    81–83, 84, 86, 90, 100
  orthodox, Malcolm's embrace of,
    300–301, 308–10, 311–12, 328–29,
    366, 391, 402, 481, 484–86
  orthodox, Nation of Islam and,
    117–19, 165, 168, 169, 223–24, 252,
    271, 284, 285, 361, 366, 397
  Prophet Muhammad, 79–80, 81, 85,
    88, 117, 119, 271, 301, 430
  Qur'an in, 79, 82, 84, 118, 119, 142,
    146, 154, 165, 224, 235, 271, 301
  race and, 167–68, 225, 301, 369
  Sunni, 3, 8, 117, 118, 165, 266, 328
  ummah (global brotherhood) of, 80,
    118, 119–20, 167, 225, 402
  women and marriage as viewed in,
    142, 146
Islamic Center, 368
Islamic Federation of the United States
    and Canada, 366
Islamic University of Madinah, 370
Israel, 12, 120, 367–38

Jack, Hulan, 54, 108, 158
Jackson, George, 13
Jackson, James E., 284
Jackson, Jesse, 484
Jackson, Miss., 177
James, C. L. R., 317, 399
James, William M., 169
Japan, 339–40, 400
Jarvis, Malcolm "Shorty," 42–43, 45, 47,
    59, 67, 68, 71, 90, 93
Jews, Judaism, 79, 80, 100–101, 134,
    169–70, 179, 200, 223, 224, 229,
    246–47, 299, 318, 370, 386, 398,
    407
  Zionism, 368
Johnson, Alvin, 438
Johnson, Lyndon, 3, 11, 304, 335, 341,
    367, 383, 387, 406, 411
Johnson, Thomas 15X, 197–98, 205, 243,
    244, 290, 398, 416, 419, 425–27, 448,
    451–54, 463–65, 473–74
Jones, Clarence, 342, 343, 362
Jones, Claudia, 54
Jones, LeRoi (Amiri Baraka), 159, 465,
    481
Jones, Robert, 78

Kalamazoo State Hospital, 35–36, 37
Kamal, Ahmad, 252
Kamboda, Otim, 371
Kaminska, Richard, 38
Keeley, John J., 444
Kennedy, Bob, 300
Katzenbach, Nicholas, 366–67
Kelly, Carolyn F., 476
Kennedy, John F., 133, 177, 184, 241, 250,
    253, 256, 258, 304
  assassination of, 7, 269, 272, 273–74,
    277
  Malcolm's "chickens" remark and,
    272–74, 277, 322
  Malcolm's criticisms of, 240, 254, 255,
    267
Kennedy, Robert, 217
Kennedy, Stephen P., 189
Kenner, Curtis and Susie, 110
Kenya, 372–74, 413, 467
Kenyatta, Charles 37X (Charles Morris),
    144–45, 196–97, 207, 279, 294, 300,
    327, 359, 362, 376, 379–82, 388, 428,
    461, 462–63, 464, 467
  Betty Shabazz and, 380–81, 388,
    392–93, 394, 428
Kenyatta, Jomo, 372–73, 389
Khavan, Nazim el-, 364
Kholy, Hassan Sabn al-, 361
Khomeini, Ayatollah, 486
Khrushchev, Nikita, 172
Kiernan, Joseph, 150–51
Killens, John Oliver, 159, 338, 341, 378,
    461, 465
King, Coretta Scott, 412
King, Martin Luther, Jr., 7, 113, 123, 133,
    136, 156, 159, 175, 177, 184, 211,
    212, 215, 237, 238, 250–52, 255–57,
    260, 297, 301–3, 323, 324, 332–33,
    342, 357, 367, 378, 405, 411–12, 414,
    480, 484–85
  assassination of, 7, 13
  "I Have a Dream" speech of, 257–58
  Malcolm compared with, 480, 482,
    483–84
  Malcolm's assassination and, 456, 458
  Malcolm's criticisms of, 238, 252, 254,
    264–65, 300, 312, 405, 406, 413, 414
  Malcolm's meeting of, 302
King, Preston, 314
Kingsley, Bryan, 349–50
Kissinger, Henry, 348
Kochiyama, Yuri (Mary) Nakahara, 340,
    439

Kofsky, Frank, 63
Korean War, 95, 103–4
Ku Klux Klan (KKK), 21–23, 25, 169, 194,
	357, 403, 411, 420, 485
	Garvey and, 22
	Louise Little and, 22–23
	Malcolm's meeting with, 13, 178–79,
		180, 184, 189, 200, 201
Kunstler, William, 169, 474
Kuwait, 367, 370

Lacy, Leslie, 315, 316, 318
Lagos, 313
LaGuardia, Fiorello, 55, 56, 57, 58, 59
Lahoris, 83
Lamb, Thomas W., 1
Lansing, Mich., 27–28, 305
	Malcolm in, 25, 50–51, 64
Latty, Ernest B., 171
Laviscount, Samuel L., 95–96
Lawson, James, 131, 192
Lebanon, 312, 370, 486
Lee, Spike, 8, 144, 471, 486
Leeks, Sylvester, 341
Lennon, Bernard, 65
Lennon, Nellie F., 65
Lennon, William Paul, 65–66, 72, 73, 75,
	96
Lenoir, John, 365
Levison, Stanley, 156
Lewis, John, 250, 257, 263, 297, 333, 372,
	458
Liberia, 384
Liberty Party, 20
Licorish, David N., 109
Lightfoot, Claude, 284
Lincoln, C. Eric, 162–63, 190–91, 207,
	218
Lindh, John Walker, 486
Liston, Sonny, 280, 286, 287, 468
Little, Daisy Mason, 15–16
Little, Earl, Jr. (half-brother), 15, 37, 40,
	42, 63
Little, Earl, Sr. (father), 15–16, 24–25, 27,
	30, 41, 42, 48, 52, 77, 78, 225
	birth of, 15
	burning of house of, 25–26
	death of, 30–32
	Louise's marriage to, 16
	UNIA and, 20–23, 27, 28
Little, Ella (half-sister), *see* Collins, Ella
	Little
Little, Hilda (sister), 22, 32, 36, 37, 38, 50,
	64, 74, 77, 78, 98

Little, Louise (mother), 16, 24–25, 30,
	32–36, 48, 92
	burning of house of, 25–26
	Earl's death and, 30–32
	institutionalization of, 35–36, 37, 265
	KKK and, 22–23
	marriage of, 16
	UNIA and, 20–23
Little, Mary (half-sister), 15, 37
Little, Philbert (brother), 22, 31, 44, 64,
	72, 75, 77, 78, 92, 94, 96, 118, 145,
	265, 305, 458
Little, Reginald (brother), 24, 44–45, 50,
	61–63, 64, 75–77, 92, 93, 122, 175
	expelled from Nation of Islam, 92–93,
	122, 175
Little, Robert (brother), 35
Little, Wesley (brother), 32, 77
Little, Wilfred (brother), 20, 25, 26, 28–38,
	50, 64, 75, 77, 78, 98, 100, 106,
	116–17, 118, 134, 145, 305, 448,
	458
Little, Yvonne (sister), 32–33, 78
Lobster Pond, 63–64
Logan, Arthur, 405
Lomax, Louis, 160–63, 188, 212, 224–25,
	252, 257, 277, 285, 303, 332
Los Angeles, Calif., 149, 205–9, 211–12,
	217, 230, 238–39, 334, 409, 431
Los Angeles Dispatch, 132–33
Los Angeles Herald-Dispatch, 227, 237, 340
Los Angeles Times, 238, 274, 333, 363–64,
	415
Lost-Found Nation of Islam, *see* Nation
	of Islam
Lumumba, Patrice, 172, 189, 315
Luqman, Anas M., 5, 290–91, 294, 298,
	398, 410, 454, 468
Luthuli, Albert, 415
Lynn, Conrad, 350
Lynn, Winfred W., 59

MacDonald, Bill, 286
Maged, Muhammad Abdul Azziz, 308,
	362
Maki, Ibrahim, 319
Malcolm X:
	arrest and sentencing of, 67–68
	assassination of, 4–6, 7, 9, 11–12, 283,
		289, 410, 423, 427, 429–49, 450–57,
		460, 462–65, 473–76
	autobiography of, *see Autobiography of
		Malcolm X, The*
	autopsy of, 450–51, 458

Malcolm X (*cont.*)
  becomes minister, 103, 104
  birth of, 23
  change in racial attitudes of, 319,
    328–29, 333, 342, 386, 400–401, 427
  childhood of, 27, 30–38
  childhood house burned, 25
  children of, *see* Shabazz, Attallah;
    Shabazz, Gamilah Lumumba;
    Shabazz, Ilyasah; Shabazz,
    Qubilah
  column written by, 130
  criminal activities of, 11, 43, 49, 50, 51,
    60–62, 64–68, 70, 71, 74, 78, 96, 132,
    260
  death threats and plots against, 289,
    290–91, 295, 298, 299, 332, 341,
    343–44, 347–48, 358–59, 360,
    379–80, 382, 401–2, 405, 409, 410,
    423–29, 479
  in debates, 169, 172, 176–77, 186,
    224–25, 332–33, 482
  drug and alcohol use of, 43, 50, 61, 64,
    71–72, 73, 78, 96
  economic philosophy of, 336–37,
    369–70, 399
  education of, 36–38, 39, 45, 74, 91
  evangelizing work of, 102, 105, 111,
    114, 122–23, 124, 129, 136
  eviction case against, 295, 296, 305,
    335, 337, 344–47, 366, 415, 416, 419,
    420, 426, 447
  father's death and, 31–32
  firebombing of home of, 3, 416–17,
    418–21, 433, 434, 443, 462, 470
  funeral of, 458–59
  homosexual encounters of, 66, 78
  interviews with, 172, 178, 218–19,
    222–23, 231–32, 246–47, 277, 285,
    295, 299, 326, 365, 367, 371, 384,
    406–7, 409, 410, 412, 415, 418,
    420–21
  jobs held by, 43, 46–47, 48, 49–50, 51,
    61, 63–64, 98, 100–4, 107
  magazines and newspapers
    published by, 163–64
  marriage of, 145–50; *see also* Shabazz,
    Betty
  marriage as viewed by, 140–42,
    144–45
  military service avoided by, 59–60,
    103–4
  mother's illness and, 36
  name of, 96, 135, 193, 397

  named national minister of Nation of
    Islam, 258–59, 346
  nicknames of, 11, 37, 46, 49, 51–52, 71
  physical appearance of, 30, 45, 50–51,
    410
  in prison, 70–77, 90–99, 311
  radio and television appearances of,
    169, 172, 176–77, 178, 186, 222–23,
    224–25, 255, 299, 300, 341, 342, 358,
    371, 401, 404, 407, 410
  speaking style and abilities of, 91, 95,
    104, 113, 116, 138, 186, 306
  wife of, *see* Shabazz, Betty
  women as viewed by, 36, 47, 68–69,
    116, 142, 143, 374–75
Malcolm X: speeches, lectures, and
    sermons, 135–38, 143, 153, 168,
    178, 190, 201–4, 254–55, 261–62,
    268, 299, 305, 306, 312, 335–36,
    347–48, 395–96, 405, 407–8, 411,
    418–19, 427
  "The Ballot or the Bullet," 44, 133,
    302, 303–4, 306–7, 484
  excerpts from, 115–16, 130–31,
    132–33, 216, 229, 264
  "The Farce on Washington," 256, 262,
    264
  "God's Judgment of White America,"
    269–73
  in Great Britain, 390, 391
  at Harlem Freedom Rally, 170–71
  at Harvard Law School, 398–99
  at Hotel Theresa, 192–93, 216
  at London School of Economics,
    413–14
  "Message to the Grassroots," 133,
    264–65, 270, 272, 302, 303, 304, 306,
    461, 483
  at Mosque No. 1, 132–34, 306
  at Mosque No. 7, 130–31, 193–94,
    228–29, 262
  at Philadelphia temple, 115–16
  "There's a Worldwide Revolution
    Going On," 419
  at universities, 184–88, 202, 218, 221,
    229, 230, 262–63, 266–67, 314–17,
    371, 391, 408, 421, 428
  at Williams Church, 399, 400
Mallory, Willie Mae, 305
Malloy, Lorenzo and Helen, 138–39, 144,
    145, 147
Mandela, Nelson, 415, 485
Mao Zedong, 340, 399, 400
Manchester Guardian, 391

Mansur, Yaqub al-, 80
Marcello, Warren X, 471
Marderosian, Kora, 67
Marks, Charles, 463, 464–65
Marshall, Paule, 350
Marshall, Thurgood, 184
Marxism, 155, 158, 263, 305, 317, 354, 407
Mason, Jackie, 72, 75
Massachusetts Reformatory at Concord, 74–76, 98, 132
Matthews, George, 451
Mayfield, Julian, 159, 314, 315, 316, 318, 362, 383
Mboya, Tom, 361, 372
McCormick, Kenneth, 261, 331, 352
McGuine, Cyril, 32
McKinley, Wilbur X, 425, 436, 475
McKissick, Floyd, 257, 403
McKnight, Sammy, 60, 61
Mecca, 88, 100, 106, 119, 271, 327, 369, 390, 391, 397
    Elijah Muhammad's journey to, 168–69, 420
    Malcolm's pilgrimage to, 3, 9, 281, 301, 307–9, 314, 321, 324, 328–29, 334, 360, 366, 373
Mendi, Mohammad T., 149
Meredith, James, 223
Message to the Blackman in America (Elijah Muhammad), 89, 142, 165
Messenger Magazine, 163
Michaux, Lewis, 192
Michigan:
    racial housing restrictions in, 26–27, 28
    see also Detroit, Mich.; Lansing, Mich.
Michigan State University, 229
Middle East, 327, 332, 343
    Malcolm's travels in, 165–68, 305, 307–13, 319, 360–74, 384, 386, 392, 397
Militant, 263, 302, 304
Militant Labor Forum, 305
Milwaukee, Wisc., 24
Mitchell, Sara, 348, 427–28, 434, 435, 441
Mohammed V, Sultan, 120
Molette, John X, 151, 153, 160
Molette, Yvonne X, 151, 153, 160
Monitor, 21
Montgomery, Ala., 123, 136, 156, 297
Monthly Review, 299
Moore, Archie, 225, 227, 280
Moore, Carlos, 404, 412

Moorish Science Temple of America, 81–83, 84, 86, 90, 100
Morocco, 120
Morris, Charles 37X, *see* Kenyatta, Charles 37X
Morton, Kenneth, 398
Moses, Bob, 403
Moslem Sunrise, 83, 109–10
Mosque No. 1 (Detroit), 101, 102, 103, 104, 106, 132, 134, 306, 448
Mosque No. 4 (Washington, D.C.), 236, 237, 262, 345
Mosque No. 7 (Harlem), 2, 5, 12, 105, 107–8, 110–13, 120, 121, 124–26, 140, 141, 164, 168, 170, 171, 173–74, 189–91, 193–97, 210, 215, 221–23, 228–29, 236, 242, 244–45, 254, 256, 289, 294–95, 324, 325, 333–34, 339, 344, 347, 355, 356, 358, 397, 425, 426, 474
    firebombing of, 457, 459, 477–78
    Malcolm named minister of, 107
    Malcolm's eviction case and, 305, 335, 337, 346
    Malcolm's marriage and, 146
    Malcolm's suspension and, 274–76, 278, 279
    Malcolm's talks at, 130–31, 193–94, 228–29, 262
    rallies organized by, 211, 216, 251
    renaming of, 469
Muhammad, Abdur-Rahman, 410–11, 417, 476
Muhammad, Akbar, 168, 169, 251–52, 153–54, 276, 363, 364, 381, 402, 423
Muhammad, Augustus, 87
Muhammad, Clara (Clara Poole), 77–78, 86, 87, 88, 104, 144
    Elijah's infidelity and, 182
Muhammad, Elijah (Elijah Poole), 9, 86–90, 92, 95, 100, 101, 103, 108, 110, 112, 115, 119, 121, 122, 124, 125, 127, 130, 132, 136, 140, 154, 164, 173, 176–78, 186, 193, 198, 211, 213, 215, 217–18, 223–25, 231, 234, 240, 241, 254, 255, 270–73, 276, 285, 297–98, 300, 305, 338–39, 345, 366, 370, 392, 397, 402, 411, 420, 457–58, 477
    apolitical philosophy of, 109, 133–34
    authority of, 168, 169, 171, 181–82, 202
    Autobiography of Malcolm X and, 247, 249, 260, 276
    civil rights and, 208–9, 227

Muhammad, Elijah (Elijah Poole) *(cont.)*
Clay and, 225, 226, 280, 288, 292, 293
death of, 119, 216, 469
Ella Collins and, 175
extramarital affairs and illegitimate
children of, 181–83, 195, 232,
233–34, 235, 236, 247, 258, 265–66,
277–78, 279, 285, 290, 311, 326, 338,
340–42, 344, 347, 355, 358, 363, 397,
407, 408–9, 420, 423, 470
Fard and, 86–90, 93, 118, 135
Farrakhan and, 113, 114
FBI and, 88, 182, 183
gender relations as viewed by, 142–43
global Islamic community and,
117–19, 165
Haley and, 447–48
Harlem speech of, 191–92
Kennedy and, 254, 255, 269, 273–74,
277
KKK and, 178–79
Little family's first connection to,
77–78
Malcolm's assassination and, 423–24,
426, 432, 446–47, 457, 478
Malcolm's correspondence with,
78–79, 88, 90, 92, 93, 96–97, 101,
141, 185, 190–91, 194–95, 202
Malcolm's early visits to, 101–2, 124
Malcolm's marriage and, 144–45, 146,
150
Malcolm's open letter of conciliation
to, 349–50
Malcolm's preparation for ministry
and, 104
Malcolm's speeches and, 187–88, 202,
221, 228
Malcolm's split with, 3, 12, 129,
208–9, 265, 291, 293–96, 304, 305,
311, 326
Malcolm's suspension and, 274,
276–79, 282–83, 293, 329
March on Washington and, 258
Message to the Blackman in America, 89,
142, 165
police incidents and, 159–60, 208–9,
211
Rockwell and, 199, 200–201
second home of, 182–83, 195
threats against, 244
"What the Muslims Believe"
statement of, 216
"What the Muslims Want" statement
of, 215–16

white journalists and, 161, 162
Williams and, 146, 181, 183, 266, 292,
358, 408–9, 423
Muhammad, Elijah, Jr., 105, 118, 195,
214, 221, 244, 273
Muhammad, Harriet, 251
Muhammad, Herbert, 105, 118, 168, 195,
258, 273, 284, 471
Muhammad, Kallat, 87
Muhammad, Prophet, 79–80, 81, 85, 88,
117, 119, 271, 301, 430
Muhammad, Wallace (son of Elijah),
118, 131, 173–74, 232–33, 235,
245, 265, 283, 284, 285, 341,
381, 391–92, 402, 458, 469–71,
477
name changed by, 469
as Nation of Islam leader, 119, 173,
469
Muhammad, Wallace D. Fard, 84–90, 93,
105, 118, 135, 255, 285, 334, 482
Muhammad Speaks, 163–64, 165, 173, 195,
201, 204, 206, 213–16, 220, 221, 226,
228, 236, 237, 242, 256, 258, 267,
269, 275, 284, 291, 295, 327, 348,
397–98, 471
Mulligan, Bernard, 442
Murphy, Michael, 228, 298
Murray, Albert, 50
Murray, Pauli, 158
music, 62
bebop, 62–63, 110, 116
jazz, 37, 43, 45, 50, 51, 62–63, 91, 110,
113, 465
musicians, 110, 113–14, 465
Muslim Brotherhood, 312, 368–69, 385,
486
Muslim Girls Training (MGT), 87, 104–5,
123, 124, 139, 140, 143, 147, 150,
249, 279, 321
Muslim Mosque, Inc. (MMI), 3, 6, 295,
296, 298–300, 305–6, 316, 318, 320,
321, 324, 325, 326–28, 332–34,
337–42, 344–46, 348, 350, 358–59, 3
60, 363, 364, 366, 370, 374–79,
381–82, 388–93, 398, 401, 411, 413,
421–23, 426–28, 430, 431, 433, 453,
454, 460–62, 467, 470
Muslims, 80, 484–86
in prisons, 90, 93–95, 97, 98, 123,
146–47, 240–41
see also Islam
Muslim World League, 361, 368, 390,
391

Nairobi, 371–74
Nasser, Gamal Abdel, 12–13, 120, 165,
   166, 361, 365, 368, 369, 390, 396, 486
Nation, 465
National Association for the
   Advancement of Colored People
   (NAACP), 17, 20, 21, 24, 27, 89,
   109, 123, 156, 157, 158, 169, 170,
   171, 177, 185, 192, 203, 212, 215,
   227, 241–42, 246, 250, 251, 264, 284,
   303, 354, 456
National Urban League, 170, 212, 250,
   251, 343
Nation of Islam (NOI), 2, 9, 12, 79, 86–90,
   100, 184, 310, 469–70
   American Nazi Party and, 199,
      200–201, 267, 275
   apolitical philosophy of, 109, 133–34,
      155, 159, 177, 188, 189–90, 202, 209,
      215, 253, 284
   "Black Muslims" phrase used for, 2,
      117
   civil rights and, 153–54, 159, 208–9,
      215–17, 255–56, 258, 260, 267, 284
   Clay and, 225–27, 280, 281, 286,
      288–89, 292–93
   contradictions in theology of, 167–68
   decision-making officers in, 104–5
   discipline in, 121–22, 181, 242–44, 298,
      424, 425–26
   Elijah Muhammad's leadership of, *see*
      Muhammad, Elijah
   eviction suit against Malcolm by, 295,
      296, 305, 335, 337, 344–47, 366, 415,
      416, 419, 420, 426, 447
   Faisal and, 311
   FBI surveillance of, 104, 111, 126,
      139–40, 154, 173, 212, 214, 218, 220,
      222, 231, 233, 243, 273, 277–78
   growth of, 117, 123, 129, 131, 135, 136,
      152, 154, 195, 215, 220
   The Hate That Hate Produced series
      about, 160–64, 168, 169, 212, 220
   Hinton incident and, 127–29, 153
   Kennedy assassination and, 269
   KKK and, 178–79
   Little family's conversion to, 75–79
   Malcolm's assassination attributed to,
      13, 456, 476
   Malcolm's concerns about, 167–68
   Malcolm's conversion to, 88–89, 92,
      101
   Malcolm's critics in, 171, 174, 198,
      201–2, 211, 221, 222, 326

   Malcolm's feud with, 3, 339, 341, 342,
      344, 348–50, 392, 396–98, 456
   Malcolm's house firebombed by,
      416–17, 418–21, 433, 434, 443
   Malcolm's rejection of theology of,
      310, 327–28
   Malcolm's split from, 2–3, 9, 12, 129,
      135, 193, 265, 266, 268, 283–86,
      289–96, 297–98, 305, 310, 315, 319,
      321, 323, 325–27, 331–32, 339, 342,
      360, 361, 373, 454
   Malcolm's suspension from, 273–79,
      281–83, 284, 293, 326, 329, 330–31,
      335, 346, 347
   musicians and, 113–14
   Muslim Mosque and, 3, 295, 296, 298,
      323–24, 334, 338, 392
   orthodox Islam and, 117–19, 165, 168,
      169, 223–24, 252, 271, 284, 285, 361,
      366, 397
   Reginald Little expelled from, 92–93,
      122, 175
   Saviour's Day Conventions of, 105,
      111, 112, 113, 126, 136, 152, 165,
      169, 182, 194, 200, 232–33, 286, 288,
      292, 457–58
   separatist philosophy of, 9, 77, 78,
      136, 153, 168, 171, 176–77, 178, 179,
      192, 199, 201–3, 220, 240, 251, 258,
      260, 338, 469
   in South, 136–37, 177–78
   tithing in, 124, 195, 213, 232
   threats and physical intimidation
      against Malcolm from, 289,
      290–91, 295, 298, 299, 332, 341,
      343–44, 347–48, 379–80, 382, 401–2,
      405, 409, 410, 423–29, 479
   thugs in, 242–43, 298, 398, 410
   Wallace Muhammad's leadership of,
      119, 173, 469
   "What the Muslims Believe"
      manifesto of, 216
   "What the Muslims Want" manifesto
      of, 215–16
   whites demonized in, 2, 8, 77, 86, 88,
      89, 92, 96, 105, 137–38, 167–68, 194,
      224–25, 255, 285, 407, 469
   women in, 116, 142–43, 249
   Yacub's History and, 78, 86, 96, 135,
      168, 224, 255, 285, 319, 370, 469
Nazis, 199–201, 239, 267, 275
Nebraska, 21, 23
Neal, Larry, 460
Negroes with Guns (Williams), 305

Negro March on Washington Movement, 44, 57, 250
Nehru, Jawaharlal, 157
Nelson, Truman, 465
Newark, N. J., 198, 478
New Jersey Herald, 184
Newsweek, 274
Newton, Huey P., 227
New York, N.Y., 53, 193, 206
  demonstrations in, 267–68
  Harlem, *see* Harlem
  segregation in, 108, 127
  Stuyvesant Town, 58, 59
New York Herald Tribune, 249, 438, 455
New York Police Department (NYPD), 12, 55, 56, 57, 59, 61, 131–32, 192–93, 215, 251, 268, 336, 347, 349, 357, 358, 376–77, 422, 425–26, 457, 466–67
  Bureau of Special Services and Investigation, 132, 135, 151, 171, 356, 357, 416, 422, 431, 453–56, 466–67, 473, 478
  in confrontation at Malcolm's home, 150–52, 153, 160, 164
  in Hinton incident, 127–29, 131, 134–35, 151, 152, 177, 209, 231
  Malcolm's assassination and, 3–4, 13, 430–31, 433–34, 44–46, 451–56, 462, 473, 478
New York State, 158
New York Times, 3, 9, 127, 161–62, 217, 227, 253, 274, 276, 293, 296, 305, 312, 318, 326, 328–29, 357, 362, 389, 405, 420, 451, 454, 456, 462, 465, 481
Nicholson, Joseph, 25, 26
Nielson, Thomas A., 132
Nigeria, 313–14, 315, 348, 362, 364, 373–74
Nixon, Richard, 8, 162, 262
Nketsia, Nana, 383
Nkrumah, Kwame, 167, 314, 316–17, 318, 322, 336, 365, 368, 383, 389, 406, 412, 458, 485
Norfolk Prison Colony, 76, 90, 93–94
  Malcolm in, 74–77, 88, 90–94
Norton, Eleanor Holmes, 472
Nyerere, Julius K., 371, 389, 396

Obama, Barack, 482, 485, 486
Obote, Milton, 372
O'Connell, James, 443
Odinga, Oginga, 371
Omaha, Nebr., 14, 21, 23

Organization of African Unity (OAU), 341, 360–63, 365–66
Organization of Afro-American Cadets, 381
Organization of Afro-American Unity (OAAU), 3, 5, 9, 193, 284, 328, 341–42, 348, 350, 353, 354, 356–58, 360, 363, 365, 374, 376–79, 381, 382, 383, 388–90, 392, 393, 399, 401, 403, 404, 407–8, 411, 412, 415, 419, 421–22, 426, 427–31, 433, 434, 454, 460–62, 468, 471
  Audubon rallies of, 2, 3–6, 350, 358, 377, 388, 395–96, 400, 404, 410, 431–35
  Statement of Basic Aims and Objectives, 337–38, 350–51
  tensions between Muslim Mosque and, 375
  women in, 374–75
Osman, Ahmed, 224
Osman, Omar, 408
Oweida, Muhammad Taufik, 390
Owen, Chandler, 163
Oxley, Lloyd, 39

Pacheco, Ferdie, 227
Padmore, George, 368, 406
Pakistan, 149
Palestine Liberation Organization (PLO), 12, 367, 486
Pan-Africanism, 18, 29, 81, 83, 120, 167, 168, 177, 190, 270, 284, 317, 318, 325, 358, 360, 361, 363, 365, 371, 382, 385, 389, 395, 406, 414, 415, 460, 485
Paris, 362, 412, 413
  airplane crash in, 212, 246
  Malcolm in, 362, 386
Parker, William H., 207, 217
Parks, Gordon, 421
Parks, Rosa, 136
Parrish, Richard, 192
Patterson, Floyd, 280, 469
Patterson, William, 343
Pearson, Drew, 333
People's Metropolitan African Methodist Episcopal Zion Church, 20
Peterson, Caleb, 239
Philadelphia, Pa., 20, 105, 106–7, 110, 111, 115–16, 122, 222, 236
Pittsburgh Courier, 132, 167, 168, 184, 192, 223–24, 237, 293
Poe, Reese V., 127

Poiter, Juanita, 350, 461
Poitier, Sidney, 342–43, 350, 378, 418
police, 159–60, 211–12, 230, 344
  in Los Angeles, 205–9, 211–12, 217,
    230, 238–39, 334, 409, 431
  in New York City, *see* New York
    Police Department
  in Rochester, 228, 229–31
Poole, Clara, *see* Muhammad, Clara
Poole, Elijah, *see* Muhammad, Elijah
Poole, Sharon 6X, 394, 423, 451–52
Postal Service, U.S., 8
Potts, Frankie Lee, 127, 128
Powell, Adam Clayton, Jr., 55–56, 57, 58,
    60, 108–9, 126, 127, 133, 204, 210,
    211, 241, 251, 262, 276, 303, 333,
    458
Powell, Adam Clayton, Sr., 55
Powell, James, 376
Prescott, Larry 4X, 12, 244–46, 256,
    267–68, 270, 273, 275, 326, 348–49,
    457, 459, 470
Prince, Richard, 576
prisons, 90, 123, 241
  Malcolm in, 70–77, 90–99, 311
  Muslims in, 90, 93–95, 97, 98, 123,
    146–47, 240–41
Public Enemy, 8
Purlie Victorious (Davis), 325

Qadianis, 83
Quayle, Dan, 8
Qur'an, 79, 82, 84, 118, 119, 142, 146, 154,
    165, 224, 235, 271, 301
Qutb, Sayyid, 312

"Racism: The Cancer That Is Destroying
    America" (Malcolm X), 366
railroads, 50
  Malcolm's jobs on, 48, 49–50
Rainey, Joe, 401
Ramadan, Said, 368–69, 385–86
Randolph, A. Philip, 44, 54, 163, 175,
    191–93, 209, 210, 216, 249–50, 255,
    256, 260, 343, 419
Rangel, Charles, 377
Revolutionary Action Movement
    (RAM), 353–55, 460, 462
Reynolds, Ga., 15
Reynolds, Paul, 248, 261, 329, 331, 332,
    351, 352, 402, 403, 447, 448, 465
Richardson, Gloria, 298
Riesel, Victor, 363–64
riots, 58, 109, 303

in Harlem, 54–55, 58–59, 60, 62, 359,
    376–77
Roberts, Gene X, 422, 431, 436, 438, 439,
    451
Roberts, Joan, 439
Robeson, Paul, 156–57
Robinson, Cleveland, 192
Robinson, Jackie, 276, 287
Rochester, N.Y., 228, 229–31
Rockefeller, John D., Jr., 53
Rockefeller, Nelson, 276
Rockwell, George Lincoln, 198–201,
    238–39, 267
Rogers, J. A., 91
Rogers, William X, 207
Romaine, Anne, 328
Roosevelt, Eleanor, 156
Roosevelt, Franklin D., 44, 56, 175, 250
Root, Gladys Towles, 409
Rosary, Lucille X, 181, 183, 358, 408–9,
    423
Roseland Ballroom, 43, 46
Rothwax, Harold J., 474
Rushin, James, 442–43
Rusk, Dean, 413
Rustin, Bayard, 156, 175–77, 186–87, 192,
    193, 201, 216, 230, 249–50, 253, 255,
    257, 258, 264, 458, 466, 482
Ryan, Jessie 8X, 435

Sabbatino, Peter L. F., 465
Sadat, Anwar el-, 166
Sadiq, Mufti Muhammad, 83, 84
Saghaf, Seyyid Omar el-, 369
St. Louis, Mo., 217–18
Sanders, Betty, *see* Shabazz, Betty
Sandlin, Shelman, 180
Sanford, John Elroy, 51–52
Saturday Evening Post, 231, 351, 365, 455
Saudi Arabia, 166, 168–69, 307–9, 311,
    359, 361, 362, 368, 369, 390–91, 428,
    486
Savoy Ballroom, 57–58, 60
Schlesinger, Arthur, Jr., 184
Schuyler, George, 188
Schuyler, Michael W., 21
Seale, Bobby, 403
segregation, 9, 16–17, 18, 28, 44, 57, 89,
    108, 109, 123, 127, 137, 154, 155–56,
    158, 161, 177, 202–4, 250, 353
  in Birmingham, 237, 250
  desegregation, 123, 132, 137, 156, 158,
    175, 202–4, 211, 215, 250, 258, 298,
    405, 406

Selma, Ala., 400, 411
Semrad, Elvin, 40
Shabazz:
    as surname, 135, 193
    tribe of, 2, 84, 86, 135, 229, 482
Shabazz, Attallah, 148, 164, 180, 327, 422,
    433, 473
Shabazz, Betty (Betty Sanders) (wife), 8,
    46, 138–39, 143–45, 149–50, 164,
    180, 198, 205, 216–17, 222, 275,
    280–81, 289, 292, 341, 342, 352, 359,
    362, 364, 367, 379–82, 401–2, 415,
    422, 423, 427, 429, 434, 447, 471,
    472
    assertiveness of, 147, 149
    death of, 472–73
    debts of, 148, 152
    firebombing of home of, 3, 416–17,
        418–21, 433, 434, 443, 462, 470
    interviews with, 249, 328
    Kenyatta and, 380–81, 388, 392–93,
        394, 428
    Malcolm's assassination and, 433,
        435, 439, 441, 458, 459, 460–61,
        464–65, 472
    Malcolm's marriage to and
        relationship with, 145–50, 152,
        164, 180–81, 194–95, 205, 222, 233,
        379
    and Malcolm's split from Nation of
        Islam, 296
    Muslim Mosque members and,
        326–27, 379, 380
    in NYPD incident, 151, 152, 153, 160,
        164
Shabazz, Gamilah Lumumba, 379
Shabazz, Ilyasah, 216–17, 281
Shabazz, James 3X (James McGregor),
    159–60, 278, 279, 295, 358, 419, 424,
    425, 470–71
Shabazz, John, 211–12
Shabazz, Omar, 476
Shabazz, Qubilah, 178, 180, 472
Sharrieff, Ethel, 105, 106, 118, 173, 182,
    194–95, 221, 249, 358
Sharrieff, Hassan, 358
Sharrieff, Raymond, 104, 106, 111, 118,
    124, 135, 150, 173, 183, 194–95, 213,
    217, 220, 221, 242, 244, 254, 273,
    278–79, 283, 292, 298, 339, 358, 424,
    471
Sharrieff, Willie, 105–6
Shawarbi, Mahmoud, 301, 308, 334, 361,
    367, 369

Shawarbi, Muhammad, 313
Shelton, Robert M., 179
Shepp, Archie, 465
Sheppard, Barry, 406–7
Shifflett, Lynne Carol, 322–23, 337,
    341–42, 350, 362, 375, 379, 382, 393,
    427, 428
Shukairy, Ahmed al-, 368
Simmons, Minnie, 151, 153, 160
Small's Paradise, 48–49, 51
Smith, Robert 35X, 6, 436, 437, 453, 459
Smith, Welton, 438–39, 443
Sobukwe, Robert, 415
socialism, 336–37, 370, 399
Socialist Workers Party (SWP), 263–64,
    302, 305, 336, 377, 389
Souls of Black Folk, The (Du Bois), 81,
    399–400
Southern Christian Leadership
    Conference (SCLC), 156, 157, 237,
    264, 354, 411, 480
Soviet Union, 336, 362, 368, 390
Spellman, A. B., 299
Springfield Union, 94
Stanford, Max, 353–55, 359, 460
Stern, Herbert, 444
Stevenson, Adlai, 108, 189
Stokes, Ronald X, 207–9, 211, 217, 238,
    334
Stoner, J. B., 178
Strother, Gloria, 46, 69
Student Nonviolent Coordinating
    Committee (SNCC), 175–76, 210,
    228, 250, 251, 256–57, 303, 333, 372,
    400, 403, 411–12, 456, 484
Stuyvesant Town, 58, 59
Suarez, Henry, 442
Sudan, 119
Suez crisis, 120
Sukarno, Achmed, 119
Summerford, Ruth, 148
Sunday Express, 415
Supreme Council on Islamic Affairs
    (SCIA), 361, 364, 390
Supreme Court, U.S., 55, 89, 123, 155–56,
    177–78
surnames, 85
    of Malcolm, 96, 135, 193, 397
    Shabazz, 135, 193
    X, 2, 96, 135
Surur al-Sabban, Sheikh Muhammad,
    368, 390
Sutton, Percy, 192, 305, 327, 335, 344, 377,
    461

Sweet, Gladys, 27
Sweet, Ossian, 27

Tall, Lypsie, 127, 128
Tanzania, 362, 371–72, 396
Tatum, William, 350
Taylor, Cedric, 415
Thaxton, Osborne, 122
Thomas, Benjamin X, 425, 431, 432, 452, 475
Thomas, Cary 2X, 463
Thomas, John, 214
Till, Emmett, 109
Timberlake, Ronald, 446
Time, 455
Tobias, Channing, 56
Touré, Sékou, 384, 385, 389
Traynham, William, 135
Trotsky, Leon, 302
Trotskyist Militant Labor Forum, 335–36
Trotter, William Monroe, 17
Truman, Harry, 95
Tshombe, Moise, 387, 404, 411, 412
Tubman, William, 384
Tunisia, 120
Turner, Nat, 91
Tuskegee, Ala., 156

United Auto Workers (UAW), 103, 306
United Nations, 172, 316, 337, 343, 351, 359, 360, 362, 383, 399, 412, 485
    demonstrators and, 189, 190
    Guevara's address at, 394–95
"Universal Ethiopian Anthem," 19
Universal Negro Alliance, 22
Universal Negro Improvement
    Association and African
    Communities League (UNIA),
    16–24, 28–29, 82, 83, 86, 89
    Malcolm and, 27, 28
Upshur, Walter A., 135
Ussery, Wilfred, 227

Vietnam, 119, 120, 297, 340, 404, 411, 412, 468–69
voting, 133, 155, 156, 267, 271–72, 274, 299, 302, 303–4, 306–7, 377, 400, 406, 411, 413, 484
Voting Rights Act (1965), 133

Waddell, Phil, 239
Wagner, Robert, 228
Wahl, Maurice, 344, 366
Walcott, Louis X, *see* Farrakhan, Louis

Walker, Herb, 26
Wallace, George, 240, 341
Wallace, Mike, 160–62, 212, 339, 342, 348, 476
Wallace, Tom, 325, 349, 417, 423
Warden, Donald, 227
Warden, James 67X, 5, 121, 137–38, 144, 147, 150, 194, 196, 197, 205, 208, 209, 222, 236, 262, 266, 275, 289–90, 294, 300, 302, 306, 321, 323, 327–28, 332, 334, 338, 340–42, 355, 367, 374–75, 376–81, 388–90, 393, 396, 427, 428, 429–30, 434, 441, 444–46, 453, 460–62, 468
Warren, Robert Penn, 352–53
Washington, Booker T., 16, 17
Washington, D.C., 48, 239–40
    March on (1963), 249–51, 253–58, 260, 262, 263, 265, 297, 324
    march planned for (1941), 44, 57, 250
    Mosque No. 4 in, 236, 237, 262, 345
Washington, Harold, 844
Washington Post, 172, 237, 334, 465–66
Waterman, George W., 25–26
Weese, Donald L., 238
"What the Muslims Believe," 216
"What the Muslims Want," 215–16
When the Word Is Given (Lomax), 163
White, George R., 136
White, Walter, 59
white supremacists, 137, 179, 199, 201, 294, 367
Whitney, George, 436
Wilkins, Roger, 258
Wilkins, Roy, 109, 157, 169, 184, 212, 250, 251, 256, 265, 419, 456
Williams, Betty Sue, 141
Williams, Evelyn Lorene, 72, 75, 105, 140–41, 145, 146, 183, 233, 292, 470
    pregnancy of, 181, 183, 233, 266, 292, 358, 408–9, 423, 470
Williams, Jerry, 342
Williams, Joseph, 305, 344, 345–46
Williams, Robert F., 157, 158, 159, 305, 314, 354
Williams, Robert X, 141
Williams Institutional Christian
    Methodist Episcopal Church, 399, 400
Windom, Alice, 314, 315, 316, 317, 362
Woodson, Carter G., 91, 185
Woodward, Yvonne Little (sister), 32–33, 78

World Islamic League, 369, 370
World War II, 47, 54, 56–57, 59, 62–63, 92, 103, 112, 175
Worthy, William, 159, 184
Wright, Herbert, 171
Wright, Richard, 7

X, 8, 144, 471
X, as surname, 2, 96, 135
X, Edward, 417
X, Edwina, 397–98
X, Henry, 221
X, James, 106
X, Jeremiah, 122, 178, 179, 226, 238, 242, 276, 397
X, John D., 4
X, Lloyd, 104
X, Lonnie, 276

X, Louis, *see* Farrakhan, Louis
X, Maceo, 245, 295, 305, 344
X, Malcolm, *see* Malcolm X
X, Marilyn E., 274

Yacub's History, 78, 86, 96, 135, 168, 224, 255, 285, 319, 370, 469
Yergan, Max, 56
Yorty, Sam, 217
Young, Dorothy, 72
Young, Whitney, 251, 343, 419, 458
Young Socialist, 406–7
Young Socialist Alliance, 406

Zawahiri, Ayman al-, 487
"Zionist Logic" (Malcolm X), 367–68
zoot suits, 45, 48, 51, 62–63
Zuber, Paul, 211

M anning Marable is the M. Moran Weston and Black Alumni Professor of African-American Studies, Professor of Public Affairs, Political Science, and History, and Director of the Center for Contemporary Black History (CCBH) at Columbia University in New York City. For ten years, he was the founding director of the Institute for Research in African-American Studies at Columbia, from 1993 to 2003. Under his leadership, the Institute became one of the nation's most respected African-American Studies programs in the country.

Born in 1950, Marable received his Ph.D. in American history at the University of Maryland–College Park in 1976. For thirty-five years Marable has been a major architect of outstanding African-American Studies and interdisciplinary studies university programs. In the early 1980s, he reestablished Fisk University's historic Race Relations Institute. From 1983 to 1986, Marable was founding director of Colgate University's Africana and Latin American Studies program. From 1987 to 1989 Marable headed Ohio State University's Black Studies department.

At Columbia University in 2002, Marable established the Center for Contemporary Black History (CCBH), an innovative research, publications, and new media resources center. CCBH produces Web-based educational resources designed to enhance the teaching and learning of the African-American past, for both secondary schools and colleges. CCBH produces the leading African-American Studies academic journal in the country— *Souls: A Critical Journal of Black Politics, Culture and Society.*

Marable has been the recipient of numerous awards and prizes for his scholarly work. He has received two honorary doctorates, from the State University of New York–New Paltz (2000) and the City University of New York–John Jay College (2006). His book *The Autobiography of Medgar Evers,* coedited with Myrlie Evers-Williams, was nominated for an NAACP Image Award. In 2005, he received the Ida B. Wells–Cheikh Anta Diop Award for Outstanding Scholarship from the National Council of Black Studies. His books *Beyond Black and White,* in 1996, and *W. E. B. Du Bois,* in 1987, received the Book of the Year Award from the Gustavus Myers Center for the Study of Human Rights, University of Arkansas.

A prolific writer, since 1980 Marable has produced fifteen books, thirteen edited volumes, and more than four hundred articles in academic journals, edited volumes, encyclopedias, and related publications. Marable's major works include *How Capitalism Underdeveloped Black America: Problems in Race, Political Economy, and Society* (1983); *Black American Politics* (1985); *Beyond Black and White: Transforming African-American Politics* (1995); *Black Leadership* (1998); *The Great Wells of Democracy: The Meaning of Race in American Life* (2002); *The Autobiography of Medgar Evers* (coedited with Myrlie Evers-Williams, 2005); *Living Black History: How Reimagining the African-American Past Can Remake America's Racial Future* (2006); and *Race, Reform, and Rebellion: The Second Reconstruction and Beyond in Black America, 1945–2006* (2007).